WITHDRAWN

Se

The Law of Labor Relations

THE MACMILLAN COMPANY
NEW YORK · BOSTON · CHICAGO
DALLAS · ATLANTA · SAN FRANCISCO

MACMILLAN AND CO., LIMITED
LONDON · BOMBAY · CALCUTTA
MADRAS · MELBOURNE

THE MACMILLAN COMPANY
OF CANADA, LIMITED
TORONTO

THE
Law of Labor Relations

BENJAMIN WERNE

Adjunct Professor of Industrial Relations
Graduate School of Business Administration
New York University
Member of the New York Bar

The Macmillan Company : New York

To my beloved wife and daughter

Rose R. and Mary Jane Werne

PREFACE

THE past few decades have seen the rise of labor from a subject of passing interest to one which has permeated our entire economic structure.

Legislation through judicial interpretation and administrative rulings has affected even the minutiae of employer-employee relations. Attitudes and concepts which were but a few decades ago a matter of ethics and good conscience are now regulated by administrative and judicial fiat as well as by a myriad of statutes and ordinances. The complexities of labor law are further multiplied by a constantly growing body of arbitral awards.

When it is borne in mind that thousands of decisions are rendered annually by hundreds of courts and boards, the importance of viewing the whole in proper focus becomes self-evident.

To those who deal with these problems as a part of their daily work and who must make sound decisions today upon the basis of yesterday's new rule or regulation, the legal aspects of industrial relations may well seem a maze of uncharted courses.

To the uninitiated, the subject can seem even more confusing. Yet some abiding principles are becoming apparent, rising above the mass of changing detail, and a comprehensive guide can be prepared which will offer practical assistance to those who are called upon to deal with labor problems.

In whatever grouping the reader chances to be, the material here assembled should prove helpful.

No attempt has been made to discuss the philosophy, psychology or economics of labor. These matters have been ably treated in a growing body of literature more or less familiar to all who are exposed to the subject.

The reader will, however, find adequate material for postulating his own philosophy of labor law if he will consider the changes in statutory objectives chronicled in this book. For instance before passage of the Wagner Act an employer could say:

The company does not recognize that labor organizations have any place or necessity here . . . The company fixes wages and rents, and refuses to treat with labor organizations. The laborer can work or quit on the terms offered; that is the limit of his rights. To join a labor organization in order to secure the protection of a union against wrongs, real or imaginary, is overstepping the limit and arouses hostility.

Likewise, before the enactment of the Taft-Hartley law unions could deny employment to non-members, demand pay for stand-by employees, wage a secondary boycott, subject supervisors to union regulations. When, however, the labor law is viewed as a whole, as presented here, it will be seen that both these viewpoints belong to an archaic past.

The mature view of management today is opposed to clothing the labor agreement in the "uncomfortable habiliments of the traditional contract."

The sound judgment of organized labor views industrial enterprise as a joint venture in which both management and labor have a sizeable stake.

With this approach in mind the purpose of this book is to offer an integrated guide through the apparent labyrinth of the laws governing labor relations.

The book is intended to deal systematically with what is permitted, what is prohibited, and what is desirable under the statutes, regulations, rulings and awards that both direct and limit the processes of collective bargaining. Its foremost aim is to be of practical use.

If for example, the reader should already have a union in his plant, he is not concerned with the rudimentary rules pertaining to recognition and representation. If his concern is with negotiating and drafting the agreement, or if he has a problem growing out of operation under union contract, he need not go through the massive details of Parts One, Two and Three. He may refer to Part Four in which he will find a discussion of all the points covering the law and its interpretation, pertinent to his inquiry without backtracking or cross-checking. Each part is a unit unto itself, and, thus, while the two fundamental concepts discussed in the Introduction to Part Three, namely—interstate commerce and employer-employee relationship, are referred to in Parts One and Two, their development is left to Part Three as a fitting prologue to the discussion of rights and duties of managements and unions.

Yet the business executive or student seeking an overall treatment of the subject from the first days of union organization to the problems of renewing an existing contract will find all points covered in an orderly fashion from beginning to end of the book.

With this ambitious hope stated, it is necessary only to add what must be obvious, that the book must remain an intelligent reader's aid; it cannot be, nor is it expected to be, a *deus ex machina* or an electronic brain which will solve all problems, answer all questions and insure good labor relations.

The author is indebted for their valuable suggestions to Martin I. Rose, Esq. and Mr. Alfred G. Larke and for their indefatigable assistance in typing and proofreading to Miss Ina Lifsitz and Mr. Martin Brown.

New York City, September 1950.

CONTENTS

PART ONE

Representation

CHAPTER I. WITH WHOM MUST MANAGEMENT DEAL 3

1. Nature of Proceeding for
   Investigation and Certification of
   Bargaining Representative 3
2. Petition to the Board May Be
   Filed by 4
3. The Question of Representation 5
   How the Question of Representation
   Is Raised 5
   Petition of the Union 5
   Petition of the Employer 6
   Effect of Filing Requirements 6
   When the Question of
   Representation Is Not Raised 7
   When the Question of
   Representation Must Be Heard 8
4. Who May File the Petition 8
5. The Board May Investigate 8

CHAPTER II. WHAT IS AN APPROPRIATE BARGAINING UNIT 10

1. General 10
2. The Board Has Wide Discretion 13
3. Defining the Appropriate Unit 14
   Centralization of Control 14
   Craft or Industrial Units 15
   Guards 18
   Professional Employees 18
   Nature of Work 19
   Difference in Payment of Earnings 19
   Eligibility for Union Membership 19
   History of Collective Bargaining 20
   Fringe Groups 20
   White Collar Workers 21
   Geographical Considerations 21
   Multiple Employer Unit 21
   Multi-Plant Units 22
   Part-Time, Seasonal and
   Temporary Employees 23
   Race, Sex and Nationality 23
   Confidential and Managerial
   Employees 24
   Globe Elections 24
   Extent of Union Organization 25
   Supervisors—Foremen 25
   Independent Contractors 26

CHAPTER III. EXISTING CONTRACTS AND THEIR EFFECT 27

1. Contract as Bar to Election 27
2. Extension of Existing Contract 31
3. Automatic Renewal Clause—
   Premature Extension 32
4. Effect of Subsequent Conduct 33
5. Agreement Not to Represent
   Employees 33

CHAPTER IV. HOW REPRESENTATIVES ARE ELECTED 34

1. General 34
2. Determination of Bargaining
   Representative by Election 34
3. When Election Will Be Ordered 35
4. Prehearing Election 36
5. Who May Participate 36
6. Effect of Pending Strike on
   Eligibility to Vote 37
7. Inclusion on Election Ballot 38
8. The Equality Rule—Affiliated
   and Nonaffiliated Unions 38
9. Run-off Election 39

10. Consent Election   39
11. Consent Card-Check   40
12. Invalidating the Election   40

13. Decertification of Bargaining Representative   42
14. Union Shop Election   42
15. One-Year Election Rule   43

CHAPTER V.   STATUS OF THE BARGAINING REPRESENTATIVE   44

1. Authority   44
2. Responsibilities of the Bargaining Representatives   46

To the Employees   46
To the Employer, Third Persons and the Public   47

CHAPTER VI.   PROCEDURE IN REPRESENTATION CASES   50

1. General   50
2. The Administrative Preliminary

Investigation—and Consent and Directed Elections   50
3. Formal Hearing   55

PART TWO

Prevention of Unfair Labor Practices

CHAPTER I.   AUTHORITY OF THE NATIONAL LABOR RELATIONS BOARD   59

1. Nature of Authority   59
2. Scope of Authority   61
3. To Prevent Domination and Support of a Labor Organization   63
4. To Disestablish a Successor Labor Organization   66
5. To Prevent Discriminatory Discharges   67
   By Employers   67
   By Unions   69
6. To Prevent Discrimination for Testifying or Filing Charges   69
7. To Give Limited Protection to Supervisory Employees   70
8. To Restrain Anti-Union Activity   71
9. To Restrain Coercion by Unions   73
10. To Prevent Closed Shop   73
11. To Prevent Exaction of Excessive Union Fees   74
12. To Limit Discharges under Union Shop   74
13. To Order Reinstatement   75
14. To Reinstate Strikers   75

15. To Deny Reinstatement to Strikers   76
16. To Award or Disallow Back Pay   76
17. To Order Collective Bargaining   78
   By Employers   78
   By Unions   81
18. To Nullify Settlement Agreement   81
19. To Void "Yellow Dog" Contracts   82
20. To Make Findings upon Substantial Evidence   82
21. To Draw Inferences from the Facts and Weigh Testimony   82
22. To Issue Cease and Desist Orders   83
23. To Request Punishment for Noncompliance   84
24. To Prevent Certain Strikes and Boycotts and to Obtain Court Restraint Thereof   84
25. To Obtain Court Injunction Generally   89
26. Limitation of Time upon the Board's Exercise of Powers   89

CHAPTER II.   PROCEDURE IN UNFAIR LABOR PRACTICE CASES   90

1. Nature of the Proceeding   90
2. The Charge   91
3. Administrative Dismissals— Appeals   92
4. The Complaint and Notice of Hearing   94
5. The Answer   96

6. Issuance of Subpoenas   97
7. Hearing   99
8. Rules of Evidence   100
9. Effect of Compliance   101
10. Scope of Board Order   101
11. Objections Not Raised before the Board   103

CHAPTER III.   JUDICIAL ENFORCEMENT AND REVIEW
                                              OF BOARD ORDERS 104

1. How Obtained   104   10. Scope of Court Review   109
2. The Appropriate Court   104   11. The Basis of Court Review   111
3. The Record for Review   104   Insubstantial Evidence   111
4. Jurisdiction of the Reviewing   Lack of Fair Hearing   113
                          Court 105   Question of Law   114
5. Review of Board Certification   Rules and Preponderance of
                    Proceedings 105   Evidence 115
6. Court Review Confined to Record 106   12. Interlocutory Nature of Board
7. Power over Board Orders   107   Order 117
8. Power to Remand   108   13. Contempt Proceedings   117
9. Power to Grant Temporary
             Injunctive Relief 109

PART THREE

Rights and Duties of Management and Unions

INTRODUCTION   121

1. Interstate Commerce   121   2. Employer-Employee Relationship   123

CHAPTER I.   RIGHTS OF MANAGEMENT (INCLUDING
                                          DUTIES OF UNIONS) 129

1. To Hire   129   12. To Fair Hearing   148
2. To Discharge   130   13. To Relief from Board Penalty   148
   For Cause   130   14. To Act in Concert   149
   For Economic Causes   132   15. To Latitude in the Bargaining
   For Strikes   132   Process 149
   For Union Activities   134   16. To Continue Business   151
   Discharges under Union Security   17. To Operate for Profit   151
            Provisions of Contract 135   18. To File Unfair Labor Practice
   For Filing Charges or Testifying 136   Charges against Unions 152
3. To Transfer   136   19. To Petition for an Election   153
4. To Demote   137   20. To Seek an Injunction against
5. To Free Speech   137   Unfair Labor Practices 154
6. To Injunction   141   21. To Refuse to Bargain with
   Against Economic Strike (Not   Supervisory Employees 155
       Involving a Labor Dispute) 141   22. To Refuse to Bargain with Plant
   Against Primary Boycott   141   Guards unless Separately
   Against Secondary Boycott   142   Represented 155
   What Constitutes a Labor Dispute 142   23. To Refuse to Discharge for Dual
   Against Labor-Non-Labor   Unionism 156
                     Conspiracy 144   24. To Require Nondiscriminatory
   Against Union Compulsion   Application of Union
            to Commit Illegal Acts 144   Membership Terms 156
   Against Violent Picketing   145   25. To Refuse a Compulsory
7. To Bar Solicitation   146   Check-Off 156
8. To Protection against Invasion   26. To Refuse to Insist upon an
                 of Its Property 146   Election 157
9. To Abstain from Dealing with   27. To Refuse to Consent to an
             a Minority Union 147   Election within One Year of
10. To Protection from New Charges 147   the Last Election 157
11. To Clarification of Board's Order 147 28. To Adjust Individual Grievances 157

29. To Deny Union Shop—
                    Closed Shop 158
30. To Be Responsible for the
       Conduct of His Agents Only 158
31. To Sue for Violation of the
       Collective Labor Contract 158

32. To Refuse Contribution to Union
                         Funds 159
33. To Sue for Relief from Illegal
              Strikes and Boycotts 160
34. To Judicial Relief from Unfair
                 Labor Practices 160

CHAPTER II.   DUTIES OF MANAGEMENT (INCLUDING
                                        RIGHTS OF UNIONS) 163

1. To Bargain Collectively   163
   Majority Representation by the
                         Union 164
   Majority Representation in
       Appropriate Bargaining Unit 167
   Necessity of Good Faith   168
   Individual Bargaining Discouraged 168
   Counterproposals   171
   Union Committees   172
   Transferring Operation   172
   Changes in Operations   172
2. To Disclaim Responsibility for
            Supervisors' Activities 173
3. To Maintain Neutral Attitude   175
4. To Reinstate with or without
                    Back Pay 175
   Effect of Employer's Conduct   175
   Effect of Employee's Conduct   176
   Where Neither Is Responsible   177
   Disqualification for Reinstatement 177
   Technical Violation   178

   Same or Substantially Equivalent
                           Job 179
   Refusal to Reinstate Held No
                  Discrimination 179
   Reinstatement Ordered   180
   Reinstatement Not Ordered   181
   Who May Ask for Reinstatement   182
   Evasion   183
5. In Instate   183
6. To Pay Back Pay   183
   Computation   183
   Employee's Duty to Seek Other
                         Work 185
   Strikers   186
   Bankrupt Estate Obligated to Pay
                    Back Pay 186
7. To Disestablish
       Company-Dominated Union 187
8. To Protect Union Employees
       against Nonunion Employees 187
9. To Disclose Data   188

CHAPTER III.   UNFAIR LABOR PRACTICES BY EMPLOYERS 189

1. Direct Interference with
              Employees' Rights 189
   Individual Contracts   189
   Maintaining Neutrality   189
   Speech as Interference   191
   Conduct as Interference   192
   Espionage   193
   Economic Coercion   193
   Held Direct Interference   194
2. Indirect Interference
       (by Supervisory Employees) 199
   Held Indirect Interference   200
3. Coercion   201
4. Distinction between Free
            Speech and Coercion 202
   Held Coercive under Wagner Act 203
5. Domination of a Labor
              Organization 203
   Disavowal of Dominated Union   205
   Burden of Proof   205
   Criteria of Domination   206

   Evidence of Domination   207
   Conduct Held Domination   209
   Necessity of Complete Fracture 211
   Procedure for Fracture   213
   Sanction is "Disestablishment,"
              not "Dissolution" 213
6. Discrimination   215
   Layoffs   215
   Lockouts   215
   Rehiring   215
   Discharging   217
   Runaway Shops   218
   Transfer   219
   Held Discrimination   219
   Change in Employee Status after
              Certification of Union 221
   Practices Regarded as Pretexts
            for Discrimination 222
7. Refusal to Bargain   223
   Held Refusal to Bargain   225
   Termination of Existing Contract 229

CHAPTER IV.   UNFAIR LABOR PRACTICES BY UNIONS 230

1. Restraint and Coercion   230   4. Strikes and Boycotts   237
2. Discrimination   232   5. Discriminatory Fees   242
3. Refusal to Bargain Collectively   6. Featherbedding   242
             with Employer 233   7. Filing Requirements Imposed
   Contract Termination in   on Unions 243
             Violation of Act 235   8. Time Limitation on Filing Charges 244

PART FOUR

Collective Contracts

INTRODUCTION 249

CHAPTER   I.   COLLECTIVE BARGAINING DEFINED 249

CHAPTER   II.   DUTY TO BARGAIN 251

CHAPTER   III.   STANDARDS OF PERFORMANCE 255

CHAPTER   IV.   AUTHORITY OF THE BARGAINING AGENT 256

CHAPTER   V.   EMPLOYEES ENTITLED TO BARGAIN COLLECTIVELY 259

1. The Grouping of Employees   259   2. Employees Excluded   261

CHAPTER   VI.   AREA OF COLLECTIVE BARGAINING 263

CHAPTER   VII.   REFUSAL TO BARGAIN COLLECTIVELY 266

CHAPTER VIII.   PREPARATION FOR BARGAINING 273

CHAPTER   IX.   NEGOTIATING AND DRAFTING THE COLLECTIVE
                                                           AGREEMENT 276

1. Introduction—Status of the   10. Union Responsibility   292
          Collective Agreement 276   11. Management's Rights   294
   With Respect to the Union and   12. Supervisory Employees   295
             the Employer 276   13. Discharge   297
   With Respect to the Employees   277   14. Grievance Procedure and
   With Respect to Third Parties   278   Arbitration 298
2. Purpose of Negotiation   279   15. Seniority   300
3. Standards for Drafting the   16. Transfer   302
          Collective Agreement 281   17. Promotion   304
4. Preamble   281   18. Leave of Absence   305
5. Recognition   282   19. Holidays   307
6. Wages   284   20. Vacation   309
7. Hours   288   21. Guaranteed Work   310
8. Probationary Employees   290   22. Pension Plan   312
9. No-Strike—No-Lockout   291   23. Severance Pay   317

CHAPTER X.   OPERATING UNDER THE AGREEMENT 319

1. Introduction   319   11. Transfers   335
2. Relationship of Clauses   320   12. Promotion   337
3. Management's Rights   322   13. Leave of Absence   338
4. Supervisory Employees   326   14. Holiday Pay   339
5. Discharge   327   15. Vacation   340
6. Grievance Procedure   329   16. Guaranteed Work   342
7. No-Strike—No-Lockout   331   17. Pension Plan   343
8. Union Responsibility   332   18. Severance Pay   344
9. Probationary Employees   333   19. Merit Wage Increases   345
10. Seniority   334   20. Wage Reopening   346

CHAPTER   XI.   GRIEVANCES   347

CHAPTER   XII.   ARBITRATION   349

1. Nature of the Arbitrable Issue 349   3. Judicial Review of Arbitration 353
2. Arbitration Procedure   350

CHAPTER XIII.   LITIGATION   355

CHAPTER XIV.   EFFECT OF STATE ACTS   359

1. Union Security   359   4. Strikes   361
2. Position of Board   360   5. State Regulation of Unions   362
3. Contract Responsibility   361

AUTHORITIES   365

INDEX   460

PART ONE

Representation

CHAPTER I. With Whom Must Management Deal

II. What Is an Appropriate Bargaining Unit

III. Existing Contracts and Their Effect

IV. How Representatives Are Elected

V. Status of the Bargaining Representative

VI. Procedure in Representation Cases

1

I · WITH WHOM MUST MANAGEMENT DEAL

1. Nature of Proceeding for Investigation and Certification of Bargaining Representative

Section 9(c) of the National Labor Relations Act empowers the National Labor Relations Board to investigate and certify the bargaining agent of employees in a unit appropriate for the purpose of collective bargaining. The provision also authorizes the Board to determine the appropriate bargaining unit. The proceeding may be initiated by the filing of a petition by the union, or by an employee or group of employees, or by the employer who has received a claim by an individual or labor organization for recognition as bargaining representative. The proceeding has been said to be "essentially informal, and not adversary."[1]

The employer's obligation to bargain in good faith with a labor union becomes absolute upon the union's demand for collective bargaining, provided the union, at that time, has been designated bargaining agent by a majority of the employees in a unit appropriate for purposes of collective bargaining. The employer may, in good faith, question whether the union in fact does represent a majority and disputes may arise concerning what group or groups of employees—skilled or unskilled—constitute an appropriate bargaining unit within the meaning of the statute. Such disputes may become particularly aggravated when there are rival unions making conflicting claims that they have each been designated by a majority of the employees in an appropriate bargaining unit. These questions and disputes concern the representation of the employees and, when they affect interstate commerce as defined in the Act, the Board has authority to entertain a petition for determination of the appropriate bargaining unit and to certify to the parties the name of the bargaining representative selected by a majority of the employees in such unit.[2]

The Act gives the Board this power of investigation and certification provided the question of *representation* of the employees involves a company whose activities *affect interstate commerce*. This power is discretionary and usually will be exercised where a substantial number of employees is involved.

The Board finds a question of representation to exist generally when

3

the employer declines to recognize the union as the exclusive representative either because of: (1) doubt as to its majority status;[3] (2) disagreement with respect to the composition of the appropriate bargaining unit;[4] (3) desire to secure the Board's formal opinion on the question;[5] or (4) competition by rival unions for the right of representation.[6]

The Board has held that even the willingness of an employer to recognize and negotiate a contract with the union does not necessarily defeat the existence of a question concerning representation if the union desires to obtain the benefits of a Board certification by submitting to an election.[7]

2. Petition to the Board May Be Filed by

An employee or any person or labor organization acting on behalf of an employee, for an investigation of a controversy concerning representation.[8]

An employer, when he has been presented with a claim to bargaining rights for the employees by an individual or one or more labor organizations.[9]

The Board may institute an investigation: (1) to ascertain whether it has jurisdiction of the case; (2) to determine what groups shall be combined into a unit for purposes of collective bargaining; (3) to determine what representatives have been designated by a majority of the employees in the appropriate unit.

A proceeding is instituted by the filing of a petition requesting the Board to investigate and to certify the person or labor organization designated by the majority of the employees in the appropriate bargaining unit to represent them for the purpose of collective bargaining.[10]

Disputes as to whether an exclusive representative has been selected by the employees frequently arise: e.g., because the employer doubts whether a majority of the employees have selected such a representative; on competing claims of rival unions; over a disagreement as to the classifications of employees who constitute an appropriate unit. The Act permits the Board to settle a dispute of this nature by investigating the question, determining the choice of the employees by secret ballot (election), and thereafter certifying to the parties the exclusive representative if one is designated.[11] Such a certification does not result in any order requiring the employer to take any affirmative action or to cease and desist from engaging in any conduct. It merely results in the certification of a fact determined as a result of the investigation—that a particular labor organization has been chosen by a majority of the employees in the unit found to be appropriate by the Board. If no representative is found to have been selected, the Board dismisses the proceeding.[12]

3. The Question of Representation

There are three situations to be considered: (1) in which the question of representation arises; (2) in which the question is not raised; and (3) if raised, circumstances which compel a hearing thereon.[13]

The question concerning representation need not arise prior to the filing of the petition by the union if the existence of the question appears at the hearing. The union may file a petition without making a prior demand for bargaining upon the employer if at the hearing the union is actually seeking recognition and the employer is withholding it.[14] Although the amended Act[15] provides that the union's petition should show that the employer had "declined" recognition of the union as bargaining representative, the Board has ruled that the absence of such an allegation in the union's petition does not deprive the Board of authority to proceed on the petition[16] and, as previously noted, the willingness of the employer to negotiate a contract with the union does not bar the existence of a question concerning representation if the union desires the benefits thereof.[17]

HOW THE QUESTION OF REPRESENTATION IS RAISED

Petition of the Union   The petitioning union is required to make a "substantial" showing adequate to demonstrate that there is a probability that it may be selected by a majority. This requirement is made in order to avoid proceedings by organizations that have little or no chance of being designated as the exclusive representatives by the employees.

Such a "substantial" showing consists of the submission by the petitioning union of membership cards or of cards authorizing the union to represent the employees or of some other form of documentary evidence. The Board regards the submission of such evidence to its agent as purely an administrative expedient adopted by the Board to determine for itself whether or not there is a question of representation,[18] and until recently the agent's reports on such showing were introduced in evidence. Such reports when introduced in evidence were not subject to direct or collateral attack at the hearing.[19] Although the Board still uses these reports as in the past, it has discontinued the practice of having them introduced in evidence at the hearing.[20] In cases where the company operated under a closed shop contract or some other form of union security clause, the Board accepted as substantial a smaller representation showing than in cases where no such contractual provisions existed.[21] The petitioning union is not required to show that it represents a majority of the employees. One court said:

"The Act does not require action by a majority of employees as a condition precedent to the Board's power to investigate and direct an election to determine who shall be the exclusive bargaining representative of the unit."[22]

The normal "substantial" showing consists of a showing that at least 30 per cent of the employees have indicated their desire for membership in the union or designated it as bargaining agent.[23] Where there has been a closed shop contract with another union as permitted under the Wagner Act, the Board has accepted about a 16 per cent showing by the petitioning union, depending, of course, upon the circumstances in each case.[24]

The question of representation is likewise raised by the union where (1) the petitioning union strikes, after the employer refuses a request for exclusive recognition; (2) there are conflicting claims of unions; (3) there is a dispute as to the appropriate unit; (4) the employer refuses to grant exclusive recognition to or refuses to bargain with the union prior to certification; (5) the union refuses to show the employer its evidence of majority status; (6) the employer refuses to bargain with or recognize a union when no grounds for refusal are stated.

Where a union seeks to add to an existing unit, the Board requires that it make a showing of representation among the employees sought to be added.

To avail itself of the right to petition, a union need not be formally organized with a written constitution, bylaws, etc., to be a *bona fide* "labor organization capable of being a bargaining agency."[25] But an election will not be directed if the union involved lacks the attributes of a *bona fide* labor organization.[26]

Petition of the Employer   The question may be raised on the petition of the employer although only one labor organization has demanded that the employer grant it recognition as exclusive bargaining representative of the employees.[27] The question may also be raised where it is apparent that a dispute between conflicting unions cannot be solved without resorting to the administration of the NLRB, and no other remedy is available to the employer who has petitioned for the determination of the question.

If the employer files the petition, the Board does not require the labor organization involved to present any proof of substantial interest.[28]

Effect of Filing Requirements   A union cannot petition the Board or obtain the benefits of its certification unless, and until, such union complies with the filing requirements of the Act. The Act requires the petitioning unions and the international organizations with which they are affiliated to file with the Board affidavits of their officers that they have no communist affiliations or beliefs. The petitioning union must also file certain financial and other information with the Secretary of Labor. Failure to comply with this requirement operates as an absolute bar to procedure by the Board upon the union's petition, and the petition will be dismissed.[29]

A noncomplying union cannot be a party to a representation proceeding, cannot appear on the election ballot and cannot file exceptions to the Regional Director's recommendations for the disposition of challenged ballots.[30] The noncomplying union will not even be permitted to intervene in the proceeding in the absence of a showing of its contractual interest in the employees involved.[31]

These principles have been applied by the Board to noncomplying unions when the petition was filed by an employer. If only one union is involved and that union has not complied with the filing requirements, the Board will dismiss the petition.[32]

When a petition for decertification of a previously certified union is filed, the noncompliance of the previously certified union with the aforementioned filing requirements will not serve to defeat the petition. Quite the contrary, the noncomplying union will be placed on the ballot in the decertification election, but if it wins the election, the Board will certify only the arithmetical results of the election, not the noncomplying union.[33]

Once noncommunist affidavits are filed, the Board will not permit any litigation as to the authenticity or truth of such affidavits.[34] But when it is claimed that a complying union is acting or "fronting" for a noncomplying union and thereby participating in an effort to circumvent the filing requirements of the Act, litigation of the issue will be permitted.[35] Merely receiving aid from a noncomplying union or proof of payment for such assistance does not establish "fronting."[36]

WHEN THE QUESTION OF REPRESENTATION IS NOT RAISED

1. The question of representation is not raised whenever the union is already recognized as the sole bargaining agent for the employees unless the union is willing to submit to an election in order to obtain the benefits of a Board certification.[37]
2. No appropriate unit is found within the scope of that claimed in the representation proceeding.[38]
3. The employer has been liquidated and employs no one.[39]
4. The plant was not fully completed at the time of the hearing and only between 20 per cent and 25 per cent of the number to be hired were then employed, those employed did not constitute a "representative group" of this total, and the plant would not be operating at full capacity for more than one year from the time of the hearing.[40]

5. None of the participating labor organizations presented evidence indicating representation of a substantial number of employees in the appropriate unit claimed.[41]
6. The employers involved do not employ the classification of employees that the union claims to represent.[42]
7. One of three or four participating unions is engaged in a jurisdictional dispute with the other unions affiliated with the same national labor organization concerning the representation of the employees. However, the Board will regard the question as arising when the jurisdictional dispute has not been resolved by the parent organization after it has had an opportunity to do so.[43]

WHEN THE QUESTION OF REPRESENTATION MUST BE HEARD

The question of representation cannot be prevented from arising because:
1. The collective contract is about to expire or has terminated.[44]
2. A contract has been in existence for more than a reasonable period.[45]
3. The employer refused to hold a consent election to which it had previously agreed.[46]
4. The consent election did not reflect the free and independent choice of the employees.[47]
5. The contracting union is no longer in existence and the identity of its successor is in dispute, despite the contract.[48]
6. The petitioning union failed to claim it represented a majority of employees when requesting negotiation and claimed to represent less than 50 per cent of the employees in the unit.[49]

4. Who May File the Petition

An employee or any person or labor organization acting on behalf of an employee may file a petition for investigation of a controversy concerning representation. It seems that there is nothing in the Act or the Board's rules to prevent a company union from filing a petition for investigation and certification that it is the bargaining agency.[50]

An employer may petition the Board for an election if he has been presented with a demand for recognition as bargaining agent by an individual or labor organization. (See "Filing Requirements," Part Three, Chapter IV.)

5. The Board May Investigate

The filing of the petition for investigation and certification of bargaining representatives initiates the proceeding before the Board. The staff of the

Regional Office of the Board where the petition is filed conducts an investigation for the purpose of ascertaining whether there is a question concerning representation of employees affecting interstate commerce.[51] If the proceeding is not disposed of by agreement of the interested parties (as for example by consent election) and the Regional Director has reasonable cause to believe that there is such a question concerning representation, he issues notice of a hearing at which the interested parties are afforded an opportunity to present their contentions and supporting evidence.[52]

The Board has repeatedly held that generally it is without authority to discipline unions for violations of civil or criminal law by affecting their petitions for certification or their right to certification, except in so far as the conduct of the union may constitute a violation of the Labor Act within the remedial processes of the Board.[53] The Board has said that a union will not be permitted to obtain or retain a Board certification as bargaining representative if it discriminates against employees in the bargaining unit in regard to tenure of employment, rates of pay or other conditions of employment on the ground of race, color or creed.[54]

However, the Board has not regarded the union's exclusion of employees from membership or segregation of employee membership *per se* as violating the statutory representatives' duty "to represent all members of the unit equally and without discrimination on the basis of race, color or creed."[55]

II · WHAT IS AN APPROPRIATE
BARGAINING UNIT

1. General

Under the Act the agent selected by a majority of the employees in an appropriate bargaining unit is the exclusive representative of all the employees in that unit for the purpose of bargaining with the employer.[56] The Act empowers the NLRB to determine in each case what unit of workers is appropriate for bargaining and this determination is not reviewable by the courts unless clearly arbitrary, capricious or not founded on substantial evidence.[57]

Before the NLRB can certify representatives or decide on charges of refusal to bargain collectively, the Board must determine the unit appropriate for collective bargaining; whether it is industrial, including practically all the employees of a plant; semi-industrial, including a majority of the employees; multicraft, including several groups of skilled workers; craft, including one group of skilled workers; or other group, including only part of the employees.[58] It must also decide whether the unit includes only one plant of one employer, several or all of the plants of a company, or a group of establishments of separate and independent companies.

The Board's wide discretion to determine the appropriate bargaining unit is, however, limited by specific provisions of the Act concerning professional employees, craft units and plant guards.[59] These limitations are separately discussed below at pages 15–19.

When there is no dispute between labor organizations as to the scope of the unit desired, the Board generally finds appropriate a unit broad enough to reflect the desires of the employees, provided it is justified by the form of organization and permitted by the Act.

Where unions which have a substantial interest in the case disagree as to whether the appropriate unit is a broad or a narrow one, the Board decides what unit will carry out the policies of the Act.[60] The employees' right to the full benefit of self-organization and collective bargaining is the basis upon which the Board decides. The decision is made in each case after weighing all the factors relating to the problem of the appropriate unit in the particular case.

In considering the evidence, the Board takes into consideration the degree of departmental interdependence of the plant, history of collective bargaining in the plant and in similar plants in the industry; wages, hours, working conditions, eligibility of the employees for membership in the union or other unions; the employer's organization, management and operation of the plant; and, if all these considerations are evenly balanced, the determining factor is the desire of the employees themselves.[61]

Determination of the proper unit is necessary when cases involve: (1) a petition for certification of representative; (2) petitions for decertification of a previously certified or currently recognized bargaining representative; (3) petitions for union shop elections; and (4) charges that an employer or the union has refused to bargain collectively, in violation of the Act.[62]

The Board seeks to bring together groups having mutual interests in the purposes and objectives of collective bargaining. It will not, however, impose multiplant units upon a distinct local group if that group objects, since this would not further the interests of collective bargaining.[63] The geographical location is an important factor in multiplant units because the ability of the employees to meet on a common ground to discuss labor problems is necessary.[64] Common ownership and the nature of the work to be performed are also taken into consideration in determining the appropriate bargaining agency.[65]

The Board has held that an association of employers in certain instances is an "employer" within the meaning of the Act and an employer unit or subdivision thereof may consist of all or some of the employees of several individual employing entities.[66] The Board treats as single employers companies interrelated through common ownership and management.[67]

The Board has emphasized the special skill of a given group of employees and has excluded such a group from a bargaining unit or held a skilled group to constitute a separate unit; e.g., pattern makers.[68]

The history of collective bargaining is a factor of considerable importance in ascertaining the proper unit for employees. Where no past history exists, the desire of the group is given great weight.[69] However, a court recently held that the Board's failure to designate a bargaining unit prior to an election was improper, and its polling the desire of the employees constituted an undue delegation to employees of the Board's *power* to select an appropriate unit.[70] Nevertheless, the Board continues to be guided in such instances by the results of polling the employees' desires through election.

The Board may include in the appropriate unit what are known as "fringe groups." Whether such a group is to be included in an appropriate unit will depend on the Board's finding that it constitutes a genuine fringe group. To determine this, the Board looks to (1) skill, work, working conditions and wages of the employees of this group and of the employees in the appropriate unit; (2) history of organization; (3) history of collective bargaining in the plant and industry; (4) eligibility of the employees for membership in the union; and (5) the desires of the employees.[71] Even if the group is found to be a fringe group, it may be excluded from the larger appropriate unit if it does not properly "fit in" with that unit.

Prior to March 25, 1945, the National Labor Relations Board did not grant a petition by supervisors to establish a unit for the purposes of collective bargaining.[72] This did not mean that supervisors were not entitled to the protection of the Wagner Act. The Board would not disturb the rights of supervisors under existing collective bargaining contracts and an employer might contract with a union whose membership included supervisors, but the Board would not compel the employer to do so. The same rules were applied to foremen who had the right to hire and fire. On March 25, 1945 the Board handed down the then much discussed *Packard* decision,[73] wherein it reversed its prior position on supervisory employees as established in the *Maryland Drydock* case.[74] In the *Packard* case the Board held for the first time that supervisory employees and foremen, might constitute a unit appropriate for bargaining. The Board included in the unit several levels of foremen, stating that there was no disparity of rank among the several levels. However, it should be noted that the petitioning union in the *Packard* case was an unaffiliated union admitting to membership supervisors only, and not rank-and-file employees. Collective bargaining contracts covering rank-and-file employees should expressly exclude from the unit supervisors and superintendents.[75] These decisions are now merely of historical interest since the Act, as amended, expressly provides that the term "employee" shall not include "any individual employed as a supervisor."[76] Thus, the Board is now without authority over units of supervisory employees. Accordingly, the Board has dismissed the petition of a union of rank-and-file employees in such situations as where supervisory employees comprised a majority of the membership, thereby controlling its affairs and policies, or where such a union was conceived and organized by supervisory employees or they had sponsored its membership drive.[77]

The Act defines the meaning of the term "supervisor" on the basis of the authority of such employee and the exercise of some independent judgment as distinguished from authority which is purely routine or clerical in nature.[78]

Part-time, seasonal and temporary employees may be included in the appropriate unit. However, this will depend upon the extent to which they are regularly called to work.[79] They will be included where the character and similarity of their work and their identity of interest bring them in the same classification as permanent employees.[80] The desire of the petitioning union as to their inclusion or exclusion from the unit is also a determining factor.[81]

The Board has refused to find appropriate units based upon distinction of race or sex.[82]

Who will represent employees in bargaining is obviously one of the most important questions facing management when it is about to negotiate a collective bargaining contract with its employees, since the collective agreement supersedes all individual transactions. Management is not free to deal with its employees individually; hence management's chances of successful labor relations are much greater if the union which is to represent *all* its employees is *friendly* rather than *hostile*.[83]

2. The Board Has Wide Discretion

By the Act, Congress has placed upon the Board the duty to "decide in each case whether, in order to insure to employees the fullest freedom in exercising the rights guaranteed by this Act," the unit appropriate for the purposes of collective bargaining shall be the employer unit, craft unit, plant unit, or subdivision thereof. The Board, thus, has wide discretion, in determining the grouping of employees for the purposes of collective bargaining in each case that comes before it for decision, subject to the specific limitations provided in the Act.[84]

The Board has no inflexible rules as to how it will determine whether or not a proposed unit is appropriate for collective bargaining, and will not be bound by precedent. Furthermore, it has purposely avoided any fixed formula which might hamper its discretion in determining, after a careful examination of all the particular circumstances in the individual case, the appropriate unit. The courts have consistently refused to review Board rulings on the matter of appropriate unit unless the rulings were arbitrary, capricious, or founded upon insubstantial evidence.[85]

The fact that the Board has found a bargaining unit appropriate does not mean it will not find a different unit if the later facts warrant such a change.[86]

Manifestly, since the Board is the final arbiter of the appropriate unit, it is not necessarily bound by a stipulation between the union and the employer. But the Board will give effect to such stipulations unless they are in conflict with the Board's policies on such questions.[87]

Basically, where there is a dispute concerning representation, the issue that must be determined by the Board is of the following nature:

Whether employees of the same general type, such as maintenance and production employees, should constitute the unit or whether the union should be limited to a smaller specialized group such as craft employees; whether the scope of the unit should cover employees of the same class in one plant or more than one plant of an employer or a group of employers; and what specific occupational groups should be included in the unit, for example, whether it should include such groups of employees as clerks, inspectors, helpers, etc. This last question involves the issue of whether fringe groups should be included in the unit.

3. Factors Considered by the Board

In determining what is the appropriate unit, importance will be attached to the history of collective bargaining unless this factor is outweighed by other considerations, such as the nature of the employee's work. Thus, purely clerical employees or highly trained technicians will not be merged with production and maintenance employees.[88] The best test for determining what is an appropriate unit is the prior conduct of the parties—unless to continue that arrangement would not encourage collective bargaining.

CENTRALIZATION OF CONTROL

An important consideration in determining that various plants and departments should be combined into a single bargaining unit is a centralized control of the operations, labor policies, wages, accounting and general practices of the company in a single locality.[89] If more than one of the plants of an employer operates under similar working conditions, wage scale, interchangeability of employees, centralized supervision, the Board will find a unit of one of the plants alone not appropriate for purposes of collective bargaining.[90]

The Board did find a single unit of two plants appropriate where the ultimate control of policies of a parent and subsidiary company were vested in the president of the parent concern.[91]

Where there is single supervision, interlocking directorate, central accounting system, central employment office, a national pension policy, the Board may find a single unit appropriate.[92]

Where there is no common ownership among the various plants, and no common management of the business, the Board will set up a separate bargaining unit for each one of the plants.[93]

The Supreme Court, in *Pittsburgh Plate Glass Co. v. NLRB*,[94] upheld the Board in a proceeding against an employer (under Sec. 10(e) of the Act) for an unfair practice in refusing to bargain collectively after the Board had found the appropriate unit to be six widely (area) separated plants. The employer appealed on the ground that the Board's action was arbitrary in view of the "desire" of a majority of the employees of one plant to be treated as a separate bargaining unit. In affirming the Board's action, the Supreme Court held that scattered plants need not be considered individual units when there is identity of working conditions and centralization of management. The factors considered were: an integrated business with central control of labor policies, similarity of interest of employees, similarity of wages, hours and working conditions existing among various groups, history of collective bargaining in the unit contended for (division-wide bargaining), geographical location of the various plants sought to be included, etc. When other factors afford the Board sufficient grounds for a decision, the desire of one group of employees may not be controlling.

The Board must frequently determine whether the employees of one, several or all plants of an employer, or employees in part or in all of a system of communications, transportation or public utilities constitute a unit appropriate for the purpose of collective bargaining.[95] Where a transportation company operated as a closely-knit unit, wages and working conditions were uniform throughout the entire system and transportation of freight brought employees of all terminals into close association, the Board found a system-wide unit to be appropriate.[96]

CRAFT OR INDUSTRIAL UNITS

Where a well-established and highly skilled craft group with a history of collective bargaining on a craft basis requests a craft unit, this will be granted, despite the objections of the industrial unit.[97] On the other hand, where the history of collective bargaining has been on an industrial basis and the interrelationship of the work of the employees strongly supports an industrial unit, such unit has been found appropriate despite objections of the craft union. Where the considerations between the two are substantially evenly balanced, the Board resorts to ascertaining the desires of the employees in a self-determination election.[98] However, in the *Marshall Field* [99] case rival union organizations of employees in a department store petitioned the NLRB for certification of six AFL local unions, maintaining that several separate units were appropriate, and one CIO local union claimed that all employees should be placed in a single store unit. The Board ordered a poll of the employees in seven separate groups before it determined the appropriate bargaining unit. The court held that the Board's failure to designate the bargaining units prior to the election was improper and constituted an unlawful delegation to the employees of its power to select the appropriate unit.[100] The Board, nevertheless, continues to use the results of an election as an aid in resolving the unit question in the circumstances mentioned. In fact, the results of the election are in effect determinative of the issue.

The problem of severing a craft group from an established more comprehensive unit (as for example, a plant-wide production and maintenance unit) has been considered by the Board in many cases. The applicable rules of the Board for determination were summarized in the *General Electric Company* case[101] as follows: "The group must demonstrate that it is a true craft, that it has not been a mere dissident faction but has maintained its identity as a craft group throughout the period of bargaining upon a more comprehensive unit basis, and that it has protested inclusion in the more comprehensive unit. As an alternative, a craft group may show that production and maintenance unit was established without its knowledge, or there has been no previous consideration of the merits of a separate unit."

Depending on the desires of the employees as expressed in a self-determination election, the Board will permit severance from an established larger unit where the employees involved are engaged in craft work which is of a distinctive nature, for example, pattern makers;[a] where the employees involved are a departmental group and have come to be regarded by custom and practice as of a craft nature;[b] where the proposed unit constitutes a departmental group with a craft nucleus.[c] Severance will be denied where the employees involved are not members of a traditional craft group[d] or do not have the required skills to constitute them craftsmen[e] or constitute but a part of a larger craft group employed in the plant.[f]

These rules of the Board have been modified to some extent by the amended Act which now bars it from deciding "that any craft unit is inappropriate" for collective bargaining "on the ground that a different unit has been established by a prior Board determination, unless a majority of the employees in the proposed craft vote against separate representation."[102] Thus, where a real craft unit is involved, the employees in the craft must be given an opportunity to vote on their inclusion in a larger unit. It should be noted that their inclusion in the larger unit depends on whether a majority of them vote *against* setting up a separate craft unit. The Board, however, has held that the aforementioned amendment does not limit its authority to find a craft unit inappropriate when it does not rely on the fact that a different unit had been established by prior Board determination.[a]

Where a unit has been functioning effectively, it will continue to be appropriate even though there was a modification in the character of the plant operation which changed the physical location of the departments and increased the operation from one plant to two plants.[103]

Prior to the foregoing amendment of the Act, the Board ruled that transportation employees of a gas and electric company may not form a separate bargaining agency even though they operated as a separate department in a separate building and represented a skilled, clearly identifiable and homogeneous group similar to other groups. The Board claimed that the segregation would disturb a collective bargaining arrangement based upon an industrial unit which appeared to have achieved and maintained harmony between the company and its employees for a period of five years.[104]

The Board is not bound by union requirements of eligibility for membership. It may, however, and does give these requirements some weight in making its decisions.[105] It will also consider the desires of employees themselves, especially as manifested by their efforts at self-organization. In one case, employees were excluded from a proposed bargaining unit because they expressed a preference for another unit.[106] In another case, employees were included in the same unit despite the fact that they belonged to different unions.[107]

For many years the Board refused to set up as a separate unit a maintenance department consisting of multicraft employees on the ground that such a unit lacked cohesiveness and homogeneity.[a] The Board, in later cases, departed from this policy and permitted a separate unit of maintenance employees, where such group was composed primarily of craftsmen possessing interests in common distinct from the other employees and the petitioning union sought such a unit.[b] This policy will not be applied where there is a past history of bargaining on an industrial basis.[c]

The size of a unit carries no weight generally in determining the inclusion or exclusion of employees.

Production and maintenance employees are usually treated as a single unit. Whether other employees will be included in this unit depends upon how closely allied their interests are. The following groups have not been normally included in production and maintenance units:

1. Teamsters and chauffeurs;[108]
2. Draftsmen, if their work involves special skill;[109]

3. Private secretaries, clerical office workers, etc.;[110]
4. Salesmen;[111]
5. Traveling men.[112]

Clerical employees in tool rooms and storage rooms may be included in the unit of production and maintenance employees.[113] Transportation employees, even though they owned the operating trucks (logging camp truckers), were considered an appropriate unit with production and maintenance employees.[114] However, the employees of a company carrying on mining and manufacturing operations were held to be separate units, although such a combination is common in the industry, since the two groups were *functionally* separate and not necessarily dependent upon each other.[115]

In determining whether a particular type of employee, e.g., a highly skilled technical worker, should be included or excluded, the following factors are considered by the Board.

1. The relationship of the employee to the management.[116]
2. The degree of skill or difference in work differentiating him from the other employees.[117]
3. The desires of the employees involved.[118]

GUARDS

Guards are specifically covered by provisions of the amended Act. They cannot be included in a unit with other employees, and must constitute a separate unit themselves when their duties include the enforcement of safety rules and rules to protect plant property.[119] Nor can they be represented by a union which represents employees other than guards. The Board cannot certify a union as bargaining agent for such guards if it admits to membership, or is affiliated with another organization which admits to membership, employees other than guards. The Board has held that these principles apply to watchmen who make rounds and punch clocks.[120]

PROFESSIONAL EMPLOYEES

Professional employees also receive special treatment under the Act as amended. They cannot be included in a unit with nonprofessional employees unless they vote for such inclusion.[121] The term "professional employee" is specifically defined in the amended Act on the basis of substantial specialized instruction or learning and the exercise of discretion and judgment in the performance of the job.[122]

Time study personnel exercise considerable judgment and discretion.

However, the Board regards them as professional employees rather than supervisory on the ground that they are essentially fact-finders who do not to any substantial extent formulate, determine or effectuate management policies.[123]

On the other hand, the Board has held that inspectors in production departments of a plant are neither supervisory nor professional and may be grouped with production and maintenance employees although they exercise individual judgment and discretion which affect the earnings of other employees.[124]

NATURE OF WORK

In a conflict between the AFL and CIO over representation in an aircraft factory, the AFL contended for the inclusion of production employees, while the CIO desired to add the engineering and clerical employees as well. The Board refused to include clerical employees of an aircraft factory in the same unit with production employees because of the difference in the type of work performed, the small membership of those workers in both unions, and the dissimilarity of interests.[125] In another case the Board found that the interests of mechanical employees and truck and bus operators were sufficiently diverse as to warrant two separate bargaining units.[126]

The Board, on the other hand, has held that a close interrelation in the types of work in various departments of a plant would lend support to the creation of a plant unit rather than departmental units.[127] However, craft units would not be merged with the mass production units. Only those highly integrated mass production groups would be merged.

DIFFERENCE IN PAYMENT OF EARNINGS

Where production and maintenance employees were paid on a piece and hour rate basis, and typists, clerks, sales managers, foremen and assistant foremen were paid on a salary basis, the Board held that the latter groups could not be included in the same unit with the production employees for collective bargaining.[128] But this factor alone is not necessarily determinative.[129]

ELIGIBILITY FOR UNION MEMBERSHIP

The Board has recognized minority groups as separate bargaining units when membership in the union was foreclosed to such minorities in order that they may otherwise obtain representation for the purposes of collective bargaining.

HISTORY OF COLLECTIVE BARGAINING

When other factors are equally balanced, the history of collective bargaining at the plant may be the controlling factor in determining the appropriate bargaining unit.[130] However, the nature of the prior collective bargaining will be examined for the purpose of determining whether it shall be given any effect. If the historical bargaining unit was established by dealings with an employer-dominated union, it will not be given any effect.[131] Similarly ineffective are past bargaining units established by a labor contract covering members of the union only[132] or where there was an oral contract or a contract which did not contain substantive terms concerning tenure and conditions of employment.[133]

In the absence of a plant bargaining history, the Board may consider the history of collective bargaining at other plants of the employer and at plants of other employers operating[134] similar businesses.[135] The Board, however, has on occasions refused to follow the past bargaining history even though the unit indicated thereby was not inherently inappropriate. Typical cases were those involving craft units where the Board directed "Globe" elections.[136]

FRINGE GROUPS

Cafeteria workers are excluded from an industrial unit where their duties are distinct from those of production employees.[137] But they have been included in the industrial unit where the only union involved desires such inclusion[138] or they are required to do production work.[139]

Welders could not be separated from a plant-wide bargaining unit despite the fact that failure to secure such separation had resulted in disputes which affected war production.[140]

Plant guards may constitute appropriate units whether or not militarized,[141] subject, however, to the limitations set forth under the title "Guards" (*supra*). Thus, individuals employed as guards "to enforce against employees and other persons rules to protect property of the employer or to protect the safety of persons on the employer's premises" cannot be included in the same unit with other employees. Under the decisions of the Board, plant protection employees with monitorial duties, i.e., policing and reporting infractions of rules by other employees, were grouped in a separate unit regardless of militarization.[142]

The Board has rejected employers' contentions that the following types of employees are confidential, supervisory or managerial:
1. Timekeepers[143] (generally excluded from production and maintenance unit).

2. Payroll clerks.[144]
3. Inspectors.[145]
4. Time study men.[146]

WHITE COLLAR WORKERS

Office, clerical and technical workers are normally segregated from production and maintenance employees.[147]

But clerical employees who work in the plant (plant clericals), in close contact with production employees and under the same supervision, will be grouped with production and maintenance employees.[148]

Technical employees are usually separated from clericals if their interests appear different.[149]

GEOGRAPHICAL CONSIDERATIONS

The geographical location of the various plants or departments may be an important consideration for the Board in determining whether or not to combine plants into a single unit, or to provide separate representation for each department. The ability of the employees to meet on a common ground and discuss labor problems depends to a large degree upon geography. If plants are more than one hundred miles distant from each other, in the absence of other vital factors the Board will find that separate units would be more practical.

Where an employer's business is divided into various plants, often situated in different localities or cities, the Board will determine whether separate units are preferable for each plant or whether the entire enterprise shall be included in a single unit.[150]

If the physical separation between the two plants is not sufficient to prevent effective collective bargaining among the employees of the two or more departments, the Board will not determine separate units as appropriate.[151] The mere fact that plants are located in different states is not the decisive factor if communication between the plants is easy because of their proximity.

MULTIPLE EMPLOYER UNIT

Multiple employer units are established only when the history of collective bargaining in the industry shows the necessity and desirability of such a unit and then only when there is an association of employers or agents with authority to exercise employer functions, i.e., engage in collective bargaining and enter into binding agreements with labor organizations.[152] The Board will, when conditions are suitable, find appropriate units cover-

ing employees of a group of independent and competing companies. The
Board has given effect to the desires of employers to handle their labor
relations jointly and to be bound as a group.[153]

The essential element for the establishment of multiple employer unit is
whether the employers have participated in joint bargaining negotiations,
personally or through authorized representatives, regardless of their membership or non-membership in an association.[a] Thus, employers, who in
the past orally contracted to be bound by the same contract entered into
by the union with an employer association, were not included in the multiple
employer unit because they had not actually participated in the negotiation
of contracts.[b]

In large urban industrial centers, the effect of employer associations on
nonmember employers who individually sign the association form of
contract with the union has been considered. Unions have sought an
employer-wide unit in the industry covering association member employees
as well as the employees of nonmembers. Where the nonmembers merely
signed the association form of contract and there was no semblance of
collective bargaining with respect thereto the Board held that the employees
of each nonmember constituted an appropriate unit and employees of all
association members constituted another unit.[154] Despite objections of
employer associations and individual employees, the Board has found
multiple employer units to be appropriate on the ground that the activities
of the association brought it within the definition of the term "employer."[155]

But where a member of an association indicates an intention to pursue
an individual labor policy, a single unit will be formed for the employees
of such member.[156]

A multiple employer unit may be found to be appropriate even in the
absence of an employer association. Thus, where three companies had
together bargained with the union at joint meetings for a period of
twenty-five years, their employees were grouped in a single unit.[157]

MULTI-PLANT UNITS

The Board favors the broad unit and, in the further interest of collective
bargaining, multi-plant units have been found proper, despite the objection
of a local union in one plant or district.[158] Where the facts indicate that
a single plant or a multi-plant unit may be appropriate and there are
competing unions contending that each such unit is appropriate, the Board
has resolved the issue on the basis of the results of an election in each
proposed unit.[159] If the union seeking the multi-plant unit won in each
election, the Board granted a multi-plant unit.[160]

Thus, in one case a labor organization petitioned for one unit for the company's two plants and a rival union claimed that one of the two plants constituted an appropriate unit. The Board directed separate elections for each plant, stating that if the advocates of the two-plant unit won in both elections, then they would be combined into one unit.[161] On the other hand, the Board granted a three-plant unit because the companies had been under common control, had a single labor policy, and had identical negotiations with the union, the only labor organization involved.[162]

PART-TIME, SEASONAL AND TEMPORARY EMPLOYEES

Where there is no difference in the eligibility requirement of the union between regular and temporary employees, temporary employees may be included in the appropriate unit. If the union requests their inclusion, the Board will grant it.[163] They are included in the appropriate unit where they have a mutual interest in collective bargaining with permanent employees, i.e., where the company's policy justifies the temporary employee, when laid off, in expecting recall when an increase in staff occurs.[164] However, when temporary employees are "casual" workers, the Board has excluded them from the unit.[165]

Seasonal employees are usually included if the only labor organization involved so desires.[166] However, they have also been excluded upon request of the only labor organization involved where it appeared the union has not attempted to organize them, and they had shown no interest in the union.[167] Where there is a decided difference between the interest of seasonal and permanent employees, the Board has held there is not a sufficient community of interest between the two groups for collective bargaining as a unit.[168]

Part-time employees as well as apprentices may likewise be included in the appropriate unit.[169]

Where employees in a particular unit worked overtime in an entirely different capacity, the Board held that the bargaining agent of that appropriate unit could not negotiate concerning rates of pay, specify working conditions etc. of the overtime work of those employees.[170] Thus, a bargaining representative may not be expanded beyond the particular unit for which it was certified, i.e., to cover the same employees doing a different kind of work during overtime hours.

RACE, SEX AND NATIONALITY[171]

The color or race of employees is irrelevant in considering the determination of a unit appropriate for the purposes of collective bargaining.[172] The national policy is opposed to any discrimination on racial grounds. During the war the President ordered that there should be no discrimination in war industries or in Government because of race, creed, color or national origin, and that employers must eliminate such discrimination in connection with hiring or conditions of employment. Board certification may be revoked because of union discrimination on the basis of color.[a] But employee segregation according to color into separate equally privileged locals is not condemned.[b] The Board has refused to find appropriate bargaining units based solely upon distinctions of sex,[173] except where the distinction was supported by the history of collective bargaining in the industry and the duties of the employees concerned.[174]

CONFIDENTIAL AND MANAGERIAL EMPLOYEES

Employers have repeatedly contended before the Board that certain of their employees are managerial or confidential and should, therefore, be excluded from any unit of employees. Such contentions have been made with respect to supervisors, plant guards and various types of white collar employees. The Board has defined "managerial employees" as "executive employees who are in a position to formulate, determine and effectuate management policies."[175] "Confidential employees" have been limited to "those employees who assist and act in a confidential capacity to persons who exercise 'managerial' functions in the field of labor relations."[176]

The mere fact that certain employees have access to confidential matters relating to the employer's business, but not concerning labor relations, does not confer upon such employees a confidential status in so far as the Board is concerned.[177] On the other hand, employees have been held to be confidential because of their relationship to those directing labor relations: timekeeper who serves primarily as assistant personnel manager;[178] stenographers who spend about 25 per cent of their time taking dictation from company officials;[179] secretary to department head who collaborates in formulation of labor policies.[180]

GLOBE ELECTIONS

Where the parties are in disagreement in respect to the unit, and one of the units sought could properly include the other, or alone constitute an appropriate unit, the Board, as has already been mentioned, uses the "Globe" election procedure as an aid in determining the unit; that is, separate elections are conducted in each unit for the purpose of ascertaining the unit desired by the employees themselves. This procedure has also been applied where the union seeks to enlarge an existing unit by including therein a new group of employees who have not been previously included and have not had an opportunity to elect a bargaining representative.[181]

This situation should be distinguished from the case of an increase in the number of employees in a group already within the unit.[182]

EXTENT OF UNION ORGANIZATION

The Act provides that the extent to which the employees have been organized shall not be controlling in the determination of the appropriate bargaining unit.[183] Prior to the amendment of the statute, the Board determined the appropriate unit on the basis of the extent of union organization, when other considerations were equally balanced and the unit so found appropriate involved an identifiable group of employees. While the amended Act does not prevent the Board from taking into consideration the extent of union organization together with the factors involved, it does bar resolution of the question of appropriate unit upon that consideration.[184]

SUPERVISORS—FOREMEN[185]

The amended Act completely altered the prior Board decisions which certified units of supervisory employees as appropriate for the purposes of collective bargaining. These decisions were based upon the Board's finding that supervisors were employees within the meaning of the Act. However, the amended Act provides that the term "employee" shall not include "any individual employed as a supervisor."[186] By reason of this change in definition the Board cannot find an appropriate unit of supervisory employees. But this result does not make it illegal for employers to recognize or deal with unions representing supervisory employees. The Board, however, cannot impose the obligation to bargain collectively with such unions upon a management that will not do so voluntarily.[187]

The term "supervisor" is expressly defined in the Act.[188] In general, the definition covers individuals having authority to hire, transfer, suspend, lay off, recall, promote, discharge, assign, reward or discipline employees or effectively to recommend such action, if such authority requires the exercise of judgment and is not routine or clerical. When the issue arises, the determinative question is the nature and extent of the authority of the individual alleged to have supervisory status.

The Court of Appeals for the Sixth Circuit has held that frequency or infrequency of the exercise of supervisory authority does not determine supervisory status under the Act and thereby overruled the Board's position that "sporadic and infrequent" exercise of supervisory power by an employee did not constitute such an employee a supervisor. The Court pointed out that Section 2(11) of the Act "does not require the exercise of the power described for all or any definite part of the employee's time." The

Court said, "It is the existence of that power which determines the classification."[189]

The following classifications of individuals have been held to be supervisors on the basis of their authority, and not entitled to the right of
collective bargaining under the Act:

Foremen;[190]

Assistant foremen and operating engineers;[191]

Working foremen and section men.[192]

The following individuals have been held not to be supervisory:

A non-supervisory employee who substituted for the foremen one
month during the year;[193]

Managers of chain stores;[194]

Group leaders.[195]

INDEPENDENT CONTRACTORS

Like supervisors, independent contractors are expressly excluded by
the definition of the term "employee" from coverage of the Act and the
right of collective bargaining.[196]

The Board has held that newspaper carriers who operate home delivery
routes under contract with the newspaper publishers are independent contractors and not entitled to be grouped together for the purposes of
collective bargaining.[197]

III · EXISTING CONTRACTS AND THEIR EFFECT

1. Contract as Bar to Election

An existing collective bargaining contract with a union representing a majority of the employees in an appropriate bargaining unit is a bar to an election when:[198]

1. It is written and executed both by the employer and the contracting union;[199]
2. It covers the usual subjects of collective bargaining (wages, rates of pay, seniority, hours and conditions of work, etc.) and recognizes the union as exclusive bargaining agent;[200]
3. The contracting union is not defunct;[201]
4. It has a definite and reasonable period to run and has not been in existence for too long a period (history, industry and customs may affect reasonableness of the contract term;[202]
5. It is not of indefinite duration and has been in effect for more than a year;[203]
6. It is not terminable at will;[204]
7. The contracting union is not company-dominated and has not received illegal assistance from the employer.[205]

When the contract contains provisions for automatic renewal, the renewed contract will bar an election upon the petition of a contesting union unless:

1. The contesting union makes a bargaining demand upon the employer reasonably prior to the automatic renewal date, and within ten days thereafter files a petition with the Board;[206] or
2. The contracting parties themselves, by exchange of correspondence or by their conduct, open the contract prior to the automatic renewal date or enter into a new contract to take effect upon the expiration of the existing contract.[207]

As previously noted, an existing collective bargaining contract which grants exclusive recognition to an active union that represented a majority of the employees in an appropriate bargaining unit at the time of execution and has a reasonable period to run will operate as a bar to an election. Where there is such a contract, the Board will dismiss a petition by a rival union for determination of bargaining representative for the same group of employees.[208] Ordinarily, the legality of such a contract will be presumed in a proceeding brought to determine the bargaining representative and the Board will not permit an attack upon its validity in such proceeding.[209]

The Board will carefully scrutinize the terms and provisions of the contract when it is urged as a bar to an election. To operate as a bar to such a determination, the contract must comply with certain essential prerequisites.

When the terms of the contract with a union certified by the Board vary substantially from the unit of employees found appropriate by the Board, it will not bar another election upon the petition of a rival union.[210] A contract with a union for its members only will be similarly ineffective.[211]

A contract between an employer and a union entered into prior to the hiring of employees and commencement of plant operations is no bar to a determination of bargaining representatives upon the petition of a contesting union.[212] Where, after six months of a one-year contract term, the number of employees in the bargaining unit had more than doubled, the Board held the contract no bar to an election.[213] Similarly, a valid two-year contract was held no bar to an election where, at the time the contract was signed, substantial increase in the number of the employees and expansion of the unit was contemplated and the number of employees had more than tripled at the time of the hearing.[214]

The term or duration of the contract is vital on the question of whether it bars an election. Normally, the Board is inclined to regard long-term contracts, which have been in existence for more than a year, as no obstacle to determining bargaining representatives.[215] Equally abortive as a bar to an election is an existing contract with a union that has become defunct.[216]

The Board has recognized contracts for more than the duration of one year on the basis of the history of collective bargaining and the custom of the particular industry involved.[217]

The Board formerly held that one-year contracts generally are reasonable in term and their existence barred an election upon the petition of a rival union. The same rule is now extended to contracts for a two-year term unless the petitioning union can establish that such a contract term is contrary to established custom in the industry.[218] But the rule is to the contrary with respect to a contract for a term of three years. The Board holds that a three-year contract is no bar to election unless the contracting parties definitely establish that such a contract term is in accord with the general practice in the industry involved.[219]

The NLRB, changing policy, in the interest of stabilizing labor relations, decided that contracts of two years should bar an election although the customary term of contracts in the industry was only one year.[220] The latest policy of the Board, in so far as the effect of contracts on an election is concerned, is to treat a two-year contract the same as a one-year contract. The Board explained this change in policy by stating that "the time has come when the stability of industrial relations can be better served, without unreasonably restricting employees in their right to change representatives, by refusing to interfere with bargaining relations secured by collective agreements of two years' duration."[221]

From this reasoning, the Board also concluded that a four-year contract, which on established principle was an unreasonable period, nevertheless barred an election during the first two years of the contract.[222] And similarly, a contract of indefinite duration was then found also to bar an election during its first two years.[223] However, a contract terminable at the will of either party does not bar an election at any time.[224] Nor is a contract which is about to terminate pursuant to its terms a bar.[225]

Contracts which contain a closed shop clause or union shop clause without compliance with the Act for such a union security provision do not bar an election.[226] If the contract, however, provides that the union shop clause shall not become effective until all the requirements of the Act with respect thereto have been satisfied, the contract will operate as a bar to an election.[227] Preferential shop contracts and contracts which require the employer to hire only members of the contracting union when they are available, to hire employees through the union and, when union members are not available, to hire only persons acceptable to the union and to require them to obtain union work permits and to compel them to become union members two weeks after hire, do not bar an election since such provisions are regarded as invalid in that they go beyond the union shop permitted by the Act.[228]

A contract which provides for automatic renewal in the absence of notice by one of the contracting parties of intention to alter, modify or terminate it prior to a specified period preceding the termination date, will operate as a bar to an election. However, this rule does not apply where a contesting union has given timely notice to the employer or filed a petition with the Board reasonably prior to the specified date for automatic renewal.[229] However, the conduct of the contracting parties either before or subsequent to the automatic renewal date and prior to the termination date stated in the contract (as where notice of desire to modify or terminate the contract is given, or negotiation for a new contract is requested, or the parties enter upon negotiations for a new contract), will remove the contract as a bar to an election.230

During the war period, the pendency of a National War Labor Board proceeding involving the employer and a certified union did not in itself bar a rival union from obtaining an election. But the Board did not order an election when a certified bargaining agent had not enjoyed the benefits of collective bargaining or a contract because of "unavoidable delays consequent upon its voluntary acceptance of orderly procedures established by governmental authority (National War Labor Board) for the adjustment of differences with an employer."231 When the bargaining agent or union had represented the employees for a substantial period and had a collective bargaining contract, the Board directed an election although a proceeding was pending before the War Labor Board.232 But when the delay was the result of causes other than pendency of the War Labor Board proceeding, the Board directed an election although the bargaining agent was newly certified and had never enjoyed the benefits of a contract.233

When a bargaining agent ceases to function as such and a new bargaining representative is certified, the Board will not direct the latter to assume the obligations of an unexpired contract with the defunct union.234

In the case of *General Electric X-Ray Corporation,*235 the Board announced a new time limitation policy in cases where there are rival unions and one of them completes a written collective bargaining contract with the employer. Where one union makes a naked claim of representation upon the employer, it must file a petition for investigation of the bargaining representative with the Board within ten days thereafter, otherwise a subsequent written agreement entered into by the employer and another union will bar an election. Of course, the contracting union must have majority status and the contract must meet all other requirements for validity. But a subsequent contract will not operate as a bar if the petition is filed prior to its execution even though more than ten days have elapsed since the initial claim of majority representation.236

Further limitations, however, have been placed on the doctrine of the *General Electric X-Ray Corporation* case. Thus, the doctrine does not apply when the petitioning union's claim is substantial on its face rather than naked.237 Where a series of representation claims have been made, the ten day period may be measured from the last of such claims immediately preceding the automatic renewal date.238 Even if the petition is seasonably filed so as to prevent an intervening agreement from barring an election, substantial amendment or change of the petition makes it unseasonable and the intervening agreement a bar.239

2. Extension of Existing Contract

The extension of an existing contract which contained no automatic renewal provision was held no bar to a petition for an election filed after the execution of the extension agreement but before the expiration date of the original contract.[240] The result was the same in the case of contracts with automatic renewal clauses where the petition was filed before the automatic renewal date, although after the execution of the extension agreement.[241]

However, the Board has limited the application of this doctrine of "premature extension" to existing agreements. New agreements entered into for the first time by a certified union during the year following the certification bar an election.[242] This rule is based on the Board's doctrine that in the absence of unusual circumstances a newly certified union is entitled to an undisturbed one year period in which to bargain for the employees. The doctrine has been applied to premature extensions and automatic renewals. Thus, the premature extension or automatic renewal of an existing contract within one year of the date of the Board's certification of the contracting union is a bar to an election even though the petition for an election was filed prior to execution of the extension or automatic renewal and even though the original contract was executed prior to the date of the certification of the contracting union.[243] In the *Quaker Maid Company* case[244] the Board afforded the same immunity from an election to a premature extension agreement where both the extension agreement and the original contract were executed during the certification year.

In the *Quaker Maid Company* case, the union was designated exclusive bargaining agent as a result of a consent election, on June 19, 1945, and the contract was entered into on July 3, 1945, for one year from July 30, 1945, with provision for automatic renewal, unless either party served notice of desire to change at least thirty days prior to July 30 of any year. Seven months after the designation the parties to the contract commenced negotiations for a change in wage rates and on May 13 entered into a supplemental agreement which ratified the existing contract, extended its terminal date to July 30, 1947, and repeated the automatic renewal clause. A rival union demanded of the employer on May 6, 1946, that it be granted recognition. On June 20, 1946, it filed its petition. The Board, upon holding the supplemental agreement a bar to an election, said:

Recently, in a series of cases, we laid down the rule that a collective agreement for a reasonable term entered into within the year following certification of the contracting union is a bar during its term to a petition filed by a rival union, notwithstanding the fact that the agreement is tantamount to a premature extension of a previously existing contract. We held that, during this one-year period following certification, the premature extension doctrine does not apply. It is true that in these cases the original contract to which we refused to apply the premature extension principle was executed before the certification, whereas in this case the original agreement was signed after the designation. The reason for the rule is, however, the same in both situations. The rule rests on the principle that, during the one-year period following certification, the employer has the duty of bargaining in good faith with the certified union and that it would be entirely inconsistent for the Board to require an employer to negotiate with the certified union concerning an agreement while withholding power from the parties to make an agreement for a reasonable period effective against the claim of a rival union. Inasmuch as the 1946 supplemental agreement was signed within one year of the Independent's designation and will not terminate until July 30, 1947, we find it is a bar to a present determination of representatives.

3. Automatic Renewal Clause—Premature Extension

The "premature extension" doctrine does not apply to contracts containing automatic renewal clauses if the petitioning union makes known to the employer its claim to represent the employees or files a petition with the Board prior to the operative date of the automatic renewal clause. In the absence of such timely notice or timely filing of a petition, the contract executed during the automatic renewal period and effective immediately is a bar to an election upon a petition filed thereafter although before the expiration date of the contract.[245]

If the extension agreement was executed during the automatic renewal period to become effective after the expiration date of the original contract, and the petition for election was filed between the execution of the extension and the expiration date of the original contract, the date of execution of the extension agreement governs and an election is barred.[246] An extension agreement executed and made effective prior to the automatic renewal date barred an election upon a petition filed after the automatic renewal.[247] But where the employer and contracting union entered into a new contract prior to the operative date of the automatic renewal and the petitioner filed its petition with the Board prior to such operative date but after the execution of the new contract, the new contract was held not to bar an election.[248]

The principle of the *General Electric X-Ray Corporation* case is applied by the Board to automatically renewable contracts. Thus, the union seeking an election where the contract provides for automatic renewal must not only make timely claim on the employer to represent the employees prior to the effective automatic renewal date, but also must file its petition with the Board within a ten day period.[249]

4. Effect of Subsequent Conduct

The subsequent conduct of the parties to the contract may have the effect of removing the contract as a bar to an election upon the petition of a rival union. An existing contract, which contains no provision for modification during its term, is no bar to an election if the parties enter into a collateral agreement or enter upon negotiations for substantial changes.[250] If the contract provides for modification, the contract will not be a bar to an election if the contracting parties negotiate for changes which go beyond the scope of the provision for modification.[251]

When the contract provides for automatic renewal, the contract is no bar even after the automatic renewal date if prior thereto or subsequently the union manifests its desire to negotiate a new contract or enter into negotiations for substantial changes.[252]

5. Agreement Not to Represent Employees

In *Briggs Indiana Corporation*,[253] the Board gave effect to the provision of a twelve-month contract whereby the union agreed not to accept as members of the union the employer's superintendents, foremen, assistant foreman and plant protection employees. The Board dismissed a subsequent petition of the contracting union for certification as bargaining representative of the employer's plant protection employees. This decision is a distinct reversal of prior cases wherein the Board refused to recognize the provisions of a contract disqualifying a union as bargaining representative for various groups of employees. The Board refused to apply the same doctrine in the *Jones & Laughlin Steel Corporation* case,[254] where the contract was of nation-wide · coverage. The Board distinguished the *Briggs* case on the ground that there the parent of the local union joined in the contract and that the exclusion from union membership was clearly and unambiguously stated in the written contract. The Board said it would not accept oral evidence as to the meaning and application of such a provision. The twelve-month contract period was also an important element in the *Briggs* case.

IV · HOW REPRESENTATIVES ARE ELECTED

1. General

The Act provides that the bargaining agency be selected by (1) *a majority of the employees,* (2) *in an appropriate unit,* and that the representative selected be (3) *the exclusive representative* of all the employees in the unit.[255]

The Act empowers the National Labor Relations Board, wherever interstate commerce is *affected,* to (4) *investigate* and (5) *certify* the representative chosen.[256]

Employers may not interfere by court injunctions with the administration of elections, since it is generally held that the Board has exclusive jurisdiction of such matters and the employer is not irreparably damaged by the results of an election.[257] Nor does an election involve any threat to property or contractual rights. The Board reasons that if the employer is dissatisfied and wishes a court review of an order of election, he may disobey the Board and he will then be given a *final* order to cease and desist. From this *final* order he may always appeal to the courts. In one case the Board obtained an order temporarily enjoining an employer from interfering with an election which it had scheduled.[258]

2. Determination of Bargaining Representative by Election

The Board orders an election by issuing a Direction of Election which (1) establishes the time when the election shall be held[259] and (2) defines the employees eligible to vote.

However, only one election can be conducted by the Board during the twelve-month period following the last valid election.[260]

The employees eligible to vote are those employees employed during the payroll period immediately preceding the date of the Board's Direction of Election.[261] This is the normal practice of the Board and will be varied only for cogent reasons based on proof.[262] Employees who did not work during the eligibility period because of illness, vacation or temporary layoffs are permitted to vote. But employees who have quit or been discharged for cause and have not been rehired or reinstated prior to the date of the

Direction of Election are excluded from participation in the election.[263] Employees in the armed forces who present themselves in person at the polls may vote, but the Board generally does not permit them to vote by mail. The Board has, however, on occasion departed from this rule and provided for the mailing of ballots to eligible employees in the appropriate unit provided one or more of the parties furnished the Board within a stated short period, a list of names, work, classifications and most recent address of such employees.[264] The Board has not established this practice as a general policy and whether it will be followed depends on the facts in the particular case.

The determination of representation by means of a Board election leads to the question of whether strikers may vote in the election. Under the Wagner Act, the Board treated them as eligible voters under certain circumstances.[265] The question, under the amended Act, turns on whether such strikers have been replaced[266] and whether the strike was caused by economic reasons or by the employer's unfair labor practices.[267]

Voting must be done personally in the presence of an agent of the Board, with the rare exception noted above for employees in military service.[268] The Regional Director in charge of an election may prior to the election post notices where employees are customarily informed of matters affecting them.

The outcome of an election is determined by the principle of majority rule.[269] Voting in the election is by secret ballot. "Majority" does not mean a majority of eligible voters, but simply a majority of those voting. Thus if a union receives a majority of the valid votes cast, the Board certifies that union as the exclusive bargaining representative of the employees in the bargaining unit.[270] If, however, a very substantial number of eligible voters fail to vote at the election, certification will be denied, e.g., in a case in which there were 700 eligible voters and only 125 participated.[271]

3. When Election Will Be Ordered

The NLRB will not normally direct an election where there are unremedied unfair labor practices or there are on file pending charges of unfair labor practices.[272] But the Board will proceed with the election if the union which had filed the charges waives them as a ground for objecting to the election.[273]

The Board is generally opposed to delaying an election for other reasons. Contemplated removal of the plant to a new location,[274] high labor turnover in the plant,[275] "raiding" tactics by petitioning union[276] have been held insufficient grounds for delaying the election and an immediate election has been directed by the Board. The majority of the Board has also refused to postpone an election because of the pendency of a strike, on the ground that an immediate election often results in termination of a strike.[277] In a case where it appeared that operations would be terminated in three months and there was no likelihood of continuance thereof by a successor, the Board held that the conduct of an election would be futile and dismissed the petition.[278]

The possibility of substantial increase or reduction in the number of employees will not ordinarily delay an election. However due to the influx of personnel in war industries, the Board, under the Wagner Act, entertained a petition for a new representation within a period of less than one year, but not before six months from the date of certification, upon proof that (1) the number of employees in an appropriate unit was more than double the number of employees eligible to vote in a prior election, and (2) the petitioning labor organization represents a substantial number of the employees in the expanded unit.[279]

4. Prehearing Election

The Board's practice of conducting elections prior to hearings in cases where it was of the opinion that no substantial issues were involved has been discontinued. The amended Act does not permit elections prior to hearing.[280]

5. Who May Participate

The Board uniformly declares that employees on the payroll immediately preceding the date of the Direction of Election are eligible to vote.[281] Exceptions have been made for special reasons.

The Board wishes to make eligible as many employees as possible in the unit who are interested in the choice of representatives. In one instance a payroll date immediately preceding the hearing was chosen where the employer's business was expanding, and in another a payroll period during a peak season was chosen. If a payroll of another period would be more inclusive, the Board will use the payroll date of such a period. Where there was a substantial decrease in the employment roll because of economic reasons, the Board used as an eligibility list the payroll for the period ending about four months prior to the Direction of Election and permitted employees who worked fifteen days between the payroll date and the date of the Direction of Election to vote.[282] When a plant was shut by reason of a strike, the Board selected the payroll immediately preceding the strike.[283]

Generally, employees who have quit or have been discharged for cause and have not been rehired or reinstated prior to the date of the Direction of Election are not eligible to vote. Where it is claimed that the discharges were in violation of the Act and charges are on file with the Board, the Board permits the employees to vote, but impounds the ballot until it is determined whether or not an unfair labor practice actually was committed.[284]

Regular part-time employees are eligible to vote especially if they have regular working hours.[285] Probationary employees, apprentices and trainees are also eligible to vote.[286] Employees who are not on the payroll because of illness or on vacation, leave of absence or temporarily laid off are eligible.[287] Employees in the armed forces may vote if they appear at the polls or may ballot by mail under certain circumstances.[288] But mail balloting was denied when the employer had no knowledge of the whereabouts of fifty per cent of the servicemen.[289]

Temporary or casual employees are not eligible to vote.[290] Employees who are discharged after the eligibility date and are not rehired or reinstated prior to the election cannot vote.[291] Discharged employees who file charges claiming the discharge was in violation of the Act are permitted to vote under challenge; the ballots, if needed to determine the results of the election, are held pending the determination of the charges.[292] Eligible employees transferred out of the bargaining unit before the election cannot vote, but ineligible employees transferred into the unit are eligible to vote.[293]

6. Effect of Pending Strike on Eligibility to Vote

The amended Act changes the Board's rules concerning eligibility to vote where the employees are on strike for economic reasons. Section $9(c)(3)$ provides that "employees on strike who are not entitled to reinstatement shall not be eligible to vote.[294] Economic strikers are not entitled to reinstatement until they make application. If upon such application it appears that they have been permanently replaced by others, they would not be "entitled to reinstatement" and hence would not be eligible to vote.[295] If they have not been permanently replaced, they are entitled to reinstatement, provided their jobs have not been validly eliminated, and hence are eligible to vote. With respect to employees on strike because of the employer's unfair labor practices, the prior rules of the Board would seem to be still applicable.[296] Since replacement employees must be discharged for the reemployment of unfair labor practice strikers, such strikers are "entitled to reinstatement" and are, therefore, eligible to vote.

Whether the strike was caused by the employer's unfair labor practices will not be determined in the representation case because such a determination can be made only on a complaint issued by the General Counsel who alone, under the amended Act, has authority to decide if such a complaint should issue.[a]

7. Inclusion on Election Ballot

The Board includes on the ballot all *bona fide* labor organizations having an interest in the proceedings, provided they have complied with the filing requirements of the Act. However, in order to be accorded a place on the ballot, a nonpetitioning organization must have made some showing of representation. The showing of such an organization need not be as substantial as that required of the union filing the petition.[297] Customarily the Board holds that an intervening union has demonstrated an interest sufficient to entitle it to participate in the elecion if it has recently had contractual relations with the company.[298] A union, which has failed to show any substantial representation but relies merely upon its general organizational interest in the industry, is not entitled to a place upon the ballot.[299] The Board has excluded from the ballot a union which had previously been found to be company-dominated or which was determined to be the successor of a company-dominated union,[300] although the ballot in the original election provided a space for voting against the union or unions listed on the ballot.

8. The Equality Rule—Affiliated and Nonaffiliated Unions

By specific provision, the Board is required to apply the same rules regardless of whether the petition is filed by an employer, employee or union.[301] Petitions by nonaffiliated unions must be treated the same as petitions filed by affiliated unions. The Board cannot dismiss the petition of an unaffiliated union on the ground that it has been sponsored by and received the aid and assistance of the employer in violation of Section 8(a)(2), unless it applies the same rules to the petitions of affiliated unions which have received similar illegal aid and assistance from an employer.[302] Affiliated unions in such circumstances were never in the past charged with being company-dominated but merely with receiving illegal aid and assistance. Where the charges were sustained, the affiliated union was not ordered disestablished. The employer was ordered to cease and desist from the illegal aid and to withdraw recognition until the affiliated union was certified by the Board. On the other hand, unaffiliated unions were ordered disestablished with the result that they could never act as bargaining agent.

As a result of the amended Act, the Board cannot deny an unaffiliated union found to be company-dominated, or its successor, a place on the ballot unless it applies the same rule to affiliated unions found to have received illegal employer support. Similarly, the petition of the first type of union cannot be rejected by the Board unless it rejects the petition of the latter.

9. Run-off Election

The amended Act eliminates the Board's rather complicated rules for conduct of run-off elections. Section 9(c)(3) provides that "In any election where none of the choices on the ballot receives a majority, a run-off shall be conducted, the ballot providing for a selection between the two choices receiving the largest and second largest number of valid votes cast in the election."[303]

10. Consent Election[304]

Consent elections are those in which the parties, with the approval of a Regional Director, enter into an agreement stipulating the appropriate unit, the time and place of holding an election, and the payroll to be used for determining employees eligible to vote. The amended Act authorizes consent elections.[305] Consent elections do not result in certifications by the Board, unless the parties stipulate that the Board shall certify the representative chosen, if any.[306]

Two types of consent election agreements are provided by the Board. The first type of agreement (no certification by the Board) provides for the conduct of a secret ballot election under the supervision of the Regional Director and specifically accords finality to his determination on disputes arising out of the election. The Board will not disturb his rulings unless they are shown to be arbitrary or capricious.[307] There is no direct appeal, however, to the Board from the Regional Director's determination. The issue of arbitrariness or capriciousness can only be raised by the employer collaterally, that is, by his refusing to honor the Regional Director's certification of the results of the election.[308] In a subsequent unfair labor practice case against him upon charges of refusal to bargain filed by the union, the employer can question the Regional Director's determination on the ground aforementioned.

Where an employer interferes with a consent election of the type described, the Regional Director, authorized by the consent election agreement to conduct the election, will declare it invalid.[a]

The second type of consent election agreement provides for certification by the Board upon the consent election. In such case, the procedure on objections to the election is the same as in the case where the election was directed by the Board after a hearing and decision.[309] The Regional Director issues a report on the objections to which exceptions may be filed. The Board considers the matter, and if, in its opinion, there are material and substantial issues, directs a hearing. Otherwise, it disposes of the case without a hearing. If a hearing is held on objections to the election, the evidence is presented and the Board rules thereon either sustaining the objections and setting aside the election or overruling the objections.

11. Consent Card-Check

The amended Act obligates the Board, where there is a question concerning representation affecting commerce, to conduct an election after holding a hearing.[310] Under the Wagner Act the representation question could be determined otherwise than by an election. Thus, a check of union cards against a payroll could be authorized. But, since the amended Act binds the Board to determine representation only by an election, there is no authority for a cross-check of cards. Hence, the use of that device has been abandoned.

12. Invalidating the Election

The interested parties have the right to file objections to the election or conduct affecting the results of the election.[311] The Board has the duty to afford the employees free designation of bargaining representatives. If objections are filed seasonably as prescribed by its Rules and Regulations, the Board will conduct an investigation, and if it appears therefrom that the employees were not afforded complete freedom to exercise the right to select a bargaining representative, the election will be set aside.[312]

Valid objections to the election may be directed against substantial irregularities or procedural defects, such as failure to post official notices of election where the number of votes cast was small compared to the number eligible to vote,[313] failure to give a large department the same opportunity to vote as other departments,[314] or Regional Director's error in connection with the appropriate time for opening and counting challenged ballots.[315]

Conduct by an employer which interferes with the employee's free choice of bargaining representatives is a basis for invalidating the election.[316] Such conduct may consist of the commission of unfair labor practices. Announcement by the employer of a unilateral wage increase just before an election, or continuing to check-off dues on behalf of one of the competing unions after expiration of the contract, have been held by the Board to warrant setting aside the results of an election.[317] Threatening economic reprisals against union supporters and offering reward to opponents of the union are bases for invalidating the election.[318] In a rare case, the Board, upon an employer's objection, set aside an election because of a supervisor's encouraging employees to join and vote for the only union involved,[319] where the employer had no knowledge of the supervisor's conduct. The Board warned the employers not to rely on the conduct of their supervisors as ground for setting aside an election on the basis of employer objections.

Conduct by competing unions may invalidate an election. An election has been set aside because a union distributed a marked sample ballot bearing the name of the Regional Director so that is appeared to have official sanction.[320] The union's premature announcement of War Labor Board approval of a joint application for a wage increase was held interference with an election.[321] The conduct of the union must not go beyond campaign propaganda. Thus distribution to employees by the contracting union of a new and more advantageous contract, executed by it and the employer and to become effective after the election, was held beyond the bounds of permissible campaigning.[322] But merely calling the campaign literature of a rival union "highly offensive and unethical" is no basis for invalidating an election.[323]

The Board has even held that the conduct of third persons, not attributable to the employer, may be such as to warrant setting aside an election because "the issue before us here is whether, under all the circumstances, this election was held in an atmosphere conducive to the sort of free, unintimidated choice of representatives which the Act contemplates."[324]

The Board set aside an election because of improper conduct of the union in that its organizer, three days before the election, told an employee, "if you don't vote for the union the girls will refuse to work with you," and that to "keep from causing hard feelings" she must leave the plant on the day of the election without going to the polls.[325] The majority of the Board ruled that these remarks "conveyed a threat of economic reprisal." However, where the union campaign statements were "a vote for the union will bring you these things called job security and a living in wages" and "when the election is out of the way, your demands must be granted by the company," they did not warrant setting aside the election.[326] The Board also refused to set aside an election where the union in its campaign told the employees that if the union lost the election, the employer would immediately cut wages. The Board pointed out that the employer had published a denial of this statement before the election.[327]

13. Decertification of Bargaining Representative

The amended Act establishes a procedure for the termination of the authority as bargaining representative of a union certified by the Board or currently being recognized by the employer.[328] The petition for such determination may be filed by an employee or group of employees or any individual or labor organization acting on their behalf. It cannot be filed by an employer. The petition must allege that a substantial number of employees assert that the existing bargaining agent is no longer the majority representative. The procedure on the petition is the same as in the case of a petition for determination of bargaining representative. The petitioner must make a substantial showing of interest. If the Board has reasonable cause to believe that a question of representation affecting commerce exists, it must order a hearing on due notice. If upon the basis of the hearing the Board finds that such a question concerning representation exists, it must conduct an election and certify the results thereof.

A decertification petition will be dismissed by the Board if the union whose decertification is sought makes an unqualified disavowal or disclaimer of the right to represent employees for the purpose of collective bargaining.[329] However, if the purported disclaimer by the union is not clear, unqualified and unequivocal the petition will not be dismissed.[330]

14. Union Shop Election

The amended Act, while outlawing a closed shop, permits an employer, and a union having majority status in an appropriate bargaining unit, to enter into a union shop agreement, provided the Board has certified that at least the majority of the employees *eligible* to vote have at an election for such purposes authorized the union to enter into such an agreement.[331]

Thus, a majority union may petition the Board to conduct such an election.[332] The petition must allege that 30 per cent or more of the employees desire to authorize the union to enter into the union shop agreement. If such a showing is made and there is no question concerning the representation of the employees, the Board must conduct an election and certify the results.

The election may be conducted pursuant to a consent agreement. It should be noted that the vote necessary to grant the authority to the union is the majority of the employees in the unit *eligible* to vote (as distinguished from only those voting). In similar fashion, 30 per cent or more of the employees may petition the Board for an election to rescind the authority of the union.[333] When a valid union shop election has been held, another election cannot be conducted for the next succeeding twelve-month period.[334]

The union shop election will be held in an appropriate unit, but such a unit need not be coextensive with the union established for representation purposes.[335] Where the parties have by their labor contracts established a bargaining unit, the Board may vary such a unit for the purposes of a union shop election. Thus, where the contract covered guards and supervisors, the Board will vary the unit to exclude the guards and supervisors from the election.[336] The Board will not conduct a union shop election among guards if the union representing the guards admits, or is affiliated with a union which admits, to membership employees other than guards.[337]

15. One-Year Election Rule

The Act permits only one representation election "in any bargaining unit or subdivision within which, in the preceding twelve-month period, a valid election shall have been held."[338] The method of computing of the twelve-month period has been fixed by the Board. If as a result of the last valid election no bargaining representative was selected and the petition dismissed, the twelve-month period will be computed from the date of the last balloting and not from the date the Board issues its certification of the results of the last election.[339] Under such circumstances, the Board has held that the Act does not bar it from issuing its direction of election before the twelve-month period has expired.[340] However, if as a result of the prior election the Board has certified a bargaining representative, the Board will compute the twelve-month period from the date of the certification and not from the date of the last balloting.[341]

V·STATUS OF THE BARGAINING REPRESENTATIVE

1. Authority

The principle of majority rule invests the union representing a majority of the employees in the appropriate bargaining unit with authority to bargain and contract with the employer concerning wages, rates of pay, hours and other conditions of employment of all the employees in the unit whether or not they are members of the union. It alone has authority to negotiate the collective agreement, to handle grievances and disputes through the final level of the grievance procedure within the provisions of the agreement.

The bargaining representative must be granted exclusive recognition as such and its authority cannot be limited to its members only.[342] The right to recognition is not a subject matter for bargaining.

It includes the absolute right of the union to be represented at the adjustment of grievances at the initial stage, where such grievances are presented, and management cannot insist that the employees shall have the option of determining whether the union shop steward shall be present at the adjustment of grievances by foremen who have the authority to settle them.[343] The Board pointed out that where the foreman has such authority the adjustment of the grievance by him frequently involves the interpretation and application of the terms of the contract and, consequently, such adjustments are of vital concern to the union. A different question would be presented if the foreman had no authority under the contract to dispose of grievances.

Upon individual employee authorizations, the union may obtain a check-off of union dues from the employer.[344]

Individual employees may, however, present grievances to the employer who may adjust them provided (1) the adjustment is not inconsistent with the existing collective agreement and (2) the union has been afforded an opportunity to be present at the adjustment.[345]

The authority of the bargaining representative supersedes rights obtained by employees in individual employment contracts validly entered into by employee and employer prior to the selection of the union as exclusive bargaining agent. Individual employment contracts cannot forestall or delay the collective bargaining procedure and the right of the bargaining representative fully to exercise and completely to perform its functions within the entire area of collective bargaining. The Supreme Court[346] has summarized the impact of the designation of bargaining representative upon individual contracts of employment to be that "individual contracts, no matter what the circumstances that justify their execution or what their terms, may not be availed of to defeat or delay the procedures prescribed by the National Labor Relations Act looking to collective bargaining, nor to exclude the contracting employee from a duly ascertained bargaining unit; or may they be used to forestall bargaining or to limit or condition the terms of the collective agreement."

Furthermore, the individual employee in the bargaining unit may not, by separate agreement, limit the authority of the bargaining representative to act for all of the employees in the unit as sole bargaining representative and to enter labor contracts covering wages, rates of pay, bonus and other conditions of employment.[347] The principle of majority rule requires that he yield his individual right to agree upon basic standards of employment to the right of the bargaining representative to negotiate basic standards binding on all employees in the bargaining unit.[348] In fact, even a majority of the employees cannot by-pass the bargaining representative or bargain away the right of the union to represent them.[349]

The authority of the bargaining representative, once properly designated, restricts the employer's rights as well. The employer cannot act unilaterally, and without consulting the bargaining representative, upon the subject matter of collective bargaining, and, if he does so, his conduct constitutes an unfair labor practice.[350] The principle was summarized by the Supreme Court as follows:[351]

Such unilateral action minimizes the influence of organized bargaining. It interferes with the right of self-organization by emphasizing to the employees that there is no necessity for a collective bargaining agent. If successful in securing approval for the proposed increase in wages, it might well, as the Board points out, block the bargaining representative in securing further wage adjustments.

This announcement of the Court indicates the extent to which the employer's freedom of action is restricted by the authority of the bargaining representative.

It is well established that individual employment contracts, obtained as a result of the employer's unfair labor practices, cannot limit the legitimate authority of the bargaining representative.[352] Even if these individual contracts are not the result of unfair labor practices and are entered into between employee and employer after the execution of the collective labor agreement with the bargaining representative, they do not circumscribe the authority of the bargaining agent within the legitimate sphere of collective bargaining and the provisions of the collective agreement.[353]

The employer cannot confine the authority of the bargaining representative. He cannot limit its authority to certain employees within the bargaining unit,[354] nor can he insist that any collective agreement be signed by his employees rather than by the bargaining representative.[355]

2. Responsibilities of the Bargaining Representative

Unions that acquire the status of bargaining representative by virtue of designation by a majority of the employees in an appropriate bargaining unit enjoy the rights and privileges guaranteed and protected by the Act. These rights, however, carry with them certain responsibilities with which the bargaining representative is charged. These responsibilities are inherent in the rights which flow from the assumption of majority status. They involve duties to the employees who have cloaked the union with majority rights, to the employer who must rely upon the union's constituency for the operation and success of his business, and to the public whose welfare is vitally affected by the disruption of relations between the bargaining representative and the employer resulting from industrial warfare common to such strife.

TO THE EMPLOYEES

The bargaining representative cannot discriminate against employees in the bargaining unit with respect to wages, rates of pay, hours of work and other conditions of employment on the basis of race, color or creed.[356] The Board has indicated that such discriminatory conduct will warrant revocation of its certification of a union as exclusive bargaining representative.[357] However, racial segregation into separate but equally privileged locals has been sanctioned.[358]

The bargaining representative cannot discriminate between union members and nonunion members and must represent *all* the employees in the bargaining unit.[359] It must represent nonunion members in the unit "without hostile discrimination, fairly, impartially and in good faith."[360] The duty of impartial and fair representation obligates the bargaining representative "whenever necessary toward that end, . . . the union is required . . . to consider requests of nonunion members . . . and expressions of their views with respect to collective bargaining with the employer and to give to them notice of and opportunity for hearing upon its proposed action."[361] However, the bargaining representative is not obligated to obtain the same terms of employment for all employees and differences may be justified on the bases of such matters as seniority, type of work performed, competence and skill.

In the interest of individual employees and for the benefit of the public welfare, the Act establishes certain conduct by unions as unfair labor practices. The provisions are applicable to the union that has achieved the status of bargaining representative as well as prior thereto. The bargaining representative cannot restrain or coerce employees in the exercise of their right not to join the union or to refrain from union activities, except to the extent that such right may be limited by a valid union shop agreement; and even where there is such an agreement, the union may not condition the acquisition of membership on payment of fees which the Board finds excessive.[362]

Nor can it deny membership for reasons other than those generally applicable to other members or cause the discharge of employees under the union shop contract for reasons other than the nonpayment of periodic dues and initiation fees.[363] Thus, discharges for "dual unionism" cannot be imposed upon employees. The union shop clauses cannot be used by the bargaining representative to penalize employees for their activities on behalf of a rival union prior to the execution of the agreement.[364] However, the Board's doctrine that a union security agreement cannot be used against employees who become active in a rival union when the agreement is about to expire has been overruled by the Supreme Court.[365] If there is a petition pending before the Board for an election of bargaining representative, the employees cannot be restrained in the free exercise of their choice by the execution of a collective agreement between one of the unions and the employer.[366]

If there is no union shop agreement in effect, it is an unfair labor practice for the bargaining representative to cause or attempt to cause the employer to discriminate against employees because of their failure or refusal to proffer dues to the bargaining representative.[367]

TO THE EMPLOYER, THIRD PERSONS AND THE PUBLIC

The Labor Management Relations Act, 1947, imposes upon the bargaining representative of employees in an industry affecting interstate commerce responsibility for violation of the collective agreement. Suit for such conduct may be brought against the bargaining representative in the United States District Court and the court's process may be served where the union has its principal office or an agent engaged in representing its members.[368] If a judgment is recovered against the union it must be satisfied out of the union's assets, but the assets of its members cannot be reached.[369] The Act also

declares certain conduct by unions, such as secondary boycotts and jurisdictional strikes over assignment of work, unlawful; any person injured
thereby may sue for damages resulting therefrom.[370]

In the public interest, the National Labor Relations Act makes certain
conduct by the bargaining representative, and unions generally, unfair
labor practices. Charges of such unfair labor practices may be filed by employers and employees with the Board. Such unfair labor practices of the
bargaining representative are briefly:

1. Causing or attempting to cause an employer to discriminate against
   employees in order to encourage membership in the bargaining representative or to discourage membership in a rival union (except to the
   extent that such conduct may be in accordance with the provisions of
   a valid union shop provision).[371]
2. Causing or attempting to cause discrimination against employees to
   whom union membership was denied or terminated for reasons other
   than the nonpayment of periodic dues and the usually required initiation
   fee.[372]
3. Refusal to bargain collectively with the employer.[373]
4. Secondary boycotts and jurisdictional strikes over assignment of work
   to members.[374]
5. Featherbedding, that is, exacting payment for services not performed or
   not to be performed.[375]

If the Board has reasonable cause to believe that charges of secondary
boycott are true, it must seek to enjoin the union, by application to the
United States District Court, from such conduct pending disposition of the
case by the Board.[376] In all other cases of unfair labor practices, the union
and the employer are subject to restraint therefrom if the Board issues a
complaint on the unfair labor practices, and in the public interest applies
for and obtains the court's injunction against the union's activities.[377]

The bargaining representative is also subject to restraint in connection
with the calling of strikes upon the termination or modification of the collective agreement pursuant to its provisions and must conform to a sixty day
"cooling off" period. If the bargaining representative desires to terminate or
modify the expiring contract, it must give sixty days notice thereof to the
employer, offer to negotiate a new contract or cancel the proposed modification, give thirty days notice of the dispute, if it continues, to the Federal
Conciliation Service and any comparable state agency, and continue to conform to the contract, without strike, during the sixty day period.[378] Violation of these requirements subjects the bargaining representative to a charge
of unfair labor practices; if the employees in the plant involved engage in a
strike, they lose their status as employees until rehired by the employer.

If the bargaining representative engages in a strike (threatened or actual) which affects the national health and welfare, the President may regard such conduct as a national emergency. The dispute is then subject to inquiry by a fact-finding board and the union strike is subject to temporary restraint by injunction.[379] Some states have enacted legislation restricting the conduct of bargaining representatives in the public utility industries, and imposing compulsory arbitration upon the parties.[380]

VI · PROCEDURE IN REPRESENTATION CASES

1. General

The procedure in cases involving the certification or decertification of a bargaining representative is substantially the same. The petition is filed in the regional office of the Board for the region in which the alleged bargaining unit exists.[381] This, in the ordinary case, means the region in which is located the plant where the employees involved are employed.

The Board's regional office is in charge of a Regional Director who is responsible to the General Counsel. The Regional Director is assisted by a Chief Law Enforcement Officer (formerly Regional Attorney), who acts as chief legal adviser, and a staff of attorneys and assistants known as examiners. The members of the staff in the regional office are responsible to the Regional Director.[382]

2. The Administrative Preliminary Investigation— Consent and Directed Elections

Upon the filing of the petition in the regional office, it is given a case number and assigned to an examiner for investigation.[383] The regional office usually sends notices of the filing of the petition to other unions. There is usually an arrangement whereby a central body for each labor group receives the notice so that it can circulate its affiliated international and local unions within the locale covered by the regional office.

Broadly stated, the function of the investigation is said by the Board to cover:

(1) whether the employer's operations affect commerce within the meaning of the Act, (2) the appropriateness of the unit of employees . . . . and the existence of a bona fide question concerning representation . . . . (3) whether the election would effectuate the policies of the Act, ... (4) whether, if the petitioner is a labor organization seeking recognition, there is sufficient probability, based on evidence of representation of the petitioner, that the employees have selected it to represent them.[384]

The Field Examiner to whom the case has been assigned communicates with the employer and the union. He fixes a date for a first conference with the parties. He requests the employer to furnish information concerning his business activities in connection with interstate commerce. This is usually requested in the form of a questionnaire which the employer is asked to complete. The questionnaire will also ask the employer to concede that he is engaged in commerce within the meaning of the Act and subject to the jurisdiction of the Board.

The employer is also asked to produce the current payroll covering the employees alleged in the petition to constitute the appropriate bargaining unit. The examiner may also request the production of all information which he may deem necessary for the completion of his investigation.

The petitioning union is requested to produce some evidence that at least 30 per cent of the employees desire to be represented by it for the purposes of collective bargaining. Such proof is referred to as a showing of substantial representation. Competing unions that desire to intervene in the proceeding must also show proof of interest to the examiner, but the same percentage standard is not applied. The union seeking to intervene must show an interest which is more than academic or theoretical. A recently-expired contract with the employer covering the same employees involved in the petition has been regarded as sufficient to warrant intervention.

The proof of interest submitted by the union may be membership application cards, signed cards designating the union as bargaining representative, or dues records. There is no formal requirement.

The investigation of substantial interest is informal and no attempt is made at certainty. Normally, the examiner, or the clerical staff under his supervision, checks the names or signatures on the cards submitted by the union against the payroll records obtained from the employer. The check has even been made on a "sampling" or on a "spot" basis. The aim is to secure an overall idea of the extent of union representation, rather than accuracy.

The investigation of substantial interest of the petitioning union is regarded by the Board purely as an administrative function. If the union cannot meet the requirements, it will be advised to withdraw its petition and the petition will be dismissed if it fails to do so.

The Board will not permit the employer or a rival union to contest the showing of interest, and the results of the investigation will not be introduced at the hearing, nor will any party be permitted to offer proof on the question.[385] The examiner will not disclose to the other parties the extent of the showing of interest.

There is no obligation on the part of the employer to furnish the commerce information concerning his business or the payroll requested. However, if he refuses them, his records may be subpoenaed for production at the hearing and his payroll records may be subpoenaed for the election. Obedience to the Board's subpoena may be enforced by proceedings instituted in the United States District Court by the Board.

The commerce questionnaire signed by the employer will be introduced at the hearing to establish the Board's jurisdiction. A naked concession, unsupported by any evidence, that the employer is engaged in commerce will not be regarded as sufficient, since it has been the Board's legal position that jurisdiction must be predicated upon facts rather than consent. If the employer contests the Board's jurisdiction, the commerce questionnaire cannot be furnished and the issue must be tried at a hearing.

The conference arranged by the examiner is usually conducted by him with all parties present. In special circumstances, he may conduct separate conferences. Such factors as geographical location of the parties, their availability, the nature of the dispute and the parties involved will determine the nature of the conference.

The conference is conducted (1) to ascertain the nature of the dispute, (2) to seek an amicable adjustment on a consent basis, and (3) if no consent disposition is possible, to complete or make arrangements to complete the investigation by (a) ascertaining the nature and area of dispute and the position of the parties with respect thereto and (b) obtaining as many facts as possible bearing on the issues. Additional conferences with each of the parties may be necessary for the purpose of achieving these objectives.

At the outset, the principal aim of the examiner is to persuade the parties to agree upon a consent election.

Two types of consent elections are made available by the Board.[386] The first type leads to the issuance by the Regional Director of Consent Determination of Representatives. While the election is held and conducted in accordance with the Rules and Regulations of the Board, the determination of the Regional Director upon any question involved or that may arise is final and binding upon the parties. There is no recourse to the Board, and no Board hearing upon objections will be held. The parties, for the purpose of such consent election, must agree upon and stipulate as to the following basic matters:

1. The unit appropriate for the purpose of collective bargaining, and the employees included within and excluded from the unit. This point should be covered as specifically as possible and general descriptions should be avoided. In this way, the possibility of disagreement as to meaning and coverage of the appropriate unit provision may be minimized.
2. The payroll to be used as a list of eligible voters.
3. The date, hours and place of the election. Several questions may arise on this point. Some unions object to the holding of the election on the em-

ployer's premises, in which event a convenient substitute place must be agreed upon. While the principal factors involved are ready accessibility of the voting place to the employees and the convenience of the hours for voting, to the end that as many eligible employees as possible will have the opportunity to vote, the employer must also consider the matter from the point of view of minimizing and, if possible, eliminating interference with production. He must, therefore, in the light of all the circumstances, determine whether the election should be held during or after or before working hours. If the election is to be held during working hours, he will have to answer the question whether he will pay the employees for the time spent by them at voting. The size of the plant and the number of employees involved in the balloting may present special problems, or influence the position and suggestion of the parties on these matters.

The second type of consent election results in a certification by the Board. While the Regional Director conducts the election and investigates objections to the election and challenged ballots, he makes no final ruling on these matters. He submits a report to the Board. Final decision is made by the Board. If the Board concludes that the objections to the election raise substantial and material issues, it will order a hearing to take the proof. Otherwise, the objections are overruled and the Board will render a final disposition of the case either by issuance of certification, or by dismissal of the petition if the union has lost the election.

In addition to the foregoing matters upon which the parties must agree for the purposes of a consent election, they are required to agree to the following for the purposes of the second type or stipulation for Board certification upon consent election:

1. That there is a question concerning representation, on the basis of the facts. This means that the parties merely stipulate that the employer refuses to recognize the union until it has been certified by the Board.
2. The parties must waive hearing and notice thereof as well as the making by the Board of a Direction of Election, Findings of Fact and Conclusions of Law prior to the election.
3. The employer must state that he is engaged in commerce within the meaning of the Act.

These additional stipulations are necessary in order to establish the jurisdiction and the basis of the procedure by the Board on the stipulation within the provisions of the Act.

Subsequent to the conference, the field examiner makes his report on the case. If an agreement for consent election has been signed by the parties, he submits it to the Regional Director for approval. If approved, he sends duplicate originals to each of the parties, and proceeds to the next steps required.

If the dispute continues, he reports concerning the commerce, activities of the employer, the issues and the evidence he has obtained. He also includes the results of investigation of the interest claimed by the union or unions involved. If any collective bargaining contracts are involved, he attaches copies which he seeks to obtain from the employer. On the basis of all these matters, he makes a recommendation—either that the case should go to hearing or the petition should be dismissed. The recommendation and file of the field examiner then go to the Regional Director who, with the assistance of the legal staff, concur in or disapprove of the recommendation. The Regional Director may seek advice on the matter from the Washington staff or issue notice of hearing.

If a consent election is agreed upon, the employer prepares payroll lists of eligible voters from the payroll agreed upon. Sufficient copies for use at the polls are prepared, the number depending on the number of employees involved, and the number of polling places necessary. The voting lists show the names of the eligible employees according to departments and their badge or check numbers. Copies thereof are submitted to the union for examination and the union may question the names appearing or omitted therefrom. The parties designate observers. Arrangements are made for enclosed voting booths and the ballot box or boxes. Shortly before the election the employer receives from the Board the notices of election, which are posted in the plant in accordance with the accompanying instructions. The ballots for the election in the form agreed upon are furnished by the Board.

The observers as well as the Board agent have the right to challenge any voter. In such instances, the voter inserts his ballot in an envelope. In the meantime the Board representative writes out on a large envelope the name of the challenger and the grounds for the challenge. Then the small envelope containing the ballot is inserted in the large envelope, which is sealed and dropped by the voter into the ballot box. The challenges are not determined and the challenged ballots are not opened unless they are necessary to determine the outcome of the election.

After the close of the polls, the ballot box is opened in the presence of the observers and the ballots are tabulated by the Board agent, who reports the results to the Regional Director. In the case of consent election, the Regional Director will issue his determination of representatives or the Board will issue its certification if the union wins the election. In the other cases, the Board will issue its certification of election if the union wins, or dismiss the petition if the union is unsuccessful.

In the first type of consent election, i.e., where the final result is the Regional Director's determination of election, objection to the election by any of the parties must be served upon the parties and filed with the Regional Director within five days after they have been furnished by the Regional Director with a tally of ballots; and his determination thereof is final and binding.

Where there is an agreement for Board certification or no agreement, the Regional Director acts in an advisory capacity. The objections together with a statement of the reasons therefor must be served and filed within the five day period mentioned. The Regional Director then investigates the objections and, if necessary, the challenges, and serves upon the parties and files with the Board his report and recommendations thereon. Exceptions to the report may be filed within five days from the date of service of the report. If the exceptions appear to the Board to raise substantial and material issues, the Board may order a hearing thereon, and further testimony is taken. Thereafter the Board proceeds to a disposition of the case. If the Board does not believe the exceptions raise substantial and material issues, it will proceed toward disposition of the case without further hearing.

Where no choice receives a majority of the valid ballots cast and no objections are filed, a run-off election may be conducted. The ballot in such an election contains the two choices receiving the largest and second largest number of votes. Only one run-off election is conducted. If the issues cannot be resolved by agreement and the Regional Director determines further action is necessary, notice of hearing is issued to the parties.[387]

3. Formal Hearing

Neither the Act nor the Board's Rules and Regulations fixes how much notice of the hearing must be given. The Act requires "an appropriate hearing upon due notice." Usually five to ten days is given, but there have been instances of only two-day notices. The Regional Director has discretion in the matter so long as there is "due notice under the circumstances."

The hearing is formal and, in general, proceeds in broad outline like a lawsuit and is part of the Board's statutory investigation of bargaining representatives.[388] Witnesses are sworn and testify, and are subjected to cross-examination; and exhibits are introduced in evidence. A stenographic record of the proceeding is made. However, the entire proceeding is regarded as non-adversary.

A Hearing Officer presides and swears the witnesses. He is usually a member of the regional staff, either an attorney or a field examiner. The Board's staff Trial Examiner handles these cases only under special and unusual circumstances. The duty of the Hearing Officer is to rule on motions made to him and on the materiality and relevancy of the testimony. He is charged with the responsibility of making a complete and useful record on all the issues involved. He will frequently examine witnesses for the purpose of bringing out information which he thinks necessary and request information from the parties. He cannot dismiss the petition and has no authority to rule on motions to dismiss the petition; he must refer them to the Board for action.

Subpoenas for the hearing (both to compel attendance of witnesses and to compel production of testimony) must be issued by the Regional Director or Hearing Officer upon the written application of any party to the proceeding.[389] *The application* may be made *ex parte*. Within five days after issuance of the subpoena, the person upon whom it has been served may move before the Regional Director or the Hearing Officer for revocation of the subpoena.

The issues for the hearing may be one or more of the following questions:
1. Whether the employer is engaged in commerce within the meaning of the Act.
2. Whether there is a question concerning representation.
3. Whether the unions involved are labor organizations within the meaning of the Act.
4. The unit of employees appropriate for purposes of collective bargaining.
5. The effect of existing labor contracts.
6. What employees, either specifically or by job classification or by nature of work, should be included or excluded from the unit.

After the presentation of the evidence, the parties may orally argue their contentions before the hearing officer.

Upon the close of the hearing, the record covering the testimony, exhibits and contentions of the parties is forwarded to the Board in Washington.[390] The Hearing Officer submits a report on the hearing but makes no recommendations for disposition of the issues. The parties may file briefs with the Board.[391] Oral argument before the Board is usually not allowed except on novel issues; the Board considers the case upon the basis of the record, oral argument and the briefs, if submitted, and will dispose of the case by decision on the issues and direction of an election or such other disposition as it may determine.

PART TWO

Prevention of Unfair Labor Practices

CHAPTER I. Authority of the National Labor
Relations Board
II. Procedure in Unfair Labor Practice
Cases
III. Judicial Enforcement and Review
of Board Orders

I · AUTHORITY OF THE
NATIONAL LABOR RELATIONS BOARD

1. Nature of Authority

The National Labor Relations Board was created for the purpose of administering the Act. It has the power to interpret the Act, to resolve questions concerning the representation of employees for the purpose of collective bargaining, and to prevent and prescribe remedies for unfair labor practices as defined in the Act.[1]

Where its authority has been challenged by lawsuits, the courts almost uniformly refuse to interfere with its operations on the ground that the statute gives the Board broad discretionary powers in the conduct of elections and hearings, and the courts will not review Board rulings until they become final orders.[2] Thus, a suit in the federal court to enjoin a Board election or hearing failed because no unlawful action by the Board and irreparable injury could be shown.[3] It has been held that a hearing conducted by the Board in a representation case causes no substantial irreparable injury.[4] The Court of Appeals for the District of Columbia has held that the federal Declaratory Judgment Act does not confer upon the federal courts power to declare a Board certification of a bargaining representative invalid.[5]

On the other hand, the orders issued by the Board are not self-enforcing and it must apply to the United States Court of Appeals for a decree directing obedience.[6] Disobedience of a court order enforcing an order of the Board is contempt of court and punishable accordingly.[7]

The Board is a "public agency," responsible for performing public functions and must represent the public interests. Under the sweeping authority granted it to take action necessary to "effectuate the policy" of the National Labor Relations Act and by virtue of the broad interpretation of this authority, the Labor Board has almost unlimited broad administrative power to interpret and apply its interpretation of the Act. It has power over the issue of representation and the determination of the appropriate bargaining unit. It is limited only by the prohibition of arbitrary or capricious conduct.[8]

Where unfair labor practices have been committed by an employer or a union, the Board may issue a "cease and desist" order which may also require the performance of corrective action.[9] The determination of whether an act on the part of the employer or union constitutes an "unfair practice" and what subsequent action the employer must take are entirely within the discretion of the Board,[10] subject to the limited review that may be obtained under the statute in the Circuit Court of Appeals. It may not, however, make a sweeping order where the unfair practice was limited.[11] The jurisdiction of the Board also extends to preventing the employer from enjoying any advantage which he may have gained as a result of his violation of the statute.[12] Where the employer refuses to bargain, the appropriate order can go no further than this: to restrain the employer from refusing to bargain and from any other acts in any manner interfering with the representative's effort to negotiate, and to order the employer to bargain with the union as well as to post notices of compliance with the order. The Board's actions may not be punitive, since the Act was intended to eliminate unfair labor practices and foster collective bargaining, and not to impose penalties.

The Board enjoys virtually paramount authority over the enforcement of rights for the purposes of collective bargaining in industries affecting interstate commerce. While management still retains various rights, it may exercise these rights only with certain limitations. Thus, it may hire, but not discriminatorily because of membership or nonmembership in a union. It may discharge, but discharges must not reflect any element of interference with union activity. It may adjust individual grievances, but only on notice to the bargaining representative and not contrary to the provisions of an existing collective agreement.[13] Even if there be an individual contract with an individual employee, that contract must give way to the collective agreement.[14]

The Board is empowered "to prevent any person from engaging in any unfair labor practice," as defined in the Act, affecting interstate commerce.[15]

While it may, in some respects, resemble a private controversy, the proceeding authorized to be taken by the Board under the Act is not for the settlement and adjustment of violations of private rights. The Board acts in a public capacity to give effect to the declared policy of the Act: to eliminate and prevent obstructions to interstate commerce by encouraging collective bargaining and by protecting the "exercise by workers of full freedom of association, self-organization, and designation of representatives of their own choosing, for the purpose of negotiating the terms and conditions of their employment. . . ."[16] The immediate object of the proceeding is to prevent unfair labor practices burdening or obstructing or affecting the free flow of goods in interstate commerce. To that end the Board is authorized to order the employer and a union to cease and desist from such practices and is given the authority to order affirmative action to achieve the objectives of the Act.[17] While courts may not enjoin the Board from holding hearings on complaints alleging these unfair practices, nor from proceeding on petitions for certifications or elections, the orders of the Board are subject to review by the United States Circuit Court of Appeals.[18]

2. Scope of Authority

Nearly all industries have been brought under the Board's jurisdiction, since their activities have been found to "affect interstate commerce."[19]

Where the National Board has taken jurisdiction of a business, a state labor board cannot assume jurisdiction over the business for purposes inconsistent with policies enunciated by the federal Board under the Act. The Supreme Court held under the Wagner Act that at the time when the federal Board denied certification of bargaining units of foremen, the state board could not take jurisdiction over two steel companies engaged in interstate commerce and certify a bargaining representative for foremen employed by these companies.[20] The Labor Management Relations Act of 1947 has enlarged the scope of the federal Board's authority. But it bans the federal Board from ceding jurisdiction to state boards if the applicable state statute and the rulings of the state board thereunder are inconsistent with the federal Act and construction thereof.[21]

Among the industries held within the jurisdiction of the Board are:

1. Businesses having incoming interstate shipments but virtually none moving out into interstate commerce,[22] e.g., the Act applies to driver-salesmen of a baking plant having no outgoing interstate sales, but only incoming interstate shipments. The employer owned and operated baking plants in other states.
2. Manufacturing or other production,[23] i.e., distribution and service industries, which receive and transmit materials in interstate commerce.
3. Mining, e.g., a mine which obtained all raw materials within the state but shipped a portion of its products to points in other states.
4. Transportation, even of a local transit company, because it transported thousands of passengers engaged in the production of goods for interstate commerce in a city which is extensively engaged in the manufacture and transportation of such goods. The fact that the vehicles of the company do not cross state lines was held irrelevant.[24]

Further examples are: a shipyard building Navy vessels, department stores, chain stores, a public utility system located wholly within a state, which supplied energy to a multitude of enterprises engaged in interstate and foreign commerce. The fact that the goods were merely being processed by the employer does not prevent the Board from taking jurisdiction when the goods move in interstate commerce.

Where the business as a whole is subject to the Act, the employees may not be departmentalized to escape jurisdiction.[25] In one case a company unsuccessfully contended that its street transportation departments were local in character and, therefore, outside the Board's jurisdiction, although the company admitted being subject to the Act with respect to its electrical operations.[26]

Generally the percentage of interstate business is immaterial, unless it is of trifling quantity, in which case, the Board will not take jurisdiction.[27] The jurisdiction of the Board did not apply over the operations of a gold mining corporation which obtained its necessary equipment from dealers within the state and disposed of its product either to local refineries or to the United States Mint, also located within the state. Although the equipment had its origin in other states, and the gold, after the refining at the Mint, moved to destinations outside the state, the court held that these transactions were not so closely related to the company's mining operations as to bring the latter within the jurisdiction of the Board.[28]

The General Counsel of the Board has contended that since the amended Act gives him "final authority" as to issuance of complaints in an unfair labor practice case, the Board, once he has issued such a complaint, has no authority to decline to assert jurisdiction over a business on policy grounds, if jurisdiction in fact exists. However, the Board has overruled this contention and asserted its authority to decline to assert jurisdiction on policy grounds. Such action, the Board has said, does not constitute a denial of the "final authority" of the General Counsel in unfair labor practice cases because "after a complaint has been issued and a hearing has been held, the 'final authority' of the General Counsel is exhausted and the case is then in the hands of the Board."[29]

The Board's jurisdiction is limited to the extent that certain classes of employers are excluded by provisions of the Act. The United States or any State or political subdivision thereof is not included as an employer, i.e., a harbor district formed under a State law providing for the formation and administration of districts for improving harbors.[30] Hospitals not operated for profit are not included under the Act. Agricultural laborers and domestic servants in homes are excluded as employees.[31] Employees who plant, fertilize, cultivate and harvest crops in the open fields under natural conditions are "agricultural laborers" although in a commercial enterprise engaged in the production, sale and distribution of fruit trees and plants, etc.[32] Fruit packers in a packing house and employees in the feed mill and feeding pens of a meatpacking plant are not "agricultural laborers," since they work away from the field.[33]

Independent contractors are excluded and in determining whether an individual is an independent contractor rather than an employee, the ordinary tests of the law of agency are applied, namely, the "right of control test" applied by the courts. Thus, it was held by the Board that the "employer-independent contractor relationship exists where the control is merely limited to the result to be accomplished and does not apply to the method and manner of the services rendered."[a] A far-reaching decision of the United States Supreme Court sustained an order of the Board under the Wagner Act that newsboys engaged in selling daily newspapers in a metropolitan area were employees of the newspaper and were not independent contractors.[34] But in a subsequent case, the Board held newspaper carriers who operate home delivery routes under contract with the newspapers were independent contractors and not employees.[35]

Individuals employed as supervisors do not fall within the term "employee" as defined in the Act.[36] Thus, foremen are not within the coverage of the Act and the Board is without authority to compel collective bargaining with respect to them.

The Board does not lose jurisdiction over a case merely by virtue of discontinuance of the unfair practice, cessation of business activities or change in business structure.[37] While the Board has on several occasions professed its lack of authority to police collective agreements, it has broad discretionary and enforcement powers which can achieve such a result. Thus, it has held that breach of a collective agreement by an employer may be a refusal to bargain in violation of the Act. In one case, the Board, moving under its authority to issue a cease and desist order, found that an employer's unilateral refusal to adhere to the closed shop provisions of a union contract, coupled with its refusal to discuss the matter with the union, was an attempt to "change" the terms of the contract without negotiating with the union. Such conduct, the Board held, constitutes modification of the contract without notice to the accredited bargaining representative and, hence, is an unfair labor practice.[38]

3. To Prevent Domination and Support of a Labor Organization

The Board has authority to disestablish old employee-representation plans and employer-approved and dominated labor organizations.[39] Such plans are barred even though they were introduced merely to provide the employees with a grievance machinery. Any organization in which employees participate and which exists, partially or entirely, for the purpose of dealing with the employer concerning grievances, labor disputes, wages, rates of pay, hours of employment or conditions of work is a labor organization and subject to the Board's ban in the event of employer sponsorship, aid, domination or interference.[40] Thus a labor-management committee organized by the employer pursuant to the War Production Board's suggestions was ordered disestablished when it undertook the functions of a labor organization, because it thereby became a labor organization under the Act tainted with illegality by reason of its employer sponsorship and support.[41] A welfare and insurance society was similarly disestablished.[42] But a social organization that did not engage in any of the functions of a labor organization was not disestablished.[43] The Board, however, ordered disestablished a social organization that was used by the employer to oppose the union,[44] and it applied the same rule to an athletic club.[45] An organization which was formed originally for social purposes and functioned primarily as such an organization fell within the statutory ban when it also sought wage increases for its members, handled grievances and discussed working conditions with the employer.[46] A "manufacturing board," organized to function like the labor-management committee formed during the war, was also held in violation of the Act, because it became active in various phases of the labor-management relationship.[47] The courts have overruled contentions that the illegality in a union, by reason of activity therein by supervisors, removes such an organization from the statutory definition of "labor organization," since the very objects of the illegal interference are labor organizations within the meaning of the Act.[48]

The Board regards the following activity of an employer as evidence of employer domination and interference:

1. Employer introduction of union to employees;[49]
2. Granting use of company time and property;[50]
3. Aid in drafting constitution and bylaws;[51]
4. Circulating supporting petitions;[52]
5. Direct financial support;[53]
6. Aid or support by permitting use of company facilities, such as bulletin boards, office space or mailing lists.[54]

The Board regards as "indirect" illegal support an employer permitting a labor organization to sell foodstuffs such as milk in the plant for a commission.[55] Discouraging membership in a rival outside union is regarded as an element of support.[56]

The fact that employees have made substantial gains by collective bargaining through a company-dominated union is no defense to a charge of domination.[57]

The Board may find that the employer has interfered with the union but may regard the facts as not sufficient to establish employer domination. In that event, the Board will not order disestablishment but will order the employer to cease and desist from recognizing the organization as collective bargaining agent for the employees until certification by the Board.[58]

The complete remedy applied by the Board under the Wagner Act, upon finding employer domination of a labor organization, was to order its complete disestablishment as a bargaining representative. Such a direction by the Board required the employer "to withhold all recognition" of the dominated organization *in perpetuo*. Hence such an organization could never be certified by the Board or recognized by the employer as bargaining representative of the employees.[59] Under the Wagner Act the full disestablishment remedy was never applied by the Board to employer-controlled or assisted labor organizations which were affiliated with a national or international organization. In such cases, the Board charged the employer with interference, restraint and coercion of employees rather than with domination, support and interference with a labor organization, and the employer, by way of remedy, was merely required to withhold recognition of the organization until it was certified by the Board. The Board then withheld certification of the organization until it was satisfied that the effects of the employer's illegal conduct were dissipated. The organization was then eligible for certification and recognition as bargaining representative.[60]

This different treatment of affiliated and nonaffiliated unions was justified by the Board on the ground that "a labor organization affiliated with a national or international federation that was outside the ambit of the employer's control could not be permanently and completely subjugated to the will of the employer."[61]

The law as amended by the Labor Management Relations Act, 1947, eliminates this difference in treatment of affiliated and nonaffiliated unions, and requires the Board to apply the same rules in the cases above mentioned to all labor organizations without regard to whether such labor organizations are affiliated or not affiliated.[62] The Board has announced that it will apply the following policies under the amended Act:[63]

In all cases in which we find that an employer has dominated or interfered with, or contributed support to a labor organization, or has committed any of these proscribed acts, we will find such conduct a violation of Section 8(a) (2) of the Act, as amended in 1947, regardless of whether the organization involved is affiliated. Where we find that an employer's unfair labor practices have been so extensive as to constitute domination of the organization, we shall order its disestablishment, whether or not affiliated.

The Board believes that disestablishment is still necessary as a remedy, in order effectively to remove the consequences of an employer's unfair labor practices and to make possible a free choice of representatives, in those cases, perhaps few in number, in which an employer's control of any labor organization has extended to the point of actual domination.

But when the Board finds that an employer's unfair labor practices were limited to interference and support and never reached the point of domination, we shall only order that recognition be withheld until certification, again without regard to whether or not the organization happens to be affiliated. Subsequent representation proceedings in such situations will be governed, of course, by the provisions of Section 9(c)(2).

4. To Disestablish a Successor Labor Organization

Where there has been domination and interference with a labor organization, the Board may find a newly formed union a successor to the old company-dominated organization and order disestablishment of the successor.[64] In determining the question, the Board will consider whether the effect of the employer's domination of the old organization was dissipated prior to the formation of the new organization so that employees were free to choose whether to join the new organization. Posting of disestablishment notices with respect to the old organization has been regarded by the Board as ineffective where the employer aided and assisted the newly formed organization.[65] The Board may order disestablished a company-dominated union formed prior to the passage of the Wagner Act if its effects have not been dissipated by reorganization after the Act.[66] Where a union was formed by the leaders of a company-dominated union and there has been no action by the employer to mark a "line of fracture" between the two unions in so far as the employees are concerned, the Board may find the employer guilty of company domination of the second union.[67]

The remedy to be applied to employer-controlled or assisted "successor" labor organizations must be the same without regard to affiliation or non-affiliation. With respect to this problem, the Board has said:[68]

Identical standards must also be applied to affiliated and unaffiliated local unions in these situations in which, following disestablishment, a new labor organization appears on the scene, and a question arises as to whether it is the "successor" of the old.

5. To Prevent Discriminatory Discharges

BY EMPLOYERS

The Board will order employees who have been discharged because of union affiliation to be reinstated with back pay.[69] The same principles have been applied to discriminatory lay-offs, transfers or demotions or other changes in the status of employees.[70] The Board does not require that employees, to be entitled to reinstatement, actually hold membership in a formal union. Other types of illegal discrimination are exclusion of union leaders from wage increases granted to other employees,[71] reduction in pay and benefits because inspectors voted to join a rank-and-file union,[72] lockout[73] and plant slow-down to stop union activity.[74] An employer has been held responsible for not restoring to their jobs union employees ejected from the plant by nonunion employees.[75]

Discrimination has been found where there was no union involved and the employees acted themselves in concert.[76] The Board has held a discharge of an employee because of the union activities of the employee's relative to be an unfair labor practice.[77]

The Supreme Court has sustained the Board's findings of unfair labor practice where employees were discharged for soliciting membership for the union on the employer's property during the employees' own time.[78] In the same case, the Court also found discriminatory discharges for wearing union steward buttons in the plant although there was no labor contract between the union and the employer.

The Board has found a refusal to hire a new employee because of his union affiliation to be a violation, provided at the time of his application for a job there was a suitable vacancy available.[79] Other evidence of discriminatory discharge was found on the basis of admissions by the employer or his supervisors, studied efforts of the employer to ascertain the identity of union leaders, and discharge allegedly on the ground of inefficiency of old employees shortly after the commencement of union activity.[80] Employees, however, who engage in a sitdown strike may be legally discharged.[81]

Delegation to a company-dominated union of power to determine who shall return to work after a strike is regarded by the Board as indicative of discrimination.[82] Discharges because of strike threats or economic pressure by a rival union are held to be discriminatory unless they are warranted by a closed shop contract.[83] In the *New York Porto Rico Steamship Company* case the Board, recognizing the helpless position of the employer under the Wagner Act when such threats and pressure were applied by a union to compel discharges, did not award back pay under such circumstances.[84] Subsequently, in the *Greer Steel Company* case,[85] the Board varied its policy and awarded back pay because the union did not take the drastic action (for example, sitdown strikes) that was applied against the employer in the earlier case. The Supreme Court has held that, because of their peculiar status, seamen who mutinied on board ship could not be reinstated.[86] Discharges under a closed shop agreement with a union assisted by unfair labor practices are illegal although such assistance occurred after the union had signed up a majority of the employees.[87]

The Board has considered whether the activity for which the employee is discharged is union activity within the meaning of the Act. Filing of individual suits by employees against the employer, to recover for alleged violations of a state wage statute without notice, has been held to be union activity, where the statute had previously authorized the employees to institute suit.[88] Complaining about an employer's overtime system and refusing to agree with the employer that working conditions were satisfactory has been held protected activity.[89] Discharge of an employee because his wife participated in a strike at the plant of another employer has been held illegal by the Board.[90] Obtaining an employee's resignation because of his union activities does not relieve an employer from the charge of discrimination.[91] The employer is liable if discrimination occurs through the medium of a company-dominated union.[92] But an employer is not liable where nonunion employees drive the union employees from the plant, unless the hostility and actions towards the union employees were provoked by him or are chargeable to him.[93] That the action of the employer was for the purpose of discouraging union membership may be based on difference in treatment of union and nonunion employees,[94] as where the employees involved were union leaders,[95] who refused to join a company-dominated union,[96] or where the employer failed to support his explanation of the discharge.[97] But where an employer who honestly but mistakenly believed an employee was engaged in a slowdown and disciplined him on that basis, no violation of the Act was found.[98]

An employer, who, after certification of the union, withheld the Christmas bonus, which had in prior years been customarily given to the employees, was guilty of discrimination. It was an illegal refusal to bargain since it was done unilaterally, without either notice to the union or affording it an opportunity to bargain with respect to the bonus.[99]

An employer who discharges employees pursuant to a union shop agreement entered into with a union having a majority either by virtue of a Board certification or otherwise, violates the Act unless a majority of the employees *eligible* to vote have voted to authorize the union to enter into such contract at an election conducted for that purpose by the Board.[100] Even when the union shop contract is authorized by the eligible employees at the Board election, a discharge for nonmembership in the union violates the Act, if the employer has reasonable grounds to believe that union membership was not made available to such employee on the same terms generally applied to other members or that such membership was denied or terminated for reasons other than nonpayment of the regular dues and initiation fees.[101]

BY UNIONS

A union commits an unfair labor practice if it attempts to force an employer to discharge an employee from employment because of his refusal to join the union or engage in its activities, or because of his membership in or activity on behalf of a competing union.[102] And an attempt by a union, where there is a valid union shop agreement authorized by the employees, to cause a discharge for nonmembership because of reasons other than nonpayment of the regular dues and initiation fees is unlawful. Thus, a union cannot compel an employer to discharge employees for "dual unionism."[103]

6. To Prevent Discrimination for Testifying or Filing Charges

Discharge of an employee because he testified in a proceeding before the Board is a violation of the Act.[104] The Board holds that an employer violates the Act if he discharges an employee for filing charges with or testifying before the Board, even though the charges are false.[105] But the mere giving of testimony, whether true or false, does not impart to the employee an immunity from appropriate disciplinary action by the employer for misconduct and breaches of duty during the course of employment. Thus, it was not violative of the Act for an employer to discharge an employee for eavesdropping on conversations between the employer's officials by secreting herself near its offices and engaging in union activity during working hours, although she had testified against the employer before the Board.[106] But conditioning the reinstatement of a striker upon withdrawal of unfair labor practice charges against the employer on file with the Board is illegal.[107] Similarly, an employer was held to be in violation of the Act by the Board because he refused to rehire an employee on the ground that he believed charges filed with the Board on behalf of the employee were false.[108]

7. To Give Limited Protection to Supervisory Employees

The Board ruled under the Wagner Act that an employer who discriminates against his supervisory employees because of their union membership in, and activities on behalf of, an unaffiliated union whose membership was confined to supervisory employees only, is illegal.[109] Similarly, the discharge of a supervisor because he refused to join a union favored by his superior was found to constitute a violation of the law.[110] But the Board did not find a violation when the employer demoted a supervisor who engaged in activities for which the employer might be held responsible.[111] However, the Board ruled discriminatory the discharge of a supervisor because he refused to campaign against the union.[112] Nor, in the case of supervisors who violate neutrality instructions, will the Board permit the employer to vary his treatment according to whether the conduct in question was for or against the union.

To what extent the Board will apply these rules under the Taft-Hartley Act, which expressly excludes supervisory employees from its coverage, remains to be seen. No doubt, the Board's attitude will be to apply them if and wherever the circumstances of the case permit it consistently with the amended law. In the *Edward G. Budd* case,[114] the Supreme Court of the United States denied an employer's petition for review of a Board order, issued prior to the enactment of the new law, requiring reinstatement with back pay of a supervisor found to have been illegally discharged for his activity in behalf of a foremen's union. The Court, however, granted *certiorari* limited to the question of the validity of the part of the Board's order directing the employer to cease and desist from discouraging membership in the Foreman's Association of America and remanded the case to the Court of Appeals for consideration of the effect of the Labor Management Relations Act on that provision of the Board's order. The Court of Appeals ruled that such provision was no longer valid because under the Labor Management Relations Act employers are "free in the future to discharge supervisors for joining a union, and to interfere with their union activities."[115] The Court of Appeals for the Sixth Circuit in the *Eastern Gas & Fuel Association* case, involving the reinstatement of a discriminatorily discharged supervisor, limited the effective period of its order to August 22, 1947, the effective date of the new law.[116] The court's decision enforcing the order of the Board had been rendered prior to that date.

Despite the exclusion of supervisors from the term "employee," the Board has held under the amended Act that it has authority to order payment of back pay to, and reinstatement of, supervisory employees where the discharge of the supervisor interfered with the rights of nonsupervisory employees guaranteed in the amended Act. The discharge of a supervisor because he refused to report to his superiors the union activities of his subordinates in connection with the employer's campaign to thwart unionization was held to be such a case.[a] The Board's view is that exclusion of supervisors from the definition of the term "employee" merely relieves the employer of the duty to bargain collectively with supervisors.

The Board has held justified the discharge of supervisors for their refusal to do certain nonsupervisory work solely to prevent serious damage to plant equipment during a strike by nonsupervisory employees. The supervisors involved refused to report for such work or left their work. The Board pointed out that "we believe the complainants owed a duty to respondent inherent in their positions to comply with all reasonable instructions designed to protect the respondent's physical plant from imminent danger or destruction."[117]

In a case which arose under the Wagner Act, and was decided after the amendment thereof, the Board held illegal an employer's refusal to hire an individual as a foreman unless he withdrew charges filed against the employer with the Board.[118] While issuing a cease and desist order, the Board did not award back pay or reinstatement to the individual who sought the supervisory position.

8. To Restrain Anti-Union Activity

The Board will order discontinuance of labor espionage, surveillance of union activities, members, and meeting places, and the use of violence against union representatives and members.[119] Interrogating employees concerning their union membership or activity is proscribed.[120] Forms of application for employees which require disclosure of union affiliation have been found to constitute a violation of the Act.[121]

Threats to close the plant if the employees joined the union, or to remove the plant to another community are regarded as coercive.[122] References to union dues as "tribute" (under Wagner Act),[123] threats of legal action against employees engaging in union activity,[124] and threats to shut off credit to individual employees have also been held to be coercive.[125]

Employers who organize to boycott another employer who is dealing with the union have been held to be in violation of the Act.[126] Employers who have encouraged hostility to the union have been held liable for physical violence against employees because of their union activity or membership.[127] Permitting anti-union employees violently to evict union employees from the plant is held to be a violation.[128] Threatening and intimidating employees if they take part in a Board election is similarly treated.[129]

Where employers refused to permit representatives of the certified bargaining agency of the employees to enter upon their vessels for the purpose of conferring with the employees, the Board found the employer guilty of coercion in violation of the Act,[130] and ordered the employer to permit the union to enter upon its vessels for discussions with employees on grievances, collection of dues, and distribution of union papers. But the Board did not authorize the union agent to go aboard the vessels to solicit membership in the union.

The employer may prohibit union activity during working hours.[131] But the Board regards a discriminatory application of such a rule as unlawful interference, without regard to whether the activity occurred on company time or on employee time.[132] Considerable discussion has occurred concerning the employer's right to ban solicitation on the employer's property outside working hours, that is, before or after work, during lunch hour or rest period. The Supreme Court has sustained the Board's rule that the employer cannot prohibit union solicitation of his employees during these times, unless the employer can show special circumstances which make such a rule necessary to maintain production or discipline.[133]

The Board cannot interfere with the employer's right of freedom of speech, and temperate statements which are not coercive or threatening are not violations of the Act.[134] The Act, as amended, provides that the expression of views, argument or opinion "shall not constitute or be evidence of an unfair labor practice . . . if such expression contains no threat of reprisal or force or promise of benefit."[135] Under the Wagner Act the Board held that employer statements were coercive and violative of the Act if they were part of "total" anti-union activities intended to thwart unionization of the employees.[136]

The Board will set aside a closed shop contract between the employer and one of two rival unions when it is entered into during the pendency of a proceeding before the Board for the determination of which union is the bargaining agent.[137] The result will be the same if the contract is entered into after a Board decision setting aside the election in which the contracting union participated.[138]

An employer who, in the midst of a known union organizational campaign and during the pendency of a proceeding before the Board for determination of bargaining representatives, attempts to have his employees sign individual contracts of employment violates the Act, although the contracts on their face contain no illegal terms. The illegality found by the Board was in the employer's timing of such activity.[139]

9. To Restrain Coercion by Unions

Unions that restrain and coerce employees in the exercise of rights guaranteed in Section 7 of the Act commit unfair labor practices.[140] Section 7 guarantees the right of employees to "refrain from any and all" union activities as well as the right to join unions. Typical illegal conduct constituting violation of this right of employees would be threats of bodily harm and violence against nonunion employees for the purpose of compelling union membership or joining in strike activity. The aforementioned unfair labor practice of the union, consisting of restraint and coercion of employees, is not to be construed to interfere with the right of the union to prescribe rules for the acquisition or retention of membership.

The Board has held the following conduct to constitute restraint and coercion of employees on the part of unions: Preventing nonstriking employees from entering or leaving a struck plant;[a] use of threatening language by strikers;[b] pickets carrying sticks on the picket line;[c] piling bricks at the picket line for use by pickets;[d] union representative's statement to nonstrikers that "when we get in with the union, you old fellows won't have a job;"[e] telling employees at an organizational meeting that those who did not join the union "would eventually lose their jobs;"[f] and barring supervisors from the plant in the presence of nonstrikers.[g]

A union that restrains or coerces an employer in the selection of his representatives for purposes of collective bargaining or adjustment of grievances violates the Act.[141] Thus, a union cannot dictate to an employer who shall represent him at the bargaining table or refuse to meet with him because of such an objection.

10. To Prevent Closed Shop[142]

The amended Act outlaws the closed shop.[143] The law, however, does permit a union shop agreement if certain conditions specified in Section 8(a)(3) are met. First, the union must have majority status in an appropriate bargaining unit and must not have received any illegal aid or assistance from the employer. Then, the Board must certify that a majority of the employees *eligible* to vote have voted to authorize the union to enter into an agreement with the employer requiring continued union membership as a condition of employment. If these conditions are met, the employer and the union may enter into a union shop agreement that employees must become members of the union as a condition of employment thirty days after the effective date of the contract or date of hiring, whichever is later. The thirty day period which must elapse between the

effective date of the contract or hiring and union membership as a condition
of employment is expressly prescribed by the Act. The mere inclusion of
a union shop clause in a labor agreement without such authority having
been voted by the employees at a Board conducted union shop election is
illegal, even though the clause is not enforced by the employer.[144] But
where the union shop clause provides that it shall not become effective
until after the union wins a union shop election, the clause is lawful.[145]

Even if the union wins the union shop election and the Board certifies
that a majority of the eligible employees have voted to authorize the union
to enter into the union shop contract, the Act does not obligate the employer to grant such a provision. The union shop clause remains a subject
for negotiation between the union and the employer.

The authority of the union to enter into a union shop contract may
be revoked by the employees. Thirty per cent of them may petition the
Board for an election to rescind the union's authority.[146] However, the
election cannot be held until at least one year has expired since the last
valid election.[147]

11. To Prevent Exaction of Excessive Union Fees

When the employees are covered by a valid union shop agreement, the
union cannot, as a condition precedent to membership, charge excessive
fees. To do so is an unfair labor practice.[148] The Board determines whether
the fee is excessive and, among other factors, must consider "the practices
and customs of labor organizations in the particular industry," and the
wages paid the employees.

12. To Limit Discharges under Union Shop

Where there is a valid union shop agreement, the Act does not permit
the discharge of employees thereunder on the broad ground that the
employee's union membership has been terminated. Discharge under the
union shop clause, for any reason other than nonpayment of periodic dues
and initiation fees, is illegal.[149] Thus, expulsion from the union for "dual
unionism" activity contrary to the best interests of the union according to
those in control of the governing committees or groups of the union, or
loss of "good standing" in the union, do not constitute grounds for discharge from employment under the union shop.[150] Where employees offered
payment of initiation fees and periodic dues but refused to comply with
the union requirements of attendance at the union meeting at which their

membership was to be voted upon and at which they were to take the obligation of membership, their discharge, upon the union's request under a valid union shop contract, was held illegal.[a] Both union and employer were held liable for the payment of back pay.

Furthermore, the union shop cannot be used as a basis for discharging an employee for nonmembership if union membership was not available to him on the same terms and conditions generally applicable to members.[151]

13. To Order Reinstatement

Where the Board finds that an employer has violated the Act by discrimination in regard to hire or tenure of employment, or any term or condition of employment, it normally orders the employer to reinstate persons who have lost their employment because of such unfair labor practice.[152] The Supreme Court has upheld the power of the Board to order reinstatement even when the discharged person has obtained regular and substantially equivalent employment elsewhere.[153] However, the Court in the *Phelps Dodge* case said that such order of reinstatement is valid only if the Board finds that the reinstatement of the employee will effectuate the policies of the Act.[154]

If the discharge is for just cause, the Board is without power to order reinstatement, for "membership in a union is not a guarantee against discharge." In short, "when real grounds for discharge exist, the management may not be prevented because of union membership" from exercising its right of discharge.[155]

14. To Reinstate Strikers

Employees who engage in a strike resulting from the employer's unfair practices must be reinstated to their jobs upon application, and persons hired to replace them during the strike must be discharged to make room for the strikers.[156] The Board applies a different rule when the strike is not caused by unfair practices. Then the strikers need be rehired only if their jobs are available when they apply for employment.[157] The application must be unconditional. Deviation from normal practices, such as giving preference to former employees when vacancies occur, to the detriment of the striker, will be treated as discrimination.[158] Discharge of an employee for refusing to act as a strike-breaker has been held to be discriminatory by the Board.[159]

15. To Deny Reinstatement to Strikers

The Board denied reinstatement to strikers who sought to compel the employer to grant the strikers wage increases without approval of the National War Labor Board. Granting the strikers' demands would have subjected the employer to the sanctions and penalties of the Wage Stabilization Act.[160] This rule, however, was held not to apply in a later case where the Board found that the strike was the result of a wage dispute and not an attempt to compel the employer to comply with an unlawful demand for violation of the Stabilization laws. The Court of Appeals disagreed and held that the strike was an attempt to compel violation of the Wage Stabilization Act within the meaning of the principles enunciated by the Board in the earlier case. For these reasons, the Court denied reinstatement of the strikers.[161]

Several Courts of Appeals have refused enforcement of Board orders directing reinstatement of employees who engaged in an unauthorized or "wildcat" strike.[162] Strikers who have been guilty of serious misconduct during a strike have been denied reinstatement.[163] Employees who strike in violation of the no-strike clause of a collective agreement have been denied reinstatement.[164] However, if the employer condones the strike by offering the strikers reinstatement, the Board will require all strikers to be treated alike and will not permit reinstatement to be withheld discriminatorily from a few of the strikers.[165]

But where the employees struck without giving the notice required by the War Labor Disputes Act, the Board did not deny reinstatement.[166]

16. To Award or Disallow Back Pay

The Board's normal award for discriminatory discharge is back pay from the date of discrimination to the date when reinstatement is offered. Earnings of the employee during that period are deducted from the award. The amount of back pay usually is measured by the difference between the amount which the discharged employee would have earned if he had not been discharged and the amount of net earnings during the period of discrimination. The Board states that it patterns the back pay award to the circumstances of the case.[167] Discharged employees are allowed expenses incurred in obtaining a new job or board and lodging in connection with a new job. In the case of a discharged maritime employee, the Board included as part of his back pay award the reasonable value of the shipboard maintenance he would have received had he not been discharged.[168] Discharged employees evicted from company-owned homes have been allowed expenses in finding a new home and the amount of rent paid in the new home in excess of the rent paid for the company-owned home.[169]

Unreasonable delay in filing charges on behalf of a discriminatorily discharged employee will diminish back pay.[170] Where a discharged employee became pregnant after her discharge, the Board excluded from the back pay period a three-month period starting two months prior and ending one month subsequent to the date of the child's birth.[171]

The Supreme Court has held that no reimbursement should be allowed when losses are wilfully incurred, as when the employee wilfully refuses to seek or accept other employment.[172] During the war period, the Board announced that registration by an employee with U. S. Employment Service will be regarded as conclusive evidence that a discharged employee has made reasonable effort to obtain new employment.[173]

Liability for back pay to employees inducted into the armed forces after discharge, has been terminated by the Board as of the date of induction. The Board requires reinstatement within ninety days which the Selective Service Act allows an honorably discharged veteran in which to make application for reemployment.[174]

"Runaway shop" employers have been ordered to reinstate employees at their old or new locations with payment to employees for expenses of transportation and of moving their families.[175]

In a typical "runaway shop" case,[176] the employer moved from New York City to Pawling, N.Y., in order to evade collective bargaining with the union. Unfair labor practices of the employer precipitated a strike. The Board ordered reinstatement of the strikers at Pawling, and payment of transportation expenses. The Board said,

Effectuation of the policies of the Act is achieved by restoration in so far as possible of the *status quo* existing before the commission of the unfair labor practices. We have found that the respondent's transfer of its plant from New York City to Pawling was the first and basic step in its scheme to rid itself of the union and that such transfer itself constituted an unfair labor practice. Many of the difficulties subsequently occurring are attributable to the transfer and to the respondent's encouragement of local hostility to the union. It is abundantly clear from the record that a return to New York City would, under ordinary circumstances, most nearly achieve the restoration of the *status quo*. However, a substantial majority of the union members employed by the respondent reside in and around Pawling, and to order the respondent to return to New York City would leave such employees without remedy. Further, counsel for the Joint Board stated at oral argument that the union makes no request that the respondent be ordered to return to New York City. We will not order the respondent to return to New York City, but in view of our findings concerning the respondent's moving to Pawling, and in view of the peculiar problems arising from the customs of the New York City union members, we shall order the respondent either to

pay for the reasonable expenses entailed in the transportation and moving of
the New York City union members and their families from New York City to
Pawling or to pay for the transportation bi-weekly from Pawling to New York
City and back for those employees who wish to visit their families, at the option
of the individual union members. Since the situation has been created by the
respondent's own unfair labor practices, the respondent cannot be permitted
to shift the burden of expenses on its employees, and, therefore, we find that by
such order, the policies of the Act will be effectuated.

Under the amended Act, the Board has authority to order a union to pay
back pay to employees as remedial action for unfair labor practices by the
union.[177]

Where nonstriking employees suffered a loss of earnings because of
restraint and coercion engaged in by a striking union and its agents, which
conduct prevented the nonstrikers from going to work, the Board held it
was without authority to issue an order requiring the union to indemnify the
nonstrikers for such loss of earnings.[178] The Board pointed out that an
award of back pay in such circumstances would be in the nature of damages
to the nonstriking employees for interference with their right of ingress to
the plant. The amended Act, according to the Board, limits an award of
back pay against a union to cases where the union is responsible for unlawful discrimination against an employee. Where a union and an employer are
both responsible for unlawful discrimination against an employee, they are
held jointly and severally liable for the payment of back pay.[a]

17. To Order Collective Bargaining

BY EMPLOYERS

The Act obligates an employer to bargain collectively upon demand with
a union representing a majority of his employees in an appropriate bargaining unit.[179] The union's majority representation is a prerequisite to compel
bargaining, and the Board upon petition by the union will conduct an election to determine that question. If the union is successful upon such an
election, the obligation to bargain arises although a majority of the eligible
voters did not cast ballots. Participation of a substantial proportion of the
eligible voters is regarded by the Board as sufficient.[180] The results of a consent election conducted by a Board Regional Director are sufficient to enable
the union to precipitate the employer's duty to bargain upon its demand
for collective bargaining, and the Board will not disturb the Director's
rulings unless they can be shown to be arbitrary, capricious or unsupported
by substantial evidence.[181]

The courts attach great weight to the results of an election and Board certifications of a bargaining agency, and hold that they must be recognized by the employer for a reasonable period of time even in the face of attempts by employees to revoke the union's authority before the lapse of such reasonable period.[182]

To determine whether there has been a refusal to bargain the Board carefully scrutinizes the employer's dealings with and treatment of the employees' designated bargaining agent in an endeavor in good faith to reach an agreement. Some of the activities of employers demonstrating bad faith, in the opinion of the Board, are:[183]

1. Shifting positions to avoid or delay a consent election.
2. Avoiding prompt bargaining conferences with the union.
3. Categorically rejecting the union's proposals without offering counterproposals or substantiating the employer's position.[184] In a recent case the employer, without justification, made counterproposals which suggested abandonment of previously obtained benefits. The Board held that the counterproposal indicated bad faith.[185]
4. Unilateral wage increases after refusing to negotiate wage increases with the union.[186]
5. Ignoring the union's request for negotiating on disputed matters.[187]
6. Permitting a minority to present and negotiate grievances falling within the scope of collective bargaining.
7. Refusing to reduce to a signed agreement the terms and provisions agreed upon.[188]
8. Dilatory tactics during negotiations.[189]
9. Engaging in unfair labor practices while bargaining with the union.[190]
10. Attempting to bargain individually with the employees over the heads of union agents.[191]
11. Requiring the union to secure an agreement from competitors before bargaining.[192]

The Court of Appeals, in the *Hughes Tool Company* case, refused to sustain the Board's finding that the grant of a check-off of dues to a minority union was a violation of the Act.[193] In that case, however, the employer had granted the charging union a check-off in prior years when it represented only a minority of the employees.

The Board holds that an employer cannot refuse to bargain with the union because the union demands a closed shop or the employees are out on a strike or a contract already exists with a union which had received the employer's aid and assistance.[194] The Board has held that the employer's statutory duty to bargain is suspended by a strike in violation of the no-strike clause of a collective agreement so long as such strike continues.[195] The matters concerning which the employer's obligation to bargain was suspended involved the issues of the strike. However, a union's refusal to bargain on one occasion does not relieve the employer of the obligation to bargain upon a later demand by the union.[196]

Bluntly refusing to have any discussion with the representative of a majority union is an illegal refusal to bargain.[197] Similarly, the mass discharge of almost all the union members upon the employer's receipt of the majority union's bargaining demand is regarded as manifesting a refusal to bargain.[198]

An employer's arbitrary insistence upon the method by which a union majority status should be established and refusing a consent election to be conducted by the Board,[199] dilatory tactics during negotiations,[200] or unilateral action and attempts to bargain with employees individually on the subject-matters of the discussion have been held to be indicative of bad-faith bargaining by the employer.[201]

The Board holds that the duty to negotiate continues, after the execution of the agreement, with respect to modification, interpretation and administration.[202] However, Section 8(d) of the amended Act relieves the parties of the duties to discuss modification of the terms of a contract, if the modification is to become effective before the terms sought to be modified can be reopened under the provisions of the contract.

The Board has held that the failure of a union representative to comply with the licensing requirements of a state statute does not relieve the employer of the duty to bargain.[203] But where the employer recognized the union, and agreement was reached on some issues but no agreement was reached on other issues, including a closed shop which was prohibited by state law, there was no illegal refusal to bargain by the employer.[204] The existence of valid individual agreements with each employee does not relieve the employer of the obligation to bargain collectively when a bargaining agency has been properly designated.[205] The Supreme Court has held that an employer refuses illegally to bargain with the duly designated bargaining agent when he yields to the request of a majority of the individual employees in the bargaining unit that he deal with them as individuals rather than with the union.[206]

When there has been an illegal refusal to bargain, the union's subsequent loss of a majority, as a result of normal employee replacements in the usual course of operations, does not relieve the employer of the duty to bargain.[207] An employer who refuses to bargain without regard to the union's representation of a majority of the employees cannot thereafter be defended on that ground. He takes the risk of what the facts show concerning the union's representation.[208]

The courts have sustained the Board's holding that neither a strike[209] nor a temporary shutdown of the plant relieves the employer of the obligation to bargain with a union representing a majority of the employees.[210]

A single incident will not be determinative of whether the employer has illegally refused to bargain; the whole course of conduct must be considered. Thus, where the employer refused to bargain with the union, because of its strike in violation of the no-strike clause of the collective agreement, and thereafter bargained in good faith in an attempt to settle the strike, the Board held there was no violation of the Act.[211] The Board has also held that when charges of refusal to bargain have been filed, the subsequent execution of a collective agreement does not make the charges moot.[212]

In the absence of findings by the Board that the party guilty of an illegal refusal to bargain acted in bad faith or in rejection of the principles of collective bargaining, the Board's order must be limited to the specific conduct found illegal. Thus, where the Board found that illegality consisted of the employer granting a wage increase substantially more than that requested by the union, after an impasse was reached in bargaining negotiations, the Supreme Court ruled that "there appears no reason for enlarging the scope of the enforcement decree beyond that feature, and little, if any, need for orders requiring either specific affirmative action to be taken by the employer or the posting of any notices by it."[213]

BY UNIONS

The Act obligates the union to bargain in good faith, and its failure to comply is an unfair labor practice.[214] The Act defines "to bargain collectively" as the "mutual obligation" of the parties.[215] Neither party is required to agree to a proposal or make a concession. This would seem to eliminate the Board's prior ruling with respect to the need for counterproposals. However, General Counsel for the Board has publicly indicated that counterproposals bear very materially on the question of good faith in bargaining as in the past. If an agreement is reached, it must be reduced to writing upon the request of a party to the negotiation. Unions are required to conform to the established requirements of good-faith negotiation and cannot resort, as has been done on some occasions in the past, to a "take-it-or-else" attitude when submitting a proposed contract to an employer.[a]

18. To Nullify Settlement Agreement

Where an unfair labor practice case is settled by agreement with the Board, it may disregard the agreement upon finding that the employer com-

ifair labor practices after the agreement, and the Board may con-
issue an order directed to the unfair labor practices that occurred
subsequent to the agreement.[216] The courts held that strict legal
uoctrines, such as *res judicata* or estoppel, are not applicable to the
board.[217] A consent election agreement in which a union participated, or
even certification of that union as bargaining agent, does not preclude the
Board from finding at a later date that the same union was illegally company-dominated.[218]

19. To Void "Yellow Dog" Contracts

The Board has authority to declare illegal and set aside a form of "yellow dog" contract with employees whereby they surrender and renounce
rights guaranteed by the Act.[219]

20. To Make Findings upon Substantial Evidence

The courts will not enforce orders of the Board unless they are based on
findings supported by substantial evidence.[220] The courts will accept the
Board's determination on conflicting evidence, reasonably warranted inferences from the facts, and the Board's expert knowledge in its field.[221]
The Supreme Court has, in addition, said that the remedies prescribed by
the Board in its orders must be accepted if they are reasonably related to
the facts and within the powers granted by the Act.[222]

Section 10(c) of the Act also requires that the Board base its conclusion
on the "preponderance" of the testimony taken.[223]

21. To Draw Inferences from the Facts and Weigh Testimony

The Act gives the Board authority to weigh testimony, draw reasonable
inferences from the facts and decide credibility when there is conflicting
testimony.[224] The Supreme Court has said that the reviewing Court of Appeals cannot substitute its judgment on disputed facts for the judgment of
the Board.[225]

The provisions making applicable to Board cases the rules of evidence,
so far as practicable, and requiring the Board to base its decision on the
preponderance of the testimony taken, would seem to broaden the scope
of court review to the extent that it would see that the Board observed these
provisions.[226] This does not mean, however, that the court would have the
duty or authority to weigh the evidence anew.

22. To Issue Cease and Desist Orders

When the Board finds an employer or a union or both guilty of unfair labor practices as defined in the Act, it issues a remedial order which directs them or any one of them to cease and desist from the practices and to take such affirmative action as the Board finds will effectuate the policies of the Act.[227] The cease and desist provisions usually include specifically the unfair practices found by the Board as well as a broad injunctive provision in general terms. Wherever possible the Board will include in the order the name of the union which has been found to be the objective of the violations.[228]

The usual affirmative actions required in the order concern the unfair labor practices found. Thus, the order may require disestablishment of a company-dominated union, reinstatement with payment of back pay to the discharged employee, or bargaining with the union upon request. All orders require the employer to post notices in the plant that the employer will not engage in the conduct which he is directed to cease and desist from and that he will take the affirmative action required. The Board has varied the affirmative action required of the employer. It will not order reinstatement of a discharged employee who does not wish his job back.[229] An employee with a substantial record of absenteeism has been denied reinstatement.[230] Discriminatorily discharged employees will be denied reimbursement for willfully incurred losses.[231] An employer who has ceased operations, if found guilty of refusal to bargain, will be ordered to bargain upon the resumption of business.[232]

In addition to the posting of notices the Board has in some circumstances required the mailing of notices individually to employees.[233] The Board has also issued precautionary orders. Thus, where the Board found that a committee established by the employer had not functioned as a labor organization, it ordered the employer not to recognize the committee in the event the latter undertook to operate as a labor organization.[234] A similar ruling was made with respect to a social club.[235] The employer's compliance with recommendations of a Trial Examiner in no way deters the Board from issuing an order if it deems an order necessary or desirable.[236] In addition to issuing orders against employers, the Board has issued orders against a State Chamber of Commerce, officers of an association, and an association.[237] In these cases, under the Wagner Act, the Board found that these organizations acted in the interests of or on behalf of the employer and thus were "employers" within the meaning of that term as defined in the Act.[238] On this principle the Board has held subject to its order an independent contractor to whom the employer transferred his operations for coercive purposes.[239] The Wagner Act included in the definition of "employer" "any person acting in the interest of an employer." The amended Act eliminated this provision and defines the term "employer" in Section 2(2) thereof as including "any person acting as an agent of an employer."[240] The ordinary rules of the law of agency would seem to be applicable and under Section 2(13) of the amended Act, whether the acts involved were actually authorized or subsequently ratified is not controlling in determining the existence of an agency relationship.[241]

Where the employer has checked off dues from wages in favor of a company-dominated union, the Board may order him to reimburse the employee for the amount checked off.[242] The Board has authority to order an employer to reopen a department temporarily shut down for anti-union reasons.[243] This situation must be distinguished from a permanent shutdown.

The Board's cease and desist order must bear some reasonable relationship to the illegal conduct found by the Board. Thus, in the *Express Publishing Company* case, the court said the Board could not issue a broad and general cease and desist order when the only illegal conduct found by the Board was a refusal to bargain.[244]

23. To Request Punishment for Noncompliance

Where the courts grant enforcement of an order of the Board, failure to comply therewith may be held a contempt of the court decree enforcing the Board's order. Whether such a contempt has occurred can only be raised before the court by the Board. The Supreme Court has held that the Board alone, and not a union, has authority under the statute to institute a contempt proceeding against an employer.[245] Offering employees a bonus, as an inducement to waive reinstatement pursuant to a court decree enforcing a Board order, may be a contempt.[246] Failure to reinstate an employee was not held contemptuous where the employer consented to a decree in ignorance of the employee's conviction for a crime.[245] No contempt was found where employees, who were ordered reinstated, failed to make application for their job.[248]

24. To Prevent Certain Strikes and Boycotts and to Obtain Court Restraint Thereof

The amended Act empowers the Board to order unions and their agents to cease and desist from engaging in, or inducing or encouraging the employees "of any employer to engage in," a strike or a "concerted refusal to" use, manufacture, transport or handle or work on any goods, or to perform services, where an object thereof is:

1. Forcing an employer or self-employed person to join a union or employer organization, or to cease using, handling or dealing in the goods of another or to cease doing business with another person.249 This provision of the Act outlaws the secondary boycott by a union.
2. Forcing "any other employer" to bargain with a union as bargaining representative of the employees, unless such union has been certified by the Board in accordance with the requirements of the Act.250 This provision outlaws the secondary boycott for purposes of compelling recognition in the absence of a certification of the union by the Board.
3. Forcing an employer to bargain with a union as majority representative of the employees if another union has been certified as such representative by the employees.251
4. Forcing an employer to assign particular work to an employee in a "particular" union or in a "particular" trade or craft rather than to employees in "another" union or in "another" trade or class unless the employer is acting in disregard of a Board certification determining the bargaining representative for employees performing such work.252 This provision covers the not uncommon type of jurisdictional dispute in the building trades, particularly, where the most powerful union involved compels assignment of work to its members, regardless of wage scales, and the ready availability and desire of the employee of the employer to do the work.

A proviso in this section of the Act exempts as lawful the refusal of an employee to enter upon the premises of an employer, other than his own employer, if the employees of such other employer are engaged in a strike authorized by their bargaining representative.

The substantive effect of these provisions of the amended Act, as established by the decided case is discussed in "Strikes and Boycotts," Part Three, Chapter IV.

If charges are filed with the Board alleging that the union is engaged in the strikes or boycotts described above under 1, 2, and 3, and the Board's Regional Director, after investigation, has reasonable cause to believe that such charges are true, he must apply to the United States District Court for a temporary injunction restraining the illegal activity of the union until the Board has rendered a decision upon the unfair labor practice.253 Two factors should be noted at this point of the discussion: (1) The application for an injunction is mandatory if the Regional Director has reasonable cause to believe that the charges are true, and (2) the application for the temporary injunction, in such event, must be made even before the Board issues its complaint against the union.

The statute authorizes the District Court to issue forthwith an *ex parte* injunction for five days, if the Board's application contains a petition alleging that "substantial and irreparable injury to the charging party will be unavoidable." Of course, the Board may proceed in the court without such an allegation and the five day *ex parte* injunction. In any event, the statute requires that notice of the proceedings be given to the union and that it have an opportunity to appear and present evidence.

The constitutionality of the provisions of the amended Act requiring the Board to proceed in the District Court for an injunction in the situations mentioned above has been sustained in the Court of Appeals.[a]

The effect of Section 8(c) of the Act, providing that expressions of "views, argument or opinion" unaccompanied by threats were not unfair labor practices, has been considered with respect to secondary boycotts. The Board held that Section 8(c) does not apply to picketing and blacklisting in furtherance of a secondary boycott.[b]

Temporary injunctions were issued against a striking union in *Douds v. Teamsters Union, Local 294*,[254] involving Conway's Express, and in another case of the same name involving Montgomery Ward & Co.[255] Both cases were decided by the United States District Court for the Northern District of New York. In the first mentioned case, Conway's Express filed charges against the union alleging that the union (1) called a strike to force Conway's Express to cease doing business with another company, (2) refused to bargain collectively, (3) demanded a closed shop to restrain the rights of employees illegally, (4) engaged in "featherbedding" attempts and (5) coerced its employees generally. The Court granted the Board's application for a temporary injunction restraining these unfair labor practices by the union pending the Board's determination of the charges. Several principles were established: (1) Under the Act, the court has jurisdiction "to grant such injunctive relief or temporary restraining order as it deems just and proper;" (2) the Norris-LaGuardia Act is not applicable to the Board's application for injunction. As to this, the Court said:[256]

Respondent contends with earnestness that the provisions of the Norris-La-Guardia Act (29 U.S.C.A. 101-115), which substantially eliminates the granting or use of the injunction in labor disputes must be applied here, or at least the bases of irreparable injury, and lack of an adequate remedy at law, must be shown before the petitioner may be granted injunctive relief. Both contentions are rejected. The relief provided is entirely statutory. The common law requirements do not apply. The statutory scheme is complete in itself.

As the issuance of an injunction in cases of this nature has statutory sanction, it is of no moment that the plaintiff has failed to show threatened irreparable injury or the like, for it would be enough if the statutory conditions for injunctive relief were made to appear. Securities and Exchange Commission v. Jones 2 Cir., 85 F. 2d 17. Securities and Exchange Commission v. Torr, 2 Cir., 87 F. 2d 446 at page 450 and see also Bowles v. Swift & Co., D. C., 56 F. Supp. 679 and cases cited.

To impose the limitations of the Norris-LaGuardia Act upon the Act would be to impute to Congress an intention to grant to the Court a jurisdiction with restrictions thereon which would prevent its exercise. No evidence of Congressional intent is drawn from the language of Sec. 10(h) which specifically excludes the limitations of the Norris-LaGuardia Act from effecting injunctive relief applied for after the making of an order by the Board. This provision was carried over from the original Act, and has no effect upon sub-divisions (j) and (1) which are new provisions in the amended Act. Neither does the phrase "notwithstanding any other provisions of law" as found in Sec. 10(1) indicate that Congress intended that a different statutory requirement must be applied to the jurisdiction of the Court under 10(j) and 10(1). When the Court is given jurisdiction without limitation, the Act means just that; the phrase may be considered as surplusage. Certainly, it can not be used to imply a limitation upon another sub-section where the phrase is not found.

(3) The Board is required, in support of its application for injunction, to show a *prima facie* case of unfair labor practices by the union. As to this the Court said:[257]

While all of plaintiff's evidence was offered and received herein, it is concluded that such detail was neither contemplated by the Act or necessary in fact. There is nothing in the statute which would prompt the Court to depart from the recognized rule of equity that interlocutory relief may be granted upon a showing of reasonable probability that the moving party is entitled to final relief. A showing of a *prima facie* case for equitable relief satisfies the statute. Bowles v. Montgomery Ward & Company, 7 Cir., 143 F. 2d 38 at page 42; Northwestern Stevedoring Company v. Marshall, 9 Cir., 41 F. 2d 28; Sinclair Refining Co. v. Midland Oil Company, 4 Cir., 55 F. 2d 42.

The requirement is the same under either 10(j) or 10(1). The provision of the latter subsection; viz: "If, after such investigation, the officer or regional attorney to whom the matter may be referred, has reasonable cause to believe such charge is true and that a complaint should issue, he shall, on behalf of the Board, petition any district court of the United States—," is the measure of the requirements which must exist before such officer is required to petition this Court for the authorized relief. It is not the measure of the proof required before this Court may grant such relief.

The requirements of a *prima facie* case are met when the factual jurisdictional requirements are shown, and credible evidence is presented which, if uncontradicted, would warrant the granting of the requested relief, having in mind the purpose of the statute and interests involved in its enforcement. Such requirement has been met in this proceeding, and petitioner is entitled to relief.

These principles were also applied by the Court in the case involving *Montgomery Ward & Company*. There was no strike against that company and no dispute between that company and its employees, none of whom were members of the union. The union in that case, upon being refused permission to enter the company premises, caused the operators of trucks, who were members of the union, to leave the company's premises and to refrain from entering thereon. The charges filed by the company alleged violation of Section 8(b)(4)(A) of the Act.

On the application for the injunction, it is not required to establish the merits of the unfair labor practice charges. It need only be shown that there is reasonable cause to believe that the charges are warranted.[a] Indeed, the court is without power to determine whether unfair labor practices have been committed.[b] While the statute requires that such reasonable belief must be on the basis of investigation, the Board need not show the extent of such investigation and where the examination of witnesses before the court showed that they had been interviewed by the Board's Regional Director that requirement was met.[c] The traditional equitable requirements for injunctive relief need not be established by the Board, and the injunction will issue in the "just and proper" discretion of the court when there is a showing of reasonable cause to believe that the conduct proscribed by the Act is being committed.[d] Even completion of the construction project, over which the secondary boycott arises does not justify withholding the injunction if a resumption of the conduct could be anticipated.[e]

The scope of the temporary injunction, issued on the application of the Board, has covered the commission or continuation of the acts complained of and like or related acts.[f] The Act indicates that the injunction should continue until the Board determines the case before it. The Court of Appeals for the Tenth Circuit has held, however, that the Court has authority to terminate the injunction sooner.[g] Another court limited the duration of the injunction to three months in anticipation of the Board's decision in the unfair labor practice case within that period.[h]

In the case of jurisdictional disputes described above which also are unfair labor practices, it is not mandatory upon the Board to proceed in the District Court for a temporary injunction. However, the Board in its discretion may apply for the injunction on the basis of the charges.

The Act does, however, empower the Board to determine such jurisdictional disputes.[258] Unless within ten days after the filing of the charges the parties adjust their dispute or agree upon a "satisfactory" method for adjustment, the Board must proceed to a decision. Upon compliance therewith, or settlement of the dispute, the charges must be dismissed. Such provision would seem to preclude the Board's application to the United States Circuit Court of Appeals for an enforcement decree where there has been compliance with its decision. In the other unfair labor practice situations, the Board can obtain an enforcement decree in the Court of Appeals although there has been complete compliance with the Board's order. The language of the Act would appear to bar such a result in the case of jurisdictional disputes, since upon compliance the charges must be dismissed.

25. To Obtain Court Injunction Generally

Under Section 10(j) of the amended Act, the Board, "upon issuance of a complaint" alleging the commission of an unfair labor practice, has discretion to apply to the United States District Court for an appropriate temporary injunction.[259] The court has power "to grant to the Board such temporary relief or restraining order as it deems just and proper." The procedure and power of the court would appear to be the same as in the cases where the statute makes it mandatory for the Board to seek the temporary injunction except, perhaps, that the five day *ex parte* injunction would not issue. The nature of the unfair labor practice involved does not limit the injunctive power of the court or the authority of the Board to seek court intervention. The constitutionality of the provision has been upheld.[260]

26. Limitation of Time upon the Board's Exercise of Powers

The amended Act limits the time within which the Board can issue a complaint upon unfair labor practice charges. Section 10(b) of the Act provides "That no complaint shall issue based upon any unfair labor practice occurring more than six months prior to the filing of the charge with the Board and the service of a copy thereof upon the person against whom such charge is made."[261] Thus, the time limitation requires the charges to be filed within six months after the alleged unfair labor practices. The statute makes only one exception and that is if the "aggrieved person" was prevented from filing the charges by reason of service in the armed forces. In that event the six months period is computed from "the day of his discharge."

However, a two-year delay by the Board in seeking enforcement of its order in the United States Court of Appeals is no defense to the Board's application for enforcement, unless injustice can be shown in granting enforcement.[262]

II · PROCEDURE IN UNFAIR
LABOR PRACTICE CASES

1. Nature of Proceeding

The National Labor Relations Act as amended provides primarily for two types of proceedings before the Board. The Board is empowered by the Act to issue orders directing employers and unions to cease and desist from unfair labor practices as enumerated therein,[263] and to certify and decertify the exclusive bargaining agent of employees in an appropriate bargaining unit whenever there is a question of representation of employees affecting commerce.[264]

The first type of proceeding results in an order of the Board, if it is found on the facts that unfair labor practices have been committed. Such an order directs the employer or the union to cease and desist from the unfair labor practices found and to take affirmative action which the Board finds will effectuate the purposes of the Act. This proceeding is a formal adversary proceeding and the incidents thereof and court review of the proceedings are considered below. The order issued by the Board is a "final" order and directly reviewable by the United States Circuit Court of Appeals in accordance with and subject to the limitations of the statutory provisions.[265]

The second type of proceeding before the Board results in a written certification or decertification by the Board of the exclusive bargaining agent. The certification is not an order and contains no injunctive provisions or directions for affirmative action by the employer. It is not directly reviewable by the courts. The proceeding is considered investigatory and nonadversary and the result is not a "final" order. It is reviewable by the courts indirectly in connection with the review of an unfair labor practice proceeding when the order of the Board in such proceeding is based upon the certification proceeding.[266] For example, the Board has issued an order directing an employer to bargain collectively with the union which it has certified as the statutory bargaining representative of the employees. That order is predicated upon the proceedings which resulted in the Board certification of the union. The court upon review of the validity of the order compelling bargaining may review the certification proceeding. However, in the absence of the order, the certification proceeding cannot be reviewed by the court.

The Act makes specific provision for the initiation of the certification or decertification proceeding, by petition of employees or a union acting on their behalf.[267] An employer may file such a petition when he has received a demand for recognition from a union or individual claiming to represent the employees.[268] The Act provides for an appropriate hearing in the proceeding upon "due" notice.[269]

The New York State Labor Relations Act, like that of other states having enacted "little Wagner Acts," follows the pattern of the national law prior to its amendment.[270] Likewise the proceedings before the state boards are substantially like those before the NLRB prior to amendment.[271] Even though the New York State Act was patterned after the Wagner Act, it nevertheless still provides that an employer may file a petition when only one union is involved.[272]

2. The Charge

The Act authorizes the Board to issue a complaint alleging the commission of unfair labor practices, "whenever it is charged that any person has engaged in or is engaging" in the unfair labor practices enumerated in the statute.[273] The language of the statute indicates that the Board is without authority to issue its complaint unless such a charge is filed with the Board.[274] No provision is made in the Act as to who may file the charge, its form or the nature or sufficiency of the charge itself. These provisions are set forth in the Rules and Regulations of the Board.[275] The charge may be made "by any person" and must be written and sworn to before a notary public or other person authorized by law to administer oaths. As to the substantive portion of the charge, it need only set forth "a clear and concise statement of the facts constituting the alleged unfair labor practices affecting commerce.[276]

The Board distinguishes between the charge that is filed with it "by any person" and the complaint which it issues and serves alleging that the respondent has committed unfair labor practices.[277] The requirement of the filing of a charge under the statute, according to the Board, was intended only to prevent the Board from initiating unfair labor practice proceedings on its own motion. It has been the practice of the Board to attach a copy of the charge to the complaint which it issues. Neither the Board's Rules and Regulations nor the statute provide for the filing of an answer to the charge. They do provide for an answer to the complaint.[278]

The Board's position has been that the charge may be general and the complaint issued on the basis of its investigation may vary in some particulars from the charge. It has been held that the charge may be general when the Board's complaint was sufficiently specific to apprise the employer of the violations with which he is charged.[279] The same result was reached where all the facts were brought out at the hearing without prejudicial surprise.[280]

The Act places a limitation upon the time within which the charge may be filed after the alleged commission of unfair labor practices. No complaint can be issued upon any unfair labor practice occurring more than six months prior to the filing of the charge and the service of a copy thereof upon the person against whom the charge is made.[281]

The Board's order may cover unfair labor practices which were committed after the filing of the charge if they are related to those alleged in the complaint. The Supreme Court has said:[282]

Whatever restrictions the requirements of a charge may be thought to place upon subsequent proceedings by the Board, we can find no warrant in the language or purposes of the Act for saying that it precludes the Board from dealing adequately with unfair labor practices which are related to those alleged in the charge and which grow out of them while the proceeding is pending before the Board. The violations alleged in the complaint and found by the Board were but a prolongation of the attempt to form the company union and to secure the contracts alleged in the charge. All are of the same class of violations as those set up in the charge and were continuations of them in pursuance of the same objects. The Board's jurisdiction having been invoked to deal with the first steps, it had authority to deal with those which followed as a consequence of those already taken. We think the court below correctly held that "the Board was within its power in treating the whole sequence as one."

It has been the practice of the Board before issuing the complaint to require the filing of an amended charge conforming generally to the allegations of unfair labor practices in the complaint.

The Board's Rules and Regulations provide where the charge may be filed: normally it is the office of the Regional Director for the region in which the alleged unfair labor practice has been committed.[283] The regional offices of the Board supply blank forms for the making of the charge.

3. Administrative Dismissals—Appeals

Upon the filing of unfair labor practice charges, the Regional Director and his staff in the office where such charges are filed investigate them. If such investigation leads them to believe that there has been no violation of the Act, the Regional Director, unless the charges are withdrawn, will dismiss them. The charging party may appeal from such dismissal to the Board's General Counsel.[284] His determination of the appeal is final and there is no appeal to the Board. The Act grants the General Counsel "final authority" in the investigation of charges and the issuance of complaints.[285] The House Conference Report points out this wide authority of the General Counsel, independently of the Board:[286]

The General Counsel is to have general supervision and direction of all attorneys employed by the Board (excluding the trial examiners and the legal assistants to the individual members of the Board), and of all the officers and employees in the Board's regional offices, and is to have the final authority to act in the name of, but independently of any direction, control, or review by, the Board in respect of the investigation of charges and the issuance of complaints of unfair labor practices, and in respect of the prosecution of such complaints before the Board. He is to have, in addition, such other duties as the Board may prescribe or as may be provided by law. By this provision responsibility for what takes place in the Board's regional offices is centralized in one individual, who is ultimately responsible to the President and Congress.

Thus, the amended Act separates the prosecuting authority from the judicial authority in unfair labor practice proceedings. The General Counsel, who has supervision of the Regional Directors in the Board's various regional offices, and their staffs, constitutes the ultimate prosecuting arm of the agency, while the Board's functions in unfair labor practice cases are restricted exclusively to decisional powers. The General Counsel has contended that once he issues a complaint in an unfair labor case, the Board has no power to decline to decide the case on jurisdictional policy grounds if in fact jurisdiction under the Act exists. On overruling the contention the Board said:[287]

It is true that the Board cannot itself issue a complaint; it cannot compel the General Counsel either to issue or refrain from issuing one; it cannot review his action in refusing to issue one. Furthermore, the legislative history shows that Congress intended the General Counsel to exercise his authority to issue or refrain from issuing a complaint independently of any direction, control or review by the Board. But after a complaint has been issued and a hearing has been held, the "final authority" of the General Counsel is exhausted, and the case is then in the hands of the Board. Any action the Board may take thereafter, either as a matter of policy or on the merits, does not constitute a review of the General Counsel's "issuance" or "prosecution" of the complaint, but is the exercise of the Board's judicial powers under the Act. No judicial or quasi-judicial power has been vested in the General Counsel by statute.

Hence where the amended Act speaks of the issuance of an unfair labor practice complaint, the reference is to the issuance of a complaint by its General Counsel since he is the statutory prosecuting authority of the Board.

Court decisions under the Wagner Act dealing with the "Board's" complaint are now applicable to the General Counsel's complaint.

On the other hand, where a petition for certification or decertification of bargaining representative is dismissed by the Regional Director, the appeal may be taken to the Board.[288]

4. The Complaint and Notice of Hearing

After the filing of the charge, the General Counsel of the Board has authority to take action with respect to the unfair labor practices alleged therein. He conducts an investigation of the charges and may dismiss them if in his opinion they are unwarranted, or seek an informal[289] settlement or issue a complaint and notice of hearing thereon.[290]

The complaint issued by the General Counsel need not meet the particularity and specifications of the requirements for a pleading in an ordinary lawsuit. The only function of the complaint is to advise the person against whom it is issued of the unfair labor practices claimed to have been committed by him and to furnish him with a plain statement of the matters constituting the alleged unfair labor practices.[291] The complaint need not specify the detailed facts of the alleged unfair labor practice nor the remedy or relief which it proposes to apply with respect to it.[292] The Sixth Circuit Court of Appeals has said, concerning the complaint:[293]

> The sole function of the complaint is to advise the respondent of the charges constituting unfair labor practices as defined in the Act, that he may have due notice and a full opportunity for hearing thereon. The Act does not require the particularity of pleading of an indictment or information, nor the elements of a cause like a declaration at law or a bill in equity. All that is requisite in a valid complaint before the Board is that there be a plain statement of the things claimed to constitute an unfair labor practice that respondent may be put upon his defense.

There is no requirement that the complaint be exact with respect to minor matters such as names and dates. Minor variances in such matters between the complaint and the Board's findings of fact will be disregarded by the courts, and amendment of the complaint to conform it to the evidence in such respects is proper.[294]

After issuance, the complaint may be amended or withdrawn and the amended complaint is subject only to the requirements already mentioned.[295]

The statute provides that the Board shall have "power to issue and cause to be served . . . . a complaint stating the charges . . . . and containing a notice of hearing . . . ."[296] The notice of hearing fixes the date, time and place of hearing on the allegations of unfair labor practice set forth in the complaint. The Act provides for a minimum of five days notice of the hearing to the employer.[297] The Board's Rules and Regulations provide for ten days notice.[298]

The only party who must be served with the complaint and notice of the hearing is the person alleged to have committed the unfair labor practice.[299] An alleged company-dominated union need not be served, since the Board order will not be directed against it.[300] But it is the practice of the Board to serve, and its Rules and Regulations provide for the service of, the complaint and notice of hearing on the alleged company-dominated union.[301] When the Board seeks to declare invalid individual contracts between the employer and employees, it need not serve each employee whose contract is attacked.[302] But when the General Counsel by his complaint, attacks the validity of a labor agreement between an employer and a legitimate or *bona fide* union, the labor organization must be served with a copy of the complaint and notice of hearing and it is a necessary party to the proceeding, with full right to participate therein; otherwise a Board order affecting the contract is invalid. In such a situation, the Supreme Court said:[303]

The Brotherhood and its locals contend that they were indispensable parties and in the absence of legal notice to them or their appearance, the Board had no authority to invalidate the contracts. The Board contests this position, invoking our decision in *National Labor Relations Board v. Pennsylvania Greyhound Lines,* 303 U.S. 261. That case, however, is not apposite as there no quesiton of contract between employer and employee was involved. The Board has found upon evidence that the employer had created and fostered the labor organization in question and dominated its administration in violation of § 8 (2). The statement that the "Association" so formed and controlled was not entitled to notice and hearing was made in that relation. Id. pp. 262, 270, 271. It has no application to independent labor unions such as those before us. We think that the Brotherhood and its locals having valuable and beneficial interests in the contracts were entitled to notice and hearing before they could be set aside.

If the Board orders the reinstatement of strikers, the persons hired by the employer to replace the strikers are not entitled to receive a copy of the complaint and notice of hearing.[304]

The Board's power to issue or refuse to issue a complaint upon charges filed with it is wholly discretionary and not subject to review by the court. The Court of Appeals for the Third Circuit has said:[305]

Assuming that all circumstances looked to by the Act are in existence, nonetheless we are of the opinion that the Board does not have to cause a complaint to be issued against the employer or proceed to prohibit any unfair labor practices complained of. The course to be pursued rests in the sound discretion of the Board, and is the concern of expert administrative policy. That discretion is not a legal discretion at least in so far that upon the abuse of it the several Circuit Courts of Appeals might compel the Board to issue a complaint.

The Board is not barred from issuing a complaint by the following types of agreements or circumstances:

1. An agreement between the employer and the union to submit a discharge of an employee to grievance procedure;[306]
2. An agreement between the union and the employer that charges by the former before the Board be dropped; [307]
3. A petition by the charging union requesting dismissal of the complaint because of the amicable settlement of the dispute with the employer;[308]
4. A settlement agreement between the Board and the employer where the latter subsequently breaches the settlement;[309]
5. The conduct by the Board of an election involving the same parties;[310]
6. The placement of a company-dominated union on the ballot in an election, when the union filing the charge had lost an election conducted by the Board;[311]
7. The pendency of a proceeding before state labor relations boards;[312]
8. Refusal by the Board to proceed on jurisdictional grounds in a proceeding at an earlier date.[313]
9. Certification by the Board of a union later charged with being company-dominated.[314]

The legal doctrine of *res judicata* is not applicable to Board proceedings.[315]

5. The Answer

The Act expressly provides that the "person so complained of shall have the right to file an answer to the original or amended complaint."[316] The employer has ten days to file his answer to the complaint under the Board's Rules and Regulations.[317] The answer should set forth "a short and simple statement of the facts which constitute the grounds of defense," and the Board requires that it be signed and sworn to.[318] The answer must be filed with the Regional Director who issued the complaint.[319] The Rules and Regulations of the Board make provision for extension of the time to answer, and amendment of the answer prior to, during and subsequent to the hearing.[320]

The Board's Rules and Regulations make no provision for the furnishing of a bill of particulars of the allegations of the Board's complaint of unfair labor practices. Motions for a bill of particulars are allowed, but the information furnished is sparingly disclosed. The practice would appear to be of limited value because the information furnished will not effectively limit the issues at the hearing. The attitude of the administrative agencies has been that their proceedings are public and the issues and proof are not strictly limited as in court actions.[321] In the event of surprise at the hearing, the employer should immediately seek a reasonable adjournment of the hearing or at least a reasonable adjournment after the Board counsel has completed introduction of his evidence, in order to prepare to meet it.

6. Issuance of Subpoenas

The Act authorizes "the Board or any member thereof" to issue subpoenas "requiring the attendance and testimony of witnesses or the production of any evidence in such proceeding or investigation."[322] The Act also provides that the Board and its agents have the right to examine and take evidence of any person being investigated that "relates to any matter under investigation or in question."[323] The only limitation upon this broad subpoena power of the Board is that the testimony sought or the evidence required to be produced pursuant to subpoena *duces tecum* must "relate" to the subject matter of the Board investigation; but this power may not be used for the purpose of generally investigating the affairs of an employer.[324]

The amended Act substantially alters prior procedure with respect to the issuance of Board subpoenas. "Any party" to the proceeding before the Board may apply for the subpoena, and upon such application, the subpoena must "forthwith issue." Within five days after service of the subpoena, the person served therewith may petition for revocation of the subpoena. The subpoena must be revoked if in the opinion of the Board (a) the evidence sought does not "relate to any matter under investigation or any matter in question in such proceedings," or (b) the subpoena "does not describe with sufficient particularity the evidence whose production is required."[325] Applications for subpoenas must be in writing and may be made *ex parte* to the Regional Director, prior to hearing, and to the Trial Examiner during the hearing.[326] Petitions to revoke the subpoena are made to the same Board officials who must promptly give notice thereof to the party who has obtained issuance thereof. The Board's power to delegate to a Trial Examiner the authority to revoke a subpoena in a complaint case has been sustained.[327]

It is prejudicial for a Trial Examiner to require the employer to comply with requirements for subpoenas without compelling similar compliance by counsel for the Board in order to obtain subpoenas.[328]

In connection with its investigation of the bargaining representative of employees, when there is a question concerning representation of the employees affecting commerce, the Board may issue a subpoena compelling the employer to produce information concerning his operations and the employees in the alleged appropriate bargaining unit.329 Likewise, the Board may issue subpoenas during its investigation of unfair labor practice charges filed.

The Seventh Circuit Court of Appeals has said that the Board may issue a subpoena to the employer, prior to the service of a complaint charging commission of unfair labor practice, for the purpose of obtaining information as to whether the employer is engaged in interstate commerce.330 Upon refusal of a witness to obey the subpoena of the Board, it may apply to the United States District Court for an order requiring obedience, and any failure to obey such a court order is punishable as a contempt of court.331 The Board, in seeking enforcement of its subpoena, is not required to commence a formal lawsuit in the District Court.332 Before issuance of the subpoena or seeking an order enforcing it, the Board need not establish that the employer is engaged in commerce within the meaning of the Act.333

When the Board applies for an order to compel obedience to its subpoena, the only jurisdiction of the court is to determine whether there is a proceeding pending before the Board and whether the evidence sought "relates" to the subject matter of the investigation, and the only defense to court proceedings that can be raised is with respect to these two issues.334 The court, however, may impose reasonable conditions so that obedience to the subpoena will not disrupt or interfere with the operation of the employer's business.335

The statute provides that a witness subpoenaed to testify or produce documents cannot refuse to comply on the ground of his constitutional privilege against self-incrimination but grants such witness, who claims the privilege, immunity from prosecution on account of the matters as to which he is compelled to testify except that he is not exempt from prosecution for perjury in his testimony.336

The Board will revoke a subpoena when the information sought thereby is regarded as immaterial. For example, under the Wagner Act, where the employer applied for subpoena to obtain evidence that a union of foremen was affiliated with a parent organization having locals admitting to membership nonsupervisory employees, the Board denied the subpoena because in its view, under that Act, the affiliation of locals of rank-and-file employees was immaterial to the alleged discriminatory discharge of the employee involved in the case.337 Similarly, under the amended Act, the Board will revoke a subpoena for the purpose of establishing "fronting" by a union for another union that has not complied with the non-Communist affidavit filing requirements, where the information sought by the subpoena will not constitute probative evidence on the issue of "fronting."338

7. Hearing

The Act provides that the person charged with the commission of unfair labor practices has the right to appear and give testimony at the hearing fixed in accordance with the notice of hearing issued with the complaint.[339] Provision is also made for the intervention of interested persons who may present testimony, but the granting of the application is discretionary with the Board or its agent.[340] The Act specifically requires that all of the testimony taken at the hearing must be reduced to writing. The hearing "so far as practicable" must be conducted in accordance with the rules of evidence applicable in the United States District Courts.[341]

The hearing may be conducted by the Board or a member thereof or a designated agent. The practice of the Board has been, except in rare cases, to designate a trial examiner, who conducts and presides at the hearing. The designated trial examiner is in charge of the hearing and he may grant or deny motions,[342] determine the length of continuances[343] and examine witnesses to bring out all relevant facts.[344] But a trial examiner may not engage in unique and disproportionate cross-examination. Unnecessary and exaggerated activity by the Trial Examiner may have the effect of denying a fair hearing.[345] The Seventh Circuit Court of Appeals has said with respect to the behavior of the Trial Examiner at the hearing:[346]

The Act authorizes the Board to enter an order upon a complaint alleging unfair labor practices, only after a "hearing." This must mean a trial by a tribunal free from bias and prejudice and imbued with the desire to accord to the parties equal consideration. There is perhaps no more important right to which litigants are entitled than that they be given such a trial. Its impairment, *ipso facto,* brings the court, and administrative bodies as well, into public disrepute, and destroys the esteem and confidence which they have enjoyed so generally. Time and experience have demonstrated that the public, as well as litigants, will tolerate the honest mistakes of those who pass judgment, but not the biased acts of those who would deprive litigants of a fair and impartial trial. Foremost among the responsibilities imposed upon a reviewing court is to make sure that this foundation of our judicial system be not undermined.

However, where the testimony sought is immaterial, the Trial Examiner may deny permission to cross-examine a witness.[347] Some of the courts have held that the Trial Examiner has wide discretion in his conduct and control of the hearing and will not review his actions in the absence of a "clear showing of abuse,"[348] and "material prejudice" must be shown before a new hearing can be obtained on the ground of bias of the Trial Examiner.[349]

The Trial Examiner is in charge of the conduct of the hearing but he does not enjoy the prerogative of punishing contemptuous conduct except by exclusion from the hearing of one guilty of such conduct. Under the Board's Rules, he may strike out testimony on related matters when a witness refuses to answer a question ruled to be proper.[350]

Following the hearing, the Trial Examiner issues an Intermediate Report which contains findings of fact, conclusions of law and recommendations as to the disposition to be made of the case. He cannot issue an order, and his report is of necessity advisory to the Board. The parties, including the union and counsel for the Board, may file with the Board exceptions to the Trial Examiner's report together with briefs in support of the exceptions.[351] Upon request, the case may be argued before the Board. After the submission of the exceptions, briefs and oral argument of the case, the Board may adopt or reject the trial examiner's findings of facts, conclusions of law and recommendations. The Board, however, must make its own findings of fact and conclusions of law and upon them issue its order dismissing the complaint or directing the cessation of unfair labor practices found and requiring affirmative action by the person charged with the violation.

If no exceptions to the Trial Examiner's Intermediate Report are filed, the amended Act provides that the Trial Examiner's recommended order "shall become the order of the Board and become effective as therein prescribed."[352]

The Board, however, cannot compel compliance with its order. In order to compel obedience, it must petition the United States Circuit Court of Appeals for a decree of enforcement. If such a decree is granted by the Court, failure to comply with the Board's order as enforced by the Court decree constitutes contempt subject to punishment by the Court.

8. Rules of Evidence

The Wagner Act expressly provided that "rules of evidence prevailing in courts of law or equity shall not be controlling." The amended Act eliminates this provision and in its place provides that "so far as practicable" the Board hearings shall "be conducted in accordance with the rules of evidence applicable in the district courts of the United States under the rules of civil procedure for such courts, adopted by the Supreme Court of the United States."[353]

The Conference Report of the House states with respect to this change in the law:[354]

The House bill provided, in section 10(b), that proceedings before the Board should be conducted, so far as practicable, in accordance with the rules of evi-

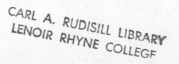

dence applicable in the district courts of the United States under the rules of civil procedure. The Senate amendment retained the language of the present act, which provides that the rules of evidence prevailing in the courts shall not be controlling. The reason for this provision in the House bill was explained in full in the committee report on the bill. If the Board is required, so far as practicable, to act only on legal evidence, the substitution, for example, of assumed "expertness" for evidence will no longer be possible. The conference agreement in section 10(c) contains this provision of the House bill.

However, whether these changes in the statute have in truth broadened the scope of court review of Board orders has yet to be determined by the Supreme Court. The Court of Appeals for the Sixth Circuit, upon remand from the Supreme Court, has held that the changes broadened the scope of review.[355] The United States Court of Appeals for the Fourth Circuit has said the changes in the amended Act have not altered the scope of judicial review of Board orders.[356]

The Board has generally held to the theories underlying the rules of evidence, because wide and unexplained departures have been regarded by the reviewing courts as insufficient to meet the substantial evidence requirements. In addition, the federal rules of civil procedure have liberalized in some measure the common law rules of evidence.

9. Effect of Compliance

After the issuance of an order by the Board, the employer against whom it is directed may comply with it, petition the court for review, or passively await the filing of a petition for enforcement by the Board and thereupon contest the validity of the order before the court. Compliance on the part of the employer does not necessarily bar the Board from seeking enforcement of its order, once issued. In a case where the Board issued an order against the domination and support by the employer of a labor organization, the Supreme Court said, "But an order of the character made by the Board, lawful when made, does not become moot because it is obeyed or because changing circumstances indicate that the need for it may be less than when made."[357] Compliance on the part of the employer with recommendations of the Board's Trial Examiner does not end the case or affect the power of the Board to make and issue its findings and direct or prevent enforcement of the Board order by the court.[358]

10. Scope of Board Order

When the Board finds that unfair labor practices have been committed, its order directs the guilty person to cease and desist therefrom and to take such affirmative steps as will dissipate the effects of such illegal acts, in order to effectuate the policies of the statute.[359] If its findings are supported by substantial evidence, the Board has authority to determine the appropriate remedy in each case, and the reviewing court is without authority to substitute its judgment on the appropriate remedy for the determination of the Board,[360] provided, of course, that the Board acts within the scope of the authority granted to it under the Act. Thus, it is for the Board to decide, upon finding that the employer had illegally refused to bargain with the designated bargaining representatives, whether the employer should be required to bargain with such representative or whether, in view of the lapse of time and changed conditions, a new election should be held.[361]

But the reviewing court has authority to limit the breadth of the Board's order so as to enjoin only violations found to have been committed or such other violations as resemble those found. The reviewing court will strike down a broad injunction order restraining violations of all the provisions of the statute unless the past conduct of the employer furnishes a basis for anticipating that such acts will be committed in the future. These principles were enunciated by the Supreme Court in the famous *Express Publishing Company* case.[362] There, the Board found that the employer had refused to bargain collectively with the bargaining representative and enjoined all violations of the Act. The Court, limiting the scope of the order to the specific violation, said:

> We hold only that the National Labor Relations Act does not give the Board an authority, which courts cannot rightly exercise, to enjoin violations of all the provisions of the statute merely because the violation of one has been found. To justify an order restraining other violations it must appear that they bear some resemblance to that which the employer has committed or that danger of their commission in the future is to be anticipated from the course of his conduct in the past.[363]

Section 10(c) requires that the Board's order be based "upon the preponderance of the testimony taken." The Conference Report states with respect to this requirement:[364]

> In section 10(c) the House bill provided that the Board should base its decisions upon the "weight of the evidence." The Senate amendment retained the present language of the act, permitting the Board to rest its orders upon "all the testimony taken." The conference agreement provides that the Board shall act only on the "preponderance" of the testimony—that is to say, on the weight of the credible evidence. Making the "preponderance" test a statutory requirement will, it is believed, have important effects. For example, evidence could not be considered as meeting the "preponderance" test merely by the drawing of "expert" inferences therefrom, where it would not meet that test otherwise. Again,

the Board's decisions should show on their face that the statutory requirement has been met—they should indicate an actual weighing of the evidence, setting forth the reasons for believing this evidence and disbelieving that, for according greater weight to this testimony than to that, for drawing this inference rather than that. Immeasurably increased respect for decisions of the Board should result from this provision.

11. Objections Not Raised before the Board

The Act expressly deprives the Circuit Court of Appeals of authority to consider, upon review of the Board proceeding, objections which have not been presented to the Board. The Act provides that "no objection that has not been urged before the Board, its member, agent or agency, shall be considered by the court, unless the failure or neglect to urge such objection shall be excused because of extraordinary circumstances."[365]

It is, thus, of vital importance that all objections be presented and argued before the Board or its Trial Examiner, because the failure to do so operates as an absolute preclusion from urging the objection before the reviewing court. While the court is granted authority to relieve the effect of such preclusion under "extraordinary circumstances," the occasion for and the facts necessary to obtain such relief may well be regarded as extremely rare.

III · JUDICIAL ENFORCEMENT AND
REVIEW OF BOARD ORDERS

1. How Obtained

If its order is not complied with, the Board is authorized by the Act to petition the United States Circuit Court of Appeals for enforcement.[366] An employer against whom the Board has entered an order may obtain a court review thereof by filing a petition for review in the United States Circuit Court of Appeals.[367] It is the practice of the Board, whenever an employer files a petition for review, to file with its answer to the employer's petition a request for enforcement of its order. Unions found to be company-dominated and unions involved in contracts which the Board has ruled to be in violation of the Act may intervene in the court proceedings.[368]

2. The Appropriate Court

Both the Board and the employer must file the petition in the Circuit Court of Appeals for the circuit in which the unfair labor practices are alleged to have occurred or where the employer resides or transacts business.[369] They may also seek court review in the Circuit Court of Appeals for the District of Columbia.

3. The Record for Review[370]

When the Board files a petition for enforcement of its order in the Court of Appeals, the Act requires that it shall certify and file in such Court a transcript of the entire proceeding before it. Such a transcript of proceedings includes the pleadings, the testimony before the Board, the exhibits, and the findings and order of the Board.[371] If the employer files a petition for review, he must file with the Court a similarly complete transcript of the proceedings certified by the Board.[372] The Court reviews the case in both instances—on the Board's petition for enforcement or on the employer's petition for review—on the basis of the transcript of the proceedings before the Board and certified by it.

4. Jurisdiction of the Reviewing Court

The Act grants exclusive jurisdiction for review of Board orders to the United States Circuit Court of Appeals and provides that its judgment shall be final, subject to review thereof, however, by the United States Supreme Court upon writ of certiorari.[373] The court does not acquire such exclusive jurisdiction over the case until the transcript of the entire proceedings before the Board has been filed in court.[374] Prior to the filing of such transcript, the Board has power to set aside, or modify, in whole or in part, its findings or order. The filing of a petition for review by the employer does not limit this power of the Board or confer exclusive jurisdiction upon the court so as to deprive the Board of power to act further in the proceeding. In a celebrated case involving these principles, the United States Court of Appeals for the Third Circuit enjoined the Board from taking any further proceedings after the Republic Steel Corporation had filed a petition for review of a Board order in that Court. The Board had given notice of its intention to enforce its order for review of which the employer had petitioned, but the transcript of the proceedings before the Board had not been filed in Court. Upon petition by the Board for relief against the action of the Court, the Supreme Court held that, under the Act, the Circuit Court of Appeals was without authority to prevent the Board from modifying its findings and order, since the transcript of proceeding had not been filed.[375] Similarly, the Board may, after filing a petition for enforcement in court, reacquire jurisdiction of the proceeding to act therein although the employer has filed a petition for review.[376]

5. Review of Board Certification Proceedings

Section 9 of the Act authorizes the Board to investigate questions affecting commerce, which concern representation of employees for purposes of collective bargaining and to certify in writing to the parties the representatives selected or designated by such employees.[377] In such a proceeding, the Board, "if it has reasonable cause to believe that a question of representation affecting commerce exists," must provide for a hearing upon "due" notice. If it finds that there is such a question of representation upon the record of the hearing, the Board must conduct an election and certify the results.[378] The certification of bargaining representative by the

Board, and its determinations in the course of such investigation or "representation proceeding," as it is commonly called, are not appealable and the Circuit Court of Appeals is without authority to review the certification proceedings,[379] except when the Board order is based upon facts certified in the representation proceedings.[380] The wide discretionary powers of the Board in a representation proceeding have been sustained as valid by the Supreme Court, and the reviewing courts will not interfere therewith, except for a procedural violation of the due process requirements, abuse of discretion by arbitrary or capricious determinations, and where the determinations of the Board are not supported by evidence.[381] The courts have refused to review the Board's dismissal of a petition for investigation and certification of bargaining representative,[382] the Board's direction of a secret ballot election,[383] and the refusal of the Board to carry out an agreement to conduct an election because the effect of unfair labor practices had not been dissipated.[384] While the Act authorizes the court to provide for the taking of additional evidence, the power applies only to unfair labor practice cases and will not be applied to a representation proceeding.[385]

6. Court Review Confined to Record

Under the statute, the reviewing court is without authority to consider matters outside the transcript or record of proceedings certified by the Board. In a case involving company domination of a union, the court considered the statements of counsel for the company that the illegal features of the union had been eliminated. This information was submitted to the court after the argument of the case before the court and did not appear in the transcript or record certified by the Board. The Supreme Court, in holding the consideration of this matter to have been error,[386] said:[387]

> The court below, in its opinion, states it was advised in a brief after the hearing in that court, that the plan had been amended by striking out the provisions in question. It concludes, therefore, that their previous existence is immaterial. The statute expressly deprives the reviewing court of power to consider facts thus brought to its attention. The case must be heard on the record as certified by the Board. The appropriate procedure to add facts to the record is prescribed in § 10 (e) of the Act.

If it is desired that the court consider facts not in the record certified by the Board, application must be made for leave to adduce such additional evidence. The applicant must satisfy the court that such evidence is material to the case and that there were reasonable grounds for the failure to introduce it before the Board. The court, then, has power to order that such additional evidence be taken by the Board and made part of the transcript or record of proceedings before the Board.[388]

7. Power over Board Orders

The power of the United States Circuit Court of Appeals over orders of the Board is specifically stated in the Act. The Court has power to grant a decree "enforcing, modifying, and enforcing as so modified, or setting aside in whole or in part" the order of the Board.[389]

Such power, however, does not authorize the Court to modify a Board order so as to provide for the inclusion of a union, which the Board excluded, on the ballot in a Board election. The *Falk Corporation*[390] case was a consolidated proceeding against the employer for alleged unfair labor practices and for an investigation and certification of bargaining representatives.[391] The unfair labor practice involved an alleged company-dominated union. The Board found the union company-dominated and excluded it from the ballot in the election directed in connection with the designation of a bargaining agent by the employees. The Board ordered the company-dominated union to be disestablished. Upon review the Court sustained the Board's findings of company domination, but modified the Board order so as to permit the employee to vote for the company-dominated union, and provided for its disestablishment unless the employees selected it as their bargaining agent. The Supreme Court held that the Court was without power under the statute to make the modifications since the Act granted the Board exclusive authority in elections. The principles stated were as follows:[392]

We think it apparent that the conditions attached by the court to the Board's order operated as a modification of the Board's Direction that Independent be omitted from the ballot in the coming election. In conditioning the Board's order, the court acted, as it said, "that the coming election shall be free, uninfluenced by the employer and unhampered by any election order which eliminates (the Independent) as a contender." In effect, the court's qualification of the Board's order judicially pronounced—in advance of the election—that election methods considered "suitable" by the courts rather than by the Board must be followed. But § 9 of the Act vests power in the Board, not in the court, to select the method of determining what union, if any, employees desire as a bargaining agent; to this end, the Board "may take a secret ballot of employees, or utilize any other suitable method to ascertain such representatives."

Nor can authority for such anticipatory judicial control of election methods be found in § 9(d) which permits a review only in those cases in which the Board makes an order relating to labor practices found to be unfair as a result of a prior certification of a selected bargaining agent. Here, the Board's order that the employer cease its unfair practices, disestablish the company union and post notices was not "based in whole or in part upon facts certified" as the result of an election or investigation made by the Board pursuant to § 9(c). The proposed election here has not even been held and consequently no certification of a proper bargaining agent has been made by the Board. Until that election is held, there can be no certification of a bargaining representative and no Board order—based on a certification—has been or can be made, so as to invoke the court's powers under 9(d).

8. Power to Remand

The Act contains no express provision which authorizes the Circuit Court of Appeals to remand a case to the Board after it has filed the transcript of the proceedings before the Board with the court. Under such circumstances the court has acquired exclusive jurisdiction over the matter.[393] The court in the general exercise of its "equity powers" may remand the case to the Board in the absence of general express statutory provision.[394] Manifestly, the exercise of such "equity powers" is discretionary with the court, and the Board cannot insist upon a remand as a matter of right. Remands have been approved under the following circumstances:

1. For the purpose of taking additional evidence;[395]
2. To permit the making of additional findings on the basis of existing evidence;[396]
3. To eliminate alleged procedural defects in the Board's proceedings;[397]
4. For clarification of a Board's order.[398]

The Court may grant the remand to the Board before deciding any of the issues in the case and without giving the Board any instructions with respect to curing any alleged defects.[399] When, upon the final hearing, questions develop upon which it is believed that further proceedings before the Board are necessary, the courts have remanded such cases for that purpose.[400] Instead of reversing the Board, the Supreme Court remanded two cases to the Board for the purpose of receiving the Board's judgment as to whether the reinstatement of discriminatorily discharged employees, who had substantially equivalent employment, would effectuate the policies of the Act.[401] Remand of a case to the Board upon its application has been denied by the court although the Board claimed that it mistakenly applied a formula for determining back pay in favor of employees found to have been discharged in violation of the Act.[402]

The Act expressly provides that either party may apply to the court for leave to submit additional evidence.[403] The applicant must satisfy the court (a) that the additional evidence is material, and (b) that there are reasonable grounds for failure to submit the evidence to the Board upon the original hearing. If the application is granted by the court, the Board must take the additional evidence and make new findings thereon or modify its prior findings and must file recommendations to the court with respect to its original order. The additional evidence becomes part of the transcript of proceedings before the court with the same effect as if taken by the Board at its initial hearing.

9. Power to Grant Temporary Injunctive Relief

After the filing of the certified transcript of proceedings by the union before the Board, the Court of Appeals has power "to grant such temporary relief or restraining order as it deems just and proper."[404] The court has similar authority when the petition for review is filed by the employer.[405]

The Court of Appeals for the Seventh Circuit exercised the power, upon motion of the Board, in a case in which it had acquired exclusive jurisdiction over the proceeding to enforce an order of the Board. The Board order before the Court enjoined general acts of interference, restraint and coercion, and cancelled the discriminatory discharge of an employee. Upon motion by the Board the Court granted a temporary order restraining the employer from interfering with an election about to be conducted by the Board, which the Board had theretofore postponed because of the alleged illegal conduct of the employer. Although the order, which the Board was seeking to enforce, did not restrain interference with an election, the Court adopted the Board's contention that the Board's general injunction against interference with an employee's right included restraint of the employer's conduct in interfering with the employee's freedom of choice of bargaining representative in an election.[406]

10. Scope of Court Review

The Act limits the authority of the reviewing court irrespective of whether the employer files a petition for review or the Board seeks enforcement of its order. The Act provides that: "The findings of the Board with respect to questions of fact, if supported by substantial evidence on the record considered as a whole, shall be conclusive."[407] Thus, review by the court is primarily limited to the legal questions and whether the facts found by the Board are supported by substantial evidence.[408] The limited authority of the reviewing court has been defined by the Supreme Court as follows:

If the Board has acted within the compass of the power given it by Congress, has, on a charge of unfair labor practice, held a "hearing," which the statute requires, comporting with the standards of fairness inherent in procedural due process, has made findings based upon substantial evidence and has ordered an appropriate remedy, a like obedience to the statutory law on the part of the Court of Appeals requires the court to grant enforcement of the Board's order.[409]

The standard of court review of Board findings has thus been stated by the Supreme Court:

It has now long been settled that findings of the Board, as with those of other administrative agencies, are conclusive upon reviewing courts when supported by evidence, that the weighing of conflicting evidence is for the Board and not for the courts, that the inferences from the evidence are to be drawn by the Board and not by the courts, save only as questions of law are raised and that upon such questions of law, the experienced judgment of the Board is entitled to great weight.[410]

The court is without power to pass upon the credibility of witnesses, to draw inferences from the facts contrary to those drawn by the Board, or to weigh the evidence; in fact, it must enforce the Board order even though its judgment on the facts differs from that of the Board and though it would have ruled otherwise had it been called upon to decide the issue in the first instance.

Findings of the Board as to the facts, if supported by evidence, are conclusive and the Court of Appeals may not:

1. Substitute its judgment on disputed facts for that of the Board;[411]
2. Determine the credibility of witnesses;[412]
3. Draw inferences of fact;[413]
4. Determine the weight to be given the testimony before the Board;[414]
5. Resolve conflicting evidence;[415]
6. Reverse the Board's findings of fact on the basis of sharp conflicts in the testimony;[416]
7. Reverse the Board's findings of fact if they are supported by substantial evidence.[417]

Where the evidence is insufficient to support the Board's finding, the reviewing court has power to deny enforcement of the order or set it aside because of such defect of proof. In a case of refusal to bargain, the Board's order, requiring the employer to bargain with the union that charged the employer with unfair labor practice, was denied enforcement because the evidence was insufficient to establish that, during a strike of the employees, the employer had been informed of the union's desire to bargain with the employer.[418]

The Board's determination of what measures should be taken by the employer to remedy unfair labor practices is treated as an inference to be drawn from the facts found; as such it cannot be disturbed by the reviewing court if such remedy ordered by the Board is supported by the evidence. Thus, where the Board has ordered disestablishment of a company-dominated union on the basis of the facts supporting its findings of company domination and support of the union, the reviewing court cannot disturb the order although it is of the opinion that disestablishment should not be ordered.[419]

The new requirements as to the rules of evidence,[420] and that the Board's decision must be "upon the preponderance of the testimony taken,"[421] would seem to broaden the extent of court review. The court would appear to have authority to consider whether these requirements of the statute have been satisfied by the Board although, presumably, it could not substitute its judgment for that of the Board. However, the Court of Appeals for the Fourth Circuit has said the changes in the amended Act have led some persons to believe "that the new Act broadened the scope of judicial review and conferred upon the courts power to correct mistakes committed by the Board in its findings of fact as well as in its conclusions of law," but such a result was not accomplished.[422] The U. S. Supreme Court has remanded a case for consideration of the scope of judicial review under the amended Act.[423] In that case, the Court of Appeals for the Sixth Circuit, upon the remand, ruled that the changes in the Act broadened the scope of review.[a] The Court of Appeals for the Fifth Circuit has regarded the amendments to the Act as giving the courts "more latitude" on review.[b] The Court of Appeals in other circuits has said that no change in the scope of court review has been accomplished by the amendments to the Act.[c] Final determination of this question awaits the ruling of the Supreme Court.

11. The Basis of Court Review

INSUBSTANTIAL EVIDENCE

The statute provides that the findings of the Board as to the facts are conclusive and cannot be altered by the reviewing court if such findings are "supported by substantial evidence on the record considered as a whole."[424]

The Wagner Act provided that the Board's findings of fact were conclusive "if supported by evidence." The courts interpreted this language to mean "supported by substantial evidence." The Supreme Court said:

We agree that the statute, in providing that "the findings of the Board as to the facts, if supported by evidence, shall be conclusive," means supported by substantial evidence. Washington V. & M. Coach Co. v. NLRB, 301 U.S. 142, 147. Substantial evidence is more than a mere scintilla. It means such relevant evidence as a reasonable mind might accept as adequate to support a conclusion[425] . . . and it must be enough to justify, if the trial were to a jury, a refusal to direct a verdict when the conclusion sought to be drawn from it is one of fact for the jury.[426]

The language of the Act, as amended, merely clarifies the former provision of the Wagner Act in the terms of the court interpretations and in accordance with the corresponding provision of the Administrative Procedure Act.[427] "The court reviews the findings of the Board as it reviews the finding of a jury on a motion n.o.v., that is to say, the findings, like the verdict, must stand if there is substantial evidence in the record to support them."[428]

When the findings of the Board as to the facts are supported by substantial evidence, the authority of the reviewing court is limited to questions of law. The Supreme Court has said:

As it did in setting up other administrative bodies, Congress has left questions of law which arise before the Board—but not more—ultimately to the traditional review of the judiciary. Not by accident, but in line with a general policy, Congress has deemed it wise to entrust the finding of facts to these specialized agencies. It is essential that courts regard this division of responsibility which Congress as a matter of policy has embodied in the very statute from which the Court of Appeals derived its jurisdiction to act.[429] The Court of Appeals' failure to enforce the Board's order resulted from the substitution of its judgment on disputed facts, for the Board's judgment, and power to do that, has been denied the courts by Congress. Whether the court would reach the same conclusion as the Board from the conflicting evidence is immaterial and the court's disagreement with the Board could not warrant the disregard of the statutory division of authority set up by Congress.[430]

Despite the provision of the Wagner Act which made inapplicable to cases before the Board the rules of evidence,[431] a mere scintilla of evidence, uncorroborated hearsay, rumor and suspicion did not constitute substantial evidence and were insufficient to support Board findings as to fact. Thus, the reviewing court has ample authority to consider whether Board findings of the facts are supported by substantial evidence and to deny enforcement of the Board order if they are based upon uncorroborated hearsay, rumor, or suspicion.[432] The Supreme Court has said:

The statute provides that "the rules of evidence prevailing in courts of law and equity shall not be controlling." The obvious purpose of this and similar provisions is to free administrative boards from the compulsion of technical rules so that the mere admission of matter which would be deemed incompetent in judicial proceedings would not invalidate the administrative order (cases cited). But this assurance of a desirable flexibility in administrative procedure does not go so far as to justify orders without a basis in evidence having rational probative force. Mere uncorroborated hearsay or rumor does not constitute substantial evidence.[433]

LACK OF FAIR HEARING

The hearing before the Trial Examiner must be conducted fairly and without any bias on his part so that all parties may be afforded a full opportunity to be heard, to present evidence and to examine and cross-examine witnesses.[434]

The announcement of the Trial Examiner of his purpose to ask and secure instructions from Washington upon a debatable point in order to save possible reversal is not necessarily prejudicial or a denial of due process.[435]

To establish grounds for reversal of the Trial Examiner on account of prejudice and bias something more than an unfavorable ruling or an unsupported finding must be shown.[436] The nature of the conduct of a Trial Examiner, sufficient to constitute bias and prejudice so as to result in denial of fair hearing, was summarized by the Circuit Court of Appeals for the Eighth Circuit in the *Montgomery Ward & Co.* case. The Court said with respect to its consideration of the record on that point:[437]

We cannot escape the conclusion that, in the hearing, the company was denied that fairness which is required by due process of law.

The responsibility for this situation rests primarily upon the examiner. It was not recognized nor corrected by the Board. It sprang from the decided partisanship of the examiner. Rather loosely classified, it manifested itself by omissions from the record of occurrences at the hearing; by unfairly restricting examination and cross-examination by counsel for the company and for the intervenor; by a hostile attitude toward witnesses (whether called by the Board or not) who might be supposed to favor the company or the intervenor; and by an obvious attitude of bias in other instances.

The Court found the ground of unfairness of the hearing so well established that, without considering the sufficiency of the evidence with respect to the findings of fact, it denied enforcement and remanded the case to the Board for a proper hearing.

Where there has been a denial of a fair and impartial hearing in accordance with the requirements of due process, the courts have refused to enforce the order of the Board, even though the record showed that there was evidence which would support the findings and order.[438] The Court of Appeals for the Fifth Circuit has said:[439]

Nor will the fact that an examination of the record shows that there was evidence which would support the judgment at all save a trial from the charge of unfairness, for when the fault of bias and prejudice in a judge first rears its ugly head, its effect remains throughout the whole proceeding. Once partiality appears, and particularly when, though challenged, it is unrelieved against, it taints and vitiates all the proceedings and no judgment based upon them may stand.

The Supreme Court has emphasized the absolute necessity for fair and open hearings by administrative agencies and not even convenience or the "natural desire to be rid of harassing delay" can justify dispensing with the "rudiments of fair play assured to every litigant by the Fourteenth Amendment."[440]

But the fact that the record shows that the Trial Examiner believed all the witnesses for the union and disbelieved all the witnesses for the employer does not establish bias and prejudice on the part of the Trial Examiner sufficient to invalidate the Board's order.[441]

QUESTION OF LAW

Nothing in the Act limits the authority of the reviewing court to consider and determine questions of law involved in cases within their exclusive jurisdiction by virtue of the Board's petition for enforcement or an employer's petition for review of the Board's order. The court is in no wise restricted by the Board's determination of such questions of law. Some courts, however, regarded the Board, under the Wagner Act, as expert in the field of labor relations and on that basis accorded its judgment in the labor field great weight, if not substantial finality, unless it was clearly shown that the judgment of the Board was erroneous. In a case involving the meaning of a provision of the Act, the Circuit Court of Appeals for the Third Circuit said:[442]

If there is foundation for the frequently reiterated phrase about the expert judgment of the administrative tribunal, this would appear to be the type of situation where that expert judgment is most appropriately exercised. A court should uphold that judgment unless it obviously is contrary to law or is contrary to the facts proven. Here it fails by neither test. We think the interpretation given by the Board was right, but even if we were doubtful we think we should support it in the absence of a showing that it is wrong.

The Board's judgment that an employer's rule prohibiting solicitation for union membership in the plant on the employees' own time was *per se* violative of the Act was accepted by the courts.[443] The point is aptly illustrated by the statement of the United States Court of Appeals for the Second Circuit in a case where the Board found a successor union company-dominated. That Court said:[444]

In this instance, that question is whether the employer's influence upon the will of his employees—which by hypothesis resulted from their past relations and his known wishes and conduct—determined their choice when they formed the new union. That concerns only human motives and of a kind with which courts are not unaccustomed to deal. At first blush it might seem, therefore, to be no different from that involved in deciding for example what actuated an employer in discharging an employee; i.e., whether he was trying to maintain discipline, or to rid himself of a troublesome union organizer. We should have a review of that question, for we should be as competent as the Board to deal with it; but the question of how deeply an employer's relations with his employees will overbear their will, and how long that influence will last, is, or at least it may be thought to be, of another sort, to decide which a board, or tribunal chosen from those who have had long acquaintance with labor relations, may acquire a competence beyond that of any court. That there can be issues of fact which courts would be altogether incompetent to decide, is plain. If the question were, for example, as to the chemical reaction between a number of elements, it would be idle to give power to a court to pass upon whether there was "substantial" evidence to support the decision of a board of qualified chemists. The court might undertake to review their finding so far as they had decided what reagents had actually been present in the experiment, for that presumably would demand no specialized skill. But it would be obliged to stop there, for it would not have the background which alone would enable it to decide questions of chemistry; and indeed it could undertake to pass upon them only at the cost of abandoning the accumulated store of experience upon the subject. It is true that to a large degree we do just that in ordinary trials when we call specialists as witnesses; but that was not always the way in which the common law met the problem (XV Harv. L.R. pp. 40-42), and in so far as we now increasingly have recourse to administrative tribunals it is no longer the way.

The same Court gave similar weight to the Board's determination that certification of a bargaining representative is conclusive on the employees and the employer for a reasonable period of time.[445]

It must be remembered, however, that the reviewing courts cannot and will not abdicate their authority. The "expert judgment" doctrine has been limited to specialized labor problems where the courts have felt the Board's judgment might be particularly important, and have applied it in the absence of a showing that such judgment was erroneous. The effect of the amended Act making the rules of evidence applicable to Board hearings or the "expertness" doctrine is discussed below.

RULES AND PREPONDERANCE OF EVIDENCE

The Act, as amended with respect to the applicability of rules of evidence and the preponderance of evidence requirement, curtails the use of the "presumed expertness" doctrine in Board cases. In the absence of definitive final court decision, the effect of these new requirements on the powers of the reviewing court, is best indicated by the following discussion in the Conference Report of the House:[446]

Under the language of section 10(e) of the present act, findings of the Board, upon court review of Board orders, are conclusive "if supported by evidence." By reason of this language, the courts have, as one has put it, in effect "abdicated" to the Board (NLRB v. Standard Oil Company, 138 Fed. (2d) 885 (1943); See also Wilson & Co. v. NLRB 126 Fed. (2d) 114 (1942); NLRB v. Columbia Products Corp. 141 Fed (2d) 687 (1944); NLRB v. Union Pacific Stages, Inc. 99 Fed. (2d) 153). In many instances deference on the part of the courts to specialized knowledge that is supposed to inhere in administrative agencies has led the courts to acquiesce in decisions of the Board, even when the findings concerned mixed issues of law and of fact (NLRB v. Hearst Publications, Inc., 322 U.S. 111; NLRB v. Packard Motor Car Co., decided March 10, 1947), or when they rested only on inferences that were not, in turn, supported by facts in the record (Republic Aviation v. NLRB, 324 U.S. 793; Le Tourneau Company v. NLRB, 324 U.S. 793).

As previously stated in the discussion of amendments to section 10(b) and section 10(c), by reason of the new language concerning the rules of evidence and the preponderance of the evidence, presumed expertness on the part of the Board in its field can no longer be a factor in the Board's decisions. While the Administrative Procedure Act is generally regarded as having intended to require the courts to examine decisions of administrative agencies far more critically than has been their practice in the past, by reason of a conflict of opinion as to whether it actually does so, a conflict that the courts have not resolved, there was included, both in the House bill and the Senate amendment, language making it clear that the act gives to the courts a real power of review.

The House bill, in section 10(e), provided that the Board's findings of fact should be conclusive unless it appeared to the reviewing court (1) that the findings were against the manifest weight of the evidence, or (2) that they were not supported by substantial evidence.

The Senate amendment provided that the Board's findings with respect to questions of fact should be conclusive if supported by substantial evidence on the record considered as a whole. The provisions of section 10(b) of the conference agreement insure the Board's receiving only legal evidence, and section 10(c) insures its deciding in accordance with the preponderance of the evidence. These two statutory requirements in and of themselves give rise to questions of law which the courts will hereafter be called upon to determine—whether the requirements have been met. This, in conjunction with the language of the Senate amendment with respect to the Board's findings of fact—language which the conference agreement adopts—will very materially broaden the scope of the courts' reviewing power. This is not to say that the courts will be required to decide any case de novo, themselves weighing the evidence, but they will be under a duty to see that the Board observes the provisions of the earlier sections, that it does not infer facts that are not supported by evidence or that are not consistent with evidence in the record, and that it does not concentrate on one element of proof to the exclusion of others without adequate explanation of its reasons for disregarding or discrediting the evidence that is in conflict with its findings. The language also precludes the substitution of expertness for evidence in making decisions. It is believed that the provisions of the conference agreement relating to the courts' reviewing power will be adequate to preclude such decisions as those in *NLRB v. Nevada Consol. Copper Corp.* (316 U.S. 105) and in the *Wilson, Columbia Products, Union Pacific Stages, Hearst, Republic Aviation,* and *Le Tourneau,* etc., cases, *supra,* without unduly burdening the courts. The conference agreement therefore carries the language of the Senate amendment into section 10(e) of the amended Act.

12. Interlocutory Nature of Board Order

In most instances, Board orders which require payment of back pay and reinstatement of employees do not specify the amount of back pay to be paid or the specific job to which the employee is to be reinstated. Such orders are general, and after enforcement is granted by the court, the Board must work out the details of the reinstatement and the amounts to be paid as back pay. This result can be accomplished, and frequently is, by negotiation between the Board's attorneys and the respondent's attorneys. If they cannot agree the Board must hold a hearing to determine the facts and make findings of fact and conclusions of law.[447] The Board may then obtain a supplemental enforcement decree setting forth the specific information found. In some cases, the Board has obtained specific authority from the reviewing courts to conduct the hearing for the purpose of determining the specific amount of back pay or the jobs to which employees are to be reinstated.[448] Several courts have ruled that the Board may conduct such hearings after enforcement is granted without obtaining additional directions from the court, but upon such a hearing the Board has no authority to take testimony on whether there has been compliance with the enforcement decree.[449] In some instances, courts themselves have determined the specific amount of back pay in the course of contempt proceedings initiated by the Board.[450] One court that followed such procedure has since disapproved of it and is of the opinion that the proper procedure is for the Board to determine the specific amount of back pay and then to secure a supplemental enforcement decree.[451]

13. Contempt Proceedings

After issuance by the court of a decree enforcing in whole or in part the Board's order, it may be alleged that the person against whom such decree issued has failed to obey or comply with its provisions. Contempt proceedings for the alleged violation of the enforcing decree may then be instituted by the Board before the court.[452] The union which filed the charges before the Board cannot institute contempt proceedings against the employer for alleged noncompliance with the enforcing decree.[453] Presumably, an employer or individual who filed unfair labor practice charges against a union would likewise be barred from instituting contempt proceedings.

The Board initiates civil contempt proceedings by filing a motion with the court that the employer be adjudged in contempt for failure to obey the court's decree. A copy of the motion papers is served upon the party alleged to be in violation of the Court's enforcement decree. Any officer or agent of a corporate employer responsible for the failure to comply may be held liable in contempt proceedings.[454] Identity of employees entitled to reinstatement and the exact amount of back pay to be paid each employee have been determined in such proceedings.[455]

Contempt proceedings by the Board have been dismissed and the Board's request that the employer be adjudged in contempt for failure to carry out the court's enforcing decree denied under the following circumstances:

1. Where the position to which the employee was required to be reinstated was abolished for valid business reasons and the employee refused an offer of a comparable position.[456]

2. Where the employees required to be reinstated had not applied for reinstatement within a specified period as provided in the decree of enforcement.[457]

3. Where the decree of the court prohibited favoritism for or discrimination against a named union or "any labor organization," and the alleged acts of favoritism were to a union not in existence at the time of the order and took place during the existence of a valid closed shop contract with that union.[458]

In a contempt proceeding the Board has the burden of establishing the violation of the court's enforcement decree, and to meet that requirement the Board must make a showing of "something more than a mere preponderance of evidence . . . . clear and convincing proof is necessary."[459]

If the question of contempt is referred to a Special Master for consideration, the courts are inclined to accept his findings unless they are clearly erroneous.[460]

PART THREE

Rights and Duties of
Management and Unions

Introduction
CHAPTER I. Rights of Management
(Including Duties of Unions)
II. Duties of Management
(Including Rights of Unions)
III. Unfair Labor Practices by Employers
IV. Unfair Labor Practices by Unions

119

INTRODUCTION

1. Interstate Commerce

The National Labor Relations Act (popularly known as the "Wagner Act"[1]) was approved and became law on July 5, 1935. It was amended by the Labor Management Relations Act, 1947, (commonly called the "Taft-Hartley Law") enacted June 23, 1947, and the amendments became effective August 22, 1947.[2] The purpose of the law is to regulate employer-employee relations "to eliminate the causes of certain substantial obstructions to the free flow of commerce" by encouraging "the practice and procedure of collective bargaining" and by protecting "the exercise by workers of full freedom of association, self-organization, and designation of representatives of their own choosing, for the purpose of negotiating the terms and conditions of their employment or other mutual aid or protection."[3] The Act is predicated upon the Congressional finding, stated in the Act, that employers have denied employees the right to organize and refused to accept the procedure of collective bargaining, resulting in the burdening of interstate commerce by reason of strikes and industrial unrest. Congress also stated in the Act that "experience has proved that protection by law of the right to organize and bargain collectively safeguards commerce from injury."[4]

The Congressional statements of policy of the Act, as amended, also recite that "certain practices by some labor organizations" burden and obstruct commerce, thereby impairing the public interest "in the free flow of such commerce" and that "the elimination of such practices is a necessary condition to the assurance of the rights herein guaranteed."[5]

The Labor Management Relations Act, 1947, states the new national policy: "to prescribe the legitimate rights of both employees and employers" and "to protect the rights of individual employees in their relations with labor organizations whose activities affect commerce."[6] In accordance with this policy, the Act, as amended, defines unfair labor practices by labor organizations, authorizes the Board to issue orders against unions to remedy such activities by unions, and provides for the right of employees "to refrain from any and all" union activities.[7]

The essential prerequisite for the applicability of the Act and the power of the National Labor Relations Board, established thereby, to issue orders for remedying unfair labor practices or certifying an exclusive bargaining agency for employees, is that the activities of the employer or a union, alleged to be engaging in unfair labor practices, as defined in the Act, affect interstate commerce or that there be a question "affecting commerce" with respect to the representation of employees.[8] The Supreme Court has said:[9]

The critical words of this provision, prescribing the limits of the Board's authority in dealing with the labor practices, are "affecting commerce." The Act specifically defines the "commerce" to which it refers (§ 2 (6)):

"The term 'commerce' means trade, traffic, commerce, transportation, or communication among the several States, or between the District of Columbia or any Territory of the United States and any State or other Territory, or between any foreign country and any State, Territory, or the District of Columbia, or within the District of Columbia or any Territory, or between points in the same State but through any other State or any Territory or the District of Columbia or any foreign country."

There can be no question that the commerce thus contemplated by the Act (aside from that within a Territory or the District of Columbia) is interstate and foreign commerce in the constitutional sense. The Act also defines the term "affecting commerce" (§ 2 (7)):

"The term 'affecting commerce' means in commerce, or burdening or obstructing commerce or the free flow of commerce, or having led or tending to lead to a labor dispute burdening or obstructing commerce or the free flow of commerce."

This definition is one of exclusion as well as of inclusion. The grant of authority to the Board does not purport to extend to the relationship between all industrial employees and employers. Its terms do not impose collective bargaining upon all industry, regardless of effects upon interstate or foreign commerce. It purports to reach only what may be deemed to burden or obstruct that commerce and, thus qualified, it must be construed as contemplating the exercise of control within constitutional bounds. It is a familiar principle that acts which directly burden or obstruct interstate or foreign commerce, or its free flow, are within the reach of the congressional power. Acts having that effect are not rendered immune because they grow out of labor disputes. See *Texas & N.O.R. Co. v. Railway Clerks,* 281 U.S. 548, 570; *Schechter Corp. v. United States, supra.,* pp. 544, 545; *Virginian Railway v. System Federation,* No. 40, 300 U.S. 515. It is the effect upon commerce, not the source of the injury, which is the criterion. *Second Employers' Liability Cases,* 223 U.S. 1, 51. Whether or not particular action does not affect commerce in such a close and intimate fashion as to be subject to federal control, and hence to lie within the authority conferred upon the Board, is left by the statute to be determined as individual cases arise. We are thus to inquire whether in the instant case the constitutional boundary has been passed.

The meaning of the terms "commerce" and "affecting commerce" have not been changed by the amendments to the Act.[10]

The jurisdiction of the Board does not necessarily depend on the volume of the employer's interstate business, and the jurisdiction of the Board has been sustained even when the volume of such business was relatively small.

The power of Congress to regulate interstate commerce is plenary and extends to all such commerce, be it great or small. . . . The amount of the commerce regulated is of special significance only to the extent that Congress may be taken to have excluded commerce of small volume from the operation of its regulatory measure by express provision or fair implication.

The language of the National Labor Relations Act seems to make it plain that Congress has set no restrictions upon the jurisdiction of the Board to be determined or fixed exclusively by reference to the volume of interstate commerce involved.[11]

In secondary boycott situations, the scope of the Act has been held to extend to small and relatively local businesses where the purpose of the boycott was to compel a cessation of business with a concern engaged in interstate commerce.[a]

Nor does the jurisdiction of the Board under the Act extend only to an employer who is himself engaged in interstate commerce business. The broad scope of the jurisdictional provisions of the Act have been interpreted to constitute a grant of power to the Board with respect to employers who are not themselves engaged in interstate commerce business, but whose activities affect such commerce as defined in the statute. The Supreme Court said:[12]

It has been settled by repeated decisions of this Court that an employer may be subject to the National Labor Relations Act although not himself engaged in commerce. The end sought in the enactment of the statute was the prevention of the disturbance to interstate commerce consequent upon strikes and labor disputes induced or likely to be induced because of unfair labor practices named in the Act. That those consequences may ensue from strikes of the employees of manufacturers who are not engaged in interstate commerce where the cessation of manufacture necessarily results in the cessation of the movement of the manufactured product in interstate commerce, has been repeatedly pointed out by this Court.

The test of the Board's jurisdiction is whether the alleged unfair labor practice, or the question concerning the representation of the employees, tends to obstruct or burden or interfere with, in a substantial manner, the free flow of interstate and foreign commerce.[13]

2. Employer-Employee Relationship

The wide scope given to the Act and the powers of the Board established thereby have infused the employee-employer relationship with rights and obligations expressed in the statute, or arising therefrom by reason of interpretation by the Board and the courts, in addition to such rights and obligations an employer may have had prior to the enactment of the statute. The term "employer" is defined in the Act, as amended, to include "any person acting as an agent of an employer."[14] By this provision, the responsibilities of the employer are limited to the activities of persons who may be found to be his agents within the established rules of agency. The prior definition and the effect of this changed provision was summarized by the House Committee on Education and Labor as follows:

The old Act included in the definition of "employer" any person acting in the interest of an employer. Under this language the Board frequently imputed to employers anything that anyone connected with an employer, no matter how remotely, said or did, notwithstanding that the employer had not authorized what was said or done, and in many cases even had prohibited it. By such rulings, the Board often was able to punish employers for things they did not do, did not authorize, and had tried to prevent.

The bill, by defining as an "employer" "any person acting *as an agent* of an employer," makes employers responsible for what people say or do only when it is within the *actual* or *apparent* scope of their authority, and thereby makes the ordinary rules of the law of agency equally applicable to employers and to union.[15]

"Employee" is defined in the Act to include "any employee" and the term is not limited "to the employees of a particular employer," except as so expressly provided.[16] However, the Act as amended restricts the right of the Board to find the existence of an employee-employer relationship on the basis of "economic facts"[17] by expressly excluding independent contractors from the definition of "employee." The House Committee said with respect to this change in definition:

An "employee," according to all standard dictionaries, according to the law as the courts have stated it, and according to the understanding of almost everyone, with the exception of members of the National Labor Relations Board, means someone who works for another for hire. But in the case of *National Labor Relations Board* v. *Hearst Publications, Inc.,* (322 U.S. 111 (1944), the Board expanded the definition of the term "employee" beyond anything that it ever had included before, and the Supreme Court, relying upon the theoretic "expertness" of the Board, upheld the Board. In this case the Board held independent merchants who bought newspapers from the publisher and hired people to sell them to be "employees." The people the merchants hired to sell the papers were "employees" of the merchants, but holding the merchants to be "employees" of the publisher of the papers was most far reaching. It must be presumed that when Congress passed the Labor Act, it intended words it used to have the meanings that they had when Congress passed the Act, not new meanings that, nine years later, the Labor Board might think up. In the law, there always has been a difference, and a big difference, between "employees" and "independent contractors." "Employees" work for wages or salaries under direct supervision. "Independent contractors" undertake to do a job for a price, decide how the work will be done, usually hire others to do the work, and depend for their income not upon wages, but upon the difference between what they pay for goods, materials, and labor and what they receive for the end result, that is, upon profits. It is inconceivable that Congress, when it passed the Act, authorized the Board to give to every word in the Act whatever meaning it wished. On the contrary, Congress intended then, and it intends now, that the Board give to words not far-fetched meanings, but ordinary meanings. To correct what the Board has done, and what the Supreme Court, putting misplaced reliance upon the Board's expertness, has approved, the bill excludes "independent contractors" from the definition of "employee."[18]

Supervisors are expressly excluded from the definition of "employee."[19] Thus, foremen are not entitled to the benefits of the Act, and it is no longer illegal for an employer to refuse to bargain collectively with a union representing foremen or other supervisory help.[20] In discussing the Board's petition for enforcement of its order (issued under the prior law) requiring an employer to bargain collectively with respect to supervisors, the United States Circuit Court of Appeals for the District of Columbia[21] said:

Before the adoption of this amendatory legislation, it was of course true, as the Supreme Court said in the Packard opinion, that there was nothing in the National Labor Relations Act which indicated that Congress intended to deny its benefits to foremen as employees. It is now unmistakably clear, however, that the 80th Congress intended to deny, and has denied, the benefits of the Act to "supervisors."

The problem and effect of these relationships become acute both to the employer and employee just as soon as a union commences a campaign to organize the employees of a particular employer, or the employees of many employers who may be related by virtue of membership in an employer association. The statute expressly limits the rights and expressly defines the obligations of the employer. Such rights and obligations of the employer are also expressly stated with respect to the successful phase of a union organizational campaign in its first instance, namely, the stage at which the union has become the exclusive bargaining agent of the employees by reason of designation or selection as such by a majority of the employees. Management still has certain rights which it may exercise either at the inception of the union's organizational campaign, or at the time when the employer is confronted with a demand for bargaining rights by the union, premised as that must be upon the ground that the union has achieved majority status. The Supreme Court, in the celebrated *Jones & Laughlin* case, said:[22]

The Act does not interfere with the normal exercise of the right of the employer to select its employees, or to discharge them.

In *Phelps Dodge Corporation* v. *National Labor Relations Board,* [23] the Supreme Court said:

The natural construction which the text, the legislative setting, and the function of the statute command, does not impose an obligation on the employer to favor union members in hiring employees. He is as free to hire as he is to discharge employees. The statute does not touch "the normal exercise of the right of the employer to select its employees or to discharge them." It is directed solely against the abuse of that right by interfering with the countervailing right of self-organization.

It is also clear that the ultimate purpose of the Act, namely, the achievement of collective bargaining, as memorialized in the written collective bargaining agreement, leaves the employer with rights which he is free to exercise, subject only to the requirement that he do not invade the proscribed unfair labor practices. Thus, his obligation to bargain does not mean that he is compelled to sign an agreement and he enjoys the right to insist upon a fair bargain so long as he bargains with an open mind and in good faith. The Supreme Court in the *Jones & Laughlin* case[24] said:

The Act does not compel agreements between employers and employees. It does not compel any agreement whatever. It does not prevent the employer "from refusing to make a collective contract and hiring individuals on whatever terms" the employer "may by unilateral action determine." The Act expressly provides in § 9(a) that any individual employee or a group of employees shall have the right at any time to present grievances to their employer. The theory of the Act is that free opportunity for negotiation with accredited representatives of employees is likely to promote industrial peace and may bring about the adjustments and agreements which the Act in itself does not attempt to compel.

While existence of the employee-employer relationship may be regarded as fundamental in any consideration of the rights and obligations imposed by the Act, its sanctions also apply even before such relationship actually comes into existence. An employer who refuses to hire an applicant for a job because of his union affiliation commits an unfair labor practice within the meaning of the Act and may be subjected to an order requiring hiring of the applicant and the payment of "back pay"[25] for the period since he was wrongfully denied employment. The Supreme Court said:[26]

It is no longer disputed that workers cannot be dismissed from employment because of their union affiliation. Is the national interest in industrial peace less affected by discrimination against union activity when men are hired? The contrary is overwhelmingly attested by the long history of industrial conflicts, the diagnosis of their causes by official investigations, the conviction of public men, industrialists and scholars. Because of the Pullman strike, Congress in the Erdman Act of 1898 prohibited inroads upon the workingman's right of association by discriminatory practices at the point of hiring. Kindred legislation has been put on the statute books of more than half the states. . . . . Discrimination against union labor in the hiring of men is a dam to self-organization at the source of supply. The effect of such discrimination is not confined to the actual denial of employment; it inevitably operates against the whole idea of the legitimacy of organization. . . .

Since the refusal to hire Curtis and Daugherty solely because of their affiliation with the Union was an unfair labor practice under § 8(3), the remedial authority of the Board under § 10(c) became operative.

The court held that the applicants, denied employment because of union affiliation, were "employees" within the meaning of Section 8(3) of the Wagner Act, since that provision defined the term as including "*any* employee" and provided further that the term "shall not be limited to the employees of a particular employer, unless the Act explicitly states otherwise." The theory has been recently restated by the Board in *Matter of Briggs Manufacturing Co.*,[27] as follows:

Section 2(3) of the Act provides that the term "employee" shall include *any* employee" and expressly states that it "shall not be limited to the employees of a particular employer, unless the Act explicitly states otherwise." The Act thus provides for the use of the term "employee" both in the broad generic sense as defined in Section 2(3) of the Act, and also in a more limited sense whenever the Act explicitly so provides. In its generic sense the term is broad enough to include members of the working class generally. (See: *Phelps Dodge Corp.* v. *N.L.R.B.*, 313 U.S. 177.) In its limited sense the term may include only the employees of a particular employer, as for example, in Section 8(5), which requires the employer "to bargain collectively" with the representatives of *his* employees subject to the provisions of Section 9(a). . . . . This broad definition covers, in addition to employees of a particular employer, also employees of another employer, or former employees of a particular employer, or even applicants for employment.

Since the definition of "employee" in this regard has been continued without change by the amendments, these authorities would remain applicable to the situation which they cover.

In addition to denying supervisory employees the benefits of the Act as amended by virtue of the statutory definition of employee, the status of certain other employees is changed. Plant guards may not be grouped by the Board with other employees for the purposes of collective bargaining, and a union cannot be certified by the Board as bargaining representative of plant guards if it admits to membership, or, is affiliated with an organization which admits to membership, employees other than plant guards.[28] Where a bargaining unit included guards and the union admitted to membership employees other than guards, the Board dismissed charges that the employer had committed unfair labor practices in refusing to bargain collectively with such union.[29]

The Board has refused to include watchmen in a bargaining unit consisting of production and maintenance employees, despite the agreement of all parties to such inclusion.[30]

Professional employees cannot be grouped with nonprofessionals unless a majority of the former vote in favor of such grouping.[31] The Board has treated time study employees as within the definition of professional employees, rather than supervisory or managerial employees, although they exercise considerable discretion and judgment. The Board held that these employees take no substantial part in the formulation and administration of management policies.[32]

The Board has said that certain editorial employees of a newspaper such as special editors, rewrite men, and out-of-town reporters are not professional employees within the statutory definition, because they were not required to undergo specialized schooling in an institution of higher learning, were not required to be licensed, and performed the same type of work and were subject to the same overall departmental supervision as other editorial employees who were not professional.[33]

The Act, as amended, requires that craft employees shall not be grouped for purposes of collective bargaining with other groups of employees on the ground that such a grouping was established by prior decision of the Board, unless the craft employees vote against separate representation.[34] Whether employees are members of a craft will depend on the skill their work involves and whether a substantial period of apprenticeship and training is required.[35]

Although employees who are inspectors exercise individual discretion and judgment and may affect the earnings of production employees, the Board has refused to classify them as supervisors or professional employees and has refused to place them in a group separate from production employees for the purposes of collective bargaining.[36]

I · RIGHTS OF MANAGEMENT
(INCLUDING DUTIES OF UNIONS)

Management long regarded the Wagner Act as one-sided, favoring labor and denying the employer many rights. Later decisions of Appellate Courts indicated a swing of the pendulum not so much toward diminishing the rights of labor, as broadening the protection afforded management.[37] The Labor Management Relations Act, 1947, was enacted to "above all recognize under law that neither party has any right in its relations with any other to engage in acts or practices which jeopardize public health, safety, or interest," "to prescribe the legitimate rights of both employees and employers," and "to define and proscribe practices on the part of labor and management."[38]

1. To Hire

The Wagner Act, as well as the amended Act, was not intended to deprive employers of the right to exercise their normal right to select their employees. However, when that right is used by employers to deny employment because of the union affiliation or activities of employees or prospective employees, it is deemed not to have been normally exercised, and constitutes interference with the employees' right of self-organization for the purposes of collective bargaining as guaranteed in the Labor Act. Thus, refusal to hire an applicant because of his membership in a union is illegal.[39] A hiring policy that is motivated by a desire to eliminate applicants for employment because of their union affiliation, union activity, or other concerted activity for the purpose of collective bargaining or mutual aid and protection is an unfair labor practice, subjecting the employer who engages in such unlawful conduct to liability for payment of back pay.[40]

The Act has been further amended with the purpose of eliminating union control over hiring of employees. Thus, the closed shop has been outlawed. Requiring union membership as a condition of employment has been limited to the union shop, provided the requirements as to certification of union authority to enter into such an agreement have been satisfied. (See

"Union Shop Election," Part One, Chapter IV.) Even where these requirements have been met, it is, nevertheless, illegal for an employer to grant preference in hiring to members of a union.[41] The hiring hall system so widely used in the maritime industry has been held illegal.[42] Under that system, the employers in the industry were obligated to obtain new employees from hiring halls operated by the unions. Since unions operated their hiring halls in such a manner as to grant preference to their members over nonmembers in sending applicants out for jobs upon receiving employers' requests, the practice was held illegal.

2. To Discharge

FOR CAUSE

An employer may discharge or refuse to reinstate employees who engaged in a wildcat strike, without being subject to a charge of unfair labor practice.[43] In one case a Circuit Court sustained the right of management to discharge employees who not only conducted a work stoppage, but prevented other employees from working. When the NLRB held that discharge constituted an unfair labor practice, the court read into the employees' action an attempt to promote the efficiency of an unauthorized strike. Management, the court concluded, may protect its property against trespass.[44]

It is unnecessary under the Labor Act for an employer to justify the discharge of an employee, so long as it is not for union activities.[45] The rule was summarized by the Sixth Circuit Court of Appeals as follows:[46]

The Act does not take from the employer the right to make and enforce reasonable rules for the conduct of the business and to take disciplinary action against employees who either violate the rules, are inefficient or malcontent, or for reasons generally are not suitable for efficient production. The Act does not authorize the Board to substitute its own ideas of discipline or Management for those of the employer, except barring discrimination or discharge for union membership.

The presumption is that the employer has not violated the law, and the burden of proof is not upon the employer, but upon the one who asserts the fact, to prove that the discharge was incurred because of union activities.[47]

An employee may not rely on his union membership and seniority standing to protect him from discharge for unjustifiable conduct.[48] Thus an employer may discharge an employee whose conduct is such that the employer is obliged to choose between repudiating the foreman or discharging the employee.[49]

An employee may be discharged for refusal to work on a new-type machine for which his foreman holds he is fitted; for refusal to perform work assigned to him; or for leaving his work.[50] An employee's refusal to report for work was held good cause for discharge,[51] as was lack of cooperation.[52] Although a union member, an employee may be discharged for repeated lateness, for excessive absence, or for failure to report absence in violation of a known company rule.[53]

An employer may discharge a helper, whose services are no longer needed, for insolent conduct and abusive remarks to his superior or for refusal to obey a legitimate order to go to work. An employer may discharge an employee who is defiant and flouts the authority of his superiors.[54] Management has the right to discharge an employee for violating a safety rule; for endangering others; for dishonesty; for quarreling; for sabotage; for talkativeness; for inefficiency including accidents, breakage, carelessness, dissipation, and horseplay; and for inability or inexperience.[55]

An employee may be discharged for profanity, despite the extreme activity of the employee in the union.[56] An employee may generally be discharged for breaking company rules, provided the rules are consistently enforced. Thus, a rule against smoking was held properly enforced where there were repeated violations and no evidence of disparate treatment of other violators.[57] Likewise, an employee may be discharged for breaking a company rule prohibiting solicitation on company time, even though the solicitation was for the union.[58] But the discharge of an employee for soliciting union membership in the plant on his own time is illegal *per se* as is an employer's rule against such solicitation on the employee's own time.[59] The validity of such a rule, when it has not been discriminatorily applied, may be established by a clear showing of real necessity, for it may be in the interest of plant production and orderly operation. The employer, however, has the burden of proof in such a case.

An employee unable to obtain a bond required of all employees was held properly discharged. An employee may also be discharged for physical defects, such as defective vision or infectious disease.[60] Likewise, he may be discharged for inability to perform work; because of change in operations, where the new system involved substantial savings and had been discussed long prior to the resultant strike; because of new methods, or for breach of a collective agreement.[61]

A plant shutdown is not discriminatory where it is a result of business exigencies, transfer of the plant (since the union refused to cut employer's operating loss), or reorganization where it was effected only after the employer's *bona fide* counterproposals had been rejected.[62] Nor was an eviction discriminatory where it was found to have been prompted by the personal anti-union activities of the nonunion workers.[63] Neither is an employer guilty of discrimination where he rehires in accordance with a valid closed shop contract or a preferential employment contract;[64] where his rejection of an employee is for just cause and not for striking or union membership or activity;[65] where the strike is an economic rather than an unfair practice strike, if there were no jobs available at the time; and where there was violence directed against plant property or company officials.[66] It should be noted, however, that the Act as amended outlaws the closed shop as well as preferential hiring clauses favoring union members, but does provide for union shop.[67]

FOR ECONOMIC CAUSES[68]

Management may institute changes for business reasons without risking violation of the Act. In one case management abolished a departmental night shift during the height of a union's organizational campaign, laying off eight employees of whom seven were union members. The change was held justified because material shortages reduced the amount of available work. In addition, the abolished shift had never been restored.[69] A decrease in business has been held a lawful reason for discharge, provided the discharges or lay-offs are of the least efficient workers or those of low seniority, and the employer's usual policy for decreasing its working force under such circumstances was followed.[70]

An employer may also discharge an employee for demand of payment contrary to the union contract.[71] An agreement with the union to discharge members in such a case was held not to constitute interference. When a dissident minority group takes action contrary to the terms of an existing contract and contrary to the wishes of the duly designated representatives chosen by the majority, disciplinary action by the employer and by the union is clearly justified.[72]

FOR STRIKES

Management has the right to refuse reinstatement to strikers who engage in a wildcat strike,[73] or strike to compel illegal action,[74] or indulge in violence, or who are guilty of trespass during a sitdown strike.[75] Where the strike causes a shutdown, such a shutdown is not discriminatory. Employees who strike in violation of the no-strike provision of the collective agreement may be discharged.[76] However, if such a strike is condoned by the employer, he cannot discriminate against the strikers.[77] Management's duty to bargain collectively with a union having a majority is suspended as to issues involved in a strike engaged in by that union in violation of a no-strike clause of an existing contract.[78] The suspension of that duty continues as long as the strike continues. Strikers who engage in serious misconduct (for example, conviction on six separate charges of assault) need not be reinstated.[79]

Foremen who refused to obey their employer's instruction to report for work during a strike of nonsupervisory employees, in order to perform work necessary for the preservation and protection of plant machinery and equipment, were held validly discharged.[80] The Board pointed out that the foremen, as supervisors, "owed a duty to" their employer "to comply with all reasonable instructions designed to protect the respondent's physical plant from imminent damage or destruction." A strike on board ship was held to be mutiny and the employer not obligated to reinstate the discharged strikers.[81] An employer may also threaten to replace economic strikers.[82]

But where the employer has agreed to a "struck" work or "hot" cargo clause in his labor contract, it was held by the Board that the refusal of employees at the instance of their steward to handle "struck" goods did not constitute insubordination, because the employer had acquiesced in such conduct by virtue of that provision of the contract.[a]

After the decision in the *American News* case,[83] the Board finally held that the employer was entitled to some relief in the not uncommon situation where the Board certifies one union and a rival union thereafter calls a strike to compel the employer to bargain with it in violation of the certification. In the case of *Thompson Products, Inc.*[84] the Board ruled that such strikers were not entitled to the protection of the Act and could validly be discharged.

Under the Act, as amended, it is an unfair labor practice for a union to strike in order to force an employer to recognize it when another union has been certified as bargaining agent.[85] If the Board's Regional Director has reasonable cause to believe that such an unfair labor practice is being engaged in by a union, upon the filing of charges to that effect, the Board must apply to the United States District Court for an order enjoining the union from engaging in such activity until the determination of the unfair labor practice case by the Board.[86]

In the *Columbia Pictures* case,[87] which did not involve unfair labor practices, a majority of the Board held eligible to participate in a Board election strikers who sought to compel bargaining with their union during the pendency before the Board of a proceeding for the determination of bargaining representatives. However, the amended Act provides that "employees on strike, who are not entitled to reinstatement, shall not be eligible to vote."[88] In the first case involving the effect of this provision, the Board directed that the replacement employees and the strikers be permitted to vote in the election, subject to challenge and left the determination of the eligibility of the strikers to a subsequent investigation.[89] Subsequently, the

Board clarified its position and held that striking employees are ineligible to vote in an election, if they have been permanently replaced by others, unless the strike was caused by the employer's unfair labor practice.[a] But whether the strike was caused by such unfair labor practices cannot be determined solely on the record made in the representation proceeding.[b]

FOR UNION ACTIVITIES

An employer may not discharge for union activity.[90] Where the discharged employee is a supervisor who has coerced subordinate workers into joining a union, the employer must make it clear to employees generally that his objection was not to union activities as such, but to union activities of a supervisor interfering with the rights of employees under the Act.[91] The Board has held that for the purpose of preserving his neutrality, an employer may require foremen or applicants for the position of foreman to withdraw from membership in a rank-and-file union which represented the nonsupervisory employees.[92] An obstreperous union member whose conduct exceeded "all necessary, reasonable and proper bounds and constituted persistent and extensive insubordination" was held properly discharged, although such behavior pertained to union activity.[93]

An employer had the right to lay off and discharge for concerted activities where the employees tampered unlawfully with the employer's premises, for example, pulled the power switch.[94] An employer also had the right to discharge a union steward who abused his position by disregarding work orders, urging other employees to slow down, and otherwise interfering with production.[95] Similarly, a union steward was legally discharged because of the overzealous performance of his duties, i.e., unduly pressing the management to take up employees' grievances or to arrange for meetings and interfering generally with the shop supervision.[96] Likewise, conduct which is definitely insubordination may not be protected as concerted activity within the meaning of the Act. In one case, an employer legally discharged a union shop steward for insubordination, although the latter's conduct was closely related to his duties as shop steward.[97]

It has been held *not* discriminatory to discharge an employee for:

1. Becoming intoxicated when such latitude is not accepted as permissible;[98]
2. Absence from work to assist another union in picketing and being arrested for breach of the peace while picketing;[99]
3. Prior to amendment of the Act, failure to belong to a union having a closed shop contract with the employer, if:
    (a) the contract was with a union not dominated or encouraged by the employer through any unfair labor practice; and

(b) the union represented the majority of employees at the time of making the contract;[100]

4. Quitting because a new workman who belonged to a rival union was employed;[101]

5. Engaging in conduct offensive to customers of the company;[102]

6. Negligently damaging equipment;[103]

7. Having a high accident record in driving a bus or truck;[104]

8. Producing defective work despite previous warnings.[105]

DISCHARGES UNDER UNION SECURITY PROVISIONS OF CONTRACT

The law as amended by the Labor Management Relations Act, 1947, no longer permits the employer and union to enter into a closed shop agreement. The proviso in Section 8(3) of the Wagner Act, which authorized closed shop contracts has been repealed so that such a contract provision is illegal.[106]

The amended Act, however, authorizes a union shop, that is, membership in the union may become a condition of employment thirty days after the effective date of the agreement or thirty days after the hiring of an employee, whichever is later.[107] But even such an agreement cannot be entered into unless "the Board shall have certified that at least a *majority of the employees eligible to vote*" in an election conducted by the Board for the purpose, "have voted to authorize such labor organization to make such an agreement."[108] The amended Act retains from the Wagner Act the former requirements that the union must not be "established, maintained, or assisted" by unfair labor practices and must be the designated representatives of the employees in a unit of employees appropriate for the purposes of collective bargaining.[109]

If these conditions of the amended Act are satisfied, the union shop agreement may be validly entered into. But, even in such event, the Act, as amended, prescribes and limits discharges under such a provision. It is an unfair labor practice for an employer to discharge an employee under the union shop provision of the contract if the employer has reasonable grounds to believe that (1) union membership was not made available to the employee on the same terms generally applied to other members, and (2) union membership of the employee was terminated for reasons other than nonpayment by the employee of the regular periodic dues and initiation fees.[110] Thus, under the new Act, the fact that an employee has been deprived of union membership for "dual unionism" affords no grounds for his discharge by the employer under the union shop provisions of the collective bargaining agreement, and an employer who discharges for such cause is subject to liability for reinstatement of the employee with back pay. The Board may also hold the union alone liable for causing the discharge.[111]

The union, under the Act, as amended, is also prohibited from the performance of certain conduct defined as unfair labor practices on its part. These include attempts by the union to cause an employer to discriminate against employees in violation of the section of the Act authorizing the union shop as described above, and for reasons other than the nonpayment by the employee of the regular periodic dues and initiation fees.[112] In addition, it is also an unfair labor practice for the union, where a valid union shop agreement has been entered into, to require as a condition precedent to becoming a member of the union the payment of fees in an amount the Board finds excessive.[113]

FOR FILING CHARGES OR TESTIFYING

The Act provides that a discharge because an employee filed charges with or testified before the Board is an unfair labor practice.[114] The Board has held that this provision is violated when the discharge is motivated by reason of the filing of charges or the giving of testimony even though the charges are false.[115] But the employer is not deprived of his right to discharge employees who have filed charges or testified, for misconduct and breaches of duty in the course of employment. The mere giving of testimony, whether true or false, does not give the employee an immunity from appropriate disciplinary action for misconduct and breaches of duty during the course of employment. Thus, it was not violative of the Act for an employer to discharge an employee for eavesdropping and engaging in union activity during working hours, although she testified falsely before the Board.[116] However, an employer was held responsible when, after pro-union employees testified before the Board, anti-union employees ejected them from the plant and the employer took no steps to restore the pro-union employees to their jobs.[117]

3. To Transfer[118]

A transfer, to prevent union talk, to a job where the employee would have less opportunity to proselytize, is not discriminatory, provided the job is no less desirable, the employee suffers no financial loss, and the employer has enforced without discrimination a rule against talking. "Working time is for work."[119] Nor was a transfer held discriminatory where the change of duties was not due to union activities.

Moreover, no discrimination is found where an employee is transferred from day to night shift if he had been formerly subject to similar transfers.[120]

Nor does discrimination necessarily result from a change in job classification in accordance with plant rules and mandatory under rulings of a government agency.[121]

4. To Demote[122]

An employer is justified in requiring employees to relinquish their supervisory functions or resign their union membership, because of the possible utilization by these men of their supervisory positions to advance the union's interest to the detriment of the employer's business. It should, however, be made clear that the employer does not discriminate against them because of their union membership and activity, but required the relinquishment of their supervisory functions because of the conflict of loyalties engendered by their union affiliation.[123] Authority for this position lies in the Act's exclusion of supervisors from the category of employees.[124]

5. To Free Speech

The Act, as amended, expressly sets forth the right of free speech. Expressions of views, arguments or opinions cannot constitute or be evidence of unfair labor practices if they contain no "threat of reprisal or force or promise of benefit."[125] For a fuller understanding of the effect of this new provision of the Act, an examination of the principles enunciated by the Board and courts under the Wagner Act is essential. Such an examination is also necessary for an understanding of the nature of expressions which are illegal because coercive.

Under the Wagner Act, not every expression of opinion on the part of management on the subject of unions or any other related subject need necessarily be considered coercive.[126] The test of whether an employer might lawfully make anti-union statements was whether such statements were threatening or coercive. The National Labor Relations Board in two cases pointed out that while management, under Supreme Court decisions, enjoyed the right to free expression, that right was of limited nature. Any expression which might be deemed to be coercive or to interfere with employees' right to self-organization would be held to be a violation of the Wagner Act.[127]

The United States Supreme Court, affirming management's constitutional right to free speech, in one of its most significant decisions since the passage of the Wagner Act, sanctioned the right of management to express "its views on labor policies or problems" without running the risk of violating the Act.[128] Since the passage of that Act, however, the Board steadily whittled away the right of management to express its opinion. The theory of the Board was that the economic superiority of management was such in regard to its employees that intimidation was implicit in the mere expression of an opinion by the employer to his employee.[129]

Today an employer may suggest that his employees would find bargaining directly with the management a better plan than bargaining through a union. He may also express his views about workers voting on union representation, provided there is no coercion and the company abides by the results. Likewise, he may offer a general opinion appealing to the intellect concerning unions, even though the opinion be adverse to unionization, but he may not threaten his employees about the consequences of forming a union.[130] He may make a fair statement of employees' rights and privileges under the Act, although under the Wagner Act it was held improper to state only the negative aspects of that Act, that is, things the employees are not obliged to do, without further stating the privileges of which the employees may avail themselves.[131]

Under the Wagner Act, emphasis had been placed upon the character of the statements made, by whom made, the manner in which they were made, the past and present condition of the employer-employee relationship (whether friendly or otherwise), the past and present antipathy shown by the employer to unions and the time, relative to unionization activity, when the statements were made.[132] An anti-union remark of a working foreman was held not to incriminate the employer, since there was no showing that the foreman either had supervisory powers or was exercising them at the time he made the remarks.[133] However, where employees making the statements were in close connection with the employer and were considered representative of management, the employer was held liable for any anti-union statements made by them.[134]

In one case, it was held that an employer could remove the taint of coercion from conduct otherwise open to interpretation as unlawful if the officials of the company, who had compared a union's wage scale unfavorably with the earnings of the employees, nevertheless made it clear that the employees could join a union and that the company would recognize the union if chosen by a majority of the employees.[135]

The following expressions by management have been held a legal exercise of the right of free speech:[136]

1. Stating to the employees that they were "blind" to pay dues and fees to a union, and that some of them "had gone to the union office to stick a knife in his back";[137]

2. The union was not interested in the employees but was out for col-

lection of dues; that the employer's understanding of the union was that, if the union got into the plant, the employees could not go to him to talk about anything but would have to take it up with a committee or some outsider;[138]

3. Arguing against unionization in letters to employees when such expressions contain no threat of reprisal or force or promise of benefit;[139]

4. Characterizing the union as "outlaw," "wildcat" and "off breed";[140]

5. The wholly isolated statement by a foreman to a single employee warning him to stay away from union meetings;[141]

6. Anti-union statements contained in letters issued by an association organized by citizens, to finance the erection of a plant, when the employer had no knowledge of such letters and did not participate in their preparation or publication;[142]

7. Letters sent to employees immediately before a Labor Board election where such letters contained statements disparaging the union as "troublemakers," and such statements as "vote 'no' against Strikers, Poison, Disunity," "Strikers, Agitators, Stifled War Production—Too Little and Too Late—Do you realize how much our Armed Forces on the battle fronts lost in war production, military equipment, guns, tanks, planes and ships by the CIO strikers, CIO labor agitations and CIO labor troubles?"[143]

8. Statements published by the employer in a local newspaper concerning the history of a local mill and mine, each of which had closed after being organized by unions, and pointing out that the employer could close his plant for good business reasons despite assertions to the contrary by the union;[144]

9. Telling employees that "The union has more money than any corporation in the United States—They have more cash, more assets than Du Pont, General Electric or any other large corporation";[145]

10. An interoffice memorandum distributed by the employer to employees urging them to vote against all of the several unions involved in an election, since it contained no threats or coercive statements.[146]

Under the Wagner Act the Board held coercive and unprotected by the free speech privilege noncoercive statements to a "captive audience" of employees. An hour before a run-off election between a CIO union and an unaffiliated union, the employees were ordered to assemble during working hours, the power and engines were shut down, and all operations were suspended. The employer's official then made anti-CIO campaign speeches. The Board did not find that the speeches in themselves were coercive. The Board concluded, however, that the employer "exercised its superior economic power in coercing its employees to listen to speeches relating to their organizational activities, and thereby independently violated Section 8 (1) of the Act."[147] The Second Circuit Court of Appeals in enforcing the Board's order pointed out that:[148]

An employer has an interest in presenting his views on labor relations to his employees. We should hesitate to hold that he may not do this on company time and pay, provided a similar opportunity to address them were accorded representatives of the union.

A different point of view was taken by the Eighth Circuit Court of Appeals when it disagreed with the Board on the "captive audience" doctrine.[149] That Court took the position that the fact that the employer's speech occurred on company time in the plant did not make it illegal, but was a convenient method of communicating with the employees. The Court, contrary to the Board, ruled that the occasion on which the employer elects to utter his thoughts is not to be considered an element of coercion.[150] The new provision of the amended Act would appear to eliminate the Board's "captive audience" doctrine. The Board, on the basis of Section 8(c) of the amended Act, has expressly overruled the "captive audience" doctrine under the Wagner Act, pointing out that "the language of Section 8(c) of the amended Act, and its legislative history, make it clear that the doctrine of the *Clark Bros.* case (captive audience doctrine) no longer exists as a basis for finding unfair labor practices."[151]

The Eighth Circuit Court of Appeals has also held that the employer need not stand mutely by, when he is attacked in union papers or leaflets as "labor's greatest enemy," "fascist-minded," or "unpatriotic and un-American;" and his officials are called "rats." The employer may answer such defamatory remarks.[152] That Court also held as privileged the employer's clearly non-coercive declared opposition to the closed shop and assurance of the employees' right of freedom of choice with respect to a bargaining representative.[153] The Board has held that an employer's statement, in response to inquiries by employees, that he would not enter into a closed shop contract, was not coercive *per se*.[154] (See "Coercion," Part Three, Chapter III.)

The Circuit Courts of Appeals have not been uniform in their determination of the effectiveness to be given the Board's finding that employer utterances were coercive and not protected by the free speech privilege. The Eighth Circuit and the Court of Appeals for the District of Columbia have applied the normal rule of review and considered whether the Board's findings on the question were supported by substantial evidence.[155] However, in two later cases the Eighth Circuit held that whether an employer's statements are coercive is a question of law to be determined by the courts upon an examination and evaluation of the evidence.[156] The Fifth Circuit seems to have applied a similar rule.[157]

6. To Injunction

AGAINST ECONOMIC STRIKE (NOT INVOLVING A LABOR DISPUTE)

The Labor Management Relations Act, 1947, provides for the issuance of injunctions against labor unions, upon the Board's initiative, in a case where it has reasonable grounds to believe that a union is engaging in a type of secondary boycott declared illegal by the Labor Act. Other provisions of that Act also subject unions to liability in damages. These problems and their impact upon the rights of employers are discussed in subsequent pages. The present considerations concern only the right of employers directly to injunctive relief from the courts.

Neither the common law nor the Fourteenth Amendment confers upon unions the absolute right to strike.[158] The lawfulness of the means used and of the objective sought must be proved in justification of the damage done.[159] The courts have varied in their application of these tests. The tendency in New York has been to adopt a *laissez-faire* attitude where the objectives of the strike involved economic benefit to the employees. The union's objective is unlawful if it bears no reasonable relation to any condition of employment. It was held that where the union by picketing sought to compel the abandonment of a labor-saving device, the objective did not bear a reasonable relation to employment.[160]

Labor unions are given preferential treatment under anti-monopoly statutes, so that they may effect their legitimate ends: improvements of wages, hours and working conditions.[161]

A court has denied an injunction against a union's bylaw prohibiting the use of spray guns, despite the fact that the war effort might be impeded. Management, the court concluded, has no right to interfere with the internal affairs of the union, and the management could, it pointed out, have used nonunion men for the spray work. The court was of the opinion that the bylaw was reasonable to protect the health and employment opportunities of the union members.[162]

AGAINST PRIMARY BOYCOTT[163]

The boycott has developed in labor disputes as one of the most effective devices by which organized labor is enabled to gain its demands. In legal consequence, distinction has been made between the primary and secondary boycott. The primary boycott, being a combination directly to refrain from dealings with the employer and being chiefly a peaceful means of persuasion, has generally been held legal.

AGAINST SECONDARY BOYCOTT

The secondary boycott, however, involves a combination to exercise definite coercive pressure upon the employer's customers and his suppliers to cause them to withhold or withdraw their patronage under fear of similar activity directed against themselves.[164] Under the amended Act, such conduct by a union may constitute unfair labor practices. (See "Strikes and Boycotts," Part Three, Chapter IV.)

WHAT CONSTITUTES A LABOR DISPUTE

So long as the activities of a labor union which restrain interstate commerce qualify as a "labor dispute" under the Norris-LaGuardia Act, they may not be enjoined by a federal court unless the rigorous preliminary requirements of the statute are met.[165] This is the case even though the activities are designed to create work for local employees at the expense of distant workers, or to prevent the use of more regular methods of work, or are incident to a jurisdictional dispute even after certification by the National Labor Relations Board.

The Norris-LaGuardia Act deprives federal courts of authority to issue injunctions in labor disputes except under conditions expressly stated in the law. Under Section 13(c) of this Act the term "labor dispute" includes a controversy concerning "terms and conditions of employment," or the representation of employees without regard to whether or not the disputants stand in the proximate relation of employer and employee.[166] A similar anti-injunction law has been enacted by various state legislators (e.g., New York Civil Practice Act, Section 876-a). An attempt to require the hiring of a special class of individuals relates to a condition of employment and involves a labor dispute.[167]

It has been held that the Norris-LaGuardia Act does not apply to the federal government where it seized property pursuant to statute (War Labor Disputes Act).[168]

The New York Court of Appeals held that a third person who suffers incidental injury from peaceful picketing may not obtain injunctive relief without complying with the provisions of Section 876-a of the Civil Practice Act, since the case grew out of a labor dispute. The facts are summarized in the syllabus of the case as follows:[169]

A builder, not a party to this action, engaged in erecting dwellings situated on private streets within a tract of land owned by it, refused to recognize defendant-respondent trades council, an association of local labor unions engaged in the building trades. A strike of union men employed on the development was thereupon called by the trades council and a peaceful picket line established at the only entrance to the development from the public highway. After the picketing began, the builder sold a dwelling to plaintiff and application was made to defendant lighting company to connect its gas and electric lines to some of the residences in the development including the one sold to plaintiff. The lighting company's employees were members of a union of electrical workers and they refused to cross the picket line on the ground that the constitution and by-laws of their union forbade their doing so.

An owner who does all his own work without any employees cannot be lawfully picketed since there is no labor dispute arising out of an employer-employee relationship.[170] But peddlers who employ no help may be picketed to compel them to become members of the union or to employ part-time union help.[171]

Where a state board or the National Board has certified one of two rival unions as bargaining agent for the employees, it has been held that there is no labor dispute when the losing union continues to picket the employer.[172] Nevertheless, some courts have refused to enjoin peaceful and truthful picketing under the foregoing circumstances despite the absence of a labor dispute, on the ground that to do so would constitute an interference with freedom of speech.[173]

In *Allen Bradley Co. v. Local Union No. 3,*[174] the boycott, imposed exclusively because plaintiff's products were manufactured outside New York City, was designed solely to assure economic security for the union members, and no change in labor policy by the plaintiffs could have lifted the barrier. But when nonlabor groups such as employers and manufacturers, joined in the boycott with the union, the combination was held illegal under the antitrust acts.

Because of the immunities granted to unions under the Clayton Act and the Norris-LaGuardia Act, unions may not be prosecuted for:

1. Permitting employers in a restricted area to use goods bearing the union label and warning builders that members should not work with materials not bearing the label;[175]
2. Striking to compel the hiring of its members instead of the members of another union affiliated with the same parent organization as the striking union;[176]
3. Refusing to admit to membership employees of a hauling company and refusing to permit its members to work for the company, thereby destroying its business.[177]

The publication of a false and malicious statement by a union, in connection with a boycott of an employer's goods moving in interstate commerce, does not render the union liable under the Sherman Act.[178] Nor do expressions of opinion by union representatives accusing the employer of unfairness ordinarily constitute "fraud" within the meaning of the Norris-LaGuardia Act sufficient to warrant issuance of an injunction, even though such opinions were inaccurate and misrepresentative in character.[179]

AGAINST LABOR-NONLABOR CONSPIRACY

The United States Supreme Court now sets a limit on the types of disputes which are covered by the Norris-LaGuardia Act.

That law, which prohibits injunctions by federal courts where labor disputes are involved, was not intended, ruled the Court, "to have application to disputes over the sale of commodities." Although there may be a labor dispute within the meaning of the Act even where the disputants "do not stand in the proximate relation of employer and employee," that term may not be expanded "to include controversies upon which the employer-employee relationship has no bearing."[180] In one case, a fish canning and processing company was held legally entitled to an injunction against a supplier's boycott conducted by a so-called fishermen's union, despite the Anti-Injunction Act and even though some employees were members of the "union," a CIO affiliate. Hence, unions are *not* immune from prosecution if they combine with nonlabor groups for the purpose of preventing the use of materials moving in interstate commerce, and if they use violence as a means of keeping such materials out of a restricted area.[181]

Management is entitled to protection from such economic pressure by a union. Thus a union was held in violation of the antitrust laws when it made an agreement with a film distributor under which the distributor refused to supply films to exhibitors unless the exhibitors employed members of the union as projectionists.[182]

AGAINST UNION COMPULSION TO COMMIT ILLEGAL ACTS

Management has the right to be protected against unwarranted aggressiveness of unions, e.g., a strike called by an outside union for recognition, which is in fact a strike against the employer's duty to deal with the majority union. In one particular case, the employer enforced, with a few minor exceptions, an attitude of neutrality toward rival unions.[183] The court will allow an injunction to protect a union against coercion by another in recruiting membership, and management is entitled to protection of a union local against an arbitrary action of the parent union.

In the *Stillwell Theatres* case,[184] however, the employer had a labor contract with the union representing the employees and agreed therein to employ only members of that union. A rival union picketed the employer with signs stating that the employer refused to employ its members. The New York Court of Appeals denied the employer's application for an injunction upon the employer's theory that the rival union was engaging in an attempt to induce breach of the labor contract. The court said there was no persuasion to break the contract and that the activity of the rival union was within the sphere of legitimate conduct overbalancing any resulting incidental injury to the employer.

AGAINST VIOLENT PICKETING

While the right to picket has been declared to be constitutionally protected, there have been certain modifications through which the court has recognized the right of management to an injunction against violent picketing. Where the picketing is marked by intimidation, threats of violence and destruction of property there is absolutely no question of management's right to restrict it.

Under the doctrine of the *Fansteel* case,[185] sitdown strikes and violence have been outlawed. But various attempts have been made, many successful, to whittle away that doctrine. Until very recently minor violence could not be curbed, because the Board ruled that such violence was not contemplated by the Supreme Court in its decision in the *Fansteel* case.[186] In view of this relaxation of the *Fansteel* doctrine, states have taken an active role in attempting to curb picketing, and courts, though upholding the right to picket as an exercise of free speech, have agreed that not only must the *objectives* be lawful, but the *means* of picketing must likewise be lawful. Where either prerequisite was lacking, courts did not hesitate to ban the picketing.[187]

On the other hand, the Supreme Court, reversing the New York Court of Appeals, which had enjoined picketing in the celebrated *Wohl* case, ruled that a labor organization had the right to picket two peddlers of bakery products in New York City, in an effort to induce them to employ a union relief driver on Sunday instead of working seven days a week themselves. The union vindicated its picketing as a protest against the "economic" and social evils of the peddler system. The Supreme Court saw no illegality in this form of picketing as would justify limiting labor's right to free speech, nor could it find any abuse of this right "through the use of excessive picketing."[188] In fact, the Court has gone so far as to deny injunctions where the pickets charged that the proprietors were unfair, the food was bad, and the customers who patronized the restaurant promoted the cause of fascism. In denying an injunction, the Supreme Court pointed out that, "to use loose language or undefined slogans that are part of the conventional give-and-take in our economic and political controversies like 'unfair' or 'fascist' is not to falsify facts."[189]

But when the business which is the object of the picketing "has no nexus" with the dispute between the union and the union's real adversary, the picketing may be enjoined and such an injunction is not violative of the free speech privilege. This principle was laid down by the Supreme Court in the *Ritter's Cafe* case.[190] In that case, Ritter made a contract with one Plaster for the construction of a building, and Plaster, under the contract, had the right to employ his own employees and employed nonunion carpenters and plasterers. There was no connection between the new building and the business of Ritter's Cafe. The carpenters and plasterers unions picketed Ritter's Cafe for the purpose of forcing Ritter to require Plaster to employ union employees. The Court sustained the right of the Texas Courts to enjoin such picketing. In differentiating the *Wohl* case the Court said,

> The dispute there related to the conditions under which bakery products were sold and delivered to retailers. The business of the retailers was therefore directly involved in the dispute. In picketing the retail establishments, the union members would only be following the subject matter of their dispute. Here we have a different situation. The dispute concerns the labor conditions surrounding the construction of a building by a contractor. Texas has deemed it desirable to insulate from the dispute an establishment which industrially has no connection with the dispute. Texas has not attempted to protect other business enterprises of the building contractor, Plaster, who is the petitioners' real adversary.

Whether mass picketing alone and in the absence of violence, untruthful signs or other unlawful acts, will be enjoined is uncertain. Recently several state courts, New Jersey, Massachusetts and Pennsylvania, have enjoined mass picketing under such circumstances.[191]

7. To Bar Solicitation

An employer may forbid solicitation during working hours provided he does not enforce the rule discriminatorily.[192] If administration of the rule is nondiscriminatory, he may prohibit the distribution and posting of union literature on his premises, despite the fact that the employees so engaged are off duty provided, however, the employer can establish the need for such a rule in the interest of plant discipline and production. He may not bar solicitation during employees' free time, even though it is done on company property.[193]

8. To Protection against Invasion of Its Property

Management is entitled to protection against invasion of its property by union representatives. In one case, although the Board ordered the companies to grant passes to their boats to union representatives, the passes were not required to be issued "without a provision therein that they shall be forfeited if the holder uses his access to the vessels either to solicit membership in the union or to collect dues."[194]

9. To Abstain from Dealing with a Minority Union

Management need not deal with a union after an economic strike if that union does not represent a majority, and may also refuse to deal with a minority union in settling a strike which the latter called.[195]

However, the United States Court of Appeals for the Second Circuit has ruled under the amended Act that minority groups in presenting individual grievances have the right to be represented by a minority union even though another union has been certified by the Board as bargaining representative of the employees. The Court held that a strike by the minority group to compel the employer to deal with their union was not an illegal attempt to compel disregard of the Board certification of the majority union. It must be noted, however, that the Court limited its decision to the special circumstances of that case which arose in a proceeding to punish the minority union for contempt of an injunction issued by a Federal District Court.[196] Management also has the right to "by-pass" a minority union and need not bargain with a union of several years' standing if it questions in good faith its majority status.[a] (See "Refusal to Bargain," Part Three, Chapter III.)

10. To Protection from New Charges

Once a Labor Board case is informally settled by a stipulation, the case is ended as far as any charges alleged in the complaint are concerned, provided, of course that the stipulations are complied with. While making this statement the Board added, however, that new charges involving other provisions of the law may be acted on, even though the charges refer to the period prior to the settlement.[197] The Board has consistently gone behind settlement agreements entered into by its agents and the employer, where the employer has subsequently continued to engage in conduct which violates the Act. In the case which occasioned this ruling, the Board dismissed charges of interference, domination of a union and discriminatory discharge, because the evidence was deemed insufficient to support the charges.

11. To Clarification of Board's Order

General equitable principles and the decision of the Court of Appeals for the Fifth Circuit indicate that management has the right to petition for clarification of a court decree enforcing the Board's order, where there is uncertainty as to what is required under the decree. In such a situation, the Court granted the petition of the Labor Board for clarification and interpretation of the Court's enforcement decree.[198]

Management should have a similar right to clarification and interpretation of an ambiguous enforcement decree, since management must comply with the decree or be subject to punishment for contempt if it does not comply with the directions contained in the decree. Management's direct interest in clarification is quite obvious. Under its general equity powers, the court has ample authority to grant clarification and interpretation of its decree when necessary.

12. To Fair Hearing

Management is entitled to a proper consideration of the evidence and the credibility of witnesses, and has the right to be judged only on substantial evidence.[199] In one case, the Court of Appeals found that the employer was denied a fair hearing in an unfair labor practice case, because the Trial Examiner assumed the functions of a prosecutor by securing from one employer a stipulation to be used against another employer and by "rashly assailing" company officials who did not obey the Board's subpoenas.[200] In another, a hearing was set aside in which the Board's Trial Examiner commented on a report which was not introduced in evidence.[201] The fact that the employer refused to put the document in evidence did not justify the Trial Examiner's comments. Such comments were regarded as prejudicial to the employer and, therefore, ground for reversing his decision.

13. To Relief from Board Penalty

The Act is remedial and not punitive. The Board has, therefore, no inherent right to order affirmative action to penalize an employer in any manner it sees fit.[202]

The Board cannot require an employer to pay over to the appropriate government agency deductions from a back pay award in the amount received by employees for work performed on "work relief projects."[203] However, the Board has authority to require an employer to reimburse employees for union dues if they were involuntarily checked off under a contract resulting from unfair labor practices or in favor of a company-dominated union.[204] In the cases where the Board applied the aforementioned rule, employees were coerced by the employer into membership in the union that received the benefit of the check-off, and the dues checked off were used in behalf of such unions. When the dues checked off were used as a welfare fund for the benefit of the employees rather than for needs of the union, the Board did not order reimbursement.[205]

14. To Act in Concert

Employers may act concertedly as a single group for the purposes of dealing with a union or unions. Such a situation commonly arises where independent and competing employers are members of an association. Where the employers, either as members of an association or otherwise, have their labor relations handled jointly and as a result of established practice negotiate uniform labor agreements with the same union, and adhere thereto, thereby indicating their desire to be bound by group rather than individual action, the Board will treat them as a single group for collective bargaining. The employees of these employers will be deemed a single bargaining unit for the purposes of collective bargaining.[206] The Board has found such a multiple employer unit, despite the opposition of the employers involved, where their history in collective bargaining demonstrated joint action and adherence to uniform labor agreements.[207] The situation is clearer where the association's power to bind the employer members to collective bargaining agreements arose by reason of duly executed powers of attorney.[208] However, the unit was limited to those employer members of the association who had delivered executed powers of attorney to the association.

The Board has recognized the right of an employer to withdraw from such a group. Thus, in one case it confined a unit to the employees of an employer who had demonstrated his intention to follow a separate and individual course in his labor relations.[209]

15. To Latitude in the Bargaining Process

The duty to bargain collectively does not require the employer's complete submission to all union demands, nor need the company accept first demands.

Under the Wagner Act, the Board eventually reached an interpretation of the law which broadly recognized that the statutory obligation to bargain collectively "does not require an employer to capitulate to the demands addressed to him."[210] It may be argued from the Board's decisions that where the subject of a demand is the all-union shop, the employer may refuse even a compromise. However, the Board has said that union security provisions as well as demands for a check-off, are "proper subjects for collective bargaining."[211] An employer is not necessarily obligated to make a counter-proposal, directly responsive to the all-union shop demand, if "good faith" is displayed in bargaining negotiations concerning other issues. The standards for testing whether the requirement of good faith has been met are broadly stated by the Board, and in each instance, the employer must be judged on the basis of the particular facts of the case.

"The extent to which the parties evidence a sincere purpose to explore the total situation and find a basis for agreement," the Board declares, "indicates the difference between the semblance and the substance of collective bargaining." Furthermore, the opinion stresses the existence of an affirmative duty on the part of the employer concerning "substance" of the bargaining: "The employer must in a very real sense undertake to discover with the union such a common ground as may exist between the parties."[212]

Refusal of an employer to capitulate to an all-union shop demand is not necessarily a refusal to bargain collectively in violation of the National Labor Relations Act. Where a union pressed for an all-union or preferential shop demand throughout extended bargaining negotiations and took the final position that it would never sign a contract without such a provision, the Board ruled that failure of the negotiations was not chargeable to the employer.[213] A company's refusal to accede to the union's nominal demand, as well as mere failure to come to terms and inability to meet wage demands, have been held not a refusal to bargain.[214] Also no lack of good faith was attributable to the company where there was a misunderstanding over contract negotiations.[215] The same was true where there was a jurisdictional dispute and a question as to the appropriate unit, and also where the employer in good faith believed that the unit was inappropriate.[216]

Where, during the discussion of a controversial point in collective bargaining negotiations, the union representative left a meeting, the company was held not guilty of refusal to bargain.[217]

Nor was there a refusal to bargain where no demand was made. An employer cannot be charged with a refusal of that which is not proffered. "In other words, the statute imposes upon the union the affirmative duty of requesting recognition before the employer can be found guilty of refusing."[218] However, the presentation of demands by a union is a basis for negotiations, and the employer, by not accepting such demands, may not contend that such refusal precludes further necessity of negotiating.

The employer also has the right to insist on proof of majority representation. The Board imposes upon the employer the obligation to cooperate with the union in resolving the question of whether the union represents a majority, when that question is reasonably and seasonably raised.[219] A union has majority status when a majority of employees in the bargaining unit have designated or selected it as their representative for the purpose of collective bargaining. If the question of union majority representation is to be determined by a Labor Board election, the results of the election are determined by the votes of a majority of those voting in the election. (By express provision of the statute, a union shop election is determined by a majority of those eligible to vote.) When the employer and the union have reached an agreement, refusal to reduce it to writing signed by the parties is a refusal to bargain.[220] These principles are, in effect, the substance of Section 8(d) of the amended Act.[221] That provision defines collective bargaining as the mutual obligation of employer and union, requires neither party to agree to a proposal or make a concession, and obligates the parties, upon demand of the other party, to enter into a signed agreement if an agreement is reached.

16. To Continue Business

Management has the right to protect and continue its business by employing new men for jobs left by strikers, and is not later bound to displace men hired to take the strikers' places in order to make positions for the strikers, provided it is not guilty of an unfair labor practice and provided the strike was not caused or prolonged by the employer's unfair labor practice.[222]

17. To Operate for Profit

It is not a violation of the Act, the National Labor Relations Board ruled, for an employer to decline to confer with a union regarding the subcontracting of manufacturing operations which are unprofitable, although the union representing the employees involved was certified as their bargaining representative.[223] On the other hand, when the employer transfers the remainder of his operations to a lower-wage town and declines to deal with the union about giving the old employees the opportunity of working at the new plant, he is guilty of violating the Act.[224]

The remedy prescribed is that the employer must place the old employees on a preferred hiring list, offering jobs as they become available to those former employees who are competent to fill them.[225] The employer has also been directed to rehire the old employees.

18. To File Unfair Labor Practice Charges against Unions

The amended Act defines unfair labor practices on the part of unions, and the Board is empowered to issue its order against unions requiring them to cease and desist from such unfair labor practices and to take affirmative action to remedy them, including the payment of back pay.[226]

There is no requirement that the party filing the charge must be a neutral third person. Thus, where there is an illegal secondary boycott, the charge alleging such unfair labor practices can be filed by the employer who is engaged in a primary dispute with the union committing the illegal acts.[227]

Under the Wagner Act, it was held that misconduct on the part of a union did not operate as a bar to its filing unfair labor practice charges against an employer.[228] However, the Board has the right to consider such misconduct for the purpose of deciding whether or not to proceed with the case. While there may be evidence which would justify the Board's refusal to proceed in such a case because of union misconduct, a reviewing court will not interfere with the Board if, in the exercise of discretion, it issues a complaint against the employer.[229] These principles should be applicable under the amended Act to charges filed by employers.

Where a union files unfair labor practice charges against an employer, and the latter files unfair labor practice charges against the union, the cases may be consolidated and tried at the same hearing.[230] The charge against the union must name the union accused of unfair labor practices, and merely naming a union representative without including the union as a "person" charged with unfair labor practices will result in dismissal of the charge.[231] The union alone or the union and "its agents" must be charged with the unfair labor practices.[232]

Before proceeding further with the discussion of employer charges, it should be noted that the filing of a charge against a union does not mean that there will be proceedings against the union. Under the present Act, the Board's General Counsel has final authority to determine whether to proceed against the union on the charges, and his exercise of such discretion is not subject to review.[233]

The amended Act authorizes the Counsel, in cases of unfair labor practices, to issue a complaint "whenever it is charged that any person has engaged in or is engaging in any such unfair labor practice."[234] The definition of the term "person" includes "labor organizations."[235] The Board's Rules provide that "any person" may file a charge and that term has the same meaning as set forth in the amended Act.[236] Thus, it is clear that like unions, employers as well as individual employees, have the right to file unfair labor practice charges against unions.

The charge of unfair labor practices must be filed with the Board, and a copy served upon the person against whom the charge is made, within six months of the occurrence of the alleged unfair labor practice; otherwise the Board is without power to issue a complaint upon the charge.[237] This time limitation applies to charges filed by unions as well as by individuals, except that in the case of an individual serving in the armed forces the six-month period does not begin to run until his discharge from such service.

19. To Petition for an Election

An employer may file a petition with the Board for investigation and certification of bargaining representatives when one or more unions have presented him with a claim to be the bargaining representative.[238] This is a marked departure from the Rule of the Board under the Wagner Act, that an employer petition would be entertained only when two or more unions claimed to be the bargaining representative. However, only one election can be conducted by the Board within a year following the last valid election.

The amended Act denies unions access to the processes of the Board unless they comply with specified filing requirements as to non-communist affidavits and register specific information.[239] They must file the non-communist affidavit with the Board and the registration information with the Secretary of Labor. Noncompliance by the union with these requirements defeats the employer's right to obtain an election, unless more than one union is involved and one of them has satisfied the filing requirements. The Board will dismiss the petition of an employer when the only union involved has not complied with the filing provisions of the amended Act.[240] The Board said:

If, as here, a labor organization that presented a claim for recognition has not complied with the provisions of Section 9(f) and (h), we would no more implement the policy of Congress if we placed it on the ballot than if we were to do so in a case in which it, or another labor organization filed the formal papers with the Board. If a non-complying union were placed on the ballot and happened to win the election, no one could expect the Board under the amended Act to issue a certification that would run in its favor. But a victory at the polls, even without later formal certification, would confer certain moral and practical advantages on the non-complying union which the basic policy of Congress appears to discountenance. Such a result can be averted with certainty only by our declining to place a non-complying union on any ballot, unless there are absolutely compelling statutory or policy reasons for doing so.

In our opinion, the fact that a petition has been filed by an employer rather than by a labor organization does not provide such compelling reasons. The question concerning representation remains a question "raised by a labor organization" which has made a claim for recognition as bargaining representative. An employer petition, like a union petition, seeks to resolve the question of who, if anyone, is the true bargaining representative of the employees. Either sets in motion the same investigative process; the same result, either of certification or of dismissal, may flow from either; and a Board election conducted on the basis of either will now preclude another Board election for 12 months. This similarity between employer and union petitions, both in purpose and in result points strongly to the conclusion that a non-complying union should derive no more advantage from the one than it does from the other. The statutory language supports the same conclusion. Sections 9(f) and (h) speak in terms of questions raised, rather than of petitions filed, by labor organizations. An employer petition must allege that he has been presented with a claim by an individual or a labor organization for recognition as bargaining representative of his employees. The distinction which Congress intended to draw by the words "raised by a labor organization" is, we believe, between a claim for recognition made by a union and a similar claim made by an individual or individuals, not between a union petition and an employer petition filed with the Board. The name of the Fur Workers, CIO, will therefore not be placed on the ballot in this case.

The Board recognizes, to be sure, that this conclusion may sometimes result in depriving an employer of information which the amended Act would permit him to secure if only a complying labor organization or organizations were affirmatively claiming representative status. Conflicting policy considerations are before us; the amended Act and its legislative history provide no sure answer as to which should prevail. We believe, however, that the exclusion of non-complying unions from the ballot in cases where employers are the petitioners is more nearly consistent with the supervening policy of denying the imprimatur of Government to such labor organizations.

20. To Seek an Injunction against Unfair Labor Practices

When the Board's Regional Director, after investigation, has reasonable cause to believe that certain unfair labor practices are being committed by a union, he must (and the statutory language makes it mandatory upon him) apply to the United States District Court for a temporary order against the union, enjoining such conduct pending the decision of the Board upon the charges.[241] The application for the injunction may be made by the Regional Director even before the issuance of the complaint.

Unfair labor practices by unions which result in the aforementioned court injunction occur when the union engages in or encourages or induces the employees of an employer to engage in a strike or concerted refusal to work for the object of:

1. Forcing an employer or self-employed person to join a union or em-

ployer organization, or to boycott or refuse to do business with another person;[242]

2. Forcing any *other* employer to recognize a union as bargaining representative unless such union has been certified by the Board;[243]

3. Forcing an employer to recognize a union, if another union has been certified by the Board.[244] This does not bar the direct strike for recognition when there is no certified union;

4. Forcing an employer to assign work to the members of the union rather than to the members of another union, unless the employer is not conforming to the certification of the Board determining the bargaining unit of the employees performing the work.[245]

In the last mentioned case, the jurisdictional strike, type 4 above, the injunction procedure is not mandatory but is within the Board's discretion.[246]

In all other unfair labor practices, whether by unions or employers,[247] the Board is empowered, after isuance of its complaint alleging the unfair labor practices, in its discretion, to apply for a court injunction.[248] The Norris-LaGuardia Act does not bar the Board's applications for temporary injunctions under the amended Labor Act. The provisions of the Act setting forth the four unfair labor practices mentioned above, are not to be construed, however, to make it unlawful for an employee to refuse to cross picket lines established against an employer other than his own, if the strike against such other employer has been approved by the bargaining agent for the employees of such other employer.[249]

21. To Refuse to Bargain with Supervisory Employees

Supervisory employees are no longer employees within the meaning of that term in the amended Act.[250] Employers cannot be compelled to bargain with a union representing supervisory employees, although it is not unlawful for these employees to be members of a union.[251]

22. To Refuse to Bargain with Plant Guards
unless Separately Represented

Guards whose duty it is "to enforce against employees and other persons rules to protect property of the employer or to protect the safety of persons on the employer's premises" cannot be included by the Board in the same bargaining unit as other employees. Nor can the Board certify a union as bargaining representative of guards if such union admits to membership, or is affiliated with an organization which admits to membership, employees other than guards.[252] Watchmen who are not uniformed, armed or deputized, and have no monitorial duties, but merely patrol the plant and punch a watch clock, have been treated as guards.[253]

23. To Refuse to Discharge for Dual Unionism

The Wagner Act authorized closed shop contracts with the bargaining representative and such contracts required employees to maintain membership in good standing in the union as a condition of employment. An employee's activity on behalf of a union other than the contracting union afforded the latter a basis for removing the employee from good standing for such activity. In that event, and even though the employee had paid all financial obligations to the contracting union, the employer was obliged to discharge the employee under the closed shop provision of the contract.

Such discharges for dual unionism are illegal under the amended Act, which outlaws the closed shop, but permits union membership as a condition of employment in the form of a union shop under specific conditions. Even where there is such a valid union shop agreement, discharge thereunder can only be effected for nonproffer by the employee of regular and periodic dues and initiation fees, and for no other reason.[254]

24. To Require Nondiscriminatory Application of Union Membership Terms

Where the employer has entered a union shop agreement which is valid under the amended Act, he cannot, upon request of the contracting union, discharge an employee for failure to join the union, if he (the employer) is chargeable with reasonable grounds for believing that union membership was not made available to such employee on the same terms and conditions generally applicable to other members of the union.[255] It is an unfair labor practice for the union to deny an employee membership under such circumstances and attempt to cause his discharge.[256] Further, when such a valid union shop agreement is in effect, the union cannot require, as a condition precedent to membership therein, fees which the Board finds are excessive.[257]

25. To Refuse a Compulsory Check-Off

The Labor Management Relations Act, 1947, outlaws the compulsory check-off of union dues by making it a criminal violation for the employer to grant such a form of check-off. The check-off may be granted in the collective bargaining contract only if each employee executes a written assignment which shall not be irrevocable for a period of more than one year or beyond the termination date of the agreement, whichever occurs sooner.[258] In authorizing such a check-off the statute mentions "membership dues" only.

26. To Refuse to Insist upon an Election

Under the Wagner Act, the Board, upon consent of the union and the employer, would resolve the question of the union's representation of a majority by a check of union cards against an agreed payroll. The Wagner Act did not prescribe any fixed method for determining the question concerning representatives, and the conduct of an election was discretionary with the Board. The amended Act provides for the determination of representation by an election, and no other method is permissible.[259] The Board has discontinued the card-check technique since the amendment of the Act.

27. To Refuse to Consent to an Election within One Year of the Last Election

The amended Act explicitly provides that only one election can be directed within the twelve-month period immediately following the last valid election.[260] The same rule would appear to apply regardless of the fact that the union seeking the election did not participate in the last election. The rule also applies to a decertification election and to elections for union shop authority or revocation of such authority.[261]

The measurement of the twelve-month period depends on the outcome of the last valid election. If that election did not result in the certification of a union, the period is measured from the date of the election.[a] If a union was certified by the Board as a result of that election, the period is measured from the date of the certification rather than the date of that election.[b]

28. To Adjust Individual Grievances

Employees or groups of employees have the right to take up and have adjusted individual grievances so long as the adjustment thereof is not inconsistent with the terms and provisions of the collective bargaining agreement in effect, and the bargaining representative has been afforded an opportunity to be present at the adjustment.[262] The bargaining agent would probably not be permitted to participate in the adjustment of the grievance, provided there was no question of conflict with the existing agreement.[263]

29. To Deny Union Shop—Closed Shop

The amended Act invalidates the closed shop by reason of the repeal of the proviso to Section 8(c) of the Wagner Act, which authorized such a union security provision. For the same reason, preferential shops or union hiring hall provisions which are discriminatory have been held to be illegal. The amended Act does permit a union shop clause provided (a) the union has majority status in the appropriate bargaining unit and (b) the Board certifies, after an election, that a majority of the employees *eligible* to vote in the election have voted to authorize the union to enter into such agreement.

When these conditions have been met, the employer may enter into a union shop arrangement, i.e., requiring as a condition of employment that employees join the union thirty days after hiring or the effective date of the agreement, whichever is later.[264]

The inclusion of the union shop clause in the agreement without prior compliance with this requirement is unlawful.[a] The execution of the contract in itself constitutes coercion of the employees by the employer[b] and the fact that the illegal clause was not put into effect is immaterial.[c] However, the provision may be included in the contract if it is expressly made subject to, and not effective until, these requirements have been met.[d] Oral assurances that a security clause will not be put into the contract until the union shop election is held are insufficient.[e] Likewise ineffective are saving clauses which merely postpone determination of validity.[f]

Authorization for the union shop may be revoked at an election if 30 per cent of the employees petition for it. Only one union shop election may be conducted in any one year following the last such election.[265]

30. To Be Responsible for the Conduct of His Agents Only

The broad definition of "employer" in the Wagner Act has been limited so as to impose liability upon the employer for the acts of his agents only.[266] The rules of the law of agency are applicable, therefore, to determine the responsibility of the employer for conduct of his subordinates. To establish the liability, the conduct of the subordinate must be within the actual or apparent scope of his authority. Actual authorization prior to commission of the acts, or subsequent ratification thereof, is not controlling.[267]

31. To Sue for Violation of the Collective Labor Contract

Where the employer and the bargaining representative have entered into a contract and the latter violates the contract, the employer has the right to an action for damages.[268] The action may be brought in the United States District Court for the district in which the union has its principal office or its authorized agents are engaged in representing employee members. Service of process upon an officer or agent of the union is sufficient.

Unlike the Norris-LaGuardia Act, the amended Labor Act does not require proof of actual authorization or subsequent ratification of the acts upon which liability of the union is based to hold the union liable for conduct of its agents. Agency for the union may be established under the usual principles of the rules of agency.

Any money judgment recovered against the union is enforceable only against the union as an entity and against its assets. Such a judgment cannot be enforced against individual members of the union or their assets.

32. To Refuse Contribution to Union Funds

Payments by an employer to the representatives of his employees (except as compensation for service and other payments of that nature specifically enumerated in the statute) are illegal and subject him to criminal penalties.[269] However, payments to trust funds are exempt from the statutory proscription, provided they meet the requirements of the statute as to both the object of the trust fund and the method of administration. This exemption legalizes payments to union welfare funds if the two prerequisites of the statute are met.

The following objects of such welfare funds are valid:[270]

1. The welfare or trust fund must be for the exclusive benefit of the employees of the employer or employers making the payments and the families and dependents of such employees;

2. Payments from the fund, either of principal or interest, must be for medical or hospital care, pensions, compensation for injuries or illness resulting from occupational illness, or insurance to provide any of the foregoing, or unemployment benefits or life insurance, disability and sickness insurance, or accident insurance.

The administration of such trust funds must be as follows:[271]

1. There must be a written agreement in which the detailed basis upon which such payments are to be made is specified;

2. The agreement must provide for equal representation of employers and employees in the administration of the fund, together with a neutral person selected by both sides, and in the event of a deadlock in the administration of the fund, the two groups must agree on an impartial umpire to make the decision, and in event of the inability to agree upon

an impartial umpire, either group may petition the United States District Court for the appointment of an umpire to decide the issue;

3. Provision for annual audit of the fund, the results thereof to be made available for inspection by interested persons;

4. Payments to pension funds or annuity funds must be segregated and the agreement must provide that such funds cannot be used for any purposes other than payment of pensions or annuities.[272]

The administrative provisions of the statute do not apply to payments to trusts established by collective agreement prior to January 1, 1946, if such trust funds are otherwise lawful. Nor do the requirements contained in the Act as to the purposes of the fund prohibit payments to such trust funds, if prior to January 1, 1947, such trust agreement contain provisions for pooled vacation benefits.[273]

33. To Sue for Relief from Illegal Strikes and Boycotts

Under the section "To Seek an Injunction against Unfair Labor Practices" there have been set forth four types of union strikes and boycotts which are specifically described in the amended Act as unfair labor practices by unions. Such conduct by a union is also declared unlawful under Title III of the Labor Management Relations Act of 1947 (in addition to describing such conduct as unfair labor practices, subject to injunction and remedial action by the Board) and persons injured in business or property by such conduct are given the right to recover damages in the United States District Court.[274] It has been held that this provision of the Act confers no right on private parties to an injunction against such conduct.[a]

34. To Judicial Relief from Unfair Labor Practices

Several decisions of lower courts tend to support the contention that both employers and unions may sue in the courts, without recourse to the Board, for relief against conduct which is an unfair labor practice within the meaning of the provisions of the amended Act. Some of these decisions attempt to distinguish between the holdings of the Supreme Court and the Circuit Courts of Appeals that the Wagner Act created no private rights and that the Board has exclusive jurisdiction of unfair labor practices, thereby excluding recourse to courts except by way of review of an order of the Board.[275]

The Wagner Act expressly provided that the Board should have "exclusive" jurisdiction over unfair labor practices. That word was eliminated from the Act.[276] On this basis the District Court has held, in the *Amazon*

Mills case, that this change eliminated the sole jurisdiction of the Board thereby giving courts concurrent jurisdiction. This Court held further that the amended Act established private rights under which the union plaintiff in the case could maintain a court action against the employer for refusal to bargain collectively, although that unfair labor practice charge had been tried before a Board Trial Examiner and was awaiting Board decision.[277] Subsequently, that Court reiterated its position and issued a temporary injunction restraining the employer from continuing its unfair labor practices.[278] The Board intervened in the case to contest the validity of the lower court's conclusions, and the case was appealed to the Fourth Circuit Court of Appeals.

The Court of Appeals reversed the District Court and held that the amendments to the Act did not give the courts jurisdiction to enjoin unfair labor practice upon the suit of a private party, and that jurisdiction to remedy unfair labor practices as defined in the amended Act still was vested exclusively in the Labor Board.[279]

In another case in the United States District Court, an employer sued to enjoin a threatened unfair labor practice—a secondary boycott within the meaning of the Labor Management Relations Act. On granting a temporary injunction against such conduct by the union, the Court relied upon the provisions of the amended Act which make the secondary boycott an unfair labor practice, and also held that the Norris-LaGuardia Act was not applicable on the ground that there was no labor dispute between the plaintiff employer and the union.[280] The Court of Appeals, however, reversed the District Court and held that the Court did not have jurisdiction to enjoin threatened unfair labor practices upon the application of a private party, since by the provision of the Labor Act such authority to seek an injunctive relief against a secondary boycott, which was an unfair labor practice, was vested exclusively in the Labor Board. The Court of Appeals also held that the dispute involved constituted a labor dispute under the Norris-LaGuardia Act and hence, was not enjoinable.[281]

The California Superior Court has held that exclusive jurisdiction over unfair labor practices still remained with the Board. That Court also held that the amended Act[282] authorized any person injured by an illegal strike or boycott to seek redress, such redress consisting of the recovery of damages, and that the amended Act did not authorize the courts to grant injunctive relief at the instance of a private party.[283]

In the *Amazon Mills* case discussed above, the Court pointed out:

The change in the statute upon which reliance is placed was clearly intended, not to vest the courts with general jurisdiction over unfair labor practices, but to recognize the jurisdiction vested in the courts by section 10, subsections (j) and (l), section 208, and section 303, to which we have heretofore made reference, as well as the power in the Board, conferred by the proviso in section 10(a) to cede jurisdiction to state agencies in certain cases. This is not only the clear meaning of the statute when its language is considered in tne light of existing law, but it is also the meaning given it by the Conference Committee of the House and Senate (See H. R. No. 510, June 3, 1947).

We do not mean to say that unusual cases may not arise where courts of equity could be called upon to protect the rights of parties created by the act. Cf. Steele v. Louisville & N. R. Co. 323 U.S. 192, 65 S. Ct. 226 89 L. Ed. 173; A. F. of L. v. N.L.R.B. 308 U.S. 401, 412, 60 S. Ct. 300, 84 L. Ed. 347. What we have here, however, is not an unusual case calling for the exercise of extraordinary jurisdiction, but an ordinary unfair labor practice case involving alleged refusal to bargain. For such a case, the plaintiff has been provided an adequate administrative remedy before the Labor Board; and certainly the extraordinary powers of a court of equity may not be invoked until this administrative remedy has been exhausted. Newport News Shipbuilding & Dry Dock Co. v. Schauffler 4 Cir. 91 F. 2d 730, 731, affirmed 303 U.S. 54, 58 S. Ct. 466, 82 L. Ed. 646.

For the same reason that plaintiff may not maintain the suit for injunction to restrain the unfair labor practice, it may not maintain the action to recover damages on account thereof. Recompense of lost wages on account of an unfair labor practice is a matter for the labor board. See Phelps Dodge Corp. v. N.L.R.B. 313 U.S. 177, 194, 61 S. Ct. 845, 85 L. Ed. 1271, 133 A.L.R. 1217; International Union etc. v. Eagle Picher Co. 325 U.S. 335, 340, 65 S. Ct. 1166, 89 L. Ed. 1649; Wallace Corp. v. N.L.R.B. 4 Cir. 159 F. 2d 952. The decree appealed from will accordingly be reversed with direction to the lower court that the case be dismissed.

II · DUTIES OF MANAGEMENT

(INCLUDING RIGHTS OF UNIONS)

1. To Bargain Collectively

The Act commands employers to "bargain collectively" and defines that obligation as follows: "To bargain collectively is the performance of the mutual obligation of the employer and the representative of the employees to meet at reasonable times and confer in good faith with respect to wages, hours and other terms and conditions of employment, or the negotiation of an agreement, or any question arising thereunder, and the execution of a written contract incorporating any agreement reached if requested by either party, but such obligation does not compel either party to agree to a proposal or require the making of a concession."[285] While it does not require an employer to reach an agreement with a union representing his employees, it *does* require that he should bargain with it in good faith.[286]

Certification of a bargaining agent by the Board or the Board's Regional Director pursuant to consent or Board-ordered election must be honored for a reasonable period and the employees' repudiation of their designated representatives during this time will not be recognized. An employer who refuses to bargain with the certified union, because six weeks or two months after these elections a majority of the employees repudiated the union, violates the Act.[287] In one case, an automobile distributor had in his employ two mechanics, both of whom joined a union, which then sought to bargain for them. The employer signed individual contracts with the two men and then informed the union that nothing remained for negotiation. "Through the use of individual contracts," the Board held, "the employer refused to bargain collectively."[288]

Refusal to bargain collectively with the representatives of a majority of the employees is an unfair labor practice. Since the parties to a labor controversy must resort to their economic strength to promote their cause, the Supreme Court pointed out that "the theory of the Act is that free opportunity for negotiation with accredited representatives of the employees is likely to promote industrial peace and may bring about the adjustments and agreements which the Act in itself does not intend to compel." Thus,

163

it has been held that an employer who enters into negotiations with representatives of his employees, without any intention of entering into an agreement, is guilty of refusing to bargain collectively and, therefore, of an unfair labor practice.[289]

The Act does not compel an employer to seek out his employees or request their participation in negotiations for purposes of collective bargaining.[290] Nor is there a duty on the part of the employer to be represented in the bargaining negotiations by a person or persons with competent authority to enter into a binding agreement with the employees. However, the character and powers of the person designated by the employer as a negotiating agent are factors which will be taken into consideration in deciding whether the employer's effort to negotiate was really made in good faith.

An employer may not have a mind "hermetically sealed" against the acceptance of the proper procedure of collective bargaining in good faith, nor may he engage in such Fabian tactics as will practically render abortive the statutory rights of the employee.

A bargaining agreement does not absolve an employer from guilt for unfair labor practices, as where officials of the company, after they entered into the collective bargaining agreement, did not cease their opposition to the union, but continued to manifest that same character of hostility that had clearly characterized their attitude prior to entering into the collective bargaining contract. The mere fact that the effectiveness of any duress had not been shown was immaterial. It is only necessary to show that the employer interfered, intimidated, or coerced, since it is the purpose of the statute to prevent the employer from interfering or intruding into the affairs of his employees.[291]

MAJORITY REPRESENTATION BY THE UNION

Before an employer is obligated to bargain with a union, or can be charged with the unfair practice of refusal to bargain, the union must, at the time, represent a majority of the employees in an appropriate bargaining unit. The Board commonly decides the question upon the basis of the following:

1. By Board certification of the union following an election after a hearing or upon the consent thereto by the parties and waiver of hearing;
2. By the Regional Director's certification of the union after the conduct of a consent election pursuant to an agreement of the parties;[292]
3. Upon hearing on charges and formal complaint that the employer has illegally refused to bargain collectively, and in the absence of Board or Regional Director's certification after election, by cross-check of union

cards or records, evidencing employee authorization against the employer's pay roll records; the documents are introduced in evidence.

The type of union card or record last referred to may be in the form of an application for membership in the union or may merely designate the union as the employee's representative for the purposes of collective bargaining. Payment of dues to the union will be immaterial to the effectiveness of the card in either form, unless such payment is, by the terms of the card itself, a condition precedent. Other types of union records that have been accepted are members' rolls, dues records[293] and records of payment of strike benefits. Payment of union initiation fees has been regarded as sufficient.[294]

Union memberships obtained as the result of a closed shop agreement are insufficient to establish the union's majority status unless the union represented a majority at the time such contract was executed.[295] Refusal of employees to cross a picket line does not aid the union's claim of majority representation in the absence of any other evidence.[296] The existence of a maintenance of membership contract and the non-payment of dues thereunder does not necessarily establish an intention on the part of the employees to withdraw from the union upon termination of the contract.[297] However, if the union loses an election, it cannot thereafter rely on cards obtained from the employees prior to the election.[298] Designation of the parent organization by the employee as bargaining agent will be counted as a valid designation of an affiliate in determining whether the latter represents a majority.[299] But designation of the union by employees who are disqualified from employment with the employer by reason of provisions of law will not be counted.[300]

The duty to bargain collectively exists only when the representatives have been selected by a majority of the employees *in a unit appropriate for the purposes of collective bargaining*. Where a union has been improperly designated, the employer need not bargain with it.[301]

The Act provides that "representatives designated or selected . . . by the majority of employees . . . shall be the exclusive representatives of all the employees . . . for the purpose of collective bargaining." The Act thus affirms by implication the right of the employer to insist that the bargaining agent be truly representative of the majority of employees. Since there is no express provision in the Act as to what kind of majority should determine the result of a representation election, the general rule applied is that if a majority of the total number of eligible employees voted, those who do not vote will be considered to assent to the will of the majority of those who do.[302]

When a union which is already the bargaining agent for one group of employees in an appropriate unit desires to extend that unit to embrace an additional group of employees, the union must make some showing of representation among the employees which it seeks to add to the unit; and where the petitioning union has no members among the employees it seeks to add to its unit, the Labor Board will dismiss the case.[303]

A union must claim a majority before an employer may be charged with refusal to bargain. Once, however, that claim is made and is based on fact, the employer refuses to deal with the union at his peril.[304] In arriving at such determination the Board will consider the employer's earlier unwillingness to meet the union and its failure to cooperate in testing whether the union's claim was based on fact.

Majority representation means over 50 per cent of the employees in the unit, and where the union receives exactly 50 per cent of the employees voting in an election, an employer who refuses to bargain cannot be charged with violating the Act.

Board certification is not a prerequisite to collective bargaining.[305] Nor may an employer question a majority of a certified union, merely because the certification is without an election. Naturally, where the Board has directed an election to determine the majority representative, the employer may refuse to bargain with either of the competing unions until there is a certification by the Board. The competing unions may not invoke the remedies of the Act in such case, because of the obvious doubt as to majority representation.

If an employer is confronted with the conflicting claims of two unions as to majority representation, but recognizes one union, the Board will find the employer guilty of unfair labor practices, particularly if a petition for an election is pending before it.[306] Nor is the employer under any obligation to decide at his peril which of the competing unions has majority status.[a] An employer may be ordered to bargain with a union that no longer has majority status, if the union did represent the majority of the employees at the time the employer unlawfully refused to bargain.[307] In one case, the court declared that the right of the majority of the employees to bargain directly is subordinated to the right of a once-designated union as collective bargaining agent where the switch in majority was the result of unfair labor practices.[308]

Where the Circuit Court of Appeals enforces an order of the Board requiring the employer to bargain collectively with a labor organization, such order does not have the result of giving the union a permanent tenure. Conditions may change and the desires of the employees may change. If the majority union has lost its majority between the time of certification and bargaining, the employer must negotiate with the union which had the original authority, provided there has been reasonable diligence by the majority union.[309]

Should an employer enter into a contract with a labor organization which does not at the time of execution represent a majority of the employees, while another union does, the Board will find a refusal to bargain a violation of the Act. So too, where the employees form an independent bargaining committee, after it becomes apparent that the employer will not deal with the union, the Board will find such a committee not to be the free choice of the employees, because of the employer's prior unfair labor practice in illegally refusing to bargain with the union. The Board will also find that the employer has refused to bargain in violation of the Act.[310] Where, however, the employer and the union were both willing to have a consent election, but the union prevented the election by withdrawing its consent, the Board found that doubt existed as to the union's majority, and would not find a refusal to bargain. An employer may not cease negotiations with a majority union merely because the union has filed charges of unfair labor practices against the employer or has gone on strike.[311]

Once the union has established that it represents a majority of the employees, there is a presumption of continuance of the majority status unless evidence to the contrary is shown.[312] The presumption is rebutted if a majority of the employees join a competing union after one year from date of certification of the certified union.[313] The presumption, however, is not destroyed by mere reduction in the employment roll.[314] But it should not, however, be relied on when rival unions are claiming to represent the employees.[315]

MAJORITY REPRESENTATION IN APPROPRIATE BARGAINING UNIT

A further prerequisite to the employer's duty to bargain collectively with a union is the requirement that the union's majority status must be in a unit appropriate for the purpose of collective bargaining.[316] The appropriate unit involves the grouping of employees in such units as will "assure" them the full benefits of collective bargaining. The Board is authorized to "decide in each case" the appropriate unit and may find appropriate "an employer unit, craft unit, plant unit or subdivision thereof."[317]

The employer may in good faith question the appropriateness of the unit asserted by the union but he does so at his peril, unless he can show that, in the exercise of reasonable judgment, he lacked knowledge of the justification of the unit asserted.[318]

· If the Board has found the appropriate unit, the issue cannot be relitigated in a case charging the employer with illegal refusal to bargain, unless the evidence offered in the unfair labor practice case is not cumulative, is material and was not available at the time the Board held its hearing on the question of appropriate unit.[319] The employer's desire to test the validity of the Board's finding of the appropriate bargaining unit does not excuse a refusal to bargain.[320]

NECESSITY OF GOOD FAITH

A *passive* attitude on the part of the employer in the collective bargaining proceeding constitutes a refusal to bargain. Thus it is the obligation of the employer to participate actively in the deliberations so as to indicate a *present intention* to find a basis for agreement, and a sincere effort must be made to reach a common ground.[321] In one case the court held that the employer's failure to give a direct answer as to whether it would sign an agreement when reached, its refusal to agree to a provision which embodied an existing company policy, its refusal to submit counterproposals, its unwillingness to take any affirmative action in the negotiations, all manifested the employer's *intention not to bargain*. While the employer is not bound to offer a counterproposal, the court stated that a counterproposal would have established the employer's willingness to bargain beyond question, and in the absence thereof the Board could not be condemned for drawing the opposite conclusion; and that, while the employees have the burden of instituting bargaining proceedings, and an employer has no burden in this respect, the employees are not required continually to present new contracts until one ultimately meets with the employer's approval.[322]

INDIVIDUAL BARGAINING DISCOURAGED

The Supreme Court has interpreted the Wagner Act to provide that a collective bargaining contract shall supersede any preexisting individual contracts with employees.[323] In one case, the Court declared that the employer may not change rates of pay through notice to individual employees, despite the latter's consent, where a collective contract provides that rates be changed only through collective bargaining.

The individual contract may still be used where (1) no union is designated by a majority; (2) the union is unable to show its majority by means prescribed by law; (3) the union loses its majority without interference by the employer.[324]

Nothing in the Act interferes with the right of individual employees "to present grievances to their employer."[325] The employer has the right to meet with individuals to adjust their grievances where the bargaining agent refuses to participate in the disposition of the grievances. In settling the grievances, the employer must act in accordance with the terms of the governing collective bargaining contract, if such exists. The bargaining agent, however, does not forfeit his right to represent individuals with respect to their grievances and may be present and bargain concerning individual grievances. The Fifth Circuit Court of Appeals has said that, where the individual grievance of an employee concerns only "some question of fact or conduct peculiar to the employee" not within the scope of the collective bargaining process, the employer may make an adjustment directly with the employee without permitting the bargaining representative to participate. But the Court also said that even if the employer believes the individual's grievance to be of such an individual nature, he must give the union notice of the hearing thereon in order that the union may have an opportunity to determine whether the grievance is of such a personal character or the subject matter of collective bargaining.[326] The Court also pointed out that a minority union has no right to participate in any of these procedures.

The amended Act provides for the adjustment of individual grievances without the intervention of the bargaining agent, so long as such adjustment is not inconsistent with the provisions of the collective bargaining agreement and the bargaining representative is afforded an opportunity to be present at such adjustment.[327]

The duty to bargain collectively with the representatives of employees is not fulfilled by merely hearing individual complaints and adjusting individual grievances. Although the negotiation of individual contracts has been declared valid by the Supreme Court, this declaration does not validate such contracts as an alternative to collective bargaining with the representative of the majority and they must give way to the collective agreement.[328]

The Board has ruled that the execution of individual contracts of employment with individual employees, following the initiation of collective bargaining negotiations with the majority representative, does not constitute a bar to collective bargaining.[329] In fact, an employer's individual bargaining with employees has been held an interference in violation of the Act.[330]

The Supreme Court has said:

Employer action to bring about changes in wage scales without consultation and negotiation with the certified representative of its employees cannot, we think, logically or realistically, be distinguished from bargaining with individuals or minorities. The fact that the application to the War Labor Board was not the actual increase of wages but a necessary preliminary does not make unilateral action, accompanied by publication of the step taken to the employees, any the less objectionable. The application to the War Labor Board marked a unilateral determination by the company that the employees of this unit should have the specific increase deemed due them by the company or none at all, if the bargaining agent should object in accordance with the letter quoted above. The employer was not getting into position to negotiate with the agent. He declared the contrary and proposed that he, as employer, would make the increase if permission were granted. . . . . By going ahead with wage adjustments without negotiation with the bargaining agent, it took a step which justified the conclusion of the Board as to the violation of § 8(1). Such unilateral action minimizes the influence of organized bargaining. It interferes with the right of self-organization by emphasizing to the employees that there is no necessity for a collective bargaining agent.[331]

While ordinarily an announcement by an employer that he would grant unilaterally certain conditions to employees, for which a union with majority status had been bargaining unsuccessfully, is deemed by the Labor Board a violation of the Act,[332] the Board held that an announcement that foremen should make every effort to handle grievances within 48 hours of complaints was primarily an instruction to foremen and not an attempt to adopt grievance procedure. Likewise, conducting a poll to learn the employees' wishes concerning changes in lunch and pay periods, where a tentative agreement called for one or the other of two pay periods but no preference had been indicated, was not a violation of the Act. Any attempt on the part of the employer to engage in individual negotiations on the subjects of collective bargaining, while there is in existence an agency representing a majority of the employees, is, however, unlawful.[333] While employees may sign individual contracts, until such time as a lawful bargaining agent is chosen, these contracts in no way limit their right to bargain collectively.[334]

From the employer's standpoint, the Board holds that he may make the contracts with individual employees, but, if he urges employees to bargain individually on the basis of these agreements, he interferes with their rights, and, if he refuses to deal with a union covering the same issues as are dealt with individually, he violates the Labor Act by his refusal to bargain.[335]

Where a union, representing a majority, calls a strike, and the employer solicits individual strikers to return to work, the employer, by so doing, may be held to have indicated his refusal to bargain collectively with the union; but whether there has been a violation of law depends on all the facts and circumstances.

Refusal to bargain with the majority union on the grievances of employees not members of the union, is an unfair labor practice if such non-union members are in the bargaining unit.[336]

The employer is not relieved of the duty to bargain with a majority union by:

1. Questioning the union's majority status or the appropriateness of the bargaining unit in bad faith;[337]
2. The union's failure to seek negotiations for three and one half months;[338]
3. Strike threat of a rival union;[339]
4. Plans of the employer to change its line of manufacture. In this case the Board held that there was a substantial area for bargaining, viz., the period until completion of the change of manufacture, retraining program and solution of the lay-off question.[340]

Alteration by the employer of existing terms and conditions of employment, without consultation with the bargaining representative, constitutes an illegal refusal to bargain.[a] Instances which are regarded as typical of such unilateral employer action in illegal derogation of the exclusive bargaining rights of the bargaining representative are:

Granting wage increases.[b]

Instituting a pension plan.[c]

Downgrading employees and changing their work week.[d]

Changing working hours.[e]

Even where genuine collective bargaining has resulted in a legitimate impasse, unilateral action may constitute an illegal refusal to bargain. It was so held where the employer, about twelve days after the impasse, unilaterally granted a wage increase substantially larger than that offered to the union during negotiations.[f] The court distinguished this situation from cases where after a *bona fide* impasse is reached, the union refuses to negotiate concerning further offers and where the employer puts into effect wage increases previously offered to and rejected by the union.

However, unilateral grant of wage increases has been permitted during a period when the union was engaged in a strike in violation of the no-strike clause of the existing contract.[g] Such wrongful strike action by the union suspends the obligation of the employer to bargain on the subject matter of the strike, so long as the strike continues.

COUNTERPROPOSALS

When a counterproposal is directly asked for it ought to be made; although ordinarily, where there is no bad faith, failure to make counterproposals does not necessarily alone constitute a refusal to bargain. However, failure to make counterproposals has been viewed as evidence of bad faith.[341] Counterproposals need not be made when the union indicates that they would be futile. Where the union sought a seniority clause to prevent further discrimination, which the company refused to consider, and the company did not offer any substitute, but refused to negotiate any issue except the hours of employment, such refusal to give any guarantee against further discriminations was deemed an indication of the company's determination to continue these practices.[342]

UNION COMMITTEES

An employer who attempts to deal directly with his employees on terms of employment and the other subjects of collective bargaining, and ignores the union committee authorized by the employees or the union representing the employees, thereby interferes with the rights of his employees to collective bargaining. The courts and the Board have repeatedly indicated that the employer's duty is to negotiate with the union representatives. That their demands may be unreasonable or beyond the economic means of the employer does not relieve him of this obligation. He must thrash out the demands with the union committee or other representative and cannot go over their heads or behind their backs to the union membership as a whole for the purpose of negotiating an agreement with them.[343]

TRANSFERRING OPERATION

If the union has established its majority status, it need not prove its majority representation again if the business is taken over by a successor employer, and the transfer of the going business does not extinguish the duty to bargain. "By its very nature and purpose, it (duty to bargain) ran with the business, and it is, therefore, binding on the successor corporation, which, with knowledge of its predecessor's obligation to bargain, took over and continued the business."[344]

After certification of a union by the Board in one case, the corporate employer transferred its plant operations to a partnership pursuant to an agreement whereby the latter also took over the employees engaged in the plant operation. The partnership agreed to manufacture products required by the corporation on a cost plus basis, the corporation to furnish the raw materials. The corporation agreed to bear the additional expense of continuing the employees' pension fund, insurance contributions and Christmas bonuses. The Board found that the corporation and the partnership had refused to bargain, holding that both were engaged in a single business enterprise under the effective control of the corporation. The Board characterized the agreement as "a scheme rigged with the purpose and intent of setting aside the certification."[345]

CHANGES IN OPERATIONS

Reconversion to peace time production may relieve the employer from the obligation to bargain collectively with the union.

Substantial changes in operations may be said so to affect the majority status of the bargaining agent as to relieve the employer of the duty imposed by the statute. In a recent case, an employer who had engaged in aircraft parts production reconverted to his normal operation of manufacturing dripcups, egg beaters and related articles. He eliminated the machine shop, established for war production, but kept his regular polishing department as in normal times; the number of employees was reduced from over 120 to 50, most of whom were employed in the polishing department. The claim of the Metal Polishers' Union that it continued to represent the unit so substantially contracted was not sustained by the Board.[346] However, the Board has warned that no general rule should be promulgated and that each case will depend on the facts. Mere reduction in the number of employees will not be enough to relieve the employer of his duty to bargain collectively.[347]

2. To Disclaim Responsibility for Supervisors' Activities

Courts as well as the Board may hold management responsible for any anti-organizational activities, not only of supervisors, but also of any employee identified with the management in other ways.[348] Added importance, is, therefore, lent to the Board's rule that an employer may not escape responsibility for anti-union acts of minor supervisors by giving them orders to remain strictly neutral. Employers to avoid involvement may adopt the practice of "openly disavowing" to the employees the anti-organizational activities of any employees who might be identified with the management.[349]

If the employer posts a notice informing his employees that he takes a neutral stand in a choice between unions, he is not held liable thereafter for statements made by his supervisors, although these statements favor a rival union to the disparagement of the certified union.[350] Where, however, the supervisors require that promotion or actual employment depend on membership in the union they favor, the employer is held liable, since it is not a mere matter of opinion but rather discriminatory action. A good example of how a company is absolved of charges of unfair labor practices by effective disavowal to the employees, of supervisory statements and conduct may be found in the typical contest between an inside and outside union. Petitions and literature hostile to the outside union may be circulated and rumors spread that the plant will shut down if the outside union obains a foothold. Minor supervisory officials may also be implicated in the campaign. Members of the outside union sometimes take the matter to top management. If the management disavows such actions and rumors to the employees, states that it is neutral and that the employees are free to exercise their right to join whatever union they desire, it relieves itself from responsibility. The disavowal, however, to be effective must be to the employees by adequate publication or at meetings with the employees.

Even though the acts of supervisors are in disobedience of the employer's instructions to them, the employer is not absolved. Instructions must be made effective.[351] An employer's responsibility for violations of the Act is not limited to conduct of those officials having any particular kind or degree of authority, such as "hiring and firing," "disciplinary power," or even "supervisory capacity." The test of the employer's liability is said to be that "If the words or deeds of the supervisory employees, taken in their setting, were reasonably likely to have restrained the employee's choice and if the supervisory employees may fairly be said to have been responsible for them, they constitute a proper basis for the conclusion that the employer did interfere."[352]

These decisions indicate a trend in the reviewing courts toward the Board's practice of imposing heavy responsibility on employers for organizational conduct by any type of employee. The Board has always ruled that an employer is responsible for the organizational activities of any supervisory employees, on the theory of *respondeat superior*.[353] But the Board adds that an employee need have no particular supervisory powers in order to charge the employer with responsibility.

However, the amendments to the Act limit the employer's, as well as the union's, responsibility to statements and conduct of persons who can be regarded as their agents by virtue of the well-established principles of agency. They are now liable for the conduct of persons acting as their agents within the scope of their actual or apparent authority.[354] The determination of whether there is such agency is not controlled necessarily by actual authorization of the acts or their subsequent ratification. (See "Employer-Employee Relationship," Part Three, Introduction.)

Subsequent interpretation of the amended law may leave little change in the established decisions, except, perhaps, to require from the Board more factual proof on the issue of agency than it has introduced under prior doctrines.

The employer is not responsible for organizational activities of a supervisor for a union which traditionally admits supervisors to membership unless it can be shown that the employer encouraged, authorized or ratified such activity or gave the employees reasonable grounds to believe that the supervisors were acting for or on behalf of management.[355]

Employer statements to supervisory employees, who are members in a rank-and-file union, have received a somewhat different treatment than the same remarks made to rank-and-file employees. Thus, where the plant superintendent interrogated two supervisory employees concerning their membership in a rank-and-file union and threatened them for such membership, the National Labor Relations Board held such conduct insufficient upon which to find a violation of the Act, because of the supervisory status of the employees, although such conduct and statements to nonsupervisory employees would have been a violation.[356]

3. To Maintain Neutral Attitude

An employer has the duty to impress effectively on supervisory employees and nonsupervisory employees his neutral attitude toward the union.[357] Failure on the part of an employer, though he announce his impartiality, to see that his attitude is effectively impressed on the management officials and effectuated by them, will result in a cease and desist order.[358]

4. To Reinstate with or without Back Pay

Where the Labor Board finds discriminatory discharges, dismissals or lay-offs of union members, it typically orders the employer to reinstate them with back pay and, in the case of an illegal lockout, the Board finds mass "discrimination" against the union employees and orders them reinstated with back pay to their former or substantially equivalent jobs together with all the rights and privileges thereof. The important consideration is not what happens to employees who have been discriminated against, but the establishment of an atmosphere in which present and future employees of the employer may be free from fear that union activity will bring reprisals upon their heads.[359] This type of order, reinstatement with back pay, is the most stringent financial sanction which the Board ordinarily applies under the Act, and it not infrequently runs into very large sums. Even though the Board may be unable to compel a runaway employer to return to a former location, it may inflict upon him heavy financial loss by exercising its authority to require reinstatement of employees with back pay.[360]

EFFECT OF EMPLOYER'S CONDUCT

Normally the employer cannot escape rehiring his discriminatorily discharged employees with back pay. The amount of the award, however, may vary considerably in proportion to the actions of the employer. After a discriminatory discharge, back pay continues to accrue until the employer makes an unconditional offer of reinstatement.[361] The amount of back pay is diminished if the employee gets another job and receives earnings. Where the employer has fired men, relying on a closed shop contract (valid under the Wagner and still legally in effect under the amended Act),[362] or where he has relied on a compromise agreement entered into with a representative of the Board, or on the report of the Trial Examiner that his actions are not unfair, he need not pay back wages. Such disallowance of back pay is regarded as fair, for it encourages reliance upon Board actions and upon contracts with its agents, and, hence, tends to facilitate successful settlement of disputes. Where, however, the employer has not attempted to bring about a peaceful settlement, he may correspondingly suffer financial loss. Thus, an employer who locks out his men must pay full back wages, even if they go on strike while locked out, which would normally prevent the award of pay during the strike.[363] In another case, the Trial Examiner reported that the Board was without jurisdiction, and the company relied on this report to fire union men indiscriminately. The Board found that it had jurisdiction and awarded back pay except that the period from the date of the Trial Examiner's Intermediate Report to the date of the Board's order was excluded from the computation of back pay.[364]

Even if the company should go out of interstate commerce after the Board's order, the Board may nevertheless still enforce its order of reinstatement. This would agree with the general rule that only an employee's conduct can deprive him of that remedy; it would also prevent borderline industries from deliberately avoiding the Board's jurisdiction.[365]

EFFECT OF EMPLOYEE'S CONDUCT

Courts have considered the employees' conduct on the issue of reinstatement and have held that by striking in violation of their agreement the men forfeited their right to reinstatement.[366]

In one case, the union threatened to strike to obtain a system of seniority which was clearly prohibited by the contract. After a *bona fide* attempt to settle the dispute, the employer discharged them and reopened the plant with new men. The court held that by their wilful breach of contract the men had forfeited their immunity to discharge during a labor dispute.[367] The Board has held that, where an employer has not breached the contract or committed an unfair labor practice, he may discharge employees who strike in violation of the no-strike clause of the contract, since by such conduct, in these circumstances, they forfeit the protection of the Act.[368] In another case, an Examiner's interpretation of "substantially equivalent" employment was rejected by the Labor Board in regard to seven employees who, after being discharged for union activity, obtained other jobs at higher hourly wages than those paid by the employer who discharged them. In requiring reinstatement, which the Trial Examiner would have withheld, the Board added that even though "substantially equivalent" employment had been obtained it would still enter such an order, since reinstatement is a necessary remedy for discrimination, "and to effectuate the policies of the Act"[369]

In a third case, the court rejected the employer's contention that, where employees strike for a reason other than that the employer engaged in unfair labor practices, they need not be reinstated if new employees have replaced them; since no replacements were made, some employees were transferred from other departments, and eventually some new people were hired in other departments. The court held that sympathy strikers are entitled to nondiscriminatory reinstatement.[370] The fact that such a strike may have been unauthorized by the union, or ill-advised, does not deprive the strikers of the protection of the Act, barring discriminatory treatment when they apply for reinstatement.

When employees engage in a strike in violation of a no-strike clause of an existing labor contract, the employer may: (a) discharge the strikers;[371] (b) refuse to bargain collectively concerning the matters involved in the strike so long as the strike continues;[372] (c) solicit the individual strikers to return to work, provided such offers are conditioned upon acceptance by a specified date;[373] (d) grant wage increases unilaterally to those who return to work;[374] (e) obtain an injunction against the continued violation of the contract.[375]

An employee who wilfully fails to seek or accept other employment affects the amount of the back pay award because he is not entitled to be made whole, by means of the back pay award, for deliberately incurred loss of earnings.[376]

WHERE NEITHER IS RESPONSIBLE

An employer may not be required to reinstate an employee in a position which, because of a loss of business, no longer exists. Especially is this true when the loss of business was caused by a strike for which the employer was not responsible. But the claim of lack of business must be substantiated.[377]

DISQUALIFICATION FOR REINSTATEMENT

Perhaps the most important problem raised in many reinstatement cases is that of demarcating the limits of the "disqualification" doctrine laid down by the Supreme Court in the sitdown strike (Fansteel) decision. The Supreme Court there held that workers who took part in a violent sitdown strike were guilty of such serious misconduct that the Board could not order their reinstatement, even though the strike had been precipitated by

the unfair labor practices of the employer.[378] An employer need not reinstate where employees have engaged in an economic strike unless, at the
time the strikers apply for jobs, there are jobs available for them. The
employer may not discriminate against strikers in hiring future employees.[379] Nor is an employer compelled to take back workers who either
confess their guilt or are proved guilty by the proper judicial authorities
of committing a felony or participation in a conspiracy to commit felony.

According to the Board, misdemeanors do not make an employee unfit
for labor; neither would the reinstatement of those guilty of such behavior
condone or encourage violence in other labor disputes. In its solution of
this problem, the Board considers such factors as the length of the strike
due to the employer's unfair practices, the amount of violence generally
occurring in the area where the strike is current, whether the violence was
solely the fault of the union members, whether the reason for the refusal
to reinstate was the violence or union activities, and the amount of property
damage resulting from the dispute.[380] Even malicious destruction of
property, not used by the employer as the reason for discharge, is no bar
to reinstatement, although there is conflict of authority between the Circuit
Courts of Appeals.[381] Sabotage, as well as physical assault in certain circumstances, has been held to be of such flagrant illegality as to warrant
severance of employment.[382]

Among the acts held not to bar reinstatement are minor offenses, violation of borough ordinances, and trespass.[383] Potential violence is no bar to
reinstatement. Excessive absenteeism may be the cause of forfeiture of
reinstatement and partial back pay although the employee was discharged
for union activity.[384]

TECHNICAL VIOLATION

For several years the National Labor Relations Board adhered to the
policy of requiring employers to reinstate with back pay employees discharged as a result of union pressure in interunion dispute situations. By
a 2 to 1 decision in the *New York and Porto Rico Steamship Company*
case,[385] the Board abandoned this doctrine when it characterized discharges
in such circumstances as amounting only to a "technical" violation of the
Act. Employers who have acted in good faith and have maintained a
neutral attitude regarding union rivalry need neither reinstate the discharged employees nor grant them back pay.

Prior to this decision, the employer had only two courses of action: to
refuse the union's demands and close down his business; or to grant the
union's demands and face charges before the Labor Board. In view of

this decision, however, employers apparently need not fear the penalty of a back pay order if they are coerced by a union into discharging rival union members, *provided they maintain strict neutrality in the interunion rivalry, and their conduct is bona fide in connection with the discharges.*

In a later decision, this doctrine was narrowly limited. Evidently the revolutionary consequences of a rule that employers need not reinstate with back pay employees discharged as a result of union pressure, did not appear to be altogether consistent with the objectives of the Wagner Act.

While the Board recognized its leniency in the *New York and Porto Rico Steamship Company* case, it justified its holding on the ground that the discharges had been made only after several sitdown strikes had occurred in the interunion dispute, and after considerable financial loss. In the *Greer Steel Company* case, the Board reverted to its earlier attitude stressing the only alternative to discharging the employees objected to by the striking union: to cease operations entirely.[386] If the employer is to avail himself of the Board's leniency in the matter of reinstatement, he must be prepared to show that there was an actual, as distinguished from a merely threatened, exercise of the union's economic power; that this union action was for the very purpose of compelling the discharges in question; and that the employer had suffered a probably substantial financial loss.

SAME OR SUBSTANTIALLY EQUIVALENT JOB

The U. S. Supreme Court has held that the Board may require an employer to reinstate an employee discharged in violation of the Labor Act although such employee had obtained substantially equivalent employment elsewhere. The Board must then find that such reinstatement will effectuate the policies of the Act.[387]

REFUSAL TO REINSTATE HELD NO DISCRIMINATION

A company did not discriminatorily refuse to reinstate some employees who had participated in a strike, not caused by its unfair labor practices, because their jobs were filled by replacements during the strike, while other employees were discriminated against in that the company failed to reinstate them to available jobs because of their participation in the strike.[388] Where employees went on strike, because of a dispute concerning the retention of a supervisor, it was held that, since the company had been presented only with a blanket demand for reinstatement of all or none of the employees, there was no unfair labor practice because of the company's refusal to reinstate the strikers on the ground that the positions had been filled.[389]

REINSTATEMENT ORDERED

1. When sabotage was not the cause of the discharge, but the discharge occurred because of the employee's union membership or activity;[390]
2. Where employees have been discharged because of their activity in an economic strike, but the employer was guilty of unfair labor practices which prolonged the strike;[391]
3. For employees who left their jobs voluntarily after the employer had tried to influence them against organizational activities;[392]
4. For employees who were discharged for engaging in a strike to compel the employer to agree with the union's demand for a wage increase, since their action was not in violation of the Economic Stabilization Act nor did they coerce the employer to put wage increases into effect unlawfully prior to War Labor Board approval. But the Board's order for reinstatement was reversed by the Court of Appeals;[393]
5. When an inefficient employee was discharged through a lay-off where a contract, establishing seniority subject to ability of the employee, was in existence and the Board found discrimination;[394]
6. Where an employee was discharged because he struck to force an employer to agree to the union's demand for a wage increase;[395]
7. Where an employer discriminatorily discharged four union employees and later announced that, irrespective of what the Board's decision should be, he was closing his plant and would not reenter the business, the Board terminated back pay for the discharged employees at the time of the closing of the plant, but ordered reinstatement of the employees if the employer should in the future reenter such business;[396]
8. Where union members were evicted from the mill forcibly and by threats of violence. The company had the affirmative duty to offer reinstatement and the evicted employees were justified in refusing to return without a definite guarantee of protection;[397]
9. The offer of an employer to reinstate strikers, on condition that they join a union found to be under his domination, had no effect on termination of back pay. The Circuit Court of Appeals for the Eighth Circuit upheld a Labor Board decision to this effect, taking the view that such tender of a job is not equivalent to a *bona fide* offer to reinstate. This ruling was held to apply even in the case of employees who did not actually apply for their jobs, since, according to the decision, they knew that the opportunity to get back their jobs was subject to this condition;[398]
10. Reinstatement was ordered of a discharged employee who had a record of appropriating goods and money of a previous employer, in view of the fact that the employee had told his employer of his earlier mis-

conduct and had received assurance that he was considered the most trustworthy man on the shift; the discharge had taken place immediately after the employee had appeared wearing a union button, and the employer was engaged in an anti-union campaign;[399]

11. Employees unlawfully discharged by a predecessor corporation are entitled to reinstatement by its successor corporation having the same managerial employees and labor policy; they are not, however, entitled to back pay, since imposition of back pay requirements would amount to a penalty, and an order for reinstatement in the circumstances is sufficient to effectuate the policies of the Labor Act;[400]

12. The fact that employees engaged in a strike without serving the notice of thirty days required by the War Labor Disputes Act did not justify denial of reinstatement or other rights guaranteed by the Wagner Act;[401]

13. Although the employees involved were not the object of discrimination, the Board ordered reinstatement, where four of the strikers entered the armed services during the time the other strikers were discriminated against. The Board declared that if these four workers had not entered the armed forces, they, too, would have been discriminated against and, therefore, were entitled to the same relief as the other strikers;[402]

14. Employees discharged to prevent the occurrence of a contemplated strike were ordered reinstated by the Board.[403]

REINSTATEMENT NOT ORDERED

1. The Board found itself unable to order an employer to reinstate strikers, although the employer had engaged in unfair labor practices, where subsequent to the strike the employer discontinued the particular line of business in which the strikers were engaged and went into another line, requiring only two machine operators of a different class of labor. It ordered the strikers put on a preferential hiring list from which they were to be offered employment should the employer again engage in his former operations;[404]

2. In the "runaway" plant situation, where an employer removes his plant to avoid bargaining, the Board normally has not gone so far as to order the employer to move back again.[405] It has, however, applied a "persuader" by ordering that the employer either return to the original location or else pay moving and transportation expenses for union members and their families. In one case the order gave the employees the option of collecting moving expenses for their families

from the employer or collecting instead pay for bi-weekly transportation to visit their families back home;[406]

3. Members of a minority union, who struck to compel their employer to bargain with the union, were not entitled to compulsory reinstatement or preferential listing, the Circuit Court of Appeals for the Eighth Circuit ruled, to this extent modifying an order of the Labor Board. The Court held that a minority union, in striking for bargaining rights, acts at its own peril so far as reinstatements are concerned.[407] On the other hand, it should be noted that the members of such a minority group are entitled to the protection of the Labor Act against acts of interference and discrimination;[408]

4. No reinstatement was ordered where a group of employees engaged in a "wildcat" strike because of dissatisfaction with the course of negotiations being conducted by the bargaining representative of the employees;[409]

5. Employees who refuse to work with a member of a rival labor union and who strike to compel his discharge are not entitled to the protection of the Act in getting their jobs back, if the employer meanwhile fills the strikers' places with new workers. This ruling by the Labor Board is conditioned on the absence of any unfair labor practice as cause of the strike. In such a situation, the Board says, the employer is entitled to continue his business and to hire whatever employees are necessary for this purpose;[410]

6. Conviction for assault and battery against a nonstriker was held by the Labor Board to be ground for denying an order of reinstatement to an unfair labor practice striker so convicted.[411] Reinstatement in such a case would not effectuate the policy of the Act;

7. Breach of a no-strike agreement was sufficient ground for denying reinstatement to striking employees;[412]

An employer was cleared of having engaged in unfair labor practices where there had been no breach of the contract or unfair labor practices by the employer.[413]

Where employees went on strike to compel an employer to grant wage increases in violation of a law (the National Wage Stabilization Act),[414] reinstatement was denied. Such strikers may be lawfully discharged.

WHO MAY ASK FOR REINSTATEMENT

A discharged employee denied reinstatement by the Labor Board's order has no recourse through the courts. A "person aggrieved" under an order of the Board may appeal to the court pursuant to the Act, but an individual coming before the court on the plea that a reinstatement order of the

Board, by omitting him from its scope, deprives him of reemployment and back wages due, does not qualify under the statute. The Act does not create any private rights in favor of the individual employee.[415]

EVASION

An employer may not defeat the purposes of the Act by reinstating an employee and subsequently discharging him without cause. The employer's offer to reinstate must be specific, unequivocal and more than a mere formality. Ambiguous offers, or those which are subject to misunderstanding by the employee, do not relieve the employer of his duty to reinstate where such an obligation is found to exist.[416] Stating generally to discriminatorily discharged employees that "their positions are open for them and there will be positions open for them at any time they are ready and willing to return to work" has been held insufficient.[417]

5. To Instate

The power to instate may be deemed to be derived from the express grant of authority to reinstate.

In a celebrated decision on this phase of labor relations, an employer refused to hire two applicants for employment solely because of their union affiliations. In affirming the Board's order, the U. S. Supreme Court agreed that such a refusal is an "unfair labor practice" and held that the rejected applicants must be employed with back pay[418] from the date of their application. The Act defines an unfair labor practice to be "by discrimination in regard to hire or tenure of employment or any term or condition of employment to encourage or discourage membership in any labor organization." It is felt that to permit such action by the Board is the only way to deter an employer from an initial violation of the Act.

In accordance with this reasoning, the Board has ordered management to offer to hire strangers or persons with whom no employer-employee relationships had ever existed, and to indemnify them by giving them back pay, up to the amount they would have earned had there been no discrimination.[a]

6. To Pay Back Pay

COMPUTATION

The Act authorizes the Board to order back pay as necessary to redress an injury previously done the employees and to assure them of proper protection if they exercise their rights.[419] The Board issues an order requiring the payment of back pay to effectuate the policies of the Act.[420] "A worker is not given 'back pay' by the Board equal to what he would have earned with the employer but for the unlawful discharge, but is given that sum less any net earnings during the time between discharge and reinstatement."[421]

The Board requires payment to the employee, discharged in violation of the Act, of the amount that such an employee would normally have earned from the date of the illegal discharge to the time of a valid and unconditional offer of reinstatement made by the employer, less the employees' net earnings during the same period. The period during which the back pay accrues can be terminated normally by valid reinstatement of the employee or by making to him a valid and unconditional offer of reinstatement.[422] In some instances, placement of the employee on a preferential list for employment when it becomes available may be sufficient.[423] If during the back pay period the plant was shut down for economic reasons or because of strike, no back pay accrues during such period.[424] Normal reductions in personnel, which would have affected the discharged employee if he had not been discharged, also reduce the amount of the award.[425]

Back pay is computed at the wage rate the employee was receiving at the time of his discharge. He is awarded the advantage of subsequent increases in the rate if such increases would have affected him had he not been discharged.[426] Even tips and bonuses are taken into consideration.[427] The Board deducts from the back pay award whatever "net earnings" the employee earned during the period of the continuance of the unlawful discharge, i.e., the back pay period aforementioned, making an exception, however, for "extra-curricular" work.[428] Back pay may not be reduced by the amount the employees might have earned in equivalent jobs if they had availed themselves of opportunities open, where it is not established that the employees were offered jobs and refused them or that they had wilfully failed to seek employment.[429] However, the employer may deduct three months for a woman employee having a child; but not for her own housework, inasmuch as such housework does not constitute employment and does not give monetary returns.[430] In one case, when the employee obtained employment, the National Labor Relations Board reduced a back pay award to him because he had fraudulently concealed his interim earnings.[431]

Deductible net earnings are decreased by the employees' expenses in seeking new employment, such as transportation costs.[432]

Employees entitled to back pay under order of the Labor Board are entitled to such pay undiminished by any state unemployment compensation which they may have received. The employer is not entitled to benefit by reason of the fact that the employee has received compensation from the state, any more than if he had received assistance from any other party. This decision hinges on the determination that unemployment compensation, paid under the state act, is not "earnings" within the meaning of the Board's order directing payment to a discharged employee of amounts equal to what they normally would have earned, less "net earnings" during the stated period.[433]

From the computation of back pay awarded to employees discriminatorily discharged, the employer may deduct only those sums received by them as wages for services performed. The value of food supplied the employee by a union while the employee was picketing is not to be counted as wages. Thus, where the employer sought to deduct from the back pay the cost of groceries furnished by the union to a discharged employee engaged in picketing during his unemployment, the court found that the groceries were supplied as a gratuity by the union and not as wages and hence their cost might not be deducted from the back pay award.[434]

Despite the prior holdings of the National Labor Relations Board, Social Security Board and Internal Revenue Bureau, withholding taxes are now deductible from a back pay award by the National Labor Relations Board to a wrongfully discharged employee. The award is now interpreted as "wages" within the meaning of Section 466(a) and 1622(a) of the Internal Revenue Code. The employee who receives the award is entitled to credit on his Old Age and Survivors Account under the Social Security Act, since the award constitutes "wages" within the meaning of that Act.[435]

In the event of the death of the discharged employee, the employer is required to pay the back pay, and any insurance benefits accruable, to his estate.[436]

EMPLOYEE'S DUTY TO SEEK OTHER WORK

It has, moreover, been held that there is a duty upon the employee to seek work elsewhere during his period of idleness and by so doing to mitigate damages. But, back pay was ordered despite the failure of employees to seek other jobs, since the failure to look for other work may have been due to such good reasons as distance of other employment from home or inexperience at other work. Back pay may be cut down if the employee fails to make a reasonable attempt to secure other employment. However, registration at the United States Employment Service by the employee is considered a reasonable attempt to secure another job. Under manpower conditions during the war, the Board regarded registration with the United States Employment Service as conclusive.[437] In one case, it was held that an employee did not forfeit back pay by waiting a reasonable period after his discharge before seeking another job.[438] Back pay was, however, denied to a discharged employee during the period he was unable to work because of a confining illness.[439]

An employee discriminatorily discharged, who wilfully failed to secure employment, is not entitled to collect back pay under an award of the Labor Board. To establish such wilful failure it is not enough to show that there was a demand for labor of the type which the employees were capable of performing. Despite the employer's claim that it was impracticable to investigate each individual case of alleged refusal to accept work, the Board takes the view that only evidence relating to each individual is acceptable. But the employer is required to reimburse the employee for expenses incurred while looking for a new job.[440] And an employer found to have moved his place of business in order to escape the employee's union must pay the traveling expenses of the employee and his family.[441]

A primary purpose of the back pay order is to undo the harm done by an unfair labor practice. Back pay is given pursuant to a public proceeding and awarded to effectuate a public policy. It is not a reward to the discharged employee; nor is it a private right. Therefore, an employee discharged would have no right to bring an action in court to initiate a proceeding for back pay or, after the issuance of the Board's order, to bring suit for its collection.

Employees may not assign their right to back pay awarded by the Board.[442] Nor is it subject to attachments or court orders while in the hands of the Board.[443]

STRIKERS

When employees voluntarily strike, no back pay accrues during the period of the strike, even if it is caused or prolonged by the unfair labor practices of the employer.[444] But where there is a lockout or a shutdown by the employer to evade collective bargaining with the employees' designated bargaining agent, back pay will run from the date of such discriminatory acts.[445] Similarly, when the employer discharges an employee during the strike back pay will run from the date of discharge to the date when he was offered reinstatement, unless the discharged employee joins the ranks of the strikers.[446]

BANKRUPT ESTATE OBLIGATED TO PAY BACK PAY

Back wages due employees pursuant to an enforced order of the Labor Board rank ahead of other wage claims against a bankrupt estate.[447] In one case, the trustee of the estate had argued that the Board's order was for the purpose of preventing unfair practices and should be enforced when and if the employer again had employees. The court, however, took the view that the purpose of the order is to effectuate the policies of the Act, explaining that the Board itself is held entitled to make the claim as a "creditor" and trustee on behalf of those employees for the benefit of whom the back pay order was entered.[448]

7. To Disestablish Company-Dominated Union

An order of the Board directing an employer to disestablish a union found to be employer-dominated must be based upon findings that such employer has sponsored, dominated or interfered with the formation or administration of such labor organization or contributed financial or other support to it.[449]

The purposes of such an order are to restore the employees to the position in which they would have been, had there been no violation of the Act, and to protect the rights of employees from further violations of the Act. Together with these purposes, the remedial order fulfills a third important function: to inculcate in the employees confidence sufficient to enable them to exercise freely their right of collective bargaining and full freedom of choice in the designation of a representative for the purposes of collective bargaining.

8. To Protect Union Employees against Nonunion Employees

A "definite guarantee of protection" is required by the Labor Board of an employer in favor of union employees evicted from his plant by a non-union group. Such an eviction is tantamount to the discriminatory discharge of the union employees by the employer. The Board rejected an employer's claim that an ouster was accomplished by nonunion employees without authority from the company and that several supervisory employees participated in the anti-union demonstration.[450] The fact that wages were paid to the employees for the time away from work because of the eviction does not cancel out the discrimination where the employees were not restored to their regular positions. The employer is obligated to restore to their jobs union employees who have been evicted from a plant by nonunion employees.[451] An employer is responsible if he discharges adherents of one union because of threats of evicting them from the plant by a rival union group, although his motive was to avoid a work stoppage.[452]

9. To Disclose Data

Not infrequently, the bargaining agent will request information from the employer for the purposes of collective bargaining. Refusal of the employer to disclose the wage history of its members, such as work done, past increases, and increases from time to time, is indicative of bad faith in bargaining.[453] The Board has attached the same significance to the refusal of the employer to disclose to the union a table of wage rates in his industry, which he admitted to the union he had in his possession. Telling the union representatives, during the bargaining negotiations, to "go out and get them", evidenced lack of good faith on the part of the employer, according to the Board.[454] However, where the union was familiar with the employer's wage incentive plan, and the employer offered to permit the union to go into the plant to make its own engineering studies, the refusal of information concerning the wage incentive plan was held not to indicate bad faith.[455] Furthermore, there must be a showing that the refusal of information impeded the bargaining. In the absence thereof, refusal to furnish some data concerning earnings and production records of certain employees is not an unfair labor practice.[456]

Where the union sought to bargain collectively concerning merit increases, the refusal of the employer to furnish a list of the employees who had received such increases, and the amounts granted, was held a refusal to bargain. Also held illegal was an employer's refusal to bargain as to merit increases, the employer's refusal having been based upon the ground that merit increases are not a bargainable issue but fall in the area of management's prerogatives. Even though the union may have surrendered its right to bargain collectively concerning merit increases by virtue of provisions of the contract, and no bargaining negotiations are pending at the time, the Board has ruled that the employer is obligated to furnish information to the union, at its request, as to merit ratings and increases so that the union can adequately "police" the administration of the contract. Failure to furnish such information constitutes an illegal refusal to bargain collectively.[457]

The New York Labor Board has said that when a union demands higher wages, the failure of the employer to substantiate its claim that it cannot afford wage increases by showing its books is indicative of a refusal to bargain in good faith.[458] On the other hand, the refusal of the union's demand for information as to the number of employees who had been hired to replace economic strikers was held by the National Labor Relations Board not to be a refusal to bargain, where the union insisted on the reinstatement of all of the economic strikers as a group, although jobs were not available for all such strikers.[459]

III · UNFAIR LABOR PRACTICES BY EMPLOYERS

1. Direct Interference with Employees' Rights

INDIVIDUAL CONTRACTS

The Act makes interference by employers with their employees' right to collective bargaining an unfair labor practice which may no longer be engaged in with impunity.[460]

In an effort to head off demands for collective contracts, employers have sometimes insisted that those who obtain or retain jobs with them should sign individual contracts. If such contracts bind the employees not to join an outside union, they are usually known as "yellow dog" contracts. Insistence on such contracts is an illegal form of interference with bargaining rights.[461]

Even when individual contracts leave the employee free to join or not to join any labor organization, they may still be set aside by the Labor Board if, in agreeing to them, the worker contracts away any of his rights under the Labor Act, including the right to authorize a union to represent him in bargaining, to request a union shop, to strike for improved working conditions or any other specific demand which might be made the subject matter of bargaining.[462]

An employer who, in the midst of a known union organization campaign and during the pendency of a proceeding before the Board for determination of bargaining representatives, attempts to have his employees sign individual employment contracts violates the Act, although the contracts on their face contained no illegal terms. The timing of such activity imparts thereto its illegality.

MAINTAINING NEUTRALITY

An employer must remain neutral in an interunion dispute.[463] The duty of the employer to keep his hands off union affairs has thus been summarized by the Court of Appeals for the Eighth Circuit: "Albeit, unwillingly, yet there is no doubt that Glueck participated in a jurisdictional labor dispute and its participation had the effect, well known to it in advance, of favoring one union over the other. It is clear that it had no purpose in the sense of animus or desire—to injure one or to help the other. Its underlying and compelling purpose was to save itself. But to accomplish this result, it consciously interfered in a labor situation by actively favoring one union over another. This was properly held by the Board to be an unfair labor practice under the Act because economic interests of an employer are not valid reasons for violation of the Act."[464]

Quiet endorsement of a union even though by a convenient unawareness on the part of an employer may be interference. The AFL was permitted to collect initiation fees and dues on company time in one case, while employees were warned by supervisors against the CIO union.[465] Even friendly cooperation, if it will enable an employer to exert influence on representatives of employees in bargaining, is forbidden by the Act, the Court of Appeals ruled, thus holding in effect that such "cooperation" is an improper means of influencing the party with whom there may be a duty to bargain.[466] However, even the requirement for maintaining strict neutrality has limitations and does not silence the employer completely.

The Court of Appeals upheld an employer's right to express himself on union matters prior to an election ordered by the Board.[467] In issuing what were concededly anti-union statements, the employer told employees that they must make their own choice; he was not coercive nor did he threaten loss of benefits or reprisals. Such statements, on their face, may appeal to employees' reason, but must not be coercive nor may they indicate there will be any loss of benefits if unionization is successful; and they must be offered only as opinions.

After the Supreme Court decision in *NLRB. v. Virginia Power* [468] (and prior to amendment of the Act) employers were permitted to:
1. Disseminate facts within the area of dispute;
2. Comment impartially on the merits of the controversy, even though it involve labor organizations, but without making any anti-labor statements or references derogatory to the union and its representatives;
3. Indicate a preference for individual dealings with employees;
4. State their policy with reference to labor matters.

These privileges, however, must be considered with the next section (see "Speech as Interference," below).

Pending an election for the determination of bargaining representative, to be conducted by the Board, the employer may not give preferential treatment to any one of the unions involved, and the execution of a closed shop agreement with one of them constitutes such illegal preference.[469] But where there was a valid preexisting closed shop agreement which had not been enforced insofar as the closed shop provision thereof was concerned, the parties to the contract might validly agree orally that such provision should be enforced during the pendency of an election proceeding before the Board, and require employees to join the contracting union, in the absence of any evidence that any one was discharged for not joining that union or that any employee's activities on behalf of the rival union were in any way restricted.[470]

SPEECH AS INTERFERENCE

In considering whether conduct or speech is a form of interference, the Board and the court will give consideration to an employer's past record of anti-unionism. It is true that "unless the right of free speech is enjoyed by employers as well as by employees, the guarantee of the First Amendment is futile, for it is fundamental that the basic rights guaranteed by the Constitution belong equally to every person;" but the Labor Act prohibits as an unfair labor practice all interference with or restraint or coercion of employees in the exercise of their rights. Unlawful statements may be patently intimidating, may be coupled with a threat to move the plant, may make use of epithets such as "racketeers" or "parasites," or depict unions as rotten or corrupt and interested only in their own monetary advancement.

Held interference under the Wagner Act were making statements disparaging unions, and intended to forestall formation of an outside union; anticipating union demands and opposing them; expressing disparaging jibes at the results of an election; and disseminating anti-union propaganda through bulletins, bulletin boards, executive letters, and articles in magazines and newspapers; stating that a wage increase can be secured only through the WLB and not through the union seeking to be the bargaining agent; stating that the employer would continue to bargain with individual employees and that the election might result in the minority imposing its will on the majority; advertising for the purpose of warning the employees against voting for the union; circulating among employees a paper which indulged in name-calling of union organizers, carrying subtle threats against employees for union membership and misleading the employees about their bargaining rights; and telling plant guards that they would cease to be guards if they sought to join the contracting union, despite the employer's belief that his statement was true.[471]

The foregoing examples reflect the law as it stood prior to the amendment of the Act. They are of importance because, although the right to express "views, argument or opinion" is stated in the amended Act, such expressions are unlawful if coercive, and the line of demarcation may not be clarified with respect to borderline expressions until a substantial body of decisions under the new Act has been evolved. Some distinction as a result of the amendment to the Act was pointed out by the Second Circuit Court of Appeals in a case involving the effect of the amended Act. That Court said ". . . statements by representatives of the respondent derogatory to unions, union members, or union organization, but falling short of threats, intimidation, or promises of favor or benefit would not be unlawful if presently made and thus could not now be forbidden."[472]

CONDUCT AS INTERFERENCE

Conduct which disproves expressed impartiality, and misplaced emphasis in notices of impartiality, have been held to be interference.[473]

The presence of employer's representatives at the polls and their expression of preference for and dislike of a particular organization precludes the casting of a ballot which registers the free and independent choice of the employees, and constitutes interference with a free election.[474] Similarly the holding of elections by an employer without the consent of all labor organizations was held to be interference, irrespective of the form of the ballot.[475] Even if the mechanics of the ballot are not impeached and the election is not motivated by any desire of the employer to aid one union and discourage another, the results of an election so conducted by an employer cannot, according to the Board, reflect an accurate and independent expression by the employees of their free choice of representatives. Although the unfavored union did not ask for permission to use the plant for organizational purposes, the use of the ballot so as to suggest adverse criticism of a union and create the implication that a nonunion vote was desired, was held an interference. However, the Court of Appeals for the Sixth Circuit held that an employer who polled his employees as to whether they were for or against the union did not violate the Act, where he told the employees that he wanted to know what they wanted before submitting bids for certain timber; and the employer expressed no threats or hostility to the union.[a]

Even though there be an open ballot, it is not indicative that the employees' choice was free. Attempts to keep employees from voting, misleading or distorted statements, or celebration of anti-union results, have all been held to constitute interference, and merely posting a notice of neutrality does not purge the prior derogatory statements of their illegality.[476] One court granted an injunction against a company to prevent its interference with an employee election. The National Labor Relations Board had cancelled one election because the company had sent voters to the polls on working time, barred them from the plant if they had not voted, told them how to vote and issued various threats in the event the CIO won the election. The purpose of the injunction was to restrain the employer from such practices in the second election.[477]

ESPIONAGE

Espionage or surveillance of union members or activities is an unfair labor practice.[478] This may be exerted by a system of reports and checks, through either nonemployees or employees, e.g., specialty salesmen to accompany regular salesmen. However, a card system utilized to check thievery is not an unfair practice, but a mere allegation to that effect is not enough.

Questioning concerning union membership or activity of employees generally constitutes a violation.[479] The fact that the interrogator was alleged to have had no authority to question or that there was no discrimination is of no avail. But where the information was voluntary, the employer is not guilty of interference.[480] Thus, interrogating prospective witnesses concerning material and necessary testimony is not deemed an interference.[481] Cessation of previous practices does not justify the conclusion that they will not be repeated; accordingly, a prohibition of discontinued espionage has been sustained.[482] Enlisting the aid of employees, attempts to disorganize the union, the use of employer's guards to accompany union organizers, and the employer's attendance at union meetings through officers or supervisors have been held to constitute interference.[483]

ECONOMIC COERCION

The exercise of economic coercion to forestall unionization, undermine a majority bargaining agency or induce adherence to or membership in a company-dominated union is an interference. This may be exerted through wage increases, particularly prior to an election; granting of bonuses, gratuities, or company stock never before given; paying a bonus to strikers who return to work while withholding it from those continuing to strike; granting participation in a stock purchase plan; promising permanent employment rather than lay-offs; threatening loss of bonus and removal of the plant, and offering as the alternative, promotions and vacations with pay; and threatening reduction of force and change in method of operation.[484]

Evictions from company houses and company towns is a form of economic coercion constituting interference.[485] Systematic undermining and destruction of employee self-organization through professional spies; hiring of employees as special police; and hiring of "missionaries," union wreckers, and police have been held to constitute interference.[486] Where the police are not controlled by the employer, their violence is not attributable to him; the employer is liable, nevertheless, where the violence was observed and encouraged by company executives. Use of civic organizations to encourage hostility toward a union in municipal administration, recourse to local ordinances, the employment of state militia, and sponsoring a back-to-work movement where the strike resulted from unfair labor practices, constituted interference.[487] The holding of a strike vote by the employer subsequent to the passage of an authorized strike resolution was held to be a violation of the law.[488]

HELD DIRECT INTERFERENCE

1. Accepting an offer by the majority of the employees to abandon their union in return for a wage increase;[489]
2. Accosting strikers on a picket line when the purpose was to persuade them to cease picketing and abandon the strike;[490]
3. Actively assisting a union in an election to determine whether an AF of L or CIO union or no union was acceptable;[491]
4. Actively assisting one of rival unions;[492]
5. Agreeing in a contract to consult with the union over individual wage increases and then acting unilaterally with respect to them;[493]
6. Sponsoring, aiding, abetting and actively assisting and cooperating with a citizens' committee in its anti-union campaign;[494]
7. Announcing that in no case will employers sign a closed shop contract with a union that has not yet asked for bargaining rights.[495] But when the announcement was in response to inquiries by employees, the statement was held proper and not coercive under the circumstances;[496]
8. Making anti-union statements during a union's organizational drive; threats to discharge; threats "to lock the doors before I have a union"; statement by the company's president that the mill would be shut; and similar statement of the company's attitude by the traffic manager;[497]
9. Appealing to employees' patriotism to forestall unionization;[498]
10. Molesting and routing of union organizers in the presence of employees;[499]
11. Asking employees about their union membership or activities;[500]
12. Assisting a nationally affiliated union in organizational efforts;[501]
13. Assisting a union in securing new members, even though a *bona fide* national organization;[502]
14. Attacking a union organizer in the presence of employees;[503]
15. Attempting to break a strike by meeting with individual employees;[504]
16. Blacklisting or threatening to blacklist employees who had filed charges with the Board;[505]
17. Bringing employees into the conference room when management and

union confer, where they remained throughout the discussion without the knowledge or consent of the union; and reading an anti-union statement;[506]

18. Urging employees not to testify at a Board hearing;[507]

19. Under the Wagner Act, conveying to employees the employer's hostile attitude toward outside unions by bulletin board notices, or circulating among employees pamphlets or newspaper editorials conveying this point of view, or misrepresenting their rights under the law;[508]

20. Under the Wagner Act, creating the impression that a labor organization is unnecessary;[509]

21. Under the Wagner Act, declaring against closed shop when none is asked;[510]

22. Warning supervisors of demotion to a nonsupervisory position because of their activity in an outside union (under the Wagner Act);[511]

23. Denying or threatening to deny employees the customary benefits and privileges if they joined the union;[512]

24. Denying organizers access to employees, e.g., the use of streets in company-owned towns;[513]

25. Depriving active union members of their status as employees and of their seniority standing, because of their participation in an economic strike;[514]

26. Discharging for participation in a wildcat strike, although in at least two such cases the courts have refused to enforce reinstatement of wildcat strikers;[515]

27. Discharging satisfactory employees for unionization;[516]

28. Discouraging union affiliation, disparaging unions and questioning of employees on union activity by supervisors;[517]

29. Discriminatory application of any alleged company rule forbidding union activities;[518]

30. Distributing literature and making statements to the employees containing veiled threats in the event the union won an election;[519]

31. Ejecting union organizers from a company-owned town or plant;[520]

32. Encouraging the formation of an independent union, by meetings and by addresses made by its officers, and granting such union special benefits as well as use of company time and property;[521]

33. Enforcing a nonsolicitation rule outside of working hours, although such activity occurs on the employer's property;[522]

34. Enlisting the aid of a citizens' committee or of an employers' association, through the employer's financial power or influence in the community, to stamp out unionism by force or other pressure;[523]

35. Evicting by nonunion employees of union members from the plant. The Board held that the company had the affirmative duty of reinstating and protecting the evicted employees;[524]

36. Exacting a promise to abstain from various lawful acts;[525]

37. Expressing of opinion hostile to unions or to a particular union, where the employer himself addressed the workers, or where supervisory officials, particularly those having the right to hire and fire, conveyed the employer's anti-union views to the employees, where the text of such statements or the circumstances under which they were made indicated coercion upon the employees;[526]

38. Financing, during the course of a strike, a back-to-work movement, and paying salaries of deputy sheriffs or supplying them with weapons to assist in breaking the strike.[527] Their acts were interpreted as those of the employer;

39. Interfering with distribution of union literature outside the plant;[528]

40. Holding a meeting of employees at a time when the employer was negotiating with the union, at which the employees were urged to take a different position from that of their designated bargaining agent;[529]

41. Ignoring a letter from the union relating to bargaining rights and offering the employees individual contracts;[530]

42. Influencing representational elections, as evidenced by making exceptional loans to employees and celebrating the defeat of the union by distributing gifts and liquor;[531]

43. Interfering in organizational campaigns of rival unions;[532]

44. Intimidating union organizers or union members;[533]

45. Investigating union affiliations, and warnings to employees by the president to watch their step and not to do anything for which they would be sorry;[534]

46. Inducing an important customer of the employer to make an anti-union speech (under the Wagner Act);[535]

47. Misrepresenting the Act, by distribution of a pamphlet emphasizing what the Wagner Act does *not* purport to do, rather than the rights established by the Act; a statement presenting a distorted concept of employees' rights thereunder, and in no part describing the purposes and policies of the Act; and explaining the Act to employees in such a manner as to underline its negative aspects;[536]

48. Notifying the employees that they should resign from the union, sending employees' letters of resignation to the union and inducing them to take concerted action along such lines;[537]

49. Inducing employees to bargain individually as to wages despite the existence of a bargaining representative;[538]

50. Withholding from union members of loans made personally by company president, where employees reasonably believed the loans were made by the company;[539]

51. Parent corporation's illegal interference with the employees of a subsidiary, through the latter, where the subsidiary is wholly owned and its labor policies and operation are conducted by the parent;[540]

52. Participating in a pre-election campaign to choose a bargaining representative, to the extent of urging all employees to vote; held by the Board to be unlawful interference with employee rights when the employer's attitude or surrounding circumstances were such as to indicate that the advice amounted to coercing employees to vote against the union or suffer possible loss of benefits enjoyed if they voted for the union;[541]

53. Executing a contract with one of two rival unions while the rival union's petition for an election was pending before the Board;[542]

54. Enforcing against union members a plant rule prohibiting conversation and not enforcing the rule against nonunion members;[543]

55. Prohibiting the discussion of union affairs on company property outside of working hours, where safety and production are not normally affected and the rule was not applied to a company-dominated committee;[544]

56. Prohibiting union solicitation when anti-union solicitation is permitted;[545]

57. Proposing to the employees an agreement with "better than union" wages, during negotiations with the bargaining representative;[546]

58. Questioning employees preparatory to a Labor Board hearing when not necessary to the defense. The employees declared at the hearing that answers given to the employer were determined by what he desired to hear. The employees surmised what would happen if they answered otherwise;[547]

59. Refusing a wage increase to the union, but later granting it to employees without any notice to the union;[548]

60. Requiring employees to execute contracts restricting their right to strike, etc.;[549]

61. Shutting down a plant to defeat efforts at organization by a union;[550]

62. Sponsoring and assisting an organization rivaling the union;[551]

63. Tendering a contract to the union, which the latter refused; whereupon the employer called a mass meeting of the employees, urged the union

president to sign and, on refusal, criticized the union's bargaining committee and suggested that the union elect another president and vote favorably on the contract;[552]

64. Threatening to close the plants if an outside union succeeded in organizing employees;[553]

65. Threatening to move the plant;[554]

66. Refusing to give former employees recommendations for other jobs because of their union activity;[555]

67. Threatening demotion, discharge, curtailed production, loss of job, deprivation of holidays, and loss of employment, unless striking employees returned to work;[556]

68. Threatening to shut down or liquidate the business, to contract out, to install labor-saving machinery to replace employees or to remove the plant, unless satisfactory labor relations could be reached.[557] But a shutdown may be beyond remedy by a Board order, since industry cannot be forced to function;

69. Timing of a bonus;[558]

70. Transferring operations involving union members to another employer where both employers had a closed shop contract with their unions and the new employer was obliged to hire only those employees who joined the rival union;[559]

71. Using employment application forms which require disclosure of union affiliation;[560]

72. Using force by company guards to prevent the distribution of union literature on the public streets near a company plant;[561]

73. Keeping under surveillance union members, union meetings and meeting places, and union organizers or leaders;[562]

74. Entering into a collective bargaining agreement with a union while a proceeding or a petition filed by a rival union for investigation and certification of bargaining representative is pending before the Labor Board;[563]

75. Discharging an employee because he filed a charge with or supplied information to or testified before the Board or its agents;[564]

76. Refusing permission to employees to leave the plant to testify as witnesses in a representation case before the Board;[565]

77. Unilateral institution of a grievance procedure, thereby precluding the certified bargaining agent from taking up grievances until the execution of a written agreement;[556]

78. Prohibiting employees from wearing union caps during working hours;[567]

79. Prohibiting collections of any sort in the plant where union activity has been restricted during nonworking hours;[568]
80. Renewing or executing an exclusive bargaining contract with one of two competing unions while a representation petition was pending before the Board.[569]

2. Indirect Interference (by Supervisory Employees)

Under the Act, as amended, a supervisory employee is generally a representative of the management if he is acting as agent of the employer, and whether his acts were actually authorized or subsequently ratified is not controlling.[570] An employer is liable for the conduct and statements of supervisory employees which might constitute interference in the circumstances, and has thus been held responsible for permitting supervisory employees to coerce employees into joining a union.[571]

In his managerial capacity, a supervisory employee is feared because of the influence that his power to hire and fire might have if used to discourage union membership. Under the Wagner Act the Board uniformly held a company responsible for any anti-union activity on the part of its supervisory personnel, whether or not such acts were known to the company, and even if done in direct defiance of orders or in the face of a declaration of neutrality on the part of the employer.[572] The Board will not inquire into the actual effect of such acts in individual cases. It is sufficient that they are inherently capable of influencing the employees' choice.[573] Thus, anti-union activity on the part of a shipping master who allegedly had no power to hire or discharge was held by the National Labor Relations Board to implicate the employer, despite the fact that the management declared that it had disavowed the anti-union statements of its representative, since the latter was retained and the disavowal was not made effective within the knowledge of the employees.[574] Furthermore, there was no evidence that other officers of the company knew of the shipping master's part in forming two inside unions. Passes were denied to representatives of this organization and it was not recognized or dealt with. The Board found, however, that the inside union would not have existed but for the acts of the shipping master, whom the employees regarded as part of the management.

Should the supervisor be a union member, he may, in certain circumstances, use his power as an instrument of company control. The Board, therefore, regards even the slightest participation by such supervisory employees in the formation or the administration of a company union as domination or interference on the part of the company. It is not enough for an employer to issue instructions to supervisors that they should not discuss union matters with employees, especially when such instructions are issued only after charges have been filed. Moreover, such instructions must be made effective and be publicized to the employees.[575]

HELD INDIRECT INTERFERENCE

1. Permitting a committee of an inside union, opposing an outside union, to pass on reinstatement of strikers who belonged to the outside union;[576]
2. Activities on behalf of an inside union by an official of a town association;[577]
3. Anti-union conduct of supervisory employees although they were warned not to engage therein, upon request of a complaining union;[578]
4. Unauthorized anti-union conduct of supervisory employees who followed pattern of employer's conduct;[579]
5. Supervisory aid to an inside union, despite company instructions not to engage in such conduct and no effective means were taken to enforce instructions;[580]
6. Supervisory conduct although employer publicly disavowed such conduct to the employees, where employer failed to enforce supervisor's widespread and continued disregard of such avowal of neutrality;[581]
7. Circulation of anti-union petition in plant, to knowledge of supervisors, and employer failed to disavow such conduct on acquiring notice thereof;[582]
8. Failure to disavow to employees conduct of supervisors in support of an employer-controlled union;[583]
9. Coercive statements of supervisor to employees who were not the immediate subordinates of such supervisor, where employees did not believe that the statements were true;[584]
10. Solicitation by foremen of membership in an inside union and discouraging membership in an outside union, despite posting of employer's notices of neutrality;[585]
11. Acquiescence by plant manager in anti-union violence;[586]
12. Anti-union conduct of local Chamber of Commerce instigated by an employer;[587]
13. Anti-union conduct by outsiders acting as agents for the employer;[588]
14. Failure to disavow statements by a trade association that employer would move plant from community if employees were unionized;[589]
15. Anti-union conduct engaged in by employee at the direction and request of employer;[590]

16. Anti-union conduct through an employer association formed for
purposes of collective bargaining.[591]

In an early case the Board pointed out that in considering the employer's
responsibility for the anti-union conduct of his supervisory staff, instructions
for neutrality to them and general announcements of neutrality to employees would not in themselves insulate the employer from responsibility,
but would be viewed in the light of (a) status of the supervisors involved,
(b) effect of their statements upon the employees, (c) action taken by the
employer to eradicate any impression created upon the employees by
the supervisors' conduct, and (d) attitude of the employer toward unionization of employees.[592] An employer is not responsible for anti-union statements made to a person not an employee and not repeated to employees.[593]
Threats of reprisal for union activity made by one supervisor to another,
but not repeated to employees, were not attributed to the employer.[594]
However, coercive statements of a supervisor to a very small number of
a large contingent of employees constituted employer interference, because
of the fact that such statements spread among the employees.[595] Somewhat
similarly, an employer was held responsible for a threat made by a supervisor jokingly, where the threat gained widespread circulation in the
plant and the employer failed to disavow it.[596] However, an employer was
not held responsible for a supervisor's isolated statement expressing his
own personal feelings or opinions.[597] But expressed personal opinions of
supervisors may be a basis for employer responsibility when viewed in
the light of an employer anti-union campaign,[598] despite testimony of
employees that they understood the statements to be personal opinion,
rather than company attitude, and that they had no effect on their relationship to the union.[599]

3. Coercion

For many years the Board gave decisive weight to the conclusion that
employees yielded to "slight" suggestions of their employers, and enforced
the Wagner Act on the assumption that any expression of opinion by an
employer on the subject of unionization was necessarily coercive.[600] The
courts, however, gave greater recognition to the privilege of free speech,
although recognizing the employer's economic superiority over the employee. As a result of these cases, the Board in its later decisions under
the Wagner Act recognized the employer's right of freedom of expression
and recognized the constitutional guaranty when, in its opinion, the employer "made no threat of any sort", and coupled his statements "with

clear expressions assuring the employees that" he "would not resort to reprisal to retaliate against any exercise of any right guaranteed in the Act."[601] The Board considered the acts of the employer in determining whether his words were merely an exercise of his right to freedom of speech or an attempt at coercing his employees. Hence anti-union words become coercive when accompanied by anti-union acts.[602] In one case the court held that an employer's speeches, when considered together with all the facts and circumstances, showed a purpose of interference, intimidation and coercion.[603]

These cases are predicated upon the theory of the Supreme Court that:

> Certainly, conduct, though evidenced in part by speech, may amount, in connection with other circumstances, to coercion within the meaning of the Act. If the total activities of an employer restrain or coerce his employees in their free choice, then those employees are entitled to the protection of the Act. And in determining whether a course of conduct amounts to restraint or coercion, pressure exerted vocally by the employer may no more be disregarded than pressure exerted in other ways. For slight suggestions as to the employer's choice between unions may have telling effect among men who know the consequences of incurring that employer's strong displeasure.[604]

It remains for court decisions to determine whether this "total activities" doctrine has been overruled by the amended Act whereunder expressions of "views, argument or opinion" cannot constitute or be evidence of an unfair labor practice "if such expression contains no threat of reprisal or force or promise of benefit."[605]

4. Distinction between Free Speech and Coercion

The distinction between an employer's freedom of speech and the use of unlawful vocal pressure is not easily drawn, since slight suggestions by the employer may have undue influence among men who know the consequences of incurring the employer's displeasure. A statement by an employer in the nature of a threat will not be countenanced, even though there is no other background of coercion; and intense or extremely forceful opinion, even in the absence of a policy of discrimination and the element of threat, has been held coercive.[606] Also interpretation of the Wagner Act which was misleading, unfair and distorted,[607] was held to be unlawful.

It is wise to remember that the court is not always the judge of what may be said or what must not be said. This is initially the function of the National Labor Relations Board. In the absence of arbitrary conduct, the Board's ruling will generally remain undisturbed if supported by substantial evidence. And this ruling has been predicated upon the background and context of the talk as well as the mere words.[608] Where the Board found that the employer, in addition to his anti-union words, also discriminatorily discharged union members and refused to recognize a majority union, management could not claim its constitutional prerogative of free speech.

HELD COERCIVE UNDER WAGNER ACT

The following types of expressions were held coercive utterances under the Wagner Act (probably allowable under present Act):

1. Union officials are more interested in dues than in the welfare of employees, and the workers would do better to leave the determination of wages to the company;[609]
2. No employee need pay tribute to a labor organization to hold his job, such organization being referred to pointedly as a group of "outsiders";[610]
3. Unions never did anybody any good;[611]
4. Unionization would create a wall and barrier between employer and employees, and employees could not gain anything thereby which they could not obtain individually;[612]
5. Informing the employees that a particular union, opposed by the employer, would impose a wage scale which would result in curtailment of work and personnel;[613]
6. Statements uttered in a context of anti-union campaign;[614]
7. Charge that union was just a bunch of racketeers trying to collect dues and it won't get you anywhere in the end;[615]
8. Publication by an employer of a circular to the effect that employees need not pay dues to outsiders to obtain collective bargaining.[616]

Not only has the employer been held for his own remarks, but in one case he was held liable for the conduct of an ordinary employee in thanking other employees for their anti-union activity, when the statement was made in the presence of the employer without any objection on his part.

5. Domination of a Labor Organization

The Act prohibits an employer from dominating or interfering with the formation or administration of any labor organization or contributing financial or other support to it.[617]

The company union clause of the Act has been broadly interpreted so as to outlaw any conduct of an employer which is designed to bring into being an organization of employees that will function as his creature.

Opinions differ widely as to the circumstances which will render an "inside" or unaffiliated union illegal under the Act.

The test in determining whether a union is employer-controlled is not an objective one but rather subjective, from the standpoint of employees. As was said in the case of *International Association of Machinists v. NLRB,* "If the employees would have just cause to believe that solicitors professedly for a labor organization were acting for and on behalf of the management, the Board would be justified in concluding that they did not have the complete and unhampered freedom of choice which the Act contemplates."[618]

The law prohibits the formation of employees' associations which, though ostensibly independent, are really influenced though *ever so slightly* by the management. An association of employees may not be recognized as representing the employees for collective bargaining purposes under the Act when it once appears that the management has had a hand in its formation, or has supported it or in any wise interfered with its administration. On the other hand, employees have the right freely to organize themselves, if they wish, into "inside" associations. It is as much the duty of the National Labor Relations Board to protect such an association as it is to destroy an employer-dominated union. In determining whether an unaffiliated labor organization has been free of employer domination, interference and support, Congress intended that criteria applicable to nationally affiliated unions should also be applied to unaffiliated or inside unions. Intimate contact between members of an inside association and the management in seeking better wages and hours may amount to no more than "the normal relations and innocent communications which are a part of all friendly intercourse, albeit between employer and employee, recognized and approved by the Supreme Court."

The fact that a union's constitution, adopted by secret vote, excludes employer participation in its affairs, is operated democratically, and a check-off arrangement with the employer is carried out at the request of individual members, is no defense to a charge of domination. The issue is, according to the Board, not what choice the employees had made, but whether their choice *was free*. The very existence of the favored inside union and its recognition by the employer are held to preclude a free choice. Even though the National Labor Relations Board has designated a union as bargaining agent, there is nothing to prevent it from later declaring the union to be company-dominated and ordering it to be disestablished.

An employer has been exonerated of charges that he dominated an inside employee organization, although in circumstances which the Labor Board declared "raises serious questions as to its independence" in view of its formation and administration and expressions by the employer that he preferred an inside union to an outside union.[619]

DISAVOWAL OF DOMINATED UNION

When a union is ordered disestablished, there must be more than a mere mechanical separation or casual dismissal. There must be a disavowal in good faith of the disqualified union under such circumstances as could reasonably be expected to convince the body of its employees that from that time on no particular union would receive the employer's favor and none would be burdened with his hostility; and that, so far as the company's interest in the matter was concerned, every employee in the plant was free to make any choice of collective bargaining representative that he might desire.[620]

BURDEN OF PROOF

The burden of establishing that a union was company-dominated is upon the Board. It must be remembered that what the statute defines as an unfair labor practice on the part of the employer is not merely an atmosphere of friendliness, a sense of mutual interest between employer and employee. Positive evidence must be produced of employer domination. Mere ineffectiveness of a union is no indication of domination on the part of the employer.

The Act prohibits the employer from interfering with, restraining or coercing employees in the exercise of their rights to self-organization, to form, join or assist labor organizations, to bargain collectively through representatives of their own choosing, and to engage in concerted activities for the purpose of collective bargaining or for their mutual aid and protection, and from interfering with the formation or organization of any labor organization, or contributing financial or other support to it. It nowhere provides, and there is no warrant in it for the view, that preference by employees for, and their selection of, an unaffiliated as against a nationally affiliated organization, raises any presumption that this preference was coerced or purchased by the employer. The statute goes on a presumption exactly the contrary of this, that employees have the intelligence and character requisite to self-organization either by joining or assisting a labor organization or forming one of their own.

The amended Act corrects the disparity of treatment between affiliated and nonaffiliated unions under the Wagner Act. In cases of illegal aid or assistance or support of a nationally affiliated union, the Board's complaint did not allege company domination and its order, consequently, did not require disestablishment of such an organization. Such disestablishment would permanently bar that union from, at any time in the future, acting as bargaining representative for the employee. However, when nonaffiliated unions were involved, the charge of company domination was made in the complaint and disestablishment was ordered, with the result that such organization never could represent employees. The amended Act expressly requires that in determining whether a complaint should be issued, and in deciding the cases, the same rules must be applied without regard to affiliation.[621]

The court, in the exercise of an informed discretion, will determine, first, whether the findings are supported by substantial evidence and second, whether the Board's orders are within the reasonably broad discretion conferred by the Act, appropriate to effectuate its policies, or constitute an abuse of that discretion.[622]

In determining when unions are company-dominated, it will be helpful to select diversified situations in which such domination has been held to exist.

CRITERIA OF DOMINATION

1. Appearance to the employees that the employer continued to show preference to the new organization. The test of successorship is the appearance of continuity and relation between the preceding illegal organization and the later organization, so that the employees were not apprised of the fact that the new organization did not carry with it the preference, domination, and interference which accompanied the prior organization;[623]

2. Cooperation, if it will enable an employer to exert influence on representatives of employees in bargaining, since it amounts to an improper means of influencing the party with whom there may be a duty to bargain. The mere fact that the employees are concurrently informed of their rights under the Act, and that there will be no discrimination against them for exercising such rights, will not clear management of the charge of domination;[624]

3. The continuation in responsible posts in a new organization of employees who were officers in two earlier company-dominated organizations (though continuation in and of itself has been held not to constitute domination);[625]

4. Contribution of financial support to a union, e.g., by extending credit, by not requiring prompt payment from it for rent of a vending machine and a place of meeting; renting of a vending machine at a nominal charge, though large profits were reaped from it;[626]

5. Permitting solicitation for members in a plant during working hours;[627]
6. The formation of an organization with employer assistance to prevent the success of outside unions;[628]
7. Supervisors' participation in the formation of an inside union;[629]
8. Employee participation limited to the annual selection of representatives who, to hold office, had to continue in employment and had to have one year of service to be eligible for nomination;[630]
9. Employer presenting a plan of organization to the employees;[631]
10. Counsel for the employer obtained a corporate charter for an inside union upon petition of employees, signed under threats of discharge, although a shop committee provided for never was designated and never functioned.[632]

EVIDENCE OF DOMINATION

The following situations have been held evidence of company domination:
1. Employer aid through financial contribution;[633]
2. Automatic membership;[634]
3. Absence of dues;[635]
4. Presenting an unrequested contract to an inside union and pressing for negotiations;[636]
5. Company retaining power to terminate the tenure of an employee representative by discharge, transfer or promotion;[637]
6. Company reserving equal number of votes with employee representatives on the Joint Committee, and veto of employees' action;[638]
7. Lack of a contract with the organization and employer's breach of one made with a committee of the organization, without protest from the organization;[639]
8. Company suggestion of an inside union at a time when an outside union began its organizational drive;[640]
9. Dominant membership of supervisors or control by supervisors;[641]
10. Domination by virtue of rules;[642]
11. Employers limiting employees to the choice of fellow employees as representatives on the Joint Committee and thereby depriving them of an opportunity to select expert outside representatives whom they might desire;[643]
12. Giving employees to understand that their jobs depended upon their joining the "independent" union;[644]
13. Granting of various privileges, such as the use of bulletin boards, company rooms for meeting, or the right to organize during working hours, although denying these privileges to the "outside" union;[645]
14. Hasty recognition of the "independent" union as the bargaining rep-

resentative without proof that it represented a majority of the workers;[646]

15. Permitting the union to hold annual elections on company time and property and furnishing physical equipment necessary for the election;[647]

16. Representation of departments only by employees in such departments, thus making it possible for the company to remove individual representatives by transferring them to new departments;[648]

17. Requirement that officers must be employees for a specific length of time;[649]

18. Furnishing a legal adviser to an inside union.[650]

Thus, the Board has castigated an employee representation plan, a goodwill club, a collective bargaining committee, a department council, and an organization designed to get striking employees "back to work."[651]

In some cases disestablishment was ordered, even though evidence existed of the employees' preference.

If the organization purports to function as a collective bargaining agency, the employer must in no wise interfere with it or support it.

In *NLRB v. Newport News Company,* the Supreme Court stated:[652]

The Board has concluded that the provisions embodied in the final revision, whereby action of the Committee requires, for its effectiveness, the agreement of the company, and whereby amendment of the plan can become effective only if the company fails to signify its disapproval within fifteen days of adoption, still give the respondent such power of control that the plan is in the teeth of the expressed policy and the specific prohibitions of the Act. The respondent argues that these provisions affect only the company and not the employes; that, in collective bargaining, there is always reserved to the employer the right to qualify or to reject the propositions advanced by the employes. Whatever may be said of the first mentioned provision, this explanation will not hold for the second. The plan may not be amended if the company disapproves the amendment. Such control of the form and structure of an employe organization deprives the employes of the complete freedom of action guaranteed to them by the Act, and justifies an order such as was here entered.

In the *Southern Bell Company* case, the Supreme Court summarized some of the evidence indicative of company domination, as follows:[653]

There is testimony that in April and May, 1935, just before the passage of the National Labor Relations Act, the Association's president, Askew, in anticipation of the passage of the act, successfully canvassed the membership for fifty cent contributions so that the Association would have its own funds and be able to operate after the bill became a law. The Company aided the solicitation with advice, automobile transportation and expenses for the solicitors. Over five thousand dollars was raised. Three Association officials actively engaged in the fund raising. Askew, the President, Weil, the vice-president and soon to be president, and Wilkes, the acting treasurer, were employees having close touch with the company management. Askew was a state cashier, Wilkes was secretary to key officials, and Weil, plant practice supervisor, a position described by him as covering the distribution and explanation to the proper employees of printed routine job instructions.

In short, a labor organization is found to be company-dominated when a series of acts of an employer, when taken as a whole, reveal that the organization is not a freely functioning association truly representative of the employees. No single act is generally regarded as determinative of company domination. However, the National Labor Relations Board has indicated that the factors of substantial continuity of constitution and bylaws and *identity of officers* might be sufficient to establish company domination.[654]

Where the employer not only participated in considering any action which the governing body under a "Representation Plan" might desire to take, but finally determined what that action should be, the employer was held never to have afforded his employees freedom of choice for purposes of collective bargaining, and the "Plan" was held to be dominated.[655]

Where a labor organization is company-dominated, it may be disestablished, and the contract made between it and an employer may be set aside, although neither the organization nor its members is made a party to the proceeding.[656]

The Rules and Regulations of the National Labor Relations Board under the Wagner Act required that a copy of its complaint, alleging company-domination, and notice of hearing be served on the alleged company-dominated organization and that that organization might, on application, receive full rights to participate in the proceedings on the issue of company-domination if it so desired.[657]

The Rules and Regulations of the Board, issued under the amended Act, achieve substantially the same result by including within the definition of the term "party" any labor organization alleged to be illegally dominated, supported or assisted.[658] They also require service of a copy of the complaint upon all parties.[659]

In addition, the alleged company-dominated labor organization has the right, under the Board's Rules and Regulations, to file a motion for leave to intervene in the proceeding for the purpose of contesting the issue of its illegality under the Act.[660]

CONDUCT HELD DOMINATION

1. Although the company posted notices of its neutrality and instructed supervisors to observe it, the action was insufficient, ineffective and too long delayed;[661]

2. At employer's instigation, supervisory employees formed an association in opposition to union activity, and donated time and money toward its establishment;[662]

3. Despite a Board order disestablishing a company union, and the company's posting of a notice accordingly, the union on the same day called a meeting and established another union, which was dominated and was a continuance of the old one except for a change of name;[663]

4. Company established employees' association in 1919 and gave it financial support. After enactment of the Wagner Act, the company announced that the association would exist, but that its financial support would be withdrawn. This action did not sever the company from the association. Because of the prior domination, nothing less than "an explicit announcement to the employees that the respondent (employer) would no longer recognize or deal with the association" would do. The fact that the association procured benefits for the employees is immaterial;[664]

5. Company originated and set up an "Employee's Plan" in 1933, without any election or determination by the employees of their preferences. Election of representatives took place on company time and property. Employees were limited in their choice of representatives. No general meetings were held. All expenses were met by the company. On passage of the Act, the company should have publicly and unequivocally declared that it was severing all connection with the "Plan" and was disestablishing it "in order that there can be no doubt in the minds of the men as to the respondent's (employer's) absolute neutrality in respecting the form of employee organization." The fact that 525 of the company's 635 employees would testify that they were satisfied with the "Plan" would not relieve an employer from a finding that the "Plan" was dominated;[665]

6. Company permitted use of company time and property for organizational activities and meetings;[666]

7. Company assisted in drawing a constitution and bylaws;[667]

8. Employees' association which was concededly company-dominated, did not lose that character by mere change of name. Consequently, a stipulation between the company and the CIO union providing that the company union be disestablished had not been complied with, and a contract entered into with such company-dominated union, after a consent election wherein the CIO lost, was invalid "because it was made with a labor organization dominated, interfered with, and supported by the respondent (employer);[668]

9. Company gave vending machine privileges to a union;[669]
10. Employer suggested formation of inside union during a strike by a nationally affiliated union;[670]
11. Successor to company-dominated "Association" was itself held company-dominated where personnel was carried over; and formation of the new organization was under the direction of the officers of the former association;[671]
12. Employer contributed financial support to a successor organization;[672]
13. Successor organization took over and used assets of the prior company-dominated organization;[673]
14. Union's self-disestablishment was held insufficient to cure an alleged domination. Nothing less would suffice, according to the Board, than action by the employer which made it clear that he removed his stamp of approval from the inside union, thus leaving the way open for an uninfluenced expression of opinion by the employees.[674]

NECESSITY OF COMPLETE FRACTURE

When does a union cease to be company-dominated? It is difficult to draw the line in the transition from a company-dominated union under an "Employee Representation Plan" subject to management's control to a stage wherein the employees bargain through a union freely chosen. The cardinal issue in ascertaining whether the transition has been complete is the factor of continuity or lack of continuity in the organizations, that is, whether there has been a clear line of cleavage between the organizations. A new union which continues indistinguishable from the old betrays a continuity of domination.[675] It has frequently been pointed out that participation by the leaders of the earlier organization in the formation of the new one raises the presumption that there is no sharp break between the two. For this reason, a line of fracture between the dominated union and the successor is essential if the latter is to escape the taint of domination. In one case, the test was whether employees might reasonably have inferred that the employer favored the organization, in view of the fact that an illegal inside organization had existed for some years in the plant and this association had not been disestablished until the later one was organized.[676]

In all such cases the courts may analogize from the law of criminal conspiracy.[677] The burden of proof rests with a participant in a conspiracy to show that he is no longer a party. Whether a disavowal constitutes proof is a question of fact for a jury to decide. As mentioned above, in seeking to determine whether the employer has disavowed support of the new organization, the National Labor Relations Board looks to the attitude of the employees. Where the Board finds that management has not convinced employees of its severance this finding will be accepted and the Board's order of disestablishment upheld.[678]

The court in the *Sperry Gyroscope Corporation* case[679] said, quoting the Supreme Court, that "the fact-findings of an administrative agency like the Board, must be accorded an even higher dignity than that of a jury, because the findings of such agencies are those of specialists in a particular field advised by experts." The Board's findings are generally conclusive and it is for it, under the statutory scheme, to determine how the effect of unfair labor practices must be expunged.[680] Thus, any appeal for consideration must really be directed to the Board, which means that there is no appeal.

The designation of a company-dominated union by the majority of employees is utterly ineffective and will not validate a contract between the employer and such dominated union.[681] Nor do differences arising in negotiations with such union indicate freedom from domination.[682] There may be domination within the meaning of the Act without complete subservience to the desires of the employer.

Distinctive aids in determining the approximate point at which company domination ceases may be found in the following situations: The Circuit Court on the one hand found a successor union dominated by the employer where the organization was formed immediately after company officials had suggested a continuation of the former "plan" but without employer representatives; organizers of the new union were closely identified with management; no dues, membership meetings or applications for membership were provided for; solicitation of membership and conduct of elections were permitted on company time and property.[683] In another case, the Supreme Court upheld a Board's ruling that a successor organization to an employee association was company-dominated, since there was no sharp cleavage between the successor union and the employee association and the same employees had been active as officers in both.[684] Another successor union was held to be free of employer domination where the structure of the new union differed substantially from that of the predecessor "plan;" organizers were not identified with the management; provision was made for membership applications, payment of dues, calling of strikes and regular elections; and the employer recognized it only after proof of majority status.[685]

Three considerations have been laid down by the Eighth Circuit Court of Appeals for guidance in deciding whether the successor to a dominated labor organization is also dominated.[686] These are:

1. Were employees informed before the new organization was established that all recognition of the old one had been terminated?
2. Were employees told that they were free to join or not join any organization?
3. Were employees told that the employer was completely indifferent to their choice of organization?

All three questions must be answered in the affirmative if the successor organization is to be found free of employer domination.

PROCEDURE FOR FRACTURE

The disestablishment of a company-dominated union need not follow any formal or mechanical procedure. In one case, the Board failed to find a sufficient distinction between a prior employees' representation plan and the later union which accepted all of the officers of the earlier organization. The court, however, took into account the fact that the employer told the employee representatives that he was completely divorced from their organization.[687] It was the court's opinion that the evidence supported the employer's statement. In a contempt proceeding by the Board, the court ruled that the employer may purge himself of contempt by withdrawing recognition from the dominated union and by posting, and keeping posted for a specified time, notices stating he has withdrawn such recognition; that he has abrogated his contract with the organization; that employees may form or join any labor organization, local or affiliated; that the employer does not favor or disfavor either an independent labor organization or any other labor organization but is completely neutral; and that employees will not incur the favor or disfavor of the employer regardless of what choice they may make.[688]

If the provisions of the notice are adhered to, the withdrawal of such recognition, the abrogation of such contract, the posting of such notice, and the elapsing of the specified period will constitute a complete fracture between the dominated union and another labor organization if any should be formed, and the employees may then exercise complete freedom of choice to form or join any organization, whether it be purely local or affiliated with a parent body.

SANCTION IS "DISESTABLISHMENT," NOT "DISSOLUTION"

Should an employer be found to have dominated a labor organization, either through giving it aid or otherwise, the employer may be ordered to withdraw all recognition from such an organization and completely disestablish it as representative of the employees.[689] The remedy which the

Labor Board ordinarily prescribes, and the courts have ordered enforced, is that all recognition be withdrawn in so far as the union is treated as a bargaining agent, and that plant notices be posted by the management to the effect that this will be done. The organizations, however, may continue to fulfill other purposes, such as those of a social club or group insurance plan. In one case, the court construed a "disestablish" order to mean that the employer may not now recognize the union as bargaining agent for his employees.[690]

Half-way measures for divesting company unions of employer domination will not satisfy the requirements of the Act. In one case, employees who had been active in a defunct employee representation plan organized the new union upon the employer's statement of its desirability. Membership was solicited on company time and property and company representatives urged employees to attend the meetings. The union was found employer-dominated.[691] In another, employees in no way identified with the management organized a new union which had dues, regular meetings, strike calls and referenda on acceptance of contracts. The company rendered no aid not afforded also to outside unions and deferred exclusive recognition until there was proof of majority status. Here there was no finding of employer domination.[692]

A labor organization ordered disestablished can never be certified by the Board as bargaining representative or recognized as such by the employer. Nor can it be designated effectively as bargaining representative by the employees.[693] If the evidence falls short of establishing domination and establishes no more than illegal interference and support, the Board will not direct disestablishment, but will order only withdrawal of recognition from the labor organization until certified by the Board.

Under the Wagner Act, the Board applied this distinction in cases involving affiliated unions. The employer was charged with illegal interference and support, and the affiliated union was qualified to act as bargaining representative after the Board was satisfied that effects of the unfair labor practices had been dissipated. The difference in treatment between the affiliated and nonaffiliated unions was justified by the Board on the ground that the former "would not be permanently and completely subjugated to the will of the employer."[694] This distinction was eliminated by the amendments to the Act.[695] The Board has held thereunder that dominated unions will be ordered disestablished regardless of whether such union is affiliated. Where the evidence establishes no more than illegal interference and support, only withdrawal of recognition will be ordered regardless of whether the union involved is affiliated.[696]

6. Discrimination

LAY-OFFS

A lay-off is not necessarily an unfair labor practice and only becomes such upon a finding that the lay-off was motivated by a purpose forbidden by the Act.[697] A lay-off is discriminatory where it is imposed because of union activities or as the alternative to joining a company-dominated union. Where a disproportionate number of union members was found among the workers laid off, the employer's defense, curtailment of production, was not accepted.[698]

LOCKOUTS

Lockout through shutdown or mass discharge, because of union membership or activity, is discrimination.[699] But where, instead of proving that the plant was closed for the purpose of discouraging the employees' first efforts to bargain collectively, the records proved the exact opposite, there was no illegal lockout.[700]

Held discriminatory were lockouts for refusal to come to work at an earlier hour, when coupled with a refusal of the employer to attempt to negotiate a compromise; for absence from work, where it was not proved that the absence was without permission; for a seasonal shutdown, where it was not genuine; for inventory and business conditions or lack of funds, where the primary reason was to discourage union membership and activity.[701] Similarly, closing down operations after employees joined the union and demanded bargaining rights (thus discharging the employees involved), constituted a discriminatory lockout.[702]

REHIRING

In an effort to determine whether an unlawful anti-union policy has been followed, the Board has resorted to comparing treatment of union and nonunion employees. Accordingly, there was discriminatory rehiring where a company was found, in taking back two-thirds of its working force, to have called back only two out of fifty-nine union employees.[703] While the burden of proof remains on the Board, the burden of showing which of those not returned to their jobs would have been returned in the absence of an anti-union policy is placed on the company, which, if unable to show that certain ones would not otherwise have been called back, is required to reinstate all the union employees.[704]

Delayed reinstatement is a form of discrimination in rehiring, as is having the machinery of reinstatement in the hands of employees hostile to the strikers, and reinstating a union official, who formerly worked in a unionized plant, to a job in another mill, which was imperfectly organized.[705] Conditional reinstatement, e.g., requiring the renunciation of union affiliation, acceptance of a "yellow dog" contract, imposition of an illegal closed shop contract, on application where such application would be an idle gesture, and conditioning the application, e.g., promise not to picket, or to reveal union membership, have been held discriminatory.[706]

Lack of an established rehiring policy, combined with apathy on the part of an employee, may afford an employer a valid defense against a charge of discriminatory refusal to reinstate a laid-off union leader. The National Labor Relations Board ruled that, although other laid-off employees were rehired and no new employees were taken on to do the same type of work as the laid-off worker, the employer's failure to recall her was not discriminatory. The employee had made no effort to obtain re-employment and the evidence did not disclose that the employer followed any established practice of recalling laid-off employees to fill vacant jobs.[707]

By-passing a former economic striker in filling new jobs has been held discriminatory. While as a rule economic strikers are not entitled to reinstatement if their places have been taken by replacement employees, their employer may not pass them over when they apply for their jobs and hire new or former employees in their places because of his resentment against the strike.[708] The reasons assigned by the employer for his choice (superior efficiency or desire to train new workers) were held not to be the actual reasons but an attempt to penalize employees for their concerted activity. The refusal to bargain may convert an economic strike into an unfair practice strike. The mere fact that the strike would have occurred had the employer been willing to bargain is no defense. The employer's responsibility entails rehiring the strikers with back pay from the time they asked *unconditionally for reinstatement and were not reinstated.*[709]

An economic strike has been held to become an unfair labor practice type of strike where it was prolonged by the employer's refusal to bargain with the union.[710] Refusal to reinstate employees who engaged in a sympathy strike was held discriminatory.[711] While the company was not under a duty to displace workers in order to make place for striking employees on their application, the company was obligated not to discriminate against them where there were vacancies which such employees could have filled, and the refusal to so reinstate them was held to be discriminatory.

Refusal to reinstate employees who had made application through the union, despite the fact that such employees had participated in a sitdown strike, and there had been a mutual settlement of claims, was held discriminatory.[712] An employer is not necessarily justified in refusing reinstatement to an employee who is an alien, even though the employer is engaged in defense work.[713] A company could not refuse to reinstate an employee, discriminatorily laid off, because the AFL union, with which the company had a contract, objected to the employee's CIO activity and the company did not wish any further labor trouble.[714] In reinstating employees who have gone on strike, an employer may not distinguish between an economic striker whose concerted activities are more or less objectionable to him and give preference accordingly.[715]

DISCHARGING

The dividing line between insubordination and concerted activity for mutual aid is not always readily discernible. It can best be understood by an examination of illustrative situations. While employers may lawfully discharge employees who decline to perform certain unusual work, unless they receive guarantees that nonunion employees will not be given the regular work, one employer was held prohibited from discharging other employees who struck in protest against the first discharges. The Board held that the first discharges were for insubordination. To discharge employees for striking, however, is ruled to be unlawful in that the strike is a form of concerted activity protected by the law.[716]

Discharge of nonunion employees, who refused to do work previously performed by union employees engaging in an unfair labor practice strike, was held by the Board to be discriminatory. The employer's contention that the refusal was insubordination was rejected. In so ruling, the Board asserted that the refusal to do this work was in the nature of a partial strike, a form of concerted activity held to be protected by the Wagner Act. Reinstatement of the discharged employees having been refused, the Board awarded them back pay from the date of refusal.[717] Even though an employee was guilty of serious misconduct, his dismissal because of hostility to an inside company-dominated union constituted discrimination.

Inducing an employee, on notice of prospective discharge, to sign a resignation card did not suffice to avert a finding of unlawful discharge, under a Labor Board ruling. The employee involved, who was shop chairman of the union, was told, according to the findings, that he should seek employment elsewhere, since the company was giving regular employment only to those who stood by it. He was promised, however, that if he resigned his job he would be given a letter of recommendation.[718]

Permission to work overtime at premium wage rates assumes greater prominence as a possible form of unlawful discrimination with the stepping up of hours of work. The Labor Board has found that an employer who restricted the privilege of overtime work to those who had not signed applications for membership in an outside union thereby violated the Act.[719] The employer's later rectification of such discrimination did not save him from a cease and desist order where there were other unfair labor practices, the effects of which had not been completely erased. But in the absence of direct evidence that an employer knew of the union membership of employees discharged, a Pennsylvania court decided that the Pennsylvania Labor Board was in error in finding that the discharges were discriminatory.[720]

Where a discriminatory policy is adopted, individual discrimination is presumed. The Board need not consider the basis for the lay-off of each of the persons affected. One worker's protest against the employment of another worker has been held by the Labor Board to be a valid basis for subsequent discharge of the second employee. The Board refused to find discrimination in the discharge of a union member following his transfer from one department of a plant to another during a period when operations were declining. Justification for the discharge was found in the fact that a regular employee of the second department protested such transfer on the ground that other regular employees of the department were currently being laid off.[721]

While an employer who shuts down a plant to discourage the activities of a union may, under certain conditions, be found by the Labor Board to have engaged in a discriminatory lockout (a serious matter because the sequel is usually back pay for all employees from the time of the shutdown), there is no discrimination where there was a sound business reason for the shutdown, even though the occasion was used to discourage the union.[722] But a discharge as well as a lockout occasioned by illegal "interference" may also result in a back pay award.[723] The importunities of a bargaining agent will not excuse a union-motivated discharge.[724] On the other hand, a discharge which hinged upon the interpretation of a seniority clause of a contract was held to be within the lawful discretion of management.[725] If the discriminatory discharge was occasioned by the company's removal of the plant to another location, the employer may be compelled to bear the expense of the employees in obtaining and maintaining new living quarters at the new plant location.[726]

RUNAWAY SHOPS

Prior to the passage of the Wagner Act, the only existent legal sanction against runaway shops was by injunction, which was granted only where the flight was in violation of a union contract forbidding removal. Since 1935, however, the Board has been empowered to deal with runaways by virtue of its remedial authority in cases where an employer is found to have engaged in intimidating or discriminatory labor practices.[727]

Relocation to obtain cheaper rent, materials, or labor, or lower taxes or more accessible markets is privileged.[728] Such transfer of the plant violates the Act, however, where it is caused by the employer's antipathy to the organization of his employees or to avoid bargaining with their representative. Prior labor difficulties are evidence of unlawful intent although they are not conclusive, while proof is strengthened by the absence of substantial economic gains. A nominal change of factory ownership (frequently a concomitant of plant removal) does not aid the employer, since it will be disregarded as not in good faith.

Closely analogous to the runaway shop are transfer of production to other existing branches, contracting work out and temporary plant shutdown.[729]

TRANSFER

Discrimination exists when an employee is transferred from one job to another, even though it carries the same wage rate, if the new job is considered by the employee to be less desirable and the purpose is discouragement of union activity.[730] In one case, the employee disliked the change because of its claimed effect on his health. Although the original transfer was not discriminatory, it became discriminatory when subsequently the employer became aware of the employee's union membership and then refused to give the employee his old job again, when it was feasible to do so. Transfer to an isolated spot, where the job is more perilous or involves more strenuous or less desirable work, or intolerable conditions; transfer for alleged mistakes; transfer which would impair seniority; or transfer to temporary work or work of less responsibility have been held to constitute discrimination.[731] The mere fact that the transfer was effected on the demand of a rival labor organization does not justify the violation. Discrimination was found when an employee was removed from his machine and, although kept idle at full pay, isolated in a room near the president's office. Demotion to the status of a "spare hand," because of union activity, was held to be a discrimination as was reinstatement to a lesser rank or being relieved of many duties.[732]

HELD DISCRIMINATION

1. Changing seniority rating because of union activity;[733]
2. Depriving newspaper employees of their by-lines, that is, the privilege of signing articles, because of the fact that they had engaged in a strike;[734]

3. Discharge of active union employees for absence from work to go deer hunting where other employees did the same thing without being discharged or subjected to disciplinary action;[735]
4. Discharge of active union members;[736]
5. Discharge for disobeying a rule against union solicitation during work hours when the rule itself was discriminatorily enforced;[737]
6. Discharge of an employee allegedly because of trouble with his foreman, growing out of the employee's unstable temperament, where it was shown that his foreman had arranged a pay increase and the employee was actively supporting a union opposed by his employer;[738]
7. Discharge of an employee who had been assigned to work, at which it was known that she was inefficient, while another employee was assigned to work at which the discharged employee was efficient;[739]
8. Discharge of an employee who had been most active in union affairs, allegedly for spreading false rumors, but where the employer had made only a superficial investigation of the employee's connection with the alleged rumors;[740]
9. Discharge of a nonunion member who sought a raise and attempted to induce others to join him in the demand where the employer's motive was to discourage concerted activity for the benefit of the employee;[741]
10. Discharge of employees immediately after they openly distributed union membership cards to other employees;[742]
11. Discharge imposed on employee because of his intoxication and neglect of work, where such neglect had been condoned by the company on the part of members of a company-dominated union;[743]
12. Discharge pursuant to a valid closed shop contract where the expiration date was near and the employees had changed their affiliation, but maintained membership in good standing in the contracting union;[744]
13. Discharge of workers who refused to sign individual employment contracts; of salesmen who refused to ride in trucks driven by strikebreakers (concerted action); of union members for distribution of union literature where there was no rule forbidding it; of employees who acted in concert to aid another union; and of employees who refused to do the work of an employee discriminatorily discharged;[745]
14. Discrimination against union members as to amount, type and duration of employment of seasonal employees;[746]
15. Announcing to strikers that to retain their jobs they must report to work by a certain date and join an employer-assisted or -dominated

union, after employer had made a closed shop contract with that union, although the employer later gave notice that the closed shop clause would not be enforced.[747]

16. Failure of employer to follow his usual seniority plan in lay-offs, where union activity and not business decline was the reason for the discharges, even though there was a decrease in business;[748]

17. Inciting to insubordination by means of labor-baiting;[749]

18. Locking out employees pursuant to an illegal closed shop contract;[750]

19. Matching dues for a union, even under a mutual consideration pact;[751]

20. Discharging an employee for severing his union affiliations, where a preferential shop agreement was in effect (valid under Wagner Act);[752]

21. Reducing hours of work of an employee because of union activity and his testimony at a Board hearing;[753]

22. Refusing a job to an applicant unless he changed his name and social security number so as to conceal the fact that he had participated in a strike;[754]

23. Shutdown for which "good reason" exists may be discriminatory if unprecedented. Closing down a lumber camp because of unusually heavy rains, but at a time when a union had obtained a foothold among employees and was seeking to bargain for them, was held by the Labor Board to have been a discriminatory lockout. A governing consideration was the fact that the camp had never previously closed down completely for such a reason even when precipitation had been greater;[755]

24. Forcing a resignation by discriminatory treatment;[756]

25. Threats to close the plant; permitting the refusal of admission to union employees unless they destroyed membership cards; bribery; transfer of union members to other plants;[757]

26. Unexplained hiring of inexperienced nonunion employees in preference to union employees active in the affairs of the union, held sufficient to create a reasonable inference of discrimination;[758]

27. Unilaterally transferring salaried employees to hourly status without notice to the bargaining agent, resulting in loss to the employees.[759]

CHANGE IN EMPLOYEE STATUS AFTER CERTIFICATION OF UNION

Three days after employees in one plant selected a union as bargaining representatives, the employer unilaterally altered their terms and conditions of employment, including wage rates. The employer asserted that the change was necessary because the employees involved were inspectors who inspected the work of rank-and-file employees whose union the inspectors designated as their bargaining agent. Under those circumstances, the employer argued that the change in status was necessary, but the Board ruled that the change was illegal.[760]

PRACTICES REGARDED AS PRETEXTS FOR DISCRIMINATION

1. Abolition of employees' jobs where the real motive was the employer's desire to rid himself of an irritating nucleus of union members and sympathizers, and discharge for violation of a safety[761] rule, where the primary motive was found to be antipathy to the union;
2. Discharge allegedly for neglect of work but actually for union activity;[762]
3. Discharge of CIO secretary on the pretext that the employee had allowed a vibrator to burn up, although the immediate supervisor who was responsible for operation of the machine had not been questioned at all about this, and a nonunion employee, whose failure to oil the machinery was primarily responsible, had not been discharged;[763]
4. Discharge of employees for failure to join a labor organization in the absence of a closed shop contract;[764]
5. Suspension for distributing union bulletins in the parking lots of employer;[765]
6. Discharge for not remaining a member of the company-dominated union as required by the contract;[766]
7. Discharge for fighting, where the company was lax in discipline;[767]
8. Discharge through enforcement of a rule which had never been previously enforced;[768]
9. Discontinuance of a department in the business to avoid collective bargaining with a union chosen by the employees discharged;[769]
10. Discrimination against a union under the guise of eliminating delays in production, where the delays were found not to have been occasioned by the activities of the discharged employees;[770]
11. Discriminatory disregard of a seniority clause under pretense of adopting a new employment policy;[771]
12. Charging employee with spoilage of material, talking to others, stopping work, etc., where the spoilage was not greater than that of other employees and there was no rule against talking;[772]
13. Discharge of employee for criticism of management policies, where criticism was a basis of organizing activities;[773]
14. Discharge of an employee only after he had joined the union despite the employer's knowledge of the employee's bad record, and fact that employee's work had been unsatisfactory for many months, and others who had produced less sales were not discharged;[774]

15. Discharge of an inspector, found to be the first so penalized, for passing defective material, where her discharge came ten days after her election as an officer of the union was discovered.[775]

16. Discharge of worker motivated by the refusal of the employee to join a company-dominated union;[776]

17. Discharge where employees were not customarily disciplined for the same type of conduct;[777]

18. Discharge on grounds of physical defect, when the record indicates that the claim of physical defect was a mere pretext to get rid of unionists;[778]

19. Reducing the force after the rush period so that there was a marked disparity in the proportion of union members before and after the rush period;[779]

20. Refusal to rehire, because of union activity, after proper lay-off;[780]

21. Discharge for theft from former employer where dereliction was known to the employer, who had accepted the worker as an honest and capable employee for two and one-half years. Only when he joined the union, ruled the Board, did the employer take action allegedly on this past record, and such action was solely to procure plausible justification for discharge with the intention of destroying the majority membership then claimed by the union;[781]

22. Discharge for use of obscene language, where the Board found that the use of such language was very common.[782]

7. Refusal to Bargain

The duty to bargain collectively is the process of negotiation between management and the freely designated representative of the majority of employees in whom is vested the combined bargaining power of the employee unit.[783] The subject matter of collective bargaining comprises wages, hours, and other working conditions. It is not for the Board to pass upon the subject of the union agreement nor to direct who will conduct negotiations. Its function is to order elections and certify the duly elected bargaining agent. Refusal to bargain may be manifested through many forms of employer conduct which may be interference, coercion, domination or discrimination. It may be evidenced by failure to cooperate, by bad faith in insisting upon an election, by denial of recognition to the duly elected bargaining agent, or by the mere semblance of negotiation for ulterior purposes.

The duty to bargain may be channelized by the terms and provisions of the contract between the employer and the union. Breach of the no-strike clause of the contract or resorting to a strike to compel adjustment of complaints instead of following the grievance procedure provided in the contract, suspends the employer's duty to bargain on the subject of the strike so long as such illegal conduct continues.[784] A company was found to have satisfied the duty to bargain collectively where it agreed to the union's proposed provisions for union recognition, in good faith made counterproposals which the union repeatedly rejected without receding from its original position, refused to permit the union's auditors to examine its books as to its inability to pay the wage increase demanded, but made available to the union its profit and loss statements for a number of years as well as its tax returns.[785]

Competitive disadvantages, uncertainty, which is not genuine, of union status, or alleged prior union misconduct will not justify refusal to bargain.[786]

Management may not insist on a contract clause giving the individual employee the right to determine whether or not the union steward shall be present at the adjustment of his grievances by the foreman—the initial step in the grievance procedure. A company, during negotiations, insisted upon the inclusion of the following provision in the contract:

Any matter which in the opinion of the Union or any Employee at any yard requires adjustment may be taken up by such Employee, *with or without* the steward of the Union or for the department in which such employee works, as such *Employee shall elect,* with the foreman of such department and, if it shall not be satisfactorily disposed of by the foreman, it may then be taken up as a grievance in the manner hereinafter set forth. (Emphasis added.)

The Board ruled that the company was guilty of an illegal refusal to bargain collectively because it conditioned its signing of an agreement upon the union's acceptance of the above clause. The Board's view is that the statutory right to recognition of the union having majority status includes the right to be present at all grievance adjustments.[a] The Board said:

The Respondents contend, nevertheless, that the Act does not prohibit them from demanding in good faith an agreement containing the disputed clause. In effect, they argue, first, that this clause does not derogate from the Union's exclusive representative status, which only relates to collective bargaining concerning rates of pay, wages, hours of employment, and other conditions of employment, but not to the adjustment of grievances; and, secondly, that a grievance procedure and a reasonable definition of grievances for such purposes are proper matters for collective bargaining.

The short answer to the first argument is that, whatever may be the majority representative's authority with respect to the adjustment of grievances, a question not now before us, the fact is that the disputed clause limits the right secured to the Union as the bargaining representative to attend the adjustment. Grievances are usually more than mere personal dissatisfactions or complaints of employees and their adjustment frequently involves the interpretation and application of the terms of a contract or otherwise affects the terms and conditions of employment not covered by a contract. For this reason, these matters are unquestionably the concern of the bargaining representative.

It should be noted that in the *Bethlehem Steel Company* case[b] the *foreman* had authority to settle grievances, which settlement was final unless appealed by the employee or the union. The Board pointed out that:

> The entirely different question of the right of the Union to be present at purported adjustments of grievances by minor supervisors *who have no authority under the contract* to dispose of grievances is not here presented, and we do not pass on that question. (Emphasis added.)

It is noteworthy from this statement that the Board indicates that unions may waive their right to attend grievance adjustments. To this extent, there would seem to be some area for negotiation with regard to that right, although the employer cannot refuse to sign an agreement unless that right is waived.

HELD REFUSAL TO BARGAIN

1. Accepting offer of union members to sell out;[787]
2. Alleging that the union is irresponsible;[788]
3. Appealing to union members over the head of the bargaining committee;[789]
4. Attempting to destroy the union's majority while negotiating with the union by inducing employees to renounce the union and form an inside union;[790]
5. Accepting a contract from the business agent of a union competing with the union designated as bargaining representative by a majority of the employees in the appropriate bargaining unit;[791]
6. Untimely challenging of certification;[792]
7. Confining counterproposals to the proposition that existing relationships be continued where there was in the past no history of collective bargaining;[793]
8. Contending in bad faith that a unit different from that sought by a union is appropriate;[794]
9. Transferring operation to elude the union;[795]
10. Announcing that all grievances must be presented in writing when they were previously presented orally;[796]
11. Declining the request of a union to write into a contract, already agreed upon, a clause granting the majority union exclusive bargaining rights.[797] The Board stresses the value to the union of such express

recognition and holds that the full measure of the employer's duty is not fulfilled unless the clause is incorporated in the agreement. Recognition of the sole bargaining agent as such is not subject matter for bargaining;

12. Declining to deal with a certified union on the ground that the unit was not appropriate;[798]

13. Declining to meet union representatives, though the Board had certified that union, until a court had determined that the Board had jurisdiction;[799]

14. Declining to discuss an agreement when a union asked to bargain, though when the union offered to request an election, if its claim to majority status was questioned, the company terminated the meeting on the ground the union had failed to establish its majority status;[800]

15. Delaying meeting the union representatives for four months, when it was the president's duty to appoint a fully authorized representative to negotiate in his place;[801]

16. Delaying the process of negotiation beyond justifiable limits;[802]

17. Demanding a list of union members rather than accepting the NLRB's Field Examiner's word that a union represents a majority of employees, in violation of an agreement that the Field Examiner's conclusion should be final.[803]

18. Delaying negotiations by discussion of unrelated matters;[804]

19. Disturbing the union's efforts to arrange for a conference outside working hours;[805]

20. Excluding the union in considering a wage adjustment;[806]

21. Failing to ask for proof of majority status and then later demanding it;[807]

22. Failing to cooperate in the determination of a union's claim of majority status;[808]

23. Finding dilatory successive objections;[809]

24. Granting of concession to dominated organization while a *bona fide* union was attempting to negotiate;[810]

25. Granting of wage increase following employees' suggestion that they withdraw from the union;[811]

26. Imposing, as a condition to executing a contract with a union, the requirement that the union either should become incorporated so as to be amenable to legal process or should post a performance bond;[812]

27. Imposing a limitation on the employee committee, insisting on the absence of two of the seven members; and delay in questioning the appropriateness of the bargaining unit;[813]

28. Imposing on the union an undue obstacle to collective bargaining by requiring the union to re-establish its majority after the commision of unfair labor practices;[814]
29. Negotiating individually during a strike and passive attitude of employer with respect to the union;[815]
30. Insisting on a clause in the contract that the contract is ineffective until competitors enter into a similar agreement;[816]
31. Insisting that the established policy of a wage revision precluded collective bargaining on that subject;[817]
32. Maintaining that the right to lay off employees is solely within employer's own discretion instead of abiding by formulated rules;[818]
33. Misrepresenting bargaining conditions;[819]
34. Questioning a union's majority status after having conceded that the union represented a majority of employees in a unit;[820]
35. Questioning a unit when evidence of bad faith was found through untimely raising of the question, and intimidation;[821]
36. Recognizing officers of a company-dominated union as bargaining representatives;[822]
37. Refusal of the authorized company representative to negotiate with the union;[823]
38. Refusing to accept requests to bargain;[824]
39. Refusing to bargain with a union no longer representing a majority, though it had a majority at the time of the original refusal, was no defense to a charge before the Board, where the employer's unfair labor practices had caused defections from the union;[825]
40. Refusing to bargain with a union which had been certified by the National Labor Relations Board but had not obtained a required state license;[826]
41. Refusing to bargain with a union which had been chosen in an employee election, on the ground that the majority of employees later signed affidavits declaring that they had not intended to vote for the union. The Board held that results of an employee election are binding upon the parties since they reflect the employees' desires at the time of the election. Certification of representatives must be honored for a reasonable period even though there has been a repudiation of a certified union by a majority of the employees concerned;[827]
42. Refusing to bargain with a union which had lost its majority or whose membership had been depleted by employees leaving the company subsequent to an unlawful refusal to bargain;[828]
43. Refusing to cooperate in an election;[829]

44. Refusing to enter into *written* and *signed* contracts containing any understandings they reach on the subject of wages, hours, or other conditions of employment;[830]

45. Refusing to make commitments because of uncertainties in business conditions.;[831]

46. Refusing to negotiate with the union the matter of hiring employees who would be laid off as a result of a removal;[832]

47. Refusing to cooperate with mediation agencies toward an adjustment of a strike at the plant;[833]

48. Adamantly refusing to make any kind of concession to the union in connection with its bargaining demands and taking an unsupportable negative position with respect to them;[834]

49. Refusing to discuss anything but grievances;[835]

50. Refusing to reveal wage data to a union;[836]

51. Refusing to sign a written agreement embodying conditions presently existing in the business;[837]

52. Rejecting specific proposals of the union as unnecessary because they are already legal obligations of the company or a part of the company's policy;[838]

53. Rejecting a union's offer to prove its majority claim;[839]

54. Removal of plant to evade the union;[840]

55. Sending persons to conferences who were not authorized to make any kind of agreement;[841]

56. Shutdown to avoid bargaining;[842]

57. Stalling in arranging a conference until the close of the season, and otherwise exhibiting a hostile attitude toward a certified union;[843]

58. Stalling in bargaining, as distinguished from permissible delay;[844]

59. Unilateral installation of vacation plan;[845]

60. Unilateral action on individual merit increases and refusal to disclose information with respect thereto;[846]

61. Unilaterally transferring salaried employees to an hourly status without consulting the bargaining agent and despite its protest;[847]

62. Refusal to bargain concerning merit increases since they are not within the sole prerogative of management;[848]

63. Insistence on including in a contract a stringent anti-strike clause which severely penalized the union in the event of violation thereof;[849]

The amended Act defines to bargain collectively as the "performance of the mutual obligation" of the employer and the union and imposes upon them the following rights and duties which, insofar as the employer is concerned, continue to be the same as under the Wagner Act:[850]

1. To meet at a reasonable time;

2. To confer in good faith on employment terms and conditions and on the negotiation of an agreement or any question arising thereunder;
3. To incorporate into a written instrument any agreement reached if requested.
4. Neither party is obligated to agree to a proposal.
5. Neither party is required to make a concession.

This definition outlaws the "take it or else" attitude assumed by some unions upon the submission of their proposed contract. Such a position at the bargaining table would preclude good faith bargaining and, under the amended statute, would appear to be an illegal refusal to bargain collectively on the part of the union.[851]

TERMINATION OF EXISTING CONTRACT

When an existing contract is about to expire and the parties desire its termination or modification, the party desiring such termination or modification is obligated to comply with the "sixty day cooling off" requirements of the Act, during which period the union cannot strike nor the employer lock out the employees. Failure by either union or employer to comply with the notice requirements is a breach of the statutory duty to bargain collectively. (See "Existing Contracts and Their Effect," Part One, Chapter III.)

IV · UNFAIR LABOR PRACTICES BY UNIONS

1. Restraint and Coercion

It is an unfair labor practice for unions or their agents to restrain or coerce employees in the exercise of their right to form, join or assist labor organizations for purposes of collective bargaining or their right to refrain from any and all such activity.[852] The evil sought to be remedied covers such union conduct as threats of reprisals against employees and their families during the course of an organizational campaign, direct interference by mass picketing and other violent conduct and duress of employees by unions.[853] The Board has held that a strike by a dissident group during the existence of a collective agreement containing a no-strike clause does not in itself constitute restraint and coercion of employees; and the mere fact that a strike may violate other provisions of the Act does not in itself make such a strike coercive, since the prohibition of restraint and coercion of employees by unions was intended to restrain only acts of violence and coercion rather than the calling of a strike.[854] The Board has held that picketing to compel organization of the employees was not coercive of nonunion employees in the absence of actual violence or physical coercion even though it was in aid of an illegal secondary boycott.[855] The following discussion by the Board of the point is significant:

The most that can be said . . . . is that the picketing was intended to demonstrate to the nonunion workers that it was to their advantage to become union members. It did not constitute restraint and coercion of those employees in the exercise of their rights guaranteed under the Act, nor did it have that effect.

The legislative history of the amendment to the Wagner Act with which we are here concerned shows that the Congress intended to prohibit the use by unions in organizational efforts of "goon squads," threats of violence as well as other types of threats, and mass picketing; that it sought to make unions liable for the same type of restraint and coercion against employees that would be an unfair labor practice if used by employers against employees. . . . .[856]

In a recent case, the Board reviewed the legislative history of the provisions of the amended Act which make union restraint and coercion of employees an unfair labor practice. The Board held that it was intended to eliminate physical violence and intimidation by unions as well as the use of threats of economic action against specific individuals to compel them to join the union.[857] In the same case, the Board made two other significant rulings with respect to union restraint and coercion: (1) that a union's unlawful refusal to bargain collectively did not *per se* constitute illegal restraint and coercion of employees in the exercise of rights guaranteed in the Act; and (2) that a strike, peaceably conducted, to compel employers to agree to an illegal hiring hall clause, and not directed primarily at compelling employees to forego rights guaranteed in Section 7 of the Act, did not constitute union restraint and coercion of employees within the meaning of the Act.

The Board has held the following types of conduct on the part of unions and their agents to be illegal restraint and coercion of employees:[858]

1. Preventing employees who do not desire to join in a union strike from going to and from work during the strike.
2. Pickets threatening with physical violence employees who desire to enter the plant.
3. A superior force of strikers following an outnumbered group of nonstrikers for some distance from the plant. This conduct constituted a threat of bodily harm.
4. Union agent pushing a nonstriker against a wall and threatening him with a beating.
5. Obstructing nonstrikers' ingress to the plant by standing in the way of their automobiles and threatening them with physical violence.
6. Union agent ordering pickets to "pull" nonstrikers out of the automobiles in which they were going to work.
7. Mass picketing which forcibly blocked ingress of nonstrikers to the plant.

However, in the same case the Board held that the conduct of pickets in daring one of the nonstrikers to come out of the automobile in which he was riding was too trivial to constitute restraint and coercion.

While the Board has ruled that mass picketing accompanied by violence and threats of violence constitutes restraint and coercion, it has not as yet decided "whether peaceful picketing by a large number of persons without more is constitutionally privileged or *per se* unlawful under the Act."[859]

Other conduct by unions and their agents held to be restraint and coercion of employees is as follows:

1. Damage to plant property caused by pickets hurling stones and other objects at plant windows, which were broken so that the machinery and equipment were exposed to damage by the elements. Such conduct, the Board held, constitutes a threat of physical violence to employees who would attempt to work.[860] The fact that the strike was for union recognition did not justify such conduct.

2. Keeping nonstrikers from entering the plant.[861]

3. Imprisoning nonstrikers in the plant.[862]

The amended Act expressly excludes from the prohibition against union restraint and coercion the right of unions to prescribe their own rules for the acquisition or retention of membership in the union; and on this ground the Board refused to hold coercive the threat of an international union to expel locals that did not follow its order to pursue conduct which was violative of the Act.[a]

Coercing an employer in designating who shall represent him for collective bargaining or in the handling and adjustment of grievances is also an unfair labor practice.[863] Thus, unions cannot dictate or compel the removal of a personnel director or a supervisor from such functions.

The free speech provision of Section 8(c) of the Act which guarantees the right to express "views, argument or opinion" without "threat of reprisal or force or promise of benefit" is applicable to unions as well as employers.[864] Thus, the abuse of strikebreakers by name calling alone does not constitute restraint and coercion.[865] Because of this provision, the Board has reversed its captive-audience doctrine enunciated under the Wagner Act.[866] Instead, the Board holds that, under the amended Act, an employer who compels his employees to gather during working hours and listen to his speeches against the union does not commit a violation of the Act in the absence of coercive statements.[867] (See "Direct Interference with Employee's Rights," Part Three, Chapter III.)

2. Discrimination

Unions cannot attempt to cause employers to discharge employees for dual unionism or failure to join the union, even where there is in effect a valid union shop agreement which satisfies all the requirements of the amended Act, except when such employees fail to offer to pay the regular union dues and initiation fees.[868] The employee is free at all times to become active in behalf of a rival union so long as he proffers dues and initiation fees of the contracting union. If the contracting union succeeds in securing his discharge, despite payment of dues and initiation fees, it commits an unfair labor practice and is subject to the remedial order of the Board, including liability to reimburse the aggrieved employee his lost pay.[869] In the absence of a valid union shop clause, it is an unfair labor practice for unions to cause or attempt to cause employers to discriminate against employees in order to encourage or discourage membership in any union.

The following types of conduct have been held to constitute illegal attempts by unions to cause an employer to discriminate against employees because of nonmembership in the union:

1. Insistence by the union, during negotiations for a collective bargaining agreement, that provision for hiring through the union hiring hall be included in any agreement, and engaging in a strike to enforce such a demand where the practice in the union's hiring was to give preference in jobs to union members over nonmembers.[870] The Board said in this connection:

Beyond the peradventure of doubt, the hiring-hall in practice has involved discrimination in the hire and tenure of employment of unlicensed seamen to encourage membership in NMU. It is a discrimination which has been initiated by NMU, and acquiesced in by the Companies. Moreover, it is clear from the record in this case that what NMU was demanding in its negotiations, and in its strike, was not merely a continuation of the form of the hiring-hall clause in its agreements with the Companies, but a continuation of the practice outlined above, by which preference in job assignment and job retention was given to NMU members. But the Act as now amended no longer permits employers to discriminate against employees who are not members of labor organizations, except pursuant to a "union-shop" agreement under certain specified conditions which have not here been met. The Respondents in their negotiations and in their strike were engaged in an "attempt to cause" the Companies to discriminate against employees in a manner which is prohibited by Section 8(a) (3) of the Act. By so doing the Respondents have violated Section 8(b) (2) of the Act.

2. Insistence upon a closed shop and striking to compel agreement thereto.[871]
3. Insistence upon a union shop without compliance with the requirements of the Act for validating such a union security clause.[872]

3. Refusal to Bargain Collectively with Employer

Unions are obligated under the amended Act to bargain collectively in good faith with employers and the failure of a union to do so is an unfair labor practice on its part.[873] To bargain collectively, both with respect to unions and employers, is defined as "the performance of the mutual obligation of the employer and the representative of the employees to meet at reasonable times and confer in good faith with respect to wages, hours, and other terms and conditions of employment, or the negotiation of an agreement, or any question thereunder, and the execution of a written contract incorporating any agreement reached if requested by either party, but such obligation does not compel either party to agree to a proposal or require the making of a concession."[874]

The vast body of authorities, both Board and court, holding that employers who engage in negotiation with "hermetically sealed minds" toward the process of collective bargaining fail to bargain in good faith would now appear to be applicable to unions that assume the "take-it-or-leave-it" attitude with respect to their demands.[875] Thus, it was an unlawful refusal to bargain for a union to insist, as a condition precedent to entering into an agreement, that the employer agree to an illegal hiring clause.[876] The Board pointed out that:

It was the purpose of Congress to impose upon labor organizations the same duty to bargain in good faith which had been imposed upon employers in Section 8(5) of the Wagner Act, and continued in Section 8(a) (5) of the amended Act. Moreover, the standards and tests set forth in Section 8(d), applicable to both employers and unions, closely paraphrase those established in decisions of the Board and the courts in recent years. Such decisions, although they dealt primarily with employers' responsibility to bargain collectively under the Wagner Act, are nevertheless significant guide posts in determining the collective bargaining obligations of unions under Section 8(b) (3).[877]

Likewise, the union committed the same unfair labor practice when it conditioned the execution of an agreement upon the employer's consent to a closed shop, which is outlawed by the amended Act,[878] or a union shop without compliance with preliminary requirements established by the amended Act.[879]

The union must also meet the standards of good faith in negotiations. Thus, if the facts show that the union's position at a collective bargaining negotiation was not taken in good faith, it is guilty of a refusal to bargain collectively. In the *Great Atlantic & Pacific Tea Company* case,[880] the Labor Board pointed out:

In several of these cases, this very International, as a petitioner, asserted that the A & P and other chain organizations were engaged in commerce. It is difficult to believe that Swan, Henderson, and their legal advisers were unaware of these decisions. Moreover, on October 27, 1947, Schoen showed (Swan) a letter from the Board's General Counsel giving the opinion that the Company's operations were covered by the Act and that any collective bargaining contract had to be made in conformity therewith. Finally, the fact that the A & P grocery chain is a huge organization operating on a nationwide scale is a matter of common knowledge, probably even better known to the Respondents than to the public generally. To accept the explanation, under such circumstances, that Local 421 in good faith believed the Company was not subject to the Act is to strain our credulity. The jurisdictional point was, we believe, used by Local 421 to justify non-compliance with the amended Act. Accordingly, we find, contrary to the Trial Examiner, that Local 421 did not raise the issue of jurisdiction in good faith.

The duty to bargain, which rests alike on the employer and the representative of the employees, involves the obligation to bargain in good faith concerning terms and conditions of employment which are permitted by law. Neither party may require that the other agree to contract provisions which are unlawful. And when, as here, one of the parties creates a bargaining impasse by insisting, not in good faith, that the other agree to an unlawful condition of employment, that party has violated its statutory duty to bargain. Accordingly, we find, as did the Trial Examiner, that from on or about October 21, 1947, Local 421, as bargaining representative of the employees, refused to bargain collectively with the Company in violation of Section 8 (b) (3) of the Act.

CONTRACT TERMINATION IN VIOLATION OF ACT

When an existing collective agreement is about to expire, both union and employer parties thereto are required to take certain specific steps and observe a sixty day "cooling off" period before either a strike or lockout can occur. Failure to do so is an unfair labor practice.[881]

The steps required are imposed upon the party desiring to terminate or modify the contract and are as follows:

1. Serve written notice upon the other party of the proposed termination or modification sixty days prior to the termination of the contract or proposed modification.
2. Notify the other party of its willingness to meet and negotiate.
3. Within thirty days after the notice of such dispute notify the Federal Conciliation Service and any State Mediation Board of the existence of the dispute if no agreement has been reached by that time.
4. Continue in full force and effect, without strike or lockout, all the terms and conditions of the contract for a period of sixty days after such notice is given or until the expiration of the contract, whichever is later.

The Board has pointed out[882] that "Section 8(d)(1) of the amended Act defines one aspect of the obligation to bargain collectively, but automatic renewal of an existing contract does not result from failure to meet this obligation." The United States Circuit Court of Appeals for the District of Columbia has held that a strike called by a union without compliance with the aforementioned provisions of Section 8(d) of the amended Act is illegal.[883]

The provisions of Section 8(d) of the amended Act are inapplicable in the event that in the intervening period the Board certifies a new bargaining agent, or the authority of an existing bargaining agent is revoked.

These provisions do not mean that either of the parties is obligated to discuss or agree to a proposed modification of any of the terms of a contract for a fixed period if the modification is to become effective before such terms can be reopened under the provisions of the contract.

Employees who strike prior to the expiration of the sixty day period lose their status as employees until re-employed by the employer involved.

The Board has considered the meaning of subsection (4) of Section 8(d) of the amended Act insofar as it limits the right to strike "for a period of sixty days after such notice is given or until the expiration date of such contract, whichever occurs later." In the *Wilson & Company, Inc.*[a] case, the existing collective agreement was for a two-year period and contained a wage reopening clause after one year. Within the one-year period, the union gave notice of reopening for wage adjustment and a form of sixty-day notice under Section 8(d). After the lapse of the sixty days, the union went on strike. The employer contended that under the above quoted language of Section 8(d) the union could not strike until the expiration of the contract a year later and that the strike, consequently, violated Section 8(d). The contract did not contain a no-strike clause. Although agreeing that employer's position fell within the literal language of subsection (4) of Section 8(d), the Board overruled the employer's contention. The Board concluded, on the basis of the legislative history of the statutory provisions involved, that Section 8(d) did not bar strikes in support of demands made in accordance with reopening clauses of agreements. The Board said:

It cannot be denied that the result reached by the Trial Examiner is supported by a purely literal reading of Section 8(d) (4), for the strike occurred before the termination date of the contract and that date "occurred later" than the end of the 60-day notice period. In our opinion, however, the results which follow from such a literal reading are patently unreasonable, and at variance not only with the broad policy of the Act, but also with the specific purpose of the proviso to Section 8(d). If Section 8(d) (4) is read so as to prohibit a strike for modification of a contract until that contract expires, the concept of contract modification is rendered almost meaningless, and the act will have destroyed the effectiveness of provisions contained in hundreds of collective bargaining agreements whereby the parties have agreed to consider wage and similar adjustments during the term of the agreement, and, in the absence of a no-strike clause, have further recognized that demands made pursuant to reopening clauses may be supported by the traditional modes of economic pressure. Such a result would constitute a serious deterrent to the execution of collective bargaining agreements of any substantial duration, and would thereby remove a most important encouragement to stability in industrial relations.

As to the purpose of Section 8(d), the Board said:

It is apparent that the prime purpose of Section 8(d) was to prevent so-called "quickie" strikes designed to secure termination or modification of collective bargaining agreements. To accomplish this purpose, Congress in Section 8(d) provided for a mandatory 60-day "cooling off" period during which a labor organization that is a party to a collective bargaining agreement is forbidden to strike to enforce its demands to modify or terminate the contract. Nowhere in the legislative history is there any indication of an intent to extend the statutory waiting period beyond the 60 days to which reference is repeatedly made. Quite the contrary, the statements quoted above, in our opinion, serve to emphasize that once the 60-day period has elapsed, so far as the statutory requirements are concerned, unions and employers are free to take economic action.

4. Strikes and Boycotts

While the amended Act expressly reserves undiminished the right of unions to strike,[884] certain conduct of that kind as well as boycotts are defined as unfair labor practices. To constitute such unfair labor practice two elements must exist, namely:

1. The union must engage in, or induce or encourage employees to engage in, a strike or a concerted refusal in the course of their employment to use, manufacture or transport goods or work on any goods, articles or materials, or to perform services.
2. An object of such conduct must be any of the objectives banned by the amended Act.

The proscribed objectives of such strike or refusal to work are:[885]

1. To force an employer to join an employer organization or to force a self-employed individual to join any labor organization, or to force any employer or person to cease using, selling or handling products of any person or doing business with any other person. This provision bars the secondary boycott.[886]
2. To force any other employer to recognize the union as bargaining representative, unless such union has been certified by the Board as collective bargaining agent of employees of the other employer.[887]
3. To force an employer to recognize the union if another union has been certified by the Board as bargaining representative.[888]
4. To force an employer to assign work to the members of the union in preference to the members of another union, unless the employer is failing to conform with a Board certification determining the bargaining representative of the employees performing the work.[889]

These provisions of the amended Act, however, do not restrict the right of employees to refuse to cross the picket lines against another employer if the strike against such other employer has been approved by the union with which such other employer is required to deal as the representative of such other employees.

A union that engages in proscribed types of strikes and boycotts may be enjoined from activity by the United States District Court pending the determination of the unfair labor practice case by the Board. If charges of such unfair labor practices are filed with the Board and its Regional Director has reasonable cause to believe that the union is engaging in such illegal conduct, the Board's Regional Director must make application to the court for the temporary injunction except in the case of a jurisdictional strike as designated in point 4 above.[890] In this type of unfair labor practice, the application by the Board for temporary injunction is discretionary with the Board.

The United States District Court for the Southern District of California has sustained the constitutionality of the provision of the amended Act making the secondary boycott an unfair labor practice.[891]

Picketing and the distribution of "we do not patronize" lists have been enjoined under this provision against secondary boycotts.[892]

This rule was subsequently limited by the Board so that the placing on the union's unfair list of the name of the employer who is involved in a primary labor dispute with the union is not violative of the Act.[a] Thus, the Board has confined the violation to the use by the union of unfair lists against the secondary employer, although the effect of such lists—inducement and encouragement to boycott—would seem to be the same whether the primary employer's name or the secondary employer's name is placed on the union's unfair list.

It has been held that the Norris-LaGuardia Act does not apply to the Board's application for an injunction to restrain union unfair labor practices pending decision by the Board thereon, and to obtain the injunction the Board is not required to show irreparable injury and the inadequacy of the remedy at law.[893]

However, another District Court denied the Board an injunction when the union ceased its secondary boycott after the filing of the petition for the injunction with the Court, the Court pointing out that under the circumstances there was no reasonable likelihood of substantial and irreparable injury to the flow of commerce.[894] The Court kept the case on the docket in the event there were further unfair labor practices by the union.

To establish a secondary boycott within the meaning of the amended Act, two factors must appear: (1) the union conduct must have as an object the forcing of an employer to cease using the products of any manufacturer or to cease doing business with any person; and (2) the union's conduct must constitute inducement and encouragement of employees within the meaning of Section 8(b) (4) (A) of the amended Act. That the picketing for the purposes may be peaceful does not relieve the union of liability for violating the Act; the Board has held that peaceful picketing in aid of a secondary boycott is illegal.[895] Similarly, union "do not patronize" lists used to induce employees not to aid in the secondary boycott are not protected by the free speech provision of the amended Act and are illegal when used to enforce a secondary boycott.[896] "Product boycotts"—picketing any employer who uses the product of a manufacturer with whom the union has its principal dispute—is no defense to a charge of an illegal secondary boycott by the union.[897] Likewise illegal is the conduct of the union in following the shipments of the employer with whom the union has its primary dispute to freight terminals where the merchandise is unloaded for transportation, and in setting up picketing at the unloading points. The picketing at such points seeks to induce the employer of the transportation companies not to handle the merchandise of the primary employer.[898]

An important limitation on the secondary boycott provisions of the Act has been established by the Board. Thus, if a union engages in a primary dispute with an employer and pickets him, the fact that such picketing has the incidental effect of inducing employees of other employers not to handle the goods of another does not make the primary picketing illegal.[899] Similarly, the Board also held in the same case that it was not illegal for the striking union to advise other unions that the employer's product at the premises where the picketing occurred was "hot."

These decisions indicate that in the Board's view the place where the union's activities occur can be crucial and they are limited by the prohibition against secondary boycotts if confined to the immediate vicinity of the struck employer's premises.

On the basis of its view of the motor transportation industry as of "roving nature" so that the employer's trucks constitute his place of business and the place of employment of the employees, the Board has held that the picketing of such trucks at the premises of the customers or consignees of the struck motor carrier is not an unlawful boycott, although such conduct may have the incidental effect of inducing and encouraging the employees of the customers and consignees not to handle the struck carrier's freight.[900] The Board regarded such union conduct as primary action against the struck carrier since the picketing of its terminal and dispatcher's office would be futile for the reason that the customers and consignees rarely had occasion to contact those points.

Where the union threatens a secondary employer through an officer that it will picket that secondary employer unless he ceases doing business with the firm with whom he has a primary dispute, there is no violation of the anti-boycott section of the Act, because such conduct does not constitute inducement or encouragement of employees.[901]

"Struck work" or "hot cargo" provisions of a labor contract, whereby unions reserve the right not to handle goods from concerns engaged in a labor dispute, have been held not to violate the secondary boycott ban.[902] The Board's view is that nothing in the Act prevents an employer from pledging himself by contract to assist unions in their disputes. The provision of the Act outlawing secondary boycotts, according to the Board, is designed to prevent unions from involving neutral employers in a labor dispute through their employees and not otherwise. Thus, where the neutral employer has agreed to the "struck work" clause, his employees may take action to enforce it, and their conduct in so doing is not insubordination. As a result of the decision, it would seem that union efforts to obtain the "struck work" clause in negotiations would be intensified.

A District Court denied an injunction to the Board because the subcontractor who was subjected to the boycott took over a substantial amount of work from the employer with whom the union had its primary dispute, and performed such additional work under the supervision of the employer. The Court said that by such conduct the subcontractor made himself a primary party to the dispute with the union and that the relationship between the subcontractor and the employer did not constitute "doing business" within the meaning of the provisions against secondary boycotts embodied in the Act.[903] This holding has become known as the "ally" doctrine. However, the mere existence of a normal contractor and subcontractor relationship is in itself insufficient to warrant application of the "ally" doctrine and something more must be shown.[904] Concerns which have substantially common ownership, management and control would be regarded as allies in a secondary boycott situation.[905]

Illegal union action against employers to force recognition by another employer was described by the Board[906] as follows:

Local 145 picketed the Read, Howland, and Meigs Companies and thereby induced and encouraged the employees of these companies and the employees of companies supplying transportation service to these companies to engage in a concerted refusal to perform services required by their employment, that is, to make deliveries to and from the Read, Howland, and Meigs Companies. Similarly, Local 191, by its instructions to the employees of Read not to cross the picket line, induced and encouraged the employees of the Read Company to engage in a strike or concerted refusal in the course of their employment to make deliveries to and from the Read Company. An object of this encouragement and inducement was to force Delivery Company to recognize Local 145 as the representative of its employees, although Local 145 had not been certified as the bargaining representative of the employees of Delivery Company under the provisions of Section 9 of the Act.

In other words, the employers being picketed (Read, Howland, and Meigs Companies) are the "any" employers in the terms of the statute; the employees of Read, Howland, and Meigs Companies are likewise "the employees of any employer." They have been induced or encouraged by Locals 145 and 191 "to engage in, a strike or a concerted refusal in the course of their employment to * * * transport * * * or to perform any services." The object of the activities of Locals 145 and 191 was not to force the Read, Howland, and Meigs Companies (the "any" employers in this case) to recognize "a labor organization," but, on the contrary, to force or require the Delivery Company (the "any other employer" in this case) to recognize "a labor organization" (Local 145), which had not been certified by the Board. It seems clear to us that the activities of the Respondents are proscribed by the very terms of Section 8 (b) (4) (B) of the Act.

We are not persuaded, as is our colleague, Member Murdock, that we are precluded from finding that Local 191 violated Section 8 (b) (4) (B) because of lack of proof that Local 191 was actually aware that Local 145's dispute with Delivery Company was one over the recognition of an uncertified union. We do not believe that knowledge is a necessary factor in finding a violation by Local 191 of Section 8 (b) (4) (B). Local 191 assisted Local 145 in unlawful activity and, thereby, became responsible for Local 145's unlawful objective.

The ban against secondary boycott does not apply where the union seeks to induce a boycott by railroad employees who are subject to the Railway Labor Act since, by definition, they are not employees within the meaning of the National Labor Relations Act.[907] Similarly, the picketing of a school building to compel a board of education to cease doing business with a certain contractor was held not within the secondary boycott because he is not an employer within the Act.[908]

Nor does the ban apply where the union seeks to induce and encourage one employee to strike since the Act contemplates group or concerted activities of employees.[909] Nor does violence on the primary picket line to prevent employees of another employer from entering the struck plant constitute a secondary boycott.[910]

When a union pickets an employer's premises and otherwise seeks to induce his employees not to work unless he bargains with that union, despite the Board's certification of another union as bargaining representative of the employees, it engages in unfair labor practice in violation of the Act.[911] In such a situation, the Board will not permit the noncertified union to attack the validity of its certification of the other union.

In reliance on Section 10(k) of the Act, the Board has established a preliminary procedure which is investigatory and non-adversary.[912] Under this procedure the Board's Regional Director investigates charges of violation of the Act in the nature of jurisdictional disputes and if proceedings are necessary, he brings the parties involved before him by the issuance of a notice of hearing which sets forth briefly the issues. Ten days notice of hearings are given. If the parties have adjusted the dispute or agreed upon methods for adjustment, the Regional Director may permit withdrawal of the charge or dismiss it.

If the dispute is not adjusted by this procedure, a hearing is held before a

Hearing Officer and the parties present their evidence and arguments. The function of the Hearing Officer is to make a complete record of the facts and contentions of the various parties. The dispute then goes to the Board for determination. If the parties fail to comply with the Board's determination of the dispute, a complaint of unfair labor practice may be issued and the proceeding is then the same as in other unfair labor practice cases. The record of the preliminary procedure and the Board's determination of the dispute on that record is made a part of the record in the unfair labor practice proceeding.

As to the principles involved in the determination of jurisdictional disputes, the Board will consider such factors as the relevant collective bargaining history, the effect of labor contracts involved including their status, and validity under the Act, the practices, customs and traditions in the industry, applicable policies of management involved and the "bargaining or representative status" of the unions.[913]

5. Discriminatory Fees

When there is a valid union shop agreement in effect, that is, when the requirements of Section 8(a) (3) of the amended Act have been satisfied, it is an unfair labor practice for the union to require, as a condition precedent to becoming a member, the payment of fees which the Board finds excessive.[914] In determining whether a fee is excessive, the Board is required to consider among all the factors (a) practice and customs of labor organizations in the industry; (b) wages paid the employees affected.

6. Featherbedding

The amended Act declares it to be an unfair labor practice for a union to exact or attempt to exact from an employer payments for services not performed.[915] The Board has placed definite limitations on the extent to which featherbedding is outlawed by the Act. Where there exists an employee-employer relationship, a demand by the union or the continuance of payment of employees for non-production time was held not to fall within the ban against featherbedding.[916] In another case, the Board held there was no illegal featherbedding where the union demanded a payment "under a color of right in the nature of a claim for damages for breach of contract."[917] The union, claiming violation of a contract because the employer had hired a nonunion employee, demanded as one of the conditions for settling a strike that the employer pay to it an amount equal to the wages earned by the nonunion employee.

7. Filing Requirements Imposed on Unions

If unions desire to have the advantages of Board action they must comply with the filing requirements of the amended Act.[918] The union must file with the Board affidavits by all its officers denying Communist affiliation, and with the Secretary of Labor certain detailed information. If the requirements are not met by the union, the Board cannot issue a complaint upon the charge of such union, or entertain its petition for investigation and certification or for a union shop election. Thus, the noncomplying union is barred from all relief or aid through the Board.

The filing requirements apply not only to the local union filing the petition or charges but also to the international with which it is affiliated. Both must be in compliance before the local union can proceed before the Board.

When the union is not in compliance, the Board will not:

1. Entertain its charges of unfair labor practices;
2. Conduct an election on its petition;[919]
3. Certify it as bargaining agent, even though the election occurred prior to the effective date of the amendments;[920]
4. Permit it to appear on an election ballot when the petition was filed by a complying union;[921]
5. Permit it to appear on an election ballot on the petition of an employer;[922]
6. Compel an employer to bargain collectively with a noncomplying union.[923] A noncomplying union cannot petition for a union shop election[924] or for decertification.[925] If the only union involved has not complied with the filing requirements, the employer's representation petition will be dismissed.[926] Nor will the noncomplying union be permitted to intervene in a proceeding unless it has an existing contract covering the employees involved in the proceeding.[927] A noncomplying union cannot receive the benefit of a write-in vote in an election or contest the validity of an election.[928]

The Board has held that although its local union is not in compliance, the international may petition for an election and have its name, only, on the ballot.[929]

The Board has also held that the terms "national or international" in the provisions of the Act, setting forth the filing requirements, do not include the parent AFL and CIO federations and that these organizations as such are not required to comply.[930]

The Board has ruled that when non-Communist affidavits have been filed "it is not the purpose of the Act to require the Board to investigate the authenticity or truth of affidavits which have been filed in accordance with Section 9(h) of the Act."[931] In a later case a majority of the Board took the same position although, according to newspaper reports, an officer signing and swearing to the non-Communist affidavit was reputed to have said that he still believed in the principles and doctrines of the Communist Party.[932]

While a noncomplying union has no right to file objections to an election conducted to determine the bargaining representative of the employees, the Board has ruled that such a union may file objections to a decertification election. The Board's basis for this view is that in the decertification proceeding the noncomplying union "is not attempting to avail itself of the Board processes, but is made a necessary party by virtue of the petitioner's claim that the union no longer represents a majority of the employees in the appropriate unit."[933]

A noncomplying union that does not allege a contractual interest in the proceeding will not be permitted to become a party to a proceeding for the determination of bargaining representatives of the employees.[934]

A noncomplying union that seeks to obtain the benefits of Board processes by having an individual or a committee or another union act as a "front" for it, will be barred from such proceeding upon proof of such "fronting."[935] Evidence that the petitioner, a *bona fide* labor organization, has received assistance and even paid a noncomplying union for such assistance, is not sufficient to convince the Board of "fronting" so as to cause dismissal of a petition.[936]

The filing requirement does not affect the rights of individuals to file charges of discriminatory practices, and a claim that an employee filing such a charge is "fronting" for a noncomplying union is no defense to such a charge.[937] The fact that a noncomplying union assisted the employee in filing charges of discrimination does not affect his rights before the Board.[938]

8. Time Limitation on Filing Charges

Charges of unfair labor practice, whether filed by union, employer or individual employee, must be filed within six months of the occurrence of the alleged illegal acts.[939] Unless they are filed within that statutory period, the Board is without power to issue a complaint thereon. In addition, notice of the charge must be served within the specified period upon the party alleged to have committed the unfair labor practices.

However, Section 10(b) of the amended Act does not bar the issuance of a complaint based upon an amended charge where such amended charge is substantially a restatement of the original charge which itself was timely filed and served.[940] Nor does this Section have the effect of limiting the allegations of the complaint if the underlying charge was timely filed and served.[941]

The Board has ruled that the time limitation contained in Section 10(b) operates as a statute of limitation but does not affect the introduction of evidence. Relevant testimony of events occurring more than six months prior to the filing and service of the charge will be received in evidence at a hearing on a complaint alleging unfair labor practices.[942]

The time limitation does bar the Board from making any finding of unfair labor practices on the basis of events which occurred more than six months prior to the timely filing and service of the charge; and the Board's complaint may include allegations of unfair labor practices uncovered during the investigation of the original charge although such unfair labor practices are not specifically enumerated in the charge.[943] Where the original charge was timely filed and served, the Board's findings are not limited to events which have occurred during the six months period prior to the filing of an amended charge.[944]

The Board has refused to dismiss a complaint issued on an amended charge where the original charge was timely filed but the charging union thereafter changed its name and affiliation and filed an amended charge more than six months after the occurrence of the acts constituting the alleged unfair labor practices.[945]

PART FOUR

Collective Contracts

Introduction

CHAPTER I. Collective Bargaining Defined

II. Duty to Bargain

III. Standards of Performance

IV. Authority of the Bargaining Agent

V. Employes Entitled to Bargain Collectively

VI. Area of Collective Bargaining

VII. Refusal to Bargain Collectively

VIII. Preparation for Bargaining

IX. Negotiating and Drafting the Collective Agreement

X. Operating under the Agreement

XI. Grievances

XII. Arbitration

XIII. Litigation

XIV. Effect of State Acts

247

INTRODUCTION

The labor contract represents the fruition of the collective bargaining procedure; yet it is a process which must be continued even after the contract is executed by the parties. Thus the contract itself and its administration rest upon the performance of the duty of management and union to bargain collectively. The principles relating to that obligation have been considered in detail in earlier pages.

Those readers who turn immediately, however, to this Part on the Collective Contract should find integrated in it the fundamental principles on which negotiations must be based. For this reason we begin this section with a summary of these principles as they bear on the problems of Negotiating and Drafting the agreement and Operating thereunder.

The quotations from arbitration awards which appear in Part IV are reproduced from *Labor Arbitration Reports* by permission of the Bureau of National Affairs, Inc., Washington, D. C.

I · COLLECTIVE BARGAINING DEFINED

The Labor Management Relations Act defines "to bargain collectively" as:

The performance of the mutual obligation of the employer and the representative of the employees to meet at reasonable times and confer in good faith with respect to wages, hours, and other terms and conditions of employment, or the negotiation of an agreement, or any question arising thereunder, and the execution of a written contract incorporating any agreement reached if requested by either party, but such obligation does not compel either party to agree to a proposal or require the making of a concession.[1]

This definition establishes the following standards for collective bargaining:

1. The obligation to bargain collectively is mutual, that is, the union as well as the employer is under the duty to bargain.

2. The parties are required to meet at reasonable times and confer in good faith. Generally, therefore, the same tests for determining whether there has been good faith compliance with the standards prescribed by the Act would appear to be applicable to both employer and union.[2]

3. They are required in good faith to negotiate an agreement.

4. An agreement, if reached, must be reduced to writing and signed, upon the request of either party.

5. Neither party is required to agree to a proposal or make a concession. This negative portion of the definition in no way limits or detracts from the good faith standard imposed upon the parties. It does not necessarily relieve either side from making counterproposals. The extent of the "give" and attempt to meet mutual requirements on both sides of the bargaining table constitutes evidence of the good faith that each party must demonstrate in seeking to reach an agreement. The mere demand for a concession by either union or employer does not require the other party to yield thereto or make a concession. But they are required to bargain with respect to such demands.

Collective bargaining requires that the parties involved deal with each other with open and fair mind and sincerely endeavor to overcome obstacles or difficulties existing between them to the end that employment relations may be stabilized and obstruction to the free flow of commerce prevented.[3]

Mere pretended bargaining will not suffice; neither must the mind be hermetically sealed against the thought of entering into an agreement. To do less than is required by the standards of good faith and conduct is a refusal to bargain collectively and violates the spirit and intent of the Act.

Where an employer refused to bind himself contractually as to wage rates, hours of work, holidays, vacations and bonuses, insisting upon the right to grant such conditions of employment as gratuities, and rejected a clause against lockouts, he has demonstrated his bad faith and his refusal to bargain.[4] The employer cannot insist upon withdrawing these matters from the sphere of collective bargaining. Nor can he insist upon reserving to himself the right to alter, at his discretion, existing practices with respect to these matters for collective bargaining. Such an attitude shows a total want of good faith and makes genuine collective bargaining impossible.

It should be noted that the execution of the collective agreement does not complete or terminate the duty to bargain collectively. The definition specifically requires that "any question arising" under the agreement is subject to the collective bargaining process, and standards for performance of the obligation to bargain on both sides are applicable.

However, during the existence of the contract, questions may arise which are not covered by or under the agreement. Such disagreements are not questions "arising" under the agreement. While such a situation is not specifically covered by the statutory definition, it seems clear that the obligation compelling the parties to bargain in good faith would exist with respect to such questions.

There is, however, a specific exemption from the requirement to bargain collectively when there is a collective contract for a fixed term. Neither party is required to discuss or agree to any modification of such contract if the modification is to become effective before the provisions of the contract sought to be modified can be reopened pursuant to the terms of the contract.[5]

II·DUTY TO BARGAIN

Section 9(a) of the Act provides as follows:[6]

Representatives designated or selected for the purposes of collective bargaining by the *majority of the employees in a unit appropriate for such purposes,* shall be the exclusive *representatives of all the employees in such unit* for the purposes of collective bargaining in respect to rates of pay, wages, hours of employment, or other conditions of employment.

The principle of majority rule is applied in the determination of the bargaining representative with whom an employer is obligated to bargain collectively.[7] If a majority of the employees in an appropriate bargaining unit select a representative for the purposes of collective bargaining, all the employees in such unit are bound by that choice, including employees who are not members of the union and those who have either failed or refused to designate the union as bargaining representative.[8]

The duty of the employer to bargain collectively with the union does not arise until the aforementioned conditions have been met, that is, the union has been designated as bargaining representative by a majority of the employees in the appropriate bargaining unit, and the union as such representative makes a demand upon the employer for collective bargaining.[9] If no such demand is made, the obligation to bargain on the part of the employer is not crystallized. The employer is under no obligation to search out the union for the purposes of collective bargaining.[10]

The failure or refusal of an employer to bargain collectively in good faith upon demand of a union having majority status in the appropriate bargaining unit is an unfair labor practice and bargaining may be compelled by the National Labor Relations Board with the aid of an enforcement order of the United States Court of Appeals.[11] The existence of a strike does not relieve the employer of the duty to bargain.[12] Nor may he refuse to bargain because he claims the union is irresponsible.[13] Where there has been bargaining in good faith, resulting in an impasse, negotiations need not be resumed if it clearly appears that they would be futile.[14] However, the impasse does not terminate the duty to bargain and negotiations must be resumed if there is the slightest likelihood that results may be achieved by doing so.[15]

251

A union may demand that an employer bargain with it and negotiate a contract. This is a demand for recognition of the union as exclusive bargaining agent for the employees. The employer may, upon proper authority, concede that the demanding union does represent a majority. In that event, the employer recognizes the union and proceeds to negotiate a contract. On the other hand, the employer may in good faith question the majority representation by the union. He may in good faith insist that a Board election be held as proof of the union's majority.[16] He may also on the basis of "reasonable judgment," and in good faith, question whether the bargaining unit claimed by the union is appropriate.[17] In view of the vast body of decisions by the Board on questions of appropriate bargaining unit, the employer's "reasonable judgment" in raising the unit issue is subject to attack. Generally the obligation of the employer is to cooperate reasonably toward an expeditious determination of the majority status of the union.[18]

If the employer questions the union's majority representation, the union may seek resolution of the issue by filing a petition for investigation and certification of the bargaining representative by the Board.[19] If the employer is not acting in good faith, the union may file charges with the Board, claiming a refusal to bargain as an unfair labor practice.[20] In either event, the union is without recourse to the Board unless it files the non-Communist affidavits and registration statements required by amendments of the National Labor Relations Act contained in the Labor Management Relations Act of 1947.[21]

Under the amended Act, the employer may file a petition for an election although only one union has claimed to have majority status.[22] However, the Board has said the employer's petition will be dismissed if the only union involved fails to comply with the requirements for filing of non-Communist affidavits and registration information.[23]

The filing of a petition gives the Board authority to resolve the question if it has jurisdiction. Essentially two questions are presented,[24] viz:—

1. What is the appropriate bargaining unit?

2. Does the union represent a majority of the employees in such a unit?

Both questions may be resolved by agreement of the union and the employer.[25] They may stipulate the appropriate unit and agree that an election be held. Under the amended Act, the Board will not check union membership cards against a payroll even though the parties agree thereto.[26] The parties, however, may agree upon an independent check.

If the parties cannot agree upon a method for determining the question of representation, the Board must hold a hearing, determine the appropriate bargaining unit, conduct an election and certify the bargaining agent, if one is selected by the employees in the unit. The question of majority representation is then resolved.[27]

Only one election can be conducted by the Board during a twelve-month period. Thus, if the union loses the election, it cannot seek a new ballot for a year. This twelve-month bar is the result of the amendments to the Act and varies from prior practices of the Board.[28]

At the very outset of an employer's experience with union representation or on the expiration of a collective bargaining agreement, he may be faced with conflicting claims by rival unions. When an employer receives conflicting claims for bargaining rights from rival unions, he may file a petition for investigation and certification of the bargaining representative with the Board.[29] The questions raised by the employer's petition are the same as in the case of a petition filed by a union, namely, what is the appropriate bargaining unit and who is the bargaining agent. They may be answered by the consent method already mentioned or by a decision on the disputed issues and the direction of an election by the Board.

An employer who undertakes to bargain with one of the rival unions does so at his peril.[30] The other union may file a charge of unfair labor practice with the Board. If it establishes that it represents a majority in an appropriate bargaining unit, the Board will find the employer guilty of refusal to bargain, and direct the employer to bargain with the union filing the charge. The Board has also held that an employer violates the Act if he signs a contract with one of two rival unions during the existence of the dispute as to which one of them represents the employees as exclusive bargaining agent.[31] On the other hand, the employer need not determine, at his peril, which of the competing unions represents a majority of the employees.[a] When the conflicting claims arise at the expiration of a collective bargaining agreement, other considerations may be involved. The terms of the contract may be important. When a contract provides for automatic renewal as of a certain period prior to the expiration date, unless a contrary intent is stated, the rival union must make its demand on the employer prior to the commencement of the automatic renewal period and file a petition with the Board within ten days after such demand.[32] In the absence of such timely demand and petition, the contract is a bar to proceedings by the rival union. Proper notification by either party to the contract, stating its intent not to renew, opens the contract and makes claims of the rival union timely.[33] Negotiation of a new agreement or an interim agreement, after the automatic renewal date and prior to the expiration date of the contract, permits a rival union to assert its claim effectively, provided it has served notice upon the employer before the effective automatic renewal date of the contract.[34] When a union has been certified as bargaining representative by the Board, such union and the employer are relieved of claims by rival unions for a reasonable period after certification, normally one year; and an original contract as well as an extension of its term may be entered into the year following date of certification.[35] Of course if the contracting union becomes defunct or there is a substantial shift in the affiliation of the employees, a new union may step in.[36]

Where an employer has negotiated a contract with a union, and all that remains is the drawing of the written agreement, a rival union may assert a claim effectively at any time prior to the actual signing of the written agreement by the parties.[37]

Claims by rival unions affiliated with the same parent organization create a jurisdictional dispute over representation, for example, claims by unions affiliated with the AFL. The Board will afford the parent organization a limited time in which to adjust the dispute between its two unions, and upon failure of the parent organization to resolve the disagreement, will proceed to determine the bargaining representative.[38]

III · STANDARDS OF PERFORMANCE

While the Act, as amended, defines the duty to bargain collectively, it leaves to the Board and to the courts the determination of what tests shall be applied for the purpose of ascertaining whether employers and unions are performing such duty. The standard of performance is said to be negotiation in good faith to the end that agreement shall be reached with respect to wages, hours and conditions of work, and reduction of the agreement to a signed contract for a fixed reasonable period.[39] Mere gestures in such a direction do not constitute collective bargaining.[40] Nor does the requirement that the employees submit a list of demands, which are either accepted or rejected without explanation, satisfy the requirements.[41]

The submission of proposals by a union or by an employer, with a "take-it-or-else" attitude, does not constitute collective bargaining. "Negotiations with an intent only to delay and postpone a settlement until a strike can be broken" are not collective bargaining.[42]

"Interchange of ideas, communication of facts peculiarly within the knowledge of either party, personal persuasion, and the opportunity to modify demands in accordance with the total situation thus revealed at the conference is of the essence of the bargaining process."[43]

The nature of the good-faith requirement indicates that whether the standard of performance is met will depend on the facts in each case where the issue is raised. The guide posts for performance and the manifestations of non-performance are considered in connection with refusals to bargain collectively.[44]

IV. AUTHORITY OF THE BARGAINING AGENT

A union that has been selected as bargaining representative by a majority of the employees in an appropriate bargaining unit has widespread authority with respect to wages, hours and conditions of work of all the employees in the bargaining unit.[45] By virtue of the application of the principle of majority rule, the bargaining representatives, through negotiation of the collective agreement, may fix the wages, hours, and conditions of work of nonmembers of the union, and those employees in the unit who have either failed to designate it as their bargaining representative or refused to do so.[46]

If authority is obtained by reason of a union shop election conducted by the Board in accordance with the requirements of the Act, the bargaining representative, by means of the collective agreement, may require employees to become members of the union within thirty days after its effective date and new employees may be required to join the union thirty days after hiring. If employees fail to join within the period prescribed, the union may obtain their discharge from employment. Similarly, if during the contract term, employees fail to pay the periodic dues, the union may obtain their discharge.[47]

If the employees voluntarily, in writing, authorize the deduction, the union may obtain a check-off of union dues by agreement with the employer.[48] However, such authorizations cannot be irrevocable for a period of more than one year or beyond the date of termination of the contract, whichever is sooner.

When the collective agreement has been entered into, the union has the authority to police its administration, compel performance, process and secure adjustment of grievances and arbitrate all questions subject by the contract provisions to arbitration procedure.[49]

When the union has attained majority status, its right to exclusive recognition as bargaining agent of all the employees in the appropriate unit cannot be questioned. Such exclusive right is not a subject matter of collective bargaining, and any attempt by an employer to bargain with respect to it is an unfair labor practice.[50]

The authority of the bargaining representative extends to those situations where individual employees or groups of employees have the right to present grievances to the employer by virtue of the provisions of the Act. While such grievances may be adjusted without the intervention of the bargaining representative, provided the adjustment is not inconsistent with the provisions of the existing collective contract, the Act requires that the bargaining representative be afforded an opportunity to be present at such adjustment.[51] The employer cannot insist that an employee shall have the option of determining whether or not a union representative shall be present at the initial adjustment of grievances with the representative of management authorized to make such adjustments.[a] The right of recognition includes the right of the union to be present on such occasions.

The exclusive authority of the bargaining representative, once established, presumptively, at least, continues until revoked by the employees.[52] However, when a majority of the employees in an appropriate unit have designated a bargaining agent in an election conducted by the Board, they cannot shortly thereafter revoke such authority.[53] Petitions signed by a majority of the employees to cancel the authority granted by them, six months prior thereto, are ineffectual. No new election, either to revoke the union's authority or to designate another bargaining representative, can be conducted by the Board for a twelve-month period succeeding the last election.[54] The union's authority as evidenced by the Board's certification is normally valid for the period of one year. During this period the union may negotiate a two-year contract[55] and even prematurely extend an existing contract to the exclusion of demonstrably valid claims of representation by a rival union.[56]

The authority of a union is limited in certain respects by the provisions of the amended Act. Thus, unions which have failed to comply with the requirements to file non-Communist oaths by its officers and to register information specified in the Act, cannot enforce their authority to represent employees for collective bargaining, and the employer may, without violating the Act, refuse to bargain collectively with such a union.[57] A union that does not comply cannot petition the Board for certification. If the petition has been filed by a complying union, a noncomplying union will be excluded from the election.[58] As has been noted more fully under the discussion of the statutory filing requirements imposed on unions, noncompliance therewith limits the authority of the union in other respects.[59]

The fact that unions engaged in a jurisdictional dispute concerning the representation of employees are affiliated with the same International, does not necessarily divest either of them of the right to obtain certification as bargaining representative from the Board. The Board, however, will take such cases only when it appears that the parent organization has not composed the conflict. Typical are the cases where the jurisdictional dispute has existed for some years without determination by the parent organization, although the machinery within such organization for resolving the conflict has been exhausted.[60]

Where unions are engaged in a jurisdictional dispute concerning the assignment of work by the employer to their members, the authority of the rival unions in such situations may be resolved by the Board under the amended Act. Unless the rival unions settle such a dispute within ten days after filing of an unfair practice charge, the Board may decide it for them.[61]

The Act prescribes a specific method whereby employees may validly revoke the authority of a previously designated bargaining representative for purposes of collective bargaining. This procedure is commonly known as "decertification," that is, the Board certifies the results of an election conducted to determine whether the currently recognized or previously certified union still is the bargaining representative of the employees in the appropriate bargaining unit.[62] Any employee or group of employees may file the decertification petition;[63] the petition cannot be filed by an employer.

The petition must allege that a substantial number of employees assert that the union, which has been certified or is being currently recognized by the employer as bargaining representative, no longer is such representative.[64] The procedure thereafter is the same as on a petition for certification.[65] The Board investigates as to whether there is reasonable cause to believe that there is a question concerning representation. If so, a hearing must be had and if, upon the record of the hearing, the Board finds that there is a question concerning representation of the employees, it must conduct an election among the employees and certify the results. The amended Act, limiting elections to one a year, is also applicable.[66] Hence, if a union has been certified, a petition for decertification, filed within one year of the election on which the certification was issued, must be dismissed because the Board can conduct only one election during the twelve-month period following the last election.

V · EMPLOYEES ENTITLED TO

BARGAIN COLLECTIVELY

1. The Grouping of Employees

To bargain collectively, employees must be grouped in units appropriate for the purposes of collective bargaining. The Act empowers the Board to "decide in each case" the appropriate unit "in order to assure to employees the fullest freedom in exercising the rights guaranteed" by the Act.[67] Thus, the decisive question in determining the unit is whether the proposed grouping will "assure" the employees the benefits of collective bargaining.

The Board may find appropriate the employer unit, craft unit, plant unit or subdivision thereof. Some of the important factors considered in resolving the question of what is the appropriate bargaining unit are:

1. The extent and type of organization of the employees;[68]
2. History of collective bargaining among the employees at the plant involved, and at other plants of the employer, and at plants of other employers in the same industry;[69]
3. The duties, skill, wages, and working conditions of the employees;[70]
4. The desires of the employees;[71]
5. The eligibility of employees for membership in the union;[72]
6. The relationship between the proposed unit and the organization and administration of the employer's business;[73]

The extent to which the employees have been organized may be a factor in determining the appropriate unit, but it cannot be the sole justification for the establishment of a proposed unit.[74] On this principle the Board refused to set up a unit consisting only of seamers, loopers and examiners in a knitting mill, since the sole basis for establishing such unit was the fact that these employees had organized.[75] This principle has been applied also to the sales employees of a department store.[76]

In conforming with accepted practice, production and maintenance employees are grouped together.[77] Clerical employees usually constitute a separate unit. Factory clerical employees, however, are grouped with the production employees, since they work in close proximity, are usually sub-

259

ject to the same supervision and have marked similarity in wages, hours and working condition.[78] Supervisory employees, such as foremen, are not included in the same unit with nonsupervisory employees except in special industries like the printing trades, where historically such inclusion of foremen has developed.[79]

Employees who constitute a true craft unit are afforded an opportunity to vote in a so-called "Globe" election on whether they desire to be included in a larger group of plant employees or maintain a separate identity as a craft unit.[80] This principle has been applied in the case of such typical craft employees as pattern makers[81] and highly skilled electrical maintenance employees.[82] However, the employees involved must truly represent a craft by virtue of such factors as long training or apprenticeship periods and the high degree of skill involved, and must in themselves constitute a homogeneous group.[83] Craft unit severance has been denied semi-skilled or quasi-skilled employees such as painters who were recruited from the unskilled labor force,[84] and employees who performed only some of the functions of blacksmiths.[85] But where a so-called craft unit consisted of a heterogeneous commingling of various types of work, a single craft unit was denied, although all the employees involved could generally be classified as electricians.[86]

Craft employees, however, cannot be included in a larger unit merely because they were so grouped by a prior Board determination, unless a majority of them vote against separate representation.[87]

Professional employees cannot be grouped with non-professionals unless a majority of them vote for such inclusion.[88] The term "professional employee" is defined in Section 2(12) of the Act and covers employees whose work is predominantly intellectual, requiring knowledge of an advanced type in a field of science or learning, customarily acquired by a long course of study in an institution of higher learning. Typical examples are graduate engineers and chemists. The Board analyzes the nature of the position, training and work to determine whether the employees can properly be grouped as professional employees.[89]

Plant guards who "enforce against employees and other persons rules to protect property of the employer or to protect the safety of persons on the employer's premises" must be separately grouped and cannot be included with employees performing other tasks. Nor can a union be certified by the Board as bargaining representative of such employees if it, or the international organization with which it is affiliated, admits to membership employees other than guards.[90] Watchmen who make rounds and punch clocks have been held to be guards subject to the foregoing principles.[91]

Time study personnel, who are essentially fact-finders exercising considerable judgment and discretion but not to any substantial degree formulating, determining or effectuating management policies, have been held to be professional employees entitled to bargain collectively, rather than managerial employees.[92]

Although inspectors in the production departments of a plant exercise individual judgment and discretion which affect the earnings of other employees, they have been held not to be supervisory or professional employees, and may be grouped with production and maintenance employees.[93]

2. Employees Excluded

By virtue of the definition of employee, which excludes them from coverage of the Act, supervisory employees cannot insist upon the right of collective bargaining.[94] A supervisory employee is defined to mean an individual having authority to hire, transfer, suspend, lay-off, recall, promote, discharge, assign, reward or discipline other employees or effectively to recommend such action if such authority requires the exercise of judgment and is not routine or clerical.[95]

Thus, foremen with such power cannot bargain collectively as a matter of right.[96] Assistant foremen and operating engineers have been held supervisors under the aforementioned definition.[97] Section men and a working foreman whose duties involve authority of a supervisory nature have also been held supervisors.[98]

On the other hand, a rank-and-file employee who substitutes for a foreman one month during the year has been held not to be a supervisory employee.[99]

Likewise managers of a retail chain store were held to be nonsupervisory because of the lack of sufficient authority,[100] and group leaders have been similarly classified for the same reason.[101] As pointed out in a preceding chapter, time study employees and inspectors have not been regarded as having sufficient authority to bring them within the definition of a supervisory employee.

The determinative factor in these cases is the nature and extent of the authority of the employees claimed to be supervisory.

It should be noted, however, that while supervisory employees do not have the right of collective bargaining, and the refusal of an employer to bargain with them does not constitute an unfair labor practice, an employer may voluntarily undertake collective bargaining with supervisory employees. Nor does the Act bar supervisors from membership in a labor organization.[102]

Independent contractors, like supervisors, are also excluded by definition from the term "employee" and cannot claim the right of collective bargaining under the Act.[103]

The Board has held that newspaper carriers who operate home delivery routes under contract with the publishers are independent contractors and hence not entitled to be grouped as an appropriate bargaining unit.[104]

VI·AREA OF COLLECTIVE BARGAINING

While Section 8(d) of the National Labor Relations Act defines "to bargain collectively," the subject matter of the bargaining process is described only generally as "wages, hours and other terms and conditions of employment." Neither party is compelled to make an agreement with respect to these general matters,[105] and their duties have been described as requiring them to enter into discussions with open and fair minds and a sincere purpose to find a basis for agreement.[106] The specific subject matter of these responsibilities has been developed by decisions of the Board and the courts.

In considering the area of bargaining, particular stress has been laid on what are the inherent managerial fields which the union may not invade and as a matter of policy in which they should not participate. Management does have certain responsibilities to its customers and stockholders (in the event of a corporation) and to the government as well as to its employees.

Some writers prefer to speak of management functions rather than prerogatives. Whatever they are called, in essence unions have of late been more insistent on participating in them than on any other single issue. Unions have achieved such participation by advocating clauses requiring mutual consent and joint committees as a prerequisite to the adoption of any policy, and by demanding seniority and unlimited arbitration, which affect other demands, such as pensions, welfare plans, etc. The trend of Board decisions has been toward widening the scope of bargaining to include greater participation by the employees through the bargaining representative, in matters which affect them and which have been thought to be of exclusive management concern for many years.

The term "wages" has been broadly construed and the Board has said that "there is indeed an inseparable nexus between an employee's current compensation and his future benefits." Somewhat similarly, the term "conditions of work" has been held to mean more than "physical working conditions" and to include "terms or conditions under which employment status is afforded or withdrawn."[107]

Thus, the fact that a collective agreement has been negotiated without mention or inclusion of certain employee benefits such as an existing bonus, pension, or retirement plan does not remove such benefits from the area of mandatory collective bargaining, and the union has not by silence or its failure to raise the issues at negotiations waived its right to bargain collectively with respect to them. Nor is the fact that such a program is in operation a basis for the employer's refusal to bargain collectively on such matters.

Some of the specific matters as to which collective bargaining has been held mandatory are as follows:

1. Union security provisions;[108]
2. Machinery for adjustment of grievances;[109]
3. Pension and retirement plans;[110]
4. Vacations and holidays;[111]
5. Bonuses;[112]
6. Merit increases;[113]
7. Profit sharing plans;[114]
8. Work standards and loads;[115]
9. Group insurance;[116]
10. Grounds for dismissal of employees;[117]
11. Plant and employee rules;[118]
12. Hours and composition of work shifts;[119]
13. Re-employment of laid off employees;[120]
14. Subcontracting of work;[121]
15. Rest and lunch periods;[122]

However, Section 8(d) of the Act does indicate that proposed modifications of the provisions of an executed and functioning agreement cannot be the subject matter of collective bargaining during the contract term unless the contract by its terms provides for reopening. That section contains the following provision:

> ... and the duties so imposed shall not be construed as requiring either party to discuss or agree to any modification of the terms and conditions contained in a contract for a fixed period, if such modification is to become effective before such terms and conditions can be reopened under the provisions of the contract.

The same section of the statute plainly indicates that "any questions arising" under the terms of an existing collective agreement are properly the subject matter of collective bargaining. Thus, the execution of a collective contract does not end the process of collective bargaining, and the interpretation and administration of a contract already made and the settlement of disputes arising under any such contract are properly regarded as within the sphere of collective bargaining.[123] Clearly, therefore, a refusal by an employer to bargain collectively within that area might constitute an unfair labor practice within the meaning of the Act; and the existence of a collective contract between the parties does not preclude the Board from finding that unfair labor practices have taken place, and issuing an appropriate order. However, the Board has been of the view that it would not effectuate the statutory policy of "encouraging the practice and procedure of collective bargaining" for it to assume the role of policing collective contracts between employers and labor organizations by attempting to decide whether disputes as to the meaning and administration of such contracts constitute unfair labor practices under the Act.[124] On the contrary, it believes that parties to collective contracts would thereby be encouraged to abandon their efforts to dispose of disputes under the contracts through collective bargaining or through the settlement procedures mutually agreed upon by them, and to leave the interpretation and administration of their contracts to the Board. Where the parties have not exhausted their rights and remedies under the contract as to which the dispute has arisen, the Board has been reluctant to exercise its jurisdiction, and has dismissed a complaint without prejudice in so far as it charged refusal to bargain collectively.[125]

On the other hand, where the parties have litigated an issue under the contract procedure, the Board, in the exercise of discretion, has refused to permit relitigation of the same issue on the theory that an unfair labor practice was involved.

In the matter of *Timken Roller Bearing Company,*[126] the Board said:

It is evident that the Union has concurrently utilized two forums for the purpose of litigating the matter here in dispute. Although the arbitrator determined the issues before him within the framework of the 1943 agreement and expressly refrained from prejudicing the rights of either party before the Board, it would not comport with the sound exercise of our administrative discretion to permit the Union to seek redress under the Act after having initiated arbitration proceedings which, at the Union's request, resulted in a determination upon the merits. In the interest of ending litigation and otherwise effectuating the policies of the Act, we shall dismiss that portion of the complaint relating to the respondent's refusal to bargain as to the Employees' Manual.

Individual grievances of employees or groups of employees may fall outside the area of collective bargaining. Management may resolve such a dispute unilaterally provided that the adjustment thereof is in nowise inconsistent with the terms of the existing collective agreement and the bargaining representative is given an opportunity to be present at such adjustment.[127] The Act, however, does not define what would fall within the term grievance.

VII·REFUSAL TO BARGAIN COLLECTIVELY

Refusal to bargain, as it is viewed by the Boards and courts, is not necessarily limited to cases of total refusal to bargain; it may consist of refusing to bargain on certain specific matters, while agreeing to negotiate on others.

Refusal, by an employer or a union which has been designated bargaining representative of the employees in an appropriate bargaining unit, to bargain collectively constitutes an unfair labor practice under the Act.[128] The Board may compel the violator of the statute to bargain by issuing an order to that effect and obtaining enforcement thereof by decree of the United States Court of Appeals.[129] Violation of such a decree is contempt of court and subjects the offender to punishment.[130]

The illegal refusal to bargain may be manifested by dilatory and evasive tactics,[131] denial of recognition of the union as the exclusive representative of the employees,[132] disregard of the bargaining representative[133] or lack of good faith in dealing with the union.[134] "Good-faith" conduct is a fundamental requirement throughout the process of collective bargaining.[135] The nature of the obligation to bargain in good faith does not permit the establishment of a yardstick for testing whether there was compliance with the express mandate and spirit of the Act. Each case where the question is raised must be determined on the basis of the circumstances involved. It has, however, been said in general that the sincerity of the employer's efforts in negotiating with a union may be tested by the length of time involved in the negotiations, considered in the light and nature of the problems, and the persistence with which the employer offered opportunity for agreement.[136]

"Good-faith" performance of the obligation to bargain collectively can be illustrated by marking the conduct which has been characterized as illegal. Such a consideration will also chart, to some degree, the extent of the duty imposed by the statute.

An employer cannot ignore a demand by a union for a conference to negotiate a collective agreement. Failure to respond thereto in any way is an illegal refusal to bargain, if the union has been designated bargaining representative by a majority of the employees in an appropriate bargaining unit.[137]

266

Questioning in bad faith the union's majority status, or the propriety of the bargaining unit asserted by the union, constitutes refusal to bargain.[138] Management is liable for dilatory tactics in not raising the question of the union's majority status openly and in good faith. The employer must not adopt procedures of evasion and indirection, avoiding conferences and shifting his position, thereby demonstrating to employees that he intends not to negotiate and that their designation of the representative for the purposes of collective bargaining was futile.[139]

When the employer has properly raised the question of the union's majority status, he is under a duty to cooperate reasonably in resolving the question.[140] He cannot without sufficient cause refuse to cooperate in any reasonable method for determining whether the union represents a majority of the employees. He cannot arbitrarily refuse to consent to a Board election to determine the question of representation.[141]

While management may question the propriety of the bargaining unit asserted by the union, it cannot do so in bad faith or for purposes of stalling or in defiance of established and recognized principles which attest the correctness of the unit claimed.[142] For example, to contend that admittedly supervisory employees should be permitted to vote at an election in a unit of nonsupervisory employees would be patently improper in most instances, since it is now well recognized that both classes of employees can not be grouped together. On the other hand, such a contention would have been valid under the Wagner Act as to foremen in the printing industry because foremen have historically been included in the same unit with rank-and-file employees in that industry.

Refusal by management to furnish an authorized representative to participate in personal conferences with the union representatives is denial of collective bargaining. The Act cannot effectively foster and encourage collective bargaining unless the employer and the union cooperate in the "give and take" of personal conferences.[143]

While both parties may agree to bargain collectively through the mail, management cannot force such procedure upon the union. The employer situated at a distance from the plant where the dispute arises cannot insist upon negotiating long distance by letters, telephones and telegrams.[144] Such conduct, manifestly, subjects the union and the employees to undue delay and unjustifiable financial burden. Management must make its representatives available for personal conferences at the plant involved at reasonable times and places. The plant is where employees are hired, work, and are discharged; therefore, plant management is better able to understand and solve the problems in the negotiations affecting those employees.

Section 9(a) of the Act[145] requires management to recognize the bargaining agent of the employees' unfettered choice. A clause, demanded by management, which calls for the recognition of the union as the sole collective bargaining agency only for those employees who are affiliated with the union, is inconsistent with the statutory command that the union with majority status shall be the exclusive representative of all the employees in the appropriate bargaining unit for the purposes of collective bargaining.

With respect thereto the Court of Appeals for the Seventh Circuit has said:

> There is no escape from the conclusion that the words "for those employees who are affiliated with the union" place a limitation upon the recognition granted, which cannot be reconciled with the plain language of the statute.
>
> If there be any doubt in this respect, however, it is dispelled by the controversy concerning recognition which was paramount at the numerous conferences had between petitioner and the locals, including Local 226. In the first place, the recognition required by 9(a) is not a bargaining matter as petitioner (company) sought to make it. When it was disclosed to petitioner that Local 226 (the union) represented a majority of the employees in the appropriate unit (this was at no time questioned by petitioner), the obligation was then fixed upon it to recognize the local as the sole and exclusive bargaining agent, not only for the members of the union, but for all employees. In place of complying with this statutory requirement, petitioner made it the subject of a long and extended bargaining process. Subsequent to the time when demand for recognition was made, petitioner, at all times, has been in default of its statutory obligation.

Since the company insisted upon imposing this limitation upon the representative status of the union, it was guilty of a refusal to bargain, although it had bargained in good faith on all other issues.[146] The union must be treated as an equal contracting party, and the employer violates the law if he insists that any contract negotiated must be signed by his employees alone rather than by the union.[147]

Collective bargaining, as imposed by the Act, obligates the employer not to engage in conduct which is destructive of the employee's bargaining representative. He cannot go behind the back of the union and deal directly with the employees or unilaterally grant benefits. By such conduct he induces employees to abandon the union and thereby interferes with their right to bargain collectively through representatives of their own choosing. Such conduct is subversive of the procedure of collective bargaining which the Act seeks to encourage.[148] Thus, an employer by negotiating a wage increase directly with his employees, at a time when wage negotiations are pending with the union, violates the obligation to bargain with the union. He violates the Act although he negotiates directly with the employees, and grants them a wage increase at their request and instance and upon their voluntary promise to abandon the union.[149]

By virtue of the same principles of collective bargaining, unilateral action by an employer upon the subject matter of collective bargaining while negotiations are being conducted or to be commenced constitutes an illegal refusal to bargain. The unilateral grant of a wage increase during wage negotiations is a typical example of such conduct.[150] A reduction of employee benefits may be a refusal to bargain. Where an employer made a sudden reduction in wages well-timed to discourage any bargaining on the subject, he committed a refusal to bargain about wages within the meaning of the Act.[151]

The existence of individual contracts of employment with individual employees offers no obstacle to collective bargaining, although the terms of such contracts are of themselves valid. When a majority of the employees have designated a representative for the purpose of collective bargaining, the individual contracts must yield to the collective agreement, in accordance with the public policy embodied in the Act for the benefit of the majority.[152] Manifestly, if the individual contracts contain terms which are in conflict with, or contrary to the provisions of the Act, such as a provision against bargaining for a signed collective agreement with a labor organization, they are illegal. Such individual contracts cannot defeat collective bargaining.[153]

An employer who enters upon collective bargaining negotiations with the firm intent of not joining in a signed agreement or who refuses to execute a written contract, if agreement is reached, thereby illegally refuses to bargain.[154] While not obligated to take the initiative in seeking a contract or to agree, the employer cannot proceed to negotiate with his mind in adamant opposition to arriving at any agreement. He must approach the bargaining table with a reasonable and fair mind and make an honest and sincere effort to reach an agreement.[155] Where a management flatly refused the union's demand for a union shop, seniority and job security provisions and coupled its position with threats to dissolve the company and instructions to its operating officials to "work out" arrangements with individual employees, a conclusion that there was no intent to deal with the union was justified.[156]

Refusal of management to include in a signed agreement existing working conditions is evidence of refusal to bargain. It indicates an intention to reserve such conditions for unilateral employer action rather than to assume a contractual obligation to perform for a fixed term.[157]

The requirements of collective bargaining are not satisfied by merely meeting with the union. Mere discussion of grievances with the union is likewise insufficient. Both sides are obligated beyond discussion. Discussions must be with a sincere purpose to find a basis for an agreement.[158]

The existence of a strike called by the union does not justify the employer's refusal to bargain; nor can he condition bargaining upon the employees' return to work.[159]

An employer who has committed unfair labor practices by engaging in a campaign to destroy the union cannot avoid the obligation to bargain collectively by claiming that the employees no longer wish to be represented by the union.[160] Similarly, where there has been an illegal refusal to bargain by the employer, the subsequent loss of majority by the union affords the employer no basis for continuing to refuse to bargain with the union.[161] The principle underlying this ruling is that the subsequent loss of a majority by the union may reasonably be attributed to the prior unfair labor practices of the employer, who will not be permitted to take advantage of his own violations of the law. However, in one case, the court, upon the basis of the special facts presented, reached a result contrary to this principle. In that case, the employer illegally refused to bargain, but engaged in no other unfair labor practices. The facts showed the subsequent loss of majority in the small bargaining unit involved was directly attributable to economic reasons causing a reduction in force which was effectuated in good faith.[162] The court was of the opinion that these facts made the aforementioned principle inapplicable, and denied enforcement of a Board order requiring the employer to bargain with the union.

A refusal to bargain in violation of the Act, as in the case of other unfair labor practices, is not excusable on the ground that a rival union has subjected the employer to serious economic pressure in order to compel the latter not to bargain collectively with the bargaining representative.[163] The mere fact that there has been expansion of the plant does not justify a refusal to bargain. Such a factor, at best, will only be considered by the Board as one reason for making a redetermination of the bargaining unit and it will not necessarily be controlling on that question.[164]

The employer may not always insist upon a Board election and certification for the purpose of having the union establish its majority status in an appropriate bargaining unit. However, his refusal to accept membership cards proferred by the union as proof of majority designation does not necessarily indicate bad faith in raising the question.[165] He may, however, be put to his proof to show that he had an honest doubt as to the majority status of the union and that his insistence upon an election was not for the purpose of frustrating or avoiding the obligation to bargain.[166]

Similarly, the employer cannot decline to bargain on the ground that the union was never certified as bargaining representative by the Board. Certification is not a condition precedent to the union's right to demand bargaining. The controlling factor is whether the union has been designated by a majority of the employees in the proper bargaining unit. Such designation may exist without an election or Board certification.[167]

The question of the appropriate bargaining unit places the employer in a difficult position. He raises the issue in response to the union's demand for collective bargaining at his peril, unless the facts show that in the exercise of reasonable judgment he lacked knowledge of the appropriateness of the unit asserted.[168]

The amended Act excludes from the term "employee" individuals employed as supervisors.[169] By virtue of the new definition, employers are no longer obligated to bargain collectively with unions representing a majority of their foremen or other supervisors. Nor can the employer be compelled to do so although nothing in the law prohibits the employer from voluntarily undertaking such collective bargaining.[170] Prior to the amendment, the Board interpreted the term "employee" to include foremen within the coverage of the Act and compelled the employer to bargain with the union representing the foremen.[171] However, these cases fell with the amendment of the Act, and after the amendment the courts denied enforcement of a Board order compelling bargaining with a foremen's union, although the order to do so had been issued prior to the effective date of the amended Act.[172] The court felt bound by such a substantial change in the substantive provisions of the Act. It is noteworthy, however, that substantial procedural changes effectuated by the amendments have been applied prospectively and not to cases arising under the prior law.[173] One exception has been laid down by the Board. Where the order compels an employer to bargain with a union, the Board will condition the effectiveness of the order upon the union's compliance with the filing requirements of the amendments within thirty days after issuance of the order, and the courts have sanctioned this policy of the Board.[174] Thus, if the union fails to satisfy the filing requirements within the thirty day period, the bargaining order is of no effect. The Board has explained this new policy on the ground that while the filing requirements are procedural, they embody an important public policy which requires that a noncomplying union should not have the benefits of a Board order to bargain, which is tantamount to a new certification of the union. Since a noncomplying union cannot petition for certification, it should not be accorded, through an order to bargain, the same benefits accruing to a complying union.

When an existing collective bargaining agreement is about to terminate, either party thereto may be held guilty of refusal to bargain for its failure to comply with the requirements of the amended Act with respect to notice of desire to terminate or modify the contract. The amended Act[175] sets

forth procedures which the parties must follow if they wish to terminate
or modify the contract. Failure of either to comply is an unfair labor practice. A party to the contract to terminate or modify it must comply as
follows:

1. Give written notice to the other party of the proposed termination or modification sixty days before the expiration date;
2. Offer to meet and confer with the other party for the purpose of negotiating
   a new contract or a contract containing the proposed modification;
3. Within thirty days after giving such notice, notify the Federal Conciliation
   Service and the comparable state agency if no agreement has been reached;
4. Continue the contract in full force and effect for sixty days after such notice
   is given or until the expiration date of the contract, whichever is later, without
   resorting to a strike or lockout.

An employee who engages in a strike during the sixty day period loses
his status as an employee, which deprives him of the protection of the
amended Act.

Many collective labor agreements provide for automatic renewal of
their terms and provisions unless either party gives notice to the other
of desire to terminate or modify the agreement a specified number of days
prior to the termination date. Failure to give such notice has the effect of
renewing all the terms and provisions of the contract for another fixed
term as provided in the contract. Compliance with the notice requirements
set forth in the contract does not constitute compliance with the statute.
The statutory requirements as to notice requirement and the sixty day
"cooling off" period must be allowed regardless of the terms and provisions
of the contract. A strike or lockout in violation thereof is an unfair labor
practice.

The provisions of the amended law concerning contract termination
do not apply if there is an intervening certification by the Board of a new
bargaining agency or a decertification of the union which is party to the
expiring contract.

VIII·PREPARATION FOR BARGAINING

Management should insist on the requirement that demands or proposals for modification of the contract be submitted sufficiently well in advance of the termination or renewal date to allow for the requisite preliminary planning prior to the actual negotiation.

In preparing for negotiations, certain basic information should be compiled, such as (1) sample contracts and contract clauses; (2) surveys of wages and working conditions in the industry, in allied industries, in industries in the immediate area; (3) points of difference and experiences under existing contracts which require change; (4) economic arguments best calculated to insure the acceptance by the union of the particular viewpoint advocated and the objectives sought by management.

Some form of permanent administrative agency in a trade group should be charged with the duty of following the effect of contract provisions with a view to recommending necessary changes and amendments in the interest of more practicable administration; and understandings and policies should be catalogued which, while not actually written into the agreement, may be helpful in further negotiations and incorporated in a master agreement or annexed thereto, or in an agreement of interpretation designed to clarify clauses in a previously negotiated contract.

In preparing to meet the proposals of the union, meetings should be held with foremen and supervisors to review current practices and experiences under the contract about to expire (or if the contract is a first one, to consider patterns which should be avoided as a result of experiences of other companies).

Foremen should meet with management in pre-bargaining sessions so that they may gain first-hand information during the progress of negotiations, as a result of which they will be enabled to aid in the negotiation, interpretation and application of the agreement. Through such meetings, the foremen will acquire a much more accurate understanding of company policy and become equipped to handle troublesome situations which few members of management other than foremen can be expected to anticipate.

Management should have at its immediate disposal a comprehensive outline of all jobs, their classification and content, wage differentials, and the data required to justify disparity in pay, a comparable picture of the industry in and out of the area, cost of living and other economic data needed to explain or further its position, with supporting reasoning to convince union representatives and employee members of the union's bargaining committee.

Among the important data to be carefully studied as possible trend indicators are industry wage rates and wage changes in the area, in the region, or even throughout the nation.

For comparative purposes, it is advisable to marshall rates, even of other industries; fringe practices, settlements, cost of living data, productivity records, financial statements and profit reports, supplemented by economic studies.

Among the best sources of bargaining data from the union's point of view are corporation financial statements, since these give the membership an understanding of the position of the particular company and its relation to the industry. Of equal importance is the relation of the industry to the economy. To both union and management, the financial services, as *Moody, Poor,* the *Wall St. Journal,* the *Journal of Commerce;* and studies made by various administrative agencies, such as the Federal Trade Commission, Bureau of Labor Statistics of the United States Department of Labor, National Labor Relations Board, Wage-Hour Division should all prove of considerable help.

The soundness of the company's proposals will be determined, in the main, by the extent to which they are based upon the problems as they confront foremen in the shop.

The approach to bargaining should be through selected negotiators who are deliberate in judgment, know the industry and are highly skilled in moving effectively at the auspicious time. Only such conferees should be selected as can be entrusted with the delicate and arduous task of negotiating. They should be assisted by advisory committees with whom they may consult as negotiations progress. The negotiators would do well to view differences in viewpoint between management and the union as constituting a "challenge to find new solutions, rather than a threat to industrial peace."

Federal, state and local laws governing the operation of the plant should be reviewed. Reports of trade associations should be studied inasmuch as they may reflect industry-labor policies, trends and practices. These reports frequently indicate how other managements in comparable situations have met union demands and resolved disputed issues. These reports further serve to indicate the extent of the union's demands and the positions it has taken in the course of negotiations with other employers. It may even reflect some of the union bargaining strategy.

Management should inquire into the appropriateness of every provision, to make certain that none will prove ineffective, inadequate or troublesome. It should study competitive factors such as going wage rates, costs, type of management, comparative advantages, profits, prices, markets and methods of absorbing costs and give ample consideration to the correction of practices found to be unjustified. In marshalling data for bargaining conferences, the practical significance of each proposal must be weighed and its long-term effect upon the company and industry analyzed.

IX · NEGOTIATING AND DRAFTING
THE COLLECTIVE AGREEMENT

1. Introduction—Status of the Collective Agreement

WITH RESPECT TO THE UNION AND THE EMPLOYER

The collective bargaining agreement establishes the wages, hours and working conditions of the employees covered for the term of the contract, and should be an assurance of uninterrupted production for that period.[176] The agreement must be given a reasonable construction no matter how inartistically drawn and regardless of its apparent lack of any obligation upon the union. The reasonable implication would appear to be that the contract produces reciprocal obligations, that the union is obligated to do everything allowable under its constitution and bylaws to bring about compliance by its members with the provisions of the contract and abstain from any act which would conflict with any such provisions.

Union enforcement through the courts of terms and provisions of the collective agreement is now well recognized.[177] Courts have enjoined the discharge of union members and the hiring of nonmembers in violation of the closed shop provision of a contract.[178] General wage reductions and lockouts in violation of the contract, and employer attempts to "runaway" in order to avoid the agreement,[179] have been similarly treated. The contract has been held to be binding upon the legal successor of the employer who entered into the agreement.

In most jurisdictions, the employer's attempt to obtain redress for the union's breach of the contract has long been beset with insurmountable obstacles because of the rule that the union, as an unincorporated association, is not a legal entity subject to legal process.[180]

The enactment of the Labor Management Relations Act constituted a statutory recognition of the collective agreement as a valid, binding and enforceable contract. Section 301(a) thereof provides that the contracting union may be sued as a legal entity for violation of the contract.[181] Service of process upon an officer or agent of the union constitutes service upon the union. Any money judgment against the union can be satisfied only from the union's assets; union members and their assets are not answerable thereto.

Under this new provision, the union could be liable in damages for breach of a no-strike clause of the contract. Some courts have said that in the absence of express provision, a promise not to strike will be implied in the contract.[182] To establish union liability for acts in violation of the contract, it is necessary to satisfy the ordinary rules applicable for establishing an agency relationship between the actor and the union, and an express authorization or ratification need not be shown. While the union should not be liable for unauthorized strikes by its members if it acts in good faith, an obligation on the part of union officials to use union discipline to end the strike should be implied.

During the contract term, union members covered by its terms may shift their allegiance, or the contracting local union as a whole may transfer its affiliation; the authorities indicate that in all such circumstances the contracting union continues to be bound by the agreement and is entitled to its benefits.[183] If the international is not a party to the contract, it may revoke the local's charter without affecting contractual relations between local members and the employer. But if the membership of the contracting union consists entirely of employees covered by the contract and all of them withdraw from the contracting union, such a move may be tantamount to a vote to dissolve the contracting union.

The Norris-LaGuardia Act and similar state statutes restrict the right of an employer to enforce the collective agreement by injunction, since these enactments apply to controveries "involving or growing out of a labor dispute." A controversy over enforcement of the collective agreement would appear to be a "labor dispute." However, union enforcement of the agreement is not beset with such difficulties. A New York court held that the state anti-injunction statute did not bar enforcement of a contract by injunction against an employer.[184]

WITH RESPECT TO THE EMPLOYEES

Since the collective agreement is entered into by the exclusive statutory bargaining representative for all employees in the appropriate unit, they should be bound thereby regardless of their membership in the contracting union. In view of the fact that the agreement is for the benefit of the bargaining unit as a whole rather than the individual, the trend has been, within the last decade, in the light of the development of the entire concept of collective bargaining, to regard the agreement as creating no "individual" rights. The standards of wages and other conditions of work in individual employment contracts fix these matters in so far as such contracts are consistent with the collective agreement. But the individual right yields to the collective agreement. A Michigan court has held that seniority rights of an employee, acquired by virtue of the terms of a collective agreement, may be lost by virtue of another such agreement subsequently negotiated by the union.[185]

However, on the theory that the employee is a third party beneficiary of the collective agreement, courts have permitted individuals to recover any differential between the wages provided in the contract and the amount actually paid, as damages for discharge in breach of the contract or for violation of the seniority provisions thereof.[186] Consistent with this theory a court has permitted an employer to recover from employee the excess of payments erroneously made to him.[187]

In any event, if the employee has individual rights against the employer under the collective agreement or is individually obligated to the employer in any respect, these rights and obligations should be subject to the grievance and arbitration machinery of the contract. Some New York courts have held that employees covered by the contract could not maintain lawsuits against the employer upon matters covered by the contract, since they were subject to arbitration.[188] Furthermore, so long as the union acts in good faith, individual employees should have no right to invoke the arbitration machinery. A contrary rule would be destructive of the principles of collective bargaining. Some contracts expressly confine the right of arbitration to the union and the employer.

One other aspect of the individual employee's obligations under the contract should be noted in connection with the obvious principle that the agreement must bind nonunion members in the bargaining unit covered thereby as well as union members. If a group of employees who are not members of the union or a dissident group of union members strike in violation of the no-strike clause of the contract, they should be held subject to such provision and responsible for breach thereof.[189]

WITH RESPECT TO THIRD PARTIES

During the lifetime of the collective agreement, a rival of the contracting union may strike against the employer to compel his noncompliance with the contract. Some courts have enjoined strike activities by the rival union upon the request of the employer or of the contracting union, on the ground that such activity constitutes "malicious" inducement to breach the contract. The New York Court of Appeals has refused to interfere in such a situation on the theory that the interests of the rival union in furthering its own advancement justified any injury that might result.[190]

2. Purpose of Negotiation

The aim in negotiation of a collective bargaining contract should be to achieve a mutually satisfactory agreement that will establish proper labor relations and uninterrupted production for a fixed period.

Negotiations will usually be preceded by the union's submission of a proposed contract or demands for provisions in the contract. There is no reason why management may not, in the first instance, submit a proposal, and it may be advantageous for it to do so, since the initial proposal very often establishes in general the pattern of the negotiations and the final agreement.

Where negotiations follow upon the termination of a prior contract, the union usually submits its proposals for modification of the prior agreement. Management should also submit its proposals for modification. An exchange of proposals in advance of the meeting affords each party an opportunity for full preparation and may have the effect of expediting negotiations.

Management should be prepared to negotiate the proposals it presents as well as the demands of the union.

The employer cannot dictate to the union who shall act for it at the bargaining conference, regardless of how distasteful a particular individual representing the union may be. The employer must negotiate with any representatives designated by the union. Nor can the union dictate to an employer who shall represent him at negotiations. The designation of representatives to negotiate is within the exclusive authority of each party, and neither has the right to invade the other's authority to select representatives for the bargaining conference. However, if either party persists in sending to the bargaining conferences so-called representatives who are in fact mere messenger boys without power to reach even a tentative conclusion, such conduct is evidence of bad faith in bargaining.

The procedure of the bargaining conference, as a rule, involves give and take. Prior to the conference, each side formulates its demands and designates negotiators. The negotiators then meet at the appointed time and place. The conference opens with each side formally presenting its demands together with arguments and supporting reasons. Then follow clarifying discussions in which rebuttals are made and concessions granted. The employer will try to show that the economic situation does not warrant the union's demands, and the union will produce statistics to support its contentions, or may rely on statistics concerning the cost of living. Each issue is taken up, and during the conference each side may hold a private meeting to discuss the advisability of yielding or holding out. Demands may be traded and the ultimate conclusion may await the decision on two or three crucial matters. Matters may be discussed individually or in package. The final agreement is more frequently than not a compromise.

Employees should be kept informed of the progress of the collective bargaining, but in such manner as not to irritate the union or subject the employer to a charge of bypassing the bargaining representative. Instead of relying upon paid advertisements, wise management will tell its employees its side of the story through personalized communications. A communications program properly authored and administered should inform the supervisory staff, employees and, where indicated, the people of the community, of developments as bargaining proceeds.

To keep employees informed on day-to-day progress, the company should make foremen and supervisors an integral part of management and thus, enable these representatives of management to answer employee questions intelligently and accurately. Minutes of bargaining meetings should be communicated to the employees. Particular care should be exercised to avoid giving voluminous and too detailed direct information, so that the employees will not get the impression that they are being swamped with company propaganda. Information might best come from the lower echelons of supervision. On the other hand, an effort should be made to agree with the union that in the event of a breakdown of negotiations no releases should be sent to the newspapers except by mutual consent.

The mechanics of the procedure of collective bargaining preclude unilateral action by either side within the area of collective bargaining. The rule has been summarized by the Board as follows:

> It is of the essence of collective bargaining that no rupture in bargaining negotiations be created by a fait accompli in a matter then under negotiation.[191]

Thus, while wage negotiations are pending, the employer cannot, as a rule, make a unilateral wage increase or decrease. The principle is applicable to all the matters which are the subject of the pending negotiations. Nor can the employer go behind the back of the union and, while negotiations are pending, reach an agreement on the various subject matters thereof directly with the employees. Furthermore, the employer cannot engage in such conduct even though his employees voluntarily request him to do so.[192] The grant of a wage increase substantially greater than that requested by the union and over which the parties negotiated to a legitimate impasse is an unfair labor practice—refusal to bargain collectively.[193]

Every effort should be made to incorporate into the contract objective standards for settling problems. Management should submit data to unions, recess and caucus to discuss proposals, and determine its course of action.

In making its final proposal, management should consider the advantage of relations predicated on a rational and factual basis, rather than on emotion or threat of economic power.

In some industries a union-inspired form-contract is utilized in an effort to unify practices and expedite negotiations, as well as to prevent individual differentiations which may, from the union's point of view, undermine its gains. Thus the maritime, brewery, construction, coal and automotive unions point to a pattern of "multiple employer unit on an industrial basis."194

3. Standards for Drafting the Collective Agreement

Completion of negotiation of the collective agreement between the employer and the union presents the problem of drawing the agreement. The importance of the drafting of the agreement cannot be overestimated, since it involves integrating by means of the written word the agreement that has been reached in the negotiations. Poor draftsmanship of the agreement can frustrate the negotiations by failure to express the intent and understanding of the parties or by omissions which will foster disputes and litigation. The problems remain the same regardless of which party prepares the initial draft of the agreement.

In the drafting of the agreement, three factors should be borne in mind at all times:

1. The provisions should be clear and definite and should explicity cover the subject matter in accordance with the intent and agreement of the parties;

2. The language should be simple so as to be readily understood by the employees in the plant. Artistry in language may well give way to simplicity;

3. All the provisions should clearly cover the complete intentions of the parties so as to be understandable by any third party—an arbitrator or a court.

4. Preamble

The opening sentence of the contract as well as the recognition clause should state the parties to the agreement. Manifestly, the contracting local union, considered as an entity, should be bound by the agreement. The officers of the union should likewise be bound so that they are obligated by all its provisions including the no-strike clause and the provisions concerning management's rights.

The collective agreement should start with a statement of what the document is, that is, an agreement between the employer by name and the contracting union (and international if a party) by exact name, on behalf of itself, its officers, and its members.

A preamble may well recite that it is the general purpose and intent of the parties to promote and improve industrial and economic relations between them, to establish a basis of agreement concerning rates of pay, wages, hours and working conditions and to provide means for the amicable adjustment of disputes and grievances at the plant covered by the agreement. The preamble may also recite that the purpose of the agreement is to achieve uninterrupted production and to secure cooperation between the company and the employees through collective bargaining as a substitute for industrial warfare. However, the achievement of these primary purposes depends more on the attitudes and responsibility of union and management at all levels than on the bare words of the agreement.

The words of the preamble may attain particular significance when the interpretation and construction of the agreement are at issue. Where the contract is silent or its language is ambiguous, arbitrators justifiably probe the preamble for some indication of what the parties generally intended.

5. Recognition

Recognition must be granted the union representing a majority of the employees in the appropriate bargaining unit. It is not a subject matter for collective bargaining, and any attempt to bargain with respect to it is an unfair labor practice.

Upon demand of the union, the contract must include a provision whereby the employer recognizes the union as the exclusive and sole bargaining representative of the employees in the bargaining unit.

The recognition clause should state and identify the employees included within the bargaining unit and, hence, covered by the contract. It should clearly specify the employees excluded from the unit and contract coverage and specifically identify the plant where the employees, covered by the contract, are employed so that it will not be applicable to other or new plants of the employer.

In order to avoid future disagreement, the exclusions from the bargaining unit should be specifically enumerated. To make certain of these limitations it would be well for the parties to cover the list of departments in the plant as well as the job classification of employees. Thereby, "fringe" groups may be disclosed, subjected to discussion and an agreement reached with respect to them. The exclusion of foremen should be specific and a general exclusionary provision with respect to all employees who would be within the definition of the term "supervisor" should be agreed upon. In some cases, the problem may be reduced to such detail as to require reference to particular employees.

Negotiation of much of the foregoing may be eliminated by a Board certification, since the appropriate bargaining unit and the exclusions therefrom are then stated by the Board. However, even in such cases the statement of the unit and its exclusions should be carefully examined, and if any of its descriptive classifications fail to cover categories of employees that have been added since the Board certification, this fact should be brought to the union's attention for the purpose of disposition.

Where the negotiations are with a local union affiliated with an international, consideration may be required as to whether the international should be a party to the contract. It has been said that generally participation of international representatives, by reason of a broader experience, has a stabilizing effect on the relationship between the employer and the employees. The constitutions of some international unions require that they enter into the contract together with or on behalf of the local union, which is also a party to the contract. In some instances, the international may require certain "stock" clauses to be included in the contract. If such mandated clauses are undesirable, the contract should be with the local.

RECOGNITION CLAUSE

A typical clause provides:

(A) The Company recognizes the union as the exclusive bargaining agent for the employees of the Company in the designated plants subject to the inclusions and exclusions as set forth in the certifications of representatives by the National Labor Relations Board following elections, or as mutually agreed between the local plant and the local union.

It is agreed that the term employees, for the purpose of this local supplemental agreement, includes the hourly rated and piecework production, engineering and maintenance employees at the company's plants, except those employees working in the capacity of office employees, employees in full supervisory capacity, pattern-makers, and plant protection employees exclusive of fire department employees. The company agrees to meet with and bargain with the accredited representatives of the union on all matters pertaining to hours of work, rates of pay, general working conditions of employment, and all other employee-employer relations.

(B) In the event the union, at some future date is recognized or designated in accordance with the regulations of the National Labor Relations Board as the bargaining agent for a unit of production and/or maintenance employees not mentioned in the preamble of this agreement, the company agrees that it will within ten (10) days following the request of the union, negotiate the question of whether this agreement will become applicable in whole or in part to such new bargaining unit.

6. Wages

While management has the right to hire, direct operations, etc., wages are indisputably a matter of collective bargaining. In negotiating wage scales, management should stress the necessity for maintaining justifiable differentials, thereby avoiding any charge that skilled or older employees are accorded no recognition, but are treated in the same manner as are learners, probationers or common labor. Accordingly, scales should be agreed upon and adhered to which will reflect such recognition.

While specific schedules, shift differentials, minimum pay, transfer policy and waiting time are matters for negotiation, management should reserve the right to initiate adjustments, provided these are neither arbitrary nor discriminatory. Though management should consult the union on any adjustments, it must not be too rigidly bound by the union's veto power. The right to make such adjustments should be vested in management, subject to grievance procedure in the event of an alleged abuse.

The union's wage demand may be for new minimum job rates, an across-the-board increase, lump sum adjustments to be allocated among individuals or given groups, automatic progression and merit increases or combinations and variations of these. The request for new minimum rates will raise the questions of job comparability and the prevailing minima in the industry in the area in which the plant is located. Other factors, particularly with respect to the across-the-board increases, are the prevailing wage levels, increases granted by competitors, comparative benefits and working conditions, cost of living changes, productivity of the employees and their wage adjustments, and "pattern" wage increases.

To avoid freezing wages at a given level in the face of rising costs, provision is at times made for reopening for wage adjustment through an escalator clause or otherwise. Such reopening is generally limited to once in any given contract term and then is restricted to wages only and not fringe benefits, to avoid complete renegotiation.

WAGE CLAUSE

A typical clause provides:

SECTION A: Wages During Learning Period: Minimum Wages After Learning Period

1. Prior to the completion of the learning period on any job, probationary

female employees shall receive seventy-five cents (75c) an hour, and probationary male employees shall receive eighty-nine cents (89c) an hour.

2. After the completion of the learning period on any one job, minimum guarantees shall vary depending upon the method by which the employee is compensated, whether piecework, Standard Hour Plan, or hourly rated (day
work) as follows:
   a. If compensated on a piecework basis, no female employee shall receive
   less than seventy-five cents (75c) an hour, and no male employee shall
   receive less than eighty-nine cents (89c) an hour.
   b. No employee compensated under the Standard Hour Plan shall receive less
   than the base rate established for the particular job.
   c. No employee compensated on an hourly (day work) basis shall receive
   less than the hourly rate established for the particular job.

3. The employer shall have the right, in his sole discretion, with reference to
probationary employees:
   a. To waive the learning period.
   b. To begin the learning period at any time during the probationary period.

SECTION B: Military Induction Pay—All employees who enter the Armed
Forces of the United States prior to ——————————, shall at the time of induction, be paid military induction pay computed as follows:

1. Employees with six (6) months or more of employment shall receive forty
(40) hours' pay at average earnings rate.

2. Employees with one year or more of employment shall receive eighty (80)
hours' pay at average earnings rate.

SECTION C: Changes in Job Procedure and Time Standards.

1. The employer may as heretofore at any time and from time to time make
the following changes in job procedure:
   a. Change from day work to incentive work, or from incentive work to
   day work.
   b. Make changes in the motions or methods of job procedure and appropriate
   changes in incentive rates; or where, over a period of time an accumulation
   of minor changes have occurred which in total have resulted in a change
   in job time, adjustments in incentive rates may be made.
   c. The employer shall notify the union and discuss time standard changes
   with it before installation, except for minor routine changes. Minor routine
   changes may be installed without prior discussion with the union.

2. If the union and the employer differ as to the fairness of any such change,
such difference shall be resolved by the grievance and arbitration procedure
herein provided.

3. In the event that the fairness and reasonableness of a time standard change
shall be questioned, it is agreed that the operator shall make a reasonable
effort to develop incentive earnings through the application of the standard
as changed before a grievance is filed. The trial period during which the
operator will expend reasonable effort will be identical in length to the learning
period of the job, but in no event will exceed a period of two (2) weeks. If a
grievance is registered, the union shall have the right to have a qualified
time study engineer inspect and study the job in question.

4. Wage rates and time studies will be available to the union at all times.
5. If it is determined by negotiation or by arbitration that any time standard change was unfair, employees in the employ of the employer at the time such determination becomes final, shall be granted an appropriate pay adjustment retroactive to the date of such time standard change, but in no event retroactive to a date earlier than two (2) weeks prior to the date on which a grievance concerning that time standard change was filed. In such event an appropriate adjustment in average earning rate for the period in question shall also be made.

SECTION D: Transfer Wage Policy

1. Upon being transferred to a job for which a learning period has been established, an employee shall be advised of the learning period by the department foreman.
2. Average earnings rate as referred to in this Agreement is computed on a six (6) weeks basis as follows: Total pay, less shift and overtime premium pay, divided by the total number of hours worked. The six (6) weeks average is computed on the first six (6) weeks of the eight (8) weeks immediately preceding the effective date of the average.
3. When an employee is transferred from one job to another job, the following wage policies shall be applied during the established learning period for the new job:
   a. When an employee is transferred from either a piecework job or a Standard Hour Plan job to a piecework job, he shall be paid either his average earnings rate or his piecework earnings on the new job, whichever is higher.
   b. When an employee is transferred from either a piecework job or a Standard Hour Plan job to a day work job, he shall be paid either his average earnings rate or the established rate of the new job, whichever is higher.
   c. When an employee is transferred from a day work job to a piecework job, he shall be paid either the established rate of the old job, the base rate of the piecework job, or his piecework earnings on the new job, whichever is highest.
   d. When an employee is transferred from a day work job to another day work job, he shall be paid the higher of the two established rates.
   e. When an employee is transferred from any incentive job to an individual Standard Hour Plan job, he shall be paid either his average earnings rate or his incentive earnings on the new job, whichever is higher.
   f. When an employee is transferred from a day work job to an individual Standard Hour Plan job, he shall be paid either the established rate of the old job, the base rate of the incentive job, or his incentive earnings on the new job, whichever is highest.
   g. When an employee is transferred from any incentive job to a group Standard Hour Plan job (except where paragraph "i" is applicable), he shall be paid his average earnings rate.
   h. When an employee is transferred from a day work job to a group Standard Hour Plan job (except where paragraph "i" is applicable), he shall be paid the established rate for the job from which he was transferred or the base rate of the incentive job, whichever is higher.

   i. When an employee is transferred from one job to another job within the same Standard Hour Plan group, he shall be paid either the base rate established for the new job or incentive earnings on the new job, whichever is higher.
   j. These transfer wage policies shall not apply to any employee upon his retransfer to his regular job if such retransfer occurs within sixty (60) days from the date of transfer from such regular job. However, a refresher period, during which these transfer wage policies shall apply, may be granted any such employee by mutual agreement of the Department Foreman and Department Steward.
4. If an employee is again transferred prior to completing a learning period after the first transfer, he shall, for the purpose of applying the transfer wage policies set forth in paragraph "3," be deemed to have been transferred directly from the job from which he was first transferred.
5. After a transferred employee has completed a learning period on a new job, he shall be paid at the rate and in accordance with the wage policy which governs the new job.

SECTION E: Equal Pay for Equal Work—It is agreed that there shall be equal pay for equal work, regardless of sex or age.

SECTION F: Shift Premium—All employees working on the scheduled second shift operation shall receive a premium of five per cent (5%) above their rate or five cents (5c) an hour, whichever is higher. All employees working on the scheduled third shift operation shall receive a premium of ten per cent (10%) above their rate.

SECTION G: Depressed Production—Any employee whose earnings are found to be adversely affected because of waiting for supplies, materials, repairs to machines or equipment, power shutdowns, machine overhauls, or changes in work, or by reason of faulty materials, equipment or supplies,—which conditions are not of normal variation in plant operations—shall be compensated at not less than his average earnings rate for all time worked after the date on which it is ascertained that such conditions existed. Such employee shall notify his foreman at the time the delay begins.

SECTION H: Maintenance of a Balanced Wage Structure—The Employer and the union recognize as essential to their mutual welfare the continued maintenance of a balanced wage structure under which there is maintained an equitable relationship between the rates of pay or earnings of specific jobs and job classifications within the plan. Therefore, either the employer or the union shall have the right to present to the other, requests and suggestions for adjustment in the rates of pay or earnings of specific jobs when in the opinion of either such adjustments are deemed necessary to the maintenance of a balanced wage structure.

If, within three (3) weeks after any such request is presented by either party, the employer and the union have failed to reach a mutually satisfactory agreement, the dispute shall be adjusted and settled by means of the grievance and arbitration procedure set forth herein, beginning at Step "2" thereof. Any adjustment negotiated or arbitrated hereunder shall be made effective no earlier than the date on which the request for such adjustment was received.

SECTION I: General Wage Revision

1. Either party shall have the right to request a general revision of the wage scale. Any such request for general revision of the wage scale shall be made in writing, shall specify a future date on which it is proposed in the request that the revision shall be made effective, and shall be mailed by registered mail to the party of whom such request is made not less than thirty (30) days prior to the date on which it is proposed in the request that the revision shall be made effective. Within five (5) days after receipt of any such request, the parties shall meet for the purpose of considering and negotiating the proposed revision. If, within thirty-five (35) days after such request is received, the parties do not agree, either party may submit the issue to arbitration as provided in this Agreement. Any general wage revision negotiated or arbitrated hereunder shall be made effective no earlier than the effective date proposed in the written request for such general wage revision.

2. Any general revision of the wage scale shall not be made effective prior to (date). At least six (6) calendar months shall elapse between the effective dates of such general revisions of the wage scale.

7. Hours

Regular—In scheduling hours of work, particular consideration should be given management's right to alter work hours where necessary, so long as no undue hardship is imposed on the employees. Units of time should be defined and management should reserve the right to require overtime and to penalize unexcused absences by a denial of overtime work. Particular care should be exercised in crediting employees with all time worked, to comply with the Fair Labor Standards Act.

Premium Time—Whether it be for the 6th or 7th consecutive day, Saturday, Sunday or holiday, extra hazardous or onerous work, etc., premium time should be specifically defined and payment therefor should comply with the Fair Labor Standard Act, in order to avoid overtime on premium time. Provision should be made against the pyramiding of overtime.

Report Time—While employees should not be penalized when reporting for work which is not available, management should be entitled to some measure of protection where every effort to avoid such futile reporting has been exhausted. Unavailability of work, when due to work stoppages or causes beyond the control of management, generally results in no liability for report time, if the employee is notified reasonably in advance not to report for work. Every precaution should be taken to avoid unnecessary obligation to pay. In the event an employee reports for work, when his regular job is not available, and refuses work other than that regularly his own, he should not be entitled to report time.

HOURS CLAUSE

A typical clause provides:

SECTION A: Definitions

1. Workweek: The workweek shall begin at 11 p.m. on Sunday of each week and end at 11 p.m. on Sunday of the following week.
2. Workday: The workday shall be considered to begin at the time an employee is scheduled to begin work, and to continue for a period of twenty-four (24) hours thereafter.
3. Regular Hours of Work: The regular hours of work for each shift shall not exceed eight (8) hours in any one workday and forty (40) hours in any one workweek.
4. Regularly Scheduled Workweek: The regularly scheduled workweek shall consist of five (5) consecutive shifts, one each day, from Monday to Friday inclusive. For this purpose, and for the purpose of paragraph "2" of Section "B" of this Article, the shift which begins at 11 p.m. on Sunday shall be considered a Monday shift.
5. First Shift: The first shift shall be any work period starting between the hours of 6 a.m. and 9:59 a.m.
6. Second Shift: The second shift shall be any work period starting between the hours of 10 a.m. and 5:59 p.m.
7. Third Shift: The third shift shall be any work period starting between the hours of 6 p.m. and 5:59 a.m.

SECTION B: Overtime Pay

1. Employees shall be paid at the rate of time and one-half for work performed in excess of eight (8) hours in any one workday and in excess of forty (40) hours in any one workweek.
2. Any employee absent without excuse on any one or more, or any part of one or more, of the first five (5) days of his workweek may be excluded from an opportunity to share in work available in that workweek on either or both of the premium days (Saturday and Sunday).

SECTION C: Reporting Allowance

1. Four Hour Minimum Reporting Pay
   An employee who is scheduled or notified to report and who does report for work shall be provided with and assigned to a minimum of 4 hours of work on the job for which he was scheduled or notified to report or, in the event such work is not available, shall be assigned or reassigned to another job of at least equal job class for which he is qualified. In the event, when he reports for work, no work is available, he shall be released from duty and credited with a reporting allowance of 4 times the standard hourly wage rate of the job for which he was scheduled or notified to report. When an employee who starts to work is released from duty before he works a minimum of 4 hours, he shall be paid for the hours worked in accordance with Section 9—Rates of Pay—and credited with a reporting allowance equal to the standard hourly wage rate of the job for which he was scheduled or notified to report multiplied by the unworked portion of the 4-hour minimum.

2. Exceptions
   The provision of this Section C shall not apply in the event that:
   a. Strikes, work stoppages in connection with labor disputes, failure of utilities beyond the control of management, or acts of God interfere with work being provided; or
   b. An employee is not put to work or is laid off after having been put to work, either at his own request or due to his own fault; or
   c. An employee refuses to accept an assignment or reassignment within the first 4 hours as provided in Paragraph 1 above;
   d. Management gives reasonable notice of a change in scheduled reporting time or that an employee need not report. Management and the grievance committee shall promptly determine what constitutes reasonable notice.

8. Probationary Employees

Newly hired employees should be subject to a probationary period for obvious reasons. The length of the probationary period will depend on the nature of the work in the plant. Management is entitled to a reasonable trial period for such a worker in order to determine whether he is qualified for and adaptable to the job as a regular employee.

The probationary period should be fixed in specific terms which will be influenced by the prior contract, if any, the standards in the industry, and, what is most important, the requirements of the employer in the light of the foregoing factors.

During this trial period, probationary employees should be subject to discharge for any reason, in the sole discretion of management, without recourse to the grievance machinery in any respect. Otherwise, the value and effect of a probationary period is meaningless. Where such a clause cannot be had because of union objection, compromise has been reached by permitting the question of discharge of a probationary employee to be carried by the union through several of the lower levels of the grievance machinery. In no event, however, is there any reason to permit the question to be carried to arbitration, and if the first mentioned type of recourse is agreed to, it should be made clear that the discharge of the probationary employee is excluded from the scope of arbitration.

The clause should provide (a) for the length of the trial period, preferably on a workday rather than calendar basis; (b) that during such period discharge or retention of the employee shall be at the sole discretion of management; (c) that discharge of the probationary employee be without recourse; and (d) that the seniority of a probationary employee who becomes a regular employee shall be computed from date of hiring.

To differentiate further between regular and probationary employees, it is sometimes provided that the benefits of the contract, such as holiday pay, are not available to probationary employees.

PROBATIONARY EMPLOYEES CLAUSE

A form of clause covering these points is as follows:

The first thirty (30) days of employment of all new employees shall be a probationary or trial period during which probationary period the new or probationary employee may, in the exclusive discretion of management be discharged without cause or notice and without recourse. Probationary employees retained beyond the probationary period shall be regular employees and their seniority shall date from the date of hiring.

9. No-Strike—No-Lockout

During the term of the contract, management is entitled to the assurance that there will be no interruption of work by reason of a strike, sitdown, slowdown, or work stoppage of any kind. The union is entitled to management's assurance that there will be no lockout during this period.

The no-strike pledge by the union should form an important consideration for management's contractual obligations. The absence of such provision from the contract may leave management without recourse against the union in the event of a strike, because courts may be reluctant to imply a no-strike provision in the contract. Furthermore, recourse to a suit for damages under the Labor Management Relations Act may be futile.

Such a provision may raise the question of union responsibility for unauthorized strikes by union members. To establish union responsibility for a strike, it is necessary to show that its agents, to whom the strike may be attributed, acted within the scope of their express or apparent authority; but express authority or ratification of the strike need not be shown. The union, however, if it acts in good faith, is entitled to be relieved of responsibility for unauthorized strikes. However, it should be responsible for securing, or cooperating in securing, the unauthorized strikers to return to work as quickly as possible. The union, therefore, should be required immediately to order such strikers back to work and impose disciplinary action for such conduct or authorize the employer to impose disciplinary action upon the recalcitrant strikers.

NO-STRIKE—NO-LOCKOUT CLAUSE

The no-strike, no-lockout clause should unconditionally bar such conduct during the term of the agreement. The term "strike" should be defined and the definition should adequately cover all forms of interruption of production. The conduct the union is to pursue in the event of a strike in violation of the clause may be described so that its responsibility may be understood by the employees. Penalties to be imposed for unauthorized strikes may be set forth. Of course, the matter of discipline and the imposition of the specified penalty is subject to the grievance procedure, thereby assuring to the union recourse if there is a disagreement with respect to the application of the penalties in specific instances.

Proviso should be made that in the event of a strike, work in process will be completed and machinery maintained in proper condition.

A clause covering these points is as follows:

The union agrees that there shall be no strike of any or all of the employees during the life of this agreement. The employer agrees that no lockout against any or all of its employees shall take place during the life of this agreement. For the purpose of this agreement, the term "strike" shall include a sitdown, stay-in, slow-down, walk-out, curtailment of work, stoppage of work, interference with work or receipt or shipment of materials, or products, stoppage of any of the employer's operations, or picketing of any of the employer's plants or premises or sources of supply.

If any strike occurs in violation of this agreement, the union agrees immediately and publicly to disavow such strike, to use all reasonable means to prevent the conduct and continuance of such strike; to take prompt and adequate action to discipline its members or representatives who aid, abet, or participate in such a strike, to use its best endeavors to prevent picketing, boycotting, granting of financial aid, and any kind of propaganda or advertisement against the employer, or in connection with said strike.

Should a work stoppage occur in the plant, all perishable materials in process shall be worked into a non-perishable state, and shipped or delivered to destination. Necessary care shall be given the materials and supplies on the employer's premises to prevent spoilage and maintenance requirements for the proper operation of the store and units are hereby guaranteed.

In the event of such strike, any employee or employees found guilty of instigating, fomenting, actively supporting, or condoning such illegitimate strike, shall be subject to the following penalties:

> For first offense—forfeiture of holiday pay or vacation pay
> For second offense—immediate discharge or loss of seniority

10. Union Responsibility

Unions, like management, should be required to evidence their responsibility by abstaining from certain conduct harmful to good industrial relations. The law forbids any such activity on the part of management which may be construed to interfere with, coerce, or discriminate against unions. The contract should require unions to undertake similar responsibilities, such as to maintain plant morale, secure full production, cooperate with management in furthering competency, encourage good workmanship and discipline those of its members who are guilty of obstructing production.

Aside from the requirements of the contract, the union should accept other responsibilities in connection with negotiations and contract administration.

Frequently, information disclosed at negotiations, grievance or other meetings with the union or the shop committee may be of a confidential nature and the disclosure of such information to third persons may be detrimental to the employer.

Such information or portions thereof may have to be divulged by the employer in connection with negotiations on such issues as wages, standard of work, change of machinery or operations and grievances. The information may be required to be disclosed for the purpose of complying with the Labor Board's view of what constitutes bargaining in good faith.

The union should be obligated to respect such information as confidential and not to disclose it for any reason whatsoever without the consent of the employer, and such an agreement should be applicable to an arbitration proceeding. Manifestly, if such a condition is agreed upon, the arbitrator will readily agree to respect it and will omit the confidential information from his written decision.

Furthermore, it may be desirable or appropriate to request the union specifically to assume responsibility on its part for full performance of the contract and to impose such responsibility on its members.

UNION RESPONSIBILITY CLAUSE

Typical clauses are:

The union agrees that it will not publish or circulate any false or misleading remarks about the company, its products, its officers or other personnel.

The union agrees that it will cooperate with the company and support company efforts to secure a full day's work on the part of employees whom it represents and that it will actively combat absenteeism and other practices which curtail production, and will support the company in its efforts to eliminate waste and inefficiency; to improve the quality of workmanship; to prevent accidents, and to promote good will between the company and its employees.

The union expressly recognizes that a high level of wages can be maintained only by maintaining a high level of productivity. The union and its members will cooperate in attaining such a level of productivity as is consistent with the health and welfare of the employees. The union and its members will seek to assist in effectuating economies and the utilization of improved methods and machinery.

The union, cognizant of the confidences often necessary between the management of a firm and its employees, agrees to hold any and all private matters acquired by its members in their employment as confidential.

The union agrees that this contract is binding on each and every member of the union and that its individual members accept full responsibility for carrying out all of the provisions of the contract.

The union agrees that its members shall not absent themselves in groups, thereby preventing normal production. The union further agrees that its members will work at any and all times where the emergency of the office may require it, and that their allegiance to the office in which they are employed shall predominate over all ordinary obligations.

11. Management's Rights

Functions involving the operation of the plant, manufacturing and selling the product are exercised by management. They include the hiring, promotion, transfer, disciplining, discharge and lay-off of employees, administration of the business, operation of the plant, installation and change of machinery, and the scheduling of work.

The failure specifically to reserve such rights to management in the agreement (provided, of course, they are not exercised in a manner inconsistent with the terms of the contract) has not been interpreted as a waiver or surrender of such functions. By common understanding, such functions may be freely exercised by management so long as the exercise thereof is not inconsistent with the limitations imposed by the provisions of the contract.

In addition, management regards certain functions as exclusively within its sphere of control by reason of its responsibility for the conduct of the enterprise. This position is recognized to a certain extent, under the amended Act, by the denial to supervisory personnel of the right to bargain collectively. However, in most instances, it is exceedingly difficult to draw the line between the exclusive functions of management and those which may be invaded by the terms of the collective agreement.

Management is, thus, confronted with the problem of whether it should seek in the negotiation a provision of the contract reserving its rights, and the extent to which such statement should be included.

The prevailing theory that such rights will be implied in the contract makes it unnecessary to seek an all-inclusive declaration of them. However, a general provision therefor is desirable and can serve a definitely useful function in the collective agreement.

The management's rights clause, by its statement of functions, brings to the attention of the employees the responsibilities of management for the conduct of the business, and can serve as a reminder that the interpretation of the provisions must contemplate a recognition that employees' rights should be adjusted to continue and aid in the proper operation of the business. The clause can be of substantial aid in the negotiation and adjustment of grievances. It is indicative of the parties' intentions and may offer some guidance in the interpretation of other important provisions of the agreement.

In arbitration, the management's rights clause has served a definite purpose in connection with the interpretation of the agreement. The provisions of the clause have been relied upon by arbitrators in questions involving the imposition of discipline, establishment of plant rules, promotions, change of work schedules and the hiring of new employees to fill newly created jobs.

Where a management policy has been crystallized, so as to effect a substantial change in plant operation during the contract period, such as the addition or elimination of a shift or change in machinery affecting the work force, the right to effectuate such plans should be expressly covered by the negotiations and not be left to interpretation.

The value of any such clause should not be dissipated by the addition of a proviso which will negate the prerogatives and functions here reserved.

MANAGEMENT'S RIGHTS CLAUSE

The management of the plant and the direction of the working forces, including the right to hire, suspend, promote, transfer or discharge for proper cause, and the right to relieve employees from duty because of lack of work or for other legitimate reasons is vested exclusively in the company. The determination and establishment or modification of performance standards for all operations, quality of material and workmanship required, selling prices of products, methods of selling and distributing products is reserved to the management. In the event of change of equipment, management shall have the right to reduce the working force if, in the sole judgment of management, such reduction of force is fairly required; and nothing in this agreement shall be construed to limit or in any way restrict the right of management to adopt, install or operate new or improved equipment or methods of operation.

Nothing herein contained shall be intended or shall be considered as a waiver of any of the usual inherent and fundamental rights of management, whether the same were exercised heretofore or not; and the same are hereby expressly reserved to the employer.

12. Supervisory Employees

The control of the supervisory staff should remain entirely with management. This should include promotion from the bargaining unit to supervisory status. The latter question presents serious problems and, in many instances, union participation in promotions of the type mentioned has been permitted. The National War Labor Board established a policy which permitted union participation in setting the promotional standards for a supervisory position.

Since management will normally draw its lower level supervisory staff from the employees in the bargaining unit, care should be exercised to preserve seniority in the event an employee promoted to a supervisory post is returned to the bargaining unit. The absence of such a provision may result in the reluctance, if not refusal, of well qualified nonsupervisory employees who enjoy substantial seniority to risk promotion to a lower supervisory level.

The right of foremen to do production work should be explicitly provided in the contract. Such work may be necessary for instructional, testing and experimental purposes and in emergency situations. Explicit solution of these problems should be reached in negotiation; they should not be left to determination on the basis of prior practice. The fact that the union has not objected to some of management's practices in this connection in the past does not foreclose it from raising the issue at some future date; hence, tacit reliance on prior practices is not advisable.

The clause providing for the performance of certain types of work by supervisory personnel should by its terms exclude foremen from performing work so as not to deprive production employees therefrom; it should contain a statement of the work foremen may do, such as instructional, testing and experimental work and work in an emergency where such work is required by sound business practice.

A vague, ambiguous, or too general provision will be affected by past practices. Reliance on prior failure of the union to object, as proof of acquiescence or concurrence of the union in the performance of such work, is unsound when the opportunity to be specific is at hand. Thus, where the company had its supervisors do testing work, the fact that the union in the past made no objection does not bar such an objection, unless it can be said that the union's conduct constituted a waiver of the clause of the contract restricting work by supervisory personnel.

Since the effect of past practice on a contractual provision is relevant only when the provision is ambiguous, vague or general in nature, the contract should be explicit. Management should not rely upon the union's prior acquiescence as a basis for claiming that the union has waived a right under the contract. Thus, where foremen did production work, the fact that the union chose to make no objection does not bar it from raising objections at a subsequent date, unless there was mutual willingness which management relied upon as a waiver of a contract clause restricting supervisory work. In such event, the doctrine of estoppel (by which a party is barred from modifying its position) would bar the union from now altering its position. If the contract provides that a waiver is not to be deemed a waiver for all time, the union's objection at a future date to a breach of the contract will be sustained.

SUPERVISORY EMPLOYEES CLAUSE

The following is an unduly restrictive provision which does not adequately afford management reasonable latitude with sufficient definiteness:

Foremen or supervisors shall act in a supervisory capacity only and they shall not perform any work or operation performed by a regular workman or operator at any time whatsoever, except for the purpose of instructing employees and in case of extreme emergency; and in the latter case only during the interval between the summoning of production employees and their arrival for work.

A preferable clause would provide:

To avoid depriving production employees of any work, supervisors shall do only supervisory work and shall abstain from any production work except for instruction, testing or for emergency purposes, which shall include situations where the job is in conformity with sound business practices.

In the event a foreman is promoted from the ranks he shall retain his accrued seniority for a period of six (6) months or until he is demoted from the rank of foremanship, whichever is sooner.

13. Discharge

Efficient and productive operation of the plant requires that management be in a position to take reasonable disciplinary action against employees who interfere with plant operations. Toward that end, it is well to agree with the union upon the common reasons for discharge (insubordination, stealing, destruction of property, drunkenness), so that where these vices appear they may be expeditiously dealt with. In addition, enumeration of the common causes of discharge has the advantage of giving fair warning of the penalty for the forbidden conduct, and may save the time of all parties which might otherwise be wasted in consideration of unwarranted grievances. However, care should be taken to make it clear that the grounds for discharge are not limited to the common reasons enumerated and that the penalty may also be imposed for other reasons.

Such discharges for cause will be subject to the grievance machinery; in order to clear the situation as quickly as possible, the filing of a grievance with respect to a discharge should be subject to a brief time limitation.

Provisions requiring management to give notice of discharge to the union prior thereto are deemed objectionable, since they unduly restrict management's right in the case of the common grounds for discharge. It is advisable, however, in the interest of better employee relations for management voluntarily to give such prior notice whenever it can practically do so.

DISCHARGE CLAUSE

A typical clause reads as follows:

The employer reserves the right to discharge probationary employees regardless of cause. Regular employees may be discharged for incompetency or other cause in the discretion of management, subject, however, to the grievance procedure herein set forth.

The discharge of an employee for incompetency or other reasons shall be reported by the employer to a union representative forthwith upon the occurrence of the discharge, and at that time an opportunity shall be afforded the union representative to investigate the cause thereof. Discharges for incompetency shall be objected to by the union within twenty-four (24) hours from the date of notification, and discharge for any other cause shall be objected to within three (3) days of the date thereof; otherwise, such discharge shall not be subject to the grievance procedure provided for in this agreement. If the union claims that an employee has been discharged without proper cause, the matter shall be submitted as a grievance in accordance with the grievance procedure herein set forth, and the arbitrator is empowered (1) to uphold the discharge, or (2) to reinstate the employee with or without back pay for all or part of the period since discharge; provided, however, that no back pay award in case of discharge shall exceed the number of hours worked by other employees actually performing the same type of work within the period during which the employee would have worked had the employer not discharged him.

In the event that back pay is awarded, the amount earned by the employee since the date of discharge shall be deducted therefrom.

14. Grievance Procedure and Arbitration

Grievance procedure is the machinery instituted for the handling and adjustment of grievances and disputes under the contract. The steps or levels of the procedure will vary according to the union, the industry and the requirements of the plant by reason of the size of the employment roll. These matters are factors to be considered in working out the most advantageous method for expeditious handling and resolution of such problems as may arise under the contract. The procedure should cover disputes between the employees and the employer and disputes between the union and the employer. In addition, it may be advisable to have some phase of the machinery cover the submission thereto of disputes raised by management, that is, to have the procedure adapted so that it may operate for the benefit of both sides.

Other problems raised in connection with establishing the grievance procedure involve such matters as the extent to which, if at all, management is willing to permit its time to be used for the activities of shop stewards in performance of their duties with respect to grievances and otherwise. The adjustment of grievances, and the holding of grievance or shop committee meetings with management must also be provided for.

The final step in the grievance procedure is arbitration; in a carefully drafted contract provision is made for separate arbitration.

The first consideration with respect to the arbitration clause is its scope. A decision must be made as to whether it shall cover disputes between the parties, or shall be limited to disputes arising under the contract, and whether it shall cover interpretation, construction, performance or non-performance of the contract.

Further problems are whether the contract should designate a permanent arbitrator for the contract term, and how to select such an arbiter; or whether arbitration should be before a board with an agreed method for selection of the board; how expenses incident to the arbitration are to be shared. It should be agreed that the arbitrator cannot vary, alter or modify the contract, and he should not have authority to impose upon the parties obligations not expressly or impliedly assumed by the parties. It is important to consider the effect of the arbitration on all other substantive provisions of the contract. In this connection, it should be observed, that the arbitration provision may be the basis for submitting any and possibly all the contract provisions to interpretation and construction by a third person—an arbitrator—who is not familiar wiah the history of the negotiations and the requirements essential to the operation of the plant. This clause and the substantive contract provisions will be his only guides in connection with the testimony that is presented to him. It is important, therefore, that all provisions of the contract be made to fit the specific requirements of the company as accurately as foresight permits.

It should be recalled that under the amended Act, individuals have the right to process grievances, provided union representatives are accorded an opportunity to be present and provided further that any adjustment be not inconsistent with the collective agreement.

GRIEVANCE PROCEDURE AND ARBITRATION CLAUSE

Some of the more basic requirements of provisions setting up the grievance procedure and the arbitration of disputes may be found in the following clauses:

In order to insure amicable relations between the company and the union, every effort shall be made expeditiously to settle disputes arising out of the interpretation of the terms and conditions of this agreement.

Should any such dispute or difference under the contract arise between the company and the union or any regular employee, such dispute or difference shall be considered in the following manner:

1. Any employee or group of employees and shop steward shall first attempt to settle the grievance with the manager.
2. In the event the grievance cannot be adjusted with the plant manager, it should be reduced to writing on the proper form, numbered, and, if approved by the union grievance committee, submitted in writing to the departmental superintendent.
3. In the event the grievance cannot be settled by Paragraph 2 above, the employment manager in company with the management grievance committee shall consider the grievance at the next meeting with the union grievance committee. Either the management grievance committee or the union grievance committee may call in any employee covered by this agreement, for the purpose of testifying on a grievance.
4. In the event the grievance cannot be adjusted by Paragraph 3, the union grievance committee may appeal it to the general manager who may hold a meeting with the union grievance committee and within one week from submission of the grievance, or the meeting, he shall deliver the employer's answer, unless a longer period is mutually agreed upon.
5. The union or the company, but not an individual employee, may take to arbitration any dispute that cannot be settled by the procedure above set forth. The arbitrators shall be selected, one by the company, one by the union, and the third by the other two arbitrators. In the event that the latter two cannot agree upon a third, the third shall be selected by the American Arbitration Association. The decision of a majority shall be final and binding upon all the parties. The company and the union shall share equally the cost of the arbitration.

   The arbitrators shall be limited to the issues presented to them and shall have no power to add to, detract from, or modify any of the terms of this agreement, nor to establish and change any wage rate, unless the same is subject to change in accordance with this agreement, or to decide matters which are properly the subject of collective bargaining.

15. Seniority

In negotiating a seniority clause, management should consider the scope of seniority and should not permit the doctrine of seniority to extend to an illogical extreme.

Because of the hardship on management in maintaining operations with help of questionable ability, it is exceedingly important that seniority be sharply defined and reasonably circumscribed. While length of service should be an important factor in determining whether an employee should be kept on the job, ability, skill, aptitude and amenability should all be properly considered. For this reason, seniority should be department-wide, not plant-wide, restricted to occupational group and not enjoyed until such time as the individual passes a probationary period.

Failure to return on recall or accept suitable transfer in event of reduction in forces, three absences within a six month period, or discharge should result in loss of seniority.

While seniority should be considered in employee choice of vacation, it should be more a matter of agreement between management and the employees affected than strictly a contractual obligation.

Seniority should be forfeited when there is a break in continuity of employment.

If shop steward and committeemen are to be acorded top seniority, it is desirable that they shall have been in the company employ for a reasonable period of time.

The seniority clause is generally made applicable to rehire and lay-off exclusively, not to promotion, transfers, choice of shifts, etc. It should be designed to establish the factors which are determinative in situations where continued employment of the most efficient employees is essential for the operation of the business. Clauses which make length of service the sole determinative factor when a reduction of force is economically necessary may leave the plant improperly staffed with employees who are not qualified to do particular jobs. Such a result may cripple the plant.

SENIORITY CLAUSE

A typical clause reads as follows:

1. It is mutually agreed that seniority shall be departmental and not plant-wide, and shall prevail in and be limited to lay-offs and reemployment, provided that the worker retained or returned can qualify to fill the position.
2. Seniority shall not apply in the case of promotions or demotions.
3. Seniority shall depend on the following factors:
   a. Continuous service, as defined in paragraph six (6) below
   b. Qualifications and competency
   c. Physical fitness
   Provided, however, that competency shall be of primary importance in the determination of an employee's right to employment or right to promotion where a vacancy exists. Competency shall be interpreted to mean ability to do an available job in a workmanlike manner, and in the event an employee, because of inability, whether due to lack of experience, physical fitness, or otherwise, is unable to perform available work in a workmanlike manner, the employer shall have the right to give the available work to the employee next in seniority having the requisite qualifications. The employer shall be the judge of competency of its employees, subject to review in accordance with the provisions of this agreement.
   The company reserves the right to transfer an employee who has suffered injury and is unable to continue at his usual occupation, or an employee who has been in the service of the company and becomes physically unable to

perform the duties of his usual occupation, regardless of his length of service. Any grievance arising out of such transfer shall be settled in accordance with the procedure set forth in this agreement.

4. The company is entitled to retain a specified percentage of employees even if other workers with greater length of service must be laid off, in order to permit the company to retain enough persons of exceptional ability, both for current service and as potential supervisors and executives.

5. It is further recognized that certain positions involve special knowledge, training and abilities, and management may, where necessity arises, introduce specially qualified personnel, or promote with due regard to potential ability of employees. Should an employee be promoted from the ranks to an executive or administrative job for a temporary period, he shall not forfeit his seniority rights upon his return to his former job.

6. Length of continuous service shall be computed on the basis of the aggregate of the time during which an employee was actually on the payroll of the company (the period during which an employee actually worked for the company and received wages for his service, or the period during which an employee received compensation for an injury sustained in the course of his employment by the company, but not exceeding the period for which statutory compensation is payable) calculating from the date he was first hired by the company subject, however, to the mutual understanding and agreement that the personnel records of the company shall be accepted as being correct, and further subject to the following provision:

An employee's continuous service shall be broken so that no prior period or periods of employment shall be counted and his seniority shall cease upon:

a. Justifiable discharge
b. Voluntary quitting
c. Absence for five (5) working days, unless excused by the company by reason of illness or other disability or other reasonable cause.
d. Leave of absence for a period of more than three (3) months.
e. Failure of an employee to return to work upon recall within forty-eight (48) hours after written notice is sent to him by the company at his last known address appearing on its records.

Seniority shall not require the lay-off of any employee unless there is present in the plant a duly qualified and competent employee to perform his job in a manner satisfactory to management.

16. Transfer

If seniority must be followed, it is frequently contended that it should not be extended to transfer, for efficiency may be impaired, incentive stifled and opportunity for building up an effective work force seriously impeded. It is further reasoned that the determination of an individual's skill should not be a matter of negotiation, arbitration or litigation.

Union demands for seniority in transfers are usually based on the contention that qualifications of workers cannot be mathematically equated, and that management is influenced by factors of favoritism and discrimination. In rebuttal it may be pointed out that in a non-seniority transfer system the union may always have recourse to the grievance procedure to challenge any abuse and make whole the aggrieved employee.

Consulting with the union in advance of management action is always a desirable policy, if practicable, but the consultation should be a courtesy (not a duty) at management's discretion, eventually becoming an established practice. Any practice going beyond a discretionary act may attain the force of an obligation. There should be no appeal from management's appraisal of an individual's ability except where the union charges discrimination, violation of the agreement or a grievance under the contract.

In the event of a transfer at management's initiative, seniority of the transferred employee should be protected, if not permanently, at least for a period during which his adaptability to the transferred job may be ascertained and the transference made final.

As a matter of good relations, the company should encourage promotion from the ranks, give its own older qualified employees preference in filling vacancies, canvas all eligibles within its employ before making jobs available to outsiders, and consider union recommendations, but it should place a time limit beyond which an employee's application would not be considered.

TRANSFER CLAUSE

A typical clause provides:

When an employee is required to transfer temporarily from his regular job to a job where his wages will be impaired, he shall be paid his past average hourly earnings for two (2) weeks next preceding the transfer. In case of permanent transfer, the employee shall be paid the rate of the job to which he is transferred. Any employee transferred temporarily to a job having a rate of pay higher than his past earnings shall receive the higher rate. If he accepts a transfer in lieu of lay-off he shall receive the lower rate of the new job.

Employees transferred interdepartmentally or transferred in lieu of lay-off shall retain their seniority rights in their former departments for a period of one (1) year, after which time their company seniority shall be applied to their new department. Employees transferred interdepartmentally or transferred in lieu of lay-off, shall retain their seniority rights in their original department until such time as they will have been employed in a department for a continuous period of one (1) year, after which time their company seniority shall be applied to such new department. In the event of lay-off in any new department within the one (1) year period the company may temporarily transfer such employees to other operations within the company for one (1) month. At the end of the (1) month period, or upon failure of the company to have available jobs open for such employees during the one (1) month period, or no work becomes available in the new department, such employees may claim their seniority rights in their original department.

Employees transferred in lieu of lay-off shall be entitled to their former position if such position reopens on the basis of their seniority within the one (1) year period.

In the event that such employees transferred in lieu of lay-off are offered their former position, however, and refuse such position, they shall be deemed to have forfeited their right to reinstatement in their former department.

17. Promotion

In providing for promotions, management should be especially concerned with reserving to itself the right to determine the factors entering into consideration of a promotion as well as the standards expected of the employee to be promoted. Promotion should not be restricted by the rule of seniority, although length of continuous service should be given proper cognizance.

Distinction should be drawn between promotion in the bargaining unit and advancement outside the unit. In either case, the promotion must be initiated by management, subject, if at all, to grievance procedure only if the promotion is within the bargaining unit.

In the event a member of the bargaining unit is promoted to foremanship or outside the unit, he should be permitted to retain his seniority for a reasonable period (for example, not to exceed six months).

Ability should be unilaterally determined by any reasonable means in the discretion of management, as by a written or oral test, a try-out, etc. Whatever means is to be used by management in thus ascertaining ability, it should in no wise constitute a binding precedent to be followed in other cases.

While hiring from within is good personnel policy, management should also have the right to hire an outside employee if there are no qualified employees in the plant.

PROMOTION CLAUSE

A typical clause provides:

The parties recognize that promotional opportunity and job security in event of promotions, decrease of forces, and rehiring after lay-offs should increase in proportion to length of continuous service, and that in the administration of this section the intent will be that wherever practicable full consideration shall be given continuous service in such cases.

In recognition, however, of the responsibility of management for the efficient operation of the works, it is understood and agreed that in all cases of:

Promotion (except promotions to positions excluded under the definition of "employees" in the agreement) the following factors as listed below shall be considered; however, only where factors "a" and "b" are relatively equal shall length of continuous service be the determining factor:
(a) ability to perform the work
(b) physical fitness
(c) continuous service

18. Leave of Absence

To be considered in negotiating a leave of absence clause are such questions as whether the absentee should retain accrued seniority rights, vacation benefits, other incidents of continued length of service, rights to reinstatement and renewal of benefits on his return. The number of leaves of absence to be granted at any one time, eligibility and penalties imposed for abuse as well as extension and procedures to be followed in granting leaves should be clearly defined.

If the leave is for illness, it should be stated whether a medical certificate is required; where illness is related to occupational disability, the limit of time should be specified; if the leave is for union duties, what they shall comprise, i.e., to attend convention, hold union office, etc., and the duration should be defined.

The clause designed to cover leaves of absence should provide for three situations:

1. Where the employee desires the leave for union business.
2. Where the leave is for an individual health problem.
3. Where the leave is desired for personal reasons.

The provision should not grant leave of absence automatically. Written applications should be made stating grounds for request and time desired.

Absence for union business, such as meetings and conventions, may be granted on a reasonable basis provided it does not result in the absence of too many key men. The number of persons to be excused may be limited or a general provision covering reasonableness should be used. Needless to say, the business should be *bona fide* union business, not, for example, to include picket duty at another plant.

Leaves of absence for health should be based on the production of a physician's certificate setting forth the need for it. The physician's justification for the leave or any absence from the plant should state what the employee's illness is and how and why it disables him from work and for what period the disability will continue.

Leave of absence for personal reasons should be entirely at the discretion of management; it should not, however, be arbitrarily denied.

LEAVE OF ABSENCE CLAUSE

A comprehensive clause provides:

A leave of absence may be granted for personal reasons for a period not to exceed thirty (30) days, upon application of the employee to and approval by his foreman. Such leaves of absence shall not be renewed and seniority will accumulate during the leave.

Formal Leaves of Absence for Personal Reasons
Application for Leave
Employees requesting formal leave of absence shall first make application in writing to their foreman on the form provided. Such leave of absence will be granted to an employee for not more than ninety (90) days on approval of the local management when the services of the employee are not immediately required and there are employees available in the plant capable of doing his work.

Extension of Leaves
Such leaves of absence may be extended but the approval of the general management of the division is required in such cases. Seniority will not accumulate during the period of formal leave of absence for personal reasons. Such formal leaves of absence will not be granted an employee who is laid off, and will not be extended if the employee would have been laid off had he been working during his leave.

Sick Leave of Absence Credits
Temporary employees without seniority shall not receive credit in excess of fifteen (15) days for time off for sick leave toward the ninety (90) days of continuous employment required to acquire seniority and in no case shall a temporary employee's name be placed on the seniority list while away from work on sick leave.

Compensable Cases
In compensable injury and legal occupational disease cases, sick leave will be granted automatically and seniority will accumulate for the full period of legal temporary disability.

Leave of Absence for Union Activity
Any employee elected to a permanent office in, or as a delegate to, any labor activity necessitating a leave of absence, shall be granted such leave for a minimum of one day and not to exceed one year and shall, at the end of the term in the first instance, or at the end of the mission in the second instance, be guaranteed reemployment if there is sufficient work for which he is in line at the then current rate of pay. Written notice for such leaves, giving the length of leave, shall be given the local plant management as far in advance as possible but in no event later than the day prior to the day such leave is to become effective. Seniority will accumulate during the period of such leaves.

Accrual of Seniority During Leave
Leaves of absence may be granted to employees for other union activities and seniority shall accumulate during such leaves. Such leaves will be granted

only when requests are made in writing to the personnel staff of the corporation by the president of the international union or the head of the department of the international union which handles matters under this Agreement.

Conditions Governing

All of the above leaves of absence including sick leaves are granted subject to the following conditions:

(a) Any employee on leave may return to work in line with his seniority before the expiration of his leave, providing not less than seven (7) days notice is given to management. The return within the seven day period is at the option of management. Any employee who fails to return to work in accordance with the notice as given shall be considered as having voluntarily quit unless he has a satisfactory reason.

(b) Any employee who fails to report for work within three working days after the date of expiration of the leave shall be considered as having voluntarily quit unless he has a satisfactory reason.

(c) If upon the expiration of a leave of absence there is no work available for the employee in line with his seniority, or if the employee would otherwise have been subject to lay-off according to seniority during the period of the leave, the period which breaks seniority shall start from the date of expiration of the leave.

Leave of Absence for Military Service

Any employee who enters into active service in the armed forces of the United States, as defined below, will be given leave of absence for the period of his service. Seniority will accumulate during such period. Upon termination of such service, the employee shall be offered re-employment in his previous position or a position of like seniority, status and pay, unless the circumstances have so changed as to make it impossible or unreasonable to do so, in which event he will be offered such employment in line with his seniority as may be available, which he is capable of doing, at the current rate of pay for such work, provided he meets the following requirements:

(1) Has not been dishonorably discharged.

(2) Is physically able to do the work.

(3) Reports for work within ninety (90) days of the date of such discharge, or ninety (90) days after hospitalization continuing after discharge for not more than one (1) year.

As used in this Section "active service in the armed forces of the United States" is defined as and limited to:

Volunteering or being called into service as a member of the Army, Air Forces, Navy, or Marine Corps, provided that in time of peace such service, for the purposes of this agreement, and any military leave of absence issued pursuant to the terms thereof, shall not exceed one year.

19. Holidays

When the number of holidays with pay (although not worked) have been agreed upon, several problems remain to be considered. Parties should agree on who are eligible for holiday benefits. For example holiday benefits should be limited to employees who have been on the active payroll for a stated time, and migratory workers and "floaters" should be excluded. Whether employees on sick leave, laid off or on vacation are entitled to holiday pay should be stated. Employees on sick leave who are compensated by sickness disability insurance, financed by the employer or financed partially by employer and employee, have less reason to claim holiday pay since this insurance is intended as complete compensation during the sickness disability. The clause should be specific if it is the intent of the parties that pay be granted only for holidays which fall within the regular work week.

Some contracts also attempt to meet the problem of absence on the day before and the day after a holiday by requiring work on these days as a prerequisite to eligibility for holiday pay unless such work was excused by management. If such a qualification is agreed upon, the meaning of work "on" the day before and the day after should be defined. The contract should specifically spell out the requirement of a full day's work on those days unless excused.

Such provisions substantially aid in the maintenance of normal production on work days near holidays and counteract a common tendency to "stretch" holidays. Forfeitures are not looked upon with favor by courts or arbitrators and will be imposed only when clearly required by the instrument which creates them.

The holiday clause may be improved by specific provision to cover the situation in the event the holiday falls outside the regular work week, or during a vacation. The clause should also provide for the effect of lay-offs immediately before the holiday. With respect to absences that disqualify for holiday pay, the term has been defined in some contracts to cover absence for any work day or fraction thereof.

Management should reject clauses which bar work on the agreed holidays, because exigencies of operations may require such work on occasion. This point has not been the source of serious dispute and the principal question has been the amount of compensation for holiday work. First, the amount of pay for a holiday not worked should be stated. Then the premium pay for work on the holiday should be specified. It should be agreed that there will be no pyramiding of premium pay rates. If a holiday which is worked falls on a premium pay day, such as a Saturday, the employee should not receive the premium pay for work on a holiday plus the premium pay for work on a Saturday. By express proviso he should receive only one premium. Failure to provide against pyramiding overtime may result in the imposition by an arbitrator of such premium pay.

HOLIDAY CLAUSE

A typical holiday clause is as follows:

(1) New Year's Day, Decoration Day, Independence Day, Labor Day, Thanksgiving Day, and Christmas shall be considered as holidays.

(2) Whenever such holidays fall on a regularly scheduled work day, any work performed shall be paid for at time and one-half the regular rate; when no work is performed, eight (8) hours at the regular rate shall be paid. The payments provided for in this Paragraph (2) shall not be made to any employee who does not work all scheduled days during the work week in which any one of the holidays hereinabove mentioned in this Paragraph (2) shall occur, except, however, that absence from work during such period with the prior permission of the company, evidenced by a written memorandum, shall not disqualify any employee from receiving holiday pay.

Another clause used to discourage pre- and post-holiday absences is:

There shall be no pay for holidays not worked if employees are absent on the work day preceding the holiday or on the work day following the holiday.

20. Vacation

Vacation clauses should particularly cover the questions of eligibility, length, time, extra compensation for holiday, methods of computing and rules governing payment. Whether employees who quit their jobs should receive pro-rated vacation, whether employees laid off or on leave of absence are entitled to vacation, whether compensation should be on the basis of rate of pay prevailing at the time vacation is taken or as of the new contract, where one is negotiated, during which the vacation is taken— are questions which have frequently invited arbitrators to rewrite the contract for the parties. These matters should be decided and clarified in the agreement.

Continuity of service and presence on the active payroll of the company should be prerequisites to eligibility. The time of vacation should be a matter for management to decide and not one determinable by seniority status or consent of the union. To avoid any impairment of the production schedule, management should, in the first instance, decide on the vacation period, but should consider the desires of employees, giving preference to employees in the order of seniority.

VACATION CLAUSE

A typical clause provides:

Employees shall be entitled to vacations as follows:

(a) One week—those employees who were employed after August 31 of the preceding year and before January 1 of the current year.

(b) Two weeks—those employees who were in the employ of the company on or before August 31 of the preceding year.

(c) Three weeks—those employees who have completed fifteen years of service as of January 1 of the current year.

Neither an extra day nor an additional day's pay shall be allowed because a holiday falls within the vacation period, except that in the case of an employee required by the company to schedule his vacation during a period in which a holiday falls, an additional day off, not necessarily contiguous to his vacation period, shall be allowed. An employee shall be deemed to have been required by the company to schedule his vacation during a particular period in any case in which he is limited to a choice between a vacation period in which a holiday occurs and any number of out-of-season vacation periods, i.e., during the months of October through April.

Wherever practicable, the company agrees to grant vacations on a consecutive basis and at the time desired by the employee.

Vacations shall be taken in the year in which they are due and may not be accumulated. Employees shall not be permitted to forfeit their vacations for additional pay from the company.

21. Guaranteed Work

Provisions of the contract which set forth the schedule of hours of work are not normally regarded as a guaranty of hours of work. To avoid the possibility of a claim that such a clause should be interpreted as such a guaranty, it is well to provide explicitly that it merely defines the hours of work and is not to be construed as a guaranty of hours of work per day or per week.

In some instances it is impractical or inadvisable, because of the nature of plant operations, to state specifically in the contract the exact starting and quitting time. Regular work schedules, however, can be provided for in the contract to the extent that the company agrees to maintain regular schedules of work, the starting and quitting times being subject to determination by the company. Provision can also be made for a stated prior notice of changes in the schedule with exceptions in cases of emergency. Here, again, in preparing such a clause care should be exercised so that the undertaking to maintain and furnish regular work schedules should not be construed as a guaranty of work for such regular schedules.

The true guaranteed work clauses have been developed in those situations where employer and union intend that the amount of annual wages or the extent of employment shall be stabilized by guaranty thereof on the part of the employer. Such guarantees, manifestly, are practical only in those businesses where employment has been and can continue to be regular and steady over a substantially fixed period.

Where the guaranteed work clause provides for steady employment the period during which work is guaranteed must be explicitly stated and may cover a year or a shorter time. This clause usually does not guarantee the amount of wages during such guaranteed work period, since the guarantee is directed at steady employment for the stated period. Where the clause guarantees wages over a stated period, regardless of fluctuation in employment, the total earnings guaranteed for the stated period must be set forth. A stated weekly wage may be guaranteed for the express period agreed upon.

The maximum period of the guarantee should be no longer than the term of the contract. If the contract term is more than one year the feasibility of the guarantee for such a term must be carefully considered.

Furthermore, practical limitations upon the guarantee must be included in the clause and methods should be set forth whereby the company can in event of urgent necessity, as in cases of substantial business decline, relieve itself from the continuing obligation of the guarantee by reasonable lump sum payments or payment of reasonable severance pay in lieu of what has been guaranteed. The guarantee must not be permitted to tie the company irretrievably in cases of emergencies of the type mentioned or where operations are stopped by strikes, floods, general disasters and other similar circumstances beyond the control of the company.

Another important factor to be considered in drafting the guaranteed work clause is what employees should be covered by its provisions. In some instances, it is made applicable only to key employees or particular craftsmen. In any event, it should apply only to regular employees. Probationary employees should be excluded. New employees may reasonably be excluded for a period longer than the probationary period provided in the contract.

GUARANTEED WORK CLAUSE

Periods of Employment Guaranteed

Subject to the terms and conditions hereinafter set out, the Company hereby guarantees as follows:

1. To provide not less than fifty (50) payroll weeks of employment during the work year for all workers in Group One, who have been continuously employed by the Company for less than one year.

2. To provide not less than fifty-one (51) payroll weeks of employment during the work year for all workers in Group One who have been continuously employed by the Company for one year or more and less than five years. One week of vacation time, paid or unpaid, is included as a part of this guaranteed time.

3. To provide not less than fifty-two (52) payroll weeks of employment during the work year for all workers in Group One who have been continuously

employed by the Company for five years or more. Two weeks of vacation time, paid or unpaid, are included as a part of this guaranteed time.

4. To provide not less than the remaining payroll weeks of the work year, beginning with the first work week in January, annually, for all workers in Group Two.

5. All holidays on which no work is performed and for which wages are paid under the Company-Union contract, and all days on which, by Company-Union agreement, no work is performed, shall be included as a part of this guaranteed time as a part of the week in which they occur.

6. Time lost due to sickness, injury, voluntary absence or suspension of manufacturing operations by reason of epidemic, fire, tornado, flood, jury service, court attendance or military service is included as part of this guaranteed time.

7. Time lost by reason of extreme emergency making it impossible for the Company to operate its plant or any part of its plant may be included as a part of this guaranteed time.

8. Time so lost shall not be considered as an interruption of continuous and regular employment in determining any worker's eligibility to receive payments under this plan.

9. In the event the presently existing straight-time work week maximum of forty (40) hours hereafter shall be changed by federal or state legislation, the guaranty herein provided shall be adjusted, concurrently therewith, so that the guaranteed number of hours in each payroll week and each week of employment hereby guaranteed shall be the number of hours per week prescribed by such legislation as the maximum for which straight time is to be paid.

Unemployment Payment

In order to qualify to receive any unemployment compensation payment under this plan, the employee must

1. Be a production worker covered by the Company-Union contract.
2. Be an eligible worker with his or her determined rate of pay.

Termination of Service

1. In the event of any unauthorized strike, an agreement of the Company and the Union or a decision through arbitration shall determine the nature and extent of any forfeiture of the rights of any worker or workers hereunder.

2. Separation from service by resignation by a worker or discharge for just cause of a worker by the Company shall forfeit and terminate all rights hereunder of said worker as of the date of such resignation or discharge, unless said employee shall be rehired within twenty (20) regular working days from the date of separation from service.

22. Pension Plan

Though the subject of serious dispute, the issue has been finally resolved by the courts that pension and retirement plans are an integral part of the wage structure and, therefore, properly the subject for mandatory collective bargaining. Pension payments are regarded as coming within the statutory term "wages," since the contributions to any plan for employees are part of the compensation received by him for his labor. The courts agree with union reasoning that collective bargaining is dynamic, not static, and the term "wages . . . or other conditions of employment," must not be limited in scope to the precise conception of bargaining Congress had in mind when it passed the Wagner Act in 1935. In fact, it has been copiously pointed out that the legislative history of the Labor Management Relations Act of 1947 strongly indicates that the Eightieth Congress in revising the Labor Law, intended to include pension and retirement plans within the ambit of compulsory collective bargaining.

In pressing for more welfare provisions union negotiators are utilizing the Steel Panel's conclusion that plans should be non-contributory, since they tend to bring more employees under their protective benefits; that they promote stability in view of the fact that costs can better be integrated in the labor cost schedule; that they enable management to purchase more insurance, inasmuch as the employer deducts his contributions before taxes, whereas the employee deducts his contribution after income taxes.

In many cases the plans call for benefits in the event of disability, whether through accident or illness; establish the manner in which the benefits are to be paid; and provide for loans from funds to cover extraordinary expenses arising from an employee's own illness or the illness of a member of his family.

The more serious problems raised center principally on types of benefits, when granted, by whom financed and how administered. Unions generally claim that benefits should be paid for by employers with no contribution by the employee. Employers insist that employees can genuinely benefit from such plans only when they make their adequate contribution.

Under the Labor Management Relations Act of 1947, employers may not make money payments to union representatives for the operation of a health and welfare fund, unless (a) such payments are held in trust for specific types of benefits for the employees, their families or dependents; (b) the basis of the fund is specified in writing; (c) there is tripartite representation in administering the fund; (d) it is annually audited; and (e) pensions and annuities are provided in separate trusts.

In offering benefits particular caution must be exercised to avoid conflict with the Internal Revenue Code, attack by minority stockholders or charges of discrimination under the Labor Law.

Proviso should be made requiring that the employee bear his proportionate share in the expense, so that he may assume some responsibility and not merely accept the benefits as additional compensation.

Further provisions should be made covering the qualification requirements, length of service allowance, graduation of payments, waiting period, length of compensable disability, disposition of unused allowance, deductions for holiday pay and workmen's compensation, the duration of the plan and how it is to be enforced.

PENSION CLAUSE

A typical clause provides:

1. The Retirement Plan shall be non-contributory, financed completely by the Company.
2. For the duration of the pension agreement beginning March 1, 1950, the Company agrees to pay into a pension fund 8¾ cents for every hour for which an hourly rated employee covered by the contract receives compensation, for the purpose of providing the benefits set forth herein. Since the Company assumes the responsibility to make contributions from time to time to the pension fund in an amount sufficient, based upon estimates made by a duly qualified actuary, to provide the monthly benefits specified in Section 5, taking into consideration as therein provided primary (old age) insurance benefits under the Federal Social Security Act (as now in effect or as hereafter amended), it may vary these payments accordingly. Past service benefits shall be funded in such manner as the Company in its sole discretion shall determine.
3. The benefit structure of the Retirement Plan shall be administered within the framework of the Pension Agreement by a Joint Board of Administration, having three members each from the Company and the Union. Suitable provisions shall be made for the breaking of any deadlocks by an impartial chairman selected by mutual agreement by the Company and Union representatives on the Board.
4. The Board of Administration shall be empowered to administer the Plan as it relates to development of administrative policy and procedure, for such functions as:
   a. Verifying and establishment of service credits;
   b. Methods of handling and paying claims and benefits;
   c. Interpretation of the rights of employees under the Plan;
   d. Reviewing and acting on appeals;
   e. Collection and analysis of administrative statistics;
   f. Authorization to the Bank or Trust Company acting as Trustee for the Pension Fund, for proper payments from the Pension Fund; and
   g. Similar and related functions and duties that are inherent in proper administration of benefits and operation of the Plan.
   Decisions of the Board of Administration shall be by majority vote with the impartial chairman empowered to cast the deciding vote. Decisions of the Board shall be final and binding.
5. (a) There shall be payable, on retirement at normal retirement, age 65, or older, with 30 years or more of credited service, a benefit of $100 a month including primary (old age) insurance benefits under the

Federal Social Security Act (as now in effect or as hereafter amended), payable to the employee, or at age 65, or older, with less than 30 years of credited service, a pension equal to the same proportion of $100 as the number of years of credited service bears to 30, including primary Federal Social Security benefits as before.

(b) There shall be payable on retirement after age 60, but before age 65 and after 30 years of credited service, including 10 years credited service after the effective date of the Plan, a benefit reduced to equate for all factors so as not to increase the cost of the plan or impair the benefits payable under other sections.

(c) Benefits payable under Social Security shall be deducted from the pension benefit payable after retirement under the Plan whether or not such Social Security payment is lost by the individual through acceptance of covered employment or otherwise.

6. *Disability Retirement.* Retirement for total and permanent disability after 30 years of credited service at age 55 or older shall be at a flat retirement benefit of $50 a month less any Federal Social Security benefit receivable by the employee for disability.

7. Any future increase in the old age benefits payable under the Federal Social Security Act shall reduce by the amount of such increase the portion of the benefit payable under this plan.

8. *Crediting of Service.* (a) "Past Service" shall be credited at the rate of one year of seniority as defined in the Collective Bargaining Agreement, excluding seniority credited for military service prior to employment by the Company provided, however, that there shall be added thereto a year of past service for each year by which the total years of accumulated active service prior to June 20, 1941, exceed by more than five years total seniority for that period.

(b) "Future Service" shall be credited at the rate of one year for each calendar year prior to attainment of age 65 in which the employee receives pay for 1,800 or more hours, ¾ of a year for 1,300 to and including 1,799 hours, ½ of a year for 750 to and including 1,299 hours, with no credit for less than 750 hours in a calendar year.

9. *Retirement Age.* The normal retirement age shall be 65. Retirement shall be automatic at age 68 but there shall be no increase in benefits after age 65. An employee may retire early with the consent of the Company between age 60 and 65, provided he has at least 30 years of credited service. Retirement upon total and permanent disability is permitted between ages 55 and 65 provided the employee has at least 30 years of credited service. The Company at its sole discretion may retire any employee at age 65 or older by reason of employee's inability to perform efficiently work assigned to him. Employees age 67 or more as of July 16, 1949, shall be automatically retired on the date of their first birthday following January 1, 1951. No employee shall be subject to automatic retirement prior to April 1, 1952, if, at the time he reaches normal retirement age, he has more than ten years of service and would receive a pension (including Social Security) of less than $75.00

a month. This problem will be reviewed by the parties 30 days in advance of April 1, 1952.

10. *Effective Date.* (a) The liability of the Company for payments to the "pension trust fund" as specified herein shall accrue beginning on March 1, 1950, which shall be the "effective date" of the program:

   (b) Benefit payments shall commence on April 1, 1950. Employees who retire during March, 1950, or who are to be considered retired under subparagraph (c) below, shall commence to receive benefits on April 1, 1950, if living.

   (c) Employees whose employment by the Company terminated on or after July 16, 1949, but before the effective date of the program, who would have qualified for benefits under the program had it been in effect at the time of such termination of employment, shall be treated as having retired.

11. *Vesting.* No employee shall have any vested right under the program except as to such rights as accrue to him in connection with retirement as provided for under the program.

12. The Company shall have the sole right to select and contract with a qualified Bank or Trust Company to act as the Trustee of the Pension Fund. Such Trustee shall hold, and be solely responsible for, the investment of the Pension Fund. Benefits shall be payable only from the Trust Fund; and the Trustee shall make such benefit payments from the Pension Trust Fund as are specifically authorized by the Board of Administration.

13. *Approval of Plan.* All of the foregoing shall be subject to the approval by the Commissioner of Internal Revenue as a qualified pension trust under Section 165 of the Internal Revenue Code, and in the event that any revision of the foregoing is necessary to meet the requirements for qualification, the Board, but only upon consent of the parties to this Agreement, is authorized to make such necessary revisions, adhering as closely as possible to the intent of the parties hereto as expressed in this pension agreement.

14. The Pension Agreement shall continue in effect for a period of five years from March 1, 1950. Either party may request renegotiation of the provisions of the pension agreement upon sixty-day written notice to the other party in advance of March 1, 1955. During the period of five years from March 1, 1950, neither the Company nor the Union shall demand any change in this pension agreement nor shall either party be required to bargain with respect to this pension agreement, nor shall a change in or addition to any feature in this pension agreement be an objective of or be stated as reason for any strike or lockout or other exercise of economic force or threat thereof by the Union or the Company.

15. The Company shall not be obligated to make additional payments to the fund to make up deficiencies in any year arising from depreciation in the value of the securities in the Fund resulting from abnormal conditions.

16. It is understood that the foregoing is intended to set forth the principal provisions of the Pension Plan. The Company and the Union, within two weeks following notification hereof, shall each appoint a committee of three who shall draw up an agreement which shall incorporate and implement in sufficient detail, the framework established by the foregoing provisions.

23. Severance Pay

Few contracts contain provision for severance pay in case of lay-offs, occasional lack of work or involuntary termination of employment or for reasons other than misconduct. Such clauses cover special circumstances such as employee displacement due to technological changes or permanent closing of departments. In some instances the clause has been written in the contract in exchange for management's free right to cut the working force in case of the need for substantial retrenchment and economies.

In case of technological changes or closing of departments, management should reserve the right to transfer the employees to other departments and to train the displaced employees for new jobs, before becoming liable for severance pay. In addition, management should be permitted to offer displaced employees a furlough status with retention of full rights and privileges, as well as preference in employment, in lieu of severance pay.

Severance pay is usually proportionate to the period of continuous service. Thus, some plans provide for two weeks severance pay for employees with two but less than three years of service, three weeks severance pay for employees with three but less than four years of service, etc. Under this plan, terminated employees with less than two years service may not be entitled to any severance pay.

In some instances, provision is made for deduction of unemployment compensation from severance pay.

In cases where severance pay is paid on lay-off, provision is often made for repayment of a sum equal to the unemployment compensation received, upon rehiring of the employee. If such repayment is required, provision should also be made for a method of computing severance pay for an employee, laid off for a second time, who has already received such pay for an initial lay-off.

SEVERANCE PAY CLAUSE

A typical clause provides:

A. In all cases of lay-offs or discharge, except "summary discharge," should the Union consent to a discharge, lay-offs, or reduction of working hours, or should the arbitrator sustain the Employer in any such discharge or lay-off, the employee involved shall be entitled to one week's notice or its monetary equivalent.

B. If the Employer because of adverse business conditions desires to lay-off or discharge an employee, he shall do so only with the consent of the Union. Should the Union refuse to give its consent to such lay-off or discharge, and the Employer deems himself aggrieved, the matter shall be submitted to arbitration as hereinafter provided, and if the arbitrator sustains the Employer in such discharge or lay-off, the employee involved shall be entitled to the following severance pay dependent upon the length of service with the Employer or his predecessors:

Length of Service	Severance Pay
More than 6 mos. and less than 1 yr.	1 week
1 yr. or more but less than 2 yrs.	2 weeks
2 yrs. or more but less than 3 yrs.	3 weeks
3 yrs. or more	4 weeks

C. If the Employer because of the *bona fide* sale of his business or because of taking in of a partner desires to discharge or lay-off any employee he shall do so only with the consent of the Union. If the Union refuses such consent, the Employer may submit the matter to arbitration as hereinafter provided, if he deems himself aggrieved. Should the arbitrator sustain the Employer in such discharge or lay-off because of the *bona fide* sale of his business or because of taking in of a partner, the employee involved shall be entitled to the following pay, dependent upon the length of service with the Employer or his predecessor:

Length of Service	Severance Pay
Less than 1 yr.	1 week
1 yr. but less than 2 yrs.	3 weeks
2 yrs. but less than 3 yrs.	4 weeks
3 yrs. or longer	6 weeks

In case of sale of business both Seller and Buyer shall be responsible for severance pay.

X · OPERATING UNDER THE AGREEMENT

1. Introduction

When the employer and the union have entered into the collective labor agreement, they have established the rules and regulations under which the employer must operate with respect to labor. The contract establishes the basic labor standards for the term of the agreement. The Supreme Court has pointed out the effect of the labor agreement as follows:

> The negotiations between union and management result in what often has been called a trade agreement, rather than in a contract of employment. Without pushing the analogy too far, the agreement may be likened to the tariffs established by a carrier, to standard provisions prescribed by supervising authorities for insurance policies, or to utility schedules of rates and rules for service, which do not of themselves establish any relationships but which do govern the terms of the shipper or insurer or customer relationship whenever and with whomever it may be established. Indeed, in some European countries, contrary to American practice, the terms of a collectively negotiated trade agreement are submitted to a government department and if approved become a governmental regulation ruling employment in the unit. (*J. I. Case Co.* v. *National Labor Relations Board,* 321 U.S. 332 at 335).

The employer is free to hire employees and make use of his working force to the fullest extent except in so far as he is limited by the terms of the labor agreement and the applicable provisions of the labor laws barring discrimination and other unfair labor practices.

Hence, the employer, upon execution of the agreement, is faced with the problem of operating effectively and efficiently within the terms of the agreement. Primarily the problems may be classified in these categories:

1. Interpreting the agreement consistently with management's rights and exercising such rights within the agreement so as to attain the most productive operation with maximum efficiency and minimum cost.
2. Handling and disposition of grievances submitted by the union and employees under the grievance procedure. In this category, management may also consider its grievances for submission to the union.
3. Arbitration of disputes. These are disputes and grievances arising under the contract which fail of adjustment in the grievance procedure and reach the final step for determination by an arbitrator.

2. Relationship of Clauses

In considering the meaning to be given to the various provisions of the collective bargaining agreement, it must be remembered that each provision is a definite part of the whole pattern of the employer-employee relationship thereby established. The meaning of each provision may be colored and affected by other provisions of the contract and no clause thereof can be considered as standing alone. It may be that after consideration has been given to a clause in the light of the entire contract, it will be concluded that its meaning must be derived from the intentions of the parties as expressed in such clause unaffected by other provisions. But such a result can be achieved safely only after the clause to be interpreted has been considered with the other provisions. Thus, even the absence of a relationship between clauses is arrived at by weighing the possibilities of a relationship with other provisions. In many instances, however, it will be found that clauses are related, and the meaning of a clause is determined on the basis of a consideration of related clauses. Some typical cases illustrating these principles are as follows:

A contract contained the following separate provisions:

All provisions and conditions must remain the same as at present except as hereinafter provided.
Management has the right to relieve employees from duty because of lack of work, or for proper cause . . . .

At the time the contract was signed a certain group of employees was regularly receiving overtime. Management thereafter eliminated the overtime for the group. The union claimed this action was a violation of the contract, and management asserted it was a valid exercise of managerial functions. The arbitrator sustained management, pointing out that:

A general "catch-all" provision, designed to freeze general working conditions, cannot be construed to nullify an express provision of the contract. By rearranging its methods, the company effected an economy, and the employees were relieved of eight hours of overtime which they had been getting every two weeks. This clearly was an exercise of the right to relieve employees from duty because of lack of work. The employees involved still get the 48 hours a week guaranteed by the contract; they have lost only an extra eight hours that the contract did not guarantee them.

In another case,[195] the contract contained the following provisions:

The terms "employee", "worker", and "help", when used in this agreement, include all of the employees of the employer except executives, general manager, a confidential secretary and managers of stores which the employer may hereafter open.

The employer recognizes the union as the exclusive collective bargaining agency for all of its employees in the city of New York, except executives, general manager, a confidential secretary and managers of new stores which the employer may hereafter open.

The term "regular employee" includes any employee on the regular seniority list and does not include part-time employees or any employees hired on a probation or trial period.

The union claimed that under the union security clause, all part-time employees should become members of the union as of the date of their employ, and that such part-time employees should be covered by the contract. The union argued that if the employer were to be permitted to hire part-time employees who were not required to become union members and who were not covered by the agreement, then and in that event the employer would be able to circumvent the terms of the collective bargaining agreement by hiring non-union part-time employees to displace union men.

The employer contended that part-time employees were not required to become union members and were not covered by the agreement. The employer claimed that the advantages and benefits set forth in the third contract clause quoted above were intended to apply only to "regular employees," and not to "part-time" employees. He argued that if the benefits and advantages set forth in the contract were limited in application to "regular employees," then the contract did not cover "part-timers," and that therefore there was no need for "part-timers" to become members of the union.

The arbitrator in holding that part-time employees are covered by the contract, pointed out that the only issue before him was not whether part-time employees are entitled to receive the benefits set forth in the agreement, but whether or not part-time employees fall within the definition of "employees" as set forth in the first quoted clause above. He said:

The parties' definition of the term "employee" does not exclude part-time employees. If the parties intended such exclusion, it would have been a relatively simple matter so to provide, as was done in the parties' definition of the term "regular employee," where part-time employees were specifically excluded. There is nothing repugnant about these two definitions.[196]

A report time clause was found by reason of its language not related for purposes of interpretation to the premium pay provisions of the contracts. The report time clause[197] was as follows:

In the event employees are notified to report for work and upon so doing find that less than four (4) hours work is available for them, they shall be paid for four (4) hours work at the rate of pay then in force for the job for which they were notified to report.

The union claimed this clause covered both regular hours of work and off-schedule or off-shift work of an irregular or unusual nature. The company contended the clause covered only regular hours of work. The arbitrator ruled that the union had the burden of proving that the language was intended by the parties to cover the unusual as well as the usual situation and sustained the company's position. According to the arbitrator, if the parties intended to cover the unusual situations they would have done so by clear language; otherwise they can be said to have covered only the usually common situation.

In another case, however, it was held that a report time clause cannot be considered separate and apart from the rest of the contract, and the clause was construed, in view of such other provisions, to require premium pay. The clause provided as follows:

Any employee called to work or permitted to come to work without having been properly notified that there will be no work shall receive a minimum of four hours' pay at the regular hourly rate, except in case of labor disputes or other conditions beyond the control of the local management.

The arbitrator's reasoning was as follows:

Section 2 (Report Time) must not be read with enervating literalness and apart from the rest of the contract. Its relation to the premium pay provisions is not specifically stated and may not have been contemplated. It is quite probable that the parties were thinking only of the regular work days. For it is highly unusual to call an employee to work on an extra premium day and then send him home for lack of work.

Heavy emphasis on the phrase "regular hourly rate" diverts attention from the real issue. It is true that the phrase normally denotes the established straight time rate for the classification. That can hardly be disputed. But the question here is not as to the meaning of that phrase. The question here is as to the relation between Section 2 (Report Time) and Sections 3 (Night Shift Differential) and 4 (Overtime).

A fair interpretation of the Section in its context requires that call-in pay be computed at the employee's regular hourly rate with the proper premium for the day as stated in Section 4 and with the night shift differential provided by Section 3.[198]

3. Management's Rights

Management has the right to function for the purpose of operating the business efficiently and for a profit. Its managerial rights, however, are limited or may even be surrendered in some measure by reason of the terms and provisions of the agreement. Managerial rights which are not circumscribed or surrendered in the agreement are deemed reserved to management. In no event can these rights be exercised in a manner which is inconsistent with the agreement or so as to deprive the employees of the benefits of the agreement. These principles govern the extent to which management may exercise its managerial rights during the term of the agreement.

A company, relying upon the residual rights of management to make changes in the working force in the interest of economy and efficiency, subcontracted its plant protection and transferred its former guards to other jobs in the bargaining unit. The contract contained no clause concerning the subcontracting of work by the employer. The union claimed that the change could not be made without agreement and that the company's right to direct the working force and manage operations referred only to the flow of production and not to the abolition of jobs. An arbitrator of the dispute sustained the right of the company to effectuate the changes in the absence of a clause barring subcontracting of work, and further relied upon the point that there was no showing that the employer acted in "bad faith." The arbitrator pointed out:

> The Union had a right to have this change discussed in all steps of the grievance procedure, but "this right" to discuss cannot be considered as a "veto right" in the absence of explicit language to that effect in the contract.[199]

In another case the contract provided:

> The management of the works and the direction of the working forces, including the right to hire, suspend, or discharge for proper cause, or transfer, and the right to relieve employees from duty because of lack of work or for other legitimate reasons, is vested exclusively in the company: Provided that this will not be used for the purposes of discrimination against any member of the union.

The union claimed that the employer did not have the right to reschedule hours of work.

The company contended that it had an inherent right to make such a shift in the schedule in the interest of efficient management, even without consulting the union about it, and certainly that it had such a right in the present case in view of the fact that the rescheduling had been approved by the president of the union.

The arbitrators held:

> In view of the fact that the parties to this agreement have throughout emphasized the right and obligation of management and the responsibility of management for the efficient operation of the plant, and that the parties have not seen fit at any place in the agreement to specifically restrict the function of Management in the matter of scheduling men who are working a short time in one department for work in another department which requires more than a normal work week, the arbitrator has no right to insert such a clause in the agreement.

The bulk of arbitration decisions dealing with management functions has to do with the interpretation of management function clauses such as the ones appearing in the present agreement. The decisions hold uniformly that management has general managerial rights in the absence of a collective agreement, and that when such an agreement is made these managerial rights are given up only to the extent evidenced in the contract. Management functions not surrendered in a collective agreement are reserved to management.

It is, of course, a basic rule of interpretation that management functions may not be exercised inconsistently with the provisions of a collective bargaining agreement or in a manner to deprive the employees of rights secured to them under the terms of such agreement. We are unable to conclude from a reading of the agreement that management has exercised its function in the case we are considering inconsistently with the provisions of the agreement. Nowhere in that agreement is there any provision which would deprive management of the right to schedule the employees of the plant in such a manner as to give all an equal opportunity to work the normal work week.

We think it is fair that as to such a vital subject as the exercise of essential management functions, restrictions upon them should appear in the agreement with more than a bare measure of clarity. The union is not justified in contending that the absence of provision authorizing the scheduling of overtime work proves its contention. No express authorization is necessary as this is a basic management function which may be exercised unless restricted by fairly clear factual provisions. The right to schedule the weekly working hours is an essential management function, even though exercised to avoid the payment of overtime or other premium rates.[200]

In another dispute, the issue of overtime was involved. The contract provided:

> The company may request any employee to work overtime. In such event, the employee and the steward shall be notified as far in advance as possible. When it becomes necessary to work overtime or extra time, the work shall be divided as equally as possible between all employees in the job classification within the department in which the overtime or extra time occurs, provided such employees are qualified to do the type of work required.

The company contended that it properly suspended an employee for refusal to work overtime. The company further contended that employees are bound to work overtime when reasonably directed so to do by the company and when there is no evidence that the overtime work will result in endangering health, safety or other essential interests of the employees. The company pointed to the clause above which provides that when overtime work becomes necessary, "the work shall be divided as equally as possible," and therefore inferred that this section recognizes its authority to require overtime work, "since the decision whether overtime is necessary must be exclusively that of management."

The union insisted that the matter of working overtime should be regarded as optional with employees. The union maintained that the use of the word "request" indicates that "the company had no right to direct or command the working of overtime, but only to invite or request the same, leaving the ultimate decision within the option of the employees."

In upholding the company's right to require overtime, the arbitrator said:

The privilege of the company to require overtime work would be empty of meaning if every worker by unproven verbal claim of pain, illness or discomfort could be privileged to walk off the job without penalty.

In the contract at hand, the provisions for overtime payment recognize the function of management to direct overtime work on condition that it be paid for at the rate of time and a half when it runs to more than eight hours per day or forty hours per week. The position that the company "may request" the working of overtime seems to require a somewhat different interpretation than that suggested by the union. It is a cardinal rule of documentary interpretation that no sentence in case of doubt shall be given a meaning which reduces it to complete ineffectiveness. It certainly adds nothing to the agreement between the parties to recite that "the company may request any employee to work overtime." The company could make such "request" if the contract were silent on that matter. Its right to request or require overtime work exists in the absence of statutes prohibiting it, and in the absence of any contract provision expressly excluding it.[201]

Where, on the other hand, the contract clause labelled the right of "scheduling production" an "exclusive function of management," management's right to compel overtime was denied.

The company in that case contended that it had the right to require employees to work overtime on Saturday. The company relied on the clause and argued that scheduling of certain workers for Saturday is a necessary concomitant of the "scheduling of production," and that since there is no restriction on the scheduling right elsewhere in the contract the right to schedule Saturday overtime is absolute. The union maintained that management was not justified in requiring employees to work overtime.

In holding that management may not compel overtime, the arbitrator said:

If in managerial fields, "scheduling of production" carries with it ipso facto—in the absence of any specific limitation or restraint in the contract itself—the compelling of Saturday overtime, certainly the phrase would give to the ordinary layman's mind no inkling of such plenary control over what are commonly regarded as an employee's off hours.

A more reasonable interpretation of the scheduling of production, so far as work hours are concerned, would seem to involve the scheduling of the basic workweek, night shifts, and even Saturday overtime, but without as a necessary concomitant, the obligatory aspect. . . . A claim that a particular contract further obligates the employees does not seem well grounded when its only substantiation rests on a general phrase—of more or less uncertain connotation and this is still true even in the absence of any specific reservation by the union protecting employees against compulsory overtime.202

4. Supervisory Employees

The extent to which supervisory employees may engage in production work will depend on the provisions of the agreement in this regard, if any, as well as on the nature of the production work which they undertake, and past practices in the plant involved.

In the absence of a contract ban on production work by supervisors, an arbitrator ruled that the union could not object to the fact that a group of six supervisors, including top executives, performed some manual work during an occasion on which they were investigating reasons for the unsatisfactory flow of materials from the warehouse.203 Furthermore, he indicated the manual work of the supervisors was not intended to displace production workers, but was necessary and incidental to their main task.

Despite the fact that a contract gave management the right to assign work and direct the working force, an employer was held not justified in assigning to a foreman certain duties which were a regular part of the work of a job covered by the contract. The arbitrator ruled that such action on the part of management in reassigning work constituted a unilateral change in the content of a job whose duties had previously been fixed by collective bargaining.204

Under a contract permitting supervisors to perform "a reasonable amount of production work, as heretofore," management was not guilty of violating the contract where it allowed the foremen to perform more production work during a seasonal slump than during a busy period when the contract was signed.205 The arbitrator pointed out that the union failed to show that the foremen were doing more work than in previous slack seasons. Comparison with the amount of work performed by the foremen during a busy season was not appropriate.

On the ground that supervisors had always been required to do some production work and were not in the bargaining unit or on the applicable seniority list, a company laid off employees with greater seniority than a supervisor and permitted the supervisor to do the small amount of work then available. The union protested. The contract contained no provision barring supervisors from production work and provided:

The company shall have the right to hire, transfer, assign, reassign, promote, layoff, demote and discharge employees for lawful cause; *** and to relieve employees from duty because of lack of work or breach of discipline.

The arbitrator held[206] that since available production work had fallen so low, the company action in permitting the remaining work to be done by a supervisor was justified in view of its past practice in assigning some work to supervisory employees.

5. Discharge

When management has exercised its right to discharge or discipline members of the working force, the employees involved should not be permitted to question such action except through the grievance procedure as provided in the contract. Disregard of such procedure has the effect of throwing into discard the basic purposes of the contract and in a large measure reduces to futility the painstaking and time-consuming effort to establish orderly procedures through collective bargaining negotiations. Nor should discharged or disciplined employees be permitted to short-cut the grievance procedure by seeking arbitration without first exhausting the various steps of the grievance procedure. Recognition of these fundamental principles requires that the right to discharge and discipline employees should be wisely and reasonably exercised in the first instance.

If discharged employees are reinstated upon an arbitrator's award with back pay, the earnings of such employees elsewhere, from the date of discharge, should be deducted from the back pay. Such a contention should be urged upon the arbitrator regardless of the contract provisions, when back pay is sought and the arbitrator has the authority to award it.

In cases of discharge for inefficiency or faulty work, management should be prepared to justify its position on the basis of factual records which have been regularly maintained. The arbitrator should not be permitted to substitute his judgment of what constitutes inefficiency for the judgment of management.

The refusal of employees to perform jobs assigned by management frequently results in management's exercise of the right of discharge. It is clear that in the interest of efficient and orderly plant operations management must have the right to assign members of the working force to tasks that must be performed, and that employees must perform such assignments. While the employee may question the propriety of the assignment, he is obligated to perform the task provided it does not endanger his life or health. The appropriate method by which the employee may dispute assignments is to pursue the controversy under the grievance procedure. He is not justified in adamantly refusing to do the work. Management's action when such a refusal occurs must, however, be appropriate in the light of past practices. Such past practices may make the imposition of the penalty of discharge too severe. In one case, the employer for two years failed to assign a particular employee to a specific job because it knew the employee's strong dislike for such work, although the work was regularly performed by others. Eventually, the employer assigned the task to this employee, who refused to do the work. Thereupon, the employee was summarily discharged. The arbitrator, ruling that the employee should be reinstated with a penalty for failure to resort to the grievance procedure, said: [207]

Under such circumstances, the employee was not fully justified, on the date of his discharge, again to refuse to operate the hand truck, for, under contract provisions, the employee was at liberty to raise a grievance concerning and ultimately arbitrate the Employer's request. Instead of proceeding under the grievance machinery the employee categorically declined to operate the hand truck, and thus was summarily discharged for insubordination. Though the undersigned is of the opinion that, under all the facts, the Employer was not justified in discharging the employee, yet neither was the employee justified in flouting the grievance machinery.

Long established custom can affect management's right to impose penalties even though such customs are not written into the contract. In a case where the established custom was for the employer to give notice to the union before making a discharge for dishonesty, the employer failed to give the union such prior notice before effectuating such a discharge. The dishonesty of the employee consisted of petty thievery and the contract authorized discharge for dishonesty. It was silent as to prior notice of discharge to the union. Ruling that compliance with the prior notice custom was mandatory, the arbitrator said:

A union-management contract is far more than words on paper. It is also all the oral understandings, interpretations and mutually acceptable habits of action which have grown up around it over the course of time. Stable and peaceful relations between the parties depend upon the development of a mutually satisfactory superstructure of understanding which gives operating significance and practicality to the purely legal wording of the written contract. Peaceful relations depend, further, upon both parties faithfully living up to their mutual commitments as embodied not only in the actual contract itself but also in the modes of action which have become an integral part of it.

If any of these mutually acceptable methods of effectuating the contract becomes undesirable to either party, it should obtain the consent of the other party to revise the contract, in this larger sense, accordingly. The terms of a contract cannot be unilaterally changed during the period which it covers. Certainly, an arbitrator called upon to act within the limitations imposed by the terms of the contract ought not to be expected to make any fundamental revision in the terms of the contract itself.[208]

Where a contract permitted the employer to discharge for major offenses, an employee who called the foreman a liar without provocation was regarded as properly discharged under the contract on the ground that such conduct constituted a major offense.[209]

Discharge of an employee for refusal to work overtime without excuse was held justified by an arbitrator when the overtime was occasional, had been treated as obligatory for a long time, and the nature of the work was such that occasional overtime was necessary to prevent waste. The arbitrator treated the employee's conduct as insubordination, although the contract provided that a day's work should consist of eight hours.[210]

6. Grievance Procedure

Administration of the grievance procedure involves matters which affect the daily lives of employees in relation to their job, the place where they work, their working conditions, and their reactions to their supervisors. Adequate handling of the procedure can serve as a means for keeping in contact with the employees and learning their reaction to company policies. Nevertheless, the adjustment of grievances should not become a technique whereby the union is permitted to question or alter the basic standards established by the provisions of the contract. The question in grievance matters is the application and interpretation of an existing contract, not the writing of new provisions to meet grievances as they arise.

The role of the foreman in the handling of grievances must be appreciated since he meets the complaint in the first instance. His conduct can go far toward eliminating incipient grievances. His action may be decisive of whether management's decision shall stand or fall before an arbitrator. Hence, he must be thoroughly familiar not only with production requirements but also with the requirements of the labor contract.

Employees who desire to press grievances should be required to rely on their bargaining representative. They should not be permitted to seek grievance adjustment beyond the first step of the grievance without their bargaining representative unless they are presenting individual grievances not inconsistent with the requirements of the contract.

A provision requiring prompt filing of grievances will usually be held binding by an arbitrator. But if management is responsible for any delay, compliance will sometimes be excused. Where there was a ten-month delay in the filing of a grievance because of the conduct of management, consideration of the grievance was not barred. The arbitration board pointed out that unreasonable delay in filing would usually bar consideration of the grievance. However, since the conduct of management contributed in part to the delay, the tardiness of the grievance would be disregarded.[211]

In another case,[212] the contract provided:

Should differences arise between the company and the union or employees as to the meaning and application of the provisions of this agreement, or as to the compliance of either party with any of its obligations under this agreement, or should there be any complaint or grievance by an employee or the union under this agreement, earnest effort shall be made to settle such differences immediately under the prescribed procedure.

Should an employee feel that he has not been given fair treatment in layoff or discharge, he may take the matter up as a grievance as provided in the grievance procedure.

The employer suspended an employee, after his arrest for receiving stolen merchandise, pending the outcome of his trial, and contended that the employee's suspension was not an arbitrable issue. The company claimed that since the agreement between the parties did not specifically provide for suspension, it could not be taken up as a grievance. The company referred to the difference between lay-off and discharge on the one hand, and suspension on the other. It pointed to the second paragraph quoted above and argued that its action did not constitute a discharge or even a lay-off; that in taking this action it was using its best judgment; and that the arbitrator should not, therefore, substitute his discretion for that of management.

The union maintained that regardless of whether the company designated its action as a lay-off or a suspension, it resulted in laying off the employee and in not permitting him to work. The union charged that this action was improper and a violation of the rights of the employee in view of the subsequent failure of the grand jury to indict him for wrong-doing.

The arbitrator could not accept the employer's contention that, since the contract did not refer to suspension, management had the unrestricted right in its sole discretion to suspend the employee without the employee having any right to take this action up as a grievance.

In ruling that the matter was an arbitrable one, the arbitrator said:

To hold that because the words "layoff" and "discharge" are specifically used in the contract and not the word "suspension" the Company has the unrestricted right to suspend, would constitute so narrow a construction of the agreement between the parties as to make a mockery of the provision for arbitration of disputes.

Such a holding would leave the door wide open to suspension of employees for indefinite periods without even the slightest cause and would leave the employee without any recourse in the event of such unjustified suspension. In the opinion of this arbitrator, such a holding would do violence to the spirit and intent and purpose of the agreement of the parties and would be in violation of the grievance section of the contract.

7. No-Strike—No-Lockout

Where the contract provides against strikes and imposes penalties for violations of the clause, the question of the imposition of such penalties under varied circumstances may arise during the contract term. Whether a participant in a strike may be discharged will depend on the language of the contract.

The discharge of a shop steward with eight years of service was held justified where he ordered a work stoppage engaged in by the employees in violation of the contract.[213]

A clause interdicting the "fomenting, aiding, abetting, or obstructing of orderly and efficient operation" was held sufficiently broad coverage to permit discharge of any participant.[214]

The president of a local union was held punishable for a strike where, knowing that it was to start, he did nothing to stop it, failed to order employees to return to work and participated in picketing.[215]

If a discharge of an employee for threatening those who did not slow down production is to be sustained, it was held in another case, evidence must be produced showing that actual decrease in production followed such threats.[216]

A discharge for striking against a change in the method of doing a job was sustained where the contract contained a no-strike clause and a grievance procedure. Unless the employees had some reasonable basis for believing that the change resulted in danger to life and limb, there was no justification for resorting to a strike rather than filing a grievance.[217]

Discharges for attacking supervisors during a strike were upheld in another arbitration. But where a group participated in the assault, two could not be singled out for penalty unless it could be shown they instigated the attack.[218] The fact that the employer may have recourse to legal remedies outside the contract for misbehavior of employees during a strike does not necessarily bar him from imposing penalties where such misconduct clearly affects the employer-employee relationship.[219]

A so-called union meeting which went on for eleven days was held a strike, and the president of the union who stood at the entrance to the plant urging employees to attend the meeting instead of going to work was properly discharged where the contract prohibited strikes.[220]

8. Union Responsibility

Once the collective agreement has been consummated, management, by virtue of its terms and provisions, should be entitled to operate in reliance upon union responsibility to prevent interruptions of production. Union responsibility căn be insured in the contract by adequate provisions against strikes and stoppages. The administration of such clauses during the contract requires thorough knowledge of their meaning and application.

The National Labor Relations Board has ruled that employees who engage in a strike in violation of the no-strike clause of the contract may be discharged.[221] In addition, where a strike, authorized by the contracting union, constitutes a breach of the no-strike clause, the employer is under no duty to bargain collectively concerning matters involved in the strike, so long as such strike continues.[222] The contract provisions against strikes in that case were as follows:

It is hereby agreed that the union will not initiate, authorize sanction, support nor engage in any strike, stoppage, or slowdown of work and that the employer will not lock out any employee or group of employees, since this agreement provides for the orderly and amicable settlement and adjustment of any and all disputes, differences and grievances. In case of an unauthorized strike, the union agrees that it will loyally and in good faith endeavor to secure a return of the strikers to work to the end that the dispute may then be settled peaceably in accordance with the procedure set up herein.

The right to discharge employees shall remain in the sole discretion of the employer, except that no discharge shall be made without just cause—just cause to mean, among other things, inefficiency, insubordination or persistent or serious infraction of rules relating to the health or safety of other employees, or of rules reasonably promulgated by the management relating to the actual operation of the plant, or engaging in a strike or group stoppage of work of any kind, slowdown strike, sabotage, picketing or failure to abide by the terms of this agreement or by the award of arbitration.

The Board interpreted these clauses to mean that the union was responsible for the strike action of the employee-members even before it was officially authorized by the union. Furthermore, the Board ruled that as a consequence of the wrongful strike, the employer was entitled to solicit the return to work of individuals, provided such offers of work were conditioned upon acceptance by a specified date, and to grant wage increases to those employees who returned to work.

The United States Court of Appeals for the District of Columbia has held that a strike in violation of a no-strike clause and on twenty-four hours' notice in violation of the sixty day "cooling off" requirements of the amended Labor Act is illegal. Under such circumstances, the court ruled, an employer cannot be found guilty of an illegal refusal to bargain collectively with the union.[223]

9. Probationary Employees

Management's right to hire and direct the working force is seriously impaired unless adequate provision has been made with respect to new employees, who should be required to serve a probationary period before being permitted to achieve the status of regular employees. Merely insuring a probationary period for the new employee in connection with the acquisition of seniority rights is insufficient for the purpose of adequate administration of the rights of management.

Thus, where the contract failed to provide expressly for management's right to discharge probationary employees without recourse to any of the remedies of the contract to test the justice of management's action, an arbitrator ruled that a discharged probationary employee had the right to resort to the grievance procedure, including the final step of arbitration.[224] Lacking this protection, management does not have the unqualified right to discharge new employees during the probationary period.

If no probationary period is provided in the contract, new employees acquire seniority immediately on hiring. Thus, an employee discharged for loafing within the first ten days of his employment, was awarded full reinstatement with back pay, where it appeared that he was waiting for materials rather than loafing, and the contract contained no probationary period clause.[225]

Where the contract provided that "departmental seniority shall prevail from the date of last hiring, provided the employees appear satisfactory during a probationary period of ninety calendar days, acquired within a period of twenty-four consecutive months," an employee who worked more than ninety days, then quit and returned to work within the twenty-four month period, was not required to serve another probationary period.[226]

After completion of the probationary period, an employer, according to an arbitrator's decision, cannot be discharged on the ground that he initially lacked the qualifications for the job. The arbitrator regarded as proof of the employee's qualifications the fact that he was retained beyond the probationary period.[227]

Where a probationary period clause provided that new employees could be placed in jobs for which they were best suited, an arbitrator ruled that the company had the right to place a probationary employee in a clerk's position, which became vacant, in preference to a production employee, although the contract also provided that seniority and ability should govern in transfers from one department to another.[228]

10. Seniority

The seniority clause must be given a reasonable interpretation with the intent of effectuating its purposes, without unduly restricting the efficient functioning of management. Seniority status may be lost under such circumstances as discharge for cause, prolonged lay-off or voluntary quitting. Unless the contract provides to the contrary, an employee holding an exempt position has been held to have lost his seniority status. This principle can best be understood by consideration of a case in which it was applied.

A seniority clause provided as follows:

Seniority shall be considered broken or terminated when an employee quits or is discharged for proper cause; or, he fails upon proper notice to return to work within three (3) days, unless he has a satisfactory reason which is approved in writing by the Grievance Committee and the Foreman of the Division.

It is understood and agreed between the company and the union that any employee transferred by the direction of the working forces (sic) to a lower rated job shall carry with him his regular rate of pay.

The union's interpretation of this clause was that employees on lay-off from higher-rated jobs may refuse recall to lower-rated jobs without jeopardizing their seniority rights. The union contended that the recall of the employees to work at lower-rated jobs constituted a transfer within the meaning of the transfer clause. The union further claimed that there was nothing in the contract which denied an employee, recalled after a lay-off, the right to refuse a lower-rated job, and that he might in fact do so, without losing his seniority rights.

The company denied that the recall of the above mentioned employees to a lower rated job after a one-year lay-off constituted a transfer of jobs within the meaning of the contract.

The company further claimed that since the contract imposed upon it the duty of offering all available jobs to its laid-off employees on a straight seniority basis, it likewise obligated the recalled employees to accept the jobs offered, even if they were different jobs and paid a lower rate than the jobs held at the time of lay-off; and if they refused, the employee's seniority rights under the contract must be deemed lost.

The arbitrator said:

Under the seniority provision of the contract, as indeed under all labor contracts which recognize the rights of seniority, an employee who is laid off is secured in the same seniority rights as when he is at work and the only grounds upon which his seniority can be terminated are those which would terminate his seniority if he were at work. In the instant case, neither of the employees involved would have lost their seniority rights if, at the time of their lay-off, they had been offered and had refused the lower-rated helpers' jobs. . . . Indeed there is nothing in the entire contract between the parties which subjects a laid off employee to the risk of losing his seniority rights if he rejects a lower-rated job when recalled to work. . . . Nor is it a valid objection that the construction made here would result in maintaining laid off employees on the company's seniority lists indefinitely. If this consequence be deemed objectionable, it can surely be cured by express contract provision. Indeed, collective bargaining contracts frequently provide a cut-off date for seniority rights if laid off employees are not recalled to work and if the parties here desire to amend their contract to provide similarly they are, of course, free to do so.[229]

11. Transfers

The right to transfer employees must be reserved for the efficient operation of the plant and use of the working force. Since transfers frequently affect seniority rights of employees upon which may depend their jobs, rates of pay, promotion and other benefits, the exercise of the right to transfer must be consistent with these employee rights in the manner provided in the contract. The importance of such employee rights has been emphasized by an arbitrator who ruled that employees transferred from one laboratory of the employer to another laboratory of the same employer were entitled to severance pay provided in the contract because they were treated in the second laboratory as new employees.[230]

Where a single contract covered two plants of a company, specifying the two plants as separate employers, and the work was not interchangeable at each plant, employees had no right to exercise seniority for the purpose of transferring between plants in the absence of a contract provision to that effect.[231] Standard practice in cases involving multiple plants of the same company is to assume that seniority rights for the purposes of transfers, promotions, etc., apply to each plant separately unless the contract specifically provides for, or the past practice has been, interplant application of such rights.

The transfer of employees out of the bargaining unit to supervisory or office positions creates a problem when the occasion arises to require their transfer back to the bargaining unit. In one case, the contract provided that "an employee who starts in, or at some later date is transferred to, an office or salaried position, shall accumulate seniority for a maximum of six months while employed at this class work." An employee was employed in the bargaining unit for thirteen years and was then transferred to a clerical position. She worked at that job for almost a year, when a machine was installed to do her clerical work. She requested retransfer to the bargaining unit and the company complied, crediting her with total earned seniority to the date of her transfer to the office, plus six months. The union claimed that the question of her retransfer was a subject matter for negotiation and that the company did not have the sole right to determine when office employees should be transferred back to the bargaining unit. The Board of Arbitration overruled the union's contention on the ground that nothing in the contract required negotiation of the transfer back, and that the clause quoted in part above implied the "right to return to the bargaining unit either voluntarily or upon transfer by the company."[232]

Where the contract makes no provision for the accumulation of seniority or transfer outside the bargaining unit, an employee transferred to a supervisory position does not accumulate seniority while performing such service. When it is necessary because of business exigencies to transfer foremen back to a nonsupervisory position, they are not entitled to any preferential treatment in the absence of a contract provision to that effect. Thus, a contract provided that transferred employees who desire to return to their former departments must await a vacancy and, if transferred back, must go to the bottom of the promotional line without accumulated seniority. Their departmental seniority accrues from the date of their last assignment in the department. Under this provision foremen could not be placed in the last jobs they held within the bargaining unit in the particular department to which they were transferred back.[233]

In another case, a contract provided for plant-wide seniority, and in the event of lay-offs, the laid off employees were to be allowed to exercise their seniority in other classifications provided they had the ability and qualifications. Three employees lost their jobs because of improvements in machinery, but they were not laid off because several other employees voluntarily quit, and the former were transferred to these vacancies. An arbitrator ruled, however, that although there was in fact no lay-off, these transferred employees had the right to take jobs in classifications where they had greater seniority, provided they possessed the ability and qualifications to do such jobs.[234]

Where the contract provides that the employer shall have the exclusive right to make transfers, an intra-department transfer cannot be questioned by the union if such right was not discriminatorily used against a union member.[235]

An arbitrator ruled that a provision that transfers were to be made only when vacancies occur did not prohibit a company from making a temporary transfer in an emergency.[236] Where past practice permits, there can be no doubt of management's right.

12. Promotion

Where the contract is silent on the question of promotion from within, management does not violate its contract when it hires an outsider instead of promoting one of its employees.

In one case the contract gave management the exclusive right to control operations, and direct working forces, including the right to hire and to determine qualifications and job requirements, except as modified by the terms of the agreement. By the terms of the agreement "seniority shall be given due consideration in promotions"; promotions were to be based on seniority and qualifications, with seniority prevailing when qualifications were "sufficient"; and employees assigned to vacancies or new positions were to have a reasonable opportunity to demonstrate their qualifications. A further clause provided:

The company agrees to bulletin all vacancies or new jobs not filled by seniority excluding executive, office and supervisory vacancies. The company further agrees to hold such jobs open for at least ten (10) days, and to consider employees' applications in the selection of a person to fill such vacancies. The right of final selection of such employee, however, is reserved by the company.

In upholding the company, the arbitrator pointed out that the contract provided for promotion on the basis of seniority only when management has decided that the senior man is qualified. "The determination of the employer, under the terms of the agreement, when honestly arrived at, is final and binding on the parties." Said the arbitrator:

The contract gives to the employer complete control in the determination of the qualifications and job requirements in the various classifications of its employees. When the employer gives consideration to the qualifications of employees who are applicants for promotions or for assignments to vacant positions and in its opinion finds the applicants not qualified, the contract does not require the employer to assign such vacant positions to the senior applicants.[237]

In another dispute a promotion clause provided:

For the purpose of promotion, demotion and transfer of employees covered by this agreement, the company will give due regard to length of service and ability of the employees involved; and the general practice will be followed of promoting those who, by length of service and ability, shall be deemed to have earned promotion. . . .

The company in refusing to promote a helper to a pipefitter job on the ground that he declined to take a written test, contended that it may test "ability" by any reasonable means including a written test.

The union claimed that since written examinations had never been given in the past and men had been promoted to vacancies on a length-of-service basis with a tryout period, management could not establish a written test requirement unilaterally, but should negotiate such a matter with the union.

In determining on a promotion, the arbitrator ruled, management may test ability by any reasonable means, including a written test, despite the fact that no written examinations had been given in the past, and that men had been promoted to vacancies on a length-of-service basis with a tryout period.

In the absence of any specific provision for means of ascertaining "ability," it must be held, consistently with general custom and established practice, that any reasonable means which the company chooses to adopt may be applied.[238]

13. Leave of Absence

Operating under a leave of absence clause will vary with the extent to which such clauses establish the procedure for obtaining a leave, the number of permissible reasons for granting the leave, term of leave and the effect of such leave on employee status, benefits and privileges.

When an employee goes on proper leave of absence, his job is not considered a vacancy, and a clause dealing with the filling of permanent vacancies is not applicable.[239] If the contract provides the method for filling temporary vacancies such a provision is applicable.

Employees who obtain a job elsewhere when they are about to be laid off, frequently claim they were on a leave of absence, when rehirings occur. When, under such circumstances, the employee obtained a separation-from-employment slip and did not comply with the requirements of the contract in connection with leaves of absence, an arbitrator ruled he had quit rather than taken a leave of absence.[240]

Provisions for leaves of absence to employees who become officials of the union cover only the contracting union and do not require such leaves in cases where employees become officials in another union.[241]

In the absence of specific provision to such effect in the contract, time spent on a leave of absence does not constitute continuous service for the purpose of determining vacation rights.[242] In a case where a sick leave clause covered maternity leave, an arbitrator ruled that the time on maternity leave should be included in computing vacation eligibility rather than be treated under a general leave of absence clause for which the employee would not receive vacation credit.[243]

The fact that the contract contains a leave of absence clause does not make it mandatory to grant all requests for leaves. They must be granted as stated in the clause, that is, if the clause provides for leaves for union business or sickness, they must be granted in such instances. Other requests may be granted or denied by management, it would appear, in accord with reasonable requirements of scheduling and exercise of discretion.[244]

While the employer is entitled to some latitude in reinstating an employee who returns from a six month leave, if rearrangement of work schedules and operations is necessary to make room for the employee, an arbitrator ruled that a two week period for such purposes was excessive and awarded the employee one week back pay.[245]

14. Holiday Pay

A dispute, involving the following clause, occurred as to whether employees who were on temporary lay-off at the time of a paid holiday should be paid for the holiday:

The legal holidays on which double time shall be paid in the event the employee works on said days are New Year's Day, Lincoln's Birthday, Washington's Birthday, Memorial Day, Independence Day, Labor Day, Election Day, Columbus Day, Thanksgiving Day and Christmas Day.

The above mentioned holidays shall be paid for at straight time for the hours in the regular work day, as above provided, when an employee does not work on such holiday.

Nothing in the contract provided eligibility requirements for holiday pay, such as a requirement of work on the day prior to or subsequent to the holiday. The union claimed that, since there were no restrictions, employees on temporary lay-off were entitled to holiday pay. The company contended that those laid off were not employees. The arbitrator held that holiday pay is considered as part of the annual perquisites of the job and awarded holiday pay to those temporarily laid-off employees who were reemployed by the company within the two month period following the lay-off.[246]

Another type of holiday dispute arose where the employees covered by a contract refused to cross a picket line established by a related craft union against the same employer. The union claimed the employees were entitled to holiday pay for holidays which occurred during the period the employees stayed away from work. The union argued the employees involved would have been laid off anyway because of the strike by the auxiliary craft employees and pointed out that the employer had not requested the employees to report for work during the strike. The contract provided:

There shall be no strikes, stoppages of work or slowdowns by the employees nor any lockouts by the employers during the life of this agreement. In the event that this provision is violated by any employees, the union shall immediately order such employees to return to work and no dispute of any kind shall be taken up for adjustment until all such employees are back to work.

The company resisted the claim for holiday pay on the ground that the employees engaged in a sympathetic work stoppage in violation of the contract and as a result forfeited the benefits of the contract. While agreeing that the employees would have been laid off in a few days because of the strike, the company pointed out that the employees quit work before work actually ran out and that their failure to report for work was due to a work stoppage rather than loss of employment on account of the strike of the other employees. The arbitrator held that the employees who refused to cross the picket line were not entitled to holiday pay. He reasoned that the absence of the employees must be considered a violation of the contract and said, "Neither fairness nor logic supports the union's claim that holidays falling during the period in which this violation took place should be paid by the employer. Employees cannot claim the benefits of the contract during a time when by their own choice it was inoperative in an important respect."[247]

In another case, a holiday clause deprived employees of holiday pay if they failed to work the full shift on the working day before and after the holiday except when prevented from doing so for reasonable cause. The regular hours of work were Monday through Friday, eight hours per day and forty hours per week. A specified paid holiday fell on a Monday. The employer refused payment to employees who failed to work the regularly scheduled overtime day immediately preceding the holiday, Saturday, although the employees did work the scheduled straight time day before and after the holiday. The arbitrator held (1) that employees who, though scheduled for the Saturday work, were permitted by the company not to work, should not be denied holiday pay; (2) that employees with reasonable excuses for the failure to work should not be denied holiday pay.[248]

15. Vacation

Paid vacations, when provided in the contract, are considered part of earned compensation, and any consideration of vacation problems under a labor contract must be on that basis.[249]

The obligation to grant vacations arises by reason of the labor agreement, which controls the terms and conditions of employment. The vacation clause will be applied in favor of part time employees unless there is a limitation provided in the contract.[250] Furthermore, vacation rights will be determined by virtue of the provisions of the contract in force when the vacation is taken rather than the provisions of the contract at the time it is earned.[251]

Vacation clauses are not ordinarily given retroactive effect. Thus, where employees had taken their vacations under an old contract, the increase in benefits under a new contract were not given retroactive effect.[252]

The employer is allowed some latitude in the scheduling of vacations. Where the contract authorized the employer to schedule vacations in the interest of plant operations, he was entitled to continue the policy of scheduling vacations to start on Monday even though that was not the beginning of the work week for all employees. The evidence established the need for such a policy.[253]

Determination of the employees' eligibility for vacation rights may present problems where there has been an interruption of employment. In one case, the union contended certain employees were eligible for vacation on the basis of their aggregate period of employment, whereas the employer contended that continuous service was required under the vacation clause. The employees involved had interrupted rather than continuous service. The vacation clause set forth that the cessation of work for certain causes should not interfere with the accrual of vacation rights, but periods of cessation of work on account of discharge for cause or voluntary termination were not to be included in determining eligibility for vacation. The arbitrator ruled that under such a vacation provision aggregate periods of service were the proper basis for the computation of vacation rights because "Had the parties intended to require continuous employment, it would have been simple enough for them to have said so."[254] In another case, the union sought vacation credit on the aggregate basis for an employee where there had been a substantial interruption of service by reason of lay-off with a consequent loss of seniority rights. The arbitrator overruled the union's contention on the basis of existing plant practice pointing out:

Continuity of service (for vacation benefits) must be based upon some sort of an established set of conditions. If the collective agreement is silent in this matter, but a general company policy and practice is and was in effect, then the existing practice is the controlling factor.[255]

Where the contract denied vacation benefits to those employees "not in the employ" of the company on the vacation eligibility date, an arbitration board ruled that maternity leave, under the provisions of the contract, did not terminate employment and, hence, an employee on maternity leave on the vacation eligibility date was entitled to vacation benefits if the other contract requirements for such benefits were satisfied.[256]

16. Guaranteed Work

The guaranteed work plan written into several contracts has given rise to a number of disputes such as one growing out of the existence and meaning of an escape clause by which the guarantee is made inapplicable. Thus a contract provided:

The company guarantees to each employee at least thirty-six (36) hours' pay in each week of employment subject to the following rules for eligibility:

Except as hereinafter provided, all hourly paid employees are guaranteed thirty-six (36) hours' pay in weeks when they are present each day for the full time worked by the gang in which they are employees.

An employee who is absent from work on any day that his gang works shall have his thirty-six (36) hour guarantee reduced by the number of hours that the gang worked on the day when he was absent.

The union contended that the employees were entitled to the full thirty-six hours' pay for a week in which they failed to work two days because of a severe snowstorm, in reliance upon an erroneous broadcast, not authorized by the company. The union pointed out that those employees who called the plant after hearing the announcement were told by the watchman that the company would not be working that day. Finally, the union argued that the demand for the guarantee pay was consistent with the intent of the guarantee pay clause.

The company contended that the contract language is not ambiguous. The third paragraph quoted above (the escape clause) uses the single word "absent" and is not modified by any adverb or phrase such as "unavoidably" or "through no fault of his own." The broadcast was not authorized by the company and the announcement was untrue, since the plant was open and operating. Only if the broadcast had been authorized by the company might the union argue that this act had made it unnecessary for those employees who relied on the broadcast to be present for work on each day of the week.

The arbitrator held that the employees were not entitled to pay for the days they failed to report because of the snowstorm, since the contract permitted escape from the guarantee for absences.

He reasoned that the arbitrator has no authority to impose an obligation upon the company over and above those specifically called for in the agreement. Although the circumstances which deprived many employees of the thirty-six hour guarantee were unfortunate, only the broadcasting station could be held responsible for the error. The union made no effort to prove that the company had authorized the broadcast, and only in the event such authorization had been made would the company assume an obligation under the guarantee clause. "The terms of the contract are explicit and the arbitrator refuses to stretch the meaning of the contract beyond what the language will tolerate."[257]

17. Pension Plan

In determining the meaning and intent of a disputed portion of an arbitrator's award in a pension case, a court held that the language stating: "The company proposes to provide payment of pensions to its employees during their lives in accordance with the plan hereinafter set forth," meant that the company intended to provide pension payments for life for all employees who became entitled thereto during the employment contract period, that is, between July 1, 1947, and January 31, 1948. The union contended that the arbitration award granted a pension for life to the employees of the company who became eligible therefor during that same period. The company maintained, on the other hand, that the arbitral award granted to such eligible employees the right to receive, after retirement, periodic payments only up to the termination date of the current contract on January 31, 1948.

The court, in sustaining the union's position, pointed out that all the arbitrator meant was that pension rights should accrue to the employees only so long as the contract term continued; but that, once accrued, those pension rights should continue during the respective lives of the pensioners. According to the company's construction, the court pointed out, no pension rights could vest after the contract period had expired. Furthermore, it was shown by the court, one provision of the arbitration award stated that no pensioner—once he had been retired—might reenter the service of the company, which provision is consistent only with retirement upon a pension for life. Said the court, "it would clearly inflict cruel hardship upon a pensioner if he were entitled, upon retirement, only to a maximum of seven monthly pension payments (as the companies seek to interpret the award) and then left with neither pension nor job."[258]

In another dispute, the company claimed it had the right to retire four employees under the provisions of a compulsory retirement plan, since the plan was in effect prior to the execution of the current contract with the union, the terms of the plan were known to the members of the union prior to the negotiation of the contract, and the plan was not modified in any way by the contract.

The company had introduced the pension plan, which was entirely financed by the employer, prior to the time when all of the four employees here involved were working for the company. Due to the emergency caused by the war, the involuntary retirement provisions of the plan were not enforced, but after the cessation of hostilities, an announcement was made of the reinstatement of this policy of compulsory retirement.

The union maintained that the company's action in "laying off" the four men involved violated the seniority clause of the contract.

The arbitrator ruled that since the contract contained no provision to the contrary, management had the right to establish a retirement plan. Said the arbitrator:

> The union has no proper ground to complain when the company is carrying out a plan which seeks to solve the problem of providing for persons who have grown old in the employ of the company, so long as that carrying out of the plan is not discriminatory. Particularly is this true where, as in the instant case, the union entered into a bargaining contract with the company after the announcement of the plan, and the contract as negotiated in no way mentioned the retirement plan or placed any limitation upon the company in regard to it.[259]

18. Severance Pay

Under a contract providing that the employer would grant severance pay to those employees discharged for "unsatisfactory" work performance but not to those discharged for "malfeasance," and specifically distinguishing between unsatisfactory performance and malfeasance, an employee who was discharged because of a record of excessive tardiness was denied severance pay. The union contended that the employee was discharged for unsatisfactory work performance and therefore should have been granted severance pay.

The arbitrator held that the employee, having been fired for extensive tardiness, was guilty of "malfeasance" rather than "unsatisfactory performance" and was not entitled to severance pay. Said the arbitrator:

> The distinction between unsatisfactory performance and malfeasance is the difference between inefficiency or incompetence on the one hand and, on the other, misbehavior within the individual employee's control and unrelated to the proficiency with which he discharges his assigned duties.
>
> The employer in effect promises that, if it continues the individual's employment beyond the probationary period, it will grant severance pay and related benefits if incapability is first detected at a later date. In such a case the employer has had opportunity to observe the employee's work during a trial period without incurring obligations. If a trial is deemed a satisfactory one, the employer appropriately undertakes to protect the worker against a subsequent change of opinion. Where, however, the employee after the probationary period becomes guilty of malfeasance, which includes "misconduct" but "does not include incompetence," the employer has had no opportunity to observe the employee's misbehavior and to terminate his employment before a permanent status is achieved. In cases of this description the misconduct is as a rule non-predictable, volitional, and personal. To guard the employer against large severance payments to indi-

viduals whose behavior has been objectionable, the contract expressly provides that persons dismissed for malfeasance may be denied privileges which are enjoyed by other discharged workers.[260]

19. Merit Wage Increases

The courts have ruled that merit wage increases do not fall within the sphere of exclusive managerial functions, and that employers are obligated by virtue of the Labor Act to bargain collectively with the union concerning such increases.[261] The court pointed out in the *J. H. Allison Co.* case that "the labeling of a wage increase as a gratuity does not obviate the fact that a gratuitous increase on the basis of merit does, in actuality, effectuate changes in rates of pay and wages, which are by the Act made the subject of collective bargaining."

The fact that the existing contract between the employer and the union is silent as to merit increases does not remove that subject matter from the area of mandatory collective bargaining. The contract need contain no provision against unilateral action on individual merit to entitle the union to bargain with respect thereto. Unilateral action by the employer constitutes a violation of the Act when the union seeks to bargain with respect thereto.

According to the aforementioned court decision the obligation to bargain concerning merit increases carries with it the duty on the part of the employer to furnish to the union, upon its request, "full information with respect to merit wage increases, including the number of such increases, the amount of such increases, and the standards employed in arriving at such increases."

In the *Aluminum Ore Company* case, the union, upon insistence of the employer, was willing to consider increases in wages for individual members of certain groups of employees instead of a general increase to all employees in proportional amounts. In accordance with its practice in prior years, the employer advised the union that it was making certain wage increases and that objections thereto could be taken up as a grievance. The Board and the court held that such unilateral procedure by the employer in the face of the union's demand for bargaining on the restricted increases constituted an illegal refusal to bargain collectively.[262] They also ruled that the refusal of the employer to supply the wage history of the employees involved impeded negotiations, made intelligent collective bargaining on the subject impossible and hence was illegal. The information the employer should have disclosed was "full information as to the work done by the respective employees, and as to the respective wages in the plant, their respective increases from time to time and all other facts bearing upon what constituted fair wages and fair increases."

Both cases cited above are similar, although in the *J. H. Allison* case the employer asserted the right to make unilateral merit wage increases, and in the *Aluminum Ore Co.* case, the employer asserted the right to make *all* wage increases unilaterally.

20. Wage Reopening

No obligation to discuss changes in wages or rates of pay exists during the term of the contract in the absence of specific provision to that effect. An employer's offer of a wage increase did not constitute a reopening of that question where his offer was upon condition that the contract be extended for an additional term.[263] Even if the offer of a wage increase were not conditioned upon an extension of the contract term, the union's rejection of the offer barred it from reopening the wage question at a later date where the contract contained no wage reopening clause.[264]

Where the reopening clause sets forth the procedure and circumstances for such occurrence, there must be compliance therewith in order to achieve the purposes of the clause. But where written notice is required within a specified time other factors may excuse the tardiness of the notice. Thus, where the union orally advised the employer of its desire to proceed to open wages but the written notice was untimely because of the pendency of a proceeding before the National Labor Relations Board, the arbitrator ruled there was sufficient compliance to open the wage question.[265]

A wage reopening clause does not permit a revision of job classifications, particularly where another provision of the contract requires that "existing differentials between various classes of workers shall be maintained for duration of agreement."[266]

An arbitrator ruled that upon a wage reopening he was not limited to considering cost of living changes since the effective date of the contract, and rates of other employees, but could also consider differences in rates between various cities in the industry.[267]

Where the wage reopening clause is conditioned upon mutual agreement of the parties to discuss the issue, the question is not raised by the desire of the union alone to discuss the matter, since there is no mutuality for reopening the issue unless the employer is also willing to enter into the discussions.[268]

XI · GRIEVANCES

The collective bargaining agreement almost always sets up some form of procedure for the handling and disposition of grievances. The disposition may be arrived at on the basis of mutual agreement. Failing such joint adjustment, provision is usually made for final determination of the dispute by a disinterested outsider through arbitration of the dispute. The dispute may involve not only a grievance but the interpretation and meaning of the agreement as well as the performance or nonperformance thereof. Whether the dispute, regardless of its nature, may be properly handled under the grievance procedure culminating, as it often does, in arbitration, in the absence of a prior adjustment, will depend on the coverage of the contract. Thus, the first question that will arise in connection with a dispute will be: Have the parties by the language of the contract agreed that the dispute which has arisen should be presented through the grievance procedure? At the arbitration level, the question will be: Is there an arbitrable issue within the provisions of the contract? Some contracts require arbitration of any dispute between the parties during the term of the contract. Other contracts have a more limited coverage in that they confine the use of the grievance procedure at all levels, including arbitration, to grievances and disputes involving the interpretation and meaning of the contract and its performance or nonperformance.

Grievances commonly concern the following types of subjects:

1. Wages, as for example, requests for individual wage increases or changes in job classifications.
2. Discharge and lay-off of employees.
3. Provisions of the agreement, such as seniority, vacations, holidays, transfer, etc.
4. Conduct of supervisory employees toward their subordinates.
5. Safety and health problems.
6. Changes or improvements in machinery and equipment.

Employee grievances, it will be observed, concern the day-to-day life of the employee in the industrial plant. They concern the employee's job, the place where he works, and the supervisors with whom he has contact in the normal course of his work.

Nevertheless, the grievance must be viewed in the light of the basic standards established by the terms of the contract between the employer and the union. It is the duty of both to see that the relief demanded does not violate or undermine these basic standards. The grievance must be limited to problems within the scope of these standards. Otherwise the agreement itself is destroyed. The same safeguards must be applied in the event of arbitration in order to preserve the basic provisions and keep the arbitrator from altering them or adding to or subtracting from them in each case presented to him for decision.

It should be noted, however, that aside from the provisions of the union agreement, the National Labor Relations Act, as amended, provides for the right of individual employees or groups of employees to have their grievances adjusted so long as the bargaining agent is offered an opportunity to be present.

An adequate and properly functioning grievance procedure can serve as a means of becoming aware of employee complaints which require attention and elimination of their causes. Thereby, better labor relations may be attained and companies' policies and rules geared to more efficient operation to the extent that they may be accommodated to employee needs.

The usual contract provides that the first level at which the grievance is presented is to the employee's foreman. The need for adequate training of this level of supervision in dealing with employees and the union steward and in handling grievances is of the utmost importance. The foreman is the front line of management and his handling of the employees, the union steward, and the grievance can make or break the company's position before the employees and the union, as well as determine the disposition of any dispute which must be carried through the final level.

Briefly summarized the technique for handling grievances is:
1. Have the grievance reduced to writing, if the contract so provides.
2. Secure all the facts and check any necessary records.
3. Meet with the steward or other union representatives and ascertain their position and contentions.
4. Check their complaint and demands against the contract and company policies.
5. Reach a decision quickly.
6. Advise the union of the decision promptly.

The disposition of the grievance establishes plant precedent. Adequate record of each case should be kept through all levels of the grievance procedure.

XII · ARBITRATION

1. Nature of the Arbitrable Issue

Before invoking arbitration machinery, the parties must consider whether the dispute can be submitted to arbitration. Since the obligation to arbitrate cannot be imposed except by reason of a contractual undertaking voluntarily assumed, the parties must look to the collective agreement to determine first, whether it provides for arbitration, and, second, whether their particular dispute is arbitrable within the meaning of the provisions contained in the contract.

In the absence of a provision for arbitration in the agreement, neither party can resort to arbitration unless both agree to the submission of the dispute to arbitration. Nor can either party compel the submission of the dispute. Arbitration statutes do not authorize courts to order disputants to submit their controversy to arbitration in the absence of a voluntary contractual undertaking by the parties to resolve the controversy by such procedure. Typical labor disputes which have been submitted to arbitration by agreement for submission, in the absence of prior contractual obligation to arbitrate future controversies, have involved such questions as the terms and provisions of a contract upon which the parties could not agree, as well as the issues of wages and wage increases.

If the collective agreement provides for arbitration, the parties must consider whether the particular dispute is covered by such provisions and, therefore, is arbitrable. The contract may broadly provide for arbitration of all disputes between the parties without regard to whether or not the controversy arises under the agreement. On the other hand, the contract may limit arbitrable disputes to those arising under the contract or relating to the interpretation, construction, meaning, performance or nonperformance of the agreement. If the controversy does not fall within the terms of the contract provisions requiring arbitration, it is not an arbitrable issue and courts will not direct arbitration, unless the parties voluntarily agree thereto. Thus, the scope of the arbitration clause in the collective agreement is crucial at the outset and may become the subject of dispute and litigation.

It is a cardinal principle in the construction of arbitration agreements that only such matters as are clearly within its terms are subject to arbitration.[269] The courts, and not the arbitrator, have the power to construe the agreement in order to determine what controversies the parties agreed to submit to arbitration. Only *bona fide* disputes are subject to arbitration. The mere contention that a dispute exists does not create an arbitrable issue. The New York Appellate Division has said:[270]

> While the contract provides for arbitration of disputes as to the "meaning, performance, non-performance or application" of its provisions, the mere assertion by a party of a meaning of a provision which is clearly contrary to the plain meaning of the words cannot make an arbitrable issue. It is for the court to determine whether the contract contains a provision for arbitration of the dispute tendered, and in the exercise of that jurisdiction the court must determine whether there is such a dispute. If the meaning of the provision of the contract sought to be arbitrated is beyond dispute, there cannot be anything to arbitrate and the contract cannot be said to provide for arbitration.

In that case the collective agreement provided for the arbitration of disputes as to the meaning, performance, non-performance or application of the provisions of the contract. The agreement also provided that the employer would meet with the union to "discuss the payment of a bonus." The parties met but could not agree upon payment of a bonus. The union applied to the court to compel arbitration, contending that the contract provision concerning the bonus meant that a bonus must be paid, the discussion being only as to the amount thereof, and, since the parties disagreed, an arbitrator should determine the amount in accordance with the arbitration provision. The Court, denying the application, overruled the union's contention, holding that the bonus provision meant only that payment of a bonus would be discussed and that the meaning of the bonus provision was so clear as to present no arbitrable issue.

2. Arbitration Procedure

The procedure for the submission of disputes to arbitration will be governed by the provisions of the contract and the applicable arbitration statute. The procedure should be accommodated to the requirements of both contract and statute. The contract may set up its own requirements in many respects or adopt the applicable rules of the American Arbitration Association or a governmental mediation agency. If the contract does not cover procedural requirements entirely or in some particulars, the provisions of the applicable statute must be followed.

In the first place, the contract may require exhaustion of the grievance procedure before arbitration is reached. This may depend on the nature of the controversy, but, if necessary, the controversy should first be processed through the grievance machinery.

Notice of desire to arbitrate should be given if required by the contract, and if it imposes a time limitation, that condition should be met; otherwise the right to arbitrate may be waived.[271] The notice should concisely state the controversy and the remedy claimed. The applicable statute may require a demand for arbitration and should be carefully examined for the purpose of compliance with respect to form, procedure, time requirements, and substantive provisions. Failure to give a proper and timely notice under the statute may result in forfeiture of statutory remedies. If compliance with or applicability of arbitration provisions is questioned by one of the parties, the other party may seek court redress to compel arbitration or to stay the proposed arbitration.

The arbitrator is selected in accordance with the arbitration provision or the statute, if the contract makes no provision with respect thereto. A single arbitrator or tri-partite panel may be provided for by the agreement. If the contract so provides, the arbitrator will be selected from lists submitted by the American Arbitration Association and if the parties cannot agree, the association may designate the arbitrator pursuant to its rules, or it may be necessary to apply to a court for the appointment of the arbitrator in accordance with the statute.

After the selection of the arbitrator, the parties will attend a hearing at the time and place fixed by him. He has power to conduct and postpone the hearing, upon application of either party, for good cause. Whether a stenographic transcript of the hearing is taken will depend upon the desires of the parties, and either party may obtain the same if willing to assume the expense.

At the hearing the arbitrator takes his oath of fair and impartial conduct and determination. The parties present their evidence and witnesses, with each side afforded full opportunity to present evidence, to examine and cross-examine witnesses, and to be heard. Technical rules of evidence and procedure are not applicable and hearsay evidence may be used. Opinions, affidavits and even unsworn statements may be received by the arbitrator unless the arbitration statute makes applicable the technical rules of evidence obtaining in courts of law. The parties have the right to introduce statements and admissions made by the other party in the course of attempts to settle and compromise the dispute. Since breach of confidence can only serve to destroy settlement attempts in the future, confidential statements and admissions should be used only with mutual consent.

However, the evidence and testimony offered should be material and relevant to the issues and of some probative value thereon. The arbitrator has the responsibility for conducting the hearing within such limitation. The American Arbitration Association provides a printed set of rules applicable to arbitrations and hearings that are conducted under its auspices. While considerable latitude is allowed the parties at the hearing with respect to procedure and the kind of testimony introduced, the arbitrator should rely on such evidence as may be persuasive to the reasonable mind.

In the absence of statutory provision therefor, an arbitrator is without power to issue subpoenas. However, most statutes grant such authority, and the arbitrator may issue subpoenas *duces tecum* for the production of books and records. The parties may apply to the arbitrator for the subpoena. The application should show that the documents sought are material and relevant to the issues. He may call upon the parties to produce documents and witnesses under their control.

The party instituting the arbitration must proceed first at the hearing by offering its evidence and witnesses. After cross-examination of these witnesses and upon completion of all matters desired to be presented to the arbitrator, the other party then presents its case. However, the order for the presentation of proof may be varied by the arbitrator, whose authority to conduct the hearing includes the power to determine the order of proof. It has been said that the rules requiring establishment of a *prima facie* case and the "burden of proof" are not applicable. There has been, however, disagreement on the point as to burden of proof. At the close of the hearing, the parties may arrange for the submission of briefs to the arbitrator.

The arbitrator may determine contentions of parties that there is no arbitrable issue, that the issue is outside his jurisdiction to hear and determine, and that it is beyond the scope of the contract or submission agreement.

After the arbitrator then has the completed case before him for decision, the contract or the applicable procedural provisions may require him to issue his decision within a specified time. His authority to decide the issues should be defined in the contract which should exclude any power to alter, add to or detract from the obligations of the contract. The arbitrator's decision is called the award and usually consists of a statement of the controversy, a summary and discussion of the contentions and evidence of both sides, and the remedy granted, which may be a denial of relief or a statement of the relief awarded. The award is final and binding on the parties and may be enforced under the applicable statute, depending, of course, on the pertinent provisions of the statute and the nature of the award.

Courts are not inclined to examine into the merits of the issue after the arbitrator has issued his award. Arbitration statutes usually deprive the courts of power to decide the merits of the award, although there have been cases requiring the court to construe the award.[272] It may be assumed, however, that after issuance of the award further consideration of the merits of the issue is foreclosed. Arbitration statutes usually limit attempts to set aside the award to such grounds as procuring the award by corruption or fraud, partiality or corruption of the arbitrator, misconduct of the arbitrator in denying postponement of the hearing, or any kind of misconduct prejudicial to a party, refusal of the arbitrator to hear material evidence, and any action by the arbitrator which is in excess of his authority. The question of whether there was a valid submission of the controversy may also be raised after issuance of the award if the statute so provides. Many statutes are procedural, designed to compel this issue to be raised prior to the arbitration hearing; failure to do so may constitute a waiver of that objection as a ground for vacating the award.

3. Judicial Review of Arbitration

The extent to which courts will consider the merits of an award will vary with the provisions of the arbitration statute and the attitude of the courts toward such a review. Where the court is reluctant to review the evidence, the question of whether the award is supported by evidence will not be reached.[273] However, some courts will vacate an award on the ground that there is no evidence to support the arbitrator's finding.[274]

In Pennsylvania, the court has authority to modify an award if the court would have entered judgment despite a jury verdict to the same effect as the award.[275] Under Iowa and Nebraska statutes the award has about the same effect as a jury verdict and can be rejected for any "legal and sufficient reason."[276] The Minnesota statute permits the court to vacate an award if it is contrary to "law and evidence."[277] Some courts will set aside an award where the arbitrator has made an erroneous assumption of fact, as for example where he unwittingly used incorrect weights and measures.[278] A few courts have reversed an award where their view as to the amount of damages differed substantially from that of the arbitrator.[279]

Generally, both at common law and under statute, courts will not review the wisdom of an arbitrator in applying a particular rule for the purpose of making an award unless he thereby exceeds his authority.[280] However, if the arbitrator's ruling is determined to be totally unreasonable, the award may be set aside.[281] A New York court vacated an award where the arbitrator made a mathematical error.[282]

Some courts will vacate an arbitrator's award where he intended to apply the law of the jurisdiction but reached a result which is different than the court would have reached.[283] If such a standard of judicial review is applied, an award is subject to being vacated because the arbitrator applied the wrong rule of law or because he improperly applied a correct legal rule.

Where the agreement to arbitrate establishes the standards to which an arbitrator must conform, courts will upset an award which does not conform to the stipulated standards.[284]

What effect will be given to stipulations against judicial review of the award, is not yet clear. They have seldom been declared invalid.[285] One court simply ignored the stipulation.[286] The Oregon statute invalidates such stipulations.[287]

XIII·LITIGATION

Section 301 of the Labor Management Relations Act, 1947, establishes a basis for court litigation by employers and unions over the collective labor agreement. That section authorizes suits in the United States District Court for violations of collective agreements covering employees in an industry affecting interstate commerce, without regard to the amount involved or the citizenship of the parties. The District Courts are deemed to have jurisdiction in the district in which the union maintains its principal office or in any district in which the union officials or agents are engaged in acting for employees. Legal process may be served upon a union official or agent in such capacity.

The statutory provision establishes the contracting union as a suable legal entity and eliminates the common law ground which operated in many instances as a bar to enforcing the collective agreement against the contracting union.

The right of the union to enforce the contract by court litigation against the employer was well established prior to the enactment of section 301. Unions were successful in the courts in enforcing the following clauses of the labor agreement:

1. No-lockout clause: injunction against threatened lockout granted.[288] Employers have been ordered to put back to work locked-out employees and to move back to the agreed area in the case of a runaway shop.[289]
2. Preferential hiring clauses and the several varieties of closed shop provisions.[290]
3. Provision for the establishment of an arbitration board to settle suits and disputes.

Unions have also been held entitled to recover damages for breach of contract.[291]

Individual employees covered by a collective contract have long been permitted by the courts to enforce its terms on the theory that the union contracted as agent for the employee,[292] or that the collective agreement was by implication part of the individual contract of employment,[293] or that the employee was a third party beneficiary of the contract.[294] Such lawsuits involved seniority,[295] wages,[296] discharge,[297] and improper classification.[298]

While seniority rights of union members under a collective agreement by the employer and the union are regarded as vested property rights, courts have been reluctant to act in disputes over such rights arising within the union. In the absence of fraud, arbitrary action, contravention of law or public policy, courts will respect the decision of union tribunals operating under the union constitution and bylaws, if they do not exceed their jurisdiction.[299] Thus, it has been held that a member of a union cannot obtain judicial relief in a dispute within the union concerning his seniority rights if, without adequate excuse, he has failed to exhaust all his remedies within the union, including appeal to union tribunals available for such purposes under the constitution, bylaws, and rules.[300] If, however, exhaustion of the remedies within the union would be futile or unreasonable or tantamount to a denial of justice, the courts will assume jurisdiction of the seniority dispute without requiring the union member to exhaust the remedies within the union.[301]

There is authority for the proposition that seniority rights acquired by the individual union member under the collective agreement may be subsequently modified or rescinded by agreement of the collective bargaining representative with the employer if the union acts in good faith toward all the employees. A Michigan court said, "The Brotherhood had the power by agreement with the railway to create seniority rights, and it likewise by the same method has the power to modify or destroy those rights in the interest of all of the members."[302] It would appear from the cases that the rights of the individual employee created by the collective agreement are subject to being vacated or modified by subsequent agreement between the parties to the contract—the collective bargaining representative of the employees and the employer.[303] The New York Court of Appeals has pointed out:

The objects sought by a union and the "unity of action" to achieve them cannot be attained without some harm to the individual. The tests of whether the law affords redress for such harm are the legality, good faith and freedom from malice of the union.[304]

The Supreme Court has upheld the right of an individual employee, not a member of the union, to sue the union and the employer for injunction and damages where they were about to enter into a collective agreement which discriminated against the individual employee with respect to the terms and conditions of employment on the basis of race. The Court pointed out that the union was liable in damages for breach of its duty, as collective bargaining representative, to represent all employees impartially and fairly. The employer, the Court remarked, would not be bound by, or entitled to the benefits of, an agreement made by the union in breach of its duty.[305]

While the collective agreement fixes wages, hours of work and other terms and conditions of employment for the period of the contract, it does not, in the absence of express provision, fix the length of individual employment, and the employer is free to hire and fire within the limitations of the agreement. "The employer, except as restricted by the collective agreement itself and except that he must engage in no unfair labor practice or discrimination, is free to select those he will employ or discharge."[306] The collective agreement is not a contract of employment. The Supreme Court has said, "The result is not, however, a contract of employment except in rare cases; no one has a job by reason of it and no obligation to any individual ordinarily comes into existence from it alone. The negotiations between union and management result in what often has been called a trade agreement, rather than in a contract of employment."[307] The employee cannot sue the employer for discharge upon the theory that the term of the collective agreement establishes the term of his individual employment.[308] The New York Appellate Division for the First Department has said:[309]

Assuming that plaintiff might have some enforceable rights as a third party beneficiary under this contract, as we construe the agreement it appears clear that these rights do not include the right of continuous employment for the balance of the collective bargaining period. The two year period fixed in the contract did not purport to fix the term during which member employees were to remain in the service of the defendant. It related solely to the period during which the collective agreement would be enforceable.

Nor does the termination of the collective agreement terminate individual employment.[310]

The no-strike clause of a collective agreement has been specifically enforced against a union.[311] A New York court has said:[312]

Both parties to a collective agreement must be treated upon an equal basis and if an injunction can issue against an employer to restrain him from violating a collective bargaining contract, it may issue against the union from likewise doing so.

The Wagner Act provided that the Board should have exclusive jurisdiction over unfair labor practices and it was uniformly held thereunder that the courts were without jurisdiction to redress, by injunction or otherwise, unfair labor practices.[313]

The amended Act omits the section of the Wagner Act which provided that the power of the Board to prevent persons from engaging in unfair labor practices should be exclusive. As a result, following the Act's amendment, actions were commenced in courts for redress, by way of injunction and damages, because of unfair labor practices as defined in the Act. It was contended that the aforementioned change in the Act gave the courts concurrent jurisdiction with the Board over unfair labor practices and that under Section 301 of the Labor Management Relations Act, private persons had the right to sue in a federal court because of such unfair labor practices. Several federal appellate courts have overruled this contention and have held that under the amended Act the Board still has exclusive jurisdiction over unfair labor practices and that private parties cannot maintain an action in court for an injunction or damages on account of unfair labor practices, except to the extent that the latter are expressly authorized by the statute.[314] A few state courts have followed this view.[315]

However, certain conduct by unions, such as secondary boycotts, may be the subject of a private suit to recover damages in the federal district courts although the same conduct constitutes unfair labor practices within the meaning of Section 8(b) (4) of the Act. This right of private action is expressly granted to "whoever may be injured in his business or property by reason of" such unlawful conduct, and constitutes a distinct remedy and grant of jurisdiction to the court aside from the Act.[316]

A federal district court in Missouri has held that an employer not only has the right to sue a union for damages under Section 303 of the Labor Management Relations Act because of a secondary boycott but may also sue in the federal district court for an injunction restraining such union conduct.[317] However, the United States Court of Appeals for the Eighth Circuit has held that the statutory right of a private party to recover damages from a union because of secondary boycott does not include the right to enjoin such union conduct, and the District Court is without jurisdiction to grant injunctive relief unless the requirements of the Norris-LaGuardia Act are satisfied.[318]

XIV · EFFECT OF STATE ACTS

The federal Constitution gives to Congress jurisdiction over interstate commerce. Several Supreme Court decisions under the Wagner Act indicate that, since Congress has undertaken to regulate labor relations of industries within the field of interstate commerce, state labor boards lack jurisdiction to enforce state labor relations statutes in that sphere of industry.[319] A New Hampshire court has held the federal law paramount with respect to a business engaged in interstate commerce and barred an employer in New Hampshire, whose business affected commerce, from entering into a closed shop contract, although the New Hampshire law permitted such a contract under certain conditions.[320] As a result, state agencies probably do not have jurisdiction over employers whose business affects interstate commerce within the meaning of the federal Act, unless the National Labor Relations Board cedes such jurisdiction to them, and the Board can do this only if the policies of the state agencies are consistent with the policies and principles of the federal statute. Under amendments to the Massachusetts and Connecticut Acts, their boards cannot take jurisdiction of employers subject to the federal Act unless the federal agency "has declined to assert jurisdiction thereof, or except where such federal agency has conceded to the commission jurisdiction over any such case or proceeding."[321]

However, provisions of the federal Act add special force to the requirements of state labor laws important in connection with negotiation of certain phases of the collective agreement, such as union security provisions.

1. Union Security

Despite its provisions permitting union shop clauses when authorized by a majority of the eligible employees at an election conducted by the Board, the federal Act specifically provides that where the state law prohibits union security agreements, the latter shall control.[322]

Fourteen states bar all or some forms of union security provision. Most of these states either expressly or impliedly bar agreements which in any way make membership in a union a condition of employment.[323] Maine prohibits the closed shop but allows the union shop. New Hampshire's restriction applies to employers having five or less employees. Five states have adopted constitutional amendments providing that the right to work cannot be "abridged" by membership or nonmembership in a union. Penalties for violations of these state statutes barring or limiting union security provisions vary. In some instances, the punishment is fine or imprisonment or both. Under some statutes, the person adversely affected by the illegal provision may obtain protection from it by injunction, and some of the statutes provide that the violators are civilly liable to persons damaged thereby.

Another type of statute, while generally proscribing union security provisions, permits such a provision if a specified proportion of the employees authorize the union to enter into such an agreement. The Wisconsin statute permits union security if two-thirds of the employees voting authorize it, provided this constitutes a majority of all the employees.[324] The state board is authorized to declare any union security provision terminated if it finds that the union has unreasonably refused membership to any employee subject to that provision. The Wisconsin statute is applicable to maintenance of membership provisions. The statutes are not uniform as to the proportion of the vote required to authorize the union security provision. Usually such statutes also bar arbitrary discrimination as to membership.

While not barring closed shop, there may be a state statutory regulation imposing requirements in connection with its application. In Massachusetts, discharge under a closed shop requires the union to certify that the employee was deprived of membership for the purpose of imposing discipline and the employee has the right of appeal to the State Labor Relations Commission before the discharge becomes effective.[325]

With the proscription against the closed shop, there is no basis for a system of work permits.[326] Many statutes have outlawed the selling of work permit cards. Some statutes make it unlawful to require payment of a fee or assessment as a condition of work.

2. Position of Board

The National Labor Relations Board has held that it will not conduct union shop elections under the federal Act in states which prohibit all forms of union security provision.[327]

The federal Act requires that a majority of the employees eligible to vote must authorize a union shop before the parties may negotiate a union shop agreement. The Labor Board has ruled that this federal regulation will be applied to union shop elections conducted by it in states which require a two-thirds vote of the employees for a union security clause.[328] Thus, the federal statute is applied by the Board in all cases except where the state law prohibits rather than regulates union security provision.

3. Contract Responsibility

Some state labor Acts make it an unfair labor practice for employer or union to breach the collective bargaining agreement.[329] In one state it is an unfair labor practice for the employer to violate the agreement.[330] Like the Labor-Management Relations Act, many state enactments (even before that law) provided for suit against unions in the courts.[331]

4. Strikes

A number of state statutes make strikes illegal unless approved by a majority vote prior to the cessation of work. Special legislation has recently been enacted by some legislatures in connection with public utilities. A few of these enactments impose compulsory arbitration and others authorize the governor or other state authority to take over the public utility and bar a strike after the plant has been seized. A New Jersey Court of Chancery has held such a statute constitutional.[332]

Some states authorize injunctions or suits for damages when a strike is in violation of a collective agreement. The sitdown has been expressly declared illegal in some states.[333]

Picketing, under some state statutes, is treated as actively related to a strike. In Wisconsin picketing "not constituting an exercise of constitutionally guaranteed free speech" is not permitted unless a majority of the employees have voted for the strike.[334]

Mass picketing is expressly prohibited in some states.[335] One statute defines mass picketing in terms of percentage of strikers and others limit the number of pickets.[336]

Picketing by persons other than bona fide employees of the employer against whom such conduct is directed has been proscribed in some states.[337] Eight states forbid picketing of homes of employers.[338]

Some states have also enacted legislation against the secondary boycott.[339] In several states the statutes also are directed at rival unions which seek to compel recognition by picketing, strike or boycott in disregard of the certification of another union as bargaining representative. The jurisdictional dispute has likewise been regulated or prohibited by some state statutes. Some of these statutes set up procedures for the settlement of such disputes, and violation of the procedure is subject to injunction as well as recovery of damages.

5. State Regulation of Unions

Various state statutes require the filing of registration statements by unions. A typical statute of this kind requires the union to submit a statement concerning its officers, location, salaries of officers, number of paid up members and a financial statement of receipts and expenditures and all property owned.

Some statutes bar discrimination by unions on the basis of race, color or creed and provide machinery for enforcement of this provision. One such statute bars the violating union from qualifying for collective bargaining purposes and other statutes prohibit such a union from qualifying as a labor organization for the purposes of the state act.[340]

Authorities

The superior letter refers to the note number immediately preceding it. Thus **a** appearing after a sentence with the note **100** refers to **100a,** etc.

The designation of the National Labor Relations Board Rules & Regulations in the code of Federal Regulations has changed from Part 203 (14 FR 78) to Part 102.1. Consequently, former Sec. 203.1 becomes Sec. 102.1, former Sec. 203.2 becomes Sec. 102.3 and so on as to the balance thereof. The NLRB Statements of Procedure have also been redesignated in the code as Part 101 rather than as Part 202.1 so that former Sec. 202.1 becomes Sec. 101.1 and so on as to the balance thereof. These redesignations do not include any substantive change, and the text remains unchanged.

Authorities

PART ONE: REPRESENTATION

1. Inland Empire District Council v. Millis, 325 U.S. 697, where the Court said (p. 706):
"Obviously great latitude concerning procedural details is contemplated. Requirements of formality and rigidity are altogether lacking. The notice must be 'due,' the hearing 'appropriate.' These requirements are related to the character of the proceeding of which the hearing is only a part. That proceeding is not technical. It is 'investigation,' essentially informal, not adversary. The investigation is not required to take any particular form or confined to the hearing. The hearing is mandatory— 'the Board *shall* provide for' it. But the requirement is only that it shall be provided 'in any such investigation.'"

2. Amended 29 USCA (1947, Supp.) Sec. 159(c). If no bargaining agent is selected by a majority of the employees, the Board will dismiss the proceeding. "Majority" means a majority of those employees who actually vote at the election and not a majority of those eligible to vote. NLRB v. Whittier Mills Co., 111 F. (2d) 474. Since 1939, the Board's practice has been to certify only after a secret ballot election. The Cudahy Packing Co., 13 NLRB 526; Armour & Co., 13 NLRB 567.

3. Texas Co., 4 NLRB 182; Southern Wood Preserving Co., 37 NLRB. 25.

4. Johns-Manville Products Corp., 60 NRLB. 293.

5. General Box Co., 82 NLRB No. 75.

6. American Locomotive Co., 45 NLRB 1239.

7. General Box Co., 82 NLRB No. 75.

8. NLRB Rules and Regulations, Series 5, Sec. 203.52; 29 USCA (1947, Supp.) Sec. 203.52; 29 USCA (1947, Supp.) Sec. 159(c) (1) (A).

9. NLRB Rules and Regulations, Series 5, Sec. 203.52; 29 USCA (1947, Supp.) Sec. 203.52; 29 USCA (1947, Supp.) Sec. 159(c) (1)(B).

10. 29 USCA (1947, Supp.) Sec. 159(c).

11. 29 USCA (1947, Supp.) Sec. 159(c).

12. Since the Board's direction of election and certification of bargaining representative are not orders, they are not immediately reviewable as such by the courts. American Federation of Labor v. NLRB, 308 U.S. 401. However, the certification proceeding is reviewable by the courts as part of an unfair labor practice case in which the employer has been found guilty of refusal to bargain. 29 USCA (1947, Supp.) Sec. 159(d). In American Federation of Labor v. NLRB, *supra,* the Supreme Court held that a certification under § 9(c) of the Wagner Act was not reviewable except incidentally to review orders restraining unfair labor practices under § 10. The new Act did not alter the Wagner Act with respect to Court review of Board certification. See also note 57.

13. The usual situations in which the Board finds there is a question concerning representation may be summarized as (1) where the employer questions the union's claim of majority designation, (2) where the parties are in dispute as to what constitutes an appropriate bargaining unit, and (3) where there are conflicting claims of rival unions.

14. East Texas Electric Steel Co., Inc., 72 NLRB 1144; California Metal Trades Association, 72 NLRB 624; The Jeffrey Manufacturing Co., 58 NLRB 1129; Allen

14. (*Cont.*)
and Sandilands Packing Co., 59 NLRB
724; Pacific Mills, 60 NLRB 467. In the
Jeffrey Manufacturing Co. case, the Board
said (pp. 1130, 1132):
"On or about May 15, 1944, the Company
refused to grant recognition to the Pattern
Makers as the exclusive bargaining representative of the Company's employees in
the pattern making department until certified by the Board. On June 10, 1944, at a
conference called to discuss issues raised
by the pending petition of the Pattern
Makers, the Steelworkers orally advised
the Company that it was interested in negotiating a contract, with the Company's
entire plant as a bargaining unit. The
Company gave no indication that it would
grant recognition without certification by
the Board. The Steelworkers made no further formal demand for recognition prior
to the filing of its petition on August 8,
1944. The Company's contention that the
petition should be dismissed, because the
Steelworkers made no formal demand
upon the Company for collective bargaining prior to the filing of its petition, is
without merit. For a proceeding of this
kind, it is sufficient that, as of the date of
the hearing, the Steelworkers status as a
bargaining representative is disputed and
that recognition depends upon certification by the Board."

15. Section 9(c) (1) (A) (i).

16. Advance Pattern Co., 80 NLRB 29.

17. General Box Company, 82 NLRB No.
75.

18. Matter of Buffalo Arms Corporation,
57 NLRB 1560.

19. Atlas Powder Co., Zapon Division, 43
NLRB 757.

20. O. D. Jennings Co., 68 NRLB No. 10.

21. Matter of Gibbs Gas Engine Company, 55 NLRB 492; Matter of Humble
Oil & Refining Company, 53 NLRB 116.

22. Beebe Corporation v. Millis et al., 58
F. Supp. 993.

23. NLRB Statement of Procedure, Sec.
202.17.

24. Under special circumstances the
Board has even dispensed with a current
showing of interest. Acme Brewing Com-
pany, 72 NLRB 1005. See also Imperial
Tobacco Company (of Great Britain and
Ireland), Ltd., 74 NLRB 1038.

25. The National Labor Relations Act defines the term "labor organization" very
broadly to mean any organization of any
kind in which employees participate for
the purpose of dealing with employers
concerning grievances, labor disputes,
wages, rates of pay and hours and conditions of work. The term "union" is not
used. 29 USCA (1947, Supp.) Sec. 152(5)
—Ripley Manufacturing Co., 72 NLRB
559.

26. NLRB Eleventh Annual Report, p.
11.

27. See note 9.

28. NLRB Statement of Procedure, Sec.
202.17.

29. 29 USCA (1947, Supp.) Sec. 159(f)(g)
(h). Rite-Form Corset Co., Inc., 75 NLRB
No. 19, 21 LRRM 1011. The Board has
said that in the case of unions affiliated
with the AFL or CIO, the filing provision
does not require affidavits from the officers of these parent organizations. Northern Virginia Broadcasters, Inc., 75 NLRB
No. 2, 20 LRRM 1319.

30. Sigmond Cohn & Co., 75 NLRB No.
20; Westinghouse Electric Corp., 78
NLRB No. 38; Cory Corp., 78 NLRB No.
130; R. J. Reynolds Tobacco Co., 83
NLRB No. 46.

31. Cory Corp., 78 NLRB No. 130; Oppenheim Collins & Co., Inc., 79 NLRB
No. 59.

32. Herman Lowenstein Inc., 75 NLRB
377, 21 LRRM 1032, where the Board
said (p. 382): "If, as here, a labor organization that presented a claim for recognition has not complied with the provisions
of Sections 9 (f) and (h), we would no
more implement the policy of Congress if
we placed it on the ballot than if we were
to do so in a case in which it, or another
labor organization, filed the formal papers
with the Board. If a non-complying union
were placed on the ballot and happened
to win the election, no one could expect
the Board under the amended Act to issue
a certification that would run in its favor.
But a victory at the polls, even without
later formal certification, would confer
certain moral and practical advantages on
the non-complying union which the basic
policy of Congress appears to disconte-
nance. Such a result can be averted with
certainty only by our declining to place a
non-complying union on any ballot, unless there are absolutely compelling statutory or policy reasons for doing so.
"In our opinion, the fact that a petition

has been filed by an employer rather than by a labor organization does not provide such compelling reasons. The question concerning representation remains a question 'raised by a labor organization' which has made a claim for recognition as bargaining representative. An employer petition, like a union petition, seeks to resolve the question of who, if anyone, is the true bargaining representative of the employees. Either sets in motion the same investigative process; the same result, either of certification or of dismissal, may flow from either; and a Board election conducted on the basis of either will now preclude another Board election for 12 months. This similarity between employer and union petitions, both in purpose and in result, points strongly to the conclusion that a non-complying union should derive no more advantage from the one than it does from the other.

"The statutory language supports the same conclusion. Sections 9 (f) and (h) speak in terms of questions raised, rather than of petitions filed, by labor organizations. An employer petition must allege that he has been presented with a claim by an individual or a labor organization for recognition as bargaining representative of his employees. The distinction which Congress intended to draw by the words 'raised by a labor organization' is, we believe, between a claim for recognition made by a union and a similar claim made by an individual or individuals, not between a union petition and an employer petition filed with the Board. The name of the Fur Workers, CIO, will therefore not be placed on the ballot in this case."

"The Board recognizes, to be sure, that this conclusion may sometimes result in depriving an employer of information which the amended Act would permit him to secure if only a complying labor organization or organizations were affirmatively claiming representative status. Conflicting policy considerations are before us; the amended Act and its legislative history provide no sure answer as to which should prevail. We believe, however, that the exclusion of non-complying unions from the ballot in cases where employers are the petitioners is more nearly consistent with the supervening policy of denying the imprimatur of Government to such labor organizations."

33. Harris Foundry & Machine Co., 76 NLRB No. 14.

34. Craddock Terry Shoe Corp., 76 NLRB 842.

35. Bailey Slipper Shop Inc., 84 NLRB No. 41.

36. Morrison Turning Co., 83 NLRB No. 106; Mississippi Products, Inc., 78 NLRB 873; McGraw Curran Lumber Co. Inc., 79 NLRB 705.

37. General Box Company, 82 NLRB No. 75.

38. R. J. Reynolds Tobacco Co., 33 NLRB 674.

39. N. & G. Taylor Co., 21 NLRB 1162.

40. Lukas-Harold Corp., 44 NLRB 730.

41. Houston Shipbuilding Corp., 41 NLRB 638.

42. Aluminum Line, 8 NLRB 1325.

43. U. S. Industrial Chemicals Inc., 71 NLRB 940.

44. Chrysler Motor Parts Corp., 38 NLRB 1379; Paper, Calmenson & Co., 10 NLRB 228.

45. American Radiator & Standard Sanitary Corp., 35 NLRB 172.

46. Berkeley Steel Construction Co., 9 NLRB 130.

47. Reading Batteries Inc., 19 NLRB 249.

48. Armour & Co., 12 NLRB 49; Burlington Mills, Inc., 43 NLRB 426; Public Service Gas & Electric Co., 59 NLRB 325.

49. Semon Bache & Co., 39 NLRB 1216.

50. The Board, however, will not process the petition of a union which is alleged to be company-dominated. The charge of company domination will be determined first. Where company domination is established, neither the company-dominated union nor its successor will be permitted to appear on the election ballot. Wilson & Co., 45 NLRB 831; Utah Copper Co., 49 NLRB 901.

51. Petitions are normally filed in the regional office where the contemplated bargaining unit exists. See NLRB Rules and Regulations, Series 1, Sec. 203.53, 203.64.

52. NLRB Rules and Regulations, Series 5, 29 USCA (1947, Supp.) Sec. 203.55.

53. Eppinger & Russell, 56 NLRB 1259; Wisconsin Gas & Electric Co., 57 NLRB 285; Miehle Printing Press & Manufacturing Co., 58 NLRB 1134; Land O'Lakes Creameries, Inc., 54 NLRB 468.

54. Larus & Brother Co., 62 NLRB 1075.

55. Larus & Brother Co., 62 NLRB 1075; Atlantic Oak Flooring Co., 62 NLRB 973. For discussion of the duty of statutory bargaining representative see Wallace Corp. v. NLRB, 323 U.S. 248; Steele v. Louisville & N.R. Co., 323 U.S. 192; Tunstall v. Brotherhood etc., 323 U.S. 210; Hunt v. Crumboch, 325 U.S. 821.

56. 29 USCA (1947, Supp.) Sec. 159(a).

57. Marlin-Rockwell Corp. v. NLRB, 116 F. (2d) 586. As indicated in note 12, court review of the Board's determination of the appropriate unit can be obtained only as part of a review of the Board's finding of unfair labor practice, viz., refusal to bargain. However, the United States Supreme Court has had before it the question whether the Wagner Act excludes judicial review of a Board certification by an independent suit. In American Federation of Labor v. NLRB, 308 U.S. 401, 412, the Supreme Court said: "It can be appropriately answered only upon a showing in such a suit that unlawful action of the Board has inflicted an injury on the petitioners for which the law, apart from the review provisions of the Wagner Act, affords a remedy." The Court gave the same answer in Inland Empire Council v. Millis, 325 U.S. 697, where the Court found the Board had not acted unlawfully in holding an election before the formal hearing. The amended Act does not permit prehearing elections.

58. 29 USCA (1947, Supp.) Sec. 159.

59. 29 USCA (1947, Supp.) Sec. 159(b).

60. Armour & Co. of Del., 23 NLRB 619.

61. NLRB, Third Annual Report p. 156 et seq.

62. 29 USCA (1947, Supp.) Sec. 159; 29 USCA (1947, Supp.) Sec. 158(a) (5), (b) (3).

63. DeCamp Bus Lines, 20 NLRB 250.

64. Carbide & Carbon Chemicals Corp., 64 NLRB No. 61.

65. DeCamp Bus Lines, 20 NLRB 250.

66. Sebastian Stuart Fish Co., 17 NLRB 352; Federated Fishing Boats of New England, 15 NLRB 1079; Shipowners Association of the Pacific Coast, 32 NLRB 668.

67. Gettysburg Furniture Company, 25 NLRB 1109.

68. Continental Foundry & Machine Co., 58 NLRB 213.

69. Pelican Bay Lumber Co., 23 NLRB 650.

70. Marshall Field v. NLRB, 135 F. (2d) 391.

71. NLRB Fourth Annual Report p. 93 et seq.

72. Maryland Drydock Company, 49 NLRB 733. However, the Board recognized certain historically established exceptions as in the printing and maritime industries where certain levels of supervisors have traditionally been included by the unions and the employers in units of nonsupervisory employees. See W. F. Hall Printing Co., 51 NRLB 640; Jones & Laughlin Steel Corp. v. NLRB, (CCA 5), 146 F. (2d) 833.

73. Matter of Packard Motor Car Company, 61 NLRB 4.

74. 49 NLRB 733.

75. The Board holds that supervisory employees are those with authority to hire, promote, discharge, discipline or otherwise effect changes in the status of employees or effectively recommend such action. Douglas Aircraft Company, 50 NLRB 784.

76. 29 USCA (1947, Supp.) 152(3).

77. Matter of Rochester and Pittsburgh Coal Company, 56 NLRB 1760; Matter of Toledo Stamping and Manufacturing Company, 55 NLRB 865; Matter of Douglas Aircraft Company, Inc., 53 NLRB 486.

78. Amended Act Sec. 2(11). The term "supervisor" means any individual having authority, in the interest of the employer, to hire, transfer, suspend, lay off, recall, promote, discharge, assign, reward, or discipline other employees, or responsibly to direct them, or to adjust their grievances, or effectively to recommend such action, if in connection with the foregoing the exercise of such authority is not of a merely routine or clerical nature, but requires the use of independent judgment.

79. Hillman's Inc., 69 NLRB No. 34; Raymond M. Anderson Packing Shed, 61 NLRB 1022.

80. Wilson & Co., 68 NLRB No. 84.

81. Sterling Sugars Inc., 65 NLRB No. 195.

82. U. S. Bedding Company, 52 NLRB 382. However a distinction on the basis of sex may be found where it is indicated by the history of collective bargaining in the industry and the very nature of the duties of the employees involved.

83. J. I. Case v. NLRB, 321 U.S. 332, where the Supreme Court held that contracts with individual employees must give way to the collective bargaining agreement.

84. 29 USCA (1948, Supp.) Sec. 159.

85. Pittsburgh Plate Glass Co. v. NLRB, 313 U.S. 146.

86. Pacific Greyhound Lines Inc., 9 NLRB 557; Jones & Laughlin Steel Corp., 37 NLRB 366.

87. See International Union, United Mine Workers of America, 83 NLRB No. 135.

88. E. I. DuPont de Nemours & Co., 69 NLRB No. 63.

89. Riverdale Products Co., 71 NLRB No. 174.

90. General Plate Division of Metals & Controls Corp., 71 NLRB No. 152; Dayton-Price & Company Ltd., 73 NLRB No. 25.

91. Elliott Bay Lumber Co., 8 NLRB 753; New York Post, 14 NLRB 1008.

92. Union Premier Food Stores, 11 NLRB 270; Spenser Shoe Corp., 68 NLRB No. 106; Cummer-Graham Company, 71 NLRB No. 35; Penokee Veneer Co., 51 NLRB 997; Bull-Insular Line, Inc., 56 NLRB 189.

93. Drewrys Limited U.S.A. Inc., 44 NLRB 1119; Haven-Busch Co., 45 NLRB 1302; Airparts Co., 59 NLRB 1341.

94. 313 U.S. 146. The Court held the Board's Unit determination was supported by substantial evidence.

95. General Petroleum Corp., 56 NLRB 1366 (1944); Wisconsin Power & Light Co., 6 NLRB 320; Gulf State Utilities Co., 31 NLRB 740; American Telephone & Telegraph Co., 55 NLRB 327; Rutherford Freight Lines, 35 NLRB 1322.

96. E. T. & W. N. C. Motor Transportation Co., 30 NLRB 505.

97. Webster Mfg. Co. Inc., 27 NLRB 1338; Dain Mfg. Co., 38 NLRB 528; International Harvester Co. Tractor Works, 5 NLRB 192.

98. This device for resolving the unit question is now known as the "Globe Doctrine." Sloss Sheffield Steel & Iron Company, 14 NLRB 186; U. S. Pipe & Foundry Co., 19 NLRB 1016; The Globe Machine & Stamping Co., 3 NLRB 294.

99. 135 F. (2d) 391.

100. Marshall Field v. NLRB, 135 F. (2d) 391. The Court said that the statute did not authorize the Board to delegate the unit determination to the employees by an election. However, the Board still continues the application of its "Globe Doctrine" and uses the results of the election in part for resolving the unit question.

101. 58 NLRB No. 12.

101a. American Steel Foundries, 85 NLRB No. 7; General Motors Corp., 79 NLRB 376; W. A. Jones Foundry & Machine Co., 83 NLRB No. 23; Electrician—National Carbide Corp., 85 NLRB No. 15; Gaylord Container Corp., 80 NLRB No. 181; Machinists—E. I. DuPont de Nemours Co., 83 NLRB No. 131.

101b. C. A. Swanson & Sons, 81 NLRB No. 54; Jacobson Mfg. Co., 82 NLRB No. 158 (boiler room and power house employees).

101c. International Harvester Co., 82 NLRB No. 86.

101d. Reynolds Metal Co., 84 NLRB No. 11; Frederick Loeser & Co., 85 NLRB No. 52.

101e. Irvington Varnish & Insulator Co., 84 NLRB No. 5.

101f. North American Aviation Co., 78 NLRB 142; Monsanto Chemical Co., 78 NLRB 1249.

102. 29 USCA (1947, Supp.) Sec. 159(b)(2).

102a. National Tube Co., 76 NLRB 1199.

103. Sears Roebuck & Co., 45 NLRB 961.

104. Kansas Power & Light Co., 52 NLRB 97.

105. International Nickel Co., 7 NLRB 46.

106. Globe Machine & Stamping Co., 3 NLRB 294; City Auto Stamping Co., 3 NLRB 306; Pennsylvania Greyhound Lines, 3 NLRB 622; General Steel Castings Co., 3 NLRB 779; Pacific Gas & Electric Co., 3 NLRB 835.

107. Ball Brothers Company, 57 NLRB 85; Sutherland Paper Company, 55 NLRB 38.

107a. George S. Mepham Corp., 78 NLRB 1081.

107b. Armstrong Cork Co., 80 NLRB 203.

107c. Rex Paper Co., 83 NLRB No. 33.

108. Sutherland Paper Company, 55 NLRB 38.

109. General Electric Co., 42 NLRB 833.

110. E. I. DuPont de Nemours & Co., 69 NLRB No. 63.

111. Purepac Corp., 55 NLRB 1386.

112. Minnesota Broadcasting Co., 7 NLRB 867.

113. Wichita Falls Foundry & Machine Co., 69 NLRB No. 54.

114. Connor Lumber & Land Co., 11 NLRB 776; Collins Pine Co., 54 NLRB 670.

115. Cambria Clay Products Co., 42 NLRB 980; see also Cambria Clay Products Co., 45 NLRB 1069.

116. NLRB, Third Annual Report pp. 174, 175; NLRB v. Lund, 103 F. (2d) 815, 818 (CCA 8).

117. Phelps Dodge Corp., 40 NLRB 180.

118. Globe Machine & Stamping Co., 3 NLRB 294, 299, 300.

119. 29 USCA (1947, Supp.) Sec. 159(b) (3).

120. C. V. Hill & Co., 76 NLRB No. 24.

121. 29 USCA (1947, Supp.) Sec. 159(b) (1).

122. 29 USCA (1947, Supp.) Sec. 152(12). The term 'professional employee' means:
　"(a) any employee engaged in work (i) predominantly intellectual and varied in character as opposed to routine mental, manual, mechanical, or physical work; (ii) involving the consistent exercise of discretion and judgment in its performance; (iii) of such a character that the output produced or the result accomplished cannot be standardized in relation to a given period of time; (iv) requiring knowledge of an advanced type in a field of science or learning customarily acquired by a prolonged course of specialized intellectual instruction and study in an institution of higher learning or a hospital, as distinguished from a general academic education or from an apprenticeship, or from training in the performance of routine mental, manual, or physical processes; or
　"(b) any employee who (i) has completed the courses of specialized intellectual instruction and study described in clause (iv) of paragraph (a), and (ii) is performing related work under the supervision of a professional person to qualify himself to become a professional employee as defined in paragraph (a)."

123. Worthington Pump & Machinery Corp., 75 NLRB 678.

124. Clayton Mark & Co., 76 NLRB 230, 21 LRRM 1174.

125. Ordinarily the Board will not include office and clerical employees in a unit of production and maintenance employees. Roberti Brothers, 8 NLRB 925. However, when a union seeks the inclusion of clerical employees, the Board may be guided by the desires of this group as expressed in an election. The Electric Auto-Lite Co., 9 NLRB 147; Willys Overland Motors, 9 NLRB 924. The same result has been reached when rival unions disagreed over the inclusion of clerical employees and there was a past history of collective bargaining in which they had been included. Westinghouse Electric & Mfg. Co., 21 NLRB 1150.

126. DeCamp Bus Lines, 20 NLRB 250.

127. Acklin Stamping Co., 2 NLRB 872, 876-878.

128. This difference in method of payment is only one element considered with other factors.

129. A. O. Smith Corporation, 70 NLRB No. 121.

130. E. I. DuPont de Nemours and Co., 73 NLRB 1167; Johnson & Johnson, 72 NLRB 1061; Brunswick Drug Co., 71 NLRB 309.

131. Keystone Steel & Wire Co., 65 NLRB 274.

132. Matter of Liggett Drug Co., 73 NLRB 312; Spicer Manufacturing Division of Dana Corp., 71 NLRB 1249.

133. P. Lorillard Co., 73 NLRB 596; J. A. Bisso, Receiver etc., 71 NLRB 1441; Roane-Anderson Co., 71 NLRB 266.

134. Danita Hosiery Manufacturing Co., 71 NLRB 366; Dothan Silk Hosiery Co., 70 NLRB 1350; D. O. Frost Co., 72 NLRB 900.

135. Cf. The Eclipse Lawn Mower Co., 73 NLRB 258.

136. Globe Machine & Stamping Co., 3 NLRB 294; International Minerals and Chemical Corp., 71 NLRB 878; Trimont Manufacturing Co., 74 NLRB 959; York Corp., 74 NLRB 934; Hooker Electro-Chemical Corp., 74 NLRB 618; The American Fork & Hoe Co., 72 NLRB 1025.

137. Montgomery Ward & Co. Inc., 25 NLRB 318; Blue Bell-Globe Mfg. Co., 22 NLRB 961; Caterpillar Tractor Co., 36 NLRB 1035; Wilson & Co. Inc., 52 NLRB 888.

138. Republic Aircraft Products Div. Aviation Corp., 30 NLRB 269.

139. Gerber Products Co., 59 NLRB 1362.

140. However, the Board's decisions with respect to welders has varied considerably, particularly in the later cases where in the airplane industry welders have been held to constitute an appropriate unit under certain circumstances. Essentially, the question is said to be whether they constitute a separate, identifiable, homogeneous group, and the extent of the prior history of collective bargaining, if any, on association wide basis and its extent is equally of vital importance to the Board. See Central Foundry Co., 48 NLRB 5; Northern Coal & Dock Co., 55 NLRB 764; Illinois Packing Co., 56 NLRB 221. See Solar Aircraft Co., 51 NLRB 964 ("Globe" doctrine applied to possible welders unit in aircraft engine part plant). Bethlehem Alameda Shipyards, 53 NLRB 999; Crown Zellerbach Corp., 54 NLRB 25 (Welders in shipyard "Globed"); Wilmington Boat Works, 52 NLRB 614 (Welders unit held inappropriate); Harbor Boat Building Co., 52 NLRB 658; Duke Manufacturing Co., 53 NLRB 1239.

141. Eclipse Machine Division Bendix Aviation Corp., 60 NLRB 308; Rohm & Haas Co., 60 NLRB 554; The Babcock & Wilcox Co., 61 NLRB 529.

142. Kelsey-Hayes Wheel Co., 62 NLRB 421; Ingalls Shipbuilding Corp., 59 NLRB 924; Apache Powder Co., 59 NLRB 1123; National Fireworks Inc., 62 NLRB 271.

143. Harris Seybold Potter Co., 63 NLRB 1371.

144. The Firestone Tire & Rubber Co., 73 NLRB No. 132.

145. Luminous Processes Inc., 71 NLRB No. 59.

146. Worthington Pump & Machinery Co., 75 NLRB 678.

147. Ward Leonard Electric Co., 59 NLRB 1305; Socony-Vacuum Oil Co., 60 NLRB 559.

148. Goodman Manufacturing Co., 58 NLRB 531; Chicago Rawhide Manufacturing Co., 59 NLRB 1234; Kearney & Trecker Corp., 60 NLRB 148.

149. Curtiss-Wright Corp., 63 NLRB 207.

150. Pittsburgh Plate Glass Co. v. NLRB, 313 U.S. 146; Lockheed Aircraft Corp., 58 NLRB 1188.

151. Terminal Flour Mills Co., 8 NLRB 381.

152. The Board is concerned with the authority of the association to bind effectively the individual employer-members to a collective bargaining agreement. The absence of such positive power is usually fatal to this type of unit. Whether there has been a prior history of effective collective bargaining on an association wide basis and its extent, is equally of vital importance to the Board. See Central Foundry Co., 48 NLRB 5; Northern Coal & Dock Co., 55 NLRB 764; Illinois Packing Co., 56 NLRB 221.

153. T. C. King Pipe Co., 74 NLRB 468; Foreman & Clark, 74 NLRB 77; Martinolich Shipbuilding Co., 73 NLRB 1304.

153a. Associated Shoe Industries of Southeastern Mass., Inc., 81 NLRB No. 38.

153b. Associated Shoe Industries of Southeastern Mass., Inc., 81 NLRB No. 38.

154. Advance Tanning Co., 60 NLRB 923.

155. Waterfront Employers Association of the Pacific Coast, 71 NLRB 80, 71 NLRB 121.

156. Great Bear Logging Co., 59 NLRB 701.

157. Standard Slag Co., 63 NLRB 313.

158. Pittsburgh Plate Glass Co. v. NLRB, 313 U.S. 146; Aluminum Co. of America, 6 NLRB 444.

159. Chrysler Corp., 13 NLRB 1303; 17 NLRB 737; 28 NLRB 1038.

160. Chrysler Corp., 42 NLRB 1145; Woodward Iron Co., 46 NLRB 1345.

161. Pacific Box Co., 50 NLRB 720.

162. Union Premier Food Stores, Inc., 11 NLRB 270.

163. Old Mission Packing Corp., 18 NLRB 953; Kawneer Co., 22 NLRB 995.

164. Carnegie Natural Gas Co., 53 NLRB 1331.

165. Southern Chemical Cotton Co., 3 NLRB 869.

166. R. J. Reynolds Tobacco Co., 52 NLRB 1311; Stokely Brothers & Co., Inc., 15 NLRB 872.

167. Hunt Foods Inc., 68 NLRB No. 108; Stokely Foods Inc., 66 NLRB No. 98; Libby, McNeill & Libby, 64 NLRB No. 219; California Packing Co., 48 NLRB 693.

168. Hunt Foods Inc., 68 NLRB No. 108.

169. Hillman's, Inc., 69 NLRB No. 34.

170. Carlisle & Jacquelin, 55 NLRB No. 120; See Maui Pineapple Co., 60 NLRB No. 79.

171. In Carter Manufacturing Co., 59 NLRB 804, 806, the Board said: "The Board conceives it to be the duty of a duly certified bargaining representative to provide equal representation to all employees in the unit for which it is the statutory bargaining agent, irrespective of race, color, creed or national origin. . . . However, if it is later shown, by an appropriate motion, that the union has denied equal representation to any such employee because of his race, color, creed or national origin, we will consider rescinding any certification which may be issued herein."

172. Crescent Bed Co. Inc., 29 NLRB 34; The Colorado Fuel & Iron Corp., 67 NLRB 100; Foley Lumber and Export Corp., 70 NLRB 73.

172a. Larus & Bro. Co., 62 NLRB 1075.

172b. Atlanta Oak Flooring Co., 62 NLRB 973.

173. United States Printing & Lithograph Co., 58 NLRB 453; North American Creameries Inc., 57 NLRB 795.

174. The H. W. Wilson Company, 48 NLRB 938.

175. Ford Motor Co., Chicago Branch, 66 NLRB No. 157.

176. Reed Roller Bit Co., 72 NLRB 927.

177. Cities Service Refining Corporation, 70 NLRB No. 86.

178. Albemarle Paper Co., 70 NLRB No. 15.

179. General Motors Corp., 56 NLRB 1547.

180. Southeastern Telephone Co., 70 NLRB No. 2.

181. The Hamilton Tool Co., 61 NLRB 1361; Gulf Refining Co., 62 NLRB 1385; Michigan Bell Telephone Co., 58 NLRB 622.

182. The American Steel & Wire Co., 63 NLRB 1244; The Texas Company, 63 NLRB 1334.

183. Amended Act Sec. 9(c)(5). Matter of Delaware Knitting Co. Inc., 75 NLRB 205, 206, 21 LRRM 1025, where the union petitioned for a unit of seamers, loopers and examiners of a knitting mill upon the basis of the extent of union organization. The Board said:

"All employees of the plant are under the general supervision of the plant superintendent. The 17 employees in the unit sought by the Petitioner work only during the day shift and under the supervision of the seamer-looper fixer, whereas the 35 employees of the knitting department work in two shifts, each of which is supervised by a knitter fixer.

"There has been no history of collective bargaining among any employees of the Employer. During 1945, the Petitioner made an unsuccessful effort to organize the plant on an over-all basis. The Petitioner made a second attempt, in 1946, to organize all the plant's employees, including the employees of the knitting department; however, it apparently was successful only among the seamers, loopers and examiners.

"The Petitioner apparently relies on the differences between the functions of the two groups of employees, and also on the present extent of employee organization, to support its unit contention. While the seamers, loopers, and examiners are, in many respects, distinguishable from the knitters and their helpers, it is also true that sharp distinctions also exist as between them. Thus, for example, the seamers and loopers use different types of machines, while the examiners are not machine operators. The seamers and loopers require approximately 9 months of training to qualify, whereas the examiners require only 1 month. Furthermore, none of the three classifications sought by the Petitioner falls within any recognized craft grouping. The plant is small, and in the absence of stronger evidence of homogeneity within the group sought, the arguments for breaking it up into still smaller units are not impressive.

"It is also urged that the extent of Petitioner's organization of the employees must also be considered in reaching a determination as to the appropriate unit in this case. It is true that this is one of many factors to be weighed in determining the appropriateness of a unit. But we conclude, in the light of the other facts in this record, that the extent of employee organization would actually be the sole justification for finding that the unit sought here is appropriate. It would not be a factor, but the *controlling* one. In these circumstances extent of organization cannot be the determinative element, for the Act, as amended, provides that 'the extent to which the employees have organized shall not be controlling' (Section 9 (c)(5) of the National Labor Relations Act, as amended by Labor Management Relations Act, 1947). We therefore find that the unit sought by the Petitioner is inappropriate, and will grant the Employer's motion to dismiss the petition."

184. Delaware Knitting Co. Inc., 75 NLRB No. 27; Pomeroy's Inc., 21 LRRM 1224.

185. The determining test of supervisory status according to Board decisions under the Wagner Act was the extent of the foremen's authority and powers. Exclusion or inclusion depended on whether the foreman's authority met the Board's definition of a supervisory employee. Types of supervisory employees excluded: assistant foremen; boss machine tenders; floor and shift bosses; foremen and foreladies; gang leaders; head janitors and janitresses; inspectors; overseers; paymaster; personnel directors; shareholders. Many bargaining contracts *expressly* excluded from the unit supervisory employees defined by using the Board's descriptive language.

Supervisory Units were sanctioned by the Board. In the first Packard case, 61 NLRB 4, 16 LRR 168, the Board decided that foremen in mass production industries who function primarily as "traffic cops" are employees within the meaning of the Act and may constitute an appropriate bargaining unit. In L. A. Young Spring & Wire Corp., 65 NLRB No. 59, 17 LRRM 211, the Board extended the principle of the first Packard case to non-mass production industries and to foremen whose duties and responsibilities make them more than industrial "traffic cops." The duties of the foremen and the nature of the industry in which they are engaged bear only on the question of grouping them in appropriate units for purposes of collective bargaining.

In Jones & Laughlin Steel Corp., 66 NLRB 386, the Board held that appropriate units of supervisors in the bituminous coal industry may be represented by a union which is affiliated with a labor organization that represents rank and file employees. The majority of the Board said (p. 398) that the Act did not empower the "Board to disqualify a freely chosen, legitimate labor organization, not company-dominated, as the collective bargaining representative of persons found to be 'employees' within the meaning of the Act." The majority of the Board did not regard the commingling of supervisors with rank and file unions too great a problem for management to meet. The Board said, "the unionization of foremen, particularly by affiliates of rank and file unions, raises a number of issues."

The Board held that a union representing a unit of rank and file employees may also represent a unit of foremen and assistant foremen. National Biscuit, 69 NLRB 229; L. A. Young Spring & Wire Corp., 65 NLRB 298; Baldwin Locomotive Works, 67 NLRB 168.

The principles established by the Board on the foreman question led to questions of grouping various levels of supervisors in appropriate units. In Midland Steel Products Co. (65 NLRB 997), the union sought the inclusion of departmental superintendents in a unit of foremen and assistant foremen where the superintendents had authority effectively to recommend a change in status of the foremen and assistant foremen. The Board found that both these levels of supervision had common backgrounds and interests and that "problems of the different levels of supervisors establish a community of interest." The Board held that, before deciding the issue, the department superintendents should be given an opportunity by separate voting to decide whether or not they too should be included in the same unit with their subordinates.

Aside from the question of supervisory levels, it was the policy of the Board to parallel supervisory units in so far as possible with rank-and-file units; that is, supervisors in the same departments having employees grouped in a rank-and-file unit will be similarly grouped in a supervisor's unit. Lockheed Aircraft Corp., 70 NLRB No. 53; Wheeling Steel Corp., 69 NLRB No. 19.

The Board's conclusion, unit findings and certification with respect to foremen were sustained by the Courts as within the scope and meaning of the Wagner Act. NLRB v. Packard Motor Car Co., 157 F. (2d) 80, affirmed 330 U.S. 485.

186. 29 USCA (1947, Supp.) Sec. 152(3).

187. L. A. Young Spring & Wire Corp. v. NLRB, 163 F. (2d) 905 (USCA D.C.); cert. den. 333 U. S. 837.

188. 29 USCA (1947, Supp.) Sec. 152 (11).

189. Ohio Power Co. v. NLRB, 16 Labor Cases ¶ 65, 265 (CCA 6).

190. L. A. Young Spring & Wire Corp. v. NLRB, 163 F. (2d) 905, cert. den. 333 U. S. 837; Westinghouse Electric, 75 NLRB No. 1.

191. Baker Mfg. Co., 75 NLRB 1012, 21 LRRM 1103; Andrew Jergens, 76 NLRB No. 51, 21 LRRM 1192, 1193; General Motors Corp., 76 NLRB No. 122, 21 LRRM 1253, 1254.

192. Morowebb Cotton, 75 NLRB 987, 21 LRRM 1087; Farmville Mfg. Co., 76 NLRB No. 34, 21 LRRM 1186.

193. Ironton Firebrick, 76 NLRB No. 108, 21 LRRM 1241.

194. Palace Laundry Dry Cleaning, 75 NLRB 320, 21 LRRM 1039.

195. Fred H. Cole, 75 NLRB 348; S.-P. Mfg. Corp., 75 NLRB 701.

196. 29 USCA (1947, Supp.) Sec. 152(3).

197. Kansas City Star, 76 NLRB No. 52, 21 LRRM 1185.

198. NLRB Eleventh Annual Report p. 13 et seq.

199. Gardner-Denver Company, 65 NLRB 1224.

200. Casteel Distributing Co., 76 NLRB 153; Tennessee Coal, Iron & Railroad Co., 65 NLRB 1416.

201. Kittinger Company, Inc., 65 NLRB 1215.

202. United States Finishing Co., 63 NLRB 575.

203. Hytron Radio & Electronics Corp., 66 NLRB 267.

204. Tennessee Coal, Iron & Railroad Company, 65 NLRB 1416.

205. 23 Neptune Meter Co., 67 NLRB 949.

206. General Electric X-Ray Corp., 67 NLRB 997.

207. Swift & Co., 68 NLRB 440.

208. See National Sugar Refining Co. of N. J., 10 NLRB 1410; Bon Ton Curtain Co., 20 NLRB 462; Pressed Steel Car Co., 36 NLRB 560.

209. Chrysler Corp., 13 NLRB 1303. In the case of Lamson Brothers Company, 59 NLRB 1561, the Board said (footnote 22): "It is our general practice in representation cases to refuse to admit evidence on the question whether or not a majority of employees covered by a collective bargaining contract had actually designated the contracting union as their representative at the time when the contract was made, and to presume the regularity and legality of such contracts insofar as the majority question is concerned."

210. Mathieson Alkali Works, 51 NLRB 113.

211. Pennsylvania Greyhound Lines, 3 NLRB 622; Pressed Steel Car Co., Inc., 7 NLRB 1099; Kentucky Firebrick Co., 19 NLRB 532.

212. Ball Brothers, 54 NLRB 1512. The holding of the Board was the same where the contract covered employees in a comparatively new operation which had grown substantially with the resulting tremendous increase in the number of employees since the execution of the contract. Aluminum Co. of America, 51 NLRB 1295; J. A. Zurn Mfg. Co., 48 NLRB 100.

213. Champion Motors Co., 72 NLRB 436.

214. United Parcel Service of N. Y., 74 NLRB 888.

215. M. & J. Tracy Inc., 12 NLRB 936; Rosedale Knitting Co., 23 NLRB 527; Universal Pictures, 55 NLRB 52; Twentieth Century Fox Film Corp., 56 NLRB 117.

216. Palmer Match Co., 49 NLRB 767; Rockland Light & Power Co., 49 NLRB 1398.

217. Celluplastic Corporation, 60 NLRB No. 33; West Virginia Coal & Coke Corp., 58 NLRB No. 1; Owens-Illinois Pacific Coast, 36 NLRB 990.

218. Matter of Uxbridge Worsted Company Inc., 60 NLRB 1395; Matter of Sutherland Paper Co., 64 NLRB 719; Matter of Kennecott Copper Corporation, 63 NLRB 466.

219. Matter of American Pharmaceutical Co. Inc., 67 NLRB 1152; Matter of U. S. Finishing Co., 63 NLRB 575; Matter of James E. Stark Co., 56 NLRB 1209; Matter of Chicago Curled Hair Company, 56 NLRB 1674; Matter of Omar, Incorporated, 69 NLRB 1126.

220. Reed Roller Bit Co., 72 NLRB 927.

221. Reed Roller Bit Co., *supra*, note 220.

222. Puritan Ice Co., 74 NLRB 1311.

223. Fitrol Corp., 74 NLRB 1307.

224. Potosi Tie & Lumber Co., 73 NLRB 590; General Motors Corp., 72 NLRB 1199; The Beach Company, 72 NLRB 510.

225. Flintkote Co., 85 NLRB 442; Brewster-Ideal Chocolate Co., 49 NLRB 366.

226. C. Hager & Sons Hinge Mfg. Co., 80 NLRB 163.

227. Schaefer Body Inc., 85 NLRB No. 33.

228. Broadway Pipe & Iron Co., 83 NLRB No. 136.

229. Mill B. Inc., 40 NLRB 346; Foster-Grant Co., 54 NLRB 802; Kimberly-Clark Corp., 55 NLRB 521; Portland Lumber Mills, 56 NLRB 1336.

230. C. H. Dutton, 48 NLRB 27; Dedman Foundry & Machine Co., 50 NLRB 1019; Adirondack Transit Lines, 54 NLRB 974.

231. Allis-Chalmers Mfg. Co., 50 NLRB 306; Kennecott Copper Corp., 51 NLRB 1140.

232. MacClatchie Mfg. Co., 53 NLRB 1268; Fort Dodge Creamery Co., 53 NLRB 928; Corning Glass Works, 54 NLRB 963.

233. See Yale & Towne Mfg. Co., 59 NLRB No. 187; Columbia Protektosite Co., 52 NLRB 595; Diamond Magnesium Co., 57 NLRB No. 74.

234. News Syndicate Company, 67 NLRB No. 153.

235. 67 NLRB 997.

236. Fifth Ave. Shoe Corp., 69 NLRB No. 46.

237. Acme Brewing Co., 72 NLRB 1005.

238. Consolidated Vultee Aircraft Corp., 74 NLRB 967.

239. Hyster Co., 72 NLRB 937.

240. Don Juan Inc., 71 NLRB 734.

241. Murray Leather Co., 73 NLRB 892.

242. Con P. Curran Printing Co., 67 NLRB 1419.

243. Kimberly Clark Corp., 61 NLRB 90; Omaha Packing Co., 67 NLRB 304.

244. Quaker Maid Co., 71 NLRB 915.

245. Northwestern Publishing Co., 71 NLRB 167.

246. Mississippi Lime Co., 71 NLRB 472.

247. Greenville Finishing Co., Inc., 71 NLRB No. 68.

248. Dryden Rubber Co., 71 NLRB No. 82.

249. Matter of Henry & Allen, 68 NLRB 724. The Board said that the basis for the principle was to eliminate from the bargaining relationship delay and harassment arising from dilatory tactics by rival claimants—applied with equal force to automatically renewable contracts.

250. Matter of United States Vanadium Corp., 68 NLRB 389.

251. Matter of Olin Industries, 67 NLRB 1043. See also Matter of Atlas Felt Products Company, 68 NLRB 1; Matter of Omar Incorporated, 69 NLRB 1126, where the changes were within the modification clauses.

252. Matter of The William Koehl Company, 65 NLRB 190; Matter of Miami Daily News Inc., 66 NLRB 663; Matter of Wisconsin Telephone Company, 65 NLRB 368.

253. 63 NLRB 201.

254. 66 NLRB No. 51.

255. 29 USCA (1947, Supp.) Sec. 159(a).

256. 29 USCA (1947, Supp.) Sec. 159(c).

257. 29 USCA Sec. 159(c). See Reilly v. Mills, 144 F. (2d) 259; Associated Press v. Herrick, 13 F. Supp. 897; United Employees Association v. NLRB, 96 F. (2d) 875; Madden v. Brotherhood and Union of Transit Employees of Baltimore, 147 F. (2d) 439; Inland Empire District Council v. Millis, 325 U.S. 697.

258. NLRB v. Servel Inc., 149 F. (2d) 542. A proceeding for enforcement of a Board order against the employer was pending before the Court and the temporary restraining order was issued on the theory that, if the employer were permitted to interfere with the election, irreparable damage would be done in the event enforcement of the Board order was finally decreed by the Court. The temporary restraining order was issued September 29, 1944.

259. The Direction of Election provides for the conduct of an election in the unit found appropriate under the direction and the supervision of the Board's Regional Director as quickly as possible, but not later than 30 days from the date thereof. See Direction of Election, Snowden and McSweeney Co., 55 NLRB 372; Burton-Dixie Corp., 55 NLRB 723; The Murray Company, 55 NLRB 1201; Spicer Manufacturing Co., 55 NLRB 1491; Dain Manufacturing Co., 29 NLRB 526.

260. 29 USCA (1947, Supp.) Sec. 159(c) (3).

261. Thus the employer's payroll for the payroll period immediately preceding the Direction of Election is referred to as the "eligibility list" and that payroll is often called the "eligibility date."

262. The Board has veered from this rule when the plant has been temporarily closed down by a strike or for other reasons. The last working day or the payroll period immediately preceding the strike or shutdown may be selected as the eligibility date. Carrollton Metal Products Co., 6 NLRB 564; Lenox Shoe Company, 4 NLRB 372; Seiss Manufacturing Co., 7 NLRB 481.

263. When discharged employees claim their discharges were in violation of the Act, and there is such a charge pending with the Board, they will be permitted to vote, their ballots being impounded and counted only if they would affect the election results. In that event, their tabulation must await, and depends on, the determination of the unfair labor practice charges. Williams Manufacturing Co., 6 NLRB 135; Clyde Mallory Lines, 5 NLRB 503; Irving Shoe Co., 26 NLRB 468; Rudolph Wurlitzer Co., 32 NLRB 163.

264. Because it created undue administrative problems and delay, the Board discontinued its earlier practice of permitting employees in the armed forces to vote by mail. Wilson & Co., 37 NLRB 944; Botany Worsted Mills, 56 NLRB 75; Norwalk Tire & Rubber Co., 57 NLRB 1520. The variance from cases and the provision for mailed ballots was determined in matter of Southwest Pennsylvania Pipe Lines, 64 NLRB 1384.

265. Rudolph Wurlitzer Co., 32 NLRB 163; Ideal Seating Company, 36 NLRB 166. But where there was a charge pending that the strike was caused by the employer's unfair labor practices, and the employer had refused to reinstate the strikers upon their unconditional offer to return to work, the Board held that the ballots of persons employed between the date of the strike and the offer to return to work should be impounded and, if necessary, their validity be determined after the outcome of the unfair labor practice charges. Kellburn Manufacturing Co., 45 NLRB 322.

266. Triangle Publications, Inc., 80 NLRB No. 132; Belmont Radio Corp., 83 NLRB No. 5.

267. Times Square Stores Corp., 79 NLRB No. 50.

268. Employees of a company engaged in interstate motor transportation were balloted by mail. Central Freight Lines, 58 NLRB 263; Oklahoma Transportation Co., 56 NLRB 1717 (bus company); Certain Western Union Telegraph Company employees were permitted to vote by mail. Western Union Telegraph Co., 58 NLRB 1283.

269. See 29 USCA (1947, Supp.) Sec. 159(a).

270. Postex Cotton Mills Inc., 73 NLRB 673.

271. See Weinberger Sales Co., 28 NLRB 154 (further balloting ordered where only 54 out of a unit of 540 participated). Kendall Coal Co., 41 NLRB 395 (one out of three in unit voted—certification refused).

However, the Board will certify where less than a majority but a substantial number of employees participated and all employees entitled to vote were given adequate opportunity to cast their ballots. Central Dispensary and Emergency Hospital, 46 NLRB 437. See also: A. A. Fagan, 73 NLRB 680; A. L. Mechling, 69 NLRB 838; San Fernando Heights Lemon Association, 72 NLRB 372.

272. See Condenser Corp. of America, 42 NLRB 251. Cf. Cleveland Electric Illuminating Co., 52 NLRB 518. (Union obtained court order preventing employer from complying with Board Order.)

273. A. Gross Candle Co., 72 NLRB 879; Johnson Furniture Co., 73 NLRB 1112.

274. Food Machinery Corp., 72 NLRB 483; Swan Engineering & Machinery Co., 70 NLRB 1293.

275. Philip Lewis & Sons, 71 NLRB 976.

276. The Columbia Mills Inc., 71 NLRB 1205.

277. Seneca Falls Machine Co., 71 NLRB 1106; National Silver Manufacturing Co., 71 NLRB 594.

278. International Harvester Co., Chattanooga Works, 73 NLRB 436.

279. See Aluminum Co. of America, 52 NLRB 1040.

280. See 29 USCA (1947, Supp.) 159(c). With respect to the Wagner Act and the Board's prior practice, the Supreme Court said (325 U.S. 697, 706, 707):

"We think petitioners have misconceived the effects of § 9(c). It is as follows:

'Whenever a question affecting commerce arises concerning the representation of employees, the Board may investigate such controversy and certify to the parties, in writing, the name or names of the representatives that have been designated or selected. *In any such investigation,* the Board shall provide for an *appropriate hearing upon due notice,* either in conjunction with a proceeding under section · 10 or otherwise, and *may* take a secret ballot of employees, or utilize any other suitable method to ascertain such representatives.' (Emphasis added.)

"The section is short. Its terms are broad and general. Its only requirements concerning the hearing are three. It must be 'upon due notice,' it must be 'appropriate,' and it is mandatory 'in any such investigation,' but may be held in conjunction with a § 10 (unfair practice) proceeding or otherwise.

"Obviously great latitude concerning procedural details is contemplated. Requirements of formality and rigidity are altogether lacking. The notice must be 'due,' the hearing 'appropriate.' These requirements are related to the character of the proceeding of which the hearing is only a part. That proceeding is not technical. It is an 'investigation,' essentially informal, not adversary. The investigation is not required to take any particular form or confined to the hearing. The hearing is mandatory—'the Board *shall* provide for' it. But the requirement is only that it shall be provided 'in any such investigation.' The statute does not purport to specify when or at what stage of the investigation the hearing shall be had. It may be conducted 'in conjunction with a proceeding under section 10 or otherwise.'

"Moreover, nothing in the section purports to require a hearing before an election. Nothing in fact requires an election. The hearing 'in any such investigation' is mandatory. But the election is discretionary. The Board '*may* take a secret ballot . . . or utilize any other suitable method to ascertain such representatives.' "

281. See notes 259, 262.

282. Phillips Packing Co., 73 NLRB 447.

283. Wicaco Machine Corp., 69 NLRB 741; Seneca Falls Machine Co., 71 NLRB 1106; The Chase-Shawmut Co., 71 NLRB 610.

284. See note 263.

285. F. J. Kress Box Company, 64 NLRB No. 27.

286. Saginaw Cabinet Co., 72 NLRB 951; Paragon Rubber Corp., 72 NLRB 170.

287. See Quick Industries Inc., 71 NLRB 949; Imperial Brass Manufacturing Co., 72 NLRB 513.

288. Southwest Pennsylvania Pipe Lines, 64 NLRB 1384.

289. Swift & Co., 71 NLRB 727.

290. Detroit Sheet Metal Works, 73 NLRB 475; Great Trails Broadcasting Co., 73 NLRB 396; Harrison Hardware Co., 70 NLRB 1296.

291. See Brewster Pateros Processors, Inc., 73 NLRB 833.

292. NLRB Eleventh Annual Report, p. 21 et. seq.

293. J. B. Cook Auto Machine Co., 73 NLRB 249; See Nashville Cotton Oil Mill Corp., 70 NLRB 1248.

294. 29 USCA (1947, Supp.) Sec. 159(c) (3).

295. Pipe Machinery Co., 79 NLRB No. 181.

296. NLRB Thirteenth Annual Report p. 32 et seq.

296a. Times Square Stores Corp., 79 NLRB 361.

297. American Manufacturing Co., 68 NLRB No. 36.

298. Lancaster Iron Works, 65 NLRB No. 25.

299. Thomasville Chair Co., 37 NLRB 1017.

300. Wilson & Co., 45 NLRB 831; Standard Oil Co., 48 NLRB 1291; Utah Copper Co., 49 NLRB 901.

301. 29 USCA (1947, Supp.) Sec. 159(c) (2).

302. The principles are explained in Carpenter Steel Co., 76 NLRB No. 104.

303. 29 USCA (1947, Supp.) Sec. 159(c) (3).

304. Consent elections are covered by the Board's Rules and Regulations. NLRB Rules and Regulations, Series 5, Sec. 203.54. Statements of Procedure, Sec. 202.18.

305. 29 USCA (1947, Supp.) Sec. 159(4).

306. The stipulation must provide that the parties waive a hearing before the Board and set forth sufficient facts to warrant the assumption of jurisdiction by the Board. See NLRB Rules and Regulations, cited in note 304.

307. Merrimac Hat Corporation, 85 NLRB No. 66; McMullen Leavens Co., 83 NLRB No. 138.

308. See cases cited *supra,* note 307.

309. NLRB Rules and Regulations, Series 5, Subpart G, 29 USCA (1947, Supp.) Sec. 203.32 et seq.

310. 29 USCA (1947, Supp.) Sec. 159(c) (1) (B).

311. NLRB Rules and Regulations, Series 5, 29 USCA (1947, Supp.) Sec. 203.61.

312. Where there is a consent election without certification by the Board, the Regional Director and not the Board determines the validity of the objections. See "Consent Election," Part One, Chapter IV, Sec. 10.

313. Hunt Foods Inc., 70 NLRB 1312.

314. Louis Marx Co. Inc., of Pa., 70 NLRB 1242.

315. River Raisin Paper Co., 70 NLRB 1348.

316. General Shoe Corp., 76 NLRB No. 41.

317. Shelbyville Desk Co., 72 NLRB 925; Armour & Co., 72 NLRB 1182; cf. Aurora Wall Paper Mill Inc., 72 NLRB 1035.

318. The Pure Oil Co., 73 NLRB 1.

319. Robbins Tire & Rubber Co., 72 NLRB 157.

320. Sears Roebuck & Co., 47 NLRB 291.

321. Continental Oil Co., 58 NLRB 33.

322. Acme Brewing Co., 74 NLRB 146.

323. Corn Products Refinery Co., 58 NRLB No. 263.

324. P. D. Gwaltney Jr. & Co., 74 NLRB 371.

325. G. H. Hess Co., 82 NLRB No. 52.

326. Champion Spark Plug Co., 80 NLRB No. 12.

327. The Fairbanks Co., 81 NLRB No. 132.

328. 29 USCA (1947, Supp.) Sec. 159(c) (1)(A).

329. Federal Shipbuilding & Drydock Co., 77 NLRB No. 78.

330. Art Neon Co., 84 NLRB No. 18.

331. 29 USCA (1947, Supp.) Sec. 158(a) (3).

332. 29 USCA (1947, Supp.) Sec. 159(e) (1).

333. 29 USCA (1947, Supp.) Sec. 159(e) (2).

334. 29 USCA (1947, Supp.) Sec. 159(e) (3).

335. Giant Food Shopping Center, 77 NLRB 791; Northland Greyhound Lines, Inc., 80 NLRB No. 60; Benjamin Eastwood Co., 77 NLRB 1383.

336. St. Paul & Tacoma Lumber Co., 81 NLRB No. 76.

337. Administrative Ruling in American Radiator and Standard Sanitary Corp., case No. 20-UA-1613; St. Paul & Tacoma Lumber Co., 81 NLRB No. 76.

338. 29 USCA (1947, Supp.) Sec. 159(c) (3).

339. Mallinckrodt Chemical Works, 84 NLRB No. 32.

340. Fruitvale Canning Co., 85 NLRB No. 122.

341. Armco Drainage & Metal Products, Inc., case No. 10-RM-22, issued December 13, 1948, Administrative Ruling.

342. McQuay-Norris Manufacturing Co. v. NLRB, 116 F. (2d) 748.

343. Bethlehem Steel Co., 89 NLRB No. 33.

344. 29 USCA (1947, Supp.) Sec. 185(c) (4).

345. 29 USCA (1947, Supp.) Sec. 159(a).

346. J. I. Case Co. v. NLRB, 321 U.S. 332, 337.

347. J. I. Case Co. v. NLRB, 321 U.S. 332, 339.

348. See *supra,* note 346.

349. Medo Photo Supply Corp. v. NLRB, 321 U.S. 678.

350. May Department Stores Co. v. NLRB, 326 U.S. 376.

351. May Department Stores Co. v. NLRB, 326 U.S. 376, 385.

352. National Licorice Co. v. NLRB, 309 U.S. 350.

353. "The individual hiring contract is subsidiary to the terms of the trade agreement and may not waive any of its benefits, any more than a shipper can contract away the benefit of filed tariffs, the insurer the benefit of standard provisions, or the utility customer the benefit of legally established rates." J. I. Case Co. v. NLRB, 321 U.S. 332, 336.

354. McQuay-Norris Manufacturing Co. v. NLRB, 116 F. (2d) 748.

355. NLRB v. Acme Air Appliance Co. Inc. (CCA2), 117 F. (2d) 417.

356. Steele v. Louisville & Nashville R. R. Co., 323 U.S. 192; Tunstall v. Brotherhood, 323 U.S. 210.

357. Larus & Brother Co., 62 NLRB 1075.

358. Atlantic Oak Flooring Co., 62 NLRB 973.

359. Wallace Corp. v. NLRB, 323 U.S. 248, 255, 256.

360. Steele v. Louisville & Nashville R. R. Co., 323 U.S. 192, 204.

361. Steele v. Louisville & Nashville R. R. Co., 323 U.S. 192, 204. See also, Hunt v. Crumboch, 325 U.S. 825, 826. The basic principle for responsibility of the bargaining representative was laid down in Virginian Railway v. System Federation No. 40, 300 U.S. 515. See also, Betts v. Easley, 169 P. (2d) 831 Kansas.

362. 29 USCA (1947, Supp.) Secs. 157, 158(b) (1).

363. 29 USCA (1947, Supp.) Sec. 158(b) (5).

364. Wallace Corp. v. NLRB, 323 U.S. 248.

365. Colgate-Palmolive Peet Co., v. NLRB, 25 LRRM 2095. The Board's doctrine was established in Rutland Court Owners Inc., 44 NLRB 587, supp. dec. 46 NLRB 1040.

366. Midwest Piping & Supply Co., 54 NLRB 744.

367. 29 USCA (1947, Supp.) Sec. 158(b) (2).

368. 29 USCA (1947, Supp.) Sec. 185.

369. 29 USCA (1947, Supp.) Sec. 185 (b).

370. 29 USCA (1947, Supp.) Sec. 187; See Dixie Motor Coach Corp. v. Amalgamated Assoc. etc., 74 F. Supp. 952, reversed 170 F. (2d) 902 (on other grounds).

371. 29 USCA (1947, Supp.) Sec. 158(b) (2).

372. 29 USCA (1947, Supp.) Sec. 158(b) (2).

373. 29 USCA (1947, Supp.) Sec. 158(b) (3).

374. 29 USCA (1947, Supp.) Sec. 158(b) (4).

375. 29 USCA (1947, Supp.) Sec. 158(b) (6).

376. 29 USCA (1947, Supp.) Sec. 160 (1).

377. 29 USCA (1947, Supp.) Sec. 160(j).

378. 29 USCA (1947, Supp.) Sec. 158 (d).

379. 29 USCA (1947, Supp.) Sec. 176 et seq.

380. Amazon Cotton Mill Company v. Textile Workers Union, CCA 4, 167 F. (2d) 183, 22 LRRM 2605; Gerry of California v. International Ladies Garment Workers Union (Los Angeles Superior Court, Cal.), 21 LRRM 2209. See Douds v. Wine, Liquor & Distillery Workers Union, 75 F. Supp. 447; United Packing House Workers of America v. Wilson & Co. Inc., & USDC., N.D. Ill.) July 2, 1948, 22 LRRM 2297. A federal District Court has upheld the constitutionality of Section 10(j) of the Act, which establishes the procedure whereby the Board, after issuance of its complaint, may obtain a temporary injunctive order of the federal District Court against the commission of unfair labor practices. Evans v. International Typographical Union (USDC., S.D. Ill.) 76 F. Supp. 881, 21 LRRM 2375.

381. NLRB Rules and Regulations, Series 5, Sec. 203.52; 29 USCA (1947, Supp.) Sec. 203.52.

382. 29 USCA (1947, Supp.) Sec. 153(d); see also 13 Federal Register 654, February 13, 1948.

383. NLRB Statements of Procedure, Sec. 202.17.

384. NLRB Statements of Procedure, Sec. 202.17(a).

385. Mascot Stove Co., 75 NLRB 427; Binns Passaic Iron & Brass Foundry, 77 NLRB No. 60, 22 LRRM 1016.

386. NLRB Rules and Regulations, Series 5, Sec. 203.54; 29 USCA (1947, Supp.) Sec. 203.54; NLRB Statements of Procedure, Sec. 202.18.

387. NLRB Rules and Regulations, Series 5, Sec. 203.55, 29 USCA (1947, Supp.) Sec. 203.55; NLRB Statements of Procedure, Sec. 202.19.

388. NLRB Rules and Regulations, Series 5, Secs. 203.56, 203.60, 29 USCA (1947, Supp.) Secs. 203.56, 203.60; NLRB Statements of Procedure, Sec. 202.20.

389. NLRB Rules and Regulations, Series 5, Sec. 203.58, 29 USCA (1947, Supp.) Sec. 203.58.

390. NLRB Rules and Regulations, Series 5, Sec. 203.59; 29 USCA (1947, Supp.) Sec. 203.59.

391. NLRB Rules and Regulations, Series 5, Sec. 203.60; 29 USCA (1947, Supp.) Sec. 203.60.

Authorities

PART TWO: PREVENTION OF UNFAIR
LABOR PRACTICES

1. 29 USCA (1947, Supp.) Secs. 158, 159, 160.

2. Reilly v. Millis, 144 F. (2d) 259; Associated Press v. Herrick, 13 F. Supp. 897; United Employees Association v. NLRB, 96 F. (2d) 875; The Beebe Corporation v. Millis, 58 F. Supp. 993.

3. See A.F. of L. v. NLRB, 308 U.S. 401, 412; Inland Empire Council v. Mills, 325 U.S. 697, 700; Fitzgerald v. Douds, CCA-2, 167 F. (2d) 714.

4. Morris Steinberg v. John F. Lebus et al., 71 F. Supp. 121.

5. Jones & Laughlin Steel Corp. v. United Mine Workers of America, 159 F. (2d) 18, cert. den. 331 U.S. 828.

6. 29 USCA (1947, Supp.) Sec. 160(e).

7. Great Southern Trucking v. NLRB, 139 F. (2d) 984, cert. den. 64 S. Ct. 944; NLRB v. El Paso Electric Co., 133 F. (2d) 168; NLRB v. American Manufacturing Co., 132 F. (2d) 740, cert. den. 319 U.S. 743; NLRB v. Remington Rand, 130 F. (2d) 919.

8. See notes 1 and 2.

9. 29 USCA (1947, Supp.) Sec. 160(c).

10. However, the Board's determination is subject to review by the U.S. Circuit Court of Appeals. 29 U.S. Sec. 160(e). Upon such a review the findings of the Board must be supported by substantial evidence. NLRB v. Columbian Enameling & Stamping Co., 306 U.S. 292; Consolidated Edison Co. of N.Y. v. NLRB, 305 U.S. 197; NLRB v. Standard Oil Co., 124 F. (2d) 895; NLRB v. Service Wood Heel Co., 124 F. (2d) 470. Amended Act Sec. 10(e).

11. Express Publishing Co. v. NLRB, 312 U.S. 426.

12. The Board may require the employer or union to take "such affirmative action . . . as will effectuate the policies" of the Act, 29 USCA (1947, Supp.) 160(c).

13. See Hughes Tool Co. v. NLRB, 147 F. (2d) 69; 29 USCA (1947, Supp.) Sec. 159(a).

14. J. I. Case Co. v. NLRB, 321 U.S. 332.

15. 29 USCA (1947, Supp.) Sec. 160(a).

16. See Statement of Policy in Sec. 1 of Amended Act. 29 USCA (1947, Supp.) Sec. 151. See also NLRB v. Hudson Motor Car Co., 136 F. (2d) 335; NLRB v. Condensor Corp., 128 F. (2d) 67; Agwilines Inc. v. NLRB, 87 F. (2d) 146.

17. 29 USCA (1947, Supp.) 160(c).

18. 29 USCA (1947, Supp.) Sec. 160(e) (f). See notes 1, 2 and 10.

19. "Affecting commerce" means in commerce, or burdening or obstructing commerce or the free flow of commerce or having or tending to lead to a labor dispute burdening or obstructing commerce or the free flow of commerce. 29 USCA Sec. 152(7). For the meaning of "commerce," see 29 USCA Sec. 152(b). The test of jurisdiction of the Board is the effect upon interstate commerce and not the source of the injury. Consolidated Edison Co. of New York v. NLRB, 305 U.S. 197; J. L. Brandeis & Sons v. NLRB, 142 F. (2d) 977; NLRB v. J. L. Hudson, 135 F. (2d) 380 (cert. den. 320 U.S. 740); NLRB v. Cleveland Cliffs Iron Works, 133 F. (2d) 295.

20. Bethlehem Steel Co. v. New York State Labor Relations Board; Allegheny Ludlum Steel Co. v. Kelley, 330 U.S. 767.

21. 29 USCA (1947, Supp.) Sec. 160(a).

22. Pepsi-Cola Bottling Co., 72 NLRB No. 118; Pepsi-Cola Bottling Co., 74 NLRB No. 190.

23. NLRB v. Jones & Laughlin, 301 U.S. 1.

24. Tampa Transit Lines, 71 NLRB No. 125; Wichita Transportation Corp., 73 NLRB No. 191.

25. Appalachian Electric Power Co. v. NLRB, 93 F. (2d) 985.

26. Columbus & Southern Ohio Electric Co., 36 NLRB 386.

27. J. L. Brandeis & Sons v. NLRB, 142 F. (2d) 977.

28. NLRB v. Idaho-Maryland Mines Co., 93 F. (2d) 129.

29. Local 905 of the Retail Clerks International Association (AFL). Albert E. Morgan d/b/a A-1 Photo Service, 83 NLRB No. 86, 24 LRRM 1106.

30. 29 USCA (1947, Supp.) Sec. 152(2).

31. 29 USCA (1947, Supp.) Sec. 152(3).

32. Stark Bros. Nurseries & Orchards Co., 40 NLRB 1243.

33. North Whittier Heights Citrus Assoc., 10 NLRB 1269; Tovrea Packing Co., 12 NLRB 1063.

33a. Morris Steinberg et al. d/b/a Steinberg & Company, 78 NLRB 211; Alaska Salmon Industry, Inc., 81 NLRB No. 215; Standard Oil Company, 81 NLRB No. 227.

34. Hearst Consolidated Publication v. NLRB, 322 U.S. 111.

35. Kansas City Star Co., 76 NLRB No. 52, 21 LRRM 1185.

36. 29 USCA (1947, Supp.) Sec. 152(3). §15 2(11) defines supervisor as "any individual having authority, in the interest of the employer, to hire, transfer, suspend, lay off, recall, promote, discharge, assign, reward, or discipline other employees, or responsibility to direct them, or to adjust their grievances, or effectively to recommend such action, if in connection with the foregoing the exercise of such authority is not of a merely routine or clerical nature, but requires the use of independent judgment."

37. NLRB v. Cape County Milling Co., 140 F. (2d) 543.

38. Carroll's Transfer Co., 56 NLRB No. 935.

39. 29 USCA (1947, Supp.) Sec. 158(a)(2).

40. 29 USCA (1947, Supp.) Sec. 152(5).

41. Matter of J. W. Greer Co., 52 NLRB 1341; NLRB v. Industrial Metal Fabricators, Inc., 158 F. (2d) 14; NLRB v. American Furnace Co., 158 F. (2d) 376.

42. Matter of Tampa Electric Co., 56 NLRB 1270.

43. Matter of American National Bank of St. Paul, 52 NLRB 905.

44. Matter of Donnelly Garment Co., 50 NLRB 241.

45. Matter of Essex Rubber Co., 50 NLRB 283.

46. Matter of Detroit Edison Co., 74 NLRB 267.

47. NLRB v. Jas. H. Matthews & Co., 156 F. (2d) 706.

48. E. A. Anthony & Sons, Inc. v. NLRB, 163 F. (2d) 22.

49. Superior Engraving Co., 61 NLRB 37; Poloron Products, Inc., 64 NLRB 1358.

50. Pacific Manifolding Book Co. Inc., 64 NLRB 1257.

51. Rebeson Cutlery Co. Inc., 67 NLRB 481.

52. Pacific Moulded Products Co., 76 NLRB No. 164.

53. Wilson & Co., 63 NLRB 636; Kresge Department Store, 77 NLRB No. 25.

54. Standard Oil Co. of Calif., 61 NLRB 1251; Jas. H. Matthews & Co., 63 NLRB 273; Jordanoff Aviation Corp., 69 NLRB 1189.

55. Matter of General Dry Batteries, 27 NLRB No. 169.

56. Matter of Carpenter Baking Co., 29 NLRB No. 13.

57. NLRB v. Link-Belt Co., 311 U.S. 584, 587, 600; Western Union Telegraph Co. v. NLRB, 113 F. (2d) 992, 997; Corning Glass Works v. NLRB, 118 F. (2d) 625, 629.

58. Matter of Elastic Stop Nut Corporation, 51 NLRB 694, enforced in 142 F. (2d) 371; Shenandoah Dives Mining Co., 56 NLRB 715; The Fairfield Engineering Company, 74 NLRB 827; California Canning Co., 73 NLRB 290; LaSalle Steel Co., 72 NLRB 411. Cf. Tualatin Valley Cooperative, Inc., 72 NLRB 907; Spicer Manufacturing Co., 70 NLRB 41.

59. Carpenter Steel Co., 76 NLRB No. 104.

60. Carpenter Steel Co., 76 NLRB No. 104.

61. Carpenter Steel Co., 76 NLRB No. 104.

62. 29 USCA (1947, Supp.) Secs. 160(c) 159(c) (2).

63. Carpenter Steel Co., 76 NLRB No. 104.

64. Westinghouse Electric & Manufacturing Co., 18 NLRB 300, enforced in 112 F. (2d) 657, affirmed 312 U.S. 660; NLRB v. Newport News Shipbuilding & Drydock Co., 308 U.S. 241.

65. Thompson Products Inc., 57 NLRB 925; Sperry Gyroscope Co. Inc. v. NLRB, 129 F. (2d) 922.

66. NLRB v. Southern Bell Telephone & Telegraph Co., 319 U.S. 50.

67. Westinghouse Electric & Manufacturing Co., 18 NLRB 300, enforced in 112 F. (2d) 657, affirmed 312 U.S. 660.

68. Carpenter Steel Co., 76 NLRB No. 104.

69. Matter of Atlas Mills Inc., 3 NLRB 10.

70. American Potash & Chemical Co., 3 NLRB 140 enforced 98 F. (2d) 488; Waterman Steamship Co., 7 NLRB 237. The Act specifically makes illegal discrimination in regard to hire or tenure of employment or any term or condition of employment. 29 USCA Sec. 158(3). The Alexander Milburn Company, 62 NLRB 482; Reliance Manufacturing Co., 60 NLRB 946; Irvin L. Young, 57 NLRB 1221.

71. Republican Publishing Co., 73 NLRB 1085.

72. Allis-Chalmers Mfg. Co., 70 NLRB 348, enforced 162 F. (2d) 435.

73. McLeansbow Shale Products Co., 69 NLRB 809; Port Gibson Veneer & Box Co., 70 NLRB 319.

74. Pepsi-Cola Bottling Co. of Montgomery, 72 NLRB 601.

75. Fred P. Weissman Co., 68 NLRB 1002, 71 NLRB 147.

76. Ever Ready Label Corp., 54 NLRB 551; Hymie Schwartz d/b/a Lion Brand Manufacturing Co., 55 NLRB 798; Worthington Creamery & Produce Co., 52 NLRB 121; Rockingham Poultry Marketing Cooperative, Inc., 59 NLRB 486.

77. Birdsboro Steel Foundry & Machine Co., 54 NLRB No. 1274.

78. Republic Aviation Corp. v. NLRB, 324 U.S. 793.

79. Waumbec Mills, Inc., 15 NLRB 37, enforced 114 F. (2d) 226; Montgomery Hardwood Flooring Co., 72 NLRB 113.

80. Schwarze Electric Co., 16 NLRB 246; Stover Bedding Co., 15 NLRB 635; Firestone Tire & Rubber Co., 62 NLRB 1316.

81. NLRB v. Fansteel Metallurgical Corp., 306 U.S. 240.

82. Shenandoah Dives Mining Co., 35 NLRB 1153.

83. Greer Steel Co., 38 NLRB 65; Borg-Warner Corp., 38 NLRB 866.

84. 34 NLRB 1028.

85. See note 83.

86. Southern Steamship Co. v. NLRB, 316 U.S. 31.

87. NLRB v. Electric Vacuum Cleaner Corp., 315 U.S. 685.

88. M.F.A. Milling Co., 26 NLRB 614.

89. General Shale Products Corp., 26 NLRB 97.

90. NLRB v. Ford Motor Co., 26 NLRB 34, enforced as modified 119 F. (2d) 326.

91. NLRB v. Leviton Mfg. Co., 111 F. (2d) 619.

92. NLRB v. J. Greenbaum Tanning Co., 110 F. (2d) 984, cert. den. 61 S. Ct. 18.

93. Compare NLRB v. Ashville Hosiery Co., 108 F. (2d) 288, and NLRB v. Sunshine Mining Co., 110 F. (2d) 780, cert. den. 312 U.S. 678.

94. Montgomery Ward & Co. v. NLRB, 107 F. (2d) 555; Cupples Co. Manufacturers v. NLRB, 106 F. (2d) 100.

95. American Mfg. Co. v. NLRB, 106 F. (2d) 61, affirmed as modified 309 U.S. 629; NLRB v. Leviton Mfg. Co., 111 F. (2d) 619; NLRB v. National Casket Co. Inc., 107 F. (2d) 992.

96. NLRB v. Greenbaum Tanning Co., 110 F. (2d) 984, cert. den. 61 S. Ct. 18.

97. NLRB v. Somerset Shoe Co., 111 F. (2d) 681; NLRB v. Piqua Munising Wood Products Co., 109 F. (2d) 552; M. H. Ritzwoller Co. v. NLRB, 114 F. (2d) 432.

98. Underwood Machinery Co., 74 NLRB 641.

99. Sullivan Drydock & Repair Corp., 67 NLRB 81. Similarly, an employer's unilateral transfer of employees from salary to hourly rated classifications thereby de-

99. (*Cont.*)
priving them of substantial benefits because of their designation of the union as bargaining agent is discriminatory. General Motors Corporation, 59 NLRB 1143, enforced 150 F. (2d) 201.

100. 29 USCA (1947, Supp.) Sec. 158(a) (3).

101. 29 USCA (1947, Supp.) Sec. 158(a) (3).

102. 29 USCA (1947, Supp.) Sec. 158(b) (2).

103. 29 USCA (1947, Supp.) Sec. 158(b) (2).

104. Reliance Mfg. Co., 56 NLRB 1083; The Owatonna Tool Co., 56 NLRB 1427; amended Act Sec. 8(a) (1).

105. The Kramer Company, 29 NLRB 921; Northwestern Mutual Fire Insurance Association, 46 NLRB 825; Burnside Steel Foundry, 69 NLRB 128.

106. Richmond Home Telephone Co., 70 NLRB 452.

107. St. Mary's Sewer Pipe Co., 54 NLRB 1226.

108. The Kramer Company, 29 NLRB 921.

109. Soss Manufacturing Company, 56 NLRB 348.

110. Houston Shipbuilding Corporation, 56 NLRB 1684.

111. Armour Fertilizer Works Inc., 46 NLRB 629.

112. Richter's Bakery, 46 NLRB 447.

113. Boeing Airplane Co., 46 NLRB 267.

114. Edward G. Budd Mfg. Co. v. NLRB, 332 U.S. 840.

115. NLRB v. Edward G. Budd Mfg. Co., 169 F. (2d) 571.

116. Eastern Gas & Fuel Associates v. NLRB, 162 F. (2d) 864, 866.

116a. Inter-City Advertising Co. of Greensboro, N. C., 89 NLRB No. 127.

117. Carnegie-Illinois Steel Corp., 84 NLRB No. 99, 24 LRRM 1307.

118. Briggs Mfg. Co., 75 NLRB 569.

119. Republic Steel Corp. v. NLRB, 107 F. (2d) 472, cert. den. 309 U.S. 684, modified upon rehearing as to one issue 311 U.S. 7; Montgomery Ward & Co., 107 F. (2d) 555; Fort Wayne Corrugated Paper Co. v. NLRB, 111 F. (2d) 869; NLRB v. Sunshine Mining Co., 110 F. (2d) 780, cert. den. 312 U.S. 678; NLRB v. J. Greenbaum Tanning Co., 110 F. (2d)

984, cert. den. 61 S. Ct. 18; NLRB v. Good Coal Co., 110 F. (2d) 501, cert. den. 310 U.S. 630.

120. Botany Worsted Mills v. NLRB, 106 F. (2d) 263; NLRB v. Lane Cotton Mills, 111 F. (2d) 814; North Whittier Heights Citrus Assn. v. NLRB, 109 F. (2d) 76, cert. den. 310 U.S. 632, rehearing den. 61 S. Ct. 54.

121. Brown Shipbuilding Co., 66 NLRB 1047; Grove Regulator Co., 66 NLRB 1102; Fairmont Creamery Co., 73 NLRB 1380.

122. H. J. Heinz Co. v. NLRB, 311 U.S. 514, 518; NLRB v. Link-Belt Co., 311 U.S. 584, 592–596.

123. NLRB v. Chicago Apparatus Co., 116 F. (2d) 753, 756; NLRB v. Schmidt Baking Co., 122 F. (2d) 162, 164.

124. Corning Glass Works v. NLRB, 118 F. (2d) 625, 628.

125. Colorado Fuel & Iron Corp. v. NLRB, 121 F. (2d) 165, 175.

126. Sun-Tent Luebbert Co., 37 NLRB 50.

127. NLRB v. New Era Die Co., 118 F. (2d) 500, 504; NLRB v. Elkland Leather Co., 114 F. (2d) 221, 224; NLRB v. Ford Motor Co., 114 F. (2d) 905, 909, 913.

128. NLRB v. General Motors Corp., 116 F. (2d) 306, 309, 310.

129. New York Handkerchief Co. v. NLRB, 114 F. (2d) 144, 147.

130. Richfield Oil Corp., 49 NLRB 593; General Petroleum Corp. of California, 49 NLRB 606; Cities Service Oil Co., 122 F. (2d) 149.

131. Peyton Packing Co., 49 NLRB 828.

132. Carter Carburetor Corp. v. NLRB, 140 F. (2d) 714; NLRB v. Denver Tent & Awning Co., 138 F. (2d) 410.

133. Republic Aviation Corp. v. NLRB, 324 U.S. 793; NLRB v. Le Tourneau Co. of Georgia, 324 U.S. 793.

134. NLRB v. American Tube Bending Co., 134 F. (2d) 993, cert. den. 320 U.S. 768.

135. 29 USCA (1947, Supp.) Sec. 158(c).

136. NLRB v. Crown Can Co., 138 F. (2d) 263; NLRB v. Glenn L. Martin-Nebraska Co., 141 F. (2d) 371; Elastic Stop Nut Corp. v. NLRB, 142 F. (2d) 371; NLRB v. Lettie Lee Inc., 140 F. (2d) 243; NLRB v. Trojan Powder Co., 135 F. (2d) 337, cert. den. 320 U.S. 768.

137. Midwest Piping and Supply Co., Inc., 63 NLRB 1060, 1071.

138. Flotill Products Inc., 70 NLRB 119; Lincoln Packing Co., 70 NLRB 135.

139. Port Gibson Veneer & Box Co., 70 NLRB 319.

140. 29 USCA (1947, Supp.) Sec. 158(b) (1) (A).

140a. Sunset Line & Twine Company, 84 NLRB No. 23; Smith Cabinet Manufacturing Company, 81 NLRB 886; Colonial Hardwood Flooring Company, 84 NLRB No. 69.

140b. Perry Norvell Company, 80 NLRB 225; Sunset Line & Twine Company, 84 NLRB No. 23.

140c. Smith Cabinet Manufacturing Company, 81 NLRB 886.

140d. Smith Cabinet Manufacturing Company, 81 NLRB 886.

140e. Smith Cabinet Manufacturing Company, 81 NLRB 886; Cory Corporation, 84 NLRB No. 110.

140f. Seamprufe, Incorporated, 82 NLRB 892.

140g. Smith Cabinet Manufacturing Company, 81 NLRB 886; Cory Corporation, 84 NLRB No. 110.

141. 29 USCA (1947, Supp.) Sec. 158(b) (1) (B).

142. Under the Wagner Act a closed shop contract was valid if the union at the time of the execution of the contract was the majority representative of the employees in an appropriate bargaining unit and was not assisted or maintained by unfair labor practices of the employer.

In the absence of a valid closed shop agreement, the Board held illegal any requirement that an employee join a union to hold his job (Clinton Cotton Mills, 1 NLRB 97; The Grace Company, 7 NLRB 766). A discharge because fellow employees objected to the union activities of the discharged employee is regarded by the Board as a violation of law (Edinburg Citrus Association, 57 NLRB 1145). Discharges in accordance with and at the end of the effective period of a valid closed shop contract, because the employees designated as bargaining representative for the period following the termination date of the contract a union other than the contracting union, have been held illegal by the Board when these employees continued their membership in the contracting union for the balance of the contract period (Rutland Court Owners Inc., 44 NLRB 587). Where an employer, with knowledge that the contracting union intended to deny union membership to employees active on behalf of a rival union prior to an election won by the contracting union, enters into a closed shop contract and discharges such employees pursuant to the closed shop clause at the request of the contracting union, the Supreme Court holds there has been a violation of the Act (Wallace Corp. v. NLRB, 323 U.S. 248). Collusion and fraud between the employer and a union in entering into a closed shop contract to deprive employees of their jobs and then discharging the employees pursuant to the contract is illegal (Monsieur Henri-Wines, 44 NLRB 1310).

143. 29 USCA (1947, Supp.) Sec. 158(a) (3).

144. C. Hager & Sons Hinge Mfg. Co., 80 NLRB No. 36, 23 LRRM 1044.

145. Schaefer Body Inc., 85 NLRB No. 33, 24 LRRM 1381.

146. 29 USCA (1947, Supp.) Sec. 159 (e) (2).

147. 29 USCA (1947, Supp.) Sec. 159(e) (3).

148. 29 USCA (1947, Supp.) Sec. 158(b) (5).

149. 29 USCA (1947, Supp.) Sec. 158(a) (3), (b) (2).

150. Interstate Engineering Corporation, 83 NLRB No. 26, 24 LRRM 1031.

150a. Union Starch & Refining Co., 87 NLRB No. 137.

151. 29 USCA (1947, Supp.) Sec. 158(a) (3), (b) (2).

152. Williams Motor Co., 31 NLRB 715; see also 29 USCA Secs. 158(3), 160(c).

153. Phelps Dodge Corp. v. NLRB, 313 U.S. 177; Continental Oil Co. v. NLRB, 313 U.S. 212.

154. 313 U.S. 177.

155. NLRB v. Fulton Bay & Cotton Mills, 180 F. (2d) 68.

156. Oregon Worsted Company, 3 NLRB 36, enforced 96 F. (2d) 193; Biles-Coleman Lumber Company, 4 NLRB 679, enforced 98 F. (2d) 18.

157. NLRB v. Mackay Radio & Telegraph Co., 304 U.S. 333.

158. American Bread Co., 51 NLRB 1302.

159. Pinaud Inc., 51 NLRB 235; Gardner-Denver Co., 58 NLRB 81.

160. The American News Co., 55 NLRB 1302.

161. Indiana Desk Co., 58 NLRB 10, enforcement denied, NLRB v. Indiana Desk Co., 149 F. (2d) 987.

162. NLRB v. Draper Corporation, 145 F. (2d) 199; NLRB v. Clinchfield Coal Company, 145 F. (2d) 66.

163. Mt. Clemens Pottery Co., 46 NLRB 714; Quality & Service Laundry, Inc., 39 NLRB 970; Idaho Refining Co., 47 NLRB 1127.

164. Joseph Dyson & Sons Inc., 72 NLRB 445; The Fafnir Bearing Co., 73 NLRB 1008.

165. The Fafnir Bearing Co., 73 NLRB 1008; The Carey Salt Co., 70 NLRB 1099.

166. Roanoke Public Warehouse, 72 NLRB 1281.

167. Ford Motor Co., 31 NLRB 994.

168. The Texas Co., Marine Division, 42 NLRB 593.

169. Industrial Cotton Mills Co., 50 NLRB 855.

170. American Creosoting Co. Inc., 46 NLRB 240; Holston Mfg. Co., 46 NLRB 55; Charles E. Austin Inc., 49 NLRB 1048.

171. Weiss & Geller Inc., 51 NLRB 796.

172. Phelps Dodge Corp. v. NLRB, 313 U.S. 177.

173. The Ohio Public Service Co., 52 NLRB 725.

174. The American Laundry Machinery Co., 45 NLRB 355.

175. Gerity Whitaker Co., 33 NLRB 393.

176. J. Klotz & Co., 13 NLRB 746 at 778.

177. 29 USCA (1947, Supp.) Sec. 160 (c).

178. United Furniture Workers of America (Colonial Hardwood Flooring Co.) 84 NLRB No. 69, 24 LRRM 1302.

178a. H. M. Newman et al., 85 NLRB No. 132.

179. 29 USCA (1947, Supp.) Sec. 158(a) (5).

180. The Standard Lime & Stone Co., 57 NLRB 227.

181. Aetna Fire Brick Co., 56 NLRB 849.

182. Appalachian Electric Power Co. v. NLRB, 140 F. (2d) 217; NLRB v. Century Oxford Mfg. Corp., 140 F. (2d) 541, cert. denied 323 U.S. 714.

183. Concordia Ice Co., 51 NLRB 1068, enforced 143 F. (2d) 656; The E. Bigelow Co., 52 NLRB 999, enforced 14 LRR 954; Ideal Leather Novelty Co., 54 NLRB 761; Hughes Tool Co., 56 NLRB 981, modified in 147 F. (2d) 69.

184. Montgomery Ward & Co., 37 NLRB 100.

185. Register Publishing Co. Ltd., 44 NLRB 834.

186. NLRB v. Whittier Mills, 111 F. (2d) 474; May Department Stores Co. v. NLRB, 326 U.S. 376; Benson Produce Co., 71 NLRB 888. See also NLRB v. Crompton-Highland Mills Inc., 337 U.S. 217.

187. Matter of Tomlinson of High Point Inc., 74 NLRB 681.

188. H. J. Heinz & Co. v. NLRB, 311 U.S. 514.

189. H. J. Heinz & Co. v. NLRB, 311 U.S. 514; M. H. Ritzwoller Co. v. NLRB, 114 F. (2d) 432.

190. American Mfg. Co. v. NLRB, 106 F. (2d) 61, affirmed as modified 309 U.S. 629.

191. National Licorice Co. v. NLRB, 309 U.S. 350; NLRB v. Piqua Munising Wood Products Co., 109 F. (2d) 552; Medo Photo Supply Corp. v. NLRB, 321 U.S. 678.

192. Samuel Youlin, 22 NLRB 879.

193. 147 F. (2d) 69.

194. Texas, New Mexico & Oklahoma Coaches Inc., 46 NLRB 343; M. H. Ritzwoller Co. v. NLRB, 114 F. (2d) 432.

195. United Elastic Corp., 84 NLRB No. 87.

196. Times Publishing Co., 72 NLRB 676.

197. Norwich Dairy Co., 25 NLRB 1166.

198. United Dredging Co., 30 NLRB 739.

199. NLRB v. Moltrup Steel Products Co., 121 F. (2d) 612; Solvay Process v. NLRB, 117 F. (2d) 83; NLRB v. Schmidt Baking Co., 122 F. (2d) 162.

200. NLRB v. Chicago Apparatus Co., 116 F. (2d) 753, 758, 759; Singer Mfg. Co. v. NLRB, 119 F. (2d) 131, 134, 193; NLRB v. Acme Air Appliance, 117 F. (2d) 417, 418, 421.

201. NLRB v. Pilling & Son Co., 119 F. (2d) 32, 35, 36; NLRB v. Acme Air Ap-

pliance Co., 117 F. (2d) 417, 420; NLRB v. Highland Shoe Inc., 119 F. (2d) 218, 221; Inland Lime & Stone Co. v. NLRB, 119 F. (2d) 20, 22; Oughton v. NLRB, 118 F. (2d) 486, 498.

202. George E. Carroll et al., 56 NLRB 935; Ideal Leather Novelty Co., Inc., 54 NLRB 761.

203. Eppinger & Russell Co., 56 NLRB 1259.

204. Fort Industry Co., 77 NLRB No. 205.

205. J. I. Case Co. v. NLRB, 21 U.S. 332.

206. Medo Photo Supply Corp. v. NLRB, 321 U.S. 678.

207. Franks Bros. Co. v. NLRB, 64 S. Ct. 817; Great Southern Trucking Co. v. NLRB, 139 F. (2d) 984, cert. den. 64 S. Ct. 944.

208. NLRB v. Somerset Shoe Co., 111 F. (2d) 681; NLRB v. Piqua Munising Wood Products Co., 109 F. (2d) 552; M. H. Ritzwoller Co. v. NLRB, 114 F. (2d) 432.

209. NLRB v. Piqua Munising Wood Products Co., 109 F. (2d) 552; M. H. Ritzwoller Co. v. NLRB, 114 F. (2d) 432.

210. NLRB v. Somerset Shoe Co., 111 F. (2d) 681.

211. The Fafnir Bearing Co., 73 NLRB 1008.

212. Allis-Chalmers Mfg. Co., 72 NLRB 855 (The case was dismissed for administrative reasons).

213. NLRB v. Crompton-Highland Mills, Inc., 337 U.S. 217.

214. 29 USCA (1947, Supp.) 158(b) (3).

215. 29 USCA (1947, Supp.) 158(d).

215a. National Maritime Union of America, 78 NLRB No. 137.

216. NLRB v. T. W. Phillips Gas & Oil Co., 141 F. (2d) 304; Wallace Corp. v. NLRB, 323 U.S. 248.

217. NLRB v. Baltimore Transit Co., 140 F. (2d) 51, cert. den. 64 S. Ct. 848; Wallace Corp. v. NLRB, 323 U.S. 248.

218. Wallace Corp. v. NLRB, 323 U.S. 248.

219. National Licorice Co. v. NLRB, 309 U.S. 350; American Mfg. Co. v. NLRB, 309 U.S. 629.

220. Medo Photo Supply Corp. v. NLRB, 321 U.S. 678 and cases there cited.

221. Republic Aviation v. NLRB, 324 U.S. 793; NLRB v. Le Tourneau Co. of Georgia, 324 U.S. 793; NLRB v. Standard Oil, 138 F. (2d) 885; Nevada Consolidated Copper Corp. v. NLRB, 316 U.S. 105; NLRB v. Automotive Maintenance Machinery Co., 315 U.S. 282.

222. International Association of Machinists v. NLRB, 311 U.S. 72; Phelps Dodge Corp. v. NLRB, 313 U.S. 177; NLRB v. Falk Corp., 308 U.S. 453; NLRB v. Link-Belt Co., 311 U.S. 584; NLRB v. P. Lorillard Co., 314 U.S. 512.

223. 29 USCA (1947, Supp.) Sec. 160(c).

224. NLRB v. Link-Belt Co., 311 U.S. 584.

225. NLRB v. Waterman Steamship Co., 309 U.S. 206.

226. 29 USCA (1947, Supp.) Sec. 160(b).

227. 29 USCA (1947, Supp.) Sec. 160(c).

228. The Monarch Co., 56 NLRB 1749.

229. Stewart Warner Corp., 55 NLRB 593.

230. T. A. O'Donnell, 55 NLRB 828, cert. den. *sub. nom.* Independent Association of Mill Workers v. NLRB, 322 U.S. 731.

231. The Ohio Public Service Company, 52 NLRB 725, enforced in 144 F. (2d) 252, cert. denied 324 U.S. 857.

232. Fine Art Novelty Corp., 54 NLRB 480; George E. Carroll et al., 56 NLRB 935.

233. Peter J. Schweitzer Inc., 54 NLRB 813, enforced as modified 144 F. (2d) 520; American Laundry Co., 57 NLRB 25; Cameron Can Machinery Co., 57 NLRB 1768; U.S. Automatic Corp., 57 NLRB 124; NLRB v. J. I. Case Co., 321 U.S. 332; NLRB v. Cassoff, 139 F. (2d) 397; Spalek Engineering Co., 45 NLRB 1272.

234. Rodgers Hydraulic Inc., 51 NLRB 417.

235. Ford Motor Co., 55 NLRB 897. See also the Barre Wool Co., 28 NLRB 14.

236. Angelica Jacket Co., 57 NLRB 451; Eppinger & Russell, 56 NLRB 1259.

237. American Pearl Button Co., 52 NLRB 1113, modified 149 F. (2d) 311. Compare Holtville Ice & Cold Storage Co., 51 NLRB 596, enforced in 148 F. (2d) 168; Blue Ridge Shirt Manufacturing Co. Inc., 70 NLRB 741.

238. 29 USCA Sec. 152(2).

239. NLRB v. Gleuk Brewing Co., 144 F. (2d) 847.

240. 29 USCA (1947, Supp.) Sec. 152(2).

241. 29 USCA (1947, Supp.) Sec. 152(13).

242. NLRB v. Cassoff, 139 F. (2d) 397; NLRB v. Baltimore Transit Co., 140 F. (2d) 51; cert. den. 64 S. Ct. 848; NLRB v. Virginia Electric Power Co., 319 U.S. 533.

243. NLRB v. Cape County Milling Co., 140 F. (2d) 543.

244. NLRB v. Express Publishing Co., 312 U.S. 426.

245. Amalgamated Utility Workers v. Consolidated Edison Co. of New York, et al., 309 U.S. 261.

246. NLRB v. American Potash & Chemical Corp., 113 F. (2d) 232.

247. NLRB v. Federal Bearing Co., 109 F. (2d) 945.

248. NLRB v. Eavenson & Levering Co., 4 LRRM 792.

249. Amended Act, Sec. 8(b)(4)(A), 29 USCA (1947, Supp.) Sec. 158(b)(4) (A).

250. Amended Act, Sec. 8(b)(4)(B), 29 USCA (1947, Supp.) Sec. 158(b)(4) (B).

251. Amended Act, Sec. 8(b)(4)(C), 29 USCA (1947, Supp.) Sec. 158(b)(4)(C).

252. Amended Act, Sec. 8(b)(4)(D), 29 USCA (1947, Supp.) Sec. 158(b)(4)(D).

253. Amended Act, Sec. 10(E), 29 USCA (1947, Supp.) Sec. 160(E).

253a. Douds v. Local 1250, Retail Wholesale Department Store Union (Oppenheim Collins), 170 F. (2d) 695 (CA 2); Printing Specialties Union v. LeBaron, 171 F. (2d) 331 (CA 9); United Brotherhood of Carpenters v. Sperry, 170 F. (2d) 863 (CA 10).

253b. United Brotherhood of Carpenters v. Sperry, 170 F. (2d) 863 (CA 10); Printing Specialties Union v. LeBaron, 171 F. (2d) 331 (CA 9); Styles v. Local 760, International Brotherhood of Electrical Workers, 80 F. Supp. 119, (D.C. E. Tenn.).

254. 75 F. Supp. 414.

255. 75 F. Supp. 414.

256. Douds v. Teamsters Union, Local 294, 75 F. Supp. 414, 417.

257. See note 256, *supra.*

257a. Shore v. Building & Construction Trades Council, 173 F. (2d) 678 (CA 3).

257b. LeBaron v. Kern County Farm Union, 80 F. Supp. 151, 157 (D.C. So. Cal.); See also: Styles v. Local 760, International Brotherhood of Electrical Workers, 80 F. Supp. 119 (D.C. E. Tenn.).

257c. LeBaron v. Kern County Farm Union, 80 F. Supp. 151, 157 (D.C. So. Cal.).

257d. See Douds v. Confectionery and Tobacco Jobbers Employees, 85 F. Supp. 191 (D.C. So. N.Y.); Styles v. Local 760, International Brotherhood of Electrical Workers, 80 F. Supp. 119, (D.C. E. Tenn.); Brown v. Oil Workers International Union, 15 Labor Cases ¶ 64, 820 (D.C. No. Cal.).

257e. Shore v. Building and Construction Trades Council, 173 F. (2d) 678 (CCA 3).

257f. LeBaron v. Kern County Farm Union, 80 F. Supp. 157 (D.C. So. Cal.); LeBus v. Philadelphia Coast Marine Firemen (D.C. E. La.); Styles v. Local 760, International Brotherhood of Electrical Workers, 80 F. Supp. 119 (D.C. E. Tenn.).

257g. United Brotherhood of Carpenters v. Sperry, 170 F. (2d) 863.

257h. Building and Construction Trades Council of Orange County v. Le Baron, 16 Labor Cases ¶ 65, 270 June 30, 1949 (CCA 9).

258. Amended Act, Sec. 10(k), 29 USCA (1947, Supp.) Sec. 160(k).

259. 29 USCA (1947, Supp.) Sec. 160(j).

260. Evans v. International Typographical Union, 76 F. Supp. 881.

261. 29 USCA (1947, Supp.) Sec. 160(b).

262. NLRB v. Norfolk Shipbulding & Drydock Co., 172 F. (2d) 813 (CCA 4), 23 LRRM 2312.

263. Amended Act, Sec. 8, 10(b)(c), 29 USCA (1947, Supp.) Sec. 160(b)(c). Of course the unfair labor practice must affect commerce within the meaning of the Act.

264. Amended Act, Sec. 9, 29 USCA (1947, Supp.) Sec. 159. The Board also conducts proceedings for a union shop election and to revoke the authority of the union to enter into a union shop agreement.

265. Amended Act, Sec. 10(d)(e) and (f), 29 USCA (1947, Supp.) Sec. 160(d) (e) and (f).

266. Amended Act, Sec. 9(d), 29 USCA (1947, Supp.) Sec. 159(d).

267. Amended Act, Sec. 9(c)(1)(A), 29 USCA (1947, Supp.) Sec. 159(c)(1)(A).

268. Amended Act, Sec. 9(c)(1)(B), 29 USCA (1947, Supp.) Sec. 159(c)(1)(B).

269. Amended Act, Sec. 9(c)(1), 29 USCA (1947, Supp.) Sec. 159(c)(1). No provision is made for extent of notice of hearing. It may vary according to the exigencies of the case. Ten days is the usual notice.

270. New York State Labor Relations Act, L. 1937, C. 443, Sec. 1.

271. Consolidated Laws of New York, Article 20, Sections 700–716.

272. New York State Labor Relations Board Rules and Regulations, Article II, Sections 8, 10.

273. Amended Act, Sec. 10(b), 29 USCA (1947, Supp.) Sec. 160(b).

274. NLRB v. Piqua Munising Wood Products Co., 109 F. (2d) 552.

275. Rules and Regulations, Series 5, Secs. 203.9–.12.

276. Rules and Regulations, Series 5, Sec. 203.12.

277. The Board's broad view of the charge may have some judicial support. See Texas & Pacific R.R. Co. v. Interstate Commerce Commission, 162 U.S. 197; Cincinnati H. & D. Ry. Co. v. Interstate Commerce Commission, 206 U.S. 142.

278. Amended Act, Sec. 10(b), 29 USCA (1947, Supp.) Sec. 160(b); Rules & Regulations Series 5, Sec. 203.20–.23.

279. Consumer Power Co. v. NLRB, 113 F. (2d) 38.

280. Fort Wayne Corrugated Paper Co. v. NLRB 111 F. (2d) 869.

281. Amended Act, Sec. 10(b), 29 USCA (1947, Supp.) Sec. 160(b).

282. National Licorice Co. v. NLRB, 309 U.S. 350 at page 369.

283. Rules and Regulations, Series 5, Sec. 203.10, 29 USCA (1947, Supp., foll. Sec. 2622) Sec. 203.10.

284. Board's Statement of Procedure Sec. 202.6.

285. Amended Act, Sec. 3(d), 29 USCA (1947, Supp.) Sec. 153(d).

286. House Report No. 510, 80th Congress, 1st Session p. 37.

287. Retail Clerks International Association, 83 NLRB No. 86, 24 LRRM 1106.

288. Statement of Procedure, Sec. 202.17 (c).

289. Statement of Procedure, Sec. 202.4.

290. Statement of Procedure, Sec. 202.7.

291. Consumers Power Co. v. NLRB, 113 F. (2d) 38; NLRB v. Piqua Munising Wood Products Co., 109 F. (2d) 552; Republic Steel Corp. v. NLRB, 107 F. (2d) 472, cert. den. 309 U.S. 684, modified in other respects on rehearing 311 U.S. 7.

292. See the cases cited in note 291.

293. NLRB v. Piqua Munising Wood Products Co., 109 F. (2d) 552 at p. 557.

294. M. H. Ritzwoller Co. v. NLRB, 114 F. (2d) 432.

295. Amended Act, Sec. 10(b), 29 USCA (1947, Supp.) Sec. 160(b).

296. Amended Act, Sec. 10(b), 29 USCA (1947, Supp.) Sec. 160(b).

297. Amended Act, Sec. 10(b), 29 USCA (1947, Supp.) Sec. 160(b).

298. Rules and Regulations, Series 5, Sec. 203.15, 29 USCA (1947, Supp. foll. Sec. 261) Sec. 203.15.

299. The Act makes specific provision for such service. Amended Act, Sec. 10(b), 29 USCA (1947, Supp.) Sec. 160(b).

300. NLRB v. Pennsylvania Greyhound Lines, Inc., 303 U.S. 261; Inland Steel Co. v. NLRB, 109 F. (2d) 9; American Mfg. Co. v. NLRB, 309 U.S. 629.

301. Series 5, Secs. 203.8, 203.15, 29 USCA (1947, Supp.) Secs. 203.8, 203.15.

302. National Licorice Co. v. NLRB, 309 U.S. 350.

303. Consolidated Edison Co. v. NLRB, 305 U.S. 197, at pages 232, 233.

304. NLRB v. American Mfg. Co., 106 F. (2d) 61, affirmed 309 U.S. 629.

305. Jacobsen v. NLRB, 120 F. (2d) 96 at page 100. Whether an action or proceeding may be maintained in the District Court to review the Board's refusal to issue a complaint as arbitrary or capricious is not answered by the court.

306. NLRB v. Newark Morning Ledger Co., 120 F. (2d) 262, 266, 268.

307. NLRB v. General Motors Corp., 116 F. (2d) 306, 311–312.

308. NLRB v. Prettyman, 117 F. (2d) 786, 792.

309. NLRB v. Hawk & Buck Co., 120 F. (2d) 903, 904, 905; NLRB v. Phillips Gas & Oil Co., 141 F. (2d) 304; Wallace Corp. v. NLRB, 323 U.S. 248. These principles are substantially stated in the Board's Statement of Procedure. (Secs. 202–7, 9.)

310. Magnolia Petroleum Co. v. NLRB, 115 F. (2d) 1007, 1012–1013; NLRB v. McKesson & Robbins, Inc., 121 F. (2d) 84, 92–94.

311. Wallace Corp. v. NLRB, 323 U.S. 248; Utah Copper Co. v. NLRB, 139 F. (2d) 788, cert. den. *sub. nom.* Independent Assn. of Mill Workers v. NLRB, 322 U.S. 731; NLRB v. Locomotive Finished Material Co., 142 F. (2d) 802.

312. John S. Doane Company, 63 NLRB 1403; Evenride Motors Division of Outboard Marine and Manufacturing Co., 66 NLRB No. 1142, S. G. Tilden, Incorporated, 9 SLRB 144 (N.Y. State Labor Relations Board).

However, the provisions of the Wagner Act granting the Board "exclusive" jurisdiction have been altered. Section 10(a) of the Act as amended provides as follows:

The Board is empowered as hereinafter provided, to prevent any person from engaging in any unfair labor practice (listed in Section 8) affecting commerce. This power shall not be affected by any other means of adjustment or prevention that has been or may be established by agreement, law, or otherwise: *Provided,* That the Board is empowered by agreement with any agency of any State or Territory to cede to such agency jurisdiction over any cases in any industry (other than mining, manufacturing, communications, and transportation except where predominantly local in character) even though such cases may involve labor disputes affecting commerce, unless the provision of the State or Territorial statute applicable to the determination of such cases by such agency is inconsistent with the corresponding provision of this Act or has received a construction inconsistent therewith.

In Textile Workers Union of America v. Amazon Cotton Mills (76 F. Supp. 159, 165) the United States District Court in North Carolina held that the elimination of the word "exclusive" from the grant of powers meant that, "the power to enforce the provisions of the law are not to reside solely in the National Labor Relations Board." Under the amended Act,

this Court said, it had jurisdiction upon the suit of a union to enjoin an employer from illegally refusing to bargain with the union despite the pendency of the union's unfair labor practice charges of the same nature before the Board. But the Fourth Circuit Court of Appeals on April 1, 1948 held to the contrary, reversing the District Court and remanding the case for dismissal. 167 F. (2d) 183.

313. NLRB v. Baltimore Transit Co., 140 F. (2d) 51, cert. den. 64 S. Ct. 848.

314. NLRB v. Gilfillen Bros. Inc., 148 F. (2d) 990.

315. Wallace Corp. v. NLRB, 323 U.S. 248.

316. Amended Act, Sec. 10 (b), 29 USCA (1947, Supp.) Sec. 160(b).

317. Rules and Regulations, Series 5, Sec. 203.20, 29 USCA (1947, Supp. foll. Sec. 261) Sec. 203.20.

318. Rules and Regulations, Series 5, Sec. 203.21, 29 USCA (1947, Supp. foll. Sec. 261) Sec. 203.21. An original and 4 copies must be filed.

319. Rules and Regulations, Series 5, Sec. 203.22, 29 USCA (1947, Supp. foll. Sec. 261) Sec. 203.22.

320. Rules and Regulations, Series 5, Sec. 203.23, 29 USCA (1947, Supp. foll. Sec. 261) Sec. 203.23.

321. Matter of Paragon Oil Company, Decision No. 3216 of New York State Labor Relations Board, 85 SLRB 554.

322. Amended Act, Sec. 11(1), 29 USCA (1947, Supp.) Sec. 161(1).

323. NLRB v. Northern Trust Co., 148 F. (2d) 24; Amended Act Sec. 11(1).

324. Cudahy Packing Co. v. NLRB, 117 F. (2d) 692, where the Court said (page 694): "The only limitation upon the power of the Board to compel the production of documentary or oral evidence is that it must relate to or touch the matter under investigation or in question. The Board may not go beyond this limitation and pry into the affairs of a business concern generally." NLRB v. Northern Trust Co., 148 F. (2d) 24.

325. Amended Act Sec. 11(1), 29 USCA (1947, Supp.) Sec. 161(1).

326. Rules and Regulations, Series 5, Sec. 203.31, 29 USCA (1947 Supp. foll. Sec. 261) Sec. 203.31.

327. NLRB v. International Typographical Union, 76 F. Supp. 895.

328. Inland Steel Co. v. NLRB, 109 F. (2d) 9.

329. NLRB v. Northern Trust Co., 148 F. (2d) 24.

330. In Barrett Company v. NLRB, 120 F. (2d) 583, the Court said at p. 586: "Ordinarily the Board may determine the intra- or the inter-state character of the employer's business from the employer itself. If, however, the employer refuses to give the information, the Board, in the exercise of its power to investigate, may secure the information, as here, through the issuance of the subpoena."

331. Amended Act Sec. 11(2), 29 USCA (1947, Supp.) Sec. 161(2); Cudahy Packing Co. v. NLRB, 117 F. (2d) 692.

332. Cudahy Packing Co. v. NLRB, 117 F. (2d) 692; NLRB v. Goodyear Tire & Rubber Co., 36 F. Supp. 413.

333. NLRB v. Northern Trust Co., 148 F. (2d) 24.

334. Cudahy Packing Co. v. NLRB, 117 F. (2d) 692; Goodyear Tire & Rubber Co. v. NLRB, 122 F. (2d) 450.

335. NLRB v. Northern Trust Co., 148 F. (2d) 24.

336. Amended Act Sec. 11(3), 29 USCA (1947, Supp.) Sec. 161(3).

337. Wilson Foundry & Machine Co., 70 NLRB No. 557.

338. Morrison Turning Co., 83 NLRB No. 106, 24 LRRM 1134.

339. Amended Act Sec. 10(b), 29 USCA (1947, Supp.) Sec. 160(b).

340. Amended Act Sec. 10(b), 29 USCA (1947, Supp.) Sec. 160 (b). Rules and Regulations, Series 5, Sec. 203.29, 29 USCA (1947, Supp. foll. Sec. 261) Sec. 203.29.

341. Amended Act Sec. 10(b), 29 USCA (1947, Supp.) Sec. 160(b).

342. Rules and Regulations, Series 5, Secs. 203.24–.28, 29 USCA (1947, Supp. foll. Sec. 261) Sec. 203.24–.28.

343. M. H. Ritzwoller & Co. v. NLRB, 114 F. (2d) 432.

344. Cupples Co. Manufacturers v. NLRB, 106 F. (2d) 100; Arcadia Hosiery Co. v. NLRB, 112 F. (2d) 326, cert. den. 61 S. Ct. 38; Bethlehem Steel Co. v. NLRB, 120 F. (2d) 641 at page 652.

345. Inland Steel Co. v. NLRB, 109 F. (2d) 9.

346. Inland Steel Co. v. NLRB, 109 F. (2d) 9 at page 20.

347. NLRB v. Ed. Friedrich Inc., 116 F. (2d) 888, 889.

348. NLRB v. Algoma Plywood & Veneer Co., 121 F. (2d) 602, 604, 605; Berkshire Knitting Mills v. NLRB, 121 F. (2d) 235, 237.

349. NLRB v. Ford Motor Co., 114 F. (2d) 905, cert. den. 312 U.S. 689; Bethlehem Steel Co. v. NLRB, 120 F. (2d) 641, 652.

350. Rules and Regulations, Series 5, Sec. 203.35(f), 29 USCA (1947, Supp. foll. Sec. 261) Sec. 203.35(f). This Section sets forth the "Duties and Powers of Trial Examiners."

351. Amended Act Sec. 10(c), 29 USCA (1947, Supp.) Sec. 160(c). Rules and Regulations, Series 5, Secs. 203.45–.47, 29 USCA (1947, Supp. foll. Sec. 261) Secs. 203.45–.47.

352. Amended Act Sec. 10(c), 29 USCA (1947, Supp.) Sec. 160(c).

353. Amended Act Sec. 10(b), 29 USCA (1947, Supp.) Sec. 160(b).

354. Conference Report, House Report No. 510, 80th Congress 1st Session, p. 53. With respect thereto the House Committee on Education and Labor stated (House Report No. 245, 80th Cong. 1st Sess. pp. 40–41):

"*Evidence.*—Another important change concerns the evidence before the Board. The present act (sec. 10(b)) says that rules of evidence prevailing in courts of law and equity shall not be controlling. In the circuit courts of appeals, the court must regard the Board's findings of fact as 'conclusive' if they are 'supported by evidence' (sec. 10(e) and 10(f)).

"Thus the act gives the Board great latitude in choosing the evidence that it will believe and gives great effect to findings that rest on that evidence.

"The Supreme Court has insisted that the circuit courts of appeals, in reviewing decisions of the Board, adhere strictly to those terms of the act that deal with the Board's findings and with the kind of evidence upon which the Board can rest them (Consolidated Edison Co. v. NLRB, 305 U.S. 197 (1938); NLRB v. Columbian Enameling & Stamping Co., 306 U.S. 292 (1939); International Association of Machinists v. NLRB, 311 U.S. 72, 79 (1940); NLRB v. Automotive Maintenance Mach. Co., 315 U.S. 282 (1942);

354. (*Cont.*)
Foote Bros. Gear & Machine Corp. v. NLRB, 311 U.S. 620 (1940); Link-Belt Co. v. NLRB, 311 U.S. 584 (1941).

"Anything more than a 'modicum,' a 'scintilla' of evidence is enough, or the Board may rely upon 'inferences,' 'imponderables,' 'background material,' or 'the whole congeries of facts.'

"These clauses of the act have resulted in what the courts have described as 'shocking injustices' in the Board's rulings, 'assinine reasoning' by the Board, findings 'overwhelmingly opposed by the evidence,' findings that 'strain our credulity,' and 'remarkable discrimination' on the part of the Board in believing its own witnesses and in disbelieving others. (See, for example, Wilson & Co. v. NLRB, 126 F. (2d) 114, 117 (CCA 7, 1942); Wyman-Gordon Co. v. NLRB, 17 LRRM, 823 (CCA 7, 1946); NLRB v. Columbia Products Corp., 141 F. (2d) 687 (CCA 2, 1944); NLRB v. Union Pacific Stages, Inc., 99 F. (2d) 153 (CCA 9, 1938), and cases cited therein.)

"However repugnant to the courts the Board's decisions may seem, the fact, by making the Board in effect its own Supreme Court so far as its findings of fact are concerned, renders the courts all but powerless to correct the Board's abuses.

"Courts often have deferred to the assumed expertness of the Board when their own judgment would lead them to disagree. The Board's expertness is largely theoretic. See T. R. Iserman, *op. cit.,* pp. 60–62.

"Requiring the Board to rest its rulings upon facts, not inferences, conjectures, background, imponderables, and presumed expertness will correct abuses under the act.

"The bill does this, by providing in section 10(b) of the amended Labor Act that 'so far as practicable,' the new Board's proceedings shall be conducted 'in accordance with the rules of evidence applicable in the district courts of the United States under the rules of civil procedure.' There is no such diversity in the rules of evidence among the several States as to make this clause unduly burdensome to the Board or to its trial examiners. Local lawyers and . . . regional attorneys appearing before the trial examiners can always advise them of oddities in local laws. And, in any event, an error in admitting or excluding evidence can be grounds for reversal only if it is substantial.

"To enable the courts to correct glaring errors in the Board's findings, sections 10(e) and 10(f) of the amended act, instead of making the Board's findings of fact 'conclusive,' provide that they shall have this quality only if they are not against the 'manifest weight of evidence' and are supported by substantial evidence."

355. NLRB v. Pittsburgh Steamship Co., 337 U.S. 656.

356. Eastern Coal Corp. v. NLRB (CCA-4) 176 F. (2d) 131, 24 LRRM 2211, where the Court said:

"Counsel for the company argues that this rule has been changed by certain procedural provisions of the Labor Management Act of 1947, which modified the language of the earlier National Labor Relations Act in respect to the duties of the Board in the determination of controversies and the scope of judicial review of the Board's decisions by the courts. Thereby section 10(b) of the earlier Act, which provided that the rules of evidence prevailing in courts of law or equity should not be controlling, was stricken out, and it was provided that, so far as practicable, the Board's hearings should be conducted in accordance with the rules of evidence applicable in the District Courts of the United States; and section 10 (c) was amended so as to require the Board's decisions to be supported by 'preponderance of the testimony taken'; and the review sections 10(e) and 10 (f), were modified so as to provide that 'the findings of the Board with respect to questions of fact if supported by substantial evidence on the record considered as a whole, shall be conclusive.' 29 USCA 10(b), 10(c), 10(e), 10(f).'

"These changes, as the Committee Reports clearly show (Sen. Rep. No. 105, 80th Congress, 1st Sess. 26–27 (1947); H. R. Rep. No. 500, 80th Cong. 1st Sess. 56 (1947); H. R. Rep. No. 245, 80th Cong. 1st Sess. 41 (1947), were inspired by the dissatisfaction of Congress with decisions of the Board in certain cases and with the inability of the courts to correct them; and it was believed by some persons that the new Act broadened the scope of judicial review and conferred upon the courts power to correct mistakes committed by the Board in its findings of fact as well as in its conclusions of law,

We are unable, however, to find that this result was accomplished. See NLRB v. Austin Co., 7 Cir. 165 F. (2d) 592, 595; NLRB v. Crompton-Highland Mills Inc., 337 U.S. 217 (decided Aug. 31, 1949). That the Board was cautioned to observe the usual rules of evidence and to consider the whole record and to base its findings upon the preponderance of all of the evidence is undeniable, and the courts themselves were directed to determine whether the Board's findings of fact were supported by substantial evidence in the record considered as a whole. But findings so supported are still conclusive upon the courts since the critical words selected by Congress for the guidance of the courts are the existence of 'substantial evidence' to support the Board's findings and these are the same words which the Supreme Court has defined in this very context to mean 'such relevant evidence as a reasonable man might accept as adequate to support a conclusion.' "

357. NLRB v. Pennsylvania Greyhound Lines, 303 U.S. 261 at page 271; see also NLRB v. Remington Rand, Inc., 94 F. (2d) 862, cert. den. 304 U.S. 576.

358. NLRB v. Oregon Worsted Co., 96 F. (2d) 193.

359. Amended Act Sec. 10(c), 29 USCA (1947, Supp.) Sec. 160(c).

360. NLRB v. P. Lorillard & Co., 314 U.S. 512; NLRB v. Bradford Dyeing Assn., 310 U.S. 318, 339–340; I & M v. NLRB, 311 U.S. 72, 82; NLRB v. Falk Corp., 308 U.S. 453, 458–459; Phelps Dodge Corp. v. NLRB, 313 U.S. 177, 194; NLRB v. Link-Belt Co., 311 U.S. 584, 600; Franks Bros. v. NLRB, 64 S. Ct. 817.

361. NLRB v. P. Lorillard Co., *supra.*

362. NLRB v. Express Publishing Co., 312 U.S. 426.

363. NLRB v. Express Publishing Co., 312 U.S. 426, 437. 29 USCA (1947, Supp.) Sec. 160(c). Discussion of its rulings under the Wagner Act and a statement of its policies under the amended Act were given by the Board in Carpenter Steel Co., 76 NLRB No. 670, 21 LRRM 1232.

364. House Report No. 510, 80th Congress, 1st Session, pp. 53, 54.

365. Amended Act Sec. 10(e), 29 USCA (1947, Supp.) Sec. 160(e). Marshall Field & Co. v. NLRB, 318 U.S. 253;

NLRB v. Cheney California Lumber Co., 327 U.S. 385.

366. Amended Act, Sec. 10(e); 29 USCA (1947, Supp.) 160(e).

367. Amended Act, Sec. 10(f); 29 USCA (1947, Supp.) 160(f).

368. Consolidated Edison Co. v. NLRB, 305 U.S. 197; NLRB v. Remington Rand Inc., 94 F. (2d) 862.

369. See notes 366, 367.

370. This should be distinguished from the printing of the record. The rules of the various Circuit Courts of Appeal and the Federal Rules of Civil Procedure should be consulted as to the printing of the record. Each of the Circuit Courts has established its own rules concerning printing and the rules of the Court in which review or enforcement is sought should be given careful consideration.

371. Amended Act, Sec. 10(e), 29 USCA (1947, Supp.) Sec. 160(e).

372. Amended Act, Sec. 10(f), 29 USCA (1947, Supp.) Sec. 160(f).

373. Amended Act, Sec. 10(e) (f), 29 USCA (1947, Supp.) Sec. 160(e), (f).

374. Amended Act, Sec. 10(d), 29 USCA (1947, Supp.) 160(d).

375. In re National Labor Relations Board, 304 U.S. 486.

376. Ford Motor Co. v. NLRB, 305 U.S. 364.

377. Amended Act, Sec. 9(c) (1).

378. See note 264.

379. International Association of Machinists v. NLRB, 311 U.S. 72, 81–83. Inland Empire District Council et al. v. Millis, 325 U.S. 697.

380. Amended Act, Sec. 9(d), 29 USCA (1947, Supp.) Sec. 159(d); American Federation of Labor v. NLRB, 308 U.S. 401, 406.

381. Pittsburgh Plate Glass Co. v. NLRB, 313 U.S. 146; May Department Stores Co. v. NLRB, 326 U.S. 376.

382. A. G. Workers Assn. v. NLRB, 117 F. (2d) 209, 210.

383. Wilson & Co. v. NLRB, 120 F. (2d) 913, 915; Dupont de Nemours & Co. v. NLRB, 116 F. (2d) 388, 401, cert. den. 313 U.S. 571.

384. NLRB v. Auburn Foundry, Inc., 119 F. (2d) 331, 333–334.

385. Inland Container Corp. v. NLRB, 137 F. (2d) 642.

386. NLRB v. Newport News Shipbuilding and Dry Dock Co., 308 U.S. 241, reversing 101 F. (2d) 841.

387. NLRB v. Newport News Shipbuilding and Dry Dock Co., 308 U.S. 241 at pp. 249, 250.

388. Amended Act, Sec. 10(e), 29 USCA (1947, Supp.) Sec. 160(e).

389. Amended Act, Sec. 10(e).

390. 308 U.S. 453.

391. The Board has since discontinued the practice of consolidating such proceedings.

392. NLRB v. Falk Corp., 308 U.S. 453, at pages 458, 459.

393. 29 USCA (1947, Supp.) 160(e).

394. Ford Motor Company v. NLRB, 305 U.S. 364; NLRB v. Indiana & Michigan Electric Co., 318 U.S. 9.

395. Ford Motor Company v. NLRB, 305 U.S. 364, 374; Mooresville Cotton Mills v. NLRB, 97 F. (2d) 959; NLRB v. C. A. Lund, 103 F. (2d) 815, 821.

396. Ford Motor Co. v. NLRB, *supra.*

397. Ford Motor Co. v. NLRB, *supra;* Montgomery Ward & Co. v. NLRB, 103 F. (2d) 147, 156.

398. NLRB v. Bell Oil, Burke-Divide & Reno Oil Co., 91 F. (2d) 509, 515.

399. Ford Motor Co. v. NLRB, *supra.*

400. See NLRB v. National Casket Co., 107 F. (2d) 992; NLRB v. Sterling Electric Motors, 112 F. (2d) 63; Botany Worsted Mills v. NLRB, 106 F. (2d) 263; NLRB v. Corwell Portland Cement Co., 108 F. (2d) 198; Inland Steel Co. v. NLRB, 109 F. (2d) 9; NLRB v. Somerset Shoe Co., 111 F. (2d) 681.

401. Phelps Dodge Corp. v. NLRB, 313 U.S. 177; Continental Oil Co. v. NLRB, 313 U.S. 212.

402. International Union of Mine, Mill & Smelter Workers v. Eagle-Picher Mining & Smelting Co. & NLRB, 325 U.S. 335.

403. Amended Act, Sec. 10(e), 29 USCA (1947, Supp.) Sec. 160(e).

404. Amended Act, Sec. 10(e), 29 USCA (1947, Supp.) 160(e).

405. Amended Act, Sec. 10(f), 29 USCA (1947, Supp.) 160(f).

406. NLRB v. Servel Inc. The application for the temporary restraining order is unreported. The proceeding for enforcement of the Board is reported 149 F. (2d)

542. The temporary restraining order was dated September 29, 1944.

407. Amended Act, Sec. 10(e), 29 USCA (1947, Supp.) Sec. 160(e).

408. NLRB v. Southern Bell Telephone & Telegraph Co., 319 U.S. 50.

409. NLRB v. Bradford Dyeing Assn., 310 U.S. 318 at page 342.

410. Medo Photo Supply Corp. v. NLRB, 321 U.S. 678 at page 681, footnote.

411. NLRB v. Waterman Steamship Corp., 309 U.S. 206.

412. NLRB v. Piqua Munising Wood Products Co., 109 F. (2d) 552; Cupples Company Mfrs. v. NLRB, 106 F. (2d) 100; International Assn. of Machinists v. NLRB, 110 F. (2d) 29, affirmed 311 U.S. 72.

413. NLRB v. Falk Corp., 308 U.S. 453; NLRB v. Bradford Dyeing Assn., 310 U.S. 318; NLRB v. Swank Products Inc., 108 F. (2d) 872; Montgomery Ward & Co. v. NLRB, 107 F. (2d) 555.

414. Cupples Co. Mfrs. v. NLRB, 106 F. (2d) 100.

415. NLRB v. Waterman Steamship Corp., 309 U.S. 206.

416. Southern Colorado Power Co. v. NLRB, 111 F. (2d) 539; NLRB v. Griswold Mfg. Co., 106 F. (2d) 713; Montgomery Ward & Co. v. NLRB, 107 F. (2d) 555; Republic Steel Corp. v. NLRB, 107 F. (2d) 472, cert. den. 309 U.S. 684, upon rehearing Board order modified as to work provisions only, 311 U.S. 7.

417. NLRB v. Link-Belt Co., 311 U.S. 584.

418. NLRB v. Columbian Enameling and Stamping Co., 306 U.S. 292.

419. NLRB v. Pennyslvania Greyhound Lines, 303 U.S. 261. Whether a reviewing court has any greater authority under the amended Act has yet to be determined by the Supreme Court.

420. Amended Act, Sec. 10(b), 29 USCA (1947, Supp.) Sec. 160(b).

421. Amended Act, Sec. 10(c).

422. Eastern Coal Corp. v. NLRB, 176 F. (2d) 131.

423. NLRB v. Pittsburgh Steamship Co., 337 U.S. 656.

423a. Pittsburgh Steamship Company, 180 F. (2d) 731.

423b. NLRB v. Caroline Mills, Inc., 167 F. (2d) 212, 213.

423c. NLRB v. Universal Camera Corp., 179 F. (2d) 749 (CA 2); NLRB v. Continental Oil Company, 179 F. (2d) 552 (CA 10); NLRB v. Minnesota Mining & Mfg. Co., 179 F. (2d) 323, (CA 8).

424. Amended Act, Sec. 10(e), 29 USCA (1947, Supp.) Sec. 160(e).

425. Consolidated Edison Co. v. NLRB, 305 U.S. 197 at page 229.

426. Senate Report 105, 80th Congress, 1st Session, pp. 26, 27.

427. Eastern Coal Corp. v. NLRB (CCA 4), 176 F. (2d) 131.

428. NLRB v. Columbian Enameling & Stamping Co., 306 U.S. 292, at page 299. In the same case the Court also said:
"Section 10(e) of the Act provides: '. . . The findings of the Board as to the facts, if supported by evidence, shall be conclusive.' But as has often been pointed out, this, as in the case of other findings by administrative bodies, means evidence which is substantial, that is, affording a substantial basis of fact from which the fact in issue can be reasonably inferred. Washington, V. & M. Coach Co. v. National Labor Relations Board, 301 U.S. 142; Consolidated Edison Co. v. National Labor Relations Board, 305 U.S. 197; Appalachian Electric Power Co. v. National Labor Relations Board, 93 F. (2d) 985, 989; National Labor Relations Board v. Thompson Products, Inc., 97 F. (2d) 13; Ballston-Stillwater Knitting Co. v. National Labor Relations Board, 98 F. (2d) 758, 764."
To the same effect: Hazel-Atlas Glass Co. v. NLRB, 127 F. (2d) 109; Indianapolis Power & Light Co. v. NLRB, 122 F. (2d) 757; Utah Copper Co. v. NLRB, 139 F. (2d) 788, cert. den. *sub nom.* Independent Association of Mill Workers v. NLRB, 322 U.S. 731.

429. NLRB v. Waterman Steamship Corp., 309 U.S. 206 at pages 208, 209.

430. NLRB v. Waterman Steamship Corp., *supra* at page 226.

431. The Wagner Act provided that: "In any such proceeding the rules of evidence prevailing in courts of law or equity shall not be controlling." 29 USCA Sec. 160(b).

432. NLRB v. Columbian Enameling & Stamping Co., 306 U.S. 292; Consolidated Edison Co. v. NLRB, 305 U.S. 197.

433. Consolidated Edison Co. v. NLRB, 305 U.S. 197 at pages 229, 230.

434. NLRB v. Jones & Laughlin Steel Corp., 301 U.S. 1; Morgan v. U.S., 298 U.S. 468; Valley Mould & Iron Corporation v. NLRB, 116 F. (2d) 760, cert. den. 313 U.S. 590.

435. Consumers Power Co. v. NLRB, 113 F. (2d) 38.

436. Continental Box Co. v. NLRB 113 F. (2d) 93.

437. Montgomery Ward & Co. v. NLRB, 103 F. (2d) 147, 149. See also NLRB v. Washington Dehydrated Food Co., 118 F. (2d) 980.

438. NLRB v. Phelps, 136 F. (2d) 562.

439. NLRB v. Phelps, 136 F. (2d) 562 at pages 563, 564.

440. Ohio Bell Telephone Co. v. Public Utilities Commission, 301 U.S. 292. The importance of compliance by administrative agencies with the principles of "fair and open hearing" is discussed and the cases cited by the Court at page 304.

441. NLRB v. Pittsburgh Steamship Co., 337 U.S. 656.

442. NLRB v. Hofman, 147 F. (2d) 679, 682.

443. Republic Aviation Corp. v. NLRB, 142 F. (2d) 193, affirmed 324 U.S. 793.

444. NLRB v. Standard Oil Co., 138 F. (2d) 885 at page 887.

445. NLRB v. Century Oxford Mfg. Corp., 140 F. (2d) 541. The Court said (at page 543):
"How long the employees' undoubted power to recall an elected representative may be suspended, is a matter primarily, perhaps finally, for the Board; but a period of six weeks is on any theory not the limit."

446. Conference Report, House Report 510, 80th Congress, 1st Session, pp. 55, 56.

447. Wallace Corp. v. NLRB, 159 F. (2d) 952, 954 (CCA 4).

448. NLRB v. New York Merchandise Co. Inc., 134 F. (2d) 949 (CCA 2); cf. NLRB v. Draper Corp., 159 F. (2d) 294, 298 (CCA 1).

449. Bird Machine Co. v. NLRB, 174 F. (2d) 404 (CCA 1); Home Beneficial Life Ins. Co. v. NLRB, 172 F. (2d) 62 (CCA 4).

450. NLRB v. Reed & Prince Mfg. Co., 130 F. (2d) 765, (CCA 1).

451. Bird Machine Co. v. NLRB, 174 F. (2d) 404 (CCA 1).

452. NLRB v. Hopwood Retinning Co., 104 F. (2d) 302, 305.

453. Amalgamated Utility Workers v. Consolidated Edison Co., 309 U.S. 261.

454. NLRB v. Hopwood Retinning Co., 104 F. (2d) 302.

455. NLRB v. Hopwood Retinning Co., *supra;* NLRB v. Carlisle Lumber Co., 99 F. (2d) 533, 539.
The Second Circuit Court of Appeals has required the Board to make its order precise before proceeding to contempt. The Board may obtain remand of the case for that purpose and then "move to make the enforcement order definite and final on this point." NLRB v. Sandy Hill Iron & Brass Works, CCA-2, 165 F. (2d) 660; NLRB v. New York Merchandise Co., 2 Cir., 134 F. (2d) 949, 953.

456. NLRB v. Federal Bearing Co., 109 F. (2d) 945.

457. NLRB v. Nebel Knitting Mills, 103 F. (2d) 594, (CCA-4).

458. NLRB v. Pacific Greyhound Lines Inc., 106 F. (2d) 867.

459. NLRB v. Standard Trouser Co., 162 F. (2d) 1012.

460. NLRB v. Standard Trouser Co., *supra.* The Court applied the doctrine of Rule 53(e) (2) of the Federal Rules of Civil Procedure.

Authorities

PART THREE: RIGHTS AND DUTIES OF MANAGEMENT AND UNIONS

1. 49 Stat. 449, 29 USCA Secs. 151–166.

2. Public Law 101, 80th Congress, 1st Session; See Sec. 104, Title I; 29 USCA 141 et seq.

3. Amended Act, Sec. 1; 29 USCA (1947, Supp.) Sec. 151.

4. Amended Act, Sec. 1; 29 USCA (1947, Supp.) Sec. 151.

5. Amended Act, Sec. 1; 29 USCA (1947, Supp., Sec. 151.

6. Sec. 1(b), 29 USCA (1947, Supp.) Sec. 141(b).

7. 29 USCA (1947, Supp.) Secs. 157, 158, 160(c).

8. 29 USCA Sec. 159, 160.

9. NLRB v. Jones & Laughlin Steel Corp., 301 U.S. 1, 31–32.

10. 29 USCA Sec. 152(6) and (7).

11. NLRB v. Fainblatt, 306 U.S. 601, 606.

11a. Watson's Specialty Store, 80 NLRB No. 91; Wadsworth Building, 81 NLRB No. 127. In United Brotherhood of Carpenters and Joiners of America etc. v. Sperry (170 F. (2d) 863), the Court of Appeals for the Tenth Circuit said:
"The foregoing general principles have appropriate application here. The committee hearings, the committee reports, and the language contained in the act, considered in their totality, make it plain that Congress acted in the belief that wrongful secondary boycotts directed against industrial or commercial units engaged solely in intrastate commerce for the purpose of compelling them to cease doing business with other industrial or commercial units engaged in interstate commerce could reasonably have disrup-tive adverse effect upon interstate commerce, and that it was the Congressional intent and purpose to bring boycotts of that kind within the scope of the act.

"Here, Wadsworth purchased for use in its business large amounts of raw materials which originated in other states; and it sold large amounts of manufactured products to customers in other states. Klassen was engaged in intrastate activities. The purpose of the secondary boycott against Klassen was intended solely to compel that company to cease doing business with Wadsworth. If the practice of establishing secondary boycotts against those doing business with Wadsworth were extended sufficiently in scope it could substantially reduce the flow in interstate commerce of raw materials for use by that company in the conduct of its business, and likewise it could substantially reduce the flow in interstate commerce of manufactured products to its customers in other states. And the general practice of establishing and maintaining secondary boycotts of that kind multiplied or extended throughout the country would necessarily effect a reduction in the flow in interstate commerce of both raw materials and manufactured commodities.

"Therefore, while the activities of Klassen were essentially local, they were of such character and bore such relation to interstate commerce that a secondary boycott directed against it and carried forward by blacklisting and picketing for the sole purpose of compelling it to cease doing business with Wadsworth constituted an unfair labor practice, within the scope and purpose of the act." Cf. Carpenters &

11a. (*Cont.*)
Joiners Union of America v. Ritter's Cafe, 315 U.S. 722.

12. NLRB v. Fainblatt, 306 U.S. 601, 604.

13. Consolidated Edison Co. of N.Y. v. NLRB, 305 U.S. 197.

14. 29 USCA (1947, Supp.) Sec. 152 (2).

15. House Report 245, 80th Congress, 1st Session, p. 11. The Committee report cites the following cases:

See Matter of American Steel Scraper Co., 29 NLRB 939; Matter of Schult Trailers, Inc., 28 NLRB 975, 993; Matter of Jahn & Ollier Engraving Co., 24 NLRB 896; Matter of Schwarze Electric Co., 16 NLRB 246; Matter of Swift & Co., 15 NLRB 992; Matter of American Oil Co., Inc., 14 NLRB 990; Matter of Frost Rubber Works, 23 NLRB 1071; Matter of California Walnut Growers Assn., 18 NLRB 493.

In establishing the agency relationship actual authority to perform the acts charged against the employer or the union, or subsequent ratification thereof, are not controlling. 29 USCA Sec. 152 (13). The definition of "employer" expressly excludes Federal and State Governments and political subdivisions thereof, wholly owned government corporations, Federal Reserve Bank, hospitals not operated for profit, persons covered by the Railway Labor Act and labor organizations ("other than when acting as an employer") and their agents. 29 USCA Sec. 152(2).

16. 29 USCA (1947, Supp.) Sec. 152 (3).

17. NLRB v. Hearst Publications, 322 U.S. 111.

18. House Report 245, 80th Congress, 1st Session, p. 18.

19. "Supervisor" is defined as "any individual having authority, in the interest of the employer, to hire, transfer, suspend, lay off, recall, promote, discharge, assign, reward, or discipline other employees, or responsibility to direct them, or to adjust their grievances or effectively to recommend such action, if in connection with the foregoing the exercise of such authority is not of a merely routine or clerical nature, but requires the use of independent judgment." 29 USCA Sec. 152(11). Manifestly, "straw bosses" would not fall within this definition. The following persons are also excluded from the definition of "employee": Agricultural laborers, domestics, individuals employed by parent or spouse, individuals covered by the Railway Labor Act.

20. The amended Act reverses the Board's holdings under the Wagner Act that foremen were employees within the meaning of the Act and that an employer's refusal to bargain collectively as to them was an unfair labor practice. Packard Motor Car Co. v. NLRB, 330 U.S. 485. However, the amended Act does not prohibit voluntary recognition of a foremen's union (Senate Report 105, 80th Congress, 1st Session p. 5). See 29 USCA (1947, Supp.) Sec. 164.

21. L. A. Young Spring & Wire Corporation v. NLRB, CCA D.C., 163 F. (2d) 906. In Eastern Gas & Fuel Associates v. NLRB, 162 F. (2d) 864, the Sixth Circuit Court of Appeals limited the effect of a reinstatement and back pay order to discharged foremen to the period ending August 22, 1947, the effective date of the amendments to the Act.

22. NLRB v. Jones & Laughlin Steel Co., 301 U.S. 1 at page 45.

23. 313 U.S. 177, 186, 187.

24. 301 U.S. 1 at page 45.

25. Phelps Dodge Corp. v. NLRB, 313 U.S. 177.

26. Phelps Dodge Corp. v. NLRB, 313 U.S. 177, 183, 184, 185, 187.

27. 75 NLRB 569, 570, 21 LRRM 1056.

28. 29 USCA (1947, Supp.) Sec. 159(a). Guards are defined as "any individual employed as a guard to enforce against employees and other persons rules to protect property of the employer or to protect the safety of persons on the employer's premises."

29. Matter of City National Bank & Trust Company, 76 NLRB No. 31, 21 LRRM 1168. The Board said:

". . . However, since the issuance of the Intermediate Report herein, the Act has been amended by the Labor Management Relations Act, 1947, to provide that 'no labor organization shall be certified as the representative of employees in a bargaining unit of guards if such organization admits to membership, or is affiliated directly or indirectly with an organization which admits to membership, employees other than guards.' The unit which the

Union seeks to represent comprises guards. The Union is an affiliate of an organization which admits employees other than guards into membership. Accordingly, in view of the amendments to the Act and the Union's affiliation, we do not believe that an order should be made in this case requiring the respondents to bargain on the basis of a certification issued on July 26, 1943. As the case involves only a refusal to bargain, we shall dismiss the complaint."

30. Matter of C. V. Hill & Co., Inc., 76 NLRB No. 24, 21 LRRM 1172. The Board said:

"These employees have a duty to protect property of the Employer against theft, whether by employees or by 'other persons' who might gain access to the plant. They therefore fall within the definition of the individuals whom the Board is now prohibited from including in units with other employees. In view of the terms of the declaration by Congress in Section 9 (b) (3), we have no choice but to disregard the agreement of the parties as to the watchmen, and exclude them, as well as the guards, from the production and maintenance unit."

31. 29 USCA Sec. 159(b). "Professional employee" is defined in the statute 29 USCA Sec. 152(12).

32. Matter of Worthington Pump & Machinery Corp., 75 NLRB 678, 21 LRRM 1066. The Board pointed out:

"We have reexamined our position in the representation case, together with further evidence introduced in the present proceeding concerning the duties and responsibilities of the respondent's time-study and standards employees. We conclude that the principal function of these employees is, by utilizing their training and experience, to determine the factual basis for the operation of the respondent's incentive wage plan. They are, therefore, essentially fact finders. Although it appears that they exercise considerable judgment and discretion in the performance of their duties, they do not do so to any substantial degree in the formulation, determination, or effectuation of management policies.

"We therefore affirm our earlier conclusion that the individuals here in question are employees within the meaning of Section 2 (3) of the Act, and that they may properly constitute an appropriate unit for the purposes of collective bargaining.

"We also find that time-study employees are employees within the meaning of Section 2 (3) of the Act, as amended, and that such employees, by reason of their training and responsibilities, are professional employees within the meaning of Section 2 (12) of the amended Act. The legislative history of the Labor Management Relations Act, 1947, reveals that the Congress gave specific consideration to the 'employee' status of time-study employees, professional employees, guards, foremen, and others, and that while doing so, it was conversant with the Board's decisions according bargaining rights to such employees. (See House Report No. 245, 80th Cong. 1st Sess., pp. 13–17; Senate Report No. 105, 80th Cong. 1st Sess., pp. 3–5; 11.) Time-study personnel were originally included within the supervisory category in the House Bill and, as supervisors, were denied employee status; however, they were not included within such supervisory classification in the final Conference Bill. The Conference Report indicates that, at the very least, time-study employees may be regarded as professional employees, subject to the statutory qualifications respecting a unit of such employees. (Conference Report (House Report No. 510, 80th Cong., 1st Sess., pp. 35, 36)).

"Thus, although the Act, as ultimately amended, excluded supervisors from the classification of individuals who are to be considered employees for the purposes of the Act, and imposed limitations respecting units of guards and professional employees (Section 9 (b) of the Labor Management Act), it nonetheless included professional employees within the statutory definition of employees. Finally, the statute itself refutes the respondent's contention that employees like the ones in question are to be deprived of employee status because of the nature of their duties; for, by express language, a professional employee is defined, in part, as any 'employee engaged in work . . . involving the consistent exercise of discretion and judgment in its performance.' (Section 2(12) of the Labor Management Relations Act.)"

33. Jersey Publishing Company, 76 NLRB No. 70.

34. 29 USCA (1947, Supp.) Sec. 159(b).

35. Matter of Pacific Car & Foundry Co., 76 NLRB No. 2, 21 LRRM 1161.

36. Matter of Clayton Mark & Co., 76 NLRB No. 33, 21 LRRM 1175. As to such employees, the majority of the Board said:

"The legislative history of the Labor-Management Relations Act, 1947, reveals that Congress originally gave specific consideration to the status of inspectors. As passed, however, the law only directs the Board to take particular action in representation cases with respect to three types of persons: supervisors, professional employees, and plant guards. It is silent with respect to inspectors, although enacted 8 months after the *Luminous Processes* decision had become a matter of public record.

"Inspectors were originally included within the definition of 'supervisor' in the House Bill (Section 2 (12) of H.R. 3020), and were, as such, denied employee status, but they were *not* included within the definition of 'supervisors' in the final Conference Bill. (Conference Report (House Report No. 510, 80th Cong., 1st Sess., pp. 35, 36)). It is clear, therefore, that these inspectors are not supervisors within the meaning of Section 2 (11) of the amended Act. This is not to say that there are no inspectors who are supervisors within the statutory definition. There may well be inspectors who, in the course of their duties, exercise supervisory functions within the meaning of the amended Act. It is clear from the record herein, however, that this Employer's inspectors do not have any of the supervisory duties set forth in Section 2 (11) of the Act.

"It is equally clear, in our opinion, that the amended Act and its legislative history do not authorize the classification of inspectors as 'professional employees' merely because, by the exercise of individual judgment and discretion, they may sometimes affect the earnings of production employees. Just as the duties of a particular inspector may bring him within the definition of 'supervisor' in the Act, some inspectors may be professional employees within the meaning of Section 2 (12) of the Act, if their training and duties comport with the definition therein. But that is not the situation here. The legislative history reveals that this kind of inspector was treated in the same manner as time-study employees in the original House Bill, in which both were meant to be included within the definition of 'supervisor,' and in the final Conference Bill, in which neither was included within the definition. (Matter of Clayton Mark & Company, 59 NLRB 464.) Despite the similar treatment of inspectors and time-study employees at that stage, the later Conference Report indicates that, while it was contemplated that time-study employees might be regarded as professional employees (In Matter of Worthington Pump & Machinery Corporation, 75 NLRB No. 80 (21 LRRM 1066)) and therefore entitled to representation in a separate unit, there was no intention to require similar treatment of inspectors.

"Finally, neither the amended Act nor its legislative history indicates a Congressional intent to place inspectors in the same position as plant guards, with respect to whom we may no longer certify any rank-and-file union. (Section 9(b) (3) of the amended Act.) We cannot agree with our dissenting colleagues that the Board is now under a mandate to restrict inspectors to representation by a separate unit, unaffiliated with any union that represents other employees, or that we are authorized to exercise any discretion to do so. Congress having been silent on the point, although the status of inspectors was generally considered, the legislative history bearing on congressional intent is, if anything, to the contrary. We find, accordingly, that the inspectors herein should be included in the unit of production and maintenance employees."

37. See NLRB v. American Tube Bending Co., 134 F. (2d) 993; NLRB v. Peter J. Schweitzer, 144 F. (2d) 520; Thomas v. Collins, 323 U.S. 516.

38. 29 USCA (1947, Supp.) Sec. 141(b).

39. 29 USCA (1947, Supp.) Sec. 158(a) (3); NLRB v. Waumbec Mills, 114 F. (2d) 226; Phelps Dodge Corp. v. NLRB, 313 U.S. 177.

40. NLRB v. Jones & Laughlin Steel Co., 301 U.S. 1.

41. Morley Manufacturing Co., 83 NLRB No. 60, 24 LRRM 1084; Hawley & Hoops Inc., 83 NLRB No. 50, 24 LRRM 1092.

42. National Maritime Union, 78 NLRB No. 137, 22 LRRM 1289.

43. NLRB v. Draper Corp., 145 F. (2d) 199; NLRB v. Brashear Freight Lines,

119 F. (2d) 379. See also NLRB v. Sands Mfg. Co., 306 U.S. 332, 344, cf. Western Cartridge Co. v. NLRB, 139 F. (2d) 855.

44. NLRB v. Clinchfield Coal Co., 145 F. (2d) 66; NLRB v. Fansteel Metallurgical Corp., 306 U.S. 240; See also Hazel-Atlas Glass Co. v. NLRB, 127 F. (2d) 109; Standard Lime & Stone v. NLRB, 97 F. (2d) 531.

45. See NLRB v. Goodyear Tire & Rubber Co. of Alabama, 129 F. (2d) 661, certiorari denied, 319 U.S. 776. The amended Act expressly provides that an employee discharged for cause shall not be reinstated or awarded back pay. 29 USCA Sec. 160(c).

46. NLRB v. Mylan-Sparta Co., 166 F. (2d) 485, 491, 21 LRRM 2368.

47. NLRB v. Alco Feed Mills, 133 F. (2d) 419; Interlake Iron Corp. v. NLRB, 131 F. (2d) 129; Stonewall Cotton Mills v. NLRB, 129 F. (2d) 629, certiorari denied 317 U.S. 667; Firestone Tire & Rubber Co., 67 NLRB No. 79, 18 LRRM 1031.

48. See United Biscuit Co. v. NLRB, 128 F. (2d) 771; NLRB v. National Condenser Corp., 128 F. (2d) 67; Dannen Grain & Milling Co. v. NLRB, 130 F. (2d) 321; NLRB v. West Texas Utilities Co., 119 F. (2d) 683; NLRB v. Goshen Rubber & Mfg. Co., 110 F. (2d) 432.

49. "The natural construction which the text, (National Labor Relations Act) the legislative setting and the function of the statute command, does not impose an obligation on the employer to favor union members in hiring employees. He is as free to hire as he is to discharge employees. The statute does not touch 'the normal exercise of the right of the employer to select its employees or to discharge them.' It is directed solely against the abuse of that right by interfering with the countervailing right of self-organization." Phelps Dodge Corp. v. NLRB, 313 U.S. 177, 186, 187.

50. Aurora Wall Paper Mill, Inc., 73 NLRB No. 33; Underwood Machinery Corp., 74 NLRB No. 126; Fred A. Snow, Inc., 53 NLRB 977; Industrial Metal Fabricators, Inc., 67 NLRB No. 38.

51. Atlas Steel & Tube Company, 68 NLRB No. 114; North American Refractories Co., 52 NLRB 1049.

52. Firth Carpet Company, 33 NLRB 191; Ohio Calcium Company, 34 NLRB 917.

53. Newman Machine Company, 74 NLRB No. 45; Industrial Metal Fabricators, Inc., 67 NLRB No. 38; Athens Manufacturing Co., 69 NLRB No. 75.

54. Heilig Bros. Co., 32 NLRB 505; Howard Foundry Company, 59 NLRB 60; Thompson Products, 57 NLRB 925.

55. NLRB v. Jones & Laughlin Steel Corp., 301 U.S. 1, 45, 46; Associated Press v. NLRB, 301 U.S. 103, 132; Appalachian Electric Power Co. v. NLRB, 93 F. (2d) 985, 989; Richmond Home Telephone Company, 70 NLRB No. 37; Gardner-Denver Company, 58 NLRB 81; D-N-X Engine Corporation, 57 NLRB 740; Dallas Tank & Welding Co., 51 NLRB 1315; Wennonah Cotton Mills Company, Inc., 63 NLRB 143; The Firestone Tire & Rubber Company, 67 NLRB No. 47; Williamson-Dickie Mfg. Co., 35 NLRB 1220; Hoover Co., 12 NLRB 902.

56. Holston Mfg. Co., 13 NLRB 783.

57. Textile Machine Works, 69 NLRB No. 96.

58. Scullin Steel Company, 49 NLRB 405; Dallas Tank & Welding Co., 51 NLRB 1315; The Firestone Tire & Rubber Co., 67 NLRB No. 47.

59. The National Labor Relations Board has held that the employer's discriminatory promulgation or application of a rule against solicitation for a union on the employer's property but on the employee's own time is an unfair labor practice and the courts have sustained such order when supported by substantial evidence of discrimination. NLRB v. Denver Tent Awning Co., 138 F. (2d) 410; NLRB v. Peyton Packing Co., 142 F. (2d) 1009; Carter Carburetor Corp. v. NLRB, 140 F. (2d) 714. The Board has gone further and held, in the absence of evidence of discrimination, that an employer's rule against solicitation for the union by employees on the employer's property but on their own time was *per se* an unfair labor practice unless a reasonable necessity for the existence of such a rule was established by the employer. The Board's finding against an employer because of such a rule was upheld by the Supreme Court in Republic Aviation Corp. v. NLRB, 324 U.S. 793.

60. Tex-O-Kan Flour Mills Co., 26 NLRB 765; Nevada Consolidated Copper Corp., 26 NLRB 1182; Ex Lax Inc., 34 NLRB 1095.

61. NLRB v. Sands Mfg. Co., 306 U.S. 332, 344; Joseph Dyson & Sons, Inc., 72

61. (*Cont.*)
NLRB No. 82; The Fafnir Bearing Co., 73 NLRB No. 189. See Victory Fluorspar Mining Company, 72 NLRB No. 247; Fairmont Creamery Co., 73 NLRB No. 244; See The Reardon Company, 63 NLRB 1461; W. W. Holmes et al., 72 NLRB No. 10.

62. Cf. NLRB v. Cape County Milling Co., 140 F. (2d) 543; NLRB v. Gluek Brewing Co., 144 F. (2d) 847. "It is equally well established that the Board does not have authority to impose a penalty nor to interfere with the normal exercise of the right of the employer to conduct its business." Republic Steel Corp. v. NLRB, 311 U.S. 7, 61 S. Ct. 77, 85 L. Ed. 6; Consolidated Edison Co. v. NLRB, 305 U.S. 197, 59 S. Ct. 206, 83 L. Ed. 126; NLRB v. Cape County Milling Co., 140 F. (2d) 543, 546.

63. NLRB v. Ashville Hosiery Co., 108 F. (2d) 288 (CCA 4).

64. Smith Wood Products, Inc., 16 NLRB 613.

65. Trenton Mills, Inc., 12 NLRB 241; Eagle Picher Mining & Smelting Co., 16 NLRB 727.

66. See NLRB v. Mackay Radio & Telegraph Co., 304 U.S. 333; Hazel-Atlas Glass Co. v. NLRB, 127 F. (2d) 109; Great Southern Trucking Co. v. NLRB, 127 F. (2d) 180, certiorari denied 317 U.S. 652; NLRB v. Fansteel Metallurgical Corp., 306 U.S. 240; Republic Steel Corp., 9 NLRB 219, enforced as modified Republic Steel Corp. v. NLRB, 107 F. (2d) 472.

67. Amended Act Sec. 8(a) (3); 29 USCA (1947, Supp.) Sec. 158(a) (3).

68. See note 49.

69. Gilfillan Bros. Inc., 53 NLRB 574.

70. King Ventilating Co., 60 NLRB 1.

71. David Karron, Inc., 25 NLRB 506.

72. International Envelope Co., 34 NLRB 1277.

73. NLRB v. Draper Corp., 145 F. (2d) 199.

74. In the matter of The American News Company, 55 NLRB 1302; NLRB v. Indiana Desk Co., 149 F. (2d) 987.

75. See note 66; NLRB v. Fansteel Metallurgical Corp., 306 U.S. 240.

76. The Fafnir Bearing Co., 73 NLRB 1008; Joseph Dyson & Sons Inc., 72

NLRB 445. The Court of Appeals for the Fifth Circuit has held that the employees who strike without first resorting to the grievance procedure of the contract may be discharged even in the absence of a no-strike clause. NLRB v. Dorsey Trailers, Inc., 179 F. (2d) 589.

77. The Fafnir Bearing Co., 73 NLRB 1008; The Carey Salt Co., 70 NLRB 1099.

78. United Elastic Corporation, 84 NLRB 768.

79. Roanoke Public Warehouse, 72 NLRB 1281.

80. Carnegie-Illinois Steel Corp., 84 NLRB No. 99.

81. Southern Steamship Co. v. NLRB, 316 U.S. 31.

82. NLRB v. Mackay Radio & Telegraph Co., 304 U.S. 333.

82a. Conway's Express, 87 NLRB No. 130.

83. 55 NLRB 1302.

84. 72 NLRB No. 150, 19 LRRM 1216.

85. 29 USCA (1947, Supp.) Sec. 158(b) (4) (C).

86. 29 USCA (1947, Supp.) Sec. 160(e).

87. 64 NLRB 490.

88. 29 USCA (1947, Supp.) Sec. 159(c) (3).

89. Pipe Machinery Co., 76 NLRB No. 37, 21 LRRM 1178. The Board's policy as to this problem is as follows:

"Although an economic strike (the General Counsel, on January 5, 1948, sustained the Regional Director's dismissal for lack of merit of Case No. 8-C-2172, in which the Intervenor charged the Employer with certain unfair labor practices) has been in effect at the Employer's plant, since February 17, 1947, it appears that the Employer has replaced some of the strikers and that the plant has continued to operate. All parties request an immediate election despite the currency of the strike. They differ only as to the date to be used in determining eligibility to vote in the election. The Petitioner requests that the Board use the date of the strike to determine eligibility to vote, the Intervenor urges the use of the payroll immediately before the strike, and the Employer requests the use of the payroll immediately preceding the Direction of Election, which is the customary Board eligibility date.

"Hitherto the Board has permitted both

economic strikers and their replacements to vote (Matter of The Rudolph Wurlitzer Company, 32 NLRB 163 (8 LRR Man. 191): Matter of Columbia Pictures Corporation et al., 64 NLRB 490 (17 LRR Man. 103)), irrespective of a striker's right to reinstatement, except that replacements hired after an unconditional application by the strikers to return have not been eligible to vote. (Matter of Kellburn Manufacturing Company, 45 NLRB 322 (11 LRR Man. 142)). However, Section 9 (c) (3) of the Act, as amended, now provides that 'Employees on strike who are not entitled to reinstatement shall not be eligible to vote.' Although the above quoted language clearly indicates that only those employees who are *entitled* to reinstatement shall be eligible to vote, it is apparent that we cannot accurately determine at this stage of the proceeding which of the striking employees have been validly replaced and which individuals are still entitled to reinstatement. To do so will require ascertaining the facts as of the date selected to test voting eligibility.

"Board experience in dealing with related eligibility issues has demonstrated the advisability in such circumstances of proceeding with an election forthwith, of using a current pay roll, and of permitting affected individuals to cast ballots under challenge with the proviso that their ballots shall not be counted unless the results of the election make it necessary to do so. We think the same technique is indicated here. In the event that the counting of the challenged ballots would affect the results of the election, the question as to which of these ballots shall be opened and counted must await a further investigation concerning the employment status of the individual strikers and their replacements. Accordingly, we shall direct an immediate election, permitting all employees to participate who were employed during the payroll period immediately preceding the date of this Direction. All persons hired since February 17, 1947, the date of the strike, and all strikers shall be deemed presumptively eligible to vote, subject to challenge.

"By permitting strikers and their replacements to cast ballots, as we did in the Wurlitzer case, *supra*, we are not to be taken as reiterating the doctrine in that case, upon which Section 9 (c) (3) of the amended Act has had considerable im-

pact. We are merely using this technique to lay the basis for ascertaining the active employment status of the strikers and their replacements.

"Nothing in this Direction should be construed as indicating that the Board has prejudged in any respect any of the questions which may be drawn into issue by a challenge to the eligibility of certain voters, including such questions as whether (1) a new employee is a permanent replacement, (2) a striking employee has been validly replaced, or (3) any employee's position no longer exists by reason of its permanent discontinuance for economic reasons. Matter of Longhorn Roofing Products, Inc., 67 NLRB 84 (17 LRR Man. 424); Matter of Geilich Tanning Company, 59 NLRB 1183 (15 LRR Man. 191)."

89a. The Pipe Machinery Co., 79 NLRB No. 181.

89b. Times Square Publishing Company, 79 NLRB 361.

90. 29 USCA (1947, Supp.) Sec. 158(a) (3). An employer cannot legally discharge a member of the union grievance committee because of his refusal to obey an order to come to the office alone to discuss a matter which previously had been taken up by the employer with the committee as sole bargaining agent. Ross Gear & Tool Co., 63 NLRB 1012.

91. See Tabin-Picker & Co., 50 NLRB 928; Armour Fertilizer Works Inc., 46 NLRB 629. The employer's responsibility for discrimination against his supervisory staff because of their membership or activity on behalf of a union of supervisors is a somewhat different problem. See also Soss Mfg. Co., 56 NLRB 348; Houston Shipbuilding Corp., 56 NLRB 1684; Whiting-Mead Co., 45 NLRB 987.

92. The Paraffine Cos. Inc., 76 NLRB No. 26. The Board said:

"Under facts quite analogous to those presented here, the Board held in the Climax case (66 NLRB 1359, 17 LRR Man. 396) * * * that 'the respondent, by requiring the foremen to resign from the union or suffer demotion, interfered with their right to remain members of the union (representing the production and maintenance employees),' violated Section 8 (1) and, by 'demoting them when they refused to resign from the union,' violated Section 8 (3) of the Act. In speaking of

92. (*Cont.*)
the other issue presented in the Climax case, to wit, whether the employer had the right to require a foreman to desist from wearing his rank and file union button at work, the Board said:

'In the instant case, it is true, Meyer and Engstrom (foremen) also wore buttons indistinguishable from those worn by rank and file employees, thereby superimposing upon mere passive membership an open and active support of the union among rank and file employees. We are therefore here faced with the need of balancing the right of supervisors to self-organization under Section 7 of the Act against the right of rank and file employees to be free of supervisory interference. We conclude on the facts of this case that, in contrast with mere passive membership, the wearing of union buttons by supervisors, indistinguishable from those worn by rank and file employees, may form a barrier, though no doubt a slight one, to the full exercise by subordinates of their freedom of choice. The respondent would consequently have been entitled to take appropriate steps to protect its neutrality. It would have been appropriate, for example, for the respondent to have required Meyer and Engstrom to remove and thereafter refrain from wearing the rank and file union buttons and to have demoted them if they failed to comply with its request.

"Apparently conceding the correctness of the law as stated by the Board, the respondent argues that it was merely taking necessary and appropriate steps in order to maintain and preserve its own neutrality between the numerous unions in the plant when it formulated and adhered to its policy that its supervisory foremen and candidates for that position had to give up their affiliation with the union representing the production and maintenance employees upon promotion to that position. The facts show that this condition was satisfied so far as the company was concerned when the supervisory foremen secured a withdrawal card from the union.

"The respondent points to various obligations of the union's Constitution, By-Laws and Declaration of Principles to which each member was required to adhere as being in direct conflict with the foremen's obligation to the employer and which would, of necessity, violate the respondent's policy of neutrality.

"The Constitution, By-Laws and Declaration of Principles of the Union provide for only one type of membership, whether the member be a production worker or a foreman. Every member is obligated to comply with the Constitution and Declaration of Principles of the union. By these documents he is under the 'duty to serve the local when called upon,' he is eligible for office, he must attend Union meetings and vote on measures presented there, he must wear his 'union button on the job at all times,' he must prefer charges against brother members for violations of their obligations and appear as a witness against them, he is subject to the same charges being brought against him, and to fines, suspension or expulsion upon conviction thereof. . . .

"It thus appears that these conflicting obligations imposed upon a foreman by his position with the employer and by his obligations to the union create real and present dangers to the respondent, the union and the foreman himself from the active membership role required of all union members under the present union obligations. Especially is this so with respect to the present respondent, due to the number of differently affiliated unions with which it deals. Nor does the undersigned believe that, in a case such as this is, the respondent should be required to wait patiently until its foreman have done some overt act, required by his obligation to the Union, and jeopardize the respondent's good relations with the unions before it is permitted to take the 'appropriate steps' to protect those relations."

93. In Harnischfeger Corp., 9 NLRB 676 the Board said: ". . . We do not . . . mean that it is unlawful for an employer to discharge an employee for *any* activity sanctioned by a union or otherwise in the nature of collective activity. The question is, we think, whether this particular activity was so indefensible, under the circumstances, as to warrant the respondent, under the Act, in discharging the stewards for this type of union activity."

94. Mt. Clemens Pottery Co., 46 NLRB 714.

95. Howard Foundry Co., 59 NLRB 60.

96. Fred A. Snow Company, 53 NLRB 977; Howard Foundry Co., 59 NLRB 60.

97. Fred A. Snow, 53 NLRB 977.

98. NLRB v. Dixie Motor Coach Corp., 128 F. (2d) 201 (CCA 5).

99. Emerson Electric Mfg. Co., 13 NLRB 448.

100. 29 USCA (1947 Supp.) Sec. 158(3). The amended Act, as noted elsewhere, outlaws the closed shop but permits a union shop under certain conditions. 29 USCA (1947, Supp.) Sec. 158(a)(3).

101. American Products Co., 34 NLRB 442.

102. West Texas Utilities Co., 51 NLRB 269.

103. Kilgore Mfg. Co., 49 NLRB 992.

104. Texarkana Bus Co., 26 NLRB 582; See also Cook Coffee Co., 22 NLRB 967.

105. NLRB v. Fulton Bag & Cotton Mills, 180 F. (2d) 68.

106. 29 USCA Sec. 158(3). The following principles were established by the Board under the Wagner Act in connection with the closed shop:

Where an employer discharges an employee pursuant to the provisions of a valid closed shop contract, with knowledge that the contracting union has demanded the discharge because of the employee's activities on behalf of a rival union prior to the execution of the contract, the employer commits an unfair labor practice. (Wallace Corp. v. NLRB, 323 U.S. 248.)

But when the discharge was made by the employer without knowledge that the contracting union demanded the discharge because of such activity, the Board did not find an unfair labor practice. (Spicer Manufacturing Corp. v. NLRB, 70 NLRB No. 5; Diamond T. Company, 64 NLRB 1225).

The Board said that under certain circumstances the employer was under duty to inquire into the factors which motivate the contracting union to expel the employee. The employer's failure to perform the duty made him liable for the discharge. (Diamond T. Company, 64 NLRB 1225.) The circumstances and facts under which such duty devolved upon the employer remained undefined, except in the case of maintenance-of-membership clause, when the employer appeared to be under the duty of inquiry. Thus, if the employer discharged, upon demand of the contracting union, employees who withdrew from the union during the "escape" period usually provided in the maintenance-of-membership provision, he violated the Act. (Baker & Company, 68 NLRB No. 110).

The discharge of employees, exempt from the coverage of a maintenance-of-membership contract, was illegal when it was the result of the demand of the contracting union based on activities of the employees for a rival union. (Eureka Vacuum Cleaner Co., 69 NLRB No. 107.)

Before acquiescing in the contracting union's demand for the *discharge* of an employee pursuant to the terms of the contract, the employer had to bear in mind the factors mentioned above and be sure that the contract provides for a closed shop. Essential elements of the closed shop provision are that the employee must become a member of the union and retain such membership during the contract term as a condition of employment. A provision that upon completion of a probationary period the employee shall make application for membership in the contracting union does not alone establish a closed shop, and a discharge of an employee for failure to make the application was illegal. (Iron Fireman Corp., 69 NLRB No. 4.)

Similarly, a provision in a contract that the employer will suggest to new employees that they join the contracting union did not establish a closed shop and a discharge for failure to join the union is an unfair labor practice. (Burroughs-Wellcome Co., Inc., 68 NLRB 26.)

The employer had to be careful to consider whether the employee had complied with the membership requirements of the contract because if he had, the discharge was illegal despite the demand of the contracting union. (Federal Engineering Co. Inc., 60 NLRB 592, enforced in 153 F. (2d) 233.)

107. 29 USCA (1947, Supp.) Sec. 158(a) (3).

108. 29 USCA (1947, Supp.) Sec. 158(a) (3) (ii).

109. 29 USCA (1947, Supp.) Sec. 158(a) (3) (i).

110. 29 USCA (1947, Supp.) Sec. 158(a) (3) (A) (B).

111. 29 USCA (1947, Supp.) Sec. 160(c).

112. 29 USCA (1947, Supp.) Sec. 158(b) (2).

113. 29 USCA (1947, Supp.) Sec. 158(b) (5).

114. 29 USCA (1947, Supp.) Sec. 158(a) (4).

115. The Kramer Company, 29 NLRB 921; Northwestern Mutual Fire Association, 46 NLRB 825; Burnside Steel Foundry, 69 NLRB No. 12

116. Richmond Home Telephone Co., 70 NLRB 452.

117. Fred P. Weissman Co., 71 NLRB 147.

118. The principles applicable to discharges are similarly applicable to transfers and demotions. The discrimination prohibited by the Act relates to "hire or tenure of employment or any term or condition of employment."

119. Peyton Packing Company, 49 NLRB 828 at 843.

120. American Bakeries Co., 51 NLRB 937.

121. Special Tools & Machinery Co., 64 NLRB No. 236.

122. See note 118.

123. See note 92.

124. See discussion of "Supervisory Employees," Part Three, Chapter I.

125. 29 USCA (1947, Supp.) Sec. 158(c).

126. In NLRB v. Virginia Electric & Power Co., 314 U.S. 469 at page 479, the Court said it was difficult to sustain a finding of illegality where the employer "set forth the right of the employees to do as they pleased without fear of retaliation by the Company." In NLRB v. American Tube Bending Co., 134 F. (2d) 993, 995 (cert. denied 320 U.S. 768) the Court held the following type of employer utterances protected by the free speech privilege: "The respondent professed itself willing to abide loyally by the results of the election, but did not conceal, though perhaps it made some effort to disguise, its preferences for no union whatever. But there was no intimation of reprisal against those who thought otherwise; quite the opposite. The most that can be gathered from them was an argument, temperate in form, that a union would be against the employees' interests as well as the employer's, and that the continued prosperity of the company depended on going on as they had been." Mr. Justice Jackson, concurring in a separate opinion in Thomas v. Collins, 323 U.S. 516 at page 547, said, "Free speech on both sides and for every faction on any side of the labor relation is to me a constitutional and useful right. Labor is free to turn its publicity on any

labor oppression, substandard wages, employer unfairness, or objectionable working conditions. The employer, too, should be free to answer, and to turn publicity on the records of the leaders or the unions which seek the confidence of his men. And if the employees or organizers associate violence or other offense against the laws with labor's free speech, or if the employer's speech is associated with discriminatory discharges or intimidation, the constitutional remedy would be to stop the evil, but permit the speech, if the two are separable; and only rarely and when they are inseparable to stop or punish speech or publication." See also Trojan Powder Co. v. NLRB, 135 F. (2d) 337, cert. denied 320 U.S. 768; Elastic Stop Nut Corp. v. NLRB, 142 F. (2d) 371, cert. den. 323 U.S. 722.

Employers' statements or utterances which were coercive standing alone or in their context have been held to be unfair labor practices. NLRB v. Crown Can Co., 138 F. (2d) 263; NLRB v. Glenn L. Martin-Nebraska Co., 141 F. (2d) 371; NLRB v. Lettie Lee Inc., 140 F. (2d) 243.

The Board took into consideration not only the employer's utterances by way of speech or letter but also his course of conduct with respect to unionization. American Laundry Machine Co., 57 NLRB 25; Big Lake Oil Co., 56 NLRB 684; Mississippi Valley Structural Steel Co., 56 NLRB 485; Van Raalte Company Inc., 55 NLRB 146. In M. & T. Stevens & Sons Co., 68 NLRB No. 30, the NLRB held an employer's statement in response to inquiries by employees, that he would not enter into a closed shop contract, was not coercive *per se.*

Since, under the amended Act, expressions cannot be evidence of unfair labor practice, the Board's prior theory of holding violative of the Act, on the basis of the total course of conduct of the employer, expressions which in themselves were not coercive may no longer appear applicable. The Conference Committee Report states with respect to the new provision concerning expressions:

"The practice which the Board has had in the past of using speeches and publications of employers concerning labor organizations and collective bargaining arrangements as evidence, no matter how irrelevant or immaterial, that some later act of the employer had an illegal purpose gave rise to the necessity for this change in the law. The purpose is to protect the right of free speech when what the employer says or writes is not of a threatening nature or does not promise a prohibited favorable discrimination" (House Report 510, 80th Congress, p. 45).

The protection of the new free speech provision would appear to be applicable to unfair labor practices of unions as well as employers.

127. See discussion and cases cited in note 126. In Oval Wood Dish Corp., 62 NLRB 1129, the Board said:

"By such statements, notices, letters and speeches, the respondent expressed a preference to deal directly with its employees rather than through an outside organization. However, the respondent made no threat of any sort and coupled its statement of preference with clear expressions assuring the employees that the respondent would not resort to reprisal to retaliate against any exercise of any right guaranteed in the Act. . . . Such conduct falls within the constitutional guaranty of free speech and is not a violation of the Act. We agree therefore with the Trial Examiner that the respondent's pre-election announcements . . . standing alone were privileged. . . . We shall, therefore, dismiss the complaint in its entirety."

128. NLRB v. Virginia Electric & Power Co., 314 U.S. 469.

129. See note 126. The position of the Board since the court decision on the free speech issue appears in note 127. In Agar Packing & Provision Corp., 58 NLRB 738, the Board said, "We recognize the right of an employer to answer charges directed against him by a labor organization and, under certain circumstances, to bring to the attention of his employees facts concerning that organization of which he believes the employees should be apprised. . . . However, the existence of that right does not serve as a license to engage in activities which have the effect of interfering with, restraining or coercing his employees in the exercise of rights guaranteed in Section 7, and if the employer's conduct, reasonably construed produces such an effect, it is proscribed by the Act." See the separate opinion of Board Member Reilly concurring in part and dissenting in part.

130. Agar Packing & Provision Co., 81 NLRB No. 199.

131. The employer may indicate to the employees his liberal labor policy, but in doing so he must also indicate that such liberal policies will not be withdrawn if unionization of his employees occurs. NLRB v. Peter J. Schweitzer Inc., 144 F. (2d) 520.

132. The employer's course of conduct with respect to unionization will affect the construction placed upon his utterances by letter or speech. See discussion and cases cited in note 126. Thus, an employer statement while it is proper on its face may be held illegal in view of the circumstances in which it is made, as where the employer is engaged in antiunion campaign.

133. Western Land Roller Co., 45 NLRB 638.

134. The employer is held responsible for the acts of his supervisors and the acts of those persons whom the employees may reasonably believe were acting on his behalf or represented his attitude. International Association of Machinists v. NLRB, 311 U.S. 72; NLRB v. Link-Belt Co., 311 U.S. 584. In the latter case, the Court said, "As we indicated in International Association of Machinists v. National Labor Relations Board, *supra*, the strict rules of *respondeat superior* are not applicable to such a situation. If the words or deeds of the supervisory employees, taken in their setting, were reasonably likely to have restrained the employees' choice and if the employer may fairly be said to have been responsible for them, they are a proper basis for the conclusion that the employer did interfere. If the employees 'would have just cause to believe that solicitors professedly for a labor organization were acting for and on behalf of the management, the Board would be justified in concluding that they did not have the complete and unhampered freedom of choice which the Act contemplates.' " See NLRB v. Moench Tanning Co., 121 F. (2d) 951; NLRB v. Cities Service Oil Co., 129 F. (2d) 933. However, sporadic and isolated acts are insufficient. NLRB v. Mathieson Alkali Works, 114 F. (2d) 796; Quaker State Oil Refining Corp. v. NLRB, 119 F. (2d) 631. Employer's instructions to supervisors not to interfere with unionization of his employees are not sufficient to relieve him of liability for their conduct in the absence of publication to all employees. F. W. Woolworth Co. v. NLRB, 121 F. (2d) 658. In Fulton Bag & Cotton Mills, 75

134. (*Cont.*)
NLRB No. 111, 21 LRRM 1124, the Board said:

"While the Board has, on occasion, held that the posting of a notice will relieve an employer from responsibility for acts of interference on the part of its supervisory personnel (Matter of Midwest Piping and Supply Co., Inc., 63 NLRB 1060 (17 LRR Man. 40), it is to be observed that the letter, regarded as a notice in the present instance, contains no reference to any disavowal by the respondent of the past unneutral conduct on the part of its supervisors; neither does it specifically disclaim responsibility on the part of the respondent for any future acts of like nature by such supervisors. The Board has held ineffectual to relieve an employer from responsibility for the unneutral acts of a supervisor, a notice of neutrality which contained no specific disavowal of partisan conduct by a supervisor, as would normally have dissipated the effects of his activities." (Matter of Parkchester Machine Corporation, 72 NLRB 1410 (19 LRRM 1280)).

The act as amended makes the usual rules of agency applicable to the question of the employer's responsibilities for the acts of his supervisor. See discussion of this problem under "Employer-Employee Relationship," Part Three, Introduction.

135. John H. Harland Co., 45 NLRB 76.

136. See notes 126, 127 and 129.

137. C. Pappas Co., Inc., 82 NLRB No. 90.

138. Burns Brick Co., 80 NLRB No. 85.

139. Gluck Bros., 81 NLRB No. 62.

140. U. S. Trailer Mfg. Co., 82 NLRB No. 11.

141. Sunray Oil Corporation, 82 NLRB No. 116.

142. Goodyear Footwear Corp., 80 NLRB No. 126.

143. Agar Packing & Provision Corp., 81 NLRB No. 199.

144. Mylan-Sparta Co. Inc., 78 NLRB No. 161.

145. Cookeville Shirt Co., 79 NLRB No. 88.

146. Columbia Broadcasting System, Inc., 70 NLRB No. 142. Employer statements to supervisory employees who are union members receive a somewhat different treatment than the same statements to nonsupervisory employees. Richmond Home Telephone Co., 70 NLRB No. 37; B. F. Goodrich Company, 64 NLRB 794.

147. Clark Bros. Co., Inc., 70 NLRB 802.

148. NLRB v. Clark Bros. Co., 163 F. (2d) 373, 376.

149. NLRB v. Montgomery Ward & Co., 157 F. (2d) 486.

150. NLRB v. Montgomery Ward & Co., 157 F. (2d) 486. The court said (at pages 498, 499):

"It is argued that compulsory attendance at the meetings was a species of coercion. The employees attended in groups and certainly employers have the right to meet their employees for discussion and presentation of matters of policy of mutual interests. In the instant case the employees were paid for the time spent at the meetings. The First Amendment is concerned with the freedom of thought and expression of the speaker or writer, not with the conditions under which the auditor or listener receives the message. One need not, as a condition precedent to his right of free speech under the First Amendment, secure permission of his auditor. The First Amendment does not purport to protect the right of privacy, nor does it require that the audience shall have volunteered to listen. Thus, in Martin v. City of Struthers, 319 U.S. 141, 63 S. Ct. 862, 82 L. Ed. 1313, the Supreme Court held invalid a city ordinance prohibiting the house to house distribution of handbills, although the validity of the ordinance was urged as a protection to the unwilling householder's right of privacy. It appeared in that case that handbills distributed by Martin and his fellow Jehovah's Witnesses were forced upon unwilling recipients, but the Supreme Court held the ordinance violative of the First Amendment. Speech is very frequently invoked as a means to persuade those who do not agree with the speaker and may not even wish to hear him. It was held in Thornhill v. Alabama, 310 U.S. 88, and American Federation of Labor v. Swing, 312 U.S. 321, that picketing was within the protection of the First Amendment and the protection is not lost by the misconduct or incivility of the speaker. Cafeteria Employees Union v. Angelos, 320 U.S. 293. In asking its employees to attend a meeting on company time, at which affairs of mutual interest to respondent and the employees were to be discussed, respondent was employing a convenient means of communicating with its employees. The employees were paid for attending and were not inconvenienced in the least. If they were influenced against their will by the arguments presented, this was a legitimate consequence of free speech and presumably one of its purposes. Free speech is not to be limited to ineffective speech. As said by the Supreme Court in Thornhill v. Alamaba, *supra:*

'Every expression of opinion on matters that are important has the potentiality of inducing action in the interests of one rather than another group in society. But the group in power at any moment may not impose penal sanctions on peaceful and truthful discussion of matters of public interest merely on a showing that others may thereby be persuaded to take action inconsistent with its interests.'

"The occasion on which the employer elects to utter his thoughts is not to be considered as an element of coercion. He is as free to speak at one time as another. NLRB v. American Tube Bending Co., 2 Cir., 134 F. (2d) 993; Continental Box Co. v. NLRB, 5 Cir., 113 F. (2d) 93; NLRB v. West Kentucky Coal Co., 6 Cir., 152 F. (2d) 198."

151. Babcock & Wilcox Co., 77 NLRB No. 96.

152. NLRB v. Montgomery Ward & Co., 157 F. (2d) 486, 498, where the court said:

"These few illustrations characterize the defamatory and inflammatory character of the publication which was the organ of the union, expressing its hostility and animosity toward respondent during the period referred to. Although these attacks are not considered by the Board, we think they furnish a setting which indicates that respondent was meeting and joining issue before its own employees with those who were assailing it. It confessedly had a right to defend its reputation, to speak for itself before its employees whose loyalty it had a right to ask, and the right to prove itself worthy of that loyalty. It was not required to stand mute."

Humble Oil & Refining Co. v. NLRB, 113 F. (2d) 85, where the court said:

"We do not think that the law, any more than common sense, would require the employer to stand as a sheep before the shearers dumb, not opening his mouth. The right of free speech touching his own interests was involved."

153. NLRB v. Montgomery Ward & Co., 157 F. (2d) 486, 499, 500, where the Court said:

"The Board criticizes Barr's remarks for their declared opposition to the closed shop, and it is urged that this amounted to serving notice upon the union that respondent would not bargain 'respecting this vital subject.' The only reference to the closed shop in the National Labor Relations Act is to the effect that nothing in the Act should preclude an employer from making an agreement with a labor organization, with certain exceptions not here pertinent, requiring as a condition of employment membership in a particular union, if such union is the representative of the employees as provided in the Act. In the remarks of Barr there was no refusal to bargain collectively with the bargaining agent when designated, and the statute merely authorizes but does not purport to compel the employer to recognize the closed shop. The most that can be said is that bargaining for a closed shop or for a signed agreement with the employer is a frequent subject of negotiation between employer and employees. There is no indication that there would be a refusal to negotiate, but on the contrary the right of organization and of collective bargaining by the employees is definitely and expressly recognized in Barr's remarks. Again we recur to the declaration found in NLRB v. Virginia Electric & Power Co., 314 U.S. 469, 62 S. Ct. 344, 348, 86 L. Ed. 348, that the Act does not enjoin the employer 'from expressing its views on labor policies and problems.' Reference to a policy opposed to the closed shop was not, we think, improper and it has the implied approval of other courts. Continental Box Co. v. NLRB, *supra;* NLRB v. Blossom Products Corp., 3 Cir., 121 F. (2d) 260; NLRB v. American Tube Bending Co., *supra.*"

154. M. T. Stevens & Sons Co., 68 NLRB No. 30.

155. NLRB v. Laister-Kauffman, 144 F. (2d) 9; Peter J. Schweitzer v. NLRB, 144 F. (2d) 520.

156. NLRB v. J. L. Brandeis & Son, 145 F. (2d) 556; NLRB v. American Pearl Button Co., 149 F. (2d) 311.

157. Big Lake Oil Co. v. NLRB, 146 F. (2d) 967.

158. By specific provision, the National Labor Relations Act cannot be construed "to interfere with or impede or diminish in any way the right to strike." 29 USCA 1947, Supp.) Sec. 163.

159. Before an injunction can be issued in a controversy "involving or growing out of" a labor dispute, the Federal Courts must find that unlawful acts have been threatened or will be committed. 29 USCA Sec. 107. The applicable statute is known as the Norris-LaGuardia Act and similar enactments have been adopted by many states. See 29 USCA Sections 101–115. It is significant to note that in Carpenters Union v. Ritter's Cafe, 315 U.S. 722, 725, the Court said, "The constitutional right to communicate peaceably to the public the facts of a legitimate dispute is not lost merely because a labor dispute is involved, Thornhill v. Alabama, 310 U.S. 88, or because the communication takes the form of picketing, even when the communication does not concern a dispute between an employer and those directly employed by him. American Federation of Labor v. Swing, 312 U.S. 321. But the circumstance that a labor dispute is the occasion of exercising freedom of expression does not give that freedom any greater constitutional sanction or render it completely inviolable." See also Senn v. Tile Layers Protective Union, 301 U.S. 468. Cf. Bakery Drivers Local v. Wohl, 315 U.S. 769.

160. Opera on Tour, Inc. v. Weber, 285 N.Y. 348.

161. See U.S. v. Hutcheson, 312 U.S. 219. However in Allan Bradley Co. v. Local Union No. 3, 325 U.S. 797, the court said: "United States v. Hutcheson, 312 U.S. 219, declared that the Sherman, Clayton and Norris-LaGuardia Acts must be jointly considered in arriving at a conclusion as to whether labor union activities run counter to the Anti-trust legislation. Conduct which they permit is not to be declared a violation of federal law. That decision held that the doctrine of the Duplex and Bedford cases was inconsistent with the congressional policy set out in the three 'interlacing statutes.'

"The result of all this is that we have two declared congressional policies which it is our responsibility to try to reconcile. The one seeks to preserve a competitive business economy; the other to preserve the rights of labor to organize to better its conditions through the agency of collec-

tive bargaining. We must determine here how far Congress intended activities under one of these policies to neutralize the results envisioned by the other.

"Aside from the fact that the labor union here acted in combination with the contractors and manufacturers, the means it adopted to contribute to the combination's purpose fall squarely within the 'specified acts' declared by §20 not to be violations of federal law. For the union's contribution to the trade boycott was accomplished through threats that unless their employers brought their goods from local manufacturers the union laborers would terminate the 'relation of employment' with them and cease to perform 'work or labor' for them; and through their 'recommending, advising, or persuading others by peaceful and lawful means' not to 'patronize' sellers of the boycotted electrical equipment. Consequently, under our holdings in the Hutcheson case and other cases which followed it, had there been no union-contractor-manufacturer combination the union's actions here, coming as they did within the exemptions of the Clayton and Norris-LaGuardia Acts, would not have been violations of the Sherman Act. We pass to the question of whether unions can with impunity aid and abet business men who are violating the Act. . . .

"It must be remembered that the exemptions granted the unions were special exceptions to a general legislative plan. The primary objective of all the Anti-trust legislation has been to preserve business competition and to proscribe business monopoly. It would be a surprising thing if Congress, in order to prevent a misapplication of that legislation to labor unions, had bestowed upon such unions complete and unreviewable authority to aid business groups to frustrate its primary objective. For if business groups, by combining with labor unions, can fix prices and divide up markets, it was little more than a futile gesture for Congress to prohibit price fixing by business groups themselves. Seldom, if ever, has it been claimed before, that by permitting labor unions to carry on their own activities, Congress intended completely to abdicate its constitutional power to regulate interstate commerce and to empower interested business groups to shift our society from a competitive to a monopolistic economy. Finding no purpose of Congress to immunize labor unions who aid and abet manufacturers and traders in violating the Sherman Act, we hold that the district court correctly concluded that the respondents had violated the Act."

162. Harper v. Holcherl, 153 Fla. 29, 14 So. (2d) 179, 12 LRRM 799.

163. In Goldfinger v. Feintuch, 276 N.Y. 281, the Court pointed out the Rules generally applicable as follows (p. 285) "As between an employer and an employee the right of a union to picket peacefully is generally conceded. Its purpose must be to persuade, not to intimidate." See also Senn v. Tile Layers Protective Association, 301 U.S. 468; Carpenters Union v. Ritter's Cafe, 315 U.S. 722.

164. Auburn Draying Co. v. Wardwell, 227 N.Y. 1; See Loew's Inc. v. Basson, 46 F. Supp. 66 (D.C. S.D. N.Y.).

165. 29 USCA Sec. 113.

166. 29 USCA Sec. 113(c).

167. New Nero Alliance v. Sanitary Grocery Co., 303 U.S. 552.

168. U.S. v. United Mine Workers of America, 330 U.S. 258.

169. Schivera v. Long Island Lighting Co., 296 N.Y. 26.

170. Gipps v. Osman, 170 Misc. 53, affirmed 250 App. Div. 789; Lyons v. Meyerson, 18 N.Y.S. (2d) 363, affirmed 260 App. Div. 863; Schwartz v. Fish Workers Union, 170 Misc. 566.

171. Bakery Drivers Local etc. v. Wohl, 315 U.S. 769.

172. Florsheim Shoe Store Co. v. Shoe Salesmen's Union, 288 N.Y. 188; Sachs Quality Furniture v. Hensley, 269 App. Div. 264; The Euclid Candy Co. v. Summa, 174 Misc. 19, affirmed 259 App. Div. 1081.

173. Sachs Quality Furniture v. Hensley, 269 App. Div. 264, 267, 268, where the Court said:

"We agree with the Special Term to the extent that it refused to restrain all picketing by the defendant. Notwithstanding the determination of the Labor Relations Board that Sachs Employees Association is a *bona fide* labor organization within the meaning of subdivision 5 of section 701 of the New York State Labor Relations Act (Labor Law, Art. 20), the defendant, a rival union, may, in the exercise of the right of free speech, by peaceful and truthful methods of picketing, attempt to win to itself the allegiance of members of the Association who are employees of the plaintiff. (Bakery Drivers Local v. Wohl, 315 U.S. 769; Thornhill v. Alabama, 310 U.S. 88; Carlson v. California, 310 U.S. 106; Senn v. Tile Layers Union, 301 U.S. 468; A. F. of L. v. Swing, 312 U.S. 321).

"The constitutional right of free speech, however, does not include the right to falsify the facts by means of the signs carried by pickets, which tended to create the impression the plaintiff in violation of law (New York State Labor Relations Act, Sec. 704, subd. 3) maintained a 'company union' whose members it employed. At least for the purpose of this motion for a temporary injunction, the determination of the Labor Relations Board, that Sachs Employees Association is not a company union and that it is the exclusive bargaining agent for the employees, must be accepted as correct. The statement on the signs carried by the defendant's pickets which implies that the Association is a 'company union' although found by the Labor Board not to be company-dominated; the statement that the plaintiff 're-fuses' to recognize the defendant union although by the determination of the Labor Board it is prohibited from doing otherwise (New York State Labor Relations Act, Sec. 705); and the statement, made without qualification, that 'employees of Sachs Quality Furniture, Inc. are on strike,' although less than 10% of such employees are striking, especially when considered in combination with each other, convey a wholly false impression which is detrimental to the plaintiff. (Dinny & Robbins, Inc., v. Davis, 290 N.Y. 101, 104, 105.) We do not mean to hold that the defendant must on its signs set forth all the facts relating to the proceedings before the Labor Board. We only hold that it must abstain from statements which must necessarily result in deception of the public.

"We do not consider, however, that these distortions of the truth have attained such dimensions as to require that all picketing be enjoined. (Cafeteria Union v. Angelos, 320 U.S. 293.) We think full justice may be accomplished by a temporary injunction restraining *pendente lite* the use of signs which misrepresent the facts and misrepresent, in particular, the situation resulting from the determination of the Labor Relations

173. *(Cont.)*
Board in which Sachs Employees Association was certified as the exclusive bargaining agent for the plaintiff's employees. We infringe no right of either party by enjoining statements which are false and refusing to enjoin such peaceful and truthful picketing as may ensue.

"On account of the determination of the Labor Board, no 'labor dispute' existed between the parties within the meaning of section 876-a of the Civil Practice Act, which would prevent the granting of an injunction *pendente lite* without establishing compliance with the conditions therein set forth. (Florsheim Shoe Store Co. v. Shoe Salesmen's Union, 288 N.Y. 188.)"

174. 325 U.S. 797.

175. United States v. B. Goedde (D.C., E. D. Ill.) 40 F. Supp. 523.

176. U.S. v. Hutcheson, 312 U.S. 219.

177. Hunt v. Crumboch, 325 U.S. 821.

178. Swartz v. Forward Ass'n., 41 F. Supp. 294.

179. International Ass'n. of Bridge, Structural & Ornamental Iron Workers v. Pauly Jail Building Co., 118 F. (2d) 615, cert. den. 314 U.S. 639.

180. Columbia River Packers Association v. Hinton, 315 U.S. 143.

181. In U.S. v. Hutcheson, 312 U.S. 219, the Court said, "So long as the union acts in its self-interest and does not combine with non-labor groups, the licit and the illicit under Sec. 20 are not to be distinguished by any judgment regarding the wisdom or unwisdom, the rightness or wrongness, the selfishness or unselfishness of the end of which the particular union activities are the means." The Ninth Circuit Court of Appeals in Lumber Products Association v. U.S., 144 F. (2d) 546, sustained convictions against union members where, by agreement between labor and employer groups, out of state sales of certain articles were effectively restricted. In Allen Bradley & Co. v. Local Union No. 3, 325 U.S. 797, the union and employer groups combined, thereby tainting with illegality acts which if engaged in by the union alone, would be legal.

182. See Loew's Inc. v. Basson, 46 F. Supp. 66, 10 LRRM 880.

183. Florsheim Shoe Store Co. v. Shoe Salesmen's Union. (N.Y. Court of Appeals) 288 N.Y. 188; National Labor Relations Act, Sec. 8(b)(4)(c); Oppenheim Collins & Co., 83 NLRB No. 47.

184. Stillwell Theatre Inc. v. Kaplan, 259 N.Y. 405, cert. den. 288 U.S. 606.

185. NLRB v. Fansteel Metallurgical Corp., 306 U.S. 240. Compare:—Drivers Union v. Meadowmoor Co., 312 U.S. 287; Senn v. Tile Layers Union, 301 U.S. 468; AFL v. Swing, 312 U.S. 321; Bakery Drivers Local, v. Wohl, 315 U.S. 769; Cafeteria Employees Union v. Angelos, 320 U.S. 293.

186. El Paso Electric Co., 13 NLRB 213; NLRB v. Stackpole Carbon Co., 105 F. (2d) 167; Ohio Calcium Co., 34 NLRB 917; Firestone Tire & Rubber Co., 22 NLRB 580.

187. Milk Wagon Drivers Union v. Meadowmoor Dairies Inc., 312 U.S. 287; May's Furs & Ready-to-Wear Inc. v. Bauer, 255 App. Div. (N.Y.) 643, modified 282 N.Y. 331; Kauffman v. Amalgamated Meat Cutters, Calif. Super. Ct. (1942) 10 LRRM 555; Roth v. Local Union No. 1460, Ind. Sup. Ct. 1939, 5 LRRM 966; Hoffman's Vegetarian Restaurant v. Lee, 170 Misc. 815, 10 N.Y. Supp. (2d) 287; Italian Actors Union v. Caini, N.Y., Sup. Ct. (1939) 4 LRRM 877; R. A. White Co. v. Murphy (Mass.), 38 N.E. (2d) 685.

188. Bakery & Pastry Drivers & Helpers Local 802 v. Wohl, 315 U.S. 769.

189. Bakery & Pastry Drivers & Helpers Local 802 v. Wohl, 315 U.S. 769.

190. Carpenters and Joiners Union of America, Local 213 v. Ritter's Cafe, 315 U.S. 722.

191. Carnegie-Illinois Steel Corp. v. U.S.W.A., 353 Pa. 420.

192. Peyton Packing Company, 49 NLRB 828; NLRB v. Peyton Packing Company, 142 F. (2d) 1009; Carter Carburetor Corp. v. NLRB, 140 F. (2d) 714; NLRB v. Denver Tent and Awning Co., 138 F. (2d) 410.

193. In Republic Aviation Corp. v. NLRB, 324 U.S. 793 and NLRB v. Le. Tourneau Co., 324 U.S. 793, the Supreme Court sustained the NLRB holding that prohibiting solicitation for union membership or distribution of union literature on the employer's property during the employees' own time was illegal even in the absence of discriminatory motive for, or application of, such rules. The court approved the Board's principle that such rules of an employer are presumptively illegal and absent special circumstances they constitute unlawful interference with employee's rights under the Wagner Act. The presumption is, however, rebuttable by evidence showing the need for the rule.

194. NLRB v. Cities Service Oil Co., 122 F. (2d) 149. The bargaining agent has been held entitled to have its representative board the employer's vessels for the purpose of negotiating grievances, collecting dues, and distributing union literature to union members. Richfield Oil Corporation v. NLRB, 143 F. (2d) 860.

195. Management is obligated to bargain collectively only when the union at the time of its bargaining demand represents a majority of the employees in an appropriate bargaining unit. 29 USCA (1947, Supp.) Sec. 158(a) (5). The union must convey to the employer its willingness to bargain before the obligation becomes absolute. NLRB v. Columbian Enameling and Stamping Co., 306 U.S. 292.

196. Douds v. Local 1250, Retail, Wholesale Department Store Union, 173 F. (2d) 764 (USCA2), rehearing denied April 26, 1949.

196a. Artcraft Hosiery Co., 78 NLRB 333; Continental Southern Corp., 83 NLRB 668.

197. The Board's policy with respect to agreements settling unfair labor practice charges has been sustained by the Supreme Court. Wallace Corp. v. NLRB, 323 U.S. 248. In that case the Supreme Court said (at pages 253–255):

"To prevent disputes like the one here involved, the Board has from the very beginning encouraged compromises and settlements. The purpose of such attempted settlements has been to end labor disputes, and so far as possible to extinguish all the elements giving rise to them. The attempted settlement here wholly failed to prevent the wholesale discard of employees as a result of their union affiliations. The purpose of the settlement was thereby defeated. Upon this failure, when the Board's further action was properly invoked, it became its duty to take fresh steps to prevent frustration of the Act. To meet such situations the Board has established as a working rule the principle that it ordinarily will respect the terms of a settlement agreement approved by it. It has consistently gone behind such agree-ments, however, where subsequent events have demonstrated that efforts at adjustment have failed to accomplish their purpose, or where there has been a subsequent unfair labor practice. We think this rule adopted by the Board is appropriate to accomplish the Act's purpose with fairness to all concerned. Consequently, since the Board correctly found that there was a subsequent unfair labor practice, it was justified in considering evidence as to petitioner's conduct, both before and after the settlement and certification."

198. The Solvay Process Co. v. NLRB, 122 F. (2d) 993.

199. Consolidated Edison Co. v. NLRB, 305 U.S. 197; NLRB v. Columbian Enameling & Stamping Co., 306 U.S. 292, 29 USCA (1947, Supp.) Sec. 160(c) (e).

200. NLRB v. Phelps, 136 F. (2d) 562 (CCA 5).

201. Firestone Tire & Rubber Co., 58 NLRB 630.

202. Consolidated Edison Co. v. NLRB, 305 U.S. 197, 235, 236.

203. Republic Steel Corp. v. NLRB, 311 U.S. 7.

204. NLRB v. Cassoff, 139 F. (2d) 397; Virginia Electric & Power Co. v. NLRB, 319 U.S. 533.

205. Kresge Dept. Store, 77 NLRB No. 25, 21 LRRM 1345, 1347.

206. T. C. King Pipe Co., 74 NLRB 468; Foreman & Clark, 74 NLRB 77; Martinolich Shipbuilding Co., 73 NLRB 1304.

207. Waterfront Employers Association of the Pacific Coast, 71 NLRB 80, 71 NLRB 121.

208. California Metal Trades Association, 72 NLRB 624.

209. Canada Dry Ginger Ale Inc., 73 NLRB 460; General Baking Company, 73 NLRB 44.

210. The rights and obligations of the employer were summarized by the Board in Montgomery Ward & Co., Inc., 39 NLRB 229, 240, as follows:

"The duty imposed by the Act is not limited to the recognition of the representatives of the employees, to the mere meeting and discussion of terms with them, or to the formal expression of a willingness to enter into contractual arrangements. The Board and the courts on frequent occasion have indicated that the difference between the semblance and the

210. (*Cont.*)
substance of collective bargaining may be tested by the extent to which the parties evidence a sincere purpose to explore the total situation and find a basis for agreement. The employer must in a very real sense undertake to discover with the Union such common ground as may exist between the parties. On the other hand, satisfaction of the statutory obligation does not require an employer to capitulate to the demands addressed to him."

The Board has held the employer's refusal to accede to the union's demands for preferential shop, seniority and arbitration, was not an unfair labor practice under the circumstances. M. T. Stevens & Sons Co., 68 NLRB No. 30.

211. See M. T. Stevens & Sons Co., 68 NLRB No. 30; Tampa Electric Co., 56 NLRB 1270; Cameron Can Machinery, 57 NLRB 1768.

212. Highland Park Mfg. Co., 12 NLRB 1238, enforced in NLRB v. Highland Park Mfg. Co., 110 F. (2d) 632; Art Metals Construction Co. v. NLRB, 110 F. (2d) 148.

213. In J. R. Todd d/b/a Central Minerals Company, 59 NLRB 757, the Board said: "However, we wish to point out, *obiter*, that, absent the factors comprising the total situation as outlined above, we would not have found that the respondent's failure to make detailed and specific counterproposals in itself constituted bad faith negotiations, for the union's ultimatum—'We have one contract' and 'you can take it or leave it'— would have relieved the respondent of that duty since the union's position made it clear that specific counterproposals would be unavailing."

214. Montgomery Ward & Co. Inc., 39 NLRB 229. The Board pointed out (p. 241): "It appears clear that but for the honestly taken but irreconcilable positions of the parties in regard to the preferential shop, seniority and arbitration, the negotiations would have resulted in a mutually satisfactory agreement concerning wages, hours and other terms and conditions of employment."

215. Killefer Mfg. Corp., 22 NLRB 484.

216. American Products Inc., 34 NLRB 442.

217. NLRB v. Whittier Mills, 123 F. (2d) 725 (CCA 5).

218. NLRB v. Columbian Enameling & Stamping Co., 306 U.S. 292.

219. See Chester Ward, The Mechanics of Collective Bargaining: 53 Harvard Law Review, 754.

220. H. J. Heinz Co. v. NLRB, 311 U.S. 514.

221. 29 USCA (1947, Supp.) Sec. 158 (d).

222. NLRB v. Mackay Radio & Telegraph Co., 304 U.S. 333.

223. Solvay Process Co., 47 NLRB 1113.

224. Jacob H. Klotz, 13 NLRB 746, 29 NLRB 14.

225. See Williams Motor Co., 31 NLRB 715, enforced in 128 F. (2d) 960. Cf. NLRB v. Cape County Milling Co., 140 F. (2d) 543 where there was a temporary shutdown for anti-union reasons and the employer was required to reinstate the locked out employees. The Court of Appeals said that the Williams Motor Co. case presented a distinguishable situation.

226. 29 USCA (1947, Supp.) Sec. 158 (b), 160(c).

227. Wine, Liquor & Distillery Workers Union, Local 1, etc., 78 NLRB No. 61.

228. NLRB v. Indiana & Michigan Electric Co., 318 U.S. 9.

229. NLRB v. Fred P. Weissman & Co., 170 F. (2d) 952.

230. Seamprufe, Inc., 82 NLRB No. 106.

231. Seamprufe, Inc., 82 NLRB No. 106.

232. 29 USCA (1948, Supp.) Sec. 158(b).

233. Lincourt v. NLRB, 170 F. (2d) 306.

234. 29 USCA (1947, Supp.) Sec. 160(b).

235. 29 USCA (1947 Supp.) Sec. 152(1).

236. 29 USCA (1947, Supp. fol. Sec. 262) Secs. 203.2, 203.9.

237. 29 USCA (1947, Supp.) Sec. 160 (b).

238. 29 USCA (1947, Supp.) Sec. 159 (c) (b).

239. 29 USCA (1947, Supp.) Sec. 159 (f) (g) (h).

240. Herman Loewenstein Inc., 75 NLRB 377, 382, 21 LRRM 1032.

241. 29 USCA (1947, Supp.) Sec. 160 (1).

242. 29 USCA (1947, Supp.) Sec. 158 (b) (4) (A).

243. 29 USCA (1947, Supp.) Sec. 158 (b) (4) (B).

244. 29 USCA (1947, Supp.) Sec. 158 (b) (4) (C).

245. 29 USCA (1947, Supp.) Sec. 158 (b) (4) (D).

246. 29 USCA (1947, Supp.) Sec. 160 (l).

247. 29 USCA (1947, Supp.) Sec. 160(j).

248. Evans v. Int'l Typographical Union, 76 F. Supp. 881, sustaining the constitutionality of this provision.

249. 29 USCA (1947, Supp.) Sec. 158 (b) (4) proviso.

250. 29 USCA (1947, Supp.) Sec. 152 (3).

251. 29 USCA (1947, Supp.) Sec. 164; L. A. Young Spring and Wire Corp. v. NLRB, CCA D.C., 163 F. (2d) 905.

252. 29 USCA (1947, Supp.) Sec. 159 (b) (3).

253. C. V. Hill & Co., Inc., 76 NLRB No. 24, 21 LRRM 1172.

254. 29 USCA (1947, Supp.) Sec. 158 (a) (3), (b) (2).

255. 29 USCA (1947, Supp.) Sec. 158 (a) (3) (A).

256. 29 USCA (1947, Supp.) Sec. 158 (b) (2).

257. 29 USCA (1947, Supp.) Sec. 158 (5).

258. 29 USCA (1947, Supp.) Sec. 185 (c) (4), (d).

259. Compare 29 USCA (1947, Supp.) Sec. 9(c) prior to amendment and 29 USCA (1947, Supp.) Sec. 159(c) (1) as amended.

260. 29 USCA (1947, Supp.) Sec. 159 (c) (3).

261. 29 USCA (1947, Supp.) Sec. 159 (e) (3).

261a. Fruitvale Canning Co., 85 NLRB No. 122.

261b. Armco Drainage & Metal Products, Inc. Case No. 10-RM-22, issued December 13, 1948 (23 LRRM 1220), Administrative Ruling.

262. 29 USCA (1947, Supp.) Sec. 159 (a).

263. NLRB v. Hughes Tool Co., 147 F. (2d) 60.

264. 29 USCA (1947, Supp.) Sec. 158 (a) (3).

264a. C. Hager & Sons Hinge Manufacturing Company, 80 NLRB 163.

264b. Julius Resnick Inc., 86 NLRB No. 10.

264c. Lykens Hosiery Mills, 82 NLRB No. 125; Unique Art Manufacturing Co., 83 NLRB No. 173.

264d. Reading Hardware Corp., 85 NLRB No. 112; Shaefer Body Inc., 85 NLRB No. 33; Hazel-Atlas Glass Company, 85 NLRB No. 215.

264e. Bond Stores, Incorporated, 81 NLRB No. 180; Evans Milling Company, 85 NLRB No. 71.

264f. Lykens Hosiery Mills, 82 NLRB No. 125; Unique Art Manufacturing Co., 83 NLRB No. 173.

265. 29 USCA (1947, Supp.) Sec. 159 (e).

266. 29 USCA (1947, Supp.) Sec. 152 (2).

267. 29 USCA (1947, Supp.) Sec. 152 (13).

268. 29 USCA (1947, Supp.) Sec. 185.

269. 29 USCA (1947, Supp.) Sec. 186.

270. 29 USCA (1947, Supp.) Sec. 186 (c) (5) (A).

271. 29 USCA (1947, Supp.) Sec. 186 (c) (5) (B).

272. 29 USCA (1947, Supp.) Sec. 186 (c) (5) (C).

273. 29 USCA (1947, Supp.) Sec. 186 (g).

274. 29 USCA (1947, Supp.) Sec. 187.

274a. Amalgamated Association of Street, Electric Railway and Motor Coach Employees et al. v. Dixie Motor Coach Corp., 170 F. (2d) 902.

275. Amalgamated Utility Workers v. Consolidated Edison Co., 309 U.S. 261, National Licorice Company v. NLRB, 309 U.S. 350; Agwilines Inc., v. NLRB, 87 F. (2d) 146; AFL v. NLRB, 308 U.S. 401.

276. 29 USCA (1947, Supp.) Sec. 160 (a).

277. Textile Workers Union of America v. Amazon Cotton Mills, 76 F. Supp. 159, 165, 21 LRRM 2166, 2288.

278. *Ibid.*, note 277.

279. Amazon Cotton Mill Co. v. Textile Workers Union, 167 F. (2d) 183. To same effect: International Longshoremen's and Warehousemen's Union v. Sunset Line and Twine Co., 77 F. Supp. 119.

280. Dixie Motor Coach Corp. v. Amalgamated Association etc., 74 F. Supp. 952.

281. Amalgamated Association etc. v. Dixie Motor Coach Corp., 170 F. (2d) 902 (CCA 8).

282. 29 USCA (1947, Supp.) Sec. 187.

283. Gerry of California v. International Ladies' Garment Workers, Cal. Sup. Ct., Los Angeles County, January 13, 1948, 21 LRRM 2209; See also Gerry of California v. Superior Court in and for Los Angeles County, 194 Pac. (2d) 689, denying petition to compel the Superior Court to take jurisdiction.

284. Amazon Cotton Mills Co. v. Textile Workers, 167 F. (2d) 183, 187, 190.

285. 29 USCA (1947, Supp.) Sec. 158 (d).

286. 29 USCA (1947, Supp.) Sec. 158 (a) (5). In NLRB v. Highland Park Mfg. Co., 11 F. (2d) 632, 637, the Court described the employer's duty to bargain as follows: "The requirement to bargain collectively is not satisfied by mere discussion of grievances with employees' representatives. It contemplates the making of agreements between employer and employee which will serve as a working basis for the carrying on of the relationship. The act, it is true, does not require that the parties agree; but it does require that they negotiate in good faith with the view of reaching an agreement if possible; and mere discussion with the representatives of employees, with a fixed resolve on the part of the employer not to enter into any agreement with them, even as to matters as to which there is no disagreement, does not satisfy its provisions."

287. Appalachian Electric Power Co. v. NLRB, 140 F. (2d) 217; NLRB v. Century Oxford Corp., 140 F. (2d) 541, cert. denied, 323 U.S. 714. However, where the majority status of the union has been established by an NLRB consent card check agreement, the employer may question the union's right to represent the employees when shortly after the card check they have notified him of their repudiation of the union as their bargaining agent. Joe Hearin, Lumber, 66 NLRB No. 150, 17 LRRM 399. However, in a supplemental decision in the same case, 68 NLRB No. 21, 18 LRRM 1101, the Board said it would apply the same rule to its revised form of card check agreement which provides for posting of the results on the employer's premises for five days prior to issuance of the Regional Director's Report in the cross-check. Since, under this type of Agreement, objection to the results of the cross-check may be made for a period of five days, the Regional Director's report will be given the same effect as in the case of a consent election.

288. See J. I. Case v. NLRB, 321 U.S. 322. When a bargaining agent has been selected the employer cannot enter into an agreement with his employees for a wage increase at their request and in disregard of the designated agent. Medo Photo Supply Corp. v. NLRB, 321 U.S. 678. Nor does a change in employee personnel after a refusal to bargain collectively with the designated bargaining agent relieve the employer of his duty to bargain. When there has been a refusal to bargain, subsequent loss of majority does not relieve the employer of the obligation. Franks Bros. Co. v. NLRB, 321 U.S. 202.

289. See note 286.

290. NLRB v. Columbian Enameling & Stamping Co., 306 U.S. 292.

291. George E. Carroll, 56 NLRB 935. The duty to bargain continues after the execution of the agreement. The employer continues under an obligation to bargain concerning modification, interpretation and administration of the existing agreement. See NLRB v. Sands Mfg. Co., 306 U.S. 332; Concordia Ice Co., 51 NLRB 1068, enforced 143 F. (2d) 656; Green Colonial Furnace Co., 52 NLRB 161. In the Carroll case the Board said: "By signing a trade agreement an employer does not purchase immunity from the requirements of good faith and honest negotiation which are basic to Section 8(5) of the Act."

292. The prior practice of conducting cross-check of union cards against an agreed payroll has been discontinued because of the provisions of the amended Act.

293. Consumers Lumber & Veneer Co., 63 NLRB 17.

294. Pure Oil Company, 62 NLRB 1039.

295. McGough Bakeries Corp., 58 NLRB 849.

296. McGough Bakeries Corp., 58 NLRB 849; Pure Oil Company, 62 NLRB 1039.

297. Pure Oil Company, 62 NLRB 1039.

298. Hartford Courant Co., 64 NLRB 213.

299. The Nubone Co., 62 NLRB 322.

300. John S. Doane Co., 63 NLRB 1403.

301. The statute specifically conditions the employer's obligation to bargain upon the prerequisite that the union demanding bargaining rights has been designated as bargaining agent by a majority of the employees in an appropriate bargaining unit. Only then is there an exclusive bargaining representative within the term of the statute and only then can a union so designated properly demand bargaining rights.

302. See Central Dispensary & Emergency Hospital, 46 NLRB 437; Kendall Coal Co., 41 NLRB 395.

303. Unless the petitioning union can show, prior to a hearing, that it represents a substantial number of employees in the bargaining unit it claims appropriate, the Board will dismiss the petition. The Board, however, will not permit the employer to examine into this question at a hearing and regards the subject as a matter of concern only to the Board. The extent of the showing of substantial representation required by the Board may be influenced by the circumstances. See Sayles Finishing Plants, Inc., 49 NLRB 532; Superior Coach Corp., 49 NLRB 873.

304. "There can therefore be no doubt that the employer understood that it was dealing with those who at least claimed to be acting for a union of its employees and from this the implication was that the union also claimed to represent a majority. The employer took the risk of refusal, if the claim turned out to be well founded. National Labor Relations Board v. Remington Rand, Inc., 2 Cir., 94 F. (2d) 862, 866." Art Metals Construction Co. v. NLRB, 110 F. (2d) 148, 150. See also NLRB v. Piqua Munising Wood Products Co., 109 F. (2d) 552.

305. The Act does not specify any form which the union must show to establish its bargaining authority. See Lebanon Steel Foundry v. NLRB, 130 F. (2d) 404, certiorari denied 317 U.S. 659.

306. Midwest Piping & Supply Co. Inc., 63 NLRB 1060; Flotill Products Co. Inc., 70 NLRB 119; Lincoln Packing Co., 70 NLRB 135.

306a. Crosby Chemicals, Inc., 85 NLRB No. 139.

307. Franks Bros. v. NLRB, 320 U.S. 734; NLRB v. Appalachian Electric Power Co., 140 F. (2d) 217; NLRB v. Century Oxford Corp., 140 F. (2d) 541, cert. denied 323 U.S. 714; NLRB v. Botany Worsted Mills, 138 F. (2d) 876.

308. NLRB v. P. Lorillard & Co., 314 U.S. 512.

309. NLRB v. Appalachian Electric Power Co., 140 F. (2d) 217; NLRB v. Century Oxford Corp., 140 F. (2d) 541; NLRB v. Botany Worsted Mills, 133 F. (2d) 876. In the Appalachian case, the Court said, "Accordingly, when the Board, after following the proper statutory procedure, has given certification to a unit, this certification must be honored by the company so long as it remains in force, at least for a reasonable time. To assume that the Board's certification speaks with certainty only for the day of its issuance and that a Company may, with impunity, at any time thereafter refuse to bargain collectively on the ground that a change of sentiment has divested the duly certified representative of its majority status would lead to litigious bedlam and judicial chaos. Indeed, if the Company's contention were correct, the Board's certification might even be obsolete and subject to nullification by an interim informal Gallup poll vote on the very day of its issuance."

310. Thus, the existence of a contract with an employer dominated association has been held no defense to a charge of refusal to bargain. See NLRB v. Wm. Tehel Bottling Co., 129 F. (2d) 250.

311. NLRB v. Remington Rand Inc., 94 F. (2d) 862, certiorari denied 304 U.S. 76; Hartsell Mills Co. v. NLRB, 111 F. (2d) 291; Reed & Prince Mfg. Co., 12 NLRB 944, enforced in Reed & Prince Co. v. NLRB, 118 F. (2d) 874, cert. denied, 313 U.S. 595. Here the Board speaking of the objective of the Act said, "If this objective (collective bargaining) is to be achieved it is fully as important that the bargaining process be as available during the course of a strike as prior to or subsequent to a strike."

312. Bethlehem Steel Co., 73 NLRB 277; Harris-Woodson Co. Inc., 70 NLRB 956, enforced 162 F. (2d) 97.

313. I. Spiewak & Sons, 71 NLRB 770.

314. Bethlehem Steel Co., *supra,* note 312.

315. Califruit Canning Co., 73 NLRB 290; I. Spiewak & Sons, Inc., 71 NLRB 770.

316. 29 USCA (1947, Supp.) Sec. 158 (a) (5).

317. 29 USCA (1947, Supp.) Sec. 159 (a) (b).

318. Palm Beach Broadcasting Corp., 63 NLRB 597.

319. Allis-Chalmers Mfg. Co., 70 NLRB 348, enforced 162 F. (2d) 435.

320. Craddock-Terry Shoe Corp., 73 NLRB 1339.

321. The employer cannot approach collective bargaining with his mind hermetically sealed against the subject. Great Southern Trucking Co. v. NLRB, 127 F. (2d) 180, certiorari denied 317 U.S. 652.

322. Employer's failure to make counter proposals after rejection of the union's proposals may be regarded as evidence of bad faith in bargaining. See Montgomery Ward & Co., 37 NLRB 100; Register Publishing Co., 44 NLRB 834.

323. J. I. Case Co. v. NLRB, 321 U.S. 322: "Individual contracts, no matter what the circumstances that justify their execution or what their terms, may not be availed of to defeat or delay the procedures prescribed by the National Labor Relations Act looking to collective bargaining, nor to exclude the contracting employee from a duly ascertained bargaining unit; nor may they be used to forestall bargaining or to limit or condition the terms of the collective agreement."

324. But see cases cited in note 228.

325. 29 USCA (1947, Supp.) Sec. 159 (a).

326. Hughes Tool Company v. NLRB, 147 F. (2d) 69.

327. 29 USCA (1947, Supp.) Sec. 159 (a).

328. See case cited in note 323.

329. Schierbrock Motors, 15 NLRB 1109.

330. Medo Photo Supply Corp. v. NLRB, 321 U.S. 678. See also J. I. Case Co. v. NLRB, 321 U.S. 332.

331. May Department Stores Company d/b/a Famous-Barr Company v. NLRB, 326 U.S. 376. In NLRB v. Inter-City Advertising Co., 154 F. (2d) 244, decided March 15, 1946, three months after the decision of the Supreme Court in the May Department Stores Company case, the Fourth Circuit Court of Appeals said:

"It has been suggested that it was improper for the employer to change the personnel and working conditions at the transmitter station without consultation with the union, and therefore the employer is to blame for the union's loss of majority. We do not think that this contention is tenable. The changes might indeed have become the subject of collective bargaining but it cannot be said that an employer may not make any valid change in the working conditions or personnel of his employees without consulting the union selected by its employees to represent them. In this instance the changes were made in the normal course of business, gave rise to no dispute between the management and the men, and provoked no adverse criticism from the Board. Indeed the Board expressly found that the company had not interfered with or coerced its employees by discussing and settling grievances with them without participation of the union, or by refusing to discuss grievances with the union as the exclusive representative of the men. This holding distinguishes the case from such decisions as Medo Photo Supply Corp. v. NLRB, 321 U.S. 678, 64 S. Ct. 830, 88 L. Ed. 1007; Great Southern Trucking Co. v. National Labor Relations Board, 127 F. (2d) 180; National Labor Relations Board v. George P. Pilling Co., 3 Cir., 119 F. (2d) 32, 38; Oughton v. National Labor Relations Board, 3 Cir., 118 F. (2d) 486, 498."

The Court refused to enforce an order of the NLRB requiring the employer to bargain collectively with a certified union where after the employer's wrongful refusal to bargain collectively, union membership was reduced by normal and lawful changes in personnel and without wrongful conduct by the employer to a single employee. A long line of cases would seem to indicate a contrary result, but the court distinguished these decisions as follows:

"It is apparent from this review of the facts that none of the circumstances existed which in other cases have led the courts to compel an employer to bargain with a union alleged to have lost its majority. There was no aggressive campaign against the union and no intimidation of the workers as existed in Franks Bros. Co. v. NLRB, 321 U.S. 702, 64 S. Ct. 817, 88 L. Ed. 1020; National Labor Relations Board v. Bradford Dyeing Ass'n, 310 U.S. 318, 60 S. Ct. 918, 84 L. Ed. 12,

26; and National Labor Relations Board v. P. Lorillard Co., 314 U.S. 512, 62 S. Ct. 397, 86 L. Ed. 380. There was no room for the presumption that the union majority which once existed continued in being or that the decline in union membership was due to the employer's refusal to bargain as was the case in Great Southern Trucking Co. v. National Labor Relations Board, 4 Cir., 139 F. (2d) 984 and National Labor Relations Board v. Highland Park Mfg. Co., 4 Cir., 110 F. (2d) 632; or that the loss of majority was due to unfair labor practices as was the case in National Labor Relations Board v. Cowell Portland Cement Co., 9 Cir., 148 F. (2d) 237, 242; National Labor Relations Board v. George P. Pilling & Son Co., 3 Cir., 119 F. (2d) 32; and National Labor Relations Board v. Chicago Apparatus Co., 7 Cir., 116 F. (2d) 753; and there was no ground for applying the rule that a certification of bargaining representatives must be maintained for a reasonable time on the ground that it would be impracticable to hold frequent elections upon every shift of sentiment of the employees as in National Labor Relations Board v. Appalachian Electric Power Co., 140 F. (2d) 217 and NLRB v. Century Oxford Mfr., 140 F. (2d) 541. On the contrary, the evidence in the pending case demonstrated as clearly as if an election had been held that only one union member remained at the transmitter station, and all the facts were so fully shown that no room was left for inference or speculation. The Board itself has re-examined the situation and has found in effect that the union no longer represents the men." The dissenting opinion of Judge Dobie should be noted.

332. Great Southern Trucking Co. v. NLRB, 127 F. (2d) 180, certiorari denied 317 U.S. 652; NLRB v. Barrett Co., 135 F. (2d) 959. See May Department Stores Company v. NLRB, 326 U.S. 376.

333. Medo Photo Supply Corp. v. NLRB, 321 U.S. 678.

334. See note 323.

335. The employer may not accept the voluntary offer of a majority of his employees to withdraw from the union upon the grant of wage increase. Medo Photo Supply Co. v. NLRB, 321 U.S. 678.

336. U. S. Automatic Corp., 57 NLRB 124.

337. John S. Doane Co., 63 NLRB 1403;

Bethlehem Transportation Corp., 61 NLRB 1110.

338. Motor Valve and Mfg. Co., 58 NLRB 1057, enforced 149 F. (2d) 247.

339. National Broadcasting Co. Inc., 61 NLRB 161, enforced 150 F. (2d) 895.

340. Synchro Machine Corp., 62 NLRB 985.

340a. Tower Hosiery Mills, Inc., 81 NLRB No. 120.

340b. Amory Garment Co. Inc., 80 NLRB No. 41.

340c. General Motors Corp., 81 NLRB No. 126.

340d. Bergen Point Iron Works, 79 NLRB 1073.

340e. Massey Gin and Machine Works Inc., 78 NLRB 189.

340f. NLRB v. Crompton-Highland Mills Inc., 337 U.S. 217.

340g. United Elastic Corporation, 84 NLRB No. 87.

341. Montgomery Ward & Co., 37 NLRB 100. Register Publishing Co. Ltd., 44 NLRB 834.

342. Singer Manufacturing Co., 24 NLRB 444, enforced 119 F. (2d) 131 (CCA 7).

343. Medo Photo Supply Corp., 43 NLRB 989; NLRB v. Sands Mfg. Co., 306 U.S. 332, 345; NLRB v. Hopwood Retinning Co., 98 F. (2d) 97, 100; Western Felt Works, 10 NLRB 407, 415, 416; Chesapeake Shoe Co., 12 NLRB 832; Bussmann Mfg. Co., 14 NLRB 322; Schmidt Baking Co. Inc., 27 NLRB 864; Henry McCleary Timber Co., 37 NLRB 725; Poultrymen's Service Corp., 41 NLRB 444.

344. The Northwest Glove Inc., 74 NLRB 1697; See also M. M. Joffee Co., 74 NLRB 1568; NLRB v. Fred P. Weissman, 170 F. (2d) 952 (CCA 6) cert. den. 336 U.S. 972.

345. Pioneer Electric Co., 70 NLRB No. 59.

346. See Na-Mac Products Corp., 70 NLRB 298; cf. Pioneer Electric Co., 70 NLRB 771; Simmons Co., 70 NLRB 290.

347. Na-Mac Products Corp., 70 NLRB No. 32; Electric Sprayit Co., 67 NLRB No. 101.

348. See International Association of Machinists etc. v. NLRB, 311 U.S. 72; NLRB v. Link-Belt Co., 311 U.S. 584.

349. Mere instructions to the supervisory staff not to interfere with unionization are not sufficient and an open disavowal requires adequate publication to all employees. See F. W. Woolworth Co. v. NLRB, 121 F. (2d) 658.

350. For cases illustrating the principle involved and of the type referred to in the text see Gray Envelope Mfg. Co., 45 NRLB 653; Cooper, Wells & Co., 16 NLRB 27, 31; Yale & Towne Mfg. Co., 55 NLRB 66; Sinclair Refining Co., 20 NLRB 800; Midwest Piping and Supply Co., Inc., 63 NLRB 1060.

351. See F. W. Woolworth Co. v. NLRB, 121 F. (2d) 658.

352. See International Association of Machinists v. NLRB, 311 U.S. 72; NLRB v. Link-Belt Co., 311 U.S. 584.

353. Tex-O-Kan Flour Mills Co., 26 NLRB 765, 766; Swift & Co. v. NLRB, 106 F. (2d) 87, 93 modifying 7 NLRB 269.

354. 29 USCA (1947, Supp.) Sec. 152 (2) and (13).

355. R. R. Donnelly & Sons, 60 NLRB 635; The Hartford Courant Co., 64 NLRB 213; Mississippi Valley Structural Steel, 64 NLRB 78.

356. Richmond Home Telephone Co., 70 NLRB 37.

357. See the discussion of "To Disclaim Responsibility for Supervisors' Activities," Part Three, Chapter II, Section II.

358. H. J. Heinz Co. v. NLRB, 311 U.S. 514; NLRB v. Laister-Kauffmann Aircraft Corp., 144 F. (2d) 9, (CCA 8), 14 LRRM 861; Stehli Co., 35 NLRB 44; Clinton Woolen Mfg. Co., 49 NLRB 11; Curtiss-Wright Corp., 39 NLRB 992; Boeing Airplane Co., 46 NLRB 267.

359. The Act specifically provides that upon finding unfair labor practices the Board may not only order the employer to cease and desist but also "to take such affirmative action including reinstatement of employees with or without back pay, as will effectuate the policies of the Act." 29 USCA (1947, Supp.) Sec. 160(a). Thus, the remedy for unfair labor practices is prescribed by the Board. In International Association of Machinists v. NLRB, 311 U.S. 72, the Supreme Court said: "It is for the Board not the courts to determine how the effect of unfair labor

practices may be expunged." In Phelps Dodge Corp. v. NLRB, 313 U.S. 177, 187 the Court pointed out: "Reinstatement is the conventional correction for discriminatory discharges. Experience having demonstrated that discrimination in hiring is twin to discrimination in firing, it would indeed be surprising if Congress gave a remedy for the one which it denied for the other. The powers of the Board as well as the restrictions upon it must be drawn from Sec. 10 (c), which directs the Board 'to take such affirmative action, including reinstatement of employees with or without back pay, as will effectuate the policies of this Act.' It could not be seriously denied that to require discrimination in hiring or firing to be 'neutralized,' NLRB v. Mackay Radio Co.. 304 U.S. 333, 348, by requiring the discrimination to cease not abstractly but in the concrete victimizing instances, is an 'affirmative action' which 'will effectuate the policies of this Act.' Therefore, if Sec. 10 (c) had empowered the Board to 'take such affirmative action as will effectuate the policies of this Act,' the right to restore to a man employment which was wrongfully denied him could hardly be doubted." The Court in that case held that the Board has authority to require an employer to reinstate a discriminatorily discharged employee who has found substantially equivalent employment elsewhere if such reinstatement will remedy the unfair labor practices.

360. Schieber Millinery Company, 26 NLRB 937; Klotz & Co., 13 NLRB 746.

361. The Board orders the employer to make whole the discharged men by payment to them of a sum equal to what they normally would have earned from the date of discrimination to the time of offer of reinstatement less their earning during the same period. Losses wilfully incurred by the discharged men during this period are also deductible. Phelps Dodge Corp. v. NLRB, 313 U.S. 177.

362. Labor Management Relations Act, Title I, Sec. 102.

363. Somerset Shoe Co., 12 NLRB 1057, 1059, remanded 111 F. (2d) 681; Long Lake Lumber Co., 34 NLRB 700; Ford Motor Co., 31 NLRB 994, 1104.

364. E. R. Haffelfinger Co., Inc., 1 NLRB 760, 767.

365. "In accordance with the Board's general practice, deductions were made in the present case for amounts earned during the period of the back pay award. But the deductions have been limited to earnings during the hours when the worker would have been employed by the employer in question. Matter of Pusey, Maynes & Breish Co., 1 NLRB 482; Matter of National Motor Bearing Co., 5 NLRB 409. And only "net earnings" are deducted, allowance being made for the expense of getting new employment which, but for the discrimination, would not have been necessary. Matter of Crossett Lumber Co., 8 NLRB 440.

"Even though a strike is caused by an unfair labor practice the Board does not award back pay during the period of the strike. Matter of Sunshine Hosiery Mills, 1 NLRB 664. Employees who are discriminatorily discharged are treated as strikers if during a strike they refuse an unconditional offer of reinstatement. Matter of Harter Corp., 8 NLRB 391. Originally back pay was ordered from the date of application for reinstatement, Matter of Sunshine Hosiery Mills, *supra,* but later orders have started back pay five days after application. Matter of Tiny Town Togs, Inc., 7 NLRB 54.

"If there is unjustified delay in filing charges before the Board, a deduction is made for the period of the delay. Matter of Inland Lime & Stone Co., 8 NLRB 944. Similar action is taken when a case is reopened after having been closed or withdrawn. Matter of C. G. Conn, Ltd., 10 NLRB 498. And if the trial examiner rules in favor of the employer and the Board reverses the ruling, no back pay is ordered for the period when the examiner's ruling stood unreversed. Matter of E. R. Haffelfinger Co., 1 NLRB 760; and see the order in the present case.

"The Board has refused to order any back pay where discriminatory discharges were made with honest belief that they were required by an invalid closed-shop contract. Matter of McKesson & Robbins, Inc., 19 NLRB 778.

"If the business conditions would have caused the plant to be closed or personnel to be reduced, back pay is awarded only for the period which the worker would have worked in the absence of discrimination. Matter of Ray Nichols, Inc., 15 NLRB 846. At times fluctuations in personnel so complicate the situation that a formula has to be devised for the distribution of a lump sum among the workers who have been discriminated against. Matter of Eagle-Picher Mining & Smelting Co., 16 NLRB 727.

"The rate of pay used in computing awards is generally that at the time of discrimination, but adjustments may be made for subsequent changes. Matter of Lone Star Bag & Bagging Co., 8 NLRB 244; cf. Matter of Acme Air Appliance Co., 10 NLRB 1385. Normal earnings in tips or bonuses have been taken into account. Matter of Club Troika, 2 NLRB 90; Matter of Central Truck Lines, 3 NLRB 317." Phelps Dodge Corp. v. NLRB, 313 U.S. 177, 198 (footnote 7).

366. Scullin Steel Co., 65 NLRB 1294; Joseph Dyson & Sons, Inc., 72 NLRB 445; Fafnir Bearing Co., 73 NLRB 1008.

367. NLRB v. Sands Mfg. Co., 306 U.S. 332.

368. Scullin Steel Co., 65 NLRB 1294; Joseph Dyson & Sons, Inc., 72 NLRB No. 82.

369. See notes 361 and 362.

370. Employees who strike for economic or sympathy reasons are entitled to reinstatement if their jobs have not been filled when they apply, and the employer cannot deal discriminatorily with their applications for reinstatement. NLRB v. Mackay Radio & Telegraph Co., 304 U.S. 333. But when the strike is caused by unfair labor practices of the employer the strikers must be reinstated upon their application and employees who have replaced the strikers must be discharged to make places for them. NLRB v. Grower-Shipper Vegetable Assn., 122 F. (2d) 368.

371. Joseph Dyson & Sons, Inc., 72 NLRB 445; National Electric Products Corp., 80 NLRB No. 151.

372. United Elastic Corporation, 84 NLRB No. 87.

373. United Elastic Corporation, 84 NLRB No. 87.

374. United Elastic Corporation, 84 NLRB No. 87.

375. Carroll Towing Co., Inc. v. United Marine Division. I.L.A. (N.Y. Sup. Ct. 91 N.Y. Supp. (2d) 431).

376. Phelps Dodge Corp. v. NLRB, 313 U.S. 177.

377. McKaig-Hatch Inc., 10 NLRB 33, 52; Frederick R. Barrett, 3 NLRB 513, 525, 526; Consolidated Edison Co. v. NLRB, 95 F. (2d) 390, 396, 397; E. H. Moore Inc., 40 NLRB 1058.

378. NLRB v. Fansteel Metallurgical Corp., 306 U.S. 240.

379. See note 370.

380. Republic Steel Corporation, 9 NLRB 219, Republic Steel Corp. v. NLRB, 107 F. (2d) 472. Reinstatement of strikers was required although some of them were arraigned on charges of disorderly conduct, disturbing the peace and assault and battery and some were subsequently convicted of these offenses. NLRB v. Stackpole Carbon Co., 105 F. (2d) 167, 175-6. In NLRB v. Colten (Kiddie Kover Mfg. Co.), 105 F. (2d) 179, 13 strikers were reinstated, although they were admonished by a state court judge for contempt of an injunction against violence on the picket line.

381. El Paso Electric Co. v. NLRB, 119 F. (2d) 581, 8 LRRM 660; NLRB v. Algoma Net Co., 124 F. (2d) 730, 9 LRRM 531; cf. NLRB v. Cincinnati Chemical Works, 144 F. (2d) 597, 14 LRRM 885.

382. NLRB v. Cincinnati Chemical Works, 144 F. (2d) 597, 14 LRRM 885; McGoldrick Lumber Co., 19 NLRB 887; Brown Radio Service & Laboratory, 70 NLRB No. 38; Precision Castings Co. Inc., 48 NLRB 870; Mid-Continent Petroleum Corp., 54 NLRB 912.

383. NLRB v. Reed & Prince Mfg. Co., 118 F. (2d) 874 (CCA 1); Acme Evans Co., 24 NLRB 71; Cleveland Worsted Mills Co., 43 NLRB 545; Republic Steel Corp., 9 NLRB 219; Louisville Refining Co., 4 NLRB 844, 874.

384. O'Donnell's Sea Grill, 55 NLRB 828.

385. New York and Porto Rico Steamship Company, 34 NLRB 1028.

386. In Greer Steel Company, 38 NLRB 65, the Board ordered reinstatement and back pay on the ground that there was no showing of "actual exercise by a labor organization of its economic power to the demonstrated financial detriment of the respondent for the purpose of compelling the very action of which complaint has been made." See also Marvel-Schebler Division, Borg-Warner Corporation, 38 NLRB 866.

387. Phelps Dodge Corp. v. NLRB, 313 U.S. 177.

388. NLRB v. Mackay Radio & Telegraph Co., 304 U.S. 333.

389. See Oklahoma Rendering Co., 75 NLRB No. 127, 21 LRRM 1115.

390. NLRB v. Nevada Consolidated Copper Corp., 316 U.S. 105 (1942) 10 LRRM 607; NLRB v. Algoma Net Co., 124 F. (2d) 730 (CCA 7); Norwich Dairy Co. Inc., 25 NLRB 1166; Williamson-Dickie Mfg. Co., 35 NLRB 1220.

391. Black Diamond Steamship Corp. v. NLRB, 94 F. (2d) 875; Manville Jenkes Corp., 27 NLRB 292.

392. Pacific Plastic & Mfg. Co. Inc., 68 NLRB No. 12; The Pickwick Co., 69 NLRB No. 40.

393. NLRB v. Indiana Desk Co., 149 F. (2d) 987.

394. South Carolina Granite Co., 58 NLRB 1448; Howe Scale Co., 47 NLRB 1399.

395. Home Beneficial Life Insurance Co., 69 NLRB No. 5; NLRB v. Mackay Radio & Telegraph Co., 304 U.S. 333, Wallingford Steel Co., 53 NLRB 404.

396. Ray Nichols Inc., 15 NLRB 846, 858; Surpass Leather Co., 21 NLRB 1258; Cleveland-Cliffs Iron Co., 30 NLRB 1093.

397. NLRB v. Goodyear Tire & Rubber Co. of Alabama, 129 F. (2d) 661 (CCA 5); Dow Chemical Co., 13 NLRB 993; Taylor-Colquitt Co., 47 NLRB 225; Mansfield Mills, Inc., 3 NLRB 901.

398. Eagle-Picher Mining & Smelting Co. v. NLRB, 119 F. (2d) 903.

399. Gamble-Robinson Co., 33 NLRB 351, enforced 129 F. (2d) 588 (CCA 8), 10 LRRM 856.

400. See Charles Cushman Company, 15 NLRB 90; Schieber Millinery Company, 26 NLRB No. 99; Salant & Salant Inc., 66 NLRB No. 2; South Port Petroleum Co. v. NLRB, 315 U.S. 100.

401. Republic Steel Corp., 62 NLRB 1008. However, the Third Circuit Court of Appeals has held that a strike in violation of the 30 day notice provision of the War Labor Disputes Act subjected the union to civil liability. France Packing Co. v. Dailey, 166 F. (2d) 751, 21 LRRM 2344.

402. Indiana Desk Co., 56 NLRB 76, supplemental decision 15 LRRM 21, enforcement denied 149 F. (2d) 987.

403. Volney Felt Mills, 70 NLRB No. 72.

404. N. Kiamie, 4 NLRB 808, 812, 813.

405. But see NLRB v. Cape County Milling, 140 F. (2d) 543, where the shutdown of a department was temporary for anti-union reasons.

406. J. H. Klotz & Co., 13 NLRB 746, 778.

407. NLRB v. Brashear Freight Lines, 119 F. (2d) 379.

408. See Firth Carpet Co. v. NLRB, 129 F. (2d) 633.

409. NLRB v. Draper Corp., 145 F. (2d) 199.

410. See NLRB v. Mackay Radio & Telegraph Co., 304 U.S. 333.

411. Quality & Service Laundry, Inc., 39 NLRB 970.

412. See cases cited in note 368; NLRB v. Sands Mfg. Co., 306 U.S. 332.

413. See cases cited in note 368.

414. The American News Co., Inc., 55 NLRB 1302; NLRB v. Indiana Desk Co., 149 F. (2d) 987.

415. "The Board, we have held very recently, does not exist for the 'adjudication of private rights'; it 'acts in a public capacity to give effect to the declared public policy of the Act to eliminate and prevent obstructions to interstate commerce.' " Phelps Dodge Corp. v. NLRB, 313 U.S. 177, 193. National Licorice Co. v. NLRB, 309 U.S. 350. In Amalgamated Utility Workers v. Consolidated Edison Co., 309 U.S. 261, the Supreme Court held that a union had no authority under the Act to apply to the Circuit Court of Appeals to have an employer adjudged in contempt for failure to obey the court's decree enforcing an order of the Board. Only the Board can bring such a proceeding.

The Committee on Labor of the House of Representatives stated with respect to the reinstatement of employees with or without back pay as follows: (H.R. Rep. No. 972, 74th Cong. 1st Sess. p. 21) "No private right of action is contemplated. Essentially the unfair labor practices listed are matters of public concern, by their nature and consequences, present or potential; the proceeding is in the name of the Board, upon the Board's formal complaint. The form of injunctive and affirmative order is necessary to effectuate the purpose of the bill to remove obstructions

to interstate commerce which are by the law declared to be detrimental to the public weal."

416. Ever Ready Label Corp., 54 NLRB 551; Famous-Barr Co., 59 NLRB 976.

417. NLRB v. Van Deusen, 138 F. (2d) 893, 13 LRRM 603.

418. Phelps Dodge Corp. v. NLRB, 313 U.S. 177; Continental Oil Co. v. NLRB, 313 U.S. 212.

419. 29 USCA (1947, Supp.) Sec. 160 (c).

420. 29 USCA (1947, Supp.) Sec. 160 (c).

421. Social Security Board v. Nierotko, 327 U.S. 358, 365.

422. NLRB Third Annual Report, pp. 201–202.

423. Kuehne Mfg. Co., 7 NLRB 304; Smith Wood Products Inc., 7 NLRB 950.

424. Stylecraft Leather Goods Company, 3 NLRB 920; Montgomery Ward & Co., 4 NLRB 1151.

425. Matter of Ray Nichols Inc., 15 NLRB 846.

426. Lone Star Bag & Bagging Co., 8 NLRB 244; Acme Air Appliance Co., 10 NLRB 1385.

427. Club Troika, 2 NLRB 90; Central Truck Lines, 3 NLRB 17.

428. See notes 361 and 365.

429. Phelps Dodge Corp. v. NLRB, 313 U.S. 177.

430. NLRB Ninth Annual Report, p. 65.

431. See 11 LRRM 2545.

432. NLRB Fourth Annual Report pp. 99–100.

433. Marshall Field & Co. v. NLRB, 318 U.S. 253.

434. NLRB v. Brashear Freight Lines Inc., 127 F. (2d) 198.

435. Social Security Board v. Nierotko, 327 U.S. 358.

436. NLRB v. Revlon Products Corp., 144 F. (2d) 88.

437. The Ohio Public Service Company, 52 NLRB 725.

438. Laredo Daily Times, 58 NLRB 458.

439. W. W. Rosebraugh Co., 60 NLRB 787.

440. Crossett Lumber Co., 8 NLRB 440; Hoosier Veneer Co., 21 NLRB 907.

441. J. H. Klotz & Co., 13 NLRB 746.

442. NLRB v. Stackpole Carbon Co., 128 F. (2d) 188.

443. NLRB v. Sunshine Mining Co., 125 F. (2d) 757.

444. United Biscuit Co. v. NLRB, 128 F. (2d) 771; Black Diamond Steamship Corp., 3 NLRB 84.

445. NLRB v. Long Lake Lumber Co., 34 NLRB 700, 138 F. (2d) 363.

446. NLRB Third Annual Report, p. 202.

447. NLRB v. Killoren, 122 F. (2d) 609, cert. den. 314 U.S. 696.

448. NLRB v. Killoren, 122 F. (2d) 609, cert. den. 314 U.S. 696.

449. NLRB v. Pennsylvania Greyhound Lines, 303 U.S. 261; NLRB v. Standard Oil, 142 F. (2d) 676, cert. den. 323 U.S. 791.

450. J. Greenbaum Tanning Co., 11 NLRB 300; Weirton Steel Co., 32 NLRB 1145; Clover Fork Coal Co. v. NLRB, 97 F. (2d) 331.

451. Fred P. Weissman Co., 69 NLRB 1002, 71 NLRB 147.

452. Eureka Vacuum Cleaner Co., 69 NLRB 878.

453. Aluminum Ore Co. v. NLRB, 131 F. (2d) 485.

454. NLRB v. The Sherwin-Williams Co., 34 NLRB 651, enforced 130 F. (2d) 255.

455. Crompton-Highland Mills, Inc., 70 NLRB 21 enforced on other grounds in 337 U.S. 217.

456. Pool Manufacturing Co., 70 NLRB 540.

457. J. H. Allison & Co., 70 NLRB 377, 165 F. (2d) 766, 21 LRRM 2238.

458. Hour Glass Club Restaurant Inc., Dec. No. 4533, 10 (N.Y.) SLRB 819.

459. Oklahoma Rendering Co., 75 NLRB No. 127, 21 LRRM 1115.

460. 29 USCA (1947, Supp.) Sec. 158 (a).

461. NLRB v. American Mfg. Co., 106 F. (2d) 61, modified in other respects in American Mfg. Co. v. NLRB, 309 U.S. 629. In National Licorice Co. v. NLRB, 309 U.S. 350, 360, the Supreme Court said: "By the contract each employee agreed not 'to demand a closed shop or a signed agreement by his employer with any Union.' This provision foreclosed the employee from bargaining for a closed shop or a signed agreement with the employer, frequent subjects of negotiation between employers and employees, see Consolidated Edison Co. v. National Labor Relations Board (305 U.S. 197); National Labor Relations Board v. Sands Mfg. Co., 306 U.S. 332, 342; cf. Virginian Railway Co. v. System Federation No. 40, 300 U.S. 515, 553, 555, note 7. In addition the restriction upon the employee's right to ask a signed agreement extending only to agreements with 'any union' is in plain conflict with the public policy of the Act to encourage the procedure of collective bargaining, see § 1, since it discriminates against labor organizations by forbidding signed contracts with labor unions while it permits them with the individual workers. See Consolidated Edison Co. v. National Labor Relations Board, *supra*, 236.

"It likewise forestalls collective bargaining with respect to discharged employees, first providing that a discharged employee may submit to the employer facts indicating that his discharge was unreasonable and then stipulating that the 'question as to the propriety of an employee's discharge is in no event to be one for arbitration or mediation.' The effect of this clause was to discourage, if not forbid, any presentation of the discharged employee's grievances to appellant through a labor organization or his chosen representatives, or in any way except personally." See also 29 USCA Sec. 103 providing that "yellow dog" contracts are not enforceable.

462. Even the existence of valid contracts with individual employees is not a bar to collective bargaining. When the employees designated a bargaining agent, negotiations for, and the collective agreement with, such agent, displace the individual employee agreements. J. I. Case & Co. v. NLRB, 321 U.S. 332.

463. An employer who adequately apprizes his employees of his neutrality is not responsible for the continuing and coercive statements of his supervisory staff. Houston Shipbuilding Corp., 41 NLRB 638. But the Board will hold the employer responsible if the supervisors actually discriminated against employees with respect to hire, tenure or terms or conditions of employment.

464. NLRB v. Gluek Brewing Co., 144 F. (2d) 847, 853.

465. American Smelting & Refining Co. v. NLRB, 128 F. (2d) 345.

466. American Smelting & Refining Co. v. NLRB, 128 F. (2d) 345.

467. NLRB v. American Tube Bending Co., 134 F. (2d) 993, cert. den. 320 U.S. 768.

468. 314 U.S. 469.

469. Bercut-Richards Packing Co., 65 NLRB 1052; Midwest Piping and Supply Co., 63 NLRB 1060.

470. Ellis Canning Co., 76 NLRB No. 13, 21 LRRM 1152.

471. The authorities on this subject including the position of the Board, and the material discussion above in connection with the Virginia Power Co. case are summarized in footnotes 126, 129, 132, 134.

472. NLRB v. Sandy Hill Iron & Brass Works, 145 F. (2d) 631, 21 LRRM 2021.

473. American Laundry Machinery Co., 57 NLRB 25.

474. Paragon Rubber Co., 7 NLRB 965; Metro-Goldwyn-Mayer Studios, 8 NLRB 858; Emerson Radio & Phonograph Co., 43 NLRB 613; Whiterock Quarries, Inc., 45 NLRB 165; S. H. Camp & Co., 52 NLRB 1078; Huch Leather Co., 11 NLRB 394.

475. NLRB v. Remington Rand Inc., 94 F. (2d) 862, cert. den. 304 U.S. 576; Okey Hosiery Co. Inc., 22 NLRB 792, 797; Laird, Schober Co., Inc., 14 NLRB 1152, 1155; American Steel Scraper Co., Inc., 29 NLRB 939, 945.

475a. NLRB v. Kingston, 172 F. (2d) 771.

476. New York Handkerchief Mfg. Co., 16 NLRB 532; Armour & Co., 48 NLRB 1412; Times-Picayune Publishing Co., 32 NLRB 387; Burton-Dixie Corp., 48 NLRB 621.

477. NLRB v. Servel Inc., 149 F. (2d) 542.

478. Bethlehem Steel Co. v. NLRB, 120 F. (2d) 641.

479. Texarkana Bus Co. Inc., v. NLRB 119 F. (2d) 480.

480. NLRB v. Botany Worsted Mills, 106 F. (2d) 263.

481. N. & W. Overall Co., 51 NLRB 1016.

482. Consolidated Edison Co. of N.Y. v. NLRB, 305 U.S. 197.

483. Ohio Fuel & Gas Co., 28 NLRB 667; Marshall Field & Co., 34 NLRB 1; Hearst Mercantile Co., 44 NLRB 1342; American Broach & Machine Co., 45 NLRB 241; Ridge Tool Co., 58 NLRB 1095; Lane Cotton Mills Co., 9 NLRB 952.

484. Springfield Machine & Foundry Co., 48 NLRB 974; Agar Packing & Provision Corp., 58 NLRB 738; Vincennes Steel Corp., 17 NLRB 825; Bradford Machine & Foundry Co., 44 NLRB 759; Plymouth Finishing Co., 48 NLRB 946; Davidson Granite Co., 24 NRLB 370; Serrick Corp., 8 NLRB 621.

485. Great Western Mushroom Co., 27 NLRB 352. In NLRB v. Stowe Spinning Co., 336 U.S. 226, the Supreme Court said that it was an unfair labor practice for an employer to refuse to permit the use of a meeting hall by a union where the hall was located in a company town and other organizations had been allowed to use the hall.

486. NLRB v. Fruehauf Trailer Co., 301 U.S. 49; Phelps Dodge Refining Corp., 37 NLRB 1059; Borg-Warner Corp., 23 NLRB 114; Cities Service Oil Co., 32 NLRB 1020.

487. NLRB v. Bethlehem Steel Co., 120 F. (2d) 641; NLRB v. Republic Steel Corp., 107 F. (2d) 472.

488. NLRB v. Remington Rand Inc., 94 F. (2d) 862, 870.

489. Medo Photo Supply Corp. v. NLRB, 321 U.S. 678.

490. Tidewater Express Lines, Inc., 32 NLRB 792.

491. The Serrick Corp., 8 NLRB 621, 650.

492. Southern Wood Preserving Co., 45 NLRB 230, 237, 238.

493. Highland Shoe Co. Inc., 23 NLRB 259.

494. Sunshine Mining Co., 7 NLRB 1252, 1264–1267; Bethlehem Steel Corp., 14 NLRB 539, 624; Elkland Leather Co., 8 NLRB 519, 524, 525, 530.

495. See Tampa Electric Co., 56 NLRB 1270; Cameron Can Machinery Co., 57 NLRB 1768; Comas Mfg. Co., 59 NLRB 208.

496. N. T. Stevens & Sons Co., 68 NLRB No. 30.

497. Ingram Mfg. Co., 5 NLRB 908, 922, 923; Wickwire Bros., 16 NLRB 316, 320; Tennessee Copper Co., 9 NLRB 117, 118; Ward Baking Co., 8 NLRB 558, 565.

498. Reed & Prince Mfg. Co., 12 NLRB 944.

499. Mock-Judson-Voehringer Co. of North Carolina, 8 NLRB 133, 137, 138.

500. Greensboro Lumber Co., 1 NLRB 629; Republic Steel Corp., 9 NLRB 219; Texarkana Bus Co., 26 NLRB 582.

501. Abinante & Nola Packing Co., 26 NLRB 1288.

502. John Engelhorn & Sons, 42 NLRB 866.

503. Weirton Steel Co., 32 NLRB 1145.

504. Reed & Prince Mfg. Co., 12 NLRB 944, 962.

505. See 29 USCA (1947, Supp.) Sec. 158(a) (4).

506. C. B. Cottrell & Sons, Inc., 34 NLRB 457, 463.

507. Sanco Piece Dye Works, Inc., 38 NLRB 690.

508. Ford Motor Co., 23 NLRB 548, 567; Rieke Metal Products Corp., 40 NLRB 867.

509. Union Mfg. Co. Inc., 27 NLRB 1300; Phelps Dodge Corp., 28 NLRB 540; Reliance Mfg. Co., 28 NLRB 1051; Picker X-Ray Corp., 12 NLRB 1384; Knoxville Publishing Co., 12 NLRB 1209; Lightner Publishing Corp., 12 NLRB 1255.

510. Tampa Electric Co., 56 NLRB 1270; Cameron Can Machinery Co., 57 NLRB 1768; Comas Mfg. Co., 59 NLRB 208.

511. General Motors Corp., 69 NLRB No. 17; Sherwin-Williams Co., 37 NLRB 260, 279, 280.

512. Davidson Granite Co., 24 NLRB 370; Ohio Valley Bus Co., 38 NLRB 838; Great Western Mushroom Co., 27 NLRB 352.

513. Weyerhaeuser Timber Co., 31 NLRB 258.

514. American Mfg. Concern., 7 NLRB 753, 759, 760.

515. See NLRB v. Draper Corp., 145 F. (2d) 199, NLRB v. Clinchfield Coal Co., 145 F. (2d) 66.

516. Dixie Motor Coach Corp., 25 NLRB 869; Texarkana Bus Co., Inc., 26 NLRB 582; National Lumber Mills, 37 NLRB 700.

517. Botany Worsted Mills, 4 NLRB 292, 297, 298; Union Pacific Stages, Inc., 2 NLRB 471, 478–480; Acme Air Appli-

ances Co. Inc., 10 NLRB 1385, 1390; Sorg Paper Co., 25 NLRB 946.

518. Peyton Packing Co., 49 NLRB 828; New York Times Co., 26 NLRB 1094, 1172, 1173; Times-Picayune Publishing Co., 32 NLRB 387, 394.

519. Hills Brothers Co., 62 NLRB No. 165; Union Mfg. Co., 63 NLRB 254; Young Engineering Co., 57 NLRB 1221.

520. Mock-Judson-Voehringer Co. of North Carolina, 8 NLRB 133, 137, 138; Paragon Die Casting Co., 27 NLRB 878; Harlan Fuel Co., 8 NLRB 25, 32; Sunshine Mining Co., 7 NLRB 1252, 1264–1267.

521. NLRB v. Lund, 103 F. (2d) 815; Fansteel Metallurgical Corp., 5 NLRB 930, 933–939, 943–946, modified, 306 U.S. 240; Indianapolis Power & Light Co., 25 NLRB 193, 212, 213.

522. Republic Aviation v. NLRB, 324 U.S. 793.

523. Bethlehem Steel Corp., 14 NLRB 539, 624; Jacob H. Klotz, 13 NLRB 746, 753, 759, 760; Alma Mills, 24 NLRB 1.

524. Clover Fork Coal Co. v. NLRB, 97 F. (2d) 331, 335; Weirton Steel Co., 32 NLRB 1145; J. G. Boswell Co., 35 NLRB 968, 985.

525. National Licorice Co. v. NLRB, 309 U.S. 350.

526. Peter J. Schweitzer Co., 54 NLRB No. 123; Wennonah Cotton Mills Co. Inc., 63 NLRB 143; Carl L. Norden, 62 NLRB 828; The General Fireproofing Co., 59 NLRB 375.

527. Brown Shoe Co. Inc., 1 NLRB 803, 824, 830; Chicago Casket Co., 21 NLRB 235; Alma Mills, 24 NLRB 17, 24; Bethlehem Steel Corp., 14 NLRB 539, 624; Elkland Leather Co., 8 NLRB 519.

528. Paragon Die Casting Co., 27 NLRB 878.

529. Martin Bros. Box Co., 35 NLRB 217.

530. J. H. Stone & Sons, 33 NLRB 1014.

531. Hills Brothers Co., 67 NLRB No. 165; The S. Frieder & Sons Co., 62 NLRB 880.

532. American-West African Lines Inc., 21 NLRB 691, 705; Louis F. Cassoff, 43 NLRB 1193, 1221.

533. Reliance Mfg. Co., 28 NLRB 1051.

534. The Baldwin Locomotive Works, 20 NLRB 1100, enforced 128 F. (2d) 39; Montgomery Ward & Co., 17 NLRB 191.

535. Van Dusen Dress Mfg. Co., 45 NLRB 679.

536. Mansfield Mills, Inc., 3 NLRB 901, 907; Nebel Knitting Co., 6 NLRB 284, 293; Norristown Box Co., 32 NLRB 895, 903.

537. National Mineral Co., 39 NLRB 344; Locomotive Finished Material Co., 41 NLRB 1374.

538. Charles C. Hobart, 25 NLRB 259.

539. Great Western Mushroom Co., 27 NLRB 352, 361.

540. Manville Jenckes Corp., 30 NLRB 382, 415.

541. Norfolk Shipbuilding & Drydock Corp., 70 NLRB No. 36.

542. Southern Wood Preserving Co., 45 NLRB 230, 237, 238.

543. Times-Picayune Publishing Co., 32 NLRB 387, 394.

544. The AP Parts Corp., 40 NLRB 301, 318, 320; McLain Fire Brick Co., 36 NLRB 1; Illinois Tool Works, 61 NLRB 1129.

545. Wyman-Gordon Co., 62 NLRB 561.

546. Emerson Radio & Phonograph Corp., 43 NLRB 613.

547. F. W. Woolworth Co., 25 NLRB 1362, 1371.

548. H. F. Wilcox Oil & Gas Co., 28 NLRB 79.

549. National Licorice Co. v. NLRB, 309 U.S. 350.

550. Chesapeake Shoe Mfg. Co., 12 NLRB 832; Reliance Mfg. Co., 28 NLRB 1051; Patriarca Store Fixtures, Inc., 12 NLRB 93, 97–99.

551. NLRB v. Lund, 103 F. (2d) 815, 817; Model Blouse Co., 15 NLRB 133, 143–145.

552. Martin Bros. Box Co., 35 NLRB 217.

553. NLRB v. Colten (Kiddie Kover Mfg. Co.), 105 F. (2d) 179, 181; Oregon Worsted Co., 3 NLRB 36, 46.

554. Sanco Piece Dye Works, 38 NLRB 690, 716.

555. Shenandoah-Dives Mining Co., 35 NLRB 1153.

556. John Engelhorn & Sons, 42 NLRB 866.

557. NLRB v. Colten (Kiddie Kover Mfg. Co.), 105 F. (2d) 179, 181; Pacific Gas & Electric Co., 13 NLRB 268, 291; Southern Colorado Power Co., 13 NLRB 699, 711; American Oil Co., 41 NLRB 1105.

558. Mellin-Quincy Mfg. Co., 53 NLRB 366.

559. NLRB v. Gluek Brewing Co. Inc., 144 F. (2d) 847.

560. Texarkana Bus Co., 26 NLRB 582, 586; Pacific Plastic & Mfg. Co. Inc., 68 NLRB No. 12.

561. Weirton Steel Co., 32 NLRB 1145; Ford Motor Co., 26 NLRB 322.

562. Thompson Products, Inc., 3 NLRB 332, 336; West Kentucky Coal Co., 10 NLRB 88, 112–114.

563. Flotill Products, Inc., 70 NLRB 119.

564. Friedman-Harry Marks Clothing Co. Inc., 1 NLRB 411, 428, 430, enforced 301 U.S. 58; NLRB v. Willard Inc., 98 F. (2d) 244.

565. Reliance Manufacturing Co., 60 NLRB 946.

566. Ross Gear & Tool Co., 63 NLRB 1012.

567. Agar Packing & Provision Corp., 58 NLRB 738.

568. Illinois Tool Works, 61 NLRB 1129. 65 NLRB 1181, enforced 153 F. (2d) 811, CCA 7.

569. See Phelps Dodge Copper Products Corp., 63 NLRB 686; Midwest Piping & Supply Co. Inc., 63 NLRB 1060.

570. 29 USCA Sec. 152(2), (13).

571. International Association of Machinists v. NLRB, 311 U.S. 72; NLRB v. Link-Belt Co., 311 U.S. 584.

572. See F. W. Woolworth Co. v. NLRB, 121 F. (2d) 658.

573. International Association of Machinists v. NLRB, 311 U.S. 72.

574. Cities Service Oil Co., 32 NLRB 1020.

575. North American Refractories Co., 52 NLRB 1049, Fairmount Creamery Co., 51 NLRB 651, enforced 144 F. (2d) 128.

576. Shellabarger Grain Products Co., 8 NLRB 336, 358.

577. Banner Slipper Co. Inc., 31 NLRB 621.

578. Nebraska Power Co., 19 NLRB 357, 365.

579. Schult Trailors Inc., 28 NLRB 975.

580. Curtiss-Wright Corp., 39 NLRB 992.

581. Pennsylvania Greyhound Lines, 11 NLRB 738, 746.

582. Draper Corp., 52 NLRB 1477.

583. Swift & Co., 7 NLRB 269, 284.

584. Van Raalte Co., 55 NLRB 146.

585. Inland Steel Co., 9 NLRB 783, 812.

586. Newberry Lumber & Chemical Co., 17 NLRB 795.

587. Blue Ridge Shirt Mfg. Co., 70 NLRB No. 58.

588. Zenith Optical Co., 55 NLRB 252.

589. Fred P. Weissman Co., 69 NLRB No. 125.

590. Abinante & Nola Packing Co., 26 NLRB 1288.

591. Duluth Bottling Association, 48 NLRB 1335.

592. Cooper, Wells Co., 16 NLRB 27, 32.

593. Textile Machine Works, 69 NLRB No. 96.

594. Richmond Home Telephone Co., 70 NLRB No. 37.

595. Goodall Company, 68 NLRB No. 31.

596. Burnside Steel Foundry Co., 69 NLRB No. 12.

597. Textile Machine Works, 69 NLRB No. 96.

598. Robbins Tire and Rubber Co., 69 NLRB No. 53.

599. Peter J. Schweitzer Inc., 54 NLRB 813.

600. Tennessee Copper Co., 9 NLRB 117, 118; Pennsylvania Greyhound Lines, 1 NLRB 1; Rockford Mitten & Hosiery Co., 16 NLRB 501; Ward Baking Co., 8 NLRB 558, 565.

601. Oval Wood Dish, 62 NLRB 1129.

602. See the majority and dissenting opinions in Agar Packing & Provision Corp., 58 NLRB 738.

603. Trojan Powder Co. v. NLRB, 135 F. (2d) 337, cert. denied 320 U.S. 768.

604. NLRB v. Virginia Electric & Power Co. 314 U.S. 469, 477.

605. 29 USCA Sec. 158(c).

606. NLRB v. Crown Can Co., 138 F. (2d) 263; NLRB v. Lettie Lee Inc., 140 F. (2d) 243.

607. R. R. Donnelly & Sons, 60 NLRB 635.

608. Some courts have accepted the Board's judgment as expert and controlling in certain aspects of labor relations. See NLRB v. Standard Oil Co., 138 F. (2d) 885; Republic Aviation Corp. v. NLRB, 142 F. (2d) 193, aff'd 324 U.S. 793.

609. Hoover Co., 6 NLRB 688, 691.

610. Wickwire Bros., 16 NLRB 316, 320.

611. Butler Bros., 41 NLRB 843.

612. The Glenn L. Martin-Nebraska Co., 48 NLRB 587.

613. Merchants Motor Freight Inc., 57 NLRB 1340.

614. Agar Packing & Provision Co., 58 NLRB 738.

615. International Harvester Co., 29 NLRB 456.

616. Hope Webbing Co., 14 NLRB 55.

617. 29 USCA (1947, Supp.) Sec. 158(a) (2).

618. International Association of Machinists v. NLRB, 311 U.S. 72; Sperry Gyroscope Co., Inc., v. NLRB, 129 F. (2d) 922; NLRB v. Southern Bell T. & T. Co., 319 U.S. 50; NLRB v. Pennsylvania Greyhound Lines, 303 U.S. 261; NLRB v. Falk Corp., 308 U.S. 453.

619. Chicago Molded Products Corp., 38 NLRB 111.

620. Westinghouse Electric & Mfg. Co. v. NLRB, 112 F. (2d) 657, affirmed per curiam 312 U.S. 660. The Circuit Court said at p. 660: "If the Board's order had to depend alone upon the two acts of discrimination against the local, which we have confirmed, it would somewhat tax our credulity to suppose that their effect was substantial; but we need not, and do not, put our decision upon that ground, for it seems to us that the situation is ruled by National Labor Relations Board v. Newport News Shipbuilding & Dry Dock Company, 308 U.S. 241, 60 S. Ct. 203, 84 L. Ed. 219. There also had been a 'Plan' in which company representatives had participated, and which became unlawful after the passage of the Act; there also this 'Plan' had been succeeded by an unaffiliated union; though, unlike the case at bar, the company retained some measure of control over amendments to its constitution. The court thought this factor enough to condemn the union, but it did not rest its decision upon that alone;

for it held that the successor ought to be 'disestablished,' even if this feature were removed. The reason for this was that, although the new union would be lawful, if freely formed, it had in fact arisen out of the earlier organization, and the company had done nothing to mark the separation between the two, and publicly to deprive the successor of the advantage of its apparently continued favor. It is true that in that case there was somewhat less separation between the old and the new than in the case at bar; the union was in form merely a 'revision' of the earlier 'Plan,' and its constitution had been prepared in part at any rate, by executives of the company. But that was not the circumstance which counted, as we understand it; it was rather that the employees at large had not been advised that the company was wholly indifferent whether they joined the new union, and that, as it might, and probably did, appear to be a successor of the old, the separation should have been made plain, and with it the discontinuance of any continued countenance from the employer."

621. 29 USCA (1947, Supp.) Sec. 160 (c). In the Carpenter Steel Co., 76 NLRB 670, the Board said:

"Section 10 (c) of the original National Labor Relations Act directed the Board to order employers found to have engaged in conduct violative of the Act to cease and desist from their illegal conduct. It also gave the Board power to order employers to take affirmative action to remedy the unfair labor practices committed, a power limited only by the requirement that the remedy effectuate the policies of the Act.

"For 11 years, before the 1947 amendments were incorporated in the Act by the Labor Management Relations Act, the Board found that one particular type of affirmative action would most effectively remedy the consequences of an employer's illegal control of an unaffiliated labor organization, and make possible a free choice of representatives by the employees affected. That was the complete disestablishment of the subservient organization as a bargaining representative. (See Matter of Pennsylvania Greyhound Lines, 1 N.L.R.B. 1, enforced 303 U.S. 261.) The Board invariably issued a disestablishment order, directing the employer to withhold all recognition in perpetuo, once it found a violation of Section 8 (2) of the Act

with respect to an unaffiliated organization.

"In 1947, however, the Board indicated that it would not exercise its full power to order disestablishment in all cases involving unaffiliated labor organizations which have been the beneficiary of employer unfair labor practices, but would withhold that remedy where the passage of time and other circumstances demonstrated that a less stringent order would suffice to remove the effects of the unfair labor practices that occurred. See the opinion of Chairman Herzog in Matter of Detroit Edison Company, 74 N.L.R.B. 267.

"A disestablished union could never be certified by the Board. Such orders were approved by the courts as a valid exercise of the Board's remedial powers under Section 10(c). (See, for example, N.L.R.B. v. Pennsylvania Greyhound Lines, Inc., 303 U.S. 261; N.L.R.B. v. Newport News Shipbuilding & Dry Dock Co., 308 U.S. 241.

"The Board did not, however, apply the full disestablishment remedy to employer-controlled or assisted labor organizations which were affiliated with a national or international federation. In such cases, the employer's conduct was complained against only as a violation of Section 8 (1) of the Act rather than of Section 8 (2). If a violation was found, the Board, in addition to directing the cessation of the illegal interference, merely ordered that recognition be withheld from the employer-controlled or assisted organization until it was certified by the Board. No certification would, of course, issue until the effects of the employer's illegal control or assistance had been dissipated, but thereafter it could issue to the same organization.

"This difference in treatment, as between affiliated and non-affiliated organizations, was based upon the Board's belief that a labor organization affiliated with a national or international federation that was outside the ambit of the employer's control could not be permanently and completely subjugated to the will of the employer. It was thought that complete disestablishment was therefore not required to remedy the effects of employer interference or to restore the employees' freedom of self-organization. (For the Board's original rationale, see the testimony of the Chairman before the Senate Committee on Labor and Public Welfare on March 6, 1947, and Hearings before

621. (*Cont.*)
Senate Committee on Labor and Public Welfare on S. 55 and S. J. Res. 22, 80th Cong., 1st Sess., p. 1912 (1947).)

"That Congress disagreed with the distinction drawn by the Board became apparent when the Labor Management Relations Act of 1947 was passed. In reenacting Section 10(c) of the National Labor Relations Act, Congress qualified the Board's authority to direct affirmative action by adding a proviso which required that, in deciding cases involving unfair labor practices under Section 8(a)(1) or 8(a)(2), the Board should apply the 'same regulations and rules of decision . . . irrespective of whether or not the labor organization affected is affiliated with a labor organization national or international in scope.' (Section 9(c)(2) governs the impact of this proviso upon the Board's conduct of representation proceedings.)

"This proviso constitutes, in effect, Congressional rejection of the Board's prior view that mere affiliation with a national federation places a labor organization in such a different position from an organization not so affiliated as to warrant the use of different remedies when employer assistance or control has been found. There is no evidence, however, that the proviso was intended to abolish the disestablishment remedy itself; the target was discrimination in its use.

"Both the statutory language and the debates concerning the amendment (see 93 Cong. Rec. 4150 (April 25, 1947), 4321 (April 29, 1947), 4411 (April 30, 1947), 5145 (May 12, 1947); see also Sen. Rep. No. 105, 80th Cong., 1st Sess., 3, 12 (1947)) make it wholly clear that Congress added this proviso to Section 10 (c) in order to put an end to the disparity of treatment the Board had previously applied as between affiliated and unaffiliated organizations. The Board may no longer concern itself with the affiliation of a labor organization, or the lack thereof, in framing a remedy for violations of Section 8(a)(1) and 8(a)(2). So plain a mandate must be carried out without reservation or purpose of evasion, no matter how great the practical difficulties. Upon similar facts, the Board will hereafter apply the same remedy to both affiliated and unaffiliated labor organizations. Similarity of facts must be the test.

"Henceforth the Board's policy will be as follows:

"In all cases in which we find that an employer has dominated, or interfered with, or contributed support to a labor organization, or has committed any of these proscribed acts, we will find such conduct a violation of Section 8(a)(2) of the Act, as amended in 1947, regardless of whether the organization involved is affiliated. Where we find that an employer's unfair labor practices have been so extensive as to constitute domination of the organization, we shall order its disestablishment, whether or not it be affiliated. (Identical standards must also be applied to affiliated and unaffiliated local unions in those situations in which, following disestablishment, a new labor organization appears on the scene, and a question arises as to whether it is the 'successor' of the old.)

"The Board believes that disestablishment is still necessary as a remedy, in order effectively to remove the consequences of an employer's unfair labor practices and to make possible a free choice of representatives, in those cases, perhaps few in number, in which an employer's control of any labor organization has extended to the point of actual domination.

"But when the Board finds that an employer's unfair labor practices were limited to interference and support and never reached the point of domination, we shall only order that recognition be withheld until certification, again without regard to whether or not the organization happens to be affiliated. Subsequent representation proceedings in such situations will be governed, of course, by the provisions of Section 9(c)(2)."

See also William Fogel, 82 NLRB No. 150, where the Board applied the foregoing principles to two factual situations. Illegal domination was found where the employer's representative initiated the organization, assisted in organizing and employees were paid for time spent on behalf of the organization. On the other hand illegal assistance, rather than domination, was found where the employer granted an organization prompt recognition without verifying its majority status and quickly signed a contract, providing benefits denied a nationally affiliated union during negotiations and during the pendency of a representation petition before the Board.

622. NLRB v. Southern Bell T. & T., 319 U.S. 50; NLRB v. Standard Oil Co., 138 F. (2d) 885.

623. In Sperry Gyroscope Co. v. NLRB, 129 F. (2d) 922, 927, the Court pointed out: "For in such a case as this, the crucial fact, so the Supreme Court has crisply told us, is not the company's actual purpose or intent but the effect on the employees' state of mind, i.e., what the employees might reasonably believe was the employer's attitude. This the Supreme Court made sharply clear in the language quoted above from International Ass'n. of Machinists v. NLRB, 311 U.S. 72, 80, 61 S. Ct. 83, 88, 85 L. Ed. 50: If the employees, said the court, 'would have just cause to believe' that representatives of a union were 'acting for and on behalf of the management, the Board would be justified in concluding' that the employees 'did not have the complete and unhampered freedom of choice which the Act contemplates.' Technical concepts of principal and agent, the court added, are not pertinent, because, it said, the test is whether there exists 'collective bargaining . . . (free) from all taint of an employer's compulsion, domination, or influence.' "

624. Kropp Forge Co., 68 NLRB No. 88.

625. Julius Kayser & Co., 39 NLRB 825.

626. Poultry Producers of Central Calif., 25 NLRB 347; Burson Knitting Co., 19 NLRB 806; Todd Shipyards Corp., 5 NLRB 20, 33, 34.

627. Cudahy Packing Co., 17 NLRB 302.

628. Andrew Jergens Co. of Calif., 43 NLRB 457; Emerson Radio & Phonograph Corp., 43 NLRB 613.

629. Brown Co., 65 NLRB No. 43.

630. Wyman-Gordon Co., 62 NLRB 561.

631. Wilson & Co. v. NLRB, 103 F. (2d) 243, 251.

632. NLRB v. J. Freezer & Son, 95 F. (2d) 840.

633. Wilson & Co. v. NLRB, 103 F. (2d) 243.

634. Edward G. Budd Mfg. Co., 41 NLRB 872.

635. Wilson & Co. v. NLRB, 103 F. (2d) 243.

636. Square D. Company, 41 NLRB 693.

637. Berkshire Knitting Mills, 17 NLRB 239; Western Felt Works, 10 NLRB 407.

638. Pennsylvania Greyhound Lines Inc., 1 NLRB 1, 15, enforced 303 U.S. 261.

639. Sunshine Mining Co., 7 NLRB 1252, enforced 110 F. (2d) 780; Berkshire Knitting Mills, 17 NLRB 239.

640. Lane Life Boat & Davit Corp., 60 NLRB 473.

641. Remington Arms Co. Inc., 62 NLRB 611.

642. NLRB v. Pennsylvania Greyhound Lines Inc., 303 U.S. 261.

643. NLRB v. Pennsylvania Greyhound Lines, Inc., 303 U.S. 261.

644. Hamilton Brown Shoe Co. v. NLRB, 104 F. (2d) 49.

645. NLRB v. Carlisle Lumber Co., 94 F. (2d) 138; Berkshire Knitting Mills, 17 NLRB 239; Jacobs Bros. Co. Inc., 5 NLRB 620, 630.

646. Wells-Lamont-Smith Corp., 42 NLRB 440.

647. Square D. Co., 41 NLRB 693; Food Machinery Corp., 41 NLRB 1428.

648. Berkshire Knitting Mills, 17 NLRB 239.

649. Elizabeth Arden Inc., 45 NLRB 936.

650. Industrial Rayon Corp., 7 NLRB 878, 890; Wheeling Steel Corp. 1 NLRB 699, 709.

651. However, the Board has no authority to Act unless the subject of the employer's domination is a labor organization within the meaning of the Act. See 29 USCA Secs. 152(5), 158(2).

652. 308 U.S. 241, 249.

653. 319 U.S. 50, 53, 54.

654. Keystone Steel & Wire Co., 62 NLRB 683.

655. NLRB v. Pennsylvania Greyhound Lines, 303 U.S. 261.

656. NLRB v. Pennsylvania Greyhound Lines, 303 U.S. 261; NLRB v. National Licorice Co., 309 U.S. 350.

657. 29 USCA appendix Sec. 202.5.

658. 29 USCA appendix Sec. 203.8.

659. 29 USCA appendix Sec. 203.15.

660. Virginia Electric & Power Co. v. NLRB, 319 U.S. 533; NLRB v. Cassoff, 139 F. (2d) 397; Donnelly Garment Co. v. NLRB, 165 F. (2d) 940.

661. H. J. Heinz Co., 10 NLRB 963, 974, enforced 311 U.S. 514.

662. NLRB v. J. G. Boswell Co., 136 F. (2d) 585.

663. Sperry Gyroscope Co., Inc., v. NLRB, 129 F. (2d) 922.

664. Southern Bell Telephone & Telegraph Co., 35 NLRB 621.

665. McLain Fire Brick Co., 36 NLRB 1.

666. Standard Oil Co., of Calif., 62 NLRB No. 65; American Rolling Mill Co., 43 NLRB 1020.

667. NLRB v. Pacific Greyhound Lines, 303 U.S. 272.

668. Wallace Corp. v. NLRB, 323 U.S. 248.

669. Perfection Steel Body Co., 36 NLRB 851.

670. Rock Hill Printing & Finishing Co., 29 NLRB 673.

671. NLRB v. Southern Bell Telephone & Telegraph Co., 319 U.S. 50.

672. NLRB v. Continental Oil Co., 121 F. (2d) 120 (CCA 10).

673. J. Greenbaum Tanning Co., 11 NLRB 300.

674. Neptune Meter Company, 66 NLRB No. 33.

675. Westinghouse Electric & Mfg. Co. v. NLRB, 112 F. (2d) 657; NLRB v. Southern Bell T. & T. Co., 319 U.S. 50; Sperry Gyroscope Co. v. NLRB, 129 F. (2d) 922.

676. Sperry Gyroscope Co., Inc., v. NLRB, 129 F. (2d) 922.

677. Sperry Gyroscope Co. Inc., v. NLRB, 129 F. (2d) 922, 927, 928.

678. NLRB v. Newport News Shipbuilding, 308 U.S. 241; NLRB v. Southern Bell Telephone & Telegraph Co., 319 U.S. 50.

679. Sperry Gyroscope Co., Inc., v. NLRB, 129 F. (2d) 922.

680. In NLRB v. Standard Oil Co., 138 F. (2d) 885, 887, the court said: "We need not say whether on this showing we should have come to the Board's conclusion that in November, 1941, four and a half years after the 'Association' was formed, and at a time when there can be no doubt that a very great majority of the employees still adhered to it, their adherence was a consequence of some carry-over of the respondent's earlier favor of the 'Plan,' and its well known preference for it over an alliance with any national union. We understand the law to be that the decision of the Board upon that issue is for all practical purposes not open to us at all; certainly not after we have once decided that there was 'substantial' evidence that the 'disestablished' union was immediately preceded by a period during which there was a 'dominated' union."

681. "Since we sustain the Board's findings that Brotherhood was company dominated, a closed shop agreement with it was a violation of the act, and a discharge pursuant to that agreement was improper." Sperry Gyroscope Co. v. NLRB, 129 F. (2d) 922, 931.

682. Pacific Manifolding Book Company, Inc., 64 NLRB No. 211; Supersweet Feed Company, Inc., 62 NLRB No. 9; Keystone Steel & Wire Co., 62 NLRB 683; Lane Lifeboat & Davit Corp., 60 NLRB 473.

683. Republic Steel Corp. v. NLRB, 107 F. (2d) 472.

684. NLRB v. Southern Bell Telephone & Telegraph Co., 319 U.S. 50.

685. NLRB v. Standard Oil Co., 124 F. (2d) 895.

686. NLRB v. Rath Packing Co. (CCA 8), 123 F. (2d) 684.

687. E. I. Du Pont de Nemours & Co. v. NLRB, 116 F. (2d) 388.

688. NLRB v. Rath Packing Co., 130 F. (2d) 540, 543.

689. Pacific Greyhound Lines, 2 NLRB 431, enforced in NLRB v. Pacific Greyhound Lines, Inc., 303 U.S. 272. In NLRB v. Pennsylvania Greyhound Lines, Inc., 303 U.S. 261, 271, the Court said: "In view of all the circumstances the Board could have thought that continued recognition of the Association would serve as a means of thwarting the policy of collective bargaining by enabling the employer to induce adherence of employees to the Association in the mistaken belief that it was truly representative and afforded an agency for collective bargaining, and thus to prevent self-organization. The inferences to be drawn were for the Board and not the courts. Swayne & Hoyt v. United States, *supra*. There was ample basis for its conclusion that withdrawal of recognition of the Association by respondents, accompanied by suitable publicity, was an appropriate way to give effect to the policy of the Act."

690. Cudahy Packing Co. v. NLRB, 102 F. (2d) 745.

691. NLRB v. National Tool Co., 139 F. (2d) 490.

692. NLRB v. Standard Oil Co., 124 F. (2d) 895.

693. Carpenter Steel Co., 76 NLRB No. 104.

694. Carpenter Steel Co., *supra,* note 693.

695. 29 USCA (1947, Supp.) Sec. 160 (e).

696. Carpenter Steel Co., *supra,* note 693. Virginia Electric & Power Co. v. NLRB, 319 U.S. 533; NLRB v. Cassoff, 139 F. (2d) 397; NLRB v. Baltimore Transit Co., 140 F. (2d) 51, certiorari denied 324 U.S. 795. It is significant that in the Cassoff case the check-off was in favor of a nationally affiliated union found to have been assisted by unfair labor practices rather than a union found to have been company-dominated, and in the Baltimore Transit Co. case the company-dominated union did not have a closed shop agreement.

697. 29 USCA (1947, Supp.) Sec. 158 (a) (3).

698. The crucial question is whether the layoff was "to encourage or discourage membership in any labor organization."

699. A discriminatory lockout has substantially the same effect as a discriminatory discharge, according to the Board. Hopwood Retinning Co., 4 NLRB 922, enforced as modified in other respects, NLRB v. Hopwood Retinning Co. Inc., 98 F. (2d) 97.

700. See Pepsi-Cola Bottling Co., 72 NLRB No. 118; Victory Fluospar Mining Co., 72 NLRB No. 247.

701. Bohn Aluminum & Brass Corp., 67 NLRB 847; Central Minerals Co., 59 NLRB 757; 47 NLRB 652.

702. Crystal Springs Finishing Co., 12 NLRB 1291.

703. See Montgomery Ward & Co. v. NLRB, 107 F. (2d) 555; Cupples Co. v. NLRB, 106 F. (2d) 100; Kansas City Power & Light v. NLRB, 111 F. (2d) 340; North Whittier Heights Citrus Ass'n. v. NLRB, 109 F. (2d) 76, cert. den. 310 U.S. 632. In the Montgomery Ward & Co. case, *supra* (p. 559) the Court pointed out: "At this time it should be stated that the facts also show a high percentage of union members among the employees discharged in the three departments mentioned above. To be more specific, 96% of the employees discharged therefrom belonged to the union. Stated differently, 40 of the 63 persons employed therein belong to the union, and 24 of the 25 discharged therefrom were union members (the 25th employee was a woman; there is evidence in the record that women were ineligible for union membership). Stand-

ing alone, this percentage evidence will not sustain an order based on Section 8 (3) of the Act. But, coupled with other evidence such as is present in this case, it becomes very persuasive. Hamilton-Brown Shoe Co. v. Board, 8 Cir., 104 F. (2d) 49, 53."

704. Montgomery Ward & Co. v. NLRB, 107 F. (2d) 555, 560 where the court said: "Clearly, the evidence adduced to support the complaint gives rise to an inference that is sufficient to support an order based on Section 8(3) of the Act. Unless 'destroyed and refuted by other evidence,' National Labor Relations Board v. Kentucky Fire Brick Co., 6 Cir., 99 F. (2d) 89, 92, the inference of discrimination is substantial and sufficient 'enough to justify,' if the trial were to a jury, 'a refusal to direct a verdict,' Columbian Enameling and Stamping Case, *supra,* 306 U.S. at page 300, 59 S. Ct. at page 505, 83 L. Ed. 660. See also Chamberlain v. Pennsylvania Railroad, 2 Cir., 59 F. (2d) 986, reversed 288 U.S. 333, 53 S. Ct. 391, 77 L. Ed. 819. This inference of discriminatory discharge leaves it up to the employer to give an adequate 'explanation of the discharge,' even though the burden of proof remains on the Board, since it is obvious that the reasons of the discharge 'lay exclusively within its own knowledge.' National Labor Relations Board v. Remington Rand, Inc., 2 Cir., 94 F. (2d) 862, 871, 872."

705. Sunshine Mining Co., 7 NLRB 1252; Cleveland Worsted Mills, 43 NLRB 545.

706. Carlisle Lumber Co., 2 NLRB 248; Atlas Mills Inc., 3 NLRB 10; Jacob A. Hunkele, 7 NLRB 1276; Douglas Aircraft Co. Inc., 18 NLRB 43; Swift & Co., 30 NLRB 550; Gibson County Electric Membership Corp., 74 NLRB No. 240; Califruit Canning Co., 73 NLRB No. 55.

707. Dickson-Jenkins Mfg. Co., 17 NLRB 18.

708. NLRB v. Mackay Radio & Telegraph Co., 304 U.S. 333.

709. NLRB v. Remington Rand Inc., 94 F. (2d) 862, the Court said: "But since the refusal was at least one cause of the strike, and was a tort—a 'subtraction'—it rested upon the tortfeasor to disentangle the consequences for which it was chargeable from those from which it was immune. Since it cannot show that the negotiations, if undertaken, would have broken down, it cannot say that the loss of the men's jobs

709. (*Cont.*)
was due to a controversy which the act does not affect to regulate."

710. Steward Die Casting Corp., v. NLRB, 114 F. (2d) 849 (CCA-7).

711. Firth Carpet Co. v. NLRB, 129 F. (2d) 633 (CCA-2).

712. Steward Die Casting v. NLRB, 114 F. (2d) 849.

713. Douglas Aircraft Co. Inc., 10 NLRB 242.

714. Hudson Motor Car Co., 34 NLRB 815.

715. Mackay Radio & Telegraph Co., 1 NLRB 201, enforced 304 U.S. 333.

716. Firth Carpet Co., 33 NLRB 191.

717. See Gardner-Denver Co., 58 NLRB No. 15; Pinaud Inc., 51 NLRB 235, where the strike was for economic reasons.

718. NLRB v. East Texas Motor Freight Lines, 140 F. (2d) 404.

719. Heilig Bros. Co., 32 NLRB 505.

720. See Cravis v. Pennsylvania LRB, 12 LRRM 612.

721. Hamilton v. NLRB, 160 F. (2d) 465.

722. Novelty Peanut Co., 69 NLRB 1031.

723. Pepsi-Cola Bottling Co. of Montgomery, 72 NLRB 601.

724. Bettcher Mfg. Corp., 76 NLRB No. 83.

725. Aluminum Goods Mfg. Co., 25 NLRB 1004.

726. Scheiber Millinery Co., 26 NLRB 937; Great Western Mushroom Co., 27 NLRB 352.

727. See 29 USCA (1947, Supp.) Sec. 160(c); NLRB v. Hopwood Retinning Co., 98 F. (2d) 97; NLRB v. Stackpole Carbon Co., 105 F. (2d) 167. For typical runaway shop case see Jacob H. Klotz, 13 NLRB 746.

728. Trenton Garment Co., 4 NLRB 1186; Fiss Corp., 43 NLRB 125.

729. NLRB v. Cape County Milling Co., 140 F. (2d) 543; NLRB v. Gluek Brewing Co., 144 F. (2d) 847.

730. 29 USCA (1947, Supp.) Sec. 158(a) (3).

731. Ford Motor Co., 50 NLRB 534; South Carolina Granite Co., 58 NLRB 1448; Kansas City Power & Light v. NLRB, 111 F. (2d) 340; Arrowhead Rubber Co., 56 NLRB 1618; Pulaski Veneer Corp., 10 NLRB 136.

732. Wallace Mfg. Co., Inc., 2 NLRB 1081.

733. NLRB v. Gallup American Coal Co., 131 F. (2d) 665.

734. Carrington Publishing Co., 42 NLRB 356.

735. Banner Slipper Co. Inc., 31 NLRB 621.

736. United Aircraft Corp., 67 NLRB No. 80; Industrial Metal Fabricators, 67 NLRB No. 38.

737. Johnson Bronze Co., 57 NLRB 814.

738. D. W. Onan & Sons v. NLRB, 139 F. (2d) 728.

739. NLRB v. Revlon Products, 114 F. (2d) 88.

740. Simmons Co., 54 NLRB 130.

741. Goshen Rubber & Mfg. Co., 11 NLRB 1346.

742. Central Steel Tube Co., 48 NLRB 604.

743. Edward G. Budd Mfg. Co. v. NLRB, 138 F. (2d) 86.

744. Rutland Court Owners, Inc., 44 NLRB 587, supp. dec. 46 NLRB 1040.

745. NLRB v. Bear Brand Hosiery, CCA-7 (1942), 131 F. (2d) 731; United Biscuit Co. of America, 38 NLRB 778; National Linen Service Corp., 48 NLRB 171; Club Troika Inc., 2 NLRB 90; Gardner-Denver Co., 58 NLRB 81.

746. NLRB v. Security Warehouse & Cold Storage Co., 136 F. (2d) 829.

747. Northwestern Cabinet Co., 38 NLRB 357.

748. Consolidated Edison Co. v. NLRB, 95 F. (2d) 390, modified and affirmed 305 U.S. 197.

749. National Container Corp., 57 NLRB 565.

750. Central Paint & Varnish Works, 43 NLRB 1193.

751. Cape County Milling Co., 49 NLRB 226.

752. NLRB v. Waterman Steamship Corp., 309 U.S. 206.

753. R. C. Mahon Co., 28 NLRB 619.

754. Veta Mines, Inc., 36 NLRB 288.

755. Long Lake Lumber Co., 34 NLRB 700.

756. National Linen Service Corp., 48 NLRB 171.

757. Leslie County Lumber Co., 52 NLRB 1147; Newberry Lumber & Chemical Co., 17 NLRB 795; Hopwood Retinning Co., Inc., 4 NLRB 922; New York State LRB v. Frank G. Shattuck, N.Y. Sup. Ct., 5 LRRM 980, modified in 260 App. Div. 315.

758. NLRB v. Brezner Tanning Co., 141 F. (2d) 62.

759. General Motors Corp., 59 NLRB No. 205.

760. Allis-Chalmers Manufacturing Co., 70 NLRB 348.

761. Southern Colorado Power Co., 13 NLRB 699; Central Greyhound Lines, of N.Y., 27 NLRB 976.

762. Heat Transfer Products, Inc., 52 NLRB 241.

763. Automatic Screw Machine Co., 52 NLRB 488.

764. Borg-Warner Corp., 44 NLRB 105.

765. Le Tourneau Co. of Georgia, 54 NLRB 1253, enforced 324 U.S. 793.

766. Sperry Gyroscope Co. Inc. v. NLRB, 129 F. (2d) 922.

767. Leslie County Lumber Co., 52 NLRB 1147.

768. J. Chesler & Sons Co., 13 NLRB 1.

769. Washington Mfg. Co., 4 NLRB 970.

770. Hickey Chair Mfg. Co., 41 NLRB 288.

771. Wilson & Co., Inc., 26 NLRB 297.

772. NLRB v. Grieder Machine Tool & Die Co., 142 F. (2d) 163.

773. Western Cartridge Co., 44 NLRB 1.

774. NLRB v. Schmidt Baking Co., 122 F. (2d) 162.

775. North Carolina Finishing Co. v. NLRB, 133 F. (2d) 714.

776. Thompson Products, Inc., 57 NLRB 925.

777. Midwest Steel Corp., 32 NLRB 195.

778. Taylor Trunk Co., 6 NLRB 32.

779. NLRB v. Chicago Steel Foundry Co., 142 F. (2d) 306.

780. Johnson Bronze Co., 57 NLRB 814, enforced 148 F. (2d) 818.

781. Gamble-Robinson Co., 33 NLRB 351.

782. Empire Worsted Mills, Inc., 6 NLRB 513.

783. 29 USCA (1947, Supp.) Sec. 158

(a) (5), 158(b) (3), 158(d). See also 29 USCA (1947, Supp.) Sec. 159.

784. NLRB v. Timken Roller Bearing Co., 161 F. (2d) 949 (CCA 6): United Elastic Corp., 84 NLRB 768; NLRB v. Dorsey Trailers, Inc., 179 F. (2d) 589, 25 LRRM 2333.

785. Pacific Gas Radiator Co., 21 NLRB 630.

786. Harbor Boat Building Co., 1 NLRB 349; Quality & Service Laundry, Inc., 39 NLRB 970; Chicago Apparatus Co., 12 NLRB 1002.

786a. Bethlehem Steel Co., 89 NLRB No. 33.

786b. Bethlehem Steel Co., 89 NLRB No. 33.

787. Medo Photo Supply Corp. v. NLRB, 321 U.S. 678.

788. Scripto Mfg. Co., 36 NLRB 411.

789. American Hair & Felt Co., 19 NLRB 202.

790. Paul Uhlich & Co., Inc., 26 NLRB 679.

791. Zenite Metal Corp., 5 NLRB 509.

792. Central Dispensary & Emergency Hospital, 50 NLRB 393.

793. Chambers Corp., 21 NLRB 808.

794. Max Ulman, Inc., 45 NLRB 836.

795. Schieber Millinery Co., 26 NLRB 937.

796. The E. Biglow Co., 52 NLRB 999.

797. Inland Lime & Stone Co., 24 NLRB 758.

798. May Department Stores Co. v. NLRB, 326 U.S. 376.

799. The W. H. Kistler Stationery Co., 24 NLRB 960.

800. NLRB v. Chicago Apparatus Co., 116 F. (2d) 753.

801. Martin Bros. Box Co., 35 NLRB 217.

802. Shell Oil Co. of California, 2 NLRB 835.

803. Cape County Milling Co., 49 NLRB 226.

804. Interstate Steamship Co., 36 NLRB 1307.

805. The E. Biglow Co., 52 NLRB 999.

806. Hancock Brick & Tile Co., 44 NLRB 920.

807. Golden Turkey Mining Co., 34 NLRB 760.

808. Henry Glass & Co., 21 NLRB 727.

809. Montgomery Ward & Co., 37 NLRB 100.

810. Hancock Brick & Tile Co., 44 NLRB 920.

811. Medo Photo Supply Corp. v. NLRB, 321 U.S. 678.

812. Scripto Manufacturing Co., 36 NLRB 411, 428.

813. Bingler Motors Inc., 30 NLRB 1080; Lettie Lee Inc., 45 NLRB 448.

814. Franks Bros. Co. v. NLRB, 321 U.S. 702.

815. Bingler Motors, Inc., 30 NRLB 1080.

816. Newton Chevrolet, Inc., 37 NLRB 334.

817. V-O Milling Co., 43 NLRB 348.

818. NLRB v. Westinghouse Air Brake Co., 120 F. (2d) 1004.

819. Henry McCleary Timber Co., 37 NLRB 725.

820. Dadourian Export Corp., 46 NLRB 498.

821. Lettie Lee, Inc., 45 NLRB 448.

822. Leyse Aluminum Co., 37 NLRB 839.

823. Manville Jenckes Corp., 30 NLRB 382.

824. V-O Milling Co., 43 NLRB 348.

825. NLRB v. P. Lorillard & Co., 314 U.S. 512; Franks Bros. Co. v. NLRB, 321 U.S. 702.

826. Eppinger & Russell Co., 56 NLRB 1259.

827. Century Oxford Mfg. Co., 47 NLRB 835, enforced 140 F. (2d) 541; NLRB v. Botany Worsted Mills, 106 F. (2d) 263; NLRB v. Appalachian Electric Power Co., 140 F. (2d) 217.

828. Whittier Mills Co., 15 NLRB 457.

829. National Seal Corp., 30 NLRB 188.

830. The requisite of a written signed agreement is now well established. H. J. Heinz Co. v. NLRB, 311 U.S. 514. However, the Board has held that execution of the agreement does not relieve the employer from negotiating concerning modification, interpretation and administration. Ideal Leather Novelty Co., Inc., 54 NLRB 761; George E. Carroll et al., 56 NLRB 935.

831. American Range Lines, Inc., 13 NLRB 139.

832. Brown-McLaren Mfg. Co., 34 NLRB 984.

833. The L. Hardy Co., 44 NLRB 1013.

834. S. L. Allen & Co., Inc., 1 NLRB 714.

835. Westinghouse Air Brake Co., 25 NLRB 1312.

836. Aluminum Ore Co., 39 NLRB 1286.

837. Singer Mfg. Co., 24 NLRB 444.

838. Montgomery Ward & Co., 37 NLRB 100.

839. NLRB v. Chicago Apparatus Co., 116 F. (2d) 753.

840. Gerity Whitaker Co., 33 NLRB 393.

841. Service Wood Heel Co., Inc., 31 NLRB 1179.

842. Leo L. Lowy, 3 NLRB 938.

843. Ford Motor Co., 18 NLRB 167.

844. Sigmund Freisinger, 10 NLRB 1043.

845. Inland Lime & Stone Co., 24 NLRB 758.

846. NLRB v. J. H. Allison Co., 165 F. (2d) 766.

847. General Motors Corp., 59 NLRB No. 205.

848. NLRB v. J. H. Allison Co., 70 NLRB 377, enforced 165 F. (2d) 766, 21 LRRM 2238.

849. Tower Hosiery Mills Inc., 81 NLRB 658, 180 F. (2d) 701.

850. 29 USCA (1947, Supp.) Sec. 158 (d). In the National Maritime Union case (78 NLRB No. 137) the Board said: "The legislative history of these provisions clearly indicates that it was the purpose of Congress to impose upon labor organizations the same duty to bargain in good faith which had been imposed upon employers in Section 8(5) of the Wagner Act, and continued in Section 8(a)(5) of the amended Act. Moreover, the standards and tests set forth in Section 8(d), applicable to both employers and unions, closely paraphrase those established in decisions of the Board and the courts in recent years."

851. See Times Publishing Co., 72 NLRB No. 128.

852. 29 USCA (1947, Supp.) Sec. 158 (b) (1).

853. Senate Report 105, 80th Congress, 1st Session p. 50. The Board, however, does not appear to regard mass picketing *per se* unaccompanied by violence or the blocking of access to or from a plant as constituting restraint and coercion. Thus, it has been held that the mere presence of a large number of strikers in front of the plant was not coercive. (Perry Norvell Company, 80 NLRB No. 47.) In Cory Corporation, 84 NLRB No. 110, the Board said:

"The term (mass picketing) must, therefore, be read in the context of Section 8(b) (1)(A), which simply says that labor organizations shall not 'restrain' or 'coerce' employees. So read it cannot be construed as contemplating that this Board shall affirmatively regulate the number of persons who may properly picket an establishment. That is primarily a matter for the local authorities. Our function, rather, as we see it, is limited to determining whether picketing as conducted in a given situation, whether or not accompanied by violence, 'restrained' or 'coerced' employees in the exercise of their rights guaranteed under the Act, and, if so, to enjoin such conduct."

854. Perry Norvell Company, 80 NLRB No. 47; National Maritime Union, 78 NLRB 971; American Radio Association et al., 82 NLRB No. 151, where the strike or strike threat was to compel employer consent to an illegal hiring hall clause; Great Atlantic & Pacific Tea Company, 81 NLRB No. 164, where the strike was to compel employer consent to an illegal closed shop and union shop clauses.

855. Watson's Specialty Store, 80 NLRB No. 91, 23 LRRM 1103.

856. Watson's Specialty Store, note 855, *supra.*

857. National Maritime Union, 78 NLRB No. 137, 22 LRRM 1289.

858. Sunset Line & Twine Co., 79 NLRB No. 207, 23 LRRM 1001.

859. Cory Corporation, 84 NLRB No. 110, 24 LRRM 1326.

860. North Electric Mfg. Co., 84 NLRB No. 23, 24 LRRM 1221.

861. North Electric Mfg. Co., *supra.*

862. North Electric Mfg. Co., *supra.* In Smith Cabinet Manufacturing Co., 81 NLRB No. 138, the following conduct was held coercive: Pickets carrying sticks on picket line, open piling of bricks near the picket line for use by the pickets, union telling non-strikers "when we get in with the union you old fellows won't have

a job." In Colonial Hardwood Flooring Company, Inc., 84 NLRB No. 69, union instructions to strikers "to go and get" non-strikers were held violative of the Act. Also held coercive was a statement by a union organizer at an organization meeting that employees who did not join the union "would eventually lose their jobs." Seamprufe, Incorporated, 82 NLRB No. 106.

862a. 29 USCA (Supp.) Sec. 158(b) (1). International Typographical Union, 86 NLRB No. 115, where the Board said:

"The complaint, as construed in the course of litigation, alleged the following conduct by the Respondents to be violative of Section 8(b)(1)(A): (1) all of the conduct relied upon as a basis for the 8(b)(2) allegations of the complaint; (2) refusing, or causing the subordinate ITU Locals to refuse to bargain collectively; (3) using against Local unions and their members the threat of summary expulsion when such local unions failed to follow ITU-promulgated edicts requiring Local union conduct inconsistent with the latter's statutory obligations; (4) demanding or causing local unions to demand that employers accept certain (specified) contractual terms which, if adopted and carried out, would constitute, on the employer's part, a violation of Section 8(a) (1) and a negation of the effect of other provisions of the Act; and (5) causing or supporting 'slow-downs' in production engaged in by members of subordinate local unions in an effort to force employers to comply with the terms of the 'Collective Bargaining Policy.' For various reasons, the Trial Examiner, with the one exception noted below, dismissed these allegations, which are now before us on exceptions by the parties.

"The respondents, although denying generally the commission of the conduct complained of and the sufficiency of the evidence adduced to prove the commission, have challenged all of these allegations on grounds of legal sufficiency. It is the respondents' legal position that, aside from any issue of proof, no part of the complaint states a 'cause of action' under Section 8 (b) (1) (A). Various aspects of these legal problems have been presented to us on numerous occasions since our interlocutory ruling denying, in effect, Respondents' motion for summary dismissal. We here summarize those cases to clarify

862a. (*Cont.*)
the concepts there considered and to indicate their applicability here.

"In the National Maritime Union case, the first of the series, we decided on the basis of the legislative history there cited, that, although Congress used the generic term 'restraint and coercion' on this section, the legislative scheme envisaged a narrow construction of the terms. We held its proscriptions were limited to situations involving actual or threatened economic reprisals and physical violence by unions or their agents against specific individuals or groups of individuals in an effort to compel them to join a union or to cooperate in a union's strike activities.

"Application of the foregoing principle, and its refinement in subsequent cases require the conclusion that, with one possible exception, none of the activities encompassed by the complaint constitute unfair labor practices within the meaning of Section 8(b) (1) (A). The exception is the claim that the respondents coerced segments of the membership to cooperate in the successful operation of the unlawful 'Collective Bargaining Policy' by threatening to expel recalcitrants from membership under provisions of intra-union rules granting the respondents summary expulsion power.

"It is argued by the General Counsel and the Charging Parties that, because expulsion would deprive the expelled members of certain economic perquisites of the union-membership relation, findings of 'coercion' in the statutory sense could appropriately be premised on the threat. We agree with the Trial Examiner, however, that that argument is squarely at odds with the unambiguous language of the proviso to Section 8 (b) (1) (A) and the legislative scheme as a whole, and must therefore be rejected. In our view, by including this proviso Congress unmistakably intended to, and did, remove the application of a union's membership rules to its members from the proscriptions of Section 8 (b) (1) (A), irrespective of any ulterior reasons motivating the union's application of such rules or the direct effect thereof on particular employees.

"As the respondents' legal attacks on the sufficiency of the complaint are consistent with these views, we find them meritorious. Therefore we shall dismiss all the 8 (b) (1) (A) allegations, without passing upon the sufficiency of proof. Accord-ingly, we hereby reverse the Trial Examiner's finding that 8 (b) (1) (A) violations occurred in those instances where the union had been successful in causing the employers to continue 'closed-shop' hiring practices. To the extent that the Trial Examiner's dismissal of the remaining 8 (b) (1) (A) allegations is predicated upon reasons in harmony with the views expressed above, we hereby adopt them."

863. 29 USCA (Supp. 1947) Sec. 158(b) (1) (B); Madden v. International Union, United Mine Workers of America, 79 F. Supp. 616.

864. 29 USCA (1947, Supp.) Sec. 158 (c).

865. Sunset Line & Twine Co., 79 NLRB No. 207, 23 LRRM 1001.

866. NLRB v. Clark Bros. Co., Inc., 70 NLRB 802, enforced 163 F. (2d) 373.

867. Babcock & Wilcox Co., 77 NLRB No. 96, 22 LRRM 1057.

868. 29 USCA (1947, Supp.) Sec. 158 (b) (2). In Union Starch & Refining Company, 87 NLRB No. 137, employees who had been active on behalf of a rival union tendered periodic dues and initiation fees for the purpose of membership in a union that had entered into a valid union shop contract with the employer. The union advised these employees they would be accepted as members if they attended the meeting at which they were to be voted on, took the obligation of membership and paid the initiation fees and dues. The employees refused to go beyond payment of dues and initiation fees. The union threatened a work stoppage unless these employees were discharged under the union shop clause for "failure to pay dues and initiation fees." With knowledge that the employees had tendered payment of dues and initiation fees, the employer discharged the employees. On charges and after a hearing on a complaint against the union and the employer, the Board held both guilty of illegal discrimination. The Board said:

"On these facts the issue before us is whether an employee who tenders to a union holding a valid union-shop contract an amount equal to the initiation fees and accrued dues thereby brings himself within the protection from discharge contained in the proviso of Section 8 (a) (3) and in Section 8 (b) (2) of the amended Act.

"Section 8 (a) (3) exempts from the Act's ban on discrimination, because of membership or nonmembership in a labor organization, discharges made pursuant to an authorized union shop contract which may require 'membership' in the contracting labor organization as a 'condition of employment.' This exemption, however, is circumscribed by the limitations contained in the following proviso:

" 'Provided further, That no employer shall justify any discrimination against an employee for nonmembership in a labor organization (A) if he has reasonable grounds for believing that such membership was not available to the employee on the same terms and conditions generally applicable to other members, or (B) if he has reasonable grounds for believing that membership was denied or terminated for reasons other than the failure of the employee to tender the periodic dues and the initiation fees uniformly required as a condition of acquiring or retaining membership.'

"Section 8 (b) (2) makes it an unfair labor practice for a labor organization or its agents to cause or attempt to cause an employer to discriminate against an employee in violation of subsection (a) (3) or to discriminate against an employee with respect to whom membership in such organization has been denied or terminated on some ground other than his failure to tender the periodic dues and the initiation fees uniformly required as a condition of acquiring or retaining membership.

. . . . .

"As we read the statutory language, the provisos to Section 8 (a) (3) spell out two separate and distinct limitations on the use of the type of union-security agreements permitted by the Act. Proviso (A) protects from discharge for non-membership in the contracting union any employee to whom membership is not available for some discriminatory reason, i.e., any reason which is not generally applicable. Proviso (B) protects employees who have tendered the requisite amount of dues and initiation fees and been denied membership for any other reason, even though that reason be nondiscriminatory.

"At first blush the provisos appear to involve duplication. Indeed, the respondent company argues that such a reading of the statute, when applied to employees who have never been members of the contracting union, renders meaningless proviso (A), contending that any discriminatory reason for denying an employee membership would always be a reason other than his failure to pay dues or initiation fees. More careful analysis, however, readily discloses that provisos (A) and (B) have ample independent scope, and the elementary principle of statutory construction which favors giving some meaning to each part of a statute is thereby satisfied. Thus, for example, it is clear that proviso (B) requires a tender of dues and fees, whereas proviso (A) protects any employee discriminatorily excluded from membership whether or not such tender is made.

"We therefore read proviso (B) as extending protection to any employee who tenders periodic dues and initiation fees without being accorded membership. If the union imposes any other qualifications and conditions for membership with which he is unwilling to comply, such an employee may not be entitled to membership, but he is entitled to keep his job. Throughout the amendment to the Act, Congress evinced a strong concern for protecting the individual employee in a right to refrain from union activity and to keep his job even in a union shop. Congress carefully limited the sphere of permissible union security, and even in that limited sphere accorded the union no power to effect the discharge of nonmembers except to protect itself against 'free rides.'

"We cannot say, as did the Trial Examiner, that by refusing to comply with the union's requests the employees had demonstrated that they 'were entirely unwilling to become members' and therefore that 'membership' had not been 'denied' to them. The employees were willing to comply with the only term or condition for membership which we think can, under the provisos, legally be enforced by discharge—the tender of the periodic dues and initiation fees uniformly required. Thus in the case of Rawlings, membership was 'denied' even after her application was 'favorably voted upon,' because the union imposed conditions of membership over and above the tender of dues and initiation fees. And in the case of the two Ralphs, the union, contrary to its general practice, did not even fill out applications for them; although the union

868. (*Cont.*)
agent advised them that only he could fill out applications. We cannot assume that Congress, by using the term 'denied,' intended to permit unions to forestall applications for membership and thereby circumvent the policy expressed in proviso (B).

"Nor does the legislative history which respondent company urges upon us call for a different result. Quite the contrary. Although the legislative history does establish that Congress wanted to protect from discharge an employee 'unreasonably' denied membership, Congress specified what it regarded as reasonable—the failure of the employee to tender the dues and initiation fees. The statements of Senator Taft, set forth in footnote 17 establish that he thought the bill in its final form successfully and constitutionally protected not only the union from 'free riders' but also protected those employees willing to pay for their ride. We are unable to agree with respondent company's contention that to require the tender of dues is tantamount to imposing a compulsory checkoff. The statute plainly contemplates that, under a valid union-shop contract, non-union employees may be required at least to offer to bear a fair share of the maintenance of the union. Plainly a plan under which employees pay their dues directly to the union, instead of through the employer is unlike the compulsory check-off proscribed in Section 203 of the Act.

"Finally, we note that the Trial Examiner also sought to buttress his conclusion by pointing out that a construction such as we place upon the provisos to Section 8(a)(3) 'would tend to destroy all union security,' because employees could 'choose to remain outside the union' and thereby lessen the union's effectiveness in representing the employees. The very argument the Trial Examiner advances was unsuccessfully urged upon the Congress which enacted the proviso. That decision is binding upon us, whether or not we think it wise, practical, or fair.

"Moreover, viewing the situation realistically, we believe that the Trial Examiner has overstated the case. It appears highly improbable that employees would be encouraged by our interpretation of the statute merely to tender dues and refrain from actual participation in the union. As a general rule, rather than refraining employees are likely to insist upon participating in the affairs of a union to whose treasury they are required to contribute. Indeed, without such an attitude on part of the employees involved, a union is hardly likely to obtain the vote necessary to authorize the execution of the union-security agreement.

"We conclude that the respondent company discharged the Ralphs and Rawlings, on May 13, 1948, because they were nonmembers of the respondent union. As the respondent company knew that the dischargees had tendered the periodic dues and initiation fees uniformly required as a condition of membership, without being accorded membership, we find that the respondent company discriminated in regard to hire or tenure of employment to encourage membership in the respondent union in violation of Section 8(a)(3) of the amended Act, and thereby interfered with, restrained, or coerced employees in the exercise of the rights guaranteed in Section 7, in violation of Section 8(a)(1).

"We find that the respondent union demanded the discharge of employees to whom it had not granted membership on grounds other than their failure to tender the periodic dues and the initiation fees uniformly required. As the respondent company violated Section 8(a)(3) in making the discharges which the respondent union demanded, we find that the respondent union caused the employer to discriminate against these employees, and thereby violated Section 8(b)(2). We further find that, by causing the respondent company discriminatorily to discharge such employees, through the illegal application of its contract, the respondent union restrained and coerced employees in the exercise of the rights guaranteed by Section 7, and thereby also violated Section 8(b)(1)(A) of the amended Act."

869. 29 USCA (1947, Supp.) Sec. 160 (c).

870. National Maritime Union, 78 NLRB 971, 22 LRRM 1289; American Radio Ass'n and Committee for Company & Agents etc., 82 NLRB No. 151, 24 LRRM 1006.

871. Great Atlantic & Pacific Tea Co., 81 NLRB No. 164, 23 LRRM 1464.

872. United Mine Workers of America & Jones & Laughlin Steel Corp., 83 NLRB No. 135, 24 LRRM 1153.

873. 29 USCA (1947, Supp.) Sec. 158 (b) (3).

874. 29 USCA (1947, Supp.) Sec. 158 (d).

875. See Times Publishing Company, 72 NLRB 676.

876. National Maritime Union, 78 NLRB No. 137, 22 LRRM 1289.

877. National Maritime Union, 78 NLRB No. 137.

878. Great Atlantic & Pacific Tea Co., 81 NLRB No. 164.

879. United Mine Workers of America, 83 NLRB No. 135.

880. Great Atlantic & Pacific Tea Co., 81 NLRB No. 164.

881. 29 USCA (1947, Supp.) Sec. 158 (d).

882. International Harvester Co., 77 NLRB No. 27; Crowley's Milk Co., 79 NLRB No. 81; Armstrong Cork Co., 80 NLRB No. 139.

883. Boeing Airplane Co. v. NLRB, 174 F. (2d) 988, 24 LRRM 2101.

883a. 89 NLRB No. 32.

884. 29 USCA (1947, Supp.) Sec. 163.

885. 29 USCA (1947, Supp.) Sec. 158 (b) (4).

886. 29 USCA (1947, Supp.) Sec. 158 (b) (4) (A), Wine, Liquor & Distillery Workers Union, Local 1, 78 NLRB No. 61, 22 LRRM 1222.

887. 29 USCA (1947, Supp.) Sec. 158 (b) (4) (B).

888. 29 USCA (1947, Supp.) Sec. 158 (b) (4) (C).

889. 29 USCA (1947, Supp.) Sec. 158 (b) (4) (D).

890. 29 USCA (1947, Supp.) Sec. 160 (1).

891. LeBaron v. Printing Specialties and Paper Converters Union Local 388, AFL., 75 F. Supp. 678, 21 LRRM 2268, affirmed in Printing Specialties and Paper Converters Union v. LeBaron, 171 F. (2d) 331 (CCA 9).

892. Sperry v. United Brotherhood of Carpenters etc., 21 LRRM 2244; Wadsworth Building Company, Inc., 81 NLRB No. 127; Osterink Construction Company, 82 NLRB No. 27.

892a. Denver Building and Construction Trades Council, et al., 87 NLRB No. 136.

893. Douds v. International Brotherhood of Teamsters etc., 75 F. Supp. 414, 21 LRRM 2150; see also Douds v. Local 294, International Brotherhood of Teamsters, 75 F. Supp. 414, 21 LRRM 2154.

894. Douds v. Wine, Liquor & Distillery Workers Union, 75 F. Supp. 447, 21 LRRM 2282.

895. United Brotherhood of Carpenters & Joiners of America, 81 NLRB No. 127, 23 LRRM 1403, where the Board said:

"Viewing the language of Section 8 (b) (4) (A) in the light of the manifest purpose of Congress and the interpretative meaning given to it by both the proponents and the opponents while the section was under consideration, we are impelled to the conclusion that Section 8 (b) (4) (A) embraces within its proscription peaceful picketing. Accordingly, we must find that the Respondents violated the Act by picketing Klassen, unless, as the Respondents insist, we are precluded from so doing by Section 8 (c).

"Section 8 (c) provides that the 'expressing of any views, argument, or opinion, or the dissemination thereof, . . . shall not constitute or be evidence of an unfair labor practice under any of the provisions of this Act, if such expression contains no threat of reprisal or force or promise of benefit.' Ostensibly, this section is applicable to every provision of the Act. Relying on the literal language of Section 8 (c), the Respondents argue that peaceful picketing, being a form of communication of views, is protected thereby. For reasons hereinafter to be discussed, we are unable to agree that Section 8 (c) is applicable to Section 8 (b) (4) (A) as to afford any immunity to peaceful picketing conducted in furtherance of an objective proscribed by Section 8 (b) (4) (A).

"If, as the Respondents urge, Section 8 (c) were to be read into Section 8 (b) (4) (A), not only would it limit the admissible evidence to establish a violation under Section 8 (b) (4) (A), but also it would alter substantively the express language of that section as actually to make it an unfair labor practice to 'coerce or constrain' employees by 'threat of reprisal or force or promise of benefit' rather than to 'induce or encourage' as Section 8 (b) (4) (A) provides. But, by thus circumscribing the scope of Section 8 (b) (4) (A), the manifest intention of Congress would be substantially frustrated and violence would be done to the carefully

895. (*Cont.*)
chosen language which was designed to effectuate that purpose.

"As indicated previously, Section 8 (b) (4) (A) was aimed at eliminating all secondary boycotts and their concomitant activities which Congress thought were unmitigated evils and burdensome to commerce. It was Congress' belief that labor disputes should be confined to the business immediately involved and that unions should be prohibited from extending them to other employers by inducing and encouraging the latters' employees to exert economic pressure in support of their disputes.

"It was the *objective* of the unions' secondary activities, as legislative history shows, and not the *quality of the means* employed to accomplish that objective, which was the dominant factor motivating Congress in enacting that provision. Both the proponents and opponents of the Act so interpreted Section 8 (b) (4) (A) and understood that it prohibited peaceful picketing, persuasion, and encouragement, as well as non-peaceful economic action, in aid of the forbidden objective. In these circumstances, to construe Section 8 (b) (4) (A) as qualified by Section 8 (c) would practically vitiate its underlying purpose and amount to imputing to Congress an unrealistic approach to the problem.

"For then, in no instance would this section, contrary to Congressional intent, reach peaceful picketing, though a familiar means of attaining a secondary boycott, or other peaceful forms of inducement and encouragement. (It has been held that peaceful persuasion, whether in the form of picketing or unfair lists, for an unlawful purpose constituting a violation of the anti-trust laws is enjoinable. Allen Bradley Co. v. Local Union No. 3, International Brotherhood of Electrical Workers, 325 U.S. 797 (16 LRR Man. 798). The weight of State authority also sustains the view that peaceful picketing for an unlawful objective is not privileged. Colonial Press, Inc. v. Ellis, 321 Mass. 495, 74 N.E. 2d 1 (20 LRRM 2370) (1947); Empire Storage & Ice Co. v. Giboney, 210 S.W. 2d 55 (20 LRRM 2584) (Sup. Ct., Mo., 1947); Florsheim Shoe Store Co. v. Retail Shoe Store Union, 288 N.Y. 188, 42 N.E. 2d 480 (10 LRR Man. 697) (1942).)

"And, although it is true that Section 8

(c) does not affect as such the prohibition in Section 8 (b) (4) (A) against labor organizations engaging in a strike for a proscribed objective, even that prohibition would nevertheless appear to be rendered ineffectual by Section 8 (c) in that peaceful picketing, among other things, to promote the strike would presumably be protected thereby.

"The lack of logic in importing Section 8 (c) into Section 8 (b) (4) (A) so as, in effect, to redefine inducement and encouragement of employees in terms of restraint and coercion is further cogently demonstrated by the fact that by so doing Section 8 (b) (4) (A) in that respect would duplicate and reach the same conduct as Section 8 (b) (1) (A), which makes it an unfair labor practice 'to restrain or coerce' employees, except that Section 8 (b) (4) (A) would require additional proof of object.

"As the Board has recently pointed out in the Perry Norvell case (Matter of Perry Norvell Company, 80 NLRB, No. 47 (23 LRRM 1061)):

"'The legislative history (Section 8 (b) (1) (A)) of the Act shows that, by this particular section, Congress primarily intended to proscribe the coercive conduct which sometimes accompanies a strike ... By Section 8 (b) (1) (A) Congress sought ... to insure that strikes and other organizational activities of employees were conducted peaceably by persuasion and propaganda and not by physical force, or threats of force or of economic reprisal. In that Section, Congress was aiming at means, not ends.'

"In these circumstances, we are unable to believe that Congress intended to do such a meaningless thing as to make conduct, which it had already prohibited in an earlier section in the statute (8 (b) (1) (A)), an unfair labor practice in a later section (8 (b) (4) (A)) conditioned, however, on further proof of unlawful objective. In the final analysis, it is plain from the different purposes these provisions were intended to serve in the statutory scheme that Congress contemplated that a broader scope be given to the phrase 'induce or encourage' in Section 8 (b) (4) (A) than to the phrase 'restrain or coerce' in Section 8 (b) (1) (A). By reading Section 8 (c) into Section 8 (b) (4) (A) this intention of Congress would be defeated.

"A further consideration supporting the

view that the words 'induce or encourage' in Section 8 (b) (4) (A) should be given their broad generic meaning unlimited by Section 8 (c) is the fact that such an interpretation would avoid the anomalous situation of a general provision nullifying the effectiveness of a specific provision. It is a fundamental rule of statutory construction that, where a statute contains a general and specific provision which are in apparent conflict, the former literally embracing the latter, the specific must prevail as an exception to the general. Here, Section 8 (c), which provides that the expression of views, argument or opinion, unaccompanied by threats, may not constitute an unfair labor practice is clearly inconsistent with Section 8 (b) (4) (A), which prohibits inducement and encouragement for a proscribed objective. Significantly, such inconsistency does not follow from the application of Section 8 (c) to the other provisions of the Act.

"That Congress did not intend Section 8 (c) to qualify Section 8 (b) (4) is also indicated by the fact that the original wording of Section 8 (b) (2) was changed in conference from 'persuade or attempt to persuade' to 'cause or attempt to cause,' as the provision now reads, in order to conform with Section 8(c) (93 Cong. Rec. 6600 (June 5, 1947)).

"However, it may be reasonably assumed that the House and Senate conferees refrained from rewording Section 8 (b) (4) because they did not regard that Section 8 (c) was applicable to it.

"Moreover, it is noteworthy that there is no provision in Title III comparable with Section 8 (c) purporting to qualify Section 303 which authorizes civil suit for damages arising out of the unfair labor practices defined in Section 8 (b) (4) and reenacted verbatim in Section 303. In view of the fact that the prohibited conduct is described in identical terms in both sections and that the civil relief furnished by Section 303 was designed, as legislative history shows (H. Conf. Rep. No. 510, 80th Cong. 1st Sess. (1947) p. 44), to supplement the relief afforded by Section 8 (b) (4), we are persuaded that Congress intended to give both sections the same scope and meaning. Obviously, this intention could not be effectuated should Section 8 (c) be imported into Section 8 (b) (4).

"From the foregoing discussion of the Act and its legislative history, one thing is plain: the task of choosing between the broad language of Section 8 (b) (4) (A) and the equally broad language of Section 8 (c) is not a simple or enviable one. 'Nor can canons of construction save us from the anguish of judgment' (Frankfurter, 'Some Reflections on the Reading of Statutes,' 47 Col. L. Rev. 527, 544 (1947)). But because we believe that to apply Section 8 (c) to Section 8 (b) (4) (A) would lead to 'absurd or futile results' or, at least, to 'an unreasonable one "plainly at variance with the policy of the legislation as a whole," ' we consider it our duty, as the administrative agency entrusted with the enforcement of the public policy embodied in the Act, to follow the 'purpose (of Section 8 (b) (4) (A)) rather than the literal words (of Section 8 (c))' (U.S. v. American Trucking Associations, Inc., 310 U.S. 534, 543 (1 WH Cases 64)), and thus effectuate the will of Congress.

"We therefore conclude that Section 8 (b) (4) (A) prohibits peaceful picketing, as well as other peaceful means of inducement and encouragement, in furtherance of an objective proscribed therein and that Section 8 (c) does not immunize such conduct."

896. United Brotherhood of Carpenters & Joiners of America, 81 NLRB No. 127, 23 LRRM 1403, where the Board said:

"We pass to the next question, whether the promulgation of the 'We do not patronize' list containing Klassen's name, was, like the contemporaneous picketing, a violation of Section 8 (b) (4) (A). Realistically viewed, this list, as the record indicates, was a direction or an appeal to union men not to handle any goods or perform any services for Klassen. The Trial Examiner found that the list did not offend Section 8 (b) (4) (A) because it was a 'non-coercive argument' protected by Section 8 (c). However, for the reasons discussed above which impel us to conclude that Section 8 (c) does not protect the picketing, we find that that provision does not afford any immunity to the 'We do not patronize' list. Accordingly, we find that the Respondents, in violation of Section 8 (b) (4) (A), induced and encouraged employees of any employer by means of the 'We do not patronize' list to engage in a strike or concerted refusal in the course of their employment to handle goods or perform services for Klassen." Bricklayers, Stone

896. (*Cont.*)
Masons, Marble Masons and Tile Layers
Benevolent & Protective Union, 82 NLRB
No. 27, 23 LRRM 1542.

897. See cases cited in notes 895 and 896.

898. Sealright Pacific Ltd., 82 NLRB No.
36, 23 LRRM 1573. Temporary injunction issued against the union's activities by
U. S. District Court in Le Baron v. Printing Specialties and Paper Converters
Local Union 388, 75 F. Supp. 678, aff'd.
21 LRRM 2268.

899. Pure Oil Co., 84 NLRB No. 38, 24
LRRM 1239, where the Board pointed
out:

"The complaint in this proceeding al-
leges in substance that the Union violated
Section 8 (b) (4) (A) by advocating
strike action by employees of both Pure
Oil and Great Lakes, in order to force
Pure Oil to cease doing business with
Standard Oil, and to force Great Lakes to
cease doing business with Pure Oil.

"The only evidence of such conduct by
the Union, however, consists of primary
action in support of its strike against
Standard Oil—a strike which is not alleged to be unlawful in purpose. When the
strike began, as noted above, the Union
posted pickets *at Standard Oil premises,*
including the refinery and the entrances
to the dock. The Union also sent letters to
the NMU stating in effect that the Standard Oil dock was 'hot.' Such actions represent traditional means of conveying to
fellow workers and to the public at large
the fact that a labor dispute exists with
Standard Oil.

"The General Counsel maintains,
nevertheless, that the picketing of the
dock was unlawful because it also induced
the employees of Pure Oil to engage in a
concerted refusal to handle Pure Oil products at the dock, in order to force Pure
Oil to cease doing business with Standard
Oil. We cannot agree. A strike, by its very
nature, inconveniences those who customarily do business with the struck employer. Moreover, any accompanying
picketing of the employer's premises is
necessarily designed to induce and encourage third persons to cease doing business with the picketed employee. It does
not follow, however, that such picketing is
therefore proscribed by Section 8 (b) (4)
(A) of the Act.

"It is clear from the legislative history
of the Act that Section 8 (b) (4) (A)
was aimed at *secondary* and primary action. Thus, Senator Taft said of the section:

" 'This provision makes it unlawful to
resort to a *secondary* boycott to injure the
business of a third person who is wholly
unconcerned in the disagreement between
the employer and his employees . . .
(Under) the provisions of the Norris-
LaGuardia Act, it became impossible to
stop a *secondary* boycott or any other
kind of strike, no matter how unlawful it
may have been at common law. All this
provision of the bill does is to reverse the
effect of the law as to secondary boycotts.
(93 Cong. Rec. 4323 (April 29, 1947.)
(Emphasis supplied.))' Senator Taft also
stated that primary strikes over terms
and conditions of employment were 'entirely proper' and 'throughout this bill are
recognized as completely proper strikes.'
(93 Cong. Rec. 3950 (April 23, 1947).)

"In the absence of any affirmative legislative history indicating that Section 8 (b)
(4) (A) was intended to curb traditional
primary action by labor organizations,
and because the only available legislative
history indicates the contrary, we conclude that the section does not outlaw any
of the primary means which unions traditionally use to press their demands on
employers. In this case the Union was
making certain lawful demands on Standard Oil. It was pressing these demands, in
part, by picketing the Standard Oil dock.
As that picketing was confined to the immediate vicinity of Standard Oil premises
we find that it constituted permissive primary action." (Emphasis supplied.)

900. International Brotherhood of Teamsters, Chauffeurs et al., 87 NLRB No. 82.

901. Sealright Pacific Ltd., *supra,* footnote 898. The point is also illustrated by
the Board's decision in Lumber and Saw-
mill Workers Union et al., 87 NLRB No.
135. In that case the pickets followed the
struck employer's trucks to their destinations and reported such destinations to
union officials. The union officials then
contacted the persons at such destinations,
who were customers of the struck employer, for the purpose of persuading
them not to do business with the struck
employer. The Board ruled that such conduct did violate the ban against secondary
boycotts because their union's conduct
was not directed to the employees of the
struck employer's customers.

902. International Brotherhood of Teamsters et al., 87 NLRB No. 130.

903. Douds v. Metropolitan Federation of Architects, 75 F. Supp. 672, 21 LRRM 2256.

904. Climax Machinery Company, 86 NLRB No. 142.

905. Irwin-Lyons Lumber Company, 87 NLRB No. 9.

906. The Howland Drygoods Co., 85 NLRB No. 181.

907. International Rice Milling Co. Inc., 84 NLRB No. 47.

908. Al J. Schneider Inc., 87 NLRB No. 18.

909. Gould & Preisner, 82 NLRB No. 137, where the Board said:

". . . Consistent with common usage of the word 'strike,' implying *collective* or *group* action by a number of employees, the Board has always defined a strike as a *combined* effort on the part of a body of workmen employed by the same employer to enforce a demand by withdrawal of their services. It is readily apparent from the language of the entire act that Congress did not intend to redefine the word, and that a proscribed strike must involve more than a single employee. Thus, section 8 (b) (4) (A) speaks of a 'concerted' refusal by 'employees' in the course of 'their' employment (italics added). Further, the word 'strike' is defined in section 501 of the Act as any 'concerted stoppage of work by employees . . . and a concerted slow-down or other concerted interruption of operations by employees.' We perceive nothing elsewhere in the Act warranting a departure from this unambiguous language."

910. International Rice Milling Co., Inc., 84 NLRB No. 47.

911. Oppenheim Collins & Co. Inc., 83 NLRB No. 47.

912. 29 USCA (Supp.) Sec. 160(k); Board Rules and Regulations, Series 5, and Statements of Procedure, as amended, Sections 203.74 to 203.78 inclusive and 202.29 to 202.34.

913. Moore Drydock Company, 81 NLRB No. 189; Juneau Spruce Corporation, 82 NLRB No. 71; Irwin-Lyons Lumber Company, 82 NLRB No. 107; Los Angeles Building & Construction Trades Council, 83 NLRB No. 76.

914. 29 USCA (1947, Supp.) Sec. 158 (b) (5).

915. 29 USCA (1947, Supp.) Sec. 158 (b) (6). In Cement Finishers Local, case No. 21—CB-69, July 30, 1948, 22 LRRM 1289, the parties stipulated for the following Board order against featherbedding:

Cement Finishers Local No. 627 (AFL) and R. H. Parr & Son (Los Angeles, Calif.): union, its officers, agents, successors and assigns ordered to cease and desist causing or attempting to cause any employer to pay or deliver any money in the nature of an exaction for services which are not performed or not to be performed; (2) make whole employer by the payment of any money exacted for services which were not performed; (3) post notice to all members that union will not cause or attempt to cause an employer to pay or deliver or agree to pay or deliver any money or other thing of value, in the nature of an exaction, for services which are not performed or not to be performed.

916. International Typographical Union, 86 NLRB No. 115, where the Board said:

"It is clear from the legislative history set forth in the Intermediate Report that Section 8 (b) (6) did not purport to reach all 'featherbedding' practices. The scope of the section as passed was limited to but one of the several types of featherbedding which had been encompassed in the earlier House version of the Act—exaction of payment for services 'not performed or not to be performed.' Conceding, as the proponents of the complaint urge, that the reproduction practice requires the employer to pay employees for time—equivalent to approximately 5 percent of their total work time—during which they perform no actual work in the statutory sense, it does not follow that such payment constitutes an 'exaction,' within the meaning of the section.

"Thus, Senator Taft in effect stated, as noted by the Trial Examiner, that it would not be 'in the nature of exaction' to compel employers to give employees *paid* rest or vacation periods because 'they are paid for the work they do' and the payment for rest periods, during which no work is done, is 'for valuable consideration incident to the employment itself.' It seems to us that Senator Taft's view as to what is *not an exaction* incorporates by analogy, the well-established reproduction practice in the printing industry. Thus, in the case at bar, as fully described in the Intermediate Report, all employees engage in production work for the employer's benefit,

916. (*Cont.*)
but as an incident to such employment they demand and receive payment for certain non-production time.

"In our opinion, the instant situation is unlike the only concrete examples mentioned in the legislative history as constituting an exaction. As set forth in the Intermediate Report, one such example involved a demand that the employer 'hire one orchestra and then pay for another stand-by orchestra which does no work at all'; the other example involved a union demand that the employer must have 10 musicians, 'and if you insist there is room for only 6, you must pay for the other 4 anyway.'

"The common circumstance in both examples is the fact that the stand-by or extra employees furnish no consideration whatsoever for their employment, and their entire compensation represents payment for nonproductive time; in fact, their employment relationship is created and maintained solely for the purpose of forcing payment of wages for services not to be performed.

"These examples cannot be equated with the instant situation, where the employment is for the primary purpose of doing production work—representing 95 percent of the employees' time—and the consideration for such employment includes payment, as in the case of a paid rest period, for a relatively short period of non-productive time. We are satisfied that payment for reproduction work can represent an integral part of the wage structure of workers already standing in a proximate employer-employee relationship, not unlike a guaranteed weekly or annual wage arrangement, which is generally recognized as a legal demand, although it may and often does in any given situation, involve payment for non-productive time.

"Under all the circumstances, especially the clear congressional intent to limit and restrict the application of this section, we are not convinced that the long-established and well-known reproduction practice falls within the proscription of 8 (b) (6). We shall accordingly dismiss that allegation of the complaint."

917. International Brotherhood of Teamsters et al., 87 NLRB No. 130.

918. 29 USCA (1947, Supp.) Sec. 159 (f), (g) and (h).

919. Rite-Form Corset Co., Inc., 75 NLRB 174, 21 LRRM 1011.

920. Myrtle Desk Co., 75 NLRB 226, 21 LRRM 1021.

921. Sigmund Cohn & Co., 75 NLRB 177, 21 LRRM 1015.

922. Herman Loewenstein Inc., 75 NLRB 377, 21 LRRM 1032.

923. Marshall and Bruce Co., 75 NLRB 90, 21 LRRM 1001.

924. H.C. Goodman Co., 79 NLRB 1030.

925. Advance Pattern Co., 80 NLRB No. 10.

926. Herman Loewenstein Inc., 75 NLRB 377, 21 LRRM 1032.

927. New Indiana Chair Co., 80 NLRB No. 249; Boston Consolidated Gas Co., 79 NLRB 337; Schutte & Koerting Co., 79 NLRB 599; Inspiration Consolidated Copper Co., 81 NLRB No. 226.

928. Woodmark Industries, Inc., 80 NLRB No. 171; Oppenheim Collins & Co., Inc., 79 NLRB 435; Times Square Stores Corp., 29 NLRB 361, 81 NLRB No. 46.

929. Warshawsky & Co., 75 NLRB 1291, 21 LRRM 1137.

930. Northern Virginia Broadcasters, 75 NLRB 11, 20 LRRM 1319.

931. United States Gypsum Co., 80 NLRB No. 122, 23 LRRM 1143; Craddock-Terry Shoe Corp., 76 NLRB 842.

932. American Seating Company, 85 NLRB No. 49.

933. Univis Lens Co., 82 NLRB No. 155, 23 LRRM 1679. See also Westinghouse Electric Corp., 78 NLRB No. 38, 22 LRRM 1198.

934. Oppenheim Collins & Co., Inc., 79 NLRB No. 59, 22 LRRM 1403.

935. Oppenheim Collins & Co., Inc., 79 NLRB No. 59, 22 LRRM 1403.

936. Mississippi Products, Inc., 78 NLRB 873; McGraw Curran Lumber Co. Inc., 79 NLRB 795; Morrison Turning Co., 83 NLRB No. 106, 24 LRRM 1134.

937. United Engineering Co., 84 NLRB No. 10, 24 LRRM 1213.

938. Augusta Chemical Co., 83 NLRB No. 7, 24 LRRM 1034.

939. Section 10(b) of the Act provides, in part: That no complaint shall issue based upon any unfair labor practice occurring more than six months prior to the filing of the charge with the Board and the service of a copy thereof upon the person against whom such charge is made, unless the person aggrieved thereby was prevented from filing such charge by reason of service in the armed forces, in which event the six-month period shall be computed from the day of his discharge.

940. Mason & Hughes, Inc., 86 NLRB No. 128; Jacques Power Saw Company, 85 NLRB No. 78; Erving Paper Mills, 82 NLRB 434; Dalton Telephone Co., 82 NLRB 1001.

941. Mason & Hughes, Inc., 86 NLRB No. 128; J. H. Rutter-Rex Manufacturing Co., 86 NLRB No. 68.

942. Axelson Manufacturing Company, 88 NLRB No. 155.

943. Cathey Lumber Co., 86 NLRB No. 30.

944. Lily-Tulip Cup Corporation, 88 NLRB No. 170.

945. Illinois Bell Telephone Company, 88 NLRB No. 191.

Authorities

PART FOUR: COLLECTIVE CONTRACTS

1. Sec. 8(d) of amended NLRA, 29 USCA Sec. 158(d).

2. See Times Publishing Co., 72 NLRB No. 128.

3. NLRB v. Boss Mfg. Co., 118 F. (2d) 187; NLRB v. Sands Mfg. Co., 306 U.S. 332, 342; Consolidated Edison Co. v. NLRB, 305 U.S. 197, 236; H. J. Heinz Co. v. NLRB 311 U.S. 514; NLRB v. Somerset Shoe Co., 111 F. (2d) 681; Globe Cotton Mills v. NLRB, 103 F. (2d) 91, 94; NLRB v. Sunshine Mining Co., 110 F. (2d) 780, 787; NLRB v. Whittier Mills Co., 111 F. (2d) 474, 478.

4. Singer Mfg. Co., 24 NLRB 444.

5. Sec. 8(d) of amended NLRA; 29 USCA (Supp. 1947) Sec. 158(d).

6. 29 USCA (Supp. 1947) Sec. 159(a).

7. J. I. Case Co. v. NLRB, 321 U.S. 332, 338–339; Medo Photo Supply Corp. v. NLRB, 321 U.S. 678, 683–684; Wallace Corp. v. NLRB, 323 U.S. 248, 255–256; See Virginian R. Co. v. System Federation, 300 U.S. 515, 545; Steele v. Louisville & Nashville R. Co., 323 U.S. 192, 199; Barlow-Maney Laboratories, 65 NLRB 928; Tampa Shipbuilding Co., Inc., 67 NLRB 1359.

8. Wallace Corp. v. NLRB, 323 U.S. 248, 255–256; J. I. Case Corp. v. NLRB, 321 U.S. 332; Steele v. Louisville & Nashville R. Co., 323 U.S. 192; Tunstall v. Brotherhood of Fireman, 323 U.S. 210.

9. Sec. 8(a) (5) of NLRA; 29 USCA (Supp., 1947) Sec. 158(a) (5).

10. NLRB v. Columbian Enameling & Stamping Co., 306 U.S. 292, 297–298; Barlow-Maney Laboratories, 65 NLRB 928; Bausch & Lomb Optical Co., 69 NLRB 1104.

11. Sec. 8(a) (5), 10(c), 10(e) of NLRA; 29 USCA (1947, Supp.) Secs. 158(a) (5), 160(c), 160(e); H. J. Heinz Co. v. NLRB, 311 U.S. 514; Pacific Plastic & Mfg. Co., 68 NLRB 52; May Department Stores v. NLRB, 326 U.S. 376; NLRB v. Express Publishing Co., 312 U.S. 426.

12. NLRB v. Carlisle Lumber Co., 94 F. (2d) 138.

13. Cottrell & Sons, 34 NLRB 457; Scripto Mfg. Co., 36 NLRB 411, 428.

14. Trenton Garment Co., 4 NLRB 1186.

15. Jeffery-De Witt Insulator Co. v. NLRB, 91 F. (2d) 134, 139, enforcing 1 NLRB 618, cert. den. 302 U.S. 731; S. L. Allen Inc., 1 NLRB 714, 728; Brown-McLaren Mfg. Co., 34 NLRB 984.

16. Artcraft Hosiery Co., 78 NLRB No. 43, 22 LRRM 1212, 1213; Chamberlain Corp., 75 NLRB No. 138, 21 LRRM 1122; R. J. Lovvorn, 76 NLRB No. 12, 21 LRRM 1149; Roanoke Public Warehouse, 72 NLRB 1281, 1284, 19 LRRM 1267.

17. Palm Beach Broadcasting Co., 63 NLRB 597; The France Foundry & Machine Co., 49 NLRB 122; Bethlehem Transportation Co., 61 NLRB 1110; Mahoning Mining Co., 61 NLRB 792.

18. Robeson Cutlery Co. Inc., 67 NLRB No. 64.

19. Sec. 9(c) (1) (A) of NLRA; 29 USCA (Supp., 1947) Sec. 159(c) (1) (A).

20. Consolidated Machine Tool Co., 67 NLRB No. 95; Schramm & Schmieg Co., 67 NLRB No. 120; Harris-Woodson Co. Inc., 70 NLRB No. 74; John S. Doane Company, 63 NLRB 1403.

21. Sec. 9(f) (g) and (h) of NLRA; 29

USCA (1947, Supp.) Sec. 159(f) (g) and (h); Myrtle Desk Co., 75 NLRB No. 29, 21 LRRM 1021; Rite Form Corset Co. Inc., 75 NLRB No. 19, 21 LRRM 1011; See Marshall & Bruce Co., 75 NLRB No. 13, 21 LRRM 1001, 1003, 1004.

22. Sec. 9(c) (1) (B) of NLRA; 29 USCA (Supp., 1947) Sec. 159(c) (1) (B).

23. See Herman Loewenstein, Inc., 75 NLRB No. 377, 21 LRRM 1032, 1933.

24. NLRB Statements of Procedure Sec. 202.17.

25. NLRB Rules and Regulations, Series 5, Sec. 203.54, 29 USCA (Supp., 1947 following Sec. 262) Sec. 203.54; NLRB Statements of Procedure Sec. 202.18.

26. See Sec. 9(c) (4) of NLRA; 29 USCA (Supp., 1947) Sec. 159(c) (4).

27. Sec. 9(c) (1) of NLRA, 29 USCA (Supp., 1947) Sec. 159(c)(1); NLRB Statements of Procedure Sec. 202.19.

28. Sec. 9(c) (3) of NLRA, 29 USCA (Supp., 1947) Sec. 159(c) (3).

29. Sec. 9(c) (1) of NLRB; 29 USCA (Supp., 1947) Sec. 159(c) (1).

30. Tampa Electric Company, 56 NLRB 1270; Hughes Tool Co., 56 NLRB 981 enforced as modified 147 F. (2d) 69. See cases cited in footnotes 7 and 8.

31. Midwest Piping and Supply Co., Inc., 63 NLRB 1060; Flotill Products, Inc., 70 NLRB 119.

31a. Crosby Chemicals Inc., 85 NLRB No. 139.

32. See General Electric X-Ray Corp., 67 NLRB 997; Henry & Allen, Inc., 68 NLRB 724. The doctrine is not applied where the claim of the petitioning rival union is not naked, but substantial on its face, Acme Brewing Co., 72 NLRB 1005.

33. The William Koehl Co., 65 NLRB 190; Wisconsin Telephone Co., 65 NLRB 368; Miami Daily News, Inc., 66 NLRB 663; Falcon Mfg. Co., 73 NLRB 467; Honolulu Rapid Transit Co., 71 NLRB 172.

34. When contracts are by their terms automatically renewable, the automatic renewal date specified in the contracts is the crucial date for determining the right of a rival union to petition the Board for an election. If the petition for an election is filed before the automatic renewal date, an election will be granted even though the petition was filed after the execution of a new contract prematurely extending the old contract. Murray Leather Co., 73 NLRB 892; Worth Hardware Co. Inc., 71 NLRB 684. If the new contract was executed and made immediately effective, petitions for an election filed after the automatic renewal date are barred. Greenville Finishing Co. Inc., 71 NLRB 436. During the period after the automatic renewal date, a new extension agreement effective immediately or to become effective upon the expiration date of the existing contract bars elections upon petitions filed after the execution of either of such new agreements. Northwestern Publishing Co., 71 NLRB 167; Mississippi Lime Company of Missouri, 71 NLRB 472.

35. Con P. Curran Printing Co., 67 NLRB 1419. The principle is applicable even though the prior contract was entered into before certification. Kimberly Clark Corp., 61 NLRB 90; Omaha Packing Corp., 67 NLRB 304. The principle is also applicable when the original contract and a new premature extension were entered into during the certification year. Quaker Maid Company, 71 NLRB 915.

36. Kittinger Company Inc., 65 NLRB 1215; Weil Bros. Textiles, Inc., 65 NLRB 1431; Industrial Paper Stock Company, 66 NLRB 1185; Archer-Daniels-Midland Co., 66 NLRB 246; Revere Copper & Brass, Inc., 67 NLRB 1114; Hocking Valley Mfg. Co., 68 NLRB 315; News Syndicate Co. Inc., 67 NLRB 1178; Carson Pirie Scott & Company, 69 NLRB 935.

37. Newman-Crosby Steel Corp., 73 NLRB 513; French Manufacturing Co., 72 NLRB 1467. Agreements which are oral (Hollywood Brands Inc., 70 NLRB 706) or the consequence of unfair labor practices (Kropp Forge Company, 73 NLRB 1148) or for union members only (J. F. Johnson Lumber Company, 73 NLRB 320; The Wheland Co., 72 NLRB 351), or which do not establish substantial terms and conditions of employment (Peoria Wholesale Liquor Distributors Association, 74 NLRB 208; Bell Cabinet Co., 73 NLRB 332; Mac's Equipment Co., 72 NLRB 583) do not constitute a bar to an election upon the petition of a rival union.

38. U.S. Industrial Chemicals, 71 NLRB 940. If a union not affiliated with the parent organization is a party to the proceeding, the Board will proceed upon the

38. (*Cont.*)
petition as a matter of course. National Foundry of New York, 73 NLRB 16.

39. Sec. 8(d) of NLRA; 29 USCA (Supp., 1947) Sec. 158(d).

40. Atlantic Refining Co., 1 NLRB 359; See Times Publishing Co., 72 NLRB 676; Arnolt Motor Co., 68 NLRB 868; Kalamazoo Coaches Inc., 66 NLRB 171; Winona Textile Mills, 68 NLRB 702.

41. S. L. Allen & Co. Inc., 1 NLRB 714.

42. Atlas Mills, Inc., 3 NLRB 10.

43. S. L. Allen & Co. Inc., 1 NLRB 714.

44. H. J. Heinz Co. v. NLRB, 311 U.S. 514; Sec. 8(d) of NLRA, 29 USCA (Supp., 1947) Sec. 158(d).

45. Sec. 9(a) of NLRA, 29 USCA (Supp. 1947) Sec. 159(a).

46. In Steele v. Louisville & Nashville R. Co., 323 U.S. 192, the Supreme Court said (pp. 200, 201, 202):

"The minority members of a craft are thus deprived by the statute of the right, which they would otherwise possess, to choose a representative of their own, and its members cannot bargain individually on behalf of themselves as to matters which are properly the subject of collective bargaining. Order of Railroad Telegraphers v. Railway Express Agency, 321 U.S. 342, and see under the like provisions of the National Labor Relations Act J. I. Case Co. v. Labor Board, 321 U.S. 332, and Medo Photo Supply Corp. v. Labor Board, 321 U.S. 678.

"The labor organization chosen to be the representative of the craft or class of employees is thus chosen to represent all of its members, regardless of their union affiliations or want of them. As we have pointed out with respect to the like provision of the National Labor Relations Act in J. I. Case Co. v. Labor Board, *supra*, 338, 'The very purpose of providing by statute for the collective agreement is to supersede the terms of separate agreements of employees with terms which reflect the strength and bargaining power and serve the welfare of the group. Its benefits and advantages are open to every employee of the represented unit. . . .' The purpose of providing for a representative is to secure those benefits for those who are represented and not to deprive them or any of them of the benefits of collective bargaining for the advantage of the representative or those members of the craft who selected it.

"As the National Mediation Board said, in In The Matter of Representation of Employees of the St. Paul Union Depot Company, Case No. R-635: 'Once a craft or class has designated its representative, such representative is responsible under the law to act for all employees within the craft or class, those who are not members of the represented organization, as well as those who are members.'

"Unless the labor union representing a craft owes some duty to represent non-union members of the craft, at least to the extent of not discriminating against them as such in the contracts which it makes as their representative, the minority would be left with no means of protecting their interests or, indeed, their right to earn a livelihood by pursuing the occupation in which they are employed. While the majority of the craft chooses the bargaining representative, when chosen it represents, as the Act by its terms makes plain, the craft or class, and not the majority. The fair interpretation of the statutory language is that the organization chosen to represent a craft is to represent all its members, the majority as well as the minority, and it is to act for and not against those whom it represents. It is a principle of general application that the exercise of a granted power to act in behalf of others involves the assumption toward them of a duty to exercise the power in their interest and behalf, and that such a grant of power will not be deemed to dispense with all duty toward those for whom it is exercised unless so expressed."

47. Sec. 8(a) (3) of NLRA, 29 USCA (Supp. 1947) Sec. 158(a) (3), Sec. 8(b) (2), 9(e) of NLRA, 29 USCA (Supp., 1947) Secs. 158(b) (2), 159(e).

48. Sec. 302(c) (4) of Labor Management Relations Act, 1947, 29 USCA (Supp., 1947) Sec. 186(c) (4).

49. J. I. Case Co. v. NLRB, 321 U.S. 332; See Timken Roller Bearing Co. v. NLRB, 161 F. (2d) 949.

50. McQuay-Norris Manufacturing Co. v. NLRB, 116 F. (2d) 748. The Seventh Circuit Court of Appeals pointed out in that case (p. 751):

"When it was disclosed to petitioner that Local 226 represented a majority of the employees in the appropriate unit, (this at no time was questioned by petitioner) the obligation was then fixed upon it to recognize the Local as the sole and exclusive bargaining agent, not only for the members of the union, but for all employees. In place of complying with this statutory requirement, petitioner made it the subject of a long and extended bargaining process."

51. Sec. 9(a) of NLRA, 29 USCA (Supp., 1947) Sec. 159(a).

51a. Bethlehem Steel Co., 89 NLRB No. 33.

52. Bethlehem Steel Co., 73 NLRB 277; Harris-Woodson Co. Inc., 70 NLRB 956, enforced 162 F. (2d) 97 (CCA 4).

53. NLRB v. Century Oxford Mfg. Co., 140 F. (2d) 541 (CCA 2); NLRB v. Appalachian Electric Power Company, 140 F. (2d) 217 (CCA 4).

54. Sec. 9(c) (3) of NLRA, 29 USCA (Supp., 1947) Sec. 159(c) (3).

55. Reed Roller Bit Company, 72 NLRB 927. See also Puritan Ice Company, 74 NLRB 1311 (4 year contract held of unreasonable duration but bar to an election during first 2 years thereof); Fitrol Corporation, 74 NLRB 1307 (a contract of indefinite duration bars an election during first 2 years). However, contracts terminable at the will of either party do not bar an election at any time. Potasi Tie and Lumber Company, 73 NLRB 590; General Motors Corporation, 72 NLRB 1199; The Beach Company, 72 NLRB 510.

56. Con P. Curran Printing Company, 67 NLRB 1419. See also Kimberly Clark Corporation, 61 NLRB 90; Omaha Packing Company, 67 NLRB 304.

57. Sec. 9(f) (g) and (h) of NLRA, 29 USCA (Supp., 1947) Sec. 159(f) (g) and (h).

58. Herman Loewenstein Inc., 75 NLRB No. 377, 21 LRRM 1032.

59. See Herman Loewenstein Inc., 75 NLRB No. 377, 21 LRRM 1032, 1033.

60. U. S. Industrial Chemicals, 71 NLRB 940.

61. Secs. 8(b) (4) (D), 10(k) of NLRA, 29 USCA (Supp., 1947) Secs. 158(b) (4) (D), 160(k).

62. Sec. 9(c) (1) (A) (ii) of NLRA, 29 USCA (Supp., 1947) 159(c) (1) (A) (ii).

63. NLRB Rules and Regulations, Series 5, Sec. 203.52, 29 USCA (Supp., 1947, fol. Sec. 262) Sec. 203.52.

64. NLRB Rules and Regulations, Series 5, Sec. 203.53(c), 29 USCA (Supp., 1947, fol. Sec. 262) Sec. 203.53(c).

65. NLRB Statements of Procedure, Secs. 202.16–202.20.

66. Sec. 9(c) (3) of NLRA, 29 USCA (Supp., 1947), Sec. 159(c) (3).

67. Sec. 9(b) of NLRA, 29 USCA (Supp., 1947) Sec. 159(b).

68. R.C.A. Communications, Inc., 2 NLRB 1109; Pacific Gas & Electric Co., 44 NLRB 665.

69. See E. I. DuPont de Nemours and Company, 73 NLRB 1167; Johnson and Johnson, 72 NLRB 1061; Danita Hosiery Manufacturing Co. Inc., 71 NLRB 366; Dothan Silk Hosiery Company, Inc., 70 NLRB 1350; The Eclipse Lawn Mower Co., 73 NLRB 258.

70. Phelps Dodge Corp., 40 NLRB 180; Strong, Hewat & Co. Inc., 41 NLRB 1166; Simpson Logging Co., 40 NLRB 1180; Willys Overland Motors, Inc., 42 NLRB 428.

71. Globe Machine & Stamping Co., 3 NLRB 294, 299, 300; Pacific Gas & Electric Co., 3 NLRB 835, 849, 850; Long Bell Lumber Co., 72 NLRB 890; Western Union Telegraph Company, 39 NLRB 287.

72. Carolina Marble Granite Works, 11 NLRB 249; Tovrea Packing Co., 12 NLRB 1063, 1083; Acme White Lead and Color Works, 29 NLRB 1158.

73. Western Union Telegraph Co., 39 NLRB 287, 292; Montgomery Ward & Co. Inc., 44 NLRB 694; Shevlin-Hixon Co., 33 NLRB 368; Studebaker Corp., 46 NLRB 1315.

74. Sec. 9(c) (5) of NLRA, 29 USCA (Supp., 1947) Sec. 159(c) (5).

75. Delaware Knitting Co. Inc., 75 NLRB No. 27, 21 LRRM 1025.

76. Pomeroy's Inc., 21 LRRM 1224.

77. Sturtevant Co., 8 NLRB 835; Morse Twist Drill & Machine Co., 36 NLRB 1096.

78. Electric Auto-Lite Co., 9 NLRB 147; Sheffield Steel Corp. of Texas, 43 NLRB 956; Hughes Tool Co., 33 NLRB 1089; Phoenix Iron Co., 38 NLRB 1320. However, office clerical and technical employees are usually not included in the industrial production and maintenance unit. Binyon O'Keefe Fireproof Storage Co., 65 NLRB 992.

79. Mueller Brass Co., 39 NLRB 167; Godchaux Sugars, Inc., 44 NLRB 874; Berkowitz Envelope Co., 38 NLRB 914.

80. National Container Corp., 75 NLRB No. 92.

81. Harnischfeger Corp., 75 NLRB No. 74, 21 LRRM 1064.

82. Waldorf Paper Products, 76 NLRB No. 17, 21 LRRM 1163.

83. Todd Shipyards Corporation, 63 NLRB 526; Standard Oil Company of California, 67 NLRB No. 18; International Harvester Company, 68 NLRB No. 45.

84. Pacific Car & Foundry Corp., 21 LRRM 1161, 76 NLRB No. 2.

85. General Motors Corp., 21 LRRM 1253, 1254, 76 NLRB No. 122.

86. Baldwin Locomotive Works, 21 LRRM 1263, 76 NLRB No. 124.

87. Sec. 9(b) (2) of NLRA, 29 USCA (Supp., 1947) Sec. 159(b) (2).

88. Sec. 9(b) (1) of NLRA, 29 USCA (Supp., 1947) Sec. 159(b) (1).

89. Lumbermen's Mutual Casualty Co., 75 NLRB No. 129; Worthington Pump & Machinery Corp., 75 NLRB No. 80, 21 LRRM 1066; Sigmund Cohn Mfg. Co. Inc., 75 NLRB No. 20.

90. Sec. 9(b) (3) of NLRA, 29 USCA (Supp., 1947) Sec. 159(b) (3); City National Bank & Trust Co., 76 NLRB No. 31; Macungie Silk Co., 75 NLRB No. 88; Radio Corp. of America, 76 NLRB No. 115.

91. C. V. Hill & Co., 64 NLRB 1109.

92. Worthington Pump & Machinery Co., 75 NLRB No. 80, 21 LRRM 1066.

93. Clayton Mark & Co., 21 LRRM 1174.

94. Sec. 2(3) of NLRA, 29 USCA (Supp., 1947) Sec. 152(3).

95. Sec. 2(11) of NLRA, 29 USCA (Supp., 1947) Sec. 152(11).

96. L. A. Young Spring & Wire Corp. v. NLRB, 163 F. (2d) 905, cert. den. 68 S. Ct. 607; Westinghouse Electric, 75 NLRB No. 1.

97. Baker Mfg. Co., 75 NLRB No. 122, 21 LRRM 1103; Andrew Jergens, 76 NLRB 51, 21 LRRM 1192, 1193; General Motors Corp., 76 NLRB 122, 21 LRRM 1253, 1254.

98. Morowebb Cotton Mills Co., 75 NLRB No. 118, 21 LRRM 1087; Farm-ville Mfg. Co., 76 NLRB 34, 21 LRRM 1186.

99. Ironton Firebrick Co., 76 NLRB No. 108, 21 LRRM 1241.

100. Palace Laundry Dry Cleaning Corp., 75 NLRB No. 40, 21 LRRM 1039.

101. Fred H. Cole, d/b/a Cole Instrument Co., 75 NLRB No. 44, 21 LRRM 1030; S. P. Mfg. Corp., 75 NLRB No. 83; 21 LRRM 1070.

102. Sec. 14(a) of NLRA, 29 USCA (Supp., 1947) Sec. 164(a).

103. Sec. 2(3) of NLRA, 29 USCA (Supp., 1947) Sec. 152(3).

104. Kansas City Star Co., 76 NLRB No. 52, 21 LRRM 1185.

105. NLRB v. Jones & Laughlin Steel Corp., 301 U.S. 1.

106. Globe Cotton Mills v. NLRB, 103 F. (2d) 91, 94.

107. See Inland Steel Company, 77 NLRB No. 1, 21 LRRM 1310.

108. Sec. 8(a) (3), 8(b) (2), 9(e) of amended NLRA, 29 USCA (Supp., 1947) Sec. 158(a) (3), 158(b) (2), 159(e).

109. Hughes Tool Co., 56 NLRB 981, modified on other grounds 147 F. (2d) 69.

110. Inland Steel Company, 77 NLRB No. 1, 21 LRRM 1310.

111. Athens Mfg. Co., 69 NLRB 605; Union Mfg. Co., 76 NLRB No. 47.

112. Union Mfg. Co., 76 NLRB No. 47.

113. NLRB v. J. H. Allison Co., 70 NLRB 377, enforced 165 F. (2d) 766, 21 LRRM 2238.

114. Union Mfg. Co., 76 NLRB No. 47.

115. Woodside Cotton Mills, 2 NLRB 42.

116. Consumers Lumber & Veneer Co., 63 NLRB 17.

117. Woodside Cotton Mills, 21 NLRB 42.

118. Timken Roller Bearing Co., 70 NLRB 500, enforcement denied on other grounds 161 F. (2d) 949.

119. Woodside Cotton Mills, 21 NLRB 42; Timken Roller Bearing Co., 70 NLRB 500, enforcement denied on other grounds 161 F. (2d) 949.

120. Woodside Cotton Mills, 21 NLRB 42.

121. Timken Roller Bearing Co., 70 NLRB 500, enforcement denied on other grounds 161 F. (2d) 949.

122. National Grinding Wheel Co., 75 NLRB No. 112, 21 LRRM 1095.

123. See NLRB v. Sands Mfg. Co., 306 U.S. 332, 342; NLRB v. Newark Morning Ledger Co., 120 F. (2d) 262 (CCA 3), cert. den. 314 U.S. 693; NLRB v. Highland Shoe, Inc., 119 F. (2d) 218 (CCA 1). The Board has condemned refusals by employers to bargain collectively concerning the disposition of grievances both before and after the execution of the agreement. Rapid Roller Co., 33 NLRB 557; U.S. Automatic Corp., 57 NLRB 124; The Alexander Milburn Company, 62 NLRB 482.

124. In Carroll's Transfer Company, 56 NLRB 935, 939, the Board said, "In viewing the case in this light, we do not embark upon a course of policing and enforcing trade agreements. If, after a full exchange of views and a sincere effort to compose differences, the parties to a trade agreement are left at an impasse concerning its interpretation, application or modification, the matter is outside our hands. If such a dispute involves questions of interpretation or application, it presumably can be solved by the courts, under the applicable principles of the law of contracts."

125. Consolidated Aircraft Corp., 47 NLRB 694, 706.

126. 70 NLRB 500, enforcement denied on other grounds 161 F. (2d) 949.

127. Sec. 9(a) of NLRA; 29 USCA (Supp., 1947) Sec. 159(a).

128. Sec. 8(a) (5) of NLRA, 29 USCA (Supp., 1947) Sec. 158(a) (5).

129. Secs. 10(c), 10(e) of NLRA, 29 USCA (Supp., 1947) Secs. 160(c), 160(e); NLRB v. Express Publishing Co., 312 U.S. 426.

130. NLRB v. Express Publishing Co., 312 U.S. 426, 433.

131. Newark Rivet Works, 9 NLRB 498, 513; Sigmund Freisinger d/b/a North River Yarn Dyers, 10 NLRB 1043, 1050, 1051; Atlas Mills, Inc., 3 NLRB 10.

132. Tomlinson of High Point, 74 NLRB 681; McQuay-Norris Manufacturing Co. v. NLRB, 116 F. (2d) 748 (CCA-7).

133. May Department Stores Co. v. NLRB, 326 U.S. 376.

134. The Todd Company, Inc., 71 NLRB 192; Athens Mfg. Co., 69 NLRB 605 enforced 161 F. (2d) 8 (CCA-5); Tomlinson of High Point, 74 NLRB 681; Pool

Mfg. Co., 70 NLRB 540; J. I. Case Co., 71 NLRB 1145.

135. Sec. 8(d) of NLRA, 29 USCA (Supp., 1947) Sec. 158(d).

136. NLRB v. Sands Mfg. Co., 306 U.S. 332; NLRB v. Sunshine Mining Co., 110 F. (2d) 780 (CCA-9); NLRB v. Highland Park Mfg. Co., 110 F. (2d) 632.

137. Palm Beach Broadcasting Corp., 63 NLRB 597; Barlow-Maney Laboratories, 65 NLRB 928; A. J. Showalter Company, 64 NLRB 573; Century Projector Corp., 49 NLRB 636.

138. Artcraft Hosiery Co., 78 NLRB No. 43, 22 LRRM 1212; See Russell Kingston, 74 NLRB 1484; Roanoke Public Warehouse, 72 NLRB 1281.

139. M. H. Ritzwoller & Co., 15 NLRB 15, enforced 114 F. (2d) 432 (CCA-7).

140. Burnside Steel Foundry Co., 7 NLRB 714, 723; Karp Metal Products Co., 42 NLRB 119; Sanco Piece Dye Works, Inc., 38 NLRB 690; Dahlstrom Metallic Door Co., 11 NLRB 408.

141. NLRB v. Chicago Apparatus Co., 116 F. (2d) 753 (CCA-7).

142. W. W. Holmes, 72 NLRB No. 10; France Foundry & Machine Co., 49 NLRB 122.

143. Burgie Vinegar Co., 71 NLRB No. 140; Republican Publishing Co., 73 NLRB No. 194; NLRB v. P. Lorillard Company, 117 F. (2d) 921 (CCA-6), reversed as to court's directions for an election in 314 U.S. 512.

144. NLRB v. P. Lorillard Co., 117 F. (2d) 921, 924, reversed as to court's directions for an election in 314 U.S. 512.

145. 29 USCA (Supp., 1947) Sec. 159(a).

146. McQuay-Norris Mfg. Co. v. NLRB, 116 F. (2d) 748, 751.

147. NLRB v. Griswold Mfg. Co., 106 F. (2d) 713 (CCA-3); NLRB v. Acme Air Appliance Co. Inc., 117 F. (2d) 417 (CCA-2).

148. May Department Stores v. NLRB, 326 U.S. 376, 385.

149. Medo Photo Supply Corp. v. NLRB, 321 U.S. 678.

150. May Department Stores v. NLRB, 326 U.S. 376; Benson Produce Company, 71 NLRB 888; Arnalt Motor Company, 68 NLRB 868; See also Hoppes Mfg. Co., 74 NLRB 853; Craddock-Terry Shoe

150. (*Cont.*)
Corp., 73 NLRB 1339; South Shore Packing Corp., 73 NLRB 1116.

151. NLRB v. Whittier Mills Co., 111 F. (2d) 474.

152. J. I. Case Co. v. NLRB, 321 U.S. 332.

153. National Licorice Co. v. NLRB, 309 U.S. 350.

154. H. J. Heinz Co. v. NLRB, 311 U.S. 514, See also the definition of to bargain collectively in Section 8(d) of the amended Act 29 USCA (Supp., 1947) Sec. 158(d).

155. NLRB v. The Boss Mfg. Co., 118 F. (2d) 187 (CCA-7); NLRB v. Somerset Shoe Co., 111 F. (2d) 681 (CCA-1); NLRB v. Whittier Mills Co., 111 F. (2d) 474, 478 (CCA-5).

156. NLRB v. Poultrymen's Service Corp., 138 F. (2d) 204.

157. See St. Joseph Stock Yards Co., 2 NLRB 39; Harnischfeger Corp., 9 NLRB 676; Pittsburgh Metallurgical Co., 20 NLRB 1077; Producers Produce Co., 23 NLRB 876.

158. Globe Cotton Mills v. NLRB, 103 F. (2d) 91, 94.

159. Jeffrey-DeWitt Insulator Co. v. NLRB, 91 F. (2d) 134; Virginia Ry. Co. v. System Federation, 57 Sup. Ct. 592, 598.

160. Consolidated Machine Tool Co., 67 NLRB 737; Bethlehem Steel Co., 73 NLRB 277; Jones & Laughlin Steel Corp., 72 NLRB 975; Wingert Contracting Co. Inc., 72 NLRB 244; L. B. Hartz Stores, 71 NLRB 848.

161. NLRB v. P. Lorillard Co., 314 U.S. 512; Franks Bros. v. NLRB, 321 U.S. 702.

162. NLRB v. Inter-City Advertising Co., 154 F. (2d) 244 (CCA-4).

163. NLRB v. National Broadcasting Co. Inc., 150 F. (2d) 895; National Labor Relations Board v. Isthmian S.S. Co., 2 Cir., 126 F. (2d) 598, 599; NLRB v. John Engelhorn & Sons, 3 Cir., 134 F. (2d) 553, 557–8; South Atlantic S.S. Co. v. NLRB, 5 Cir., 116 F. (2d) 480, certiorari denied, 313 U.S. 582, 61 S. Ct. 1101, 85 L. Ed. 1538; NLRB v. Goodyear Tire & Rubber Co., 5 Cir., 129 F. (2d) 661, 664; NLRB v. Hudson Motor Car Co., 6 Cir., 128 F. (2d) 528, 532; McQuay-Norris Mfg. Co. v. NLRB, 7 Cir., 116 F. (2d) 748, 752, certiorari denied, 313 U.S. 565, 61

S. Ct. 843, 85 L. Ed. 1524; NLRB v. Gluek Brewing Co., 8 Cir., 144 F. (2d) 847, 853; Warehousemen's Union v. National Labor Relations Board, 74 App. D. C. 28, 121 F. (2d) 84, certiorari denied, 314 U.S. 674, 62 S. Ct. 138, 86 L. Ed. 539.

164. Lakeshore Electric Mfg. Co., 67 NLRB No. 105, 18 LRRM 1023.

165. Roanoke Public Warehouse, 72 NLRB No. 229.

166. NLRB v. Dahlstrom Metallic Door Co., 112 F. (2d) 756.

167. Bridgeport Coat & Apron Supply Co., 18 LRRM 1035.

168. Palm Beach Broadcasting Corp., 63 NLRB 597.

169. Secs. 2(3), 2(11) of NLRA, 29 USCA (Supp., 1947) Sec. 152(3), 152(11).

170. Sec. 14(a) of NLRA, 29 USCA (Supp., 1947) Sec. 164(a).

171. See Packard Motor Car Co., 64 NLRB 1212, enforced 157 F. (2d) 80 (CCA-6), affirmed 330 U.S. 485.

172. L. A. Young Spring & Wire Co. v. NLRB, 163 F. (2d) 905, cert. den. 68 S. Ct. 607.

173. NLRB v. Sandy Hill Iron & Brass Works, 165 F. (2d) 660 (CCA-2).

174. Marshall & Bruce Co., 75 NLRB No. 13.

175. Sec. 8(d), 29 USCA (Supp., 1947) Sec. 158(d).

176. In J. I. Case Co. v. NLRB, 321 U.S. 332, 335, the Court said: "The negotiations between union and management result in what often has been called a trade agreement, rather than in a contract of employment. Without pushing the analogy too far, the agreement may be likened to the tariffs established by a carrier, to standard provisions prescribed by supervising authorities for insurance policies, or to utility schedules of rates and rules for service, which do not of themselves establish any relationships but which do govern the terms of the shipper or insurer or customer relationship whenever and with whomever it may be established.

177. Farulla v. Ralph A. Freundlich Inc., 155 Misc. 262, 279 N.Y. S. 228.

178. Goldman v. Cohen, 222 App. Div. 631 (N.Y.).

179. Dubinsky v. Blue Dale Dress Co., 162 Misc. 177, 292 N.Y. S. 898.

180. See Sec. 301 Labor Management Relations Act, 1947, 29 USCA Sec. 185.

181. 29 USCA (Supp., 1947) Sec. 185.

182. Wilson v. Airline Coal Co., 215 Iowa 855, See Moran v. Lasette, 221 App. Div. 118.

183. M & M Wood Working Co. v. NLRB, 101 F. (2d) 938; Peninsular & Occidental S. S. Co. v. NLRB, 98 F. (2d) 411, cert. den. 305 U.S. 653; Labonite v. Cannery Workers & Farm Laborers Union, 197 Wash. 543; World Trading Corp. v. Kolchin, 166 Misc. 854; Kelso v. Cavanagh, 137 Misc. 653.

184. Murphy v. Ralph, 165 Misc. 335, 299 N.Y. Supp. 270.

185. Hartley v. Brotherhood, 283 Mich. 201; See also O'Keefe v. Local 463, 277 N.Y. 300.

186. Moore v. Illinois Central R. Co., 24 F. Supp. 731, aff'd 312 U.S. 630; Yazoo & Miss. V. R. Co. v. Sideboard, 161 Miss. 4, 133 So. 669; Gulla v. Barton, 164 App. Div. 293, 149 N.Y. Supp. 952.

187. Keysaw v. Dotterweich Brewing Co., 121 App. Div. 58, 105 N.Y. Supp. 562.

188. P. S. Thorsen & Co. Inc. v. Neves, 179 Misc. 11, 37 N.Y.S. (2d) 113 (N. Y. Sup. Ct.) The National Labor Relations Board has held that employees who strike in violation of the no-strike clause of the contract may be discharged (Scullin Steel Co., 65 NLRB 1294; Joseph Dyson & Sons Inc., 72 NLRB 445), even though the strike was caused by the employer's unfair labor practices (National Electric Products, 80 NLRB 2951, 23 LRRM 1148).

189. Glen Alden Coal Co. v. Anthracite Miners of Pa., 29 Luzerne Legal Register 463 (Pa. C.P. 1935); cf. McGrath v. Norman, 221 App. Div. 864; Blum v. Landau, 23 Ohio App. 426.

190. Stillwell Theatre v. Kaplan, 259 N.Y. 405.

191. Dallas Cartage Co., 14 NLRB 411.

192. NLRB v. Medo Photo Supply Corp., 321 U.S. 678.

193. NLRB v. Crompton-Highland Mills Inc., 337 U.S. 217.

194. See Drewrys Limited U.S.A., 44 NLRB 1119, 1124.

195. Valley Dolomite Corp., 11 LA 98.

196. Swiss American Watch Hospital, 9 LA 724.

197. Plimpton Press, 8 LA 736.

198. Ford Motor Co., 8 LA 1043, 1044.

199. Ohmer Corp. & A. H. Ross Co., 11 LA 197.

200. Pittsburgh Tube Co., 9 LA 834.

201. Deene & Co., 11 LA 561.

202. Campbell Soup Co., 11 LA 715.

203. Pan American Airways, Inc., 10 LA 909.

204. Kraft Foods Corp., 10 LA 254.

205. Tenney Engineering Co., 10 LA 307.

206. D. M. Steward Mfg. Co., 11 LA 202.

207. J. Marcus & Co. Inc., 10 LA 385.

208. Coca-Cola Bottling Co., 9 LA 197.

209. Pure Oil Co., 11 LA 333.

210. Dortch Stove Works, 9 LA 374.

211. National Tube Co., 10 LA 664.

212. Wilson & Rogers, 10 LA 244, 246, 247.

213. Freuhauf Trailer Co., 1 LA 155.

214. Pittsburgh Tube Co., 1 LA 285.

215. Pittsburgh Tube Co., 1 LA 285.

216. Corn Products Refining Co., 3 LA 242.

217. Birmingham Slag Co., 12 LA 56.

218. John Morrell & Co., 12 LA 82.

219. Swift & Co., 12 LA 108.

220. Sherwin-Williams Co., 12 LA 238.

221. Joseph Dyson & Sons Inc., 72 NLRB 445; National Electric Products Corp., 80 NLRB No. 151.

222. United Elastic Corp., 84 NLRB No. 87.

223. Boeing Airplane Co. v. NLRB, 174 F. (2d) 988 (C.A. D.C.).

224. F. L. Jacobs, 11 LA 652.

225. Valley Dolomite Corp., 11 LA 98.

226. F. L. Jacobs Co., 11 LA 652.

227. Neches Butane Products Co., 5 LA 307.

228. Dayton Malleable Iron Co., 5 LA 388.

229. Service Conveyor Co., 9 LA 134.

230. Paramount Pictures, Inc., 12 LA 503.

231. C. K. Williams, 12 LA 987.

232. Square D. Company, 12 LA 777.

233. Corning Glass Co., 12 LA 103.

234. The Creamette Co., 12 LA 67.

235. McLouth Steel Corp., 1 LA 238.

236. Goodyear Clearwater Mills, 6 LA 760.

237. Dairyland Power Co-operative, 11 LA 797.

238. Standard Oil Co. & Central States Petroleum Union, 11 LA 810.

239. Link-Belt Co., 1 LA 530.

240. Inland Steel Co., 2 LA 655.

241. Swift & Co., 6 LA 422.

242. Chamberlin Co. of America, 8 LA 755.

243. Hampden Parlor Furniture Co. Inc., 8 LA 427.

244. I. Lewis Cigar Mfg. Co., 12 LA 661.

245. Crawford Clothes, 12 LA 1104.

246. Grinnell Lithographic Co., 10 LA 887.

247. New England Master Textile Engravers Guild, 9 LA 199.

248. Lonsdale Co., 10 LA 782.

249. Consolidated Vultee Aircraft Corp., 4 LA 24.

250. Carnegie Illinois Steel Corp., 5 LA 378.

251. Maxwell Bros. Inc., 5 LA 449.

252. Farberge, Incorporated, 12 LA 999.

253. Sinclair Refining Co., 12 LA 183.

254. Button Corporation of America, 12 LA 13.

255. Interlaken Iron Corp., 12 LA 79.

256. Campbell Soup Co., 12 LA 969.

257. Swift & Co., 10 LA 897.

258. New York City Omnibus Corp. v. Quill, 189 Misc. 892, aff'd 272 App. Div. 1015, aff'd 297 N.Y. 832.

259. American Salt Corp., 9 LA 124.

260. Zionist Organization of America, 11 LA 579.

261. NLRB v. J. H. Allison, 165 F. (2d) 766 (CCA-6) cert. den.

262. Aluminum Ore Co. v. NLRB, 131 F. (2d) 485 (CCA-7).

263. Equitable Gas Co., 7 LA 345.

264. Mountain States Power Co., 3 LA 6.

265. Heywood Narrow Fabrics, 6 LA 14.

266. Realty Advisory Board on Labor Relations, 12 LA 352.

267. Newspaper Publishers Association of Philadelphia, 12 LA 448.

268. Inland Waterways Corp. 2 LA 649.

269. Matter of Marchant v. Mead-Morrison Mfg. Co., 252 N.Y. 284; Matter of Bullard v. Grace Co., 240 N.Y. 388; Matter of Eagar Construction Corp. v. Ward Foundation Corp., 255 App. Div. (N.Y.) 291.

270. International Association of Machinists v. Cutler-Hammer, Inc., 271 App. Div. (N.Y.) 917, aff'd 297 N.Y. 519. See also Matter of Bullard v. Grace Co., 240 N.Y. 388; Matter of Kelley, 240 N.Y. 74; Matter of Belding Heminway Co., 295 N.Y. 541; B. Fernandez & Hnos., S. En. C., v. Rickert Rice Mills Inc., 119 F. (2d) 809.

271. In re Ketchum & Co., 70 N.Y. Supp. (2d) 476; contra: In re Rabinowitz, N.Y. Sup. Ct., 1947; 21 LRRM 2001.

272. New York City Omnibus Corp. v. Quill, 189 Misc. 892, aff'd 272 App. Div. 1015, aff'd 297 N.Y. 832.

273. Johnson v. Wells, 72 Fla. 290; Koepke v. E. Liethen Grain Co., 205 Wis. 75.

274. Barnes v. Avery, 192 Ga. 874; United Farmers Ass'n. v. Klein, 41 Cal. App. 2d 766, 769.

275. Pennsylvania Statute Tit. 5, Sec. 771 (d).

276. Iowa Code, Sec. 679, 1243; Nebraska Rev. Stat. Secs. 25–2115 to 25–2116.

277. Minnesota Stat. Sec. 572 05 (5).

278. Boston Water Power Co. v. Gray, 47 Mass. 131, 169.

279. Baldinger v. Camden Fire Insurance Ass'n, 121 Minn. 160; Perry v. Insurance Co., 137 N.C. 402.

280. Bryson v. Higdon, 222 N.C. 17.

281. Stowe v. Mutual Home Builders Corp., 252 Mich. 492; Raleigh Coal & Coke Co. v. Mankin, 83 W. Va. 54.

282. Matter of (Bossom) Kutsukian, 270 App. Div. 396.

283. Reid & Yeomans, Inc. v. Drug Store Employees Union, 29 NYS 2d 835, aff'd 265 App. Div. 870.

284. Campbell v. American Fabrics Co., 168 F. (2d) 959; Tabor v. Craft, 217 Ala. 276.

285. McCullough v. Clinch-Mitchell Construction Co., 71 F. (2d) 17, cert. den. 293 U.S. 582; where the stipulation was declared invalid; contra: Daniels v. Willis, 7 Minn. 374, held the stipulation was valid in absence of fraud or misbehavior.

286. City of Carlyle v. Village of Beckemeyer, 243 Ill. App. 460.

287. Oregon Comp. Laws Ann. Sec. 11-610.

288. Goldman v. Cohen, 222 App. Div. 631.

289. Dubinsky v. Blue Dale Dress Co., 162 Misc. 177, 292 N.Y.S. 898.

290. Ribner v. Rasco Butter & Egg Co., 135 Misc. 616, 238 N.Y. 132; Murphy v. Ralph, 165 Misc. 335, 299 N.Y.S. 270; Harper v. Local Union No. 520, Tex. Civ. App., 48 S.W. (2d) 1033; Weber v. Nasser, Cal. App., 286 Pac. 1074, aff'd 210 Cal. 607, 292 Pac. 637.

291. Farulla v. Ralph A. Freundlich Inc., 155 Misc. 262, 279 N.Y.S. 228.

292. Barnes & Co. v. Berry, 169 Fed. 225; Mueller v. Chicago & N. W. Ry. Co., 194 Minn. 83; Hall v. St. Louis-San Francisco Ry., 224 Mo. App. 431.

293. System Federation Louisiana & A. Ry., 119 F. (2d) 509; Yazoo & M.V.R. Co. v. Webb, 64 F. (2d) 902.

294. Moore v. Illinois Cent. R.R., 24 F. Supp. 731, aff'd 312 U.S. 630; Gulla v. Barton, 164 App. Div. 293.

295. Piercy v. Louisville & Nashville Ry. Co., 198 Ky. 477.

296. Yazoo & M.V.R. Co. v. Webb, 64 F. (2d) 902; Dierochow v. West Sub. Dairies Inc., 276 Ill. App. 355.

297. Lambert v. Ga. Power Co., 181 Ga. 624; Johnson v. American Ry. Express, 163 S.C. 191.

298. Robinson v. Dahm, 94 Misc. 729, 159 N.Y.S. 1053; Grosso v. General Bronze Corp., 57 N.Y. Supp. (2d) 227 (N.Y. City Ct.). (Recovery denied on merits of claim.)

299. Samuelson v. Bro. of R. R. Trainmen, 151 P. (2d) 347, Wyo.; Ry. Conductors of America v. Shaw, 119 P. (2d) 553 (Okla.).

300. Harris v. Missouri P. R. Co., 1 F. Supp. 946; Grand International Brotherhood, L. E. v. Marshall, 146 S. W. (2d) 411, Tex. Civ. App.

301. Dooley v. Lehigh Valley R. Co., 21 A (2d) 334, N.J. Eq., aff'd 25 A. (2d) 893; McClure v. Louisville & N. R. Co., 64 S. W. (2d) 538, Tenn.; Dobkowski v. Amalgamated Asso. Etc., 166 Misc. 277, 1 N.Y.S. (2d) 774.

302. Hartley v. Brotherhood, 283 Mich. 201, 277 N.W.Y. 885.

303. Shaup v. Grand International Brotherhood of Locomotive Engineers, 135 So. 327, Ala.; O'Keefe v. Local 463, 277 N.Y. 300; Aden v. Louisville & N. R. R., 276 S.W. 511, Ky.; Boucher v. Godfrey, 119 Conn. 622, 178 A. 655; Whiting Milk Companies v. O'Connell, 277 Mass. 570. See also Trailmobile v. Whirls, 331 U.S. 40.

304. O'Keefe v. Local 463, *supra,* note 240.

305. Steele v. Louisville & N. R. Co., 323 U.S. 192; Tunstall v. Brotherhood of Locomotive etc., 323 U.S. 210.

306. J. I. Case Co. v. NLRB, 321 U.S. 332, 335.

307. J. I. Case Co. v. NLRB, 321 U.S. 332, 335.

308. Cross Mountain Coal Co. v. Ault, 9 S. W. (2d) 692 (Tenn.); Volquardsen v. Southern Amusement Co., 156 So. 678 (LA. App.); Amelotte v. Jacob Dold Packing Co., 173 Misc. 477, 17 N.Y.S. (2d) 929.

309. Rotnofsky v. Capitol Distributors Corp., 262 App. Div. (N.Y.) 521, 523.

310. Barnes v. Hall, 146 S.W. (2d) 929 (Ky.).

311. Greater City Master Plumbers Association, Inc. v. Kahme, 6 N.Y.S. (2d) 589 (N.Y.); Uneeda Credit Clothing Stores Inc. v. Briskin, 14 N.Y.S. (2d) 964; Nevins Inc. v. Kasmach, 279 N.Y. 323; J. I. Hass Co., Inc. v. McNamara, 21 N.Y.S. (2d) 441.

312. Uneeda Credit Clothing Stores v. Briskin, 14 N.Y.S. (2d) 964, 968.

313. Agwilines Inc. v. NLRB, 87 F. (2d) 146, 150–151; Blankenship v. Kurfman, 96 F. (2d) 450; Myeers v. Bethlehem Shipbuilding Corp., 303 U.S. 41, Amalgamated Utility Workers v. Consolidated Edison, 309 U.S. 261, 265–266; National Licorice Co. v. NLRB, 309 U.S. 350, 362, 365.

314. Amalgamated Ass'n, etc. v. Dixie Motor Coach Corp., 170 F. (2d) 902; California Ass'n of Employers v. Building Construction Trades Council etc., 178 F. (2d) 175. Section 303(b) of the Labor Management Relations Act, 1947, authorizes private action in the federal district court to recover damages for secondary boycotts and other types of union conduct made illegal by Section 303(a) thereof, which conduct also constitutes unfair labor practices within the meaning of Section 8(b) (4) of the amended Labor Act.

315. Alonzo v. Industrial Container Corp., 193 Misc. 1008; State v. Eighth Judicial District Court, 207 P. (2d) 990, 996.

316. Section 303(a) and (b), Labor Management Relations Act, 1947.

317. Mills v. United Association of Journeymen and Apprentices of the Plumbing and Steamfitting Industry, etc., U.S. D.C. W.D. Mo., Sept. 8, 1948, 22 LRRM 2539.

318. Amalgamated Association etc. v. Dixie Motor Coach Corp., CCA-8, Nov. 26, 1948, 23 LRRM 2092.

319. Bethlehem Steel Co. v. N. Y. State Labor Relations Board, 330 U.S. 767; Hill v. Florida, 325 U.S. 538.

A state Act may declare illegal conduct by a union which has not been forbidden by the Federal Labor Act. Thus, the Supreme Court sustained an order of the Wisconsin Employment Relations Board based on a finding that repeated union meetings held during working hours for the purpose of exerting pressure on the employer was an illegal interruption of production under the Wisconsin Employment Peace Act even though the employer was engaged in interstate commerce. International Union, UAW etc., Local 232 et al. v. Wisconsin Employment Relations Board, 336 U.S. 245.

320. International Brotherhood of Teamsters v. Riley, 59 A (2d) 476 (N.H. Sup. Ct.).

321. 15 University of Chicago Law Review, 289, 290.

322. Sec. 14(b) of NLRA as amended.

323. Arizona, L. 1947, Chapt. 81; Arkansas, Statutes, 1947, Chapt. 101; Florida, Amendment to State Constitution, Sec. XII, approved Nov. 7, 1944; Georgia, L. 1947, Act. No. 140; Iowa, L. 1947, S. B. 109; Maine, L. 1947, Chapt. 305, Rev. Stat. Sec. 41–A; Nebraska, L. 1947, Chapt. 177, Bill No. 344; Nevada, Sec. 10473 of the Nevada Criminal Code and 10474; North Carolina, 1947, Session Laws, Chapt. No. 328; North Dakota, L. 1947, H. B. 151; South Dakota, S. B. 224, approved March 11, 1947; Tennessee, L. 1947, Public Chapt. No. 36; Texas, L. 1947, H. B. 23; Virginia, H. B. 5, Chapt. 2, approved Jan. 21, 1947; For tabular compilation see 24 LRRM 3078. See Millis and Katz, "A Decade of State Labor Legislation," 15 University of Chicago Law Review at page 282.

324. Wisconsin, Employment Peace Act, as amended, Sec. 111.06(1)(c) 1.

325. Massachusetts Acts, 1947, c. 657.

326. Alabama, Gen. Acts, (1943) 257 Sec. 15; Delaware, L. 1947, Chapt. 196, Sec. 20; Iowa, L. 1947, S. B. 109 Sec. 4; Massachusetts, Ann. Laws (Supp. 1946), Ch. 149 Sec. 150b; New York, see People v. Fay, 182 N.Y. Misc. 358; Texas, Ann. Rev. Civ. State, tit. 83, art. 5154a, Sec. 8a; Iowa, Act 1947, Chapt. 296, Sec. 4; New Hampshire, L. 1947, Chapt. 194, Sec. 21; North Carolina, L. 1947, Chapt. 328, Sec. 5; Tennessee, Pub. Acts 1947, S. B. 367, Sec. 3; Virginia, L. 1947, Chapt. 2, Sec. 5.

327. Giant Food Shop Center Inc., 77 NLRB No. 133, 22 LRRM 1070.

328. 21 LRRM 68.

329. Colorado, Stat. Ann. (Michie, Supp. 1946) Chapt. 97, Secs. 94(b) (2) (c), (22) (1); Minnesota, Stat. (Henderson, 1945) Sec. 179.11; Wisc. Stat. (Brossard, 1946) Sec. 111.06(2) (c).

330. e.g. California, Gen. Laws (Deering, 1941) Sec. 1126 (labor code).

331. Arizona L. 1947, Chapt. 81, Sec. 6; Florida, Gen. L. 1943, Chapt. 21968, Sec. 11; Minnesota, L. 1947, Chapt. 527; Texas, L. 1947, H. B. 73, Sec. 1.

332. State v. Traffic Telephone Workers' Federation of New Jersey, 142 N.J. Eq. 785, 61 A. (2d) 570. On appeal the judgment was reversed on the ground that the section of the New Jersey statute providing for settlement of disputes by a Board of arbitration was unconstitutional in that the legislature set forth no guiding standards for such a board. However, the Appellate Court regarded the general purport of the legislation as constitutional. State v. Traffic Telephone Workers' Federation of New Jersey, 2 N.J. 335, 66 A. (2d) 616.

333. Colorado, Peace Act, S. B. No. 183, Sec. 6(h); Florida, Chapt. 21968 (No. 334), Act of 1943, Union Regulation Law, Sec. 9 (9); Kansas, Union Regulation Act S. B. No. 264 (1943), Sec. 8(11); Maryland, Chapt. 340, Laws of 1941, adding Sec. 24A to Article 27 Annotated Code of Md., 1939 edition; Massachusetts, Labor Relations Law, Sec. 4A(1); Michigan, Public Act 176, 1939; Pennsylvania, Labor Relations Act, Sec. 6(2) (b); Utah, Labor Relations Act, Sec. 49-

1-16(2) (f); Vermont, Public Act 210, L. 1937; Washington, Rev. Stat. Sec. 2.563-4; Wisconsin, Employment Peace Act, Sec. 111.06(2)(h).

334. Wisconsin, Employment Peace Act, Sec. 111.06(2)(e).

335. e.g. Arkansas, Act No. 193 (1943) S. 65, approved March 11, 1943; Colorado, Labor Peace Act, Sec. 6(2)(f), see Table 3, 24 LRRM 3080.

336. South Dakota Laws (1947) Chapt. 93; Texas, L. (1947) Chapt. 138.

337. e.g. Pennsylvania, Labor Relations Act, Sec. 6(2)(d), see Table 3, 24 LRRM 3080.

338. e.g. Connecticut, Public Act No. 123, L. 1947, see 24 LRRM 3080. For compilation see Millis and Katz, "A Decade of State Labor Legislation," 15 University of Chicago Law Review at p. 299.

339. e.g. Colorado Stat. Ann. (Michie Supp. 1946) Chapt. 97, Sec. 96(6)(2) (g); Wisconsin Stat. (Brossard, 1943) Sec. 111.06(2)(g). For compilation see Millis and Katz, "A Decade of State Labor Legislation," 15 University of Chicago Law Review at p. 300.

340. Kan. Gen. Stat. (Corrick, Supp. 1941), Sec. 44–801; Nebraska Rev. Stat. (1943) Sec. 48–214; Pennsylvania Stat. Ann. (Purdon Supp. 1946), tit. 43, Sec. 211.3(f).

INDEX

Across-the-board increase, 284
Adjustment of grievances, *see* grievance
Administrative Procedure Act, 112
"Affecting commerce," meaning of term, 122
Agreement, *see* contract
Allen Bradley Co. v. Local Union No. 3, 143
American Arbitration Association, 350, 351, 352
American News case, 133
Amazon Mills case, 160–161
Anti-union activity, 71–72, *see* unfair labor practices, by employer
Apprentices, eligibility to vote in NLRB elections, 37
Appropriate bargaining unit, *see* collective bargaining
Arbitration, right to by individual, 278; contract clause, 298–300; arbitrable issues, 349–350; procedure, 350–353; judicial review of awards, 353–354
Arbitrator, how selected, 351; power of, 352–353
Automatic progression, 284
Automatic renewal clause, *see* contract

Back pay, award for discriminatory discharge, examples 76–78; how computed, 76–77; disallowed, 77; "runaway shop" employer, 77; union liability for, 78; interlocutory NLRB orders, 117; reinstatement with, 175–185; bankrupt estate, 186–187; strikers, 186
Bargaining, *see* collective bargaining
Bargaining conference, conduct at, 279
Bargaining representative, authority of, 44–46, 256–258, revocation of, 257, limitations on, 257; responsibility of, 46–49; liability under contract, 47–49, 158–159, 276–277, 355–358; unfair labor practices, 48–49
certification or decertification of: in general, 90–91, 251–254; how proceedings initiated, 3–9, 153–154;

determination of appropriate unit, 10–26; when existing contract bars proceedings, 27–33; preliminary investigation, questionnaire, substantial interest, 50–52; consent elections, 52–55; formal hearing, 55–56; issuance of subpoenas, 97–98; decertification, time limit, 257; procedure, 258
election for: contract as bar to, 27–33; Direction of Election, 34–35; eligibility to vote, 34–37; delay of, 35–36; inclusion on ballot, 38; petition for nonaffiliated union, 38–39; consent election, 39–40, 52–54; invalidating, 40–41; one-year rule, 43, 157; right of management to petition for, 153–154; decertification of, 258; *see also* elections
majority status: condition precedent to duty to bargain, 28, 164, 251–252; how determined, 164–167
Bargaining unit, *see* collective bargaining
Bill of particulars, 96
Bona fide labor organization, *see* labor organization
Bonuses, 264
Boycott, by employer to coerce unions, 71; distinction between primary and secondary, 141–142; *see also* secondary boycotts
Briggs Indiana Corporation, 33
Bureau of Labor Statistics, 274

"Captive-audience" doctrine, 139–141, 232
Card-check technique, 40, 157
Cease and desist order, employer interference, 34; company-dominated union 65; from unfair labor practices, 60, 83–85, 90, 101; when used, 83–84; responsibility of employer to remain neutral, 175; *see also* NLRB, orders
Certification, *see* bargaining representative

461

Charge, *see* unfair labor practices

Check-off, individual authorization, 44, 256; compulsory, 156–157

Clayton Act, 143–144

Clerical employees, grouping in bargaining unit, 18, 19, 21, 259

Closed shop, 5, 6, 29, 42, 73, 79, 129, 132, 135, 158

Coercion, examples as anti-union activity, 71–72
  by employer: economic, 193–194; speech as, 137–141, 201–203; examples, 203
  by unions: power of NLRB to restrain, 73; examples, 230–232

Collective agreement, *see* contract

Collective bargaining, multiple employer unit, 147; right of management to, 149–151; individual bargaining discouraged, 168–171; counterproposals, 171–172, 249; defined, 81, 151, 163–164, 249–254; standards for, 249; standards of performance, 253; employees entitled to, 259–261; employees excluded from, 261–262; preparation for, 273–275; *see also* bargaining representative and contract
  bargaining unit: power of NLRB to determine, 10–14, factors considered, 13–26, 259–261; employer unit, 11; inter-related companies, 11; fringe groups, 12, 20; supervisory units, 12, 25; minority groups, 19; confidential and managerial employees, 24; independent contractors, 26; majority representation, prerequisite to duty to bargain, 167–168; when challenged, 252–254; decentralization of, 258; employees included, examples, 259–261; employees excluded, examples, 261–262; *see also* clerical and craft employees
  duty, defined: 81, 151, 163–164, 249–254; NLRB interpretation of, 149–151; majority principle, 164–167, 167–168, 251–252; exemption from, 250; majority status prerequisite to, 164–168, 251–254 (*see* bargaining representative); principle of "good faith," 249–250, 252, 255, 266–267; principle of "reasonable" judgment, 252
  National Labor Relations Board: authority, 10, limitations, 10; determination of unit, 11–15; discretionary power, 13; enforcement powers, 59–60; petitions presented, 50–56; procedure, 50–56; power to compel, 78–

81, 251; power to resolve representation question, 252–254

refusal to bargain: by employer, 78–81, examples, 79, 150–151, 163, 164, 168, 170–171, 225–228, 232, 250, 251, 253, 256, 262–272; "good-faith" performance, 168, 266; by union, 233–237; dilatory tactics, 266–267; recognition of bargaining representative, 268; subject matter of, 269; raising questions of representation, 270–271; termination requirements, 271–272

subject matter for: widening scope of, 263; held mandatory, examples, 264; modification of existing contracts, 264; "any questions arising under," 264–265; interpretation, administration of contract, settlement of disputes under 264–265; pension plans, 313

Columbia Pictures case, 133

"Commerce," meaning of term, 122

Complaint, *see* NLRB

Conditions of employment, 250; construction of term, for collective bargaining, 263

Confidential employees, defined, 24

Consent determination of representatives, 52

Consent elections, *see* elections

Contempt, proceedings initiated by NLRB, 84; for failure to comply with enforcement order, 117–118, for refusal to bargain, 118

Contract, collective bargaining agreement, when bar to election, 27–33, 53; automatic renewal of, 27, 29, 31–33, 272; "premature extension" doctrine, 31–32; termination of, statutory requirements, 48–49, 235–237, 271–272; preferential employment contract, 132; modification of, 264; subject matter for, 263–264, 276; rights and obligations of union under, 276–277; rights and obligations of individuals under, 277–278; third party beneficiary, 278; standards for drafting, 281; operating under, 319–322; *see also* closed shop, union shop

clauses: preamble, 281–282; recognition, 282–283; wages, 284–288, merit wage increases, 345–346, wage reopening, 346; hours, 288–290; probationary employees, 290–291, 333–334; no-strike—no-lockout, 291–292, 331; union responsibility, 292–294, 332–333; management's rights,

294–295, 322–326; supervisory employees, 295–297, 326–327; discharge, 297–298, 327–329; grievance and arbitration, 298–300, 329–331; seniority, 300–302, 334–335; transfer, 302–304, 335–336; promotion, 304–305, 337–338; leave of absence, 305–307, 338–339; holidays, 307–309, holiday pay, 339–340; vacation, 309–310, 340–342; guaranteed work, 310–312, 342–343; pension plan, 312–316, 343–344; severance pay, 317–318, 344–345; relationship of clauses, 320–322
  enforcement of: by union, 256, 276; by employer, 276–277
  individual: rights superseded, 44–45; when permissible, 168–170; as obstacle to collective bargaining, 269
  liability under: of bargaining representative 47–49, 158–159, 276–277, 355–358; state labor laws, 361
  negotiation of: preparation for, 273–275; content of, 276; purpose of, 279–281; choice of representatives, 279; conduct during, 280
Cost-of-living data, in preparation for bargaining, 274
Counterproposals, 171–172, 249
Courts
  enforcement: of NLRB orders, 98, 104; contempt proceedings, 117–118; clarification of decree, 142–148
  power: over NLRB orders, 101–103, 107–108; to remand, 108–109; to grant injunction, 109, 142–143, 144; over duty to bargain, 255
  review (judicial review): of NLRB orders, 59–61, 90–91, 101–104, 106; jurisdiction of reviewing court, 105, 160–162; review of NLRB certification, 90–91, 105–107; confined to record of proceedings, 106–107, additional evidence, 108–109; fair hearing, 113–114; questions of law, 114–115
Craft employees, bargaining unit for, 15–17; when election held, examples, 15–16; General Electric case, 16; separate grouping of, 128, 260

Decertification, see bargaining representative
Declaratory Judgment Act, 59
Demotion, 137, see also unfair labor practices

Direction of Election, 34, see also election
Discharge, right of management, 130–136; subject matter for bargaining, 264; contract clause, 297–298, 327–329
  causes for: examples, 130–132; for filing charges, 69, 136; under union security provisions, 74–75, 135–136; for economic causes, 132; for strikes, 132–134, 331; for union activity, 134–135
  discriminatory: reinstatement, 75; back pay, 76–77; unfair labor practices, by employer, 67–71, 217–218, by union, 69, 232–233
Discrimination, because of race, color, or creed, 23–24, 46; bargaining representative, 46–47; between union and nonunion members, 46; withholding of bonus, 68, for testifying or filing charges, 69; reinstatement, 179; unfair labor practices, by employer, examples, 219–233, by unions, 232–233; see also discharge, lay-off, lockout, rehiring, "runaway shop," transfer
Disestablishment, see union, company-dominated
Doctrine of estoppel, 82, 296
Domination, evidence of, 64, 207; of affiliated and nonaffiliated unions, 65, 66, 204–206; how determined, 208–209; conduct held, 209–211; see also union, company-dominated
"Do not patronize" lists, 238
Douds v. Teamsters Union (Conway's Express), 86
Dual unionism, discharge for, illegal under LMRA, 47, 135–136, 156; definition of, 74; discharge for, under union shop, 74
Dues, fees, assessments, see union
Duty to bargain, see collective bargaining

Edward G. Budd case, 70
Election (NLRB), Direction of Election, when ordered, 34–36, eligibility date, 36–37, waiver of, 53; for union shop, 42–43, 73–74, 158
  for bargaining representative: union, showing of substantial interest, 5–6, 51, filing requirements, 6–7, 153–154, 243–244, 271; certification of, 4, 34–43, 50–54, 153–154, 252–254; petition for, 4–8, 153–154; self-determination election, 15–16; "Globe" elec-

Election (NLRB) (*Continued*)
  for bargaining representative (*Con.*)
    tion, 24–25, 260; when election
    barred, 27–33, 253; eligibility to vote
    in, 34–35, 36–38; delay of, 35–36;
    affiliated and nonaffiliated unions,
    38–39; run-off election, 39, 55; con-
    sent election, 38–40, 50–55; card-
    check, 40, 157; invalidating election,
    40–41; decertification of, 42, 252–
    258; one-year rule, 43, 148–151, 253;
    records subpoenaed, 51–52
Employees, eligibility to vote in election,
    34–37; responsibility of bargaining
    representative to, 46, 47; employ-
    ment denied because of union affilia-
    tion, 127; hiring of, 129–130; dis-
    charge of, 130–136; labor disputes,
    142–144; unwarranted aggressive-
    ness, 144–146; obligations toward
    management, 146–162; individual
    bargaining discouraged, 168; duty to
    seek other work, 185, 186; merit in-
    creases, 188; *see* also testimony
  benefits: as unfair labor practices, 193,
    269; within area of collective bar-
    gaining, 263–264
  definition: under NLRA, 124–125; un-
    der LMRA, 12, 25; excluding certain
    employees from scope of NLRA, 61–
    63, 261–262; *see* also supervisory
    employees
  rights of: presentation of grievances, 44,
    168–169; to transfer, 136–137; to
    free speech, 137–141; to collective
    bargaining, 163–168; to reinstate-
    ment, 175–183; to merit increases,
    188; interference with employees'
    rights, 189–201; to individual con-
    tracts, 189; to employer's neutrality,
    191–201; to form, join, or assist
    labor organizations, 230; under col-
    lective contract, 277–278
  unfair labor practices: unwarranted ag-
    gressiveness, 144–146, coercion, 201–
    203; forcing employer to discrimi-
    nate, 232–233; refusal to bargain, 233
  unfair labor practices of management:
    list of under NLRA, 47; denial of
    employment because of union affilia-
    tion, 127
Employer, association of, 11, 149; inter-
    ference in election, 34; restricted by
    bargaining representative, 45–46; re-
    sponsibility of representative to, 46–
    48; commerce questionnaire, 51–52;

classes excluded, 62; defined, under
    NLRA, 84, under LMRA, 84, 124;
    employer - employee relationship,
    123–128; *see* also management, rights
    and duties
Employer-employee relationship, rights
    and duties, 123–128
Enforcement, of order to compel bargain-
    ing, 252, 256; of collective agree-
    ment, by union, 276, 355–356, by em-
    ployer, 227, by individual, 356–358;
    judicial enforcement of NLRB or-
    ders, *see* NLRB
Escalator clause, 284
Espionage, 193, *see* also anti-union activ-
    ity
Evidence, of "substantial" showing by
    petitioning union, 5–6, 51, by non-
    petitioning union, 38; of appropriate
    bargaining unit, 11–13; of interstate
    commerce, 52; rules of evidence in
    unfair labor practice cases, 82, 100–
    101; required to obtain injunction,
    87–88; court review of, additional
    evidence, 106–107, 108–109, sub-
    stantial evidence, 82, 111–113, 148;
    "presumed expertness" doctrine, 115;
    rules and preponderance of evidence,
    115–117; in arbitration hearing,
    351–352; in arbitration award, 353
Executives, *see* managerial employees
Express Publishing Company case, 84,
    102

Fair Labor Standards Act, 288
Falk Corporation case, 107
Fansteel case, 145, 177
Featherbedding, 48, 242
Federal Conciliation Service, 48
Federal Trade Commission, 274
Filing requirements, union, prerequisite to
    recourse to NLRB, 6–7, 153–154,
    243–244, 252, 271
Foremen, *see* supervisory employees
Fourteenth Amendment, 141
Free speech, right of management to, 72,
    137–141, on union affairs, 190; as
    interference, 191; as coercion, 201,
    202; examples of, held coercive under
    NLRA, 203
Fringe benefits, 284
"Fringe groups," bargaining unit, 12, how
    determined, 20–21, 282
"Fronting," evidence of, 7, 244

General Electric Company case, 16
General Electric X-Ray Corporation case, 30
"Globe" election, when held, 24, 260
"Good-faith," principle of, in collective bargaining, 154, 168, 249, 250, 251, 255, 267
Great Atlantic & Pacific Tea Company case, 234
Greer Steel Company case, 68
Grievance, adjustment of, 44, 126, 157, 169, 257; subject matter, for collective bargaining, 264, 265; concerning discharge, 297; procedure, 298–300, 329–331, 347–348
Guaranteed work, contract clause, 310–312, 342–343
Guards, bargaining unit, 18, 20, 155–156, 260

Health and welfare funds, 313
Hearing, *see* NLRB, also arbitration, procedure
Hiring, when unfair labor practice, 67, 129–130; management's right to, 129–130; union control, 129–130; rehiring, when discriminatory, 215–217
Hiring hall system, 130, 158, 233
Holidays, held mandatory matter for collective bargaining, 264; contract clause, 307–309, 339–340
"Hot" cargo clause, 133
Hours, held mandatory matter for collective bargaining, 264; contract clause, 288–290
Hughes Tool Company case, 79

Independent contractors, excluded from coverage of NLRA, 26, 63, 261, 262
Individual, rights and obligations, under collective agreement, 44–45, 278, to grievance and arbitration procedure, 299, 348; enforcement of rights, 345–348
Industrial units, 10, 15–18
Industry-wide contract, 281
Injunction, to prevent interference with election, 34, 192–193; against strikes, 85, 141; against boycotts, 35, 141–142; procedure in obtaining, 86, 154–155; to restrain unfair labor practices, 85–86, 238; requirements for, 88,

under Norris-LaGuardia Act, 86, 142–144; scope of temporary injunction, 88; constitutionality upheld, 89; temporary injunction, 109; against labor-nonlabor conspiracy, 144; against violent picketing, 145–146; state anti-injunction statute, 277
Inspectors, 261
Insurance, group, held mandatory matter for collective bargaining, 264
Interference, by employer, 64; successor labor organization, 66; speech, 191–192; conduct, 192–193; examples of, 194–199; indirect, 199–200, examples, 200–201
Interim agreement, *see* collective bargaining
Intermediate Report, NLRB, 100
Internal Revenue Code, 313
International Union etc. v. Eagle Picher Co., 162
Interrelated companies, 11, 14
Interstate commerce, NLRB jurisdiction, 61–62, 121–122, 123; applicability of NLRA, 121–122

J. I. Case Co. v. NLRB, 319
Jones & Laughlin Steel Corporation case, 33, 125–126
Jurisdictional dispute, involving unfair labor practice, 85; requirements for injunctive relief, 88; power of NLRB to settle, 88, 89; how determined, 242; representation, 254, 257–258; NLRB resolution, 257–258

Labor dispute, what constitutes, 142–144; defined in NLRA, 142; enforcement of contract, 277
Labor Management Relations Act, union shop, 73–74, 129–130; injunction, 86, 141–142, 160; purpose of, 121, 129; content of, 121; "employee" defined, 124–125, *see* employees, excluded from; "employer," defined, 124; hiring, 129; discharges under union shop, 135–136, free speech, 137–141; "captive audience" doctrine, 138–141; filing requirements, 153–154, 243–244; dual unionism, 156; check-off, 156–157; grievances, 299, 348; health and welfare funds, 313

Labor Management Act (*Continued*)
  collective bargaining: bargaining unit, 12, 16, 25, 127–128, 233–235; bargaining representative, 42, 47, 257; election for, 35–40, 252; defined under, 151, 249
  contract: requirements for termination or modification of, 235–237, 272; enforceable under, 276; basis for court litigation, 355–358
  NLRB: enlarged scope of, 61; procedure, of, 89–91, 97–98, 100, 112, 116, 245; elections, 157
  unfair labor practices: by employer, 72, 191–192; by unions, 133, 136, 230, 237–242; NLRB jurisdiction over, 357–358
Labor organization, attributes of, 6, 64, included on ballot, 38; when complaint served on, 95; domination of, 203–214; *see* also union, company-dominated
Lay-off, for economic causes, 132; when discriminatory, 215; eligibility for holiday pay, 339, for vacation, 341
Leave of absence, contract clause, 305–307, 338–339
Lockout, 177, 215, 291–292, *see* also strikes
Lump sum adjustments, 284
Lunch period, 264

Maintenance employees, grouping in bargaining unit, 17–18, 259
Maintenance-of-membership, 360
Management, preparation for collective bargaining, 273–275; conduct during negotiations, 279–281; *see* also employer-employee relationship, employer
  duties of: to bargain collectively, 163–173, 249; to disclaim responsibility for supervisors' activities, 133–175; to reinstate employees, 175–183; power to instate, 183; to pay back pay, 183–187; to protect union employees against nonunion employees, 187; to disclose data, 188
  rights of: to hire, 129–130; to discharge, 130–136, 156; to transfer, 136–137; to free speech, listing of legitimate examples of, 137–141; to injunction, 141–146, 154–155; to bar solicitation, 146; to abstain from dealing with minority union, 147; to protection from new changes, 147;

to fair hearing, 148; to act in concert, 149; to latitude in the bargaining process, 149–151, 263; to operate for profit, 151; to file unfair labor practice charges against unions, 152–153; to petition for election, 153–154, 157; to refuse compulsory check-off, 156–157; to adjust individual grievances, 157; to deny union shop—closed shop, 158; liability for agents only, 158; to sue for violation of contract, 158–159; to refuse contributions to union funds, 159–160; to judicial review, 160–162; as contract clause, 294–295, 322–326
"Majority" principle, defined, 35; in run-off election, 39–40; in union shop election, 42, 135–136; in determining bargaining representative, 45, 251; proof of, 150–151; necessity of for collective bargaining, 164, 168; challenged as unfair labor practice, 270; *see* also collective bargaining
Managerial employees, bargaining unit, 24
Marshall Field case, 15
Maryland Drydock case, 12
Matter of Briggs Manufacturing Co., 127
Membership cards, 7
Merit increases, 264, 284, 345–346
Military induction pay, 285
Military service, back pay for employee in, 77; leave of absence for, 307
Minimum pay, 284
Minority unions, 147
Montgomery Ward Company case, 87, 113
Multicraft units, 10, 17
Multiple employer units, 21–22, 149
Multi-plant units, 11, 22–23

National Labor Relations Act, "employee," defined under, 26, 63, 124, 127, *see* also employees, excluded from; policy of, 60–61, 121; scope of, 61–63, 123–128; "employer," defined under, 84, 124; injunction under, 86–88; prerequisite for applicability of, 121–122; purpose of, 121–123, 126; hiring, 129; closed shop, 135, free speech, 137–141
  collective bargaining: bargaining unit, 10, 13, 25; who has right to, 26; defined, 81; duty to bargain, 149–151, 163, 234–235, 251, 267–268; latitude in, 149–151; representative, 34–37, 165, 258; subject matter, 263–264

NLRB: investigation and certification of bargaining agent, 3, 34, 106–107; powers of, 82, 84, 88; procedure of, 91, 95, 96, 97–98, 99, 100; enforcement of orders, 104, 105–106, 109–110; exclusive jurisdiction over unfair labor practices, 357; *see* also NLRB

unfair labor practices: by employer, 60; by union, 47–48; defined under, 183; *see* also individual topics

National Labor Relations Board

charge: *see* unfair labor practices

complaint: authority of General Counsel to issue, 62, 93, 152; function and content of, 94; who is served, 95; answer to, content of, time to file, where filed, 96–97; bill of particulars, 97

General Counsel: authority of, 50, 62, 93; notice of hearing, 94; investigate charge, 94; power affected by court decision, 94

hearing: notice of, 55, 94–95; conduct, 55–56, 99; issues, 56; rules of evidence, 82, 100–101; right to appear, 99; evidence, 99; Intermediate Report, 100; findings of facts and conclusions of law, 100; enforcement of order, 100; fairness of, 113, 148; for appropriate bargaining unit, 252; for decertification of bargaining representative, 258

jurisdiction: industries within, examples, 61–62; interstate commerce, 61–62, 121–122, 123; limited to certain classes of employers, examples, 62–63; when in conflict with state boards, 61, 359–361; *see* also supervisors

orders: enforcement of, *see* courts; cease and desist, 60, 83–84; scope of, 83–85, 101–103; employer response to, 101

powers: certify, investigate and determine bargaining representative, 3–4, *see* also bargaining representative, bargaining unit, collective bargaining, elections; discretionary, 13–26; scope of authority, 61–63; broadened under LMRA, 61; disestablish company-dominated labor organizations, 63–66; prevent discriminatory discharges, 67–69; protect supervisory employees, 70–71; restrain anti-union activity, 71–72; restrain coercion by unions, 73; prevent closed shop, 73–74; grant union shop, 74; prevent excessive fees, 74; limit discharges under union shop, 74, 75; order or disallow reinstatement, 75–76; award back pay, 76–78; order collective bargaining, 78–81, 251; void settlement agreement, 81–82; nullify "yellow dog" contracts, 82; make findings, 82; draw inferences from facts and weigh testimony, 82; issue cease and desist orders, 83–84; request punishment for noncompliance with order, 84; prevent strikes and boycotts, 84–89; obtain court injunction, 89; time limitation on exercise of, 89; *see* also procedure

procedure, in representation cases: preliminary investigation, 50–52; consent and directed elections, 52–55; formal hearing, 55–56, issuance of subpoenas, 97–98

procedure, in unfair labor practice cases: in general, 90–91; charge of, 91–92; dismissal of charge, 92–94; issuance of complaint and notice of hearing, 93–97; issuance of subpoenas, 97–98; hearing, 99–101; NLRB orders, 101–103

Rules and Regulations: notice of hearing, 55, 95, filing charges, 91–92; service of complaint, 95; answer to complaint, 96; disestablishment of company-dominated union, 209; *see* also elections

NLRB v. Hearst Publications, Inc., 124

NLRB v. Newport News Co., 208

NLRB v. Virginia Power, 190

National War Labor Board, 130, 169–170, 295

Negotiation, *see* contract

Negotiators, qualities of, 274

Newport News Shipbuilding & Dry Dock Co. v. Schauffler, 162

New York Civil Practice Act, 142–143

New York Porto Rico Steamship Company case, 67, 178–179

New York State Labor Relations Act, 91

Nonaffiliated unions, *see* union

Non-Communist affidavit, union filing requirements, 6–7, 153–154, 243–244, 252, 271

Noncomplying union, *see* above

Norris-LaGuardia Act, injunction, 86, 155, 238, 277; labor disputes under, 142, 144, 161; union immunity, 143–144; limited, 144

No-strike, no lockout, *see* strikes

Notice of hearing, 94–95, *see* also hearing, NLRB

One-year election rule, 43, 148–157, 253
Overtime, 289, 324–325

Packard case, 12
Part-time employees, bargaining unit, 23, eligibility to vote in elections, 37
"Pattern" wage increases, 284
Pension, retirement plans, 264, contract clause, 312–317, 343–344
Petition, for investigation and determination of bargaining representative, who may file, 4–8, 153–154, showing of substantial interest, 5–6, 38, 51, union filing requirements, 6–7, 153–154, 243–244, noncomplying unions, 7, for decertification, 11, 42, 50, 244, 257–258, "equality" rule, 38–39, consent elections, 52–55, formal hearing, 55–56; to revoke union shop, 74; for clarification of court decree, 147–148; *see* also elections and unfair labor practices, procedure
Phelps Dodge case, 75, 126
Picketing, 73, management's right to restrict, 145–146
Picket line, refusal to cross, 165
Pittsburgh Plate Glass Co. v. NLRB, 15
Plant and employee rules, subject matter for collective bargaining, 264
Plant, location, in determination of bargaining unit, 21
Plant unit, bargaining unit, 13
Preamble (to collective agreement), 281–282
Preferential hiring clauses, 132, 158
Preferential treatment, 190
"Premature extension" doctrine, 31–32
Premium pay, 288, 308
Primary boycott, legality of, 141–142
Probationary employees, eligibility to vote in elections, 37; wages for, 285; contract clause, 290–291, 333–334
Production employees, grouping in bargaining unit, 17–18, 19, 259
Professional employees, grouping in bargaining unit, 18–19, 127, 260; defined under LRMA, 130; defined under NLRA, 260
Profit sharing plan, subject matter for collective bargaining, 264
Promotion, contract clause, 304–305, 337–338
Pro-rated vacation, 309–310
"Public agency," 59

Quaker Maid Company case, 31
Quit, severance pay for, 317–318

Race, color, or creed, 9, 23, 24, 46
Railway Labor Act, 241
Rank-and-file employees, in bargaining unit, 12
Recognition, not subject matter for bargaining, 44; contract clause, 282–283; *see* also collective bargaining
Re-employment, of laid off employees, subject matter for collective bargaining, 264
Refusal to bargain, *see* unfair labor practice, collective bargaining
Rehiring, *see* hiring
Reinstatement, of discharged employee, 75, 175; of strikers, 76; of veteran, 77; "runaway shop" employer, 77–78; effect of employee's conduct, 176, 177; disqualification for, 177, 178; refusal to reinstate, 179; when ordered, examples, 180, 181, not ordered, examples, 181, 182; *see* also back pay
Report time, 288–290
Representation, how proceedings initiated, 3–9, petitions for, 4–8; how bargaining unit determined, 10–26; when election for barred, 27–33; how representatives elected, 34–42; procedure in cases, NLRB investigation, 50–85, *see* also NLRB, procedure, in representation cases; hearing, 55–56; *see* also bargaining representative, bargaining unit, elections
Res judicata, 82
Rest period, subject for collective bargaining, 264
Retirement, *see* pension plans
Ritter's Cafe case, 146
"Runaway shop," 77–78, 218–219
Run-off election, *see* elections

Schechter Corp. v. United States, 122
Scheduling of work, 323–324
Seasonal employees, bargaining unit, 23
Second Employers' Liability Cases, 122
Secondary boycott—boycott, 84–89, 123, 142–144, 148, 237–240; as unfair labor practices by unions, 154–155, 237–242; litigation, 358
Secret ballots, 4
Semi-industrial units, 10
Seniority, contract clause, 300–302, 334–335; transfer, 302–303, 337; leave of absence, 305; promotion, 337; judicial relief for violation of seniority rights, 356

Severance pay, contract clause, 317–318, 344–345
Sherman Act, union immunity, 144
Shifts, subject for collective bargaining, 264; premiums for, 287, 289
Shift differentials, 284
Shop steward, role in grievance procedure, 300, seniority for, 301
Showing of substantial representation, see election, for bargaining representative
Shutdown, 132
Sitdown strikes, 132, 145
Sixty-day "cooling off" period, 48–49, 235–237, 271–272
Southern Bell Company case, 208
Speech, see free speech
State anti-injunction statute, 277
State boards, conflict with NLRB over jurisdiction, 61, 359–361
State courts, review of arbitration awards, 353–354
State labor legislation, 359–362
Statutory filing requirements, see filing requirements
Steel panel, 313
Steele v. Louisville & N. R. Co., 162
Stillwell Theatres case, 144–145
Strikes—strikers, eligibility to vote in election under NLRA and LMRA, 35, 37–38; during sixty-day "cooling off" period, 48–49, 235–237, 271–272; as unfair labor practice by unions, 73, 154–155, 230–232, 237–242; "wildcat" strikes, 76, 130, 132; not cause for refusal to bargain, 81; NLRB cease and desist order, 84–85; injunctive relief from, under LMRA, 85–87, 141, 160; right of management to discharge for, 132–134; sitdown strike, 132, 145; right of unions to strike, 41, 237–242; by rival unions, 278; state legislation, 361–362
    no-strike—no-lockout: violation of pledge, 177, eligibility for holiday pay, 339–340; contract clause, 291–292, 331
    reinstatement of: when ordered, 75, 177–183; when denied, 76, 132–134; back pay, 186
"Struck" work, 133
Subcontracting, 151
Subpoenas, of employer records, 51–52, 97–98; attendance and testimony at NLRB hearing, 56, 97–98; issued by arbitrators, 352

Substantial evidence, 82, 111–113, 148 (for court enforcement of NLRB order)
"Substantially equivalent," 108, 176, 179
"Successor" labor organization, see union, company-dominated
Supervisory employees, defined under NLRA, 12–13, 25, 261–262; employees held to be, 25–26, 261–262; excluded from term "employee" and coverage of NLRA, 12, 25, 63, 70, 125, 127, 155, 261, 271; legitimate discharge of, 133; responsibility of management for their actions, 138, 173–175, 199, 201; unfair labor practices by, 199–201; contract clause, 295–297, 326–327; handling grievances, 329
    collective bargaining: appropriate unit, 12, 25, 260; role in, 273, 280
    rights: 261–262; NLRB, protection of, 70–71

Taft-Hartley Law, see Labor Management Relations Act
Temporary employees, bargaining unit, 23
Termination, of contract, notice requirements, 48–49, 271–272, intervening certification, 272; sixty-day "cooling off" period, 48–49, 235–237, 271–272
Testimony, discharges for, 69, 136; NLRB conclusions based on, 82; scope of court review, 82; subpoena, 97, 98
Texas & O.N.R.Co. v. Railway Clerks, 122
Thompson Products, Inc., 133
Timekeepers, bargaining unit, 20
Time study personnel, bargaining unit, 18–19, 20, 260–261
Timken Roller Bearing Company case, 265
Transfer, right of management to, 136–137; as unfair labor practice by employer, 219; when discriminatory, 219; wage policy, 284, 286; contract clause, 302–304, 335–336
Trust funds, statutory requirements, 159–160

Unfair labor practices, elections, 35, 37, 39; as applied to bargaining representative, 45–47, 49; misuse of free speech, 72, 137, 141; individual con-

Unfair labor practices (*Continued*)
tract of employment, 72; under NLRA, 123, 126; hiring policies, 129; hiring hall, 130; under NLRA, 123, 126; injunctions, 141–142, 154–155, 160; secondary boycotts, 142–144, 148; picketing, 145–146

by employer: anti-union activity, 71–72; discharge under union shop, 135–136; interference with employees' rights, 189–194, examples, 194–199; indirect interference, 199–200, examples, 200–201; coercion, 201–203, examples under NLRA, 203; domination of labor organization, 63–66, 203–214; discrimination, 67–71, 215–223, examples, 219–221, 222–223; refusal to bargain, 170–171, 223–229, 266–272, examples, 225–229

by union: featherbedding, 48, 242; in general, 48; forcing employer to discriminate, 69, 232–233; restraint and coercion, 73, 230–232; charging excessive fees, 74; hiring hall system, 130, 158; strikes and boycotts, 154–155; refusal to bargain, 233–235, 266–272; contract termination, 235–237; strikes and boycotts, 237–242; failure to comply with filing requirements, 243–244; time limitation on filing charges, 244–245

charge: time limit on filing, 89, 92, 244–245; NLRA quoted, 91; answer to, 91; by whom and how filed, 91, 153; where filed, 92; dismissal and appeal of, 92–93; distinction between charge and complaint, 92; how phrased, 92; investigation of, 92; discharge for filing, 136; rights of management and unions to file, 152–153

complaint: *see* National Labor Relations Board

hearing: *see* National Labor Relations Board

judicial relief from: rights of private parties, jurisdiction of NLRB, 160–162

procedure in cases: *see* National Labor Relations Board

remedies for: scope of NLRB authority, 59–63; domination and interference, 63–66; discharge of supervisors, 70–71; anti-union activity, 71–73; coercion by union, 73; prevention of closed shop, 73; discharges, 74; excessive union fees, 74; awards, 76; ordering collective bargaining, 78–84; void settlement agreements, 81; union activities, 87; cease and desist order, 83; noncompliance with NLRB order, 84; preventing strikes and boycotts, 84–89; *see* also back pay, cease and desist, injunction, reinstatement

Union, petition, raising question of representation, 5–6; affiliated and nonaffiliated, 38–39; liability under contract, 47–48; control over hiring, 129–130; immunities under Clayton and Norris-LaGuardia Acts, 143; access to plant, 146–147; obligations in collective bargaining, 149–150; filing requirements under LMRA, 153–154, 243–244, 252, 257, 271; strikes, 154–155, 230–232, 237–242; liability for breach of contract, 158–159, 276–277; welfare funds, 159–160; certification of, 163–167; employees, protection against nonunion employees, 189; preparation for bargaining, 274–275; officials, 281; responsibility, 292–294, 332–333; state regulations, 362; *see* also unfair labor practices, employer-employee relationship

activity: examples of, 68; NLRB authority to restrain anti-union activity, 71–72; prohibited during working hours, 72; right of management to bar, 146; discharge for, 134–135; grievance procedure, 299; leave of absence for, 305

company-dominated: excluded from election ballot, 38–39; disestablishment of, 64–66, 187, 213–214; affiliated and nonaffiliated unions, 65, 66, 205, 206; "successor" labor organizations, 66; reimbursement of employees for dues to, 148; how determined, 204–209; disavowal of, 205; burden of proof, 205–206; criteria of, 206–207; evidence of, 207–208; conduct held domination, 209–211; necessity of complete fracture, 211–213

dues, fees, assessments: as "tribute," 71; limited, 74; nonpayment of, 74, 232, under union shop, 136, 156, 256; discriminatory, 242; *see* also check-off

duties: *see* rights of management, 129–162

membership: eligibility for, 19–20, 33, 47, under union shop, 156; solicitation of, 67, when barred, 72, 146; discharge for, 69, 131; questions on,

71; under union shop, 73–75, 135; not guarantee against discharge, 75

organization: factor in determining bargaining unit, 25; drive for, 125–126

rights: to strike, 141; to picket, 145; to file unfair labor practice charges, 152–153; to judicial relief from unfair labor practices, 160–162; under LMRA, 228–229; authority as bargaining agent, 256–258; over contract, 256; limited, 257; *see* also management, duties of, 163–188

security: discharges under union security provisions, 74–75, 135–136; subject for collective contract, 264; state legislation, 359–361; *see* also union shop, closed shop, recognition

shop: bar to NLRB election, 29, election for, 42–43, 73–74, 158; discharges under, 68, 74–75, 135–136; legal requirements for under LMRA, 42, 73–74, 135, 158, 256; subject matter for negotiation, 74; dual unionism, 74; authority of union to enter into, 74; right of employer to deny, 158; nondiscriminatory application of, 156

United States Circuit Court of Appeals, jurisdiction of, 104–105, 160–162, 355–358; power over NLRB orders, 102–103, 107–108, to remand, 108–109, to grant injunctive relief, 85–87, 109, 154–155; *see* also courts

Vacation, 264, contract clause, 309–310, 340–342

Vesting rights, 316

Veterans' rights, to back pay after discharge, 77

Virginia Railway v. System Federation, 122

Wages, construction of term, for collective bargaining, 263; across-the-board increase, automatic progression, 284; reopening of clause, 284, 288, 346; contract clause, 288; merit wage increase, 345–346

Wage Stabilization Act, 76

Wagner Act, *see* NLRA

Wallace Corp. v. NLRB, 162

War Labor Disputes Act, 76, 142; thirty-day notice requirement, 181

War Production Board, 64

Watchmen, bargaining unit, 260

Welders, bargaining unit, 20

Welfare funds, statutory requirements, 159–160

White collar workers, bargaining unit, 21, 24

"Wildcat" strike, *see* strikes

Wohl case, 145–146

Workday, 289

Work standards and loads, subject matter for collective bargaining, 264

Workweek, 289

"Yellow dog" contracts, 82, 189